A Century of Painters of the English School

1890

A CENTURY OF PAINTERS

OF THE

ENGLISH SCHOOL.

A

CENTURY OF PAINTERS

OF THE

ENGLISH SCHOOL

BY

RICHARD REDGRAVE, C.B., R.A.

(SOMETIME SURVEYOR OF HER MAJESTY'S PICTURES AND ART DIRECTOR OF THE
SOUTH KENSINGTON MUSEUM),

AND

SAMUEL REDGRAVE.

SECOND EDITION,
ABRIDGED AND CONTINUED TO THE PRESENT TIME.

" THERE ARE NOT SO MANY WRONG OPINIONS IN THE WORLD AS IS GENERALLY
IMAGINED ; FOR MOST PEOPLE HAVE NO OPINION AT ALL, BUT TAKE UP WITH
THOSE OF OTHERS, OR WITH MERE HEARSAY AND ECHOES."—*Locke.*

LONDON

SAMPSON LOW, MARSTON, SEARLE & RIVINGTON, LIMITED

ST. DUNSTAN'S HOUSE, FETTER LANE, FLEET STREET, E.C.

1890.

Richard Clay and Sons, Limited,
LONDON AND BUNGAY.

PREFACE TO THE SECOND EDITION.

In publishing a Second Edition of this work it has been judged advisable to abridge it considerably and to issue it in a single volume for the convenience of Art Students who may use it as a book of reference. The parts omitted have been mostly those dealing with the foundation of the Academy, and the descriptions of pictures, which latter were considered a little too technical for the general reader.

It is difficult to shorten a book without reducing the interest, and to continue it without breaking the thread of the narrative, but it was absolutely necessary both to abridge the original matter and to add many new pages in order to bring the subject up to date and to make it useful to the reader of the present day. A quarter of a century, rich in art progress, has elapsed since the First Edition ; painters have now almost too many biographers, therefore, in adding details of the lives of those who have passed away during the last twenty-five years, a shorter account of many eminent men has sufficed, as compared with the notices of less distinguished men in the earlier part of the work. The endeavour has been made however by describing the methods of painting to keep up a connected account of the development of the British school, though this has necessarily been circumscribed by the plan of the original book, which has been rigidly adhered to, namely, not to mention the works of living painters.

A list of the numerous authorities which have been consulted would have been superfluous, as their aid is always acknowledged in the course of the work.

February, 1890.

PREFACE TO THE FIRST EDITION.

THE opinion is at last gaining ground that art is no longer an alien on English soil ; and the time appears to have arrived when some interest will be felt in a narrative of its progress among us. An artist may now without fear of presumption speak of "The English School," a school rich in fine works, whose painters are remarkable for the national character, as well as for the individual originality, of their genius.

Great progress was unquestionably made in the last generation towards a better appreciation of art. Now, all make it at least a subject of conversation, many of real interest. A desire to see works of art, if not a taste for them, has been developed by the public collections in the British Museum, the National Gallery, and more recently, in the South Kensington Museum, added to the growing attractions of the exhibitions at the Royal Academy, the Water-Colour Societies, the Suffolk Street Gallery, and other institutions.

Meanwhile we have no connected narrative in which the growth and development of our school, and the peculiarities of the artists who have been its pride and its ornament, have been critically traced. While impressed with the difficulty of obtaining reliable information concerning many of our painters and their works, it has been our aim to supply this want by such means as were within our reach. Some artists enjoy a reputation quite unsupported by the works they have left behind them, others, scarcely known in their own day, have bequeathed to us works of great merit, which should have given a reputation, but have hardly secured to them a record or a name.

All the Continental schools and their artists have had their historians ; everything connected with them has been narrated, lauded, and criticized, while of the progress of art in England, and its truly national character, the story has been left untold. When entrusted with the selection and arrangement of the works of the English school in the International

Exhibition of 1862, this neglect was made woefully apparent to us ; of our artists, of their most renowned works, and their present possessors, there was but scant record. We had long felt a deep interest in the works of our early painters. It then became our duty, in search of them, to visit the chief collections in the country, and availing ourselves of the opportunity, we added largely to the notes and information we had before possessed : and with the view of confirming our first impressions, we have since the commencement of this work, again seen many of the paintings which in the course of it we have critically noticed.

It has been the subject of remark that artists have rarely been writers upon their art ; that the judgment and criticism eschewed by them, have been left to others devoid of technical knowledge ; while the painter has been told that the pencil, not the pen, belongs to him, and that he will find the best employment for his time and thought at his easel. Of the truth of this, while devoting ourselves to this work we have been made fully sensible ; yet in the attempt to speak justly of the painter's art, to give a due place to forgotten genius, and a knowledge of our profession, founded on right principles, the labour has not been unattended by some feelings of compensation.

Our object has been to write a connected history of the art of painting, and of the institutions founded for its promotion, in the last and present century, during which time English art had its true birth, and has progressed to a healthy vigour. We have not attempted to write biographies of our artists, but to give such facts relating to those who were most distinguished as intimately connect them with their works, speaking, however, exceptionally more at large of others of whom little is known, yet in all cases confining ourselves to those who have finished their labours and have passed from us.

Our aim throughout has been to cultivate a catholic love for art, without prepossession or prejudice ; to see the merits of a great work before its defects, and never without a fair recognition of the difficulties the artist has had to overcome. By this spirit we have, we trust, always been guided.

In the selection of a painter's works for special criticism, while we have chosen those which are esteemed the most important, we have had a view also to those which are most accessible to the public, so as to afford an opportunity for examining the grounds of the opinions we have expressed.

KENSINGTON, *September*, 1865.

CONTENTS.

INTRODUCTORY CHAPTER.

CHAPTER I.

OUR NATIVE ARTISTS.

CHAPTER II.

WILLIAM HOGARTH.

CONTENTS.

CHAPTER III.

The Royal Academy.

CHAPTER IV.

Richard Wilson, R.A., and his Contemporaries.

CHAPTER V.

Sir Joshua Reynolds, P.R.A.

CHAPTER VI.

Thomas Gainsborough, R.A.

CHAPTER X.

PROGRESS OF HISTORIC ART.

CHAPTER XI.

THE SUCCESSORS OF REYNOLDS.

CHAPTER XII.

THE ANIMAL PAINTERS OF THE EIGHTEENTH CENTURY.

CHAPTER XVI.

The British Institution and the Water-Colour Societies.

CHAPTER XVII.

The Founders of the Water-Colour Society.

CHAPTER XVIII.

Sir Thomas Lawrence, P.R.A.

CHAPTER XIX.

The Contemporaries of Lawrence.

CHAPTER XX.

JOSEPH MALLORD WILLIAM TURNER, R.A.

CHAPTER XXI.

HOWARD, HILTON, HAYDON, AND ETTY.

CHAPTER XXII.

TABLEAUX DE GENRE.—WILKIE, MULREADY, AND LESLIE.

CHAPTER XXIII.

DAVID WILKIE, R.A.

CHAPTER XXIV.

WILLIAM MULREADY, R.A., AND THOMAS WEBSTER, R.A.

CHAPTER XXV.

LESLIE, NEWTON, AND EGG.

CHAPTER XXVI.

OLD CROME AND THE NORWICH SCHOOL.

CHAPTER XXVII.

RECENT PORTRAIT PAINTERS—PICKERSGILL, BOXALL, KNIGHT, MACNEE, HOLL.

CHAPTER XXVIII.

THE LANDSCAPE PAINTERS—CONSTABLE, CALLCOTT, AND COLLINS.

CHAPTER XXXIV.

INSTITUTIONS AFFECTING THE SPREAD OF ART.

CHAPTER XXXV.

FRESCO-PAINTING AND STATE PATRONAGE.

CHAPTER XXXVI.

MACLISE, WARD, EASTLAKE, PHILLIP, ELMORE, AND O'NEIL.

CHAPTER XXXVII.

WILLIAM DYCE, R.A., AND SCHOOLS OF DESIGN.

CHAPTER XXXVIII.

PRESERVATION OF PICTURES.

CHAPTER XXXIX.

THE PRE-RAPHAELITES.

A CENTURY OF PAINTERS.

ERRATA.

For " Munro," *read* " Monro," pages 140, 145, 182, 189, 230, 324.
For " Charles Shrriff," *read* " Charles Sherriff," page 154.
For "criticism : a lad," *read* "criticism : as in ' Idle Boys '—a lad," page 277.
For " of ' Old Water-Colours,'" *read* 'The Old Water-Colour,' page 356.

When a collection of English pictures was sent in 1855 to the International Exhibition in Paris, our art was almost unknown there ; and endeavours to obtain suitable space for its proper display were received with impatience—for it clearly was not deemed of much importance where the English pictures were hung. When however the cases were opened, curiosity prompted a glance at some of the pictures ; then surprise at their merits, which were generously acknowledged, attracted more admirers than were convenient to those charged with the arrangement ; and before this task was completed, the French artists admitted to their English brethren that only two schools then existed in Europe— " ours and yours." " Other schools," they said, " are founded on ours ; yours is an original school "—an opinion which, if only intended as a

B

CONTENTS.

CHAPTER XXXIX.

THE PRE-RAPHAELITES.

A CENTURY OF PAINTERS.

INTRODUCTORY CHAPTER.

IN a short account of the most eminent painters, ancient and modern, by Richard Graham, which was appended to the second edition of Du Fresnoy's *Art of Painting*, published in 1716, the writer says : " I am ashamed to acknowledge how difficult a matter I have found it to get but the least information touching some of those ingenious men of my own country, whose works have been a credit and a reputation to it." Yet this difficulty mainly refers to the notices of only four English artists who are included in Graham's work—Samuel Cooper, Dobson, Green-hill, and Riley. Horace Walpole also remarks, in his *Anecdotes of Painting in England* (1762), that this country had not then a single volume to show on the works of its painters, and he even apologizes for the title of his work.

When a collection of English pictures was sent in 1855 to the International Exhibition in Paris, our art was almost unknown there ; and endeavours to obtain suitable space for its proper display were received with impatience—for it clearly was not deemed of much importance where the English pictures were hung. When however the cases were opened, curiosity prompted a glance at some of the pictures ; then surprise at their merits, which were generously acknowledged, attracted more admirers than were convenient to those charged with the arrangement ; and before this task was completed, the French artists admitted to their English brethren that only two schools then existed in Europe— " ours and yours." " Other schools," they said, " are founded on ours ; yours is an original school "—an opinion which, if only intended as a

B

compliment, is not the less a fact and a truth. We have brought together in our National Gallery, of which we may well be proud, fine examples of the great works of the continental schools ; and we possess by gift (with a few occasional purchases) many works of our own painters ; but we want a collection selected to represent the school. The most choice works of the British artists should be purchased by the public for a *British Gallery*, which should include a good example by every artist of acknowledged eminence. Then, and not till then, can either our own citizens or their foreign visitors do full justice to the school of art, so purely national and characteristic, which has grown up in England since Walpole wrote.

The truth seems to be, that the English painters, for the better part of a century, struggled against an old prejudice—namely, that art is neither congenial to our soil nor to our nature, and cannot flourish among us. Hogarth, with all his shrewd intelligence, and not a little prejudice, held this opinion. He says : "We cannot vie with these Italian and Gothic theatres of art, and to enter into competition with them is ridiculous ; we are a commercial people, and can purchase their curiosities ready made, as in fact we do, and therefore prevent them thriving in our native clime. . . ."

It would be useless in the present day to combat the assertion that natural and political impediments opposed the success of art in our country. Who would now maintain the incompatibility of art and commerce, when the one has proved the handmaid to the other ? or, that the deficiency of taste shown by our cold manners and ungraceful costume must freeze art, when the charming works of Gainsborough, Reynolds, Lawrence, and a host of others witness that no impediments could chill their genius ? Who would say that the religion of England is opposed to art, which it has inspired, and will before long place in its temples ? or, that our climate is unfavourable, when we see the works of the great school of landscape painters founded upon its cloudy gleams of sun and shade, its glorious misty effects of sunrise and sunset, its spring freshness, and mellowed autumn richness ?

We are certainly not less a commercial people than when Hogarth wrote, but we have learnt since his day the intimate connection which exists between art and manufacture; the State has felt it a duty to provide instruction in drawing, to the profit and improvement of even the poorest of our population ; and in art-teaching, though its object may be definite, its limits must in their result be without bounds. The student who aims to become a designer for our cottons or porcelains, may be led by the development of his talents to the highest paths in art ; and he who begins his career by dreaming of Raphael or Titian, but who is never able to approach these great examples, need not despair and starve. He has a lower and a useful sphere open to him. He may find profitable employment as a portrait painter, though in the second rank, or as a copyist or a teacher; as a draughtsman and designer, his attainments may be of infinite value in connecting art with manufacture, the alliance between which is as close as between art and science, and as essential in perfecting the works of our artisans. In the most flourishing times of Italian art, the greatest artists lent their talents to manufacture; the most rare jewels, the most precious metals, the richest silks, have been trebled in value by the artist's skill. The meanest articles of our daily use may, by the same skill, not only be turned to greater profit, but be made more conducive to our enjoyment and improvement.

But we would not limit our view to the teaching of apprentices and mechanics. All have an interest in art. It gives an increased intelligence, a new pleasure, a truer love of Nature—the purest enjoyment we know. How feelingly this is described by our great statesman, Mr. Pitt, when sitting for his portrait to Owen:—"I exceedingly regret that I am entirely ignorant of the fine arts; and had I any control over the system of education of the patrician youth, I should take care that they cultivated the study of drawing, not only as one of the intelligent and generally useful arts, but as it would open to the mind, in every change of place, a new and most extensive source of delight."

Of the art of the painter, the sculptor, the architect, and the ornamental designer, as practised in this country, a history or even a record has to this time remained unwritten. This blank we have attempted to supply in the following pages, so far as relates to painting treated as an art exclusively. Whatever may have been the condition of English art prior to the commencement of the sixteenth century, its historical records are slight; they are confined to such particulars as may be found in the accounts of the Crown, the household expenses of the nobility, and the chapter records of our cathedrals, and frequently relate to the magnificent tombs, shrines, and chapels which in those times were erected to perpetuate the memory of the great. Now and then an English name, either as painter, sculptor, or architect, appears, but the majority so employed were foreigners, brought here to execute some particular work, and occasionally induced to prolong their stay.

Very few pictures of any kind painted prior to the reign of Henry VII. are now in existence in this country. The few which can be identified, are mostly portraits, and have been preserved in the royal palaces, the mansions of the nobility, and in our colleges and corporate halls; and these relics have, unhappily, been so restored and renovated, that very little of the original work can now be distinguished. There would, indeed, seem to have been a time, when it was deemed a part of domestic economy to clean the pictures with the other furniture, and they had periodically their share of polishing with the wainscot, when peripatetic renovators went from hall to hall, and from house to house, whitewashing and polishing. Such cleaners scrubbed off and laid on paint without the smallest responsibility. They made the pictures shine with new varnish, and patched and re-gilded the frames. By these authorities portraits were affiliated anew, both as to the painter and the subject of his work— much, perhaps, to the satisfaction of the owner, who was gratified by a more sounding title to his picture; but greatly to the confusion of the art-critic and the antiquary, now that such matters are made the subject of exact research.

After these scrubbers and cleaners, naturally came the repairers and restorers. Among the well-known memoranda by *R. Symonds* is this relating to the fine collection purchased of the Duke of Mantua by Charles I.:—" When the King's pictures came from Mantua, quicksilver was got in amongst them, and made them all black. Mr. Hieronymus Laniere (brother of Nicholas) told me that to cleanse them, first he tried fasting-spittle, then he mixt it with warm milk, and those would not do; and at last he cleaned them with aqua-vitæ alone, and that took off all the spots, and he says, 'twill take off the varnish." *Sanderson*, in his *Graphice*, tells of this old master of the cleaning-craft, " as the first who passed off copies for originals, by tempering his colours with soot, and then by rolling them up, he made them crackle and contract an air of antiquity." Laniere's inventions have survived to the present day.

As pictures aged and lost the freshness of their youthful complexions, this very defect came to be considered a beauty; the brown hue of successive coats of varnish was admired as an excellence: "A good picture," said Sir George Beaumont, "like a good fiddle, should be brown." If a picture came from abroad in a fine fresh state of preservation, the dealers were too wise to let it be seen until its pure tints were subdued to the established hue. Connoisseurs believed that pictures, like coins, obtained a patina from age, which mellowed their tone, and made them more valuable than in the state they left the painter's easel. Instances of the maltreatment of pictures are rife enough. A painter named *Brompton*, who practised in the latter half of the eighteenth century, a professed picture-cleaner, lives only in the bad repute of the mischief he has done. Among his other crimes, he is alleged to have had under his reckless hand, Vandyck's great picture of the Pembroke family at Wilton. Rubens's celebrated ceiling painting in the banqueting-house at Whitehall, was somewhat out of ready reach; it has not, however, escaped. Only sixty years after its completion, in the reign of James II., *Parry Walton*, a painter of still-life, then keeper of the King's pictures, was employed to repair it, and was paid 212*l.* for his work. Then *Giovanni Cipriani* received 1000*l.* for further retouchings; after him it was

" refreshed " by *John F. Rigaud, R.A.*, and the well-known *William Kent* is also named as having had a share in these sad doings.

With such doings, Hogarth had no sympathy. He called the smoked, dark, bad copies of frequently bad originals, and the skinned and re-painted realities which were sold in his day, " the works of the black masters." Nicholls tells of the incredible numbers of such which were annually sold in Langford's well-known auctions, obscured by dirt, or scumbled down by asphaltum to the taste of the so-called connoisseur.

Works of art, are, however, liable to other dangers and mischances ; numerous copies have been made of pictures, renowned either for the fame of their painter or their subject, for the collateral branches of families ; or, as was frequently the case, as presents from the sovereign. Charles I. employed *John Van Belcamp* exclusively, and *Joachim Sandrart* very largely, in copying his pictures for such purposes, and the same practice has prevailed to our own day. These copies in time are exalted into originals, while many of the originals themselves have been altered in size, enlarged or cut down at the will of the possessor to form companions to other pictures, to fill panels, or to fit spaces.

Again, as families rose to wealth and distinction, the herald was set to work to furnish them with coats-of-arms, and the painter with respectable forefathers. Many an ancient portrait by a curtailment of the ruff, or an extra curl of the wig, has changed its date from the first to the second James, and has figured in quite a new family relation. Nor have such schemes fallen into disuse ; an American agent recently in London explained his business to be to " collect ancestors," and that he had been very successful. He said he had picked up many good portraits, and that with proper attention to costume and age, and some little heraldic additions, he had matched suitable husbands and wives for two or three generations, and had exported several very well-assorted families, which being provided with full credentials, were most filially adopted, and that he was continuing his highly remunerative researches. This is no fiction.

Nor have these strange mutations been confined to the works of the portrait painters alone. Captain Baillie, famous as an etcher and an amateur, purchased for 7*l.* Cuyp's fine " View of Dort," and brought it to this country. It is known to have left the clever captain's hands as two separate pictures called " Morning " and " Evening," which were afterwards purchased for 2,200*l.*, and mechanically reunited—so this great work may be cited as one genuine specimen of restoration. Another instance is, however, pertinent, having been under the eyes of all in the International Exhibition of 1862. Crome's picture of Mousehold Heath fell into the hands of a Jew, who, by the same process of cutting in half, converted it into two upright landscapes, which, in the same manner, have fortunately been brought together again, yet not without, it is said, some loss of part of the subject.

Then, again, the fair fame of painters and the reputation of their works are undermined by frauds, and great profits are made by unscrupulous devices. It is mentioned in the *Life of Nollekens* that—"John Barnard, Esq., nicknamed Jacky Barnard, who was fond of showing his collection of Italian drawings, expressed surprise that Mr. Nollekens did not pay sufficient attention to them   'Yes, I do,' replied he; 'but I saw many of them at Jenkins's at Rome, while the man was making them for my friend Crone, the artist, one of your agents.'"   Perhaps it would be difficult to name a more fertile field from which successful fraud has reaped its large ill-gotten gains than these "drawings by the old masters."   The other story is equally pertinent.   "Nollekens was addressed by a young man: 'Well, Mr. Nollekens, how do you do? You don't know me; but you recollect my grandfather, Arthur Pond.' 'Oh, yes, very well; he used to christen old drawings for Hudson; ay, I have often seen him when I was a boy.'"

Even when a picture comes direct from the studio of the artist, is it always certainly the work of his own hand? How often are pictures painted in duplicate, triplicate, or in larger quantities for which names have not yet become common in our language. It is told of the court painter to George III. on his accession, that, having painted a popular likeness of that monarch head-size, he received such continuous commissions for repetitions of it, that his pupils and assistants were constantly employed on *stock*, and that above one hundred and fifty repetitions were made and found purchasers.

When it seemed probable that Etty's laborious life was drawing to its close, his works were purchased with avidity, particularly by dealers. Some dozens of his studies from the life had been lined or laid down on panels, and various purchasers' names, mostly dealers, were chalked upon them as they lay in his then deserted studio in London. He was, poor man, sick at York, and died there shortly after; but when the works we have mentioned—mere Academy studies—came forth, they were fitted with backgrounds and dressed up pictorially for the market, certainly not however by the hand of the master. Again, when Mr. Doo, R.A., wished to engrave one of Etty's large historical pictures which had been recently purchased by the Scottish Academy, the members, reluctant to lend their newly-acquired treasure, suggested that the engraving should be made from a copy; and for this purpose they selected the work of a talented young painter in Edinburgh. This reduced copy, which was touched upon by Etty, was afterwards sold for seven hundred guineas as the original sketch for the picture by Etty, the price originally paid for it as a copy being twenty guineas.

But paintings have other enemies; they are especially of that kind of riches "which moth and rust do corrupt." They have in great mansions been stowed away in roofs and cellars, and suffered to perish uncared-for and unseen. They have followed the fortunes of great families, and when they have decayed have, with them, been dispersed, lost, and neglected. More than any other, such treasures are liable to damage by fire, and their loss by this element has been proportionally great. The fire of London did an amount of damage to works of art which has never been estimated, though we find many individual instances of it; for then the mansions of the noble and wealthy were in its midst, not, as now, removed to the suburbs. Again, the number of the country-seats of old English families, filled with the treasures of art which have been destroyed by fire, either wholly or partially, is almost incredible; and particularly in later years, when attempts have been made to warm by modern inventions these spacious mediæval structures. Works of art, in times of war and riot, have been subject to wilful destruction, and have also perished from the morbid feelings of individual possessors. We have an instance of this in the orders of Parliament in 1645, for the disposal of King Charles's collections :—

"That all such pictures and statues there (York House) as are without any superstition, shall be forthwith sold, for the benefit of Ireland and the north.

"That all such pictures there as have the representation of the Second Person of the Trinity upon them shall be forthwith burnt.

"That all such pictures there as have the representation of the Virgin Mary upon them shall be forthwith burnt."

We have reason to rejoice that these Gothic orders were not strictly carried out. So soon as Cromwell attained to sufficient authority he took measures to preserve the royal collections, not only from parliamentary violence, but also from private rapacity. He saved many fine works, and he even detained some which had been actually sold by the orders of those whose usurped authority temporarily preceded the establishment of his own.

Walpole, with his friend Vertue, must have rescued many a work of art from most strange associations, and we cannot avoid quoting his picturesquely expressed authority how "Portraits that cost twenty, thirty, sixty guineas, and that proudly take possession of the drawing-room, give way in the next generation to those of the new-married couple, when they are slightly mentioned as my father's and my mother's pictures. When they become my grandfather's and my grandmother's, they mount to the two pair of stairs; and then, unless despatched to the mansion-house in the country, or crowded into the housekeeper's room, they perish among the lumber of garrets or flutter into rags before a broker's shop in Seven Dials." Such already has been the fate of some of those deathless beauties of whom Pope promised his friend that they should

"Bloom in his colours for a thousand years,"

This sad tale, too, is wittily confirmed by Reynolds, who, when his sister remarked that she had heard so much of the works of Jervas, to whom the poet refers, and had seen so little of them, only said, "My dear, you will find they are all removed to the attic."

As a set-off to the narrative of such destruction, it is pleasant to tell that at the end of the last century a large collection of the works of the great miniature-painters, *Isaac* and *Peter Oliver* was discovered in an old mansion in Wales, which belonged to a descendant of their family. This valuable treasure consisted of the portraits of Sir Kenelm Digby and his family. The latest were dated in 1633. They were enclosed in ivory and ebony cases, and the whole collection locked up in a wainscot box, where they had lain in safety, and were as fresh as when first painted. Walpole was so fortunate as to secure these rare works, he says, "at a great price." They were dispersed on the sale of the Strawberry Hill collection.

CHAPTER I.

WHILE works of art in England have suffered so greatly from neglect, ignorance, and fanaticism, added to accidental damage and natural decay, the names of our countrymen, to whom many of these works must be assigned, perished with them. Of the early painters we know little ; as illuminators, they introduced into their works delicate imitations of the human figure, animals, flowers, and foliage; as decorators, under the names of "steyners" or painters, they painted and gilded the carver's wooden and stone images, and the devices of heraldry ; and at a later period, probably, improved their imitations of the human face, till their representations were recognized by the name of "portraits on board." Of their works under the unassuming title of glaziers, there remain some well-authenticated painted windows of no mean art, though they may have been executed from the designs of foreigners. Sometimes the arts of the painter, sculptor, or "marbler," as he was then called, and architect were combined, as was the case with the great artists of the same period in Italy. But, as we have said, little remains of the works of the great decorators of this period to enable us to form a judgment of their merits. Of the painter's share, all has perished or been defaced.

Walpole, possessing the materials so carefully collected by Vertue, has given us the best connected account of the foreigners who, in the practice of their art here, became the teachers of our own artists. In the reign of Henry VII., *Mabuse*, a native of Hainault, a painter of great merit, and the contemporary of Albert Dürer, is reputed to have practised in this country, and to have painted the portraits of Henry and his children. If he came here, he did not receive much encouragement ; and as his stay could only have been short, his influence upon native art must have been slight. Henry VIII. came to the throne with an overflowing treasury. He was fond of magnificence, and, in rivalry with the sovereigns of France and Spain, he spent the wealth amassed by his father in liberally encouraging painters, architects, goldsmiths, and all who could foster his love of pompous display. He invited to England Raphael, Primaticcio, and Titian, and though these great men were not tempted by his munificence, several Italians, some of them pupils of Raphael, settled here and were employed by Henry, who was fortunate also in retaining *Holbein*, who had been induced to visit England by Sir Thomas More. Holbein's great talent as a colourist and a draughtsman, his originality, and the number and variety of his works during a long residence at the court, had an immediate and lasting effect upon the art of our country. We find, however, as is usually the case, where one man stands so incomparably above his compeers and successors, that they become his imitators and followers only, and that their works, if they approach his in excellence, are frequently attributed to him, and their names lost to posterity in the shadow of his. We next hear of *Sir Antonio More*, or *Moro*, who came to England with Philip II., and left with him on the death of Queen Mary. He painted a number of fine portraits, many of which, well authenticated, remain in this country, and several historic pieces. In Queen Elizabeth's reign, *Lucas de Heere*, a Fleming, was the court painter ; and after a short list of foreigners, among whom *Zucchero* stands prominent, we arrive at the name of *Nicholas Hilliard* (B. 1547, D. 1619), the first Englishman who attained a contemporary distinction which has survived to our own day. He was celebrated for his miniatures, and his works are preserved and greatly prized by collectors. Dr. Donne said of them,—

> "An hand or eye
> By Hilliard drawn, is worth a historye
> By a worse painter made."

He was followed in his art by another countryman, *Isaac Oliver* (B. 1556, D. 1617), who, if not his pupil, owed much to his friendly instruction, and surpassed him in the power and excellence of his works. His miniatures, and some drawings by him which remain, attest his skill, and are valued at high prices. Some of his works have been engraved.

Elizabeth's successor, James I., was no lover of art, yet three eminent portrait painters who came to England in his reign found employment, and their labours decorate the mansions of our old families, and perpetuate the features of many distinguished persons, in works which give equal delight to the artist, the historian, and the antiquary. These men, to whom we owe such cherished memories, were *Paul Vansomer*, a Fleming, who excelled in accuracy and in the pictorial treatment of his backgrounds ; *Cornelius Jansen*, of Amsterdam, distinguished by the careful finish and calm truth of his portraiture ; and *Daniel Mytens,* from the Hague, a good colourist, and happy in his landscape backgrounds. They also had their imitators, and their influence is apparent in the growing taste for art, and the nascent powers of the native artists who followed them. In this and the following reign, *Peter Oliver* (B. 1601, D. 1660), the son of Isaac, maintained the succession of native artists, and practised miniature painting with great talent and success. Fine examples of his numerous works exist, and, when in the market, are only obtained at very costly prices. Contemporary with him was *John Hoskins* (D. 1664), also a miniature painter, an artist of great merit and highly esteemed. But for the unhappy political events of the reign of Charles I., it is impossible to predict to how high a state the arts might have attained under his judicious patronage. Writers on art all concur in the opinion that he was singularly gifted in his knowledge and love of the fine arts—love given purely for their own sake, apart from the renown such possessions confer. Lilly, in his *Life and Death of Charles I.*, among his many fine qualities, mentions, "that in painting he had so excellent a fancy, that he would supply the defect of art in the workmen, and suddenly draw those lines and give those airs and lights which experience had not taught the painter." And Valentine Green, the engraver, in his *Letter to Sir Joshua Reynolds*, 1782, says that King Charles I. "amused himself often with drawing and designing."

These talents, founded on a true appreciation of art, made the king a purchaser of pictures. On his accession, the royal palaces contained one hundred and fifty different works collected by Henry VIII., with a few purchased by Prince Henry. These Charles inherited. They formed the commencement of the great collection which he brought together. Of its extent and value, we have evidence in the unfinished catalogue left by Vanderdort, his *custode*. This manuscript classified four hundred and sixty pictures disposed in the palace of Whitehall alone, comprising, among works of lesser note, twenty-eight by Titian, nine by Raphael, eleven by Correggio, eleven by Holbein, sixteen by Giulio Romano, seven by Parmegiano, seven by Rubens, seven by Tintoretto, three by Rembrandt, sixteen by Vandyck, four by Paul Veronese, and two by Leonardo da Vinci. For the well-known collection bought of the Duke of Mantua, Charles is reputed to have paid 80,000*l.* The Duke of Buckingham, too, moved by the royal example, was a munificent collector. He purchased for a large price— Walpole says 10,000*l.*—a collection of paintings made by Rubens, which included nineteen works by Titian, twenty-one by Bassano, thirteen by Paul Veronese, eight by Palma, seventeen by Tintoretto, three by Da Vinci, three by Raphael, and thirteen by Rubens himself. The Earl of Arundel also made large purchases, chiefly of statues and busts, many of them obtained from Asia Minor. Charles induced *Rubens* to visit his court, and to paint for him, though Rubens's stay was short—probably not above a year. *Vandyck*, under the judicious patronage of Charles, settled in England ; and these two eminent men established with great success a new style of portraiture in England, and gave birth to a native school of painters, in their pupils and imitators.

The English artists we have already mentioned rested their reputation on their miniature portrait ; now, in the higher style of art, *William Dobson* (B. 1610, D. 1646) rose to much celebrity. He is the first English painter who distinguished himself in portrait and history, if we except *Sir Nathaniel Bacon*, who scarcely finds a place in the ranks of art. Dobson painted the king, Prince Rupert, and several of the eminent men of his day. He was of great promise, but the evil times he fell upon, his love of pleasure, and his early death prevented the development of his art. There is a fine portrait of himself and his wife at Hampton Court Palace, a large, well-executed painting of the decollation of St. John at Wilton House, a family picture by him at Devonshire House, and a portrait of Cleveland, the poet, at Bridgewater House. His works approach nearly to those of Vandyck, and are scarcely inferior, except in the refinement of grace and drawing. In Scotland, *George Jamesone* (B. 1586, D. 1644), educated in the same school, attained great celebrity, and his works are still held in much esteem. These first dawnings of native art were, however, trampled out in the fierce struggles which then arose, or chilled in the asceticism by which they were followed. In the days of the Commonwealth we need only notice *Robert Walker*, who then rose into reputation, and died about the year 1660. He is chiefly noticeable as Cromwell's portrait painter, and as the most eminent of our native artists, at a time when foreigners met with but little encouragement here. Several well-known portraits by him exist, and are not without merit. One of his portraits of Cromwell is at Warwick Castle.

The Restoration did not bring with it happier times for art. Charles II. had neither the love for art nor the judgment of his unfortunate parent. He took some pains, however, to secure and collect such of the scattered works of his father's collections as came to his knowledge ; and Walpole quotes an interesting story of the king's visit, privately and unknown, to the widow of Oliver's son, to recover some of the miniatures by that great artist. *Sir Peter Lely* came to England in 1641, when twenty-four years of age, remained during the unsettled days of the Commonwealth, and painted Cromwell's portrait. He succeeded to the court favour and patronage which Vandyck had enjoyed during the previous reign, and for thirty years was the chief and most esteemed portrait-painter, particularly of female portraits, in England. He is admirably satirized by Pope in his second epistle; and Walpole, in the same strain, says, "His nymphs trail fringes and embroidery through meadows and purling streams." But art became less exclusively practised by foreigners; portraiture was largely encouraged, and native artists contended for a share of its profits. *Henry Anderton* (B. 1630, D. soon after 1665), was employed by the king and the court in portrait painting. *Isaac Fuller* (D. 1672), a man of dissolute habits, painted portraits and allegorical subjects of greater pretensions than merit or taste. *John Greenhill* (B. 1649, D. 1676), the most distinguished pupil of Lely, brought his life to an early close by his intemperance; and *Robert Streater* (B. 1624, D. 1680), who was not without merit, and was appointed serjeant-painter to Charles II. on the Restoration, practised both as a landscape painter and in history. His work in the theatre at Oxford, and several altar-pieces in the churches of that city, remain in a good state of preservation.

We have now reached a period when we find opinions and notices of the artists of the day. Streater, long since forgotten, enjoyed while living a great reputation. Indeed a poet, describing his allegorical picture at Oxford, bombastically prophesies—

> " That future ages must confess they owe
> To Streater more than Michael Angelo."

The painter is also mentioned in the gossiping pages of Pepys, a lover and a discriminating judge of art.

Contemporary with these men, Pepys also notices *Samuel Cooper* (B. 1609, D. 1672), the nephew and pupil of Hoskins, who continued and was distinguished for carrying to its highest pitch, the art of miniature-painting, already so excellent. Though seldom attempting more than the head of his sitter, Cooper's works possess a grace, beauty, and finish which render them most cherished in the cabinets of collectors. His fame was of his own time as of ours, and we read of him with true interest in the *naïve* diary of Pepys, who, speaking of Hales, an artist of that day, says, "He has also persuaded me to have Cooper draw my wife's picture, which though it cost me 30*l.* yet will I have it done." Following Cooper and his brother *Alexander Cooper*, who was of some repute, was a group of English portrait painters, who practised chiefly miniature art, in crayons, water-colours, and sometimes in oil. We need only catalogue their names, *Thomas Flatman, Richard Gibson* the dwarf, *William Gibson* his nephew, and *Edward Gibson*, supposed to be his son; *John Dixon*, a pupil of Kneller, *Alexander Marshall, William Hassel, Matthew Snelling*, and *Mary Beale. John Riley* (B. 1646, D. 1691) claims more particular notice. He was of a modest nature, and cast into shade by the presumptuous reputation of Lely, and Kneller to whom we will presently revert. He painted many excellent portraits, among them a portrait of Charles II., who is said on seeing it to have discouraged the bashful artist by exclaiming, "Is this like me? Then odd's fish I'm an ugly fellow." But if cast down, Riley regained his courage, painted James II. and his Queen, and was appointed court painter to William and Mary. We must not omit also to notice *John Michael Wright* (B. about 1655, D. 1700). He was a native of Scotland, a pupil of Jamesone, and came to England in 1672, when sixteen or seventeen years of age. He is no doubt the "one Wright," whom Pepys mentions rather contemptuously, but he deserves much higher consideration. He painted some excellent portraits.

Tempted aside to continue the succession of English artists, we must return to *Sir Godfrey Kneller,* who followed Lely, and like him, was at the head of his profession, in order that we may show more fully the great influence which these two men exercised upon our art for above half a century. Kneller came to England in 1674 in his twenty-seventh year, and was employed both by Charles II. and James II. He was the most distinguished painter of the reign of William III. and of Queen Anne; and he lived to paint the portrait of George I., who created him a baronet in 1715. He died in 1723, having gleaned a handsome fortune from his numerous sitters.

The sudden blaze of art which illumined the early years of the reign of Charles I. was soon extinguished. Among the causes of its decline —in which political events had undoubtedly for a time the chief share —was the tendency of the age to allegory. Rubens himself had initiated it in his extravagant flatteries of Mary dei Medicis in the Louvre, and in the apotheosis of James at Whitehall, but in Kneller's, and still more so in less able hands, such displays soon descended to vapid inanities.

When a symbol or implement alone sufficed to create a hero or a demi-god, the painter was delivered from the labour of thought to revel in mere bravura of execution, and he became as commonplace as the heroes he represented.

Antonio Verrio, invited to this country by Charles II., was the hero of this art. Walpole calls him "an excellent painter for the sort of subjects in which he was employed, that is without much invention and with less taste his exuberant pencil was ready in pouring out gods, goddesses, kings, emperors and triumphs over those public surfaces on which the eye never rests long enough to criticize, and where one should be sorry to place the works of a better master. I mean ceilings and staircases." For such works Verrio was ably fitted, and while we may despise the sort of art, and be tempted to repeat the sneer of Pope, we ought to do justice to the many qualities which the painter really possessed. His great facility, the ease with which his figures are posed, the appearance of motion, the freshness and decorative look of the surface, were real merits which pleased the age in which he found employment, made him eminent in his own day, and by his popularity led to the further degradation of art. Such works were considered historical, and the portrait painter, who of all men ought to seek individuality, soon began to ape the same manner in his portraiture.

Like the history painter, the portrait painter of the time had a set of stock ideas—attitudes and accessories for his sitters. The ladies, as we have said, figured as goddesses or shepherdesses—it seemed immaterial which was chosen; the men were a compromise, eking out a Roman emperor's habiliments with the large flowing wig of the time and other artistic properties, introduced sparingly or abundantly as the theme or the canvas might warrant. Thus in the portraits of the court beauties, the *innocence* of Nell Gwynne is typified by a lamb and a crook, while she is herself robed in a silken dis-array suitable to a court shepherdess. Another court beauty, perhaps with equal lack of merit, is represented by the court painter with the helmet and shield of the Goddess of Wisdom. This art of historical portraiture reached its climax about the end of the seventeenth century, and Kneller's equestrian portrait of William III. is characteristic of the class.

Thus the noble and dignified portraits of Vandyck, of Mytens and Jansen were succeeded by the affected allegories which Charles II. had learnt to admire during his long banishment to the Continent and sojourn at the French Court; and the degeneracy had culminated at the period we have now reached—the reign of George I.—of which Walpole says, "No reign, since the arts have been in any estimation, produced fewer works that will deserve the attention of posterity." Of the painters *Charles Jervas* (B. 1675, D. 1739) must be noticed, if only as the intimate friend of Pope, and the vain head of the poor mediocrities of his time, but nevertheless a scholar and a gentleman. With him was contemporary *Jonathan Richardson* (B. 1665, D. 1745), whose portraits were valued for the truth and firmness with which the heads were delineated, and *Sir James Thornhill* (B. 1676, D. 1734), whose decorations of public buildings, avoiding many of the errors of Verrio, are well known, particularly the cupola of St. Paul's Cathedral and the hall of Greenwich Hospital.

At the commencement of the reign of George II. Jervas and Richardson were at the head of their schools; before its termination Reynolds was fast rising into fame. Minor painters, whose works are now forgotten or little known, find some record in Walpole. Of these men *Francis Knapton* (B. 1698, D. 1788) was distinguished for his portraits in crayons, and was appointed painter to the Dilettanti Society, and the keeper of the king's pictures. There is a large portrait group in oil by him at Hampton Court, of the Princess of Wales and her family—a matter-of-fact work, without much painter like feeling.

Thomas Hudson (B. 1701, D. 1779), remembered as the master of Reynolds, was the pupil of Richardson, and, succeeding Jervas, then became the fashionable portrait painter of his day, though it strongly marks the degradation of art, that he, like his meaner followers, could only paint the head of his sitter. Northcote says that "after having painted the head Hudson's genius failed him, and he was obliged to employ Van Aachen (Vanhaken) to put in the shoulders and to finish the drapery, of both of which he was himself incapable." *Francis Hayman, R.A.* (B. 1708, D. 1776), linked himself with the memories of our own time by his paintings in Vauxhall Gardens. He was a scene painter, and was much employed in designs for book illustrations. Edward Edwards, in his *Anecdotes of Painting*, 1808, describes Hayman as having attained "a very considerable power in his art, and as unquestionably the best historical painter in the kingdom before the arrival of Cipriani." His work, "The Finding of Moses," which he presented to the Foundling Hospital, may be seen there. He lived to be one of the first members of the Royal Academy. *Francis Cotes, R.A.* (B. 1725, D. 1770), must be added to this short list. He, too, enjoyed a reputation in his day. Walpole says "that he arrived at uncommon perfection in crayons." He painted the Queen, with the Princess Royal, then an infant, on her lap. Hogarth, who did not love any of the portrait painters, declared, probably not without a little malice, that Cotes was a better portrait painter than Reynolds—an opinion which posterity was far from sharing. *Allan Ramsay* (B. 1709, D. 1784), the only son of the author of the *Gentle Shepherd*, merits a high place with the foregoing. His portraits are honest and manly, and, if wanting in grace, are free from all affectation, well and powerfully painted. Of the landscape painters who were contemporary with the men we have just mentioned, we propose to say a few words in a subsequent chapter as introductory to the great men of that school who succeeded them.

CHAPTER II.

WILLIAM HOGARTH.

"When things are at the worst they will mend," and truly things were at the worst, so far as art goes, when sturdy *William Hogarth* (born in London, November 10, 1697), after passing honestly through his seven years' apprenticeship as an engraver on silver plate, began to think for himself, and found that copper, under the influence of true art, far transcended silver merely graven with fine lines and dead repetitions. Began to think for himself!—here is the true master-key—began to look at the world around him instead of at dark canvases, pictures over which Time had swung his scythe, and which, if once good, men had so botched and tinkered, so toned and begrimed, that their original identity was lost and gone; began to think that gods and goddesses had had their day, and that we might have had enough, even of saints and martyrs at second hand—that even "Beer-street" and "Gin-lane" might be made to teach better morality, and would certainly lend themselves to form a fresher art; "grew so profane," he says of himself, "as to admire *nature* beyond the finest productions of art," and acknowledged he saw, or fancied, delicacies in *the life* so far surpassing the utmost efforts of imitation that when he drew comparison in his mind he could not help uttering blasphemous expressions against the divinity of even Raphael Urbino, Correggio, or Michael Angelo. For this, however, he adds, "though my brethren have most unmercifully abused me, I hope to be forgiven."

Here was the man wanted; the reformer the art needed; one who was determined not to follow, but to lead; one who had formed his art upon the observation of nature only, and who on that ground protested against schools which he called academies. His nature and character well fitted him for the task he had imposed upon himself; even his education as an artist proved the most suitable for him. A man almost of the people, mixing with the artisan, the manufacturer, and the tradesman

c

daily and hourly; watching their weaknesses and foibles, studying their dispositions and characters, and "habituating himself," as he tells us, "with a view of making new designs, which was his first and greatest ambition, to the exercise of a sort of technical memory;" and again we learn how, "by repeating in his own mind the parts of which the objects were composed, he could by degrees combine and set them down with his pencil." The materials for his "Southwark Fair," the "March to Finchley," the Election Series, the Idle and Industrious Apprentices, were found among the objects by which he was surrounded in his work and everyday life—they were the *nature* which was to be his guide and teacher. It is wonderful how long men go on repeating the thoughts of others—sometimes unconsciously, sometimes of set purpose—since few dare to be original, and there is safety in precedent. It therefore needed one who would break altogether with the old, both in subject and practice, and take a new departure in another course. And this Hogarth notably did.

Let us describe our reformer as he appears portrayed by himself, and see the man and his work together. Let us examine the life-size portrait head in the National Gallery. It shows a different school of art to that of the periwigged worthies of his predecessors—an honest, homely, matter-of-fact Englishman; not the least idealized; his short nose a little inclined to turn up; his round open face, his clear blue eye and rather firmly closed lips, are characteristic of one who might be a warm friend or a bitter enemy, and who did not shirk what he saw in his glass as he wrought to display himself for posterity. His light hair is closely cut or shaven, for no doubt in the afternoon, as he would repudiate singularity, he wears his wig with flowing curls, like other men of his time, but in the morning, and at his easel, he is more at his ease in his furred cap. Poor ill-remunerated Wilson, whose portrait hangs in the same gallery, wears a night-cap; but Hogarth, now well-to-do, for he has reached his forty-eighth year, has a furred cap and tassel. Yet in this there is no pretension; he is evidently represented as he sat at his work.

Had he been quarrelsome in his boyhood, or in his 'prentice years, and got that deep scar in his forehead? We know no mention by his biographers of how it occurred. Yet there it is, like old Oliver's warts and pimples duly and literally rendered. His favourite pursuits are also shown. Three volumes of Swift's works lie before him—Swift, whose satirical view of human nature so much resembled his own—his palette also, and painted on it "the line of beauty and of grace," of which he knew little and wrote much; and then in front of him, as plain and homely as himself, and, no doubt, given, like his master, to bark and bite occasionally—there, as large as life sits his favourite companion, his dog—no sleek spaniel or slim greyhound, but a bandy-legged black nosed pug, not without some similarity to his master. If we add to this his figure as seen in a smaller full-length portrait, he would appear to have been short and thick-set, a little inclined to bandy-leggedness himself, and altogether a man from whose outward appearance we should never expect the graceful and beautiful, or the refined in art. We have described his portrait, not solely to paint the man, but to mark the age of puerilities passing away, and truth and good sense revived by him—a new manner, which was to result in a great school of portrait painters, originating and derived from him. For as he has painted his very self in his own portraits, so it was with the portraits of others, whether of his wife, Jane, or of honest benevolent Captain Coram, whose good heart and kindly nature look forth from Hogarth's canvas as truly as from any written biography. We are told, *à propos* of his wife's portrait, that she one day observed, touching his " Analysis of Beauty," " It is one thing, my dear, to scribble about beauty, but quite another to paint it ; " which gave occasion to Garrick's pert remark, "I suppose he writes from his own ideas and paints from his wife."

As to the man we have described, he looks well calculated to stand all the revilings of his contemporaries, the goddess and shepherdess school, the Roman Emperor period of portrait painters and their patrons, the collectors of fiddle-brown saints and ropy-tendoned martyrs, of pseudo-Titians and second-hand Raphaels, for truly these did unmercifully abuse him all his days ; nor was he slack in his retaliation with both pen and graver. A man with little sense of the refined and beautiful, little feeling for form, and unfitted to revive art in that direction, but with a deep love of truth and nature, and a keen satirical vein for follies, foibles, and humbug of every kind. He had, nevertheless, his own views of art, was gifted with the power to express them, and was destined to lay the foundations of a new school, whose originality is yet distinct, and in a marked degree different from any other school of modern Europe. He thought, we are told, " that both writers and painters had, in the historical style, totally overlooked that intermediate class of subjects which lie between the sublime and the picturesque, and he wished to compose pictures on canvas similar to the representations on the stage, and that they should be tried by the same test and criticised by the same criterion," and by this criterion he must himself be judged if we would fully understand his merits.

Let us from this point of view examine his greatest work—the pictorial drama of " The Marriage à la Mode." It is divided into six acts or tableaux, depicting the sacrifice of youth to money and rank, with its sad moral. In the first pictorial act the preliminaries of the barter are arranged by the conspiring parents. On the one side the miserly worshipper of money prepares to sacrifice his daughter ; on the other the proud possessor of ancestral honours bargains for his son. In the second act the marriage has taken place, and we are introduced to the domestic life of the ill-assorted pair—the debauched husband utterly indifferent to his young wife, and she coolly contemptuous of her imbecile husband—their establishment artfully shown to be one of riot, debauchery, and waste. The third tableau represents the wife's rapid progress in all the worst vices of her new rank. She has adopted the foreign custom of receptions in her dressing-room ; foreign artists warble voluptuous airs as she sips her coffee ; mock antiquities, the costly rubbish of yesterday's auction, lie littered around ; and her paramour, a favoured lover in her ill-omened union, pours poisonous flattery into her willing ear. The fourth act is cunningly interpolated to give a glance at the vile life of the profligate husband, the betrayer of youth, himself betrayed, and suffering the foul curse of his crimes. The piece now hurries to its fearful climax. In the fifth picture, expediency and sin bear their first fruit ; the wife has been enticed by her paramour from a masked ball to a house of ill-fame ; she is followed by her husband, who, insensible to love, is sensitive to honour, and in a struggle with his wife's seducer is foully slain ; the lurid light, the escaping murderer, the arrival of the watch, all contribute to the truthful terror of the scene, and lead us to the last act of this pictorial tragedy, where the wife poisons herself on hearing that her guilty lover has died by the hands of justice.

Now it is true that serial pictures were not new to art ; religious subjects had been often so treated, as in the Seven Sorrows of the Virgin, or the several acts of the Passion of our Lord. But the novelty of Hogarth's work consisted in the painter being the inventor of his own drama, poet as well as painter, and in the way in which all the parts are made to tend to a dramatic whole, each picture dependent on the other, and all the details illustrative of the complete work ; the same characters recur again and again, moved in different tableaux with varied passions ; one moral running through all ; the beginning finding its natural climax in the end. Another novelty is the wonderful way in which all the objects in the picture tend to illustrate the story, and yet are so strictly appropriate in themselves. Appropriate backgrounds have been common in all good art, and in the Dutch school, on which Hogarth built his practice, Teniers and Ostade in low life, Terburg and Metzu in more genteel society, give us truthful glimpses of the scenery and into the dwellings of their countrymen, making us well acquainted with their home life. In Hogarth's pictures not only is the background as truly appropriate to time and place as in the best works of the Dutch masters, but it possesses the additional merit of adding to the dramatic interest of his work, illustrating in a series of episodes the current story of the piece. This may be more minutely shown by a description from the marriage series —say, the first scene.

As we have before remarked in this first picture the two conspiring parents are consulting on their mutual sacrifice. The father of the intended bride, a mean-looking vulgar citizen, with his whole soul fixed on money-getting, sits opposite the noble parent of his future son-in-law— sits uneasily on the edge of his chair, his sword between his legs, with the out-of-place appearance of a cur in a drawing-room. He carefully eyes the parchment deed of settlement drawn between "The Right Hon. Lord Viscount" and himself, purchasing rank for his child with gold, from which he unwillingly parts. Facing him the peer sits proudly erect, his coroneted crutch by his chair, his hereditary gout propped on soft cushions, his family genealogy unrolled beside him, springing from the loins of that father of untold sons, William the Conqueror. Standing behind the table is the wretched sinister-looking starved clerk of the wealthy citizen; what a miserly pittance does he pay his servants! He pushes the golden bribe towards the peer, but with it, as part payment, presents a mortgage on the lordly domains, which, appealing to the condescension he is showing, the titled beggar repudiates. On the other side of the picture the happy pair are seated on a sofa, and grouped with them the family lawyer, who has prepared the deeds. The future husband and wife sit back to back; no love is lost between them; no semblance of love is even thought necessary. He, it is true, loves himself, and glances at his own foppish appearance in the glass; his spindle shanks and patched glands tell their own tale of his debauchery and profligacy. He is striving to take a pinch of snuff with elegance, and to display the brilliant on his finger, while she, listlessly passing the wedding ring backwards and forwards on her handkerchief, looks the picture of sullen submission, and listens sulkily to the *badinage* of the lawyer, Counsellor Silvertongue. At the feet of the pair, a happy illustration of their future life, are two coupled hounds, the one ever desirous of moving when the other would be still.

So far as to the intention of the picture, with a few of its accessories; but the background, which is studiously contrived to fill its part in the drama, must also be described. The scenic walls of the apartment are covered with pictures—the noble owner is a man of taste: here are the " black masters," Hogarth so much decried; and what do they represent? Subjects surely not chosen for their beauty; not chosen as objects by which we would live surrounded; scenes of blood and crime—Cain killing Abel, Prometheus with his gnawing vulture, Judith as executioner of Holofernes, St. Lawrence roasting on his gridiron: these and like works, bearing no doubt names of high fame, and reputed of costly value, stamp the man of expensive habits. In the centre is the grandiose portrait of some noble ancestor, the very epitome of that vile school of French art which Hogarth abhorred. It is *au grand monarque*, the empty head covered with a long and flowing wig, the body clothed in a cuirass, round the neck the Order of the Golden Fleece, on the breast blue and red ribbons—the right hand so placed as to show the jewelled ring, the left clasping, not a sword—that were too mean a weapon—but the thunderbolt of Jove. In the air above this hero the winds of heaven are personified blowing east and west at the same time to do his bidding, a cannon blazes at his feet, the ball painted in its flight. Here is a picture such as the fashion-mongers of that day excelled in painting, and such as Hogarth hated and lived to put an end to. The ceiling of the room is also painted, as was often the case, in absurd defiance of sense and truth—such being frequently the work of foreigners, who palmed on the confiding barbarians of Britain the sheerest nonsense as high art. It represents—strange subject for a ceiling !—Pharaoh and his hosts overwhelmed in the Red Sea, and may have been intended by Hogarth not only to satirize the false taste of the time, but accessorily to point out the end of overweening pride. There is in the background yet another incident heightening the dramatic interest of the tale. The citizen's lawyer looks out of the window, in his hand is a " plan of the new building for the Right Hon.," and he gazes with astonishment on the structure itself—a front of portico and column, half finished, and evidently remaining so for want of the money the settlements he is making are to supply ; for the scaffold remains on the walls, yet no workmen are there, while lazy valets are grouped listlessly about the half-shapen stones.

Such, then, is Hogarth's background, cumulating its incidents and adding to the interest of the first scene of his drama, and in the succeeding pictures of the series, this power finds even stronger illustration. But it is not our purpose to extend the description of the works of Hogarth, or, indeed, of any other master, further than is essential to the elucidation of the modes of pictorial treatment and habits of thought of those who, from any cause, have influenced the formation of the British school. For this reason Hogarth has been particularly dwelt upon, in the desire to show how largely he worked a change for the better, by influencing his successors to look to nature for their art—to despise mere repetitions of stale subjects from masters long bygone, and thoughts diluted over and over again. He treated men and women as human beings, and felt that the commonest phase of existing society might be rendered pictorially interesting. This, now it has been accomplished, may be thought a small thing ; and as the courtiers sneered at Columbus, when he broke the egg to poise it, so some may now undervalue what Hogarth effected. But experience daily proves how tenaciously men cling to error, when sanctioned by high authority ; and it is well to remember that years after, Reynolds himself, so original both as a painter and thinker, held that the "Death of Wolfe," being a heroic subject, should be treated—not in the costume of the day—not as our soldiers fought on the heights of Abraham, but with classical undraped forms, and was only convinced of his error by the success of West's picture. In his other art-qualities, Hogarth, though educated as an engraver rather than as a painter, was by no means deficient. His execution, though solid, was more varied than that of his contemporaries—his handling easy and facile, from which cause, added to his having used a simple vehicle for his colours, his pictures have not greatly suffered, except perhaps by a sort of retributive justice at the hands of vampers up of "black masters," who have endeavoured by repeated varnishings to reduce the works of their old enemy to the same dark complexion as those he condemned. The composition and grouping of his figures, while eminently natural, are agreeably adapted to the display of his subject. His general colouring, never meretricious, is always sober and true, sometimes even excellent; the flesh of the individual heads, often felicitously handled, interchanging the warm tints and greys without appearance of muddiness.

The *drawing* of Hogarth, like that of all our British painters, has been unceasingly, but somewhat unfairly decried. The term drawing is used by many to express two distinct qualities, and this has led to a confusion of ideas, from which much of the abuse of our artists has arisen. It is used indifferently to define the sense of what is most refined and beautiful in form, and also the power of imitating form, that is, objects. Now in the former sense there is no doubt that Hogarth was deficient, and notwithstanding his good opinion of his own powers, he was certainly not qualified to attempt subjects of high art and pure form ; his historical pieces were worse than failures ; his "Sigismunda," perhaps, beneath criticism ; and it is doubtful even if the sense of the harmonies of fine form were not wanting in his nature, as the harmonies of music are to many ears, and the harmonies of colour are to the colour-blind. But in the other sense of the term, that is, the power of creating or imitating forms suitable to his own range of art, he was in every way a master draughtsman. Who could improve the action or motion of his figures, or their physical expression? Take as an instance, among others, that branded profligate *débauché*, the husband, in the second picture of the marriage series. Mark the debilitated curve of the body, the helpless feebleness of the outstretched legs, the poise of the head, hanging weakly on the muscles of the back of the neck, the characteristic outline of the thin emaciated legs—in short, the whole action as well as the individual parts of the figure ; and it will be acknowledged that the artist was no feeble draughtsman who could produce such a work as this, and numerous others in his pictures, which from time to time have served our lecturers on anatomy with subjects to illustrate motion, attitude, and expression.

Moreover, Hogarth's power of imitating and his memory of form and expression, whether arising from the mode in which he tells us he exercised it or not, must have been very great. For many of his most felicitous creations it is obvious he could never have used a model. It needed not that he should have told us such was his practice. The curious habit of sketching upon his nail as a help to memory could assist him but little, and he must have possessed a strong added power of retaining, combining, and reproducing the incidents he had seen, or the characters he met with and made the subjects of his study. In conclusion, it is not too much to say of this great artist, that in the subjects he treated he has had no equal among his many successors, and that he still stands alone and unrivalled, justifying every epithet of his friend Garrick's tender muse—

> " Farewell, great painter of mankind,
>   Who reach'd the noblest point of Art ;
> Whose pictur'd morals charm the mind,
>   And through the eye correct the heart.
>
> " If genius fire thee, reader, stay ;
>   If Nature touch thee, drop a tear ;
> If neither move thee, turn away,
>   For Hogarth's honour'd dust lies here."

Hogarth married clandestinely, in 1730, the daughter of Sir James Thornhill, the painter. He died childless at his house in Leicester Fields, 26th October, 1764, from an attack of dropsy, and was buried in Chiswick churchyard. That he had not amassed wealth by his art we may assume from the fact that his widow received from the Royal Academy a pension of 40*l.* a year from 1787 to 1789, when she died at the age of eighty years.

We have seen some paintings that connect themselves with the name of Hogarth which it may not be out of place to describe here. They are a curious relic of Hogarth's time, perhaps even some of the work of his hand, and are in a house, No. 75 Dean Street, Soho, once the residence of Sir James Thornhill. Entering this house from the front door, now closed, you are opposite the bottom of a flight of stairs occupying three sides of the hall, the fourth side, on the first floor, forming a passage or gallery leading past the front room to two apartments lighted from the back of the house. Up to the height of this gallery the lower floor has been painted to imitate channelled stone-work, terminating on the first floor level with a richly-ornamented stone stringing ; above that level, on the wall opposite the gallery, is a painted representation of a colonnaded corridor, having two arched openings between coupled columns with an ornamented balustrade, and a third arched opening between columns opposite the windows. The other side of the corridor is represented as open to the sky; above the entablature which the columns support is a covered ceiling, and in the centre an oval perspective of a balustrade, opening also to the sky with figures looking over it towards the spectator. But the principal interest in the work is concentrated on groups of figures looking out from the arched openings below. In each of these openings there are five figures of small life-size, painted with a free hand and much skill, and of the Thornhill period. They call to mind some of the figures in Hogarth's pictures ; one lady especially may have been Lady Thornhill, from the likeness to Mrs. Hogarth, and all have, more or less, the appearance of portraits, while they are very unlike, in treatment and execution, the works by Thornhill's hand at Greenwich and at Hampton Court. One of the figures is a black servant with a turban, such as we see in the " Marriage à la Mode."

It is traditional that Hogarth ran away with Miss Thornhill from this house. He most probably had ready access to it to enable him to win her affections, and we know that he studied in Thornhill's academy. Did he work on these paintings under her father, and do they represent any of the knight's family? These are interesting questions, and the work itself possesses much interest in relation to English art. The house is now in the occupation of a large manufacturer of tinned wares, and is used as a store for these goods, with which it is filled in every direction. The picture has been painted in oil on the walls, which have been plastered with a somewhat rough surface, then deeply saturated with oil, and painted over with a full pencil. It would be a work of great difficulty to remove the paintings, which thirty years ago were in good condition, though the browns had a little broken up. They would now require a careful restoration, partly because an injudicious endeavour has been made to preserve them by glueing brown paper over the figures, and partly because of the inevitable wear and tear they have undergone in consequence of their position.

CHAPTER III.

THE century which forms the subject of this work witnessed a wide-spread love of art among all classes, and a corresponding increase in the number of its professors, as well as a great change in the relations between the art-teacher and the art-student. The means of studying such art as was practised in England before the time of Lely and Kneller, cannot be very clearly traced; but it seems probable from such slight notices as incidentally occur, that the youth entering the profession of a painter was formally apprenticed, in the ordinary manner, to some master or artist of more or less eminence. For his master, and with him, the young pupil laboured, and was gradually initiated into all his methods—secrets as they were then deemed. He learnt the mode of preparing his canvas or panel, of grinding and tempering his colours, of mixing his tints, of executing his first and second painting, and the use of the transparent glaze in finishing. He learnt the mechanical part of his profession rather than its great principles, and thus trained, the apprentice naturally followed in the footsteps and the methods of his master.

On the Continent better principles of teaching had long prevailed. The academic system was established in the great Italian cities where art flourished, so early as the middle of the fourteenth century; and both the *atelier* system and the apprentice system had been used to train and keep up a succession of artists in all the great foreign schools. We have just described the latter system, under which the pupil commenced his teaching in the drudgery which is now the work of the artist's colourman. The *atelier* system, which arose out of it, became almost a necessity in an age when great works were usually confided to individual artists. It originated in Italy where the decoration of a church or a palace was the work of one great master, who drew around him many youths, some partly educated, others of more matured proficiency, who were employed, not on their own inventions, but in carrying out the designs of their master. Thus we learn that Raphael had in his studio five or six men of great talent, who not only enlarged his sketches into cartoons, but actually completed them on the walls. In Flanders, also, Rubens with his pupils and imitators form another remarkable example of the working of the *atelier* system ; their works in the gallery at Antwerp represent his art in many phases, mostly of degenerate extravagance. Of these systems, no one, at the time of which we write, had taken any firm root in England. Our native artists were few and unknown—they were not supposed capable of competing with foreigners—they had only just begun to stir themselves to provide some established means of study, and some link of professional union ; and in this effort they were joined by many whose art was chiefly developed in the meaner wants of manufacture. The sign-painters found full employment, and several painters who attained distinction in art arose from among them. Coach-painters, also, when the panels of carriages were decked with loves and graces, aspired to the highest walks in art, and so did pre-eminently scene-painters, who then, as in our own day, numbered many artists who have reached high distinction. Add to these, engravers, designers, modellers, and chasers, and we see how large a number of men, though filling different positions in art, must all have equally lacked the means of instruction essential to their progress.

Portraiture was early the prevailing fashion, and all had their portraits painted ; one renowned foreign artist succeeding the other, as we have already narrated, to whom all the great and distinguished resorted. They brought over their pupils and countrymen as their assistants, according to the Continental practice, and we find also, that some few of our own countrymen sought to share the advantages to be derived from the same pupilage. Jamesone had studied in the *atelier* of Rubens, at Antwerp ; Dobson, if not the pupil of Vandyck, was generously assisted by him ; Greenhill and Davenport were taught by Lely ; and Kneller, who appears to have exclusively employed foreigners, made the first practical attempt, in 1711, to found an institution, of which he was to be the head, for giving professional instruction to students in art. About the same time, also, several other short-lived societies or clubs were formed with the same object. In 1724, Sir James Thornhill, our own countryman, opened an art academy at his house, and submitted to Lord Halifax, then Prime Minister, a detailed proposal to establish a royal academy of art. Next, Vanderbank converted an old Presbyterian meeting-house into an academy, which struggled on for a short existence, owing to the attractions of the living model. William Shipley then succeeded in establishing a school, known as the St. Martin's

Lane Academy, in which, for nearly thirty years, all our best artists studied.

That the artists themselves urgently felt the want of some such institution is proved by the efforts they made to found one, no less than by the degraded art of the time. Portraiture alone flourished, and the portrait painters were unable to do more than paint the heads of their sitters, leaving the hands, draperies, figures, etc., to be added by another hand. Vanhacken, or Vanaken, a really clever man who came to London from Antwerp, and died here in 1749, was exclusively employed in this way. Finally, two rival painters agreed to retain him entirely in their service by paying him eight hundred guineas a year, to the confusion of their brother artists who could not do without his assistance.

The Dilettanti Society and the Society of Arts, by the influence of their publications and the premiums they offered, endeavoured to stimulate and reward young artists, and the former society proposed to join the artists in founding an academy which they were prepared to build. The Duke of Richmond also opened his gallery, supplied with fine casts from the antique, as a place for study, and some of the chief artists were its frequenters.

All these efforts did, no doubt, leave some impress on the state of the arts; but the artists felt another great want. They demanded something more than a nurse and a teacher; they were emulous of public applause, which they desired to seek by the exhibition of their works. Without the means of studying their profession, and without a public appreciating art, the artists seemed powerless to help themselves. But the means of exhibition, the second great impediment which barred the progress of native art, along with the proper facility for study, eventually found a solution together—the one proving the direct road to the other. In the year 1745, Hogarth and seventeen of the most reputed artists presented their best works to the Foundling Hospital, then recently established, with a view to make their powers known, though not, it would be unjust to infer, without charitable motives; and to their gratified surprise, so great was the attraction of their pictures, that the hospital, then as now out of the range of fashion, became the gay lounge of the *beau monde*. St. Bartholomew's Hospital was also gratuitously decorated in the same manner. The artists were elated by their success. They could not be expected to provide continued excitement for the public by the gift of their best works; but having discovered that there existed a large love of amusement and novelty, if not of art, they were able so far to make the experiment subservient to their purpose, that from it arose the permanent establishment of annual exhibitions.

The Society of Arts lent their great room, and in 1760 the artists opened there the first exhibition for the sale of their works. The admission

was free, and the room crowded. A second year of great success followed, and a third exhibition the next year in Spring Gardens, where a
charge of one shilling was made for admission, confirmed the scheme;
and in 1765 the artists, comprising mainly the body of painters, associated
together by their studies at Shipley's school, obtained a charter of
incorporation; and, with still increasing success and increasing receipts,
held their exhibition in 1766, and again in 1767. But with this success
the seeds of dissension were largely mixed. This was increased by the
discussion of plans for extending the objects of the young incorporation,
and by the inherent defects of its constitution, and in the end the Incorporated Society of Artists was dissolved, many members of the body
becoming foundation members of the Royal Academy. In fact the
seceders from the society were mainly instrumental in founding the new
institution, for this small though distinguished body of artists found access
to King George III., and the young monarch who looked favourably on
art encouraged them to submit a detailed plan of the academy for which
they sought his support. Of this his Majesty not only approved, but,
placing himself at its head, he assured the artists of his protection and
favour. The royal approval was, however, the private act of the King.
It conferred no legal authority or obligation. The institution then founded
is not a corporate body; it holds no charter under the Great Seal; nor
is the approval of any of its acts by the Crown, or the election of its
members, certified by the signature of a Secretary of State, which would
be necessary to give it constitutional recognition and vitality. Yet in its
character the Academy is no less a national institution and the representative of the national art, and its members cannot dissociate their
privileged position from the duties and responsibilities which it entails
upon them.

The scheme of the Royal Academy includes the maintenance of
schools free to all who have mastered the rudiments of art and are of
good character; exhibitions free to all whose works possess sufficient
merit; and to this is added the generous provision, that out of the
surplus arising from exhibitions, after defraying the expenses of the
schools and providing for future contingencies, the claims of necessitous
artists, without distinction, are liberally considered. The Academy consists
of forty-two members (though only thirty-six were appointed at the
commencement), painters, sculptors, and architects by profession, to
whom two engravers have been added; and, avoiding the error of the
Incorporated Society, the management is placed exclusively in this body,
which is self-elective. The only qualification for admission is fair moral
character, high professional reputation, the age of at least twenty-five
years, and residence in great Britain. The government is in the general
assembly, and in the President and Council of ten members, one-half

changing each year, and every academician serving in rotation. The officers comprise a secretary, a keeper, who supervises the instruction in the schools, and a treasurer and librarian, all elected by the members. Certain academicians and associates are also annually selected by the Council to superintend the teaching in the various schools, month by month, and this to a great extent represents the system adopted in Paris and elsewhere, where the various distinguished artists have *ateliers* of their own. Professors are also appointed to lecture on architecture, sculpture, painting, and anatomy. The Academy further includes a second class of members called associates, the number of whom is practically unlimited, but this body now consists of thirty-four members, four of whom are engravers, and it is only added to under exceptional circumstances. This body has no share in the government of the Academy, but enjoys all the other advantages it can offer, and from it alone the academicians are elected.

Such were some of the chief features of the original institution, which was established on the 10th December, 1768, and they have been maintained to the present time. Thus a permanent institution was founded which provided for the maintenance of efficient schools, for annual exhibitions, and, supplying a want quite as urgent in the interests of art, united the most eminent of our native professors, associated them in a generous rivalry, gave them the recognition and rank which election to such bodies professionally confers before all other distinctions, and, by the impetus thus supplied, gradually raised the arts to the foremost rank in public estimation.

The creation of the new institution seemed opportune. Our artists who had sought instruction on the Continent soon found that resource closed to them by the wars which ensued, while foreign artists were equally excluded here, and the interchange of engravings and works of art ceased. The new Academy came into existence at the very happiest possible time for the art of this country, and rapidly gained a high place in public favour ; its exhibitions were visited by all classes, and all the most eminent painters of the day were included in its ranks.

CHAPTER IV.

THE preceding chapter has sketched the circumstances leading to the foundation of the Royal Academy, thenceforth to exercise so great an influence on British art. At the time of its establishment three great native painters flourished, and already stood high in the public estimation. They each became members of the new academy, one of them, Reynolds, its first president, and their marked genius had great influence during the period in which they painted, and left an impression on the school which is only just passing away.

These three eminent men, who began a new epoch in art, are *Richard Wilson*, to whom we shall devote this chapter, *Joshua Reynolds*, and *Thomas Gainsborough.* As the first-named was fifty-four years of age, the second forty-five, and the third forty-one, on the establishment of the Royal Academy, it is evident that neither their merits nor their defects can be attributed to its teaching. It affords some insight, too, into the nature of the patronage of art at that time in England, that all the three began their career as portrait painters. Wilson lived by his portraits until his thirty-sixth year. Reynolds ended as he began. Gainsborough through life was largely indebted to portraiture for his income, and in the opinion of some of his contemporaries, as of our own, for his fame also. Two other portrait painters, eminent in their day, and considered at the top of their profession, were still in full practice—Hudson and Ramsay. Richardson had just withdrawn into a literary retirement. Of him Walpole says, "that his men want dignity, his women grace," adding—a poor compliment to the artist!—"the good sense of the nation is characterized in his portraits;" and worse still: "full of theory and profound reflections on art. he drew nothing well below the head, and was void of imagination. His attitudes, draperies, and backgrounds are totally insipid and unmeaning." It may be added that his mantle descended upon his pupil Hudson, who was all his master was, with a dash of insipidity instead of good sense. Ramsay had been appointed the Court painter the year before the foundation of the Royal Academy. His unaffected manly portraits, though their merits do not rise higher, earned him this distinction. In the International Exhibition of 1862, his portrait of the Duke of Argyll contrasted very favourably with the whole-length of Pius VII., considered to be one of Lawrence's best works ; yet hung close to Ramsay's, it appeared by comparison very thin and washy. Hogarth's portraits, as we have said, were truthful and characteristic, but neither his portrait of himself, nor that of his benevolent friend, Captain Coram, deserve higher praise as works of art, and in his female portraiture grace and refinement are entirely wanting. Mrs. Hogarth's portrait shows her simply as a good wifely person ; while Mrs. Doughty's somewhat justifies the story current in the family, that on their complaint of its want of beauty, the painter, in a fit of anger, drew his knife, of which it bears the mark, across his work, and could hardly be so far appeased by the apologies and intercessions of friends as to permit the portrait to be restored. There was then at least room for improvement in portraiture.

We have thought it well to defer till this chapter upon our first great landscape painter, that part of our summary of art which refers to the condition of landscape painting in England, and its connexion with the epoch we are now approaching.

Landscape painting was slow to receive the impulse given to its more fashionable rival, portraiture. The great change wrought by the genius of Hogarth had not yet extended to landscape. It does not appear that he had himself any particular predilection for it, or that he practised it, further than to paint backgrounds to some few of his pictures. Speaking of *George Lambert*, the scene painter, (B. 1710, D. 1765,) Walpole says :—" In a country so profusely beautified with the amenities of Nature, it is extraordinary that we have produced so few good painters of landscape." But there seems slight ground for wonder, since up to this period few original painters in any branch of art had arisen, and as was the case with regard to portrait painting, the scant encouragement given to art, of whatever class, had mostly fallen to the share of foreigners. Lambert almost always imitated Poussin, and though he was esteemed above the painters of his time, he is only remembered by his scenic reputation, and as the founder of the " Beaf-steak Club." Of this day also were *The Smiths of Chichester,* whose well-known names have lived to our own times. These three brothers, William (B. 1707, D. 1764), George, the most distinguished (B. 1714, D. 1776), and John (B. 1717, D. 1764), shared, in their lifetime, a great reputation, which was spread and sustained by the talented engravings of Woollett, Elliott, Peake, and other artists, who we now regret were not employed upon works of a higher class. The brothers formed a sort of domestic academy. William began in portrait, and later painted landscape as well as fruit and flowers. George, and his younger brother John who died in the prime of life, painted landscape. Fashion patronized them, and the critics classed them with Claude and Poussin, of whom they were mere imitators. They painted the sweet scenery surrounding Chichester, seeing Nature only by the borrowed light of these masters, and distorting her homely truths, by attempted classic compositions in their manner. George's works fetched higher prices than Richard Wilson's, and from him he successfully carried away the premium in a competition at the Society of Arts. Though he could claim no influence in the progress of landscape painting, we willingly admit that his works were often pleasing, and possessed merits which might well find admirers among his contemporaries. He is now forgotten, notwithstanding their extravagant praises.

In marine painting, a branch of the landscape painter's art which might have been supposed to appeal most directly to the national tastes, two foreigners, the Vandeveldes, found much employment under the last two sovereigns of the Stuart family, and fostered a few pupils and followers. *Peter Monamy* (B. 1670, D. 1749), if not their pupil, was an imitator of their art, which his own has been said to have equalled. His execution is good, and his knowledge of art considerable. He has an excellent traditional method, with little professional artifice. There is a picture by him at Hampton Court, which, though much cracked, is beautifully painted, showing a fine quality of texture, with great precision of touch the calm plane of the ocean level receding into the extreme distance, without that set scenic effect of passing cloud-shadows, which even the best masters have used to obtain the appearance of recession or distance : this work well deserves notice, and might puzzle the best painters of such subjects to rival. *Samuel Scott* (B. 1710, D. 1772), was another artist of the Vandevelde school, whom Walpole calls "the first painter of his age—one whose works will charm in every age;" adding, "if he was second to Vandevelde in sea-pieces, he excelled him in variety." He was indeed a good draftsman, and painted some tolerable topographical views, as well as marine pieces, but his works do not shew any original treatment; they are now little known or esteemed, and he is remembered chiefly as one of Hogarth's companions, in his jovial water-party to Gravesend, in 1732. *Charles Brooking* (B. 1723, D. 1759) is another painter of the same class of subjects, who enjoyed considerable reputation. He attained a clear manipulative excellence, with great truth of delineation, in which he was aided by much knowledge of naval tactics. At Hampton Court Palace there are some excellent specimens of his art. *Richard Paton* (died

1791), and *William James*, two landscape painters, who flourished about this period, have left works of some excellence, but of little genius—the latter, however, has evidently gone to Nature, in an imitative spirit for his subjects, but has failed to give them more than an antiquarian interest. He was in some respects a follower, if not a pupil, of Canaletti, who came to England about 1746, and stayed here two years. The works and reputation of this Italian had preceded him ; the facility and apparent certainty of his execution, and even the mechanical methods of handling displayed in his works, had a charm for those who had been accustomed to the tiresome excellence of the Dutch school, and many of his mechanical modes of imitating Nature were adopted by our landscape painters of this period. Thus we find in the series of subjects on the banks of the Thames by James, that he resorted to ruling for the lines of his buildings, and to the still more mechanically conventional treatment of the ripple in water, as expressed by Canaletti, a treatment also to be found in the works of others. *Dominic Serres, R.A.*, a native of Gascony (B. 1722, D. 1793), was another painter of this class, whose art was acquired here. He was assisted by Brooking, and became much patronized. Serres seems to have left the good old traditional modes of painting, allured probably by the richness of Reynolds's works, and those of the academic body who followed him. The result is, that his pictures are a sad wreck ; the vehicle having cracked all over. We must not, however, confound his works, as some have done, with those of his son, *John Thomas Serres*, who was the husband of the *soi-disant* Princess Olive of Cumberland, and who died in 1825. Painting the same class of subjects, his method of execution was so good that his works show neither hair nor vehicle cracks. His skies are clear and pure, the clouds have been laid on with much impasto, and every touch of the brush left without teasing or repetition.

Such were the men, and such the state of art in this country, when *Richard Wilson*, then in his thirty-sixth year, on paying a visit to Zuccarelli, whom he met at Venice, had his eyes opened by the friendly opinions of that painter as to his own landscape powers, and quitted his pursuit of portrait painting at once and for ever ; not perhaps, to his own profit, but, in so doing, he became the first of the great race of landscape painters, who have made English landscape art so pre-eminent in Europe. Wilson was born in Montgomeryshire, where his father held a small living, on the 1st of August, 1714. He came to London, and, his biographer says, was at a suitable age placed under a painter named Wright. Of Wilson's portrait art we have only seen one or two examples, which certainly rather justify the opinion of Edward Edwards, who, while commending Wilson's power of drawing a head, says that his portraits were not marked by any characteristic qualities. Yet a year or two before Wilson went to Italy, he was engaged to paint a whole-length portrait of the future monarch, and of his brother the Duke of York ; and we can hardly doubt that in an age of mediocrity, Wilson's delicate eye for colour and gradation, his feeling for breadth and power of generalization, would place him at least on a level with his fellow-painters. At any rate, up to his thirty-sixth year, he found means to live by his portraits, and even to save money for his journey to Italy ; while his after-biography shows that his works were beyond the taste of the day, and that with all his talent as a landscape painter, his art only just kept him from absolute want.

The painter whose genius was appreciated at once by Zuccarelli, and whom Vernet generously introduced to the notice of his countrymen, remained six years at Rome ; and on his return to his native country found, as was usual, a foreigner in possession of all the patronage. This was Zuccarelli himself, "whose *pleasing* and *elegant* style," Bryan tells, "was greatly admired, not only in Italy but throughout Europe." Zuccarelli came to England in 1752, and was at once full of commissions. His pictures are found everywhere ; in the Royal collections alone there are more than twenty of his works, while of Wilson's we find not one. Something of this may be due to his rugged independence ; but it is sad to look back on the neglect which awaited him, while such a mere decorative painter as Zuccarelli, whose works are a compound of facile insipidity and theatrical prettiness, with little Nature and less art, was constantly employed, and was enabled, after a few years, to return to his own country with abundant means for his old age.

Wright, his biographer, tells us, on the authority of Field, that Wilson's return excited some interest and much criticism in the art coteries of the time, and that those artists who constituted themselves a self-styled committee of taste, and led the public in art matters, sat in judgment upon him several times, and came to a resolution that his manner was not suited to the English taste, and that if he hoped for patronage he must change it for the lighter style of Zuccarelli. This they voted should be communicated to him by one of their number—Penny, R.A., then a painter of male portraits and pictures of sentiment. A very different estimate is, however, formed of the two landscape painters at the present time, and the advice rather reminds us of the anecdote of Jervas's admiration of his own copy of a picture by Titian, when he delightedly exclaimed, "What would little Tit say to this?"

Wilson sought to represent Nature's general truths as far as the limitations of our art-language permitted. "The skill and genius of the landscape painter," says Reynolds, "will be displayed in showing the *general effect*," and he adds that genius consists in the power of expressing that which employs the pencil of the artist, so that the power of the

D 2

whole may take possession of the mind, and for a while suspend the consideration of the subordinate beauties or defects. Wilson, and with him the then rising British school, despised petty details (no doubt carrying their principle too far), and endeavoured to suppress those commonplace incidents which are to be found in every subject, retaining only such as added to the sentiment of the whole. In this Reynolds, and Gainsborough also were eminently successful; and Wilson's pictures will live with theirs.

Wilson had studied both Poussin and Claude—studied, however, without copying. We do not, therefore, wonder that an eminent critic (the author of *Modern Painters*), who despises much of the art of those painters, should condemn Wilson as corrupted by such study; but, strange to say, he condemns him also as corrupted by the study of *Nature*, because he chose it in the vicinity of Rome, the great city where he first found out the bent of his genius.

But after years of toil in our city, amid the structures mean, although picturesque, Wilson suddenly opened his eyes in this classic land of solemn memories, and strange, wild grandeur. He saw clearly how the fashionable Canaletti had depicted it mechanically and by recipe, and the inane Zuccarelli lowered it to his own feebleness—saw at once how it transcended the subjects and scenery of our former teachers, the Dutch, heretofore the idols of our island painters. Here for six years he patiently laboured to imbibe the spirit of the scenery, to master its grandeur, and to fill his heart with its sublimity. And shall we blame him much if some of his language echoed the voices of those who had laboured in the same field, and who had been, if but imperfectly, lighted with the same glories? Certainly there is this praise due to our countryman; that our landscape art, which had heretofore been derived from the meaner school of Holland, following his great example, looked thenceforth to Italy for its inspiration; that he proved the power of native art to compete, on this ground also, with the art of the foreigner, and prepared the way for the coming men who, embracing Nature as their mistress, were prepared to leave all and follow her.

In treating of Wilson's art we must regard it not only for its own intrinsic excellence, but also in comparison with the art of his time. If his landscapes are what are called "compositions," rather than simply imitative or portrait scenes, such was considered the highest art in his day. How nobly he composed his pictures is shown not only by their natural impression of truth and grandeur, but by comparison with the feeble works of his competitors. Nor will the painter who understands his art ever forego such composition or arrangement of the parts as shall produce the most agreeable lines, the best accidents or contrasts of light and dark or of colour, hiding or suppressing, by these accidents or contrasts, the mean and the ignoble, so as to bring into due importance all those points which, having been strongly impressed on the painter, are likely as strongly to impress the spectator.

We have spoken of Wilson's treatment of landscape as "general" rather than individual, feeling assured that no term of art, as we have already said, is better understood than the term "generalization." By this a painter, without superseding one iota of drawing or character, may convey a simpler, truer, and higher impression of Nature than by the most minutely-detailed imitation. The eyes of all men differ in the power of seeing details ; also in many states of atmosphere all details are absorbed, as in the finest sunsets, and in all deep shadows out of doors in the blaze of a sunlighted day. Moreover the artist has to represent on a few inches of paper, or, at most, a few feet of canvas, besides a foreground where all the objects should be treated with distinctness, a middle distance extending, it may be, over miles of woodland, pasture, or corn, passing away in the far horizon into hills and downs, which in their turn melt into the clouds themselves, or into the unclouded sky. Does not, then, the very scale of his works imply generalization, which, be it remembered, does not mean an attempt to fuse the specific character of any two or more objects into one, but the omission of those details the representation of which, small in themselves, becomes mean or absolutely impossible on the reduced scale of the picture? No one will doubt that he who has thoroughly studied the details of the form will give the general impression of it more truly from that study; but mean and literal imitation certainly degrades art, as much as simple, broad, and general treatment ennobles it. Another fine quality in Wilson's art was the manliness and ease of the handling. The work looks as if he loved it for its own sake, and had moreover the most perfect mastery of his materials. These are qualities which all can appreciate.

In view of the sad failure of many of our English pictures, it would be highly interesting to know what vehicles and pigments were used by the artist, and what was the conduct of his work. How instructive it would be had this been written on the pictures at the time of their execution ; we should now be able to reject pigments and vehicles we have retained and to revive others we have neglected, simply from seeing how particular methods had stood the test of time. In this the worst painters might teach us equally with the best. How greatly it is to be desired that this practice should at once be adopted. By good fortune, we possess indirectly, through Farington, R.A., Wilson's pupil, the mode of painting which his master followed, with an account of his palette and vehicle, and are enabled to test their durability by the present state of his paintings. Respecting the palette and process adopted by Wilson, Wright, his biographer, says, "Some particulars have been communicated to me by a friend, derived, as he tells me, from a very authentic source. According to this statement, the colours used by Wilson were white, Naples yellow, vermilion, light ochre, brown ochre, dark or Roman ochre, lake, yellow lake, lampblack, Prussian blue, ultramarine, burnt sienna. Wilson dead-coloured in a very broad, simple manner, giving a faint idea of the effect and colour intended, without any very bright light or strong dark ; it was put on quite flat and with no handling ; the shadows in the foreground being kept thin and clear, air-tint prevailing. When quite dry, he went over this a second time, heightening every part with colour and deepening the shadows, but keeping them brown, free, loose, and flat, and in a state for finishing, the half-tints still without high-lights. The third time he altered what was necessary in the masses of tint, adding all the necessary sharpness and handling to the different objects, and then giving the finish to his picture. His great care was to bring all the parts of the work together, and not to finish one part before another, so that his pictures should not, as the painters term it, run away with him, and that while working in one part he should introduce that colour into other parts where it suited, or lower the tone to make it suit, so that the different parts might keep company with each other. His air-tint was blue, burnt ochre and light red, with sometimes a little vermilion ; in other cases, he made his air-tints of the lakes and blue ; with the lakes he made his glazing tints on the foreground very rich and warm, and of their full force ; but all this was moderated by tints which he laid on the glazings. If any part was hard, he restored it, by scumbling over it the air-tint suited to the distance of the part, and then he added the finishing touches and sharpness to prevent its being smoky or mealy. A magylph of linseed-oil and mastic varnish, in which the latter predominated, was his usual vehicle, and an oyster-shell served him to contain it. He dead-coloured with Prussian blue, but always finished his sky with ultramarine ; for it was his opinion that no other blue could give the beautiful effect of air."

If we look to Wilson's pictures to test the success of the process, we find that all the solid parts in which little vehicle has been used have stood well and firmly ; that the greens, probably from the use of yellow lake, have faded, and that all the darks have grown much darker than originally painted; and, from the too free use of mastic-magylph, have become very much cracked. This is the case especially in Wilson's more laboured works, as in the "Niobe" and the "Macænas' Villa" in the National Gallery ; less so in the "Apollo and the Seasons," while the "River Dee," belonging to the Duke of Westminster, which is rapidly and solidly painted, has no cracks, except two arising from injuries on the sky.

Wilson was not one of fortune's favourites. His life was a long struggle. He managed only to live, for the last four or five years preceding his retirement, by the help he received as librarian of the Royal Academy. He is represented as a rough diamond, yet he was a man of much classic taste, an accomplished scholar, and, when not suffering under a morbid depression of spirits, courteous in his address and brilliant in his conversation. We are told that he considered fifteen guineas a good price for a three-quarter landscape, yet, even at this mean sum, he found few purchasers, and one day, in a tone of despair or indignation, he asked Barry, R.A., who was much of his own stamp, if he knew any one mad enough to employ a landscape painter, and, if so, would he recommend him ; he had then literally nothing to do, and at this time, though advanced in years, he was in the full possession of his powers. It is pleasant to add that when his health was gradually declining, he was enabled to retire to Llanberis, where he had succeeded to a small property on the death of his brother. There he died suddenly in May, 1782. He had passed many years of his life in the house No. 36, Charlotte Street, Fitzroy Square, the corner of North Street, where at that time there were no houses to impede his view of the clear country beyond. Wilson took a lease of the above house because of the view it afforded of the country away to Hampstead, and of the sun declining in the west. He was accustomed on a fine evening to throw open the window, and to invite his friends to enjoy with him the glowing sunsets behind the Hampstead and Highgate hills. He and Marlowe, the water colour painter, used to sketch the old elms in front of Marylebone Gardens, the Vauxhall of the northern district, now entirely blotted out and forgotten. Woollett, the engraver, subsequently lived in the same house ; two arched windows, long since bricked up, but which then looked towards the north, were the painter's show-room and painting-room, and out of the upper one we may fancy him, with his shaved head and tasselled cap, looking from time to time from under his shading hand to refresh his eye with light—a practice, we are told, that he continually followed.

Dr. Wolcot (Peter Pindar) said, "It is worthy of observation that none of Wilson's pupils caught the manner of their master, and yet a school has arisen, which strongly partakes of it, of which the drawings of my early acquaintance, the generous and giddy Tom Girtin, is an instance." *George Barret, R.A.*, the landscape painter, is, however, a more prominent instance. He was born near Dublin, about 1728, and was probably the son of parents in humble circumstances, since he began life as a colourer of prints for a Dublin publisher, having had some previous instruction in drawing at West's academy, in that city. Introduced to Edmund Burke, a man so well qualified to direct the course of the young artist, he was advised to turn his attention to land-scape painting, and to study diligently from Nature. The locality of the Irish metropolis offers ample opportunities for such study. The city, with many noble buildings, gradually merges into garden-like suburbs, sloping away to the lonely shores of the distant bay, and the wild country at the foot of the Wicklow hills. Within reach of the pedestrian artist is the fine park through which the Dargle, a foaming torrent, forces its way amid rocky ravines and wooded dells, giving opportunities for study of the most varied character and unnumbered subjects for the painter. We may presume that it was from such material that the picture was painted which won Barret the premium of 50*l.*, offered by the Royal Dublin Society, and a wide reputation in his native city.

In 1761 or 1762, Barret left Ireland, in order to improve his art and his fortune in London. He brought with him two pictures which he had painted for his Irish patron, Lord Powerscourt, and sent them to the Exhibition in Spring Gardens. Here they were greatly admired, and the artist was so praised, that his reputation was at once established; and lucrative employment flowed in upon him. In 1764 he was again successful in a competition for a premium of 50*l.*, the first of its kind, offered by the Society of Arts for the best landscape, and Barry, R.A., in a letter to Dr. Sleigh, seems to feel it necessary to *vindicate* Claude's art against this young painter of thirty-two. Commissions flowed in upon him, constant employment induced facility, and facility its usual concomi-tant, his pictures became less thoughtful than heretofore, and more remarkable for ease of execution than for truth to Nature.

Among the patrons of art of that day was the Rev. John Lock, of Norbury, in Surrey. His house, situated on the summit of a hill, in the midst of a park, commands a noble view both up and down the valley. On the slopes of the hill are giant trees, oak, and ash, and beeches, together with a grove of ancient yews, existing before the Conquest, which may have sheltered the dark rites of the pagan Druids. Around the base of the hill flows the curious river Mole, while distant hills close in the prospect. Such a country must ever be a paradise to the landscape painter. Mr. Lock loved art, and loved to have the company of painters in his country home, and Barret, now one of the forty R.A.'s, was one of those who were frequent visitors in the happy valley.

We may presume that when the thoughts of artists were so intent upon monumental works, and when the project of the decoration of St. Paul's was under consideration, the subject was often discussed at Norbury; and when the scheme ended in disappointment, and Barry undertook the great room at the Society of Arts, Mr. Lock bethought himself of having one of the principal rooms at Norbury decorated with landscape paintings. He commissioned Barret to paint the walls from the skirting to the ceiling, with a series of scenes. This work differed from Barry's pictures at the Adelphi, in being painted in oil on the actual surface of the wall. It is still in existence, and, after some cleaning and repairing, seems to have stood well, and to retain much of its first brilliancy. It is rather a masterly specimen of scenic decoration, but it has little of the *finesse* of true landscape painting; indeed, this was hardly to be expected.

Barret's pictures are painted with the firm pencil and vigorous onceness which characterize the works of the best painters of his time ; they are often "compositions," with the painter's trees, the regulation rocks and water, of the followers of Poussin. But while we admire, at times, the ease and dexterity of their solid execution, and the agreeable lines of the general arrangement, his pictures do not touch us, since they are the offspring more of rule than of feeling, and are memories of other men's works, rather than the outcome of the painter's own observation of Nature. Sawrey Gilpin, the animal-painter, occasionally added the figures and cattle to his landscapes. Barret's works were sought after and eagerly purchased ; he was in the receipt of 2,000*l.* a year from his profession, yet such was his extravagance that he was in frequent difficulties. Towards the close of his life, his friend Burke procured him the appointment of master-painter at Chelsea Hospital, but at his death he nevertheless left his wife and family dependent upon the bounty of the Royal Academy. He died at Paddington, 29th May, 1784.

We must mention yet one more painter of the same school, *Julius C. Ibbetson* (B. 1759, D. 1817), who, if coming later on the stage, was not the less inspired in his art by Wilson. His works possess considerable merit. His manner was clear and firm, powerful, but occasionally hard ; his palette was simple, his colouring subdued but having a tendency to a clayey hue ; his landscapes were pleasing, and the figures and cattle well introduced, but his pictures did not find purchasers. He was one of the jolly friends of George Morland ; like him he lived from hand to mouth ; he was employed by an inferior class of picture-dealers, and made them his pot companions.

CHAPTER V.

SIR JOSHUA REYNOLDS, P.R.A.

JOSHUA REYNOLDS, born at Plympton on the 15th July, 1723, the year Kneller died, is the next of the trio who represent the new epoch in art. Unlike Wilson and, as we shall see, Gainsborough, Sir Joshua excelled only in portraits. The son of a clergyman, who sought to add to his income by keeping a school, young Reynolds was in a position to obtain knowledge, and as his father originally intended him to practice physic, we may presume that he endeavoured to ground him in the learning essential for that profession. If he never made great progress, his after-life proved that what he did acquire was a great help to him in the composition of his discourses.

Nature intended Reynolds for a painter, and if she denied him form and delicate execution, she endowed him with such a fine sense of colour, tone, and breadth, as well as of character and of beauty, as qualified him to gain a world-wide fame in the pursuit of art.

Reynolds's father seems to have been satisfied that his son's bent for art was too decided to be opposed, and to have determined to let him follow his own inclinations. In a county so remote at that time from the metropolis as Devonshire, it is not to be supposed that Reynolds could find much instruction in the art he adopted. Malone tells us that he copied such prints and drawings as fell in his way, and that in his mere boyhood he studied the " Jesuit's Perspective " to such purpose that he was able to astonish his father by a drawing of Plympton Grammar School ; but little real study of art could be thus obtained, and we may presume that in 1741, when on St. Luke's day, being then about nineteen years of age, Reynolds was placed under Thomas Hudson, in London, he had had small practice in drawing. Portrait painting at that time was more a trade than an art, and it is most probable that he returned to his native county and began taking portraits there, without having acquired much more than a little face-painting by his two years'

sojourn in the metropolis.   He says himself, " Not having the advantage
of an early academical education, I never had the facility of drawing the
naked figure which an artist ought to have."

Many circumstances render it fortunate for art that Reynolds stayed
but a short time with his master, and it is probably even a gain to art
that he did not study in the St. Martin's Lane Academy.   That school
was the centre of a knot of incapables, as Hogarth has sufficiently
shown us; while Hudson himself, as to any real knowledge of art,
inherited but the dregs of Lely and Kneller's traditions, handed down
through his master Richardson.

On leaving London and the tutelage of Hudson he spent five years in
practising his profession in Devonshire, it is presumed, with some
pecuniary success.   The study of Nature is the greatest source of
improvement to an artist; and portrait painting is, or ought to be, a
constant study of Nature.   The study of art had been hitherto denied
him, though Reynolds owned that the works of William Gandy, an
artist of Exeter, and a painter of much merit, made great impression on
him at that period of his life, but by the kindness of Captain Keppel in
whose ship he sailed for the Mediterranean in May, 1749, he was able at
the age of twenty-six to visit Italy.

Here at first he felt disappointed, and had the candour to allow that
he was so.   It is difficult to go back a century in art to what it was
when Richardson (who wrote so well, but painted only so respectably,)
was at the head of portraiture, and Thornhill (the Raphael of St. Paul's and
Greenwich) was considered " pre-eminent in the line of art he pursued ;"
when Verrio's gaudy staircases and halls (in the first freshness of their
production, and when dirt and smoke and oft-repeated varnish had not
improved by obscuring their beauties,) led the way to the galleries of the
" black masters," which our tourists brought home from Naples and
Bologna.   It is difficult to put ourselves in the position of one who
had heard these works lauded as masterpieces, and had seen the
representations by Lely and Kneller of the owners of such works,
enshrined as far greater than the pictures of their forerunner Vandyck,
and who then suddenly found himself in the presence of the grave and
solemn proprieties of Raphael, and the grand dreams of Michael Angelo,
painted in the dry and austere medium of fresco, without the allurements
of colour, or the blander amenities of oil.   Thus placed, should we be
more satisfied than Reynolds was, or rather should we not be less honest
and straightforward ?

He remained in Rome about two years, copying probably only for his
own improvement and making studies from Raphael's heads, while the rest
of his time was filled up no doubt by the practice of his profession.

Though Reynolds professes in his discourses the profoundest admiration for Michael Angelo and Raphael, his great desire was to add to the invention of these painters the colouring of the Venetian school. Northcote says: "Some attempts may be discovered in his practice to imitate Michael Angelo, and more to imitate Correggio; but it is evident that his whole life was devoted to finding out the Venetian mode of colouring, in the pursuit of which he risked both fortune and fame."

He also told Northcote that "he did not believe there ever would be in the world a superior portrait painter to Titian. That to procure a really fine portrait by Titian, he would be content to sell everything he possessed," adding, "I would be content to ruin myself," and for this he gives a reason far more worthy than the search into mere methods of execution. "If," says he, "I had never seen any of the fine works of Correggio, I should never, perhaps, have remarked in Nature the expression which I find in one of his pieces; or if I had remarked it, I might have thought it too difficult, or perhaps impossible to execute;" this shows that Venice and Parma were the sources of his inspiration. His stay in any of the cities north of Rome was short. In Florence about two months, in Bologna and Parma only a few days, in Venice six weeks—it was sufficient to impress him with an unending desire to excel in the field thus opened to his view. Henceforth he forsook the silvery freshness of Vandyck and the Flemings, the rosy brightness of Rubens, and sought after the golden tones of Titian and Giorgione. If "Vandyck painted with sun in his room," it was the sun shining through an atmosphere dimmed with mists and vapours; Reynolds desired rather to do as Titian had done before him, to paint in a light such as the summer sun sheds when he descends with glowing rays into the golden west.

This was why he was ever trying new pigments and new vehicles—carmine, orpiment, and the golden relics of the mummy, oils and varnishes, wax, amber, and resins, enriching his cold paintings by every art of scumbling and glazing. And wonderful indeed are some of the qualities he achieved; lustrous, glowing incarnations of beauty. Yet unlike his great prototype in this, that what Titian painted he wrought with certainty and principle, making one work—as far as the executive process, equal to another, enduring in their richness to our own day—whilst the works of Reynolds were, alas! but experiments, always giving or leaving glimpses of rare beauties, but too often fading ere the colours on the canvas were dry.

To Reynolds's study of Correggio we are indebted for some of his loveliest and most charming pictures, since there can be little doubt that many of his infantile subjects are deeply imbued with the feeling of that master, even the attitude in some cases reminding us of Correggio. Such is the child in the "Holy Family," and in the "Nymph and Cupid;" while the archness of his children's heads, arising from the peculiar drawing of the eyebrows, seems to be derived from the same source. Much, also, of the impasto of his execution is due to the study of that painter. But better far than any direct borrowing is the manner in which he followed both Raphael and Correggio in borrowing from Nature. Many of his best fancy pictures arose from his readiness in seizing the promptings and inspiration she placed before him. This we often find recorded both as to his subject-pictures and his portraits. A child sitting to him falls asleep. "Tired, tired; I am very tired, sir," was the little plaintive cry that Northcote heard as he painted in the next room. Perhaps this was the very child that, sleeping, suggested one of the children in the "Babes in the Wood." Turning in its sleep, the group was completed with an *abandon* and truth that could hardly be so well achieved as by the wearied pose of the little model. Another child, pleased with the painter's properties, suggests the principal figure in the "Infant Academy." Of his seizing a passing action we have one or two other remarkable instances. Thus we learn that when he was about to paint Mrs. Siddons as the "Tragic Muse," he requested her to seat herself in a suitable pose; but that having commenced, on her turning round to look at something on the wall, the new action struck him as more characteristic; he asked her to retain it, and we see how effective he made it in this the noblest portrait from his hand. Again, John Hunter the surgeon was sitting to him for the first time, and Sir Joshua had been making a series of ineffectual beginnings, when Hunter, in a fit of abstraction, took the highly characteristic attitude in which he is painted. How happily Reynolds adopted what might appear to others commonplace incidents is seen in the playful mother and child, the " Duchess of Devonshire and her Infant," and in the " Pick-a-back," with hosts of other examples that all will readily call to mind. How fortunate he was in seizing quaint attitudes is instanced in Lord Althorp with his hands in his pockets, Master Bunbury as Harry VIII., or that prim little bundle in a mob cap, Penelope Boothby.

Reynolds was, as we have shown, when he started for Italy, a free man, untrammelled by rules or practice, and happily fitted to choose his own methods and to run a free career. That he did so all his pictures bear witness. They are, as he tells us himself, a series of experiments. These proved sometimes unfortunate for the possessors of the work, sometimes for his own reputation, but they always gave evidence of a zealous search after new colours and new executive processes. Great was the abuse heaped upon him for indiscriminate use of fugitive colours and fading vehicles, even in his own day, but it turned him not aside. From Lely's time until Reynolds, flesh-painting was little better than house-painting, wholly mechanical and commonplace. The palette, arranged according to rule, with a recipe set of tints, served equally for all complexions. Vermilion and ochre, blue-black and Indian red, had to do duty for the young and the old, the fair and the dark—a little more of the grey or of the white constituting the only difference. The same laboured handling, made still more smooth and insipid by the use of the *sweetener*, resulted, in all cases, in the same tame and textureless surface. Merely as a flesh-painter, what a change was wrought by Reynolds !

On his return from Italy in 1753, he spent three months in his native county, and, on his arrival in London, set up his easel in St. Martin's Lane, then the haunt of art and artists. His early friend Lord Mount-Edgecumbe soon recommended sitters to the young artist's studio, and with these and the connexion he had made in Italy, he formed an extensive practice, so much so that during the year 1755 we find engagements with no less than one hundred and twenty-five sitters. Reynolds made acquaintance with Johnson very soon after his return to London, and the two remained fast friends for life ; the doctor being indebted to the painter for many acts of kindness, and, in return, abstaining, more than was his wont, from those fierce attacks which others encountered at his hands. As his sitters increased in number and importance, Reynolds removed first to Newport Street, and afterwards purchased the house No. 47 in Leicester Square, or, as it was then called, Leicester Fields ; here he built himself a studio and reception-rooms, and in this studio—now an auction-room—he painted during the remainder of his life. It so happened that the majority of Reynolds's friends belonged to the Opposition side in politics, and, whether from this or other causes, he was little employed by the Court. He painted the Duke of Cumberland in 1759, and shortly after the Prince of Wales, afterwards George III., but in 1762, on a vacancy in the office, he had the mortification of seeing Ramsay appointed Court painter, an artist of little originality, though of great respectability.

Between Ramsay and Reynolds there could have been little real rivalry for Walpole, writing to Dalrymple in 1759, says, " Mr. Reynolds and Mr. Ramsay can scarce be rivals—their manners are so different. The former is bold and has a kind of tempestuous colouring, yet with dignity and grace ; the latter is all delicacy. Mr. Reynolds seldom *succeeds with women*, Mr Ramsay is formed to paint them ;" and this was written after Reynolds had exhibited the lovely portrait of Kitty Fisher, and of him who was to leave us portraits of the Gunnings, Waldegraves, Hornecks, and Mrs. Sheridan !

Thus far we have spoken of Reynolds only as a portrait painter, but he claims attention as an historical painter also, as in this branch of the art many of his friends and contemporaries awarded him high rank, and warmly lamented that his talents as an historical painter were not more publicly called into requisition.

Farington, his biographer, after ranking Reynolds with the most distinguished geniuses who have adorned the arts, says of him, that "even to historical subjects, in many instances, he gave a charm that was before unknown."

Now it is precisely on these points we must differ. Notwithstanding the greatness of Reynolds as a portrait painter, and the beauty of his fancy subjects, he wholly fails as a painter of history. Allowing all that arises from "colour and harmony," we must assert, that, both as to form and character, the figures introduced into these solemn dramas are wholly unworthy to represent the persons of the actors therein. In his "Holy Family," the mother and St. Joseph, as painted by Reynolds, are simply country rustics, and the infant Saviour, St. John, &c., might, for all there is of character or holiness, change places with the Cupid who directs his arrow to transfix the Nymph. Where is the Holy Child, who ought to be named but with reverence, and painted, if at all, only after deep meditation, and it may be, prayer. Again, his infant "Samuel," more of a fancy portrait than an historical subject, is merely a simple child saying its nightly prayer to nurse or mother ere it sleeps—not him set apart from birth to holy offices and reverend service in the temple; and called, even while yet a child, to rebuke the laxity of the elder prophet, the head of the theocracy of Israel. Such subjects as these want more than mere colour, or light and shade; more than mere sweetness and simplicity.

Reynolds has left us many aphorisms; and many little insights into his mode of working may be obtained from his own notes, and from recollections by his sitters and his pupils. He evidently painted rather from the inspiration of the moment and of his subject, than from any set rule, varying his manner, both for experiment, and as his work led him on. Unlike his successor Lawrence, he seems not to have made any careful drawings on his canvas, but to have trusted to his brush to model out the form, changed often in the progress of his picture when any new position or expression pleased him; hence the failure of many of his pictures. He found a real pleasure in painting, and was untiring at his work. Beattie, the poet, tells that he sat five hours to him on the first sitting for the allegorical portrait, "in which time he *finished* my head, and sketched in the figure. The likeness," he adds, "is most striking, and the execution most masterly, I was not the least fatigued. I was so placed as to see in a mirror the whole progress;" and he declares that the masterly manner of the artist differed as much from that of all other painters, as the execution of Gerardini on the violin differs from that of a common fiddler. Reynolds was of opinion that a painter should look upon his subject or sitter as if it were a picture, and that he would then be the more likely to realize it as such. He seems never to have seen *outline,* but the whole as a picture; its breadth, colour, and light and dark. Thus his eye was always dwelling on the relation of parts, and of the figure to the ground. When it melted into the ground he was not seeking, as is too often the case, to find the form, but was content, with Nature, to lose it; even the light and shade seems, as he wrought, to be considered less as light and shade, than as different modifications of a coloured surface, which we may suppose him mentally matching as a lady does her silks. He used to say:—"Consider the object before you as more made out by light and shadow than by lines." Yet while he was thus mentally seizing the form through light and shade, and the light and shade even as it were through colour, he was wonderfully rendering the highest character and the noblest expression of his sitter.

Reynolds's mode of painting, and the beautiful effects he obtained, made such an impression on the practice of our schools, for evil as well as good, that it is necessary to enter somewhat at length into his methods of execution. We know that some of his pictures failed very soon after they left the easel, many during his lifetime, and that while some have retained their full beauty, numbers of those which have come down to us are but faded relics of the past.

Reynolds painted, in 1760, a picture of Sir Walter Blackett, for the Infirmary at Newcastle-upon-Tyne. In Leslie's life it is said,—"This picture stands well." But there is a very different story current. Sir Walter lived to a great age, an age beyond the three-score years and ten allotted to the common run of mankind, and as he advanced in years, found the picture which was to hand him down to posterity, so faded and perished from the fleeting pigments and unsatisfactory vehicles Sir Joshua had used, that the Newcastle knight made the following epigram on his own portrait, and was very fond of repeating it to his friends:—

> " Painting of old was surely well designed
> To keep the features of the dead in mind,
> But this great rascal has reversed the plan,
> And made his picture die before the man."

Sir Joshua, with his usual equanimity, took such sarcasms patiently and even joked himself at times on the subject, remarking that he might say of his works, that he came off with "*flying* colours." It is but fair to hear him in his own justification. "My frequent alterations," says he, "arose from a refined taste, which could not acquiesce in anything short of a high degree of excellence. I had not an opportunity of being early initiated in the principles of colouring; no man, indeed, could teach me. If I have never been settled with respect to colouring, let it at the same time be remembered that my unsteadiness in this respect proceeded from an inordinate desire to possess every kind of excellence that I saw in the works of others. My fickleness in the mode of colouring arose from an eager desire to attain the highest excellence."

The reasons of the failure of Sir Joshua's works may be ranged under three heads, and in discussing them we shall necessarily have to write on his methods of execution, for which he has left us ample notes. These causes of failure were :—

1st. The use of improper vehicles.

2nd. The mixture in the same work of various vehicles which are antagonistic to one another, such as those which are soft and fluent under those which are hard ; rapid dryers over slow dryers, and even in the same picture, watery with oily vehicles.

3rd. The use of uncertain and unstable pigments, and their improper combination either with one another or with the vehicles he added to them.

Reynolds seems to have departed from the Flemish mode of colouring, that of painting at once from a white ground, and to have adopted a method analogous to the Venetian system, preparing a ground by a first colouring in black and white, or, these with a little admixture of red, and then on this preparation completing with rich colourings and glazings ; although in his numerous experiments, he at times worked so completely at random that it is difficult to trace any systematic mode of procedure. Mason the poet, who himself dabbled in art, records that in 1754, when Reynolds was young in his practice, Lord Holderness sat to him for his portrait, which portrait he afterwards presented to the poet. Mason having been engaged in settling the preliminaries as to sitting, &c., was permitted to be present in the painting-room on every occasion when Lord Holderness sat, and he thus describes the mode in which the picture was painted :—" On a light-coloured canvas Reynolds had already laid a ground of white, and which was still wet, where he meant to place the head. He had nothing upon his palette but flake white, lake, and black ; and without making any previous sketch or outline, he began with much celerity to scumble these pigments together, till he had produced, in less than an hour, a likeness sufficiently intelligible, yet withal, as might be expected, cold and pallid to the last degree. At the second sitting, he added, I believe, to the other three colours, a little Naples yellow ; but I do not remember that he used any vermilion, neither then nor at the third trial required." Lake alone produced the carnation. " The drapery " of this three-quarter portrait was " crimson velvet, copied from a coat Lord Holderness then wore, and apparently not only painted, but glazed with lake, which has stood to this hour perfectly well, though the face, which as well as the whole picture *was highly varnished* before he sent it home, *very soon faded,* and soon after, the forehead particularly, cracked, almost to peeling off,

E

which," he adds, "it would have done long since had not his pupil Doughty repaired it." Mason afterwards says, that in 1759, when painting "Venus and Cupid," Reynolds had "laid aside his first favourite, lake, preferring Chinese vermilion, thinking it more durable. I have seen it (the ' Venus and Cupid '), during its progress," he continues, " in a variety of different hues of colouring, sometimes rosy beyond nature, sometimes pallid and blue." We saw this picture in the Institution in 1865. The flesh stands well, the colour is good, but cracked with dry hard cracks ; the browns have drawn together. It has evidently been much worked upon in parts.

Leslie says that Reynolds believed as confidently in the *Venetian secret*, as ever alchemist did in the "philosopher's stone." We ourselves were acquainted with an old painter, a pupil of West's, who in his latter days had devoted himself to repairing pictures, and who possessed portraits by both Titian and Rubens, which he said had belonged to Sir Joshua, and parts of which, to obtain this wished-for secret, had been scraped or rubbed down to the panel, to lay bare the under-paintings or dead colourings. It was this search for the Venetian secret—this constant course of experiments in his pictures, that has caused so many failures.

At one time he thought he had at length arrived at the best mode of painting, and wrote in his note-book, 1770—"I am fixed in my manner of painting. First and second painting, oil and copaiba varnish solely with black, ultramarine and white ; for the after and last paintings, yellow, black and lake, and black and ultramarine without white," but he adds, "retouched with a little white and with other colours ; " from this process, however, he soon changed, as we find in the same year, notes of quite different methods. Sometimes on this black and white ground, he added the tints of the complexion, either with copaiba varnish, or with mastic without oil. Thus, he says, of a portrait of Kitty Fisher, painted in 1766, "Face with wax, drapery with wax, and afterwards varnished," which is made clearer by the notes on Mr. Pelham's portrait of the same year. "Painted with lake and white, black and blue, varnished with green mastic dissolved in oil, with sugar of lead and rock alum, yellow lake and Naples yellow mixed with the varnish ; " from which it more clearly appears that on the cold neutral first colouring the enrichments were added in colours tempered with varnish. Thus painted, we find from many notes, that the picture was surface-varnished throughout before it was sent home. Such pictures failing from the wax-medium, the copaiba, or other vehicles used, the restorer, in taking off the outer coat of varnish, almost of necessity took off the last rich painting, which had been completed with the same kind of varnish. Here we trace the ruin caused by the improper vehicles used ; and the pictures thus destroyed are those pallid grey, but still delicately beautiful portraits by his hand, such as the "Kitty Fisher," the "Miss Hornecks," and a host of others.

These pictures, in fact, were wholly denuded of the "deep-toned brightness" which Sir Joshua sought for at the expense of durability. We extract from Cotton's *Sir Joshua and his Works*, 1856, notes by Sir William Beechey and Haydon upon Reynolds's experiments in colouring. Beechey says, "Sir Joshua's having made use of Venice turpentine and wax, as a varnish" (or vehicle), "accounts in a great measure for the pale and raw appearance of his pictures after cleaning. Rubbed over slightly with spirits of turpentine," and alas ! too often spirits of wine are used,—"the glazing colours must inevitably be removed." He tells us that Sir Joshua "loaded his pictures with Venice turpentine and wax without oil, without considering the consequences. It is," he adds, "a most delicious vehicle to use, and gives the power of doing such things and producing such effects as cannot be approached by anything else *while the pictures are fresh.*" He tells us, too, that "Rembrandt followed the same practice, but only painted his lights with a full body of colour, his shadows were always smooth, thin, and very soft. Sir Joshua loaded his shadows as much as his lights. There is a binding quality in white that always dries hard like cement. Dark colours are the reverse, and if thickly painted crack with any vehicle except oil."

We are rather inclined to think that Reynolds's darks have more often failed from the use of asphaltum, and that a picture painted throughout with pure wax properly melted into varnish will become hard and firm, and will not crack. We have a copy after Sir Joshua so painted thirty-five years ago and varnished at the time. It is as hard and firm as when first painted, and it is rather to the use of asphaltum or to heterogeneous mixtures of incongruous vehicles that the worst failures are to be imputed. Of this kind of vicious execution, the portrait of Miss Kirkman, noted October 2, 1772, is one of the worst specimens, "gum dragon and whiting, then waxed, then egged, then varnished, and then retouched—cracks," adds Sir Joshua himself, and who would doubt it? Haydon says, "Reynolds wanted to get at once what the old masters did with the simplest materials, and then left time and drying to enamel. To wax a head, then egg, then varnish it, then paint again, all and each still half dry beneath, could only end in ruin, however exquisite at the time," adding, "whilst West's detestable surface has stood from the simplicity of the vehicle, half Sir Joshua's heads are gone; though what remains are so exquisite one is willing to sacrifice them for the works we see," a sentence we concur in as far as it is possible to understand it.

E 2

Of his own portrait, painted in the same year, Reynolds notes, "Water and gum-dragon" (? tragacanth), "vermilion, lake, black, without yellow, varnished over with egg, after Venice turpentine." "Heavens, murder! murder!" cries Haydon, "it must have cracked under the brush!!" No wonder that when Reynolds complained to Northcote that he did not clean his brushes well, the pupil retorted, "How can I when they are so sticky and gummy!" And here let us give a note of warning to those who possess pictures by Reynolds, that they should avoid new German processes of restoration, processes for softening the gum of the varnish, rendering it fluid for a time, that it may subside evenly and again harden. What, under such a process, would become of the last glazing paintings made with the same varnish as a vehicle? Between taking off too much, or flowing the glazings into the varnish, there is hardly a choice of evils.

Reynolds himself said that vegetable pigments, the lakes and yellows used for the tints of his complexions, are far more brilliant than mineral pigments, and he declared to Northcote that they would not change, but might be safely used if locked up by varnish. He also seems to have felt that they were purer and fresher when used with varnish than with any oil medium, since all oils have more or less yellow of their own: hence his use of varnishes as a vehicle. These colours, fugitive in themselves, as the spirit gradually evaporated from the gum, faded entirely away, even when their departure was not hastened by the detergents of the restorer.

Then again Sir Joshua was accustomed to use mineral pigments, under conditions wholly unfavourable to their durability, such as his known use of orpiment (a preparation from arsenic), which suffers rapid change when mixed, as he mixed it, with white lead. Thus Northcote gives as extracts from Sir Joshua's notes, at the latter end of the year 1775, the following directions:—"To lay the palette: first lay carmine and white in different degrees; secondly, orpiment and white ditto; then lay blue-black and white ditto. The first sitting, for expedition, make a mixture on the palette as near the sitter's complexion as you can." This alone would account for many changes, since carmine and white have as little stability as orpiment and white. Failures from fugitive pigments are those mostly alluded to by his contemporaries, and this before the *restorer* had practised his art upon them. Such changes have, no doubt, progressed since the painter's lifetime, until some of his works appear as if they were merely grey preparations, fine in their modelling, in their roundness, in their character, and even in a modified beauty,—yet but ghosts and shadows of what they first were. Such pictures are not necessarily cracked; they may or may not have hair-cracks in the solid lights, a matter of small importance either way, but the colour is irretrievably gone, past the skill of any restorer, unless he substitutes his own colouring for that of Sir Joshua.

Sir Joshua's contemporaries do not allude to his use of bituminous pigments ; neither, strange to say, is there much reference in his notes to these preparations, whether as mummy, bitumen, or asphaltum, which to us appear among the most prominent causes of the failure of his pictures. The fact is, that the bad effects of asphaltum are often deferred until the picture is removed into some new locality, or exposed to new conditions, or to some new coating of rapidly drying varnish, when it will give way in a few weeks, after having remained for many years in apparent soundness. Beechey remarks that Hoppner painted with wax melted into mastic varnish, and yet that his pictures stand while Sir Joshua's had already failed. But since that time Hoppner's pictures have broken up even more than Sir Joshua's. This, we believe, has arisen not from wax but from asphaltum, and we may presume had not begun to show itself when Beechey wrote. When the masses of shadow or the darks of the picture are painted with these pigments the parts gradually separate, but not to the ground, rather leaving a wide pitchy shining seam. Attempts have been made in such cases to press the parts together, which succeeds for a short, and only for a short time ; permanent repair has not yet been achieved, nor does it seem possible.

Again these bituminous pigments used in the darks have in places the solid half-tints made with white, painted into them ; this partially hardens the bitumen, and a new set of cracks is the result ; they are generally wide and down to the ground, and show whitish to the eye.

Hanging side by side at Manchester House, are three of Reynolds's very finest pictures, viz., the original "Strawberry Girl"—for there are at least two repetitions—the fine sitting portrait of "Nelly O'Brien," the one with the hat shading the face, and the portrait of "Miss Bowles with her Dog." A careful inspection has convinced us without a doubt that the first and the last named works are painted with wax. No one can look at the edge of the rock where it comes against the sky in the "Strawberry Girl," and not be aware of the plentiful use of wax on the foliage ; the medium stands up with a crisp, full, semi-transparent impasto that is undeniable. And Reynolds says of it in his note-book, "*Cera. sol!*"—wholly wax. The painting of the white drapery curiously indicates the *drag* occasioned by a wax and turpentine medium, yet excepting that, perhaps when in Rogers's possession, it has been varnished with a brown varnish which has run down, it is in an uninjured state. Of the "Miss Bowles with her Dog" we are not aware that there is any note ; but here also the presence of wax as a medium is equally clear in many parts of the picture ; which, with the slight exception of a few small pieces chipped off quite down to the ground, is even in a finer state than the "Strawberry Girl." The face of the young child is lovely, the eyes swim in the laughing lustre of happy childhood ; it is one of the sweetest pictures in existence. Leslie used to relate that the parents of Miss Bowles were about to take her to Romney for her portrait, when, naming it to Sir George Beaumont, he strongly advised Sir Joshua. "But his pictures fade," said the father. "Never mind," was the reply, "a faded picture by Reynolds is better than the best of Romney's." He proposed that Sir Joshua should be invited to dinner and to see the child at her own home, and this being arranged Sir Joshua, delighted with the little lady, played such funny tricks to amuse her that the child thought it quite a holiday to go next day and see the gentleman who had conjured away her plate and made her so merry. In the picture she seems as if she feared he would conjure away her pet also, as she hugs the dog to her bosom almost to throttling, and is looking archly out at the painter, as if ready to retreat if he should advance. The "Nelly O'Brien," too, is in an excellent state, though the mode of painting is less clear. Most of the other Reynolds paintings in this fine collection, to the number of ten or twelve, are in the same condition, and happily prove that his works have not so wholly failed.

We cannot do justice to Reynolds without referring to his great abilities as a writer on art. He was the intimate associate of Dr. Johnson, Burke, Goldsmith, Dr. Percy, and other eminent men; and no name occurs more frequently than his in the pages of Boswell. Reynolds's writings comprise his three papers in the *Idler*, published 1759-60 : "False Criticisms on Painting," No. 76, from which we have quoted; "On the Grand Style in Painting," No. 79 ; and "On the True Idea of Beauty," No. 82 ; his annotations to Du Fresnoy's *Art of Painting ;* his notes on the *Art of the Low Countries ;* some brief remarks in Dr. Johnson's *Shakspeare ;* and his well-known discourses to the students of the Royal Academy.

These discourses especially possess great literary merit; simply yet elegantly expressed, they are forcibly didactic ; the work of a master, a thoughtful observer, skilled in all the works of all the schools, and himself of high professional attainment. So much were they esteemed that Reynolds was denied their authorship, which was attributed to Burke, who was asserted at least to have assisted in their composition. Yet they bear the evident impress of one mind expressed with one pen.

It is as easy to point out apparent inconsistencies in the discourses and other writings of Reynolds, and to confute separate points of his teaching, as it is to oppose separate texts of Scripture. There is no doubt that the writings of the first President have greatly influenced, and justly influenced, the practice of our schools. They are sound, practical, and were thoroughly suited for the period when they were produced. His professional brethren rely on his teaching, because he was a painter as well as a critic, and so ably illustrated on his canvas his discourses to the students. Read as a whole, they are a body of sound precepts such as no other school started with ; and unless each artist is to begin from the beginning, and ignore what has gone before, it will be no waste of time to study the art-precepts of the great President, if it is only to test their truth by trying to confute them.

Reynolds continued the practice of his art with but little intermission during his long career. Painting to him was such a real pleasure, that to paint was to enjoy life ; and after he had received his round of sitters for the day, he loved to spend the evening in society. He was a constant diner out, and gave dinners, at which a careless hospitality reigned, but which were frequented by the most intellectual people of the day. In 1764, the Literary Club was founded—a club which met once a week at the Turk's Head Tavern, in Gerrard Street, supping together, and spending the evening in convivial conversation. Reynolds, who was one of the club's foundation members—indeed it was formed at his suggestion—rarely missed being present, and took an active share in the discussions. He was what his friend Johnson called essentially a clubable man, and notwithstanding his deafness, took part, and often a very successful part, in conversations, the records of which, by Boswell and Burney, are read in our times with such continuous interest. His temper was mild and equable, and we often find him fulfilling the office of peacemaker, by the turn which he gave to a dispute, or by interposing a qualifying remark. Leslie, in his *Life*, published since this sketch was written, has fully rescued Reynolds from the insinuations and aspersions of Cunningham ; and Mr. Tom Taylor, in his additions to Leslie, has shown us the great portrait painter surrounded by his friends ; in his relations with the celebrities of his time, (almost all of whom sat to him ;) living in the political world of that troubled period, and in his relations with his brethren of art.

In 1768, after various abortive efforts, a Royal Academy of Arts was founded. Reynolds seems at first to have stood aloof from the new society. Acknowledged at all hands as holding the first place in art, his co-operation in the scheme of an academy was of the first importance to its success, and he yielded to the wishes of his brother artists by becoming its President. On his election, George III. honoured him with knighthood, which he seems to have valued highly, as he did the office of mayor of his little native village of Plympton, conferred upon him a short time previously ; to these titles, Oxford, in 1773, added that of Doctor of Civil Law.

From the first foundation of the Royal Academy, Reynolds was a constant contributor to its exhibitions ; the catalogues from 1769 to 1790 contain lists of 244 of his pictures. His life passed quietly at his easel ; though a few dissensions with envious brethren varied it at times. In 1781, and again in 1783, he made short journeys in Holland and Flanders, publishing valuable notes of the pictures he saw on those occasions, as well as of his methods of studying from them. His life was one of almost uninterrupted success and prosperity, disturbed only for a while by his difference with his colleagues and a temporary secession from the Royal Academy.

Farington tells us that while Reynolds resided in St. Martin's Lane his prices for portraits were—three quarters, ten guineas ; half length, twenty guineas ; whole length, forty guineas. His master Hudson's prices were rather higher, and were soon adopted by him. About four or five years later both raised their prices to fifteen, thirty, and sixty guineas for the three classes of portrait respectively. In 1760 Reynolds removed to Leicester Square, and then his prices were twenty-five, fifty, and one hundred guineas for the three classes of portrait. In 1781, we learn from Malone, his prices were fifty, one hundred, and two hundred guineas, and continued so till his death. For the " Mrs. Siddons as the Tragic Muse," in the Dulwich Gallery, Mr. Desenfans paid him seven hundred guineas. For the priceless " Strawberry Girl," the " Muscipula," and the "Shepherd Boy," his price was fifty guineas each. For his historical works he was paid at about the same rate—the "Death of Dido," now in the Royal Collection, two hundred guineas ; " Death of Cardinal Beaufort," five hundred guineas ; and for his Russian picture, " Hercules strangling the Serpents," fifteen hundred guineas.

Reynolds never married. When he first settled in London, his sister Frances kept his house, and afterwards his niece, Miss Palmer, fulfilled the same duty. During his long life his good health was almost uninterrupted, till the latter part of the year 1782, when he experienced a slight sensation of paralysis, from which, however, he perfectly recovered. But in 1789, his left eye, which had long been weak, failed, and fearing the total loss of sight, he at once resolved to relinquish the practice of his profession. He continued, however, to enjoy society, but was subject to fits of depression, fearing the loss of the remaining eye. Other distressing symptoms afterwards arose, which his friends ascribed to his depressed spirits ; these, however, continued to increase, and after lingering about three months, during which he bore his illness with calmness and equanimity, he died of an enlarged liver on the 23rd of February, 1792. His biographers love to tell of his lying in state at the Royal Academy—the long funeral procession—the pall, borne by dukes, marquises, and earls—and his place beside Wren in the crypt of St. Paul's. Well might the great and the noble honour him, who has made us familiar with all that were lovely, as well as most that were worthy of being known, in the age he embellished. He left behind him many pictures, finished and unfinished, a fine collection of drawings by the old masters, and about 80,000*l*., the bulk of which, on the death of his sister Frances, reverted to his niece, Miss Palmer, who became, by marriage, Marchioness of Thomond.

CHAPTER VI.

THOMAS GAINSBOROUGH, R.A.

THOMAS GAINSBOROUGH, R.A., the last and youngest of the three artists whose works characterize the period under review, was born at Ipswich in 1727, and there his early taste for art was first developed. It has already been said that he was great both in landscape and in portraiture. He seems from the first to have employed his talents on either indiscriminately, and to have continued to practise both simultaneously to the end of his life. At fifteen years of age, we are told by Fulcher, in his life of the painter, Gainsborough came to London and was lodged in the house of a silversmith, who introduced him to Gravelot, the engraver, from whom he acquired some knowledge of that art and valuable help in drawing. He was then for some time, four years it is said, under Hayman, and entered himself as a student at the St. Martin's Lane Academy, a place much frequented by the artists of that day—by the juniors for practice, by the seniors as visitors and dogmatizers. It may be presumed that there were means of study for those who chose to avail themselves of them, but that there can be no doubt that the place abounded with all the threadbare rules and traditional commonplaces of a profession in a state of senility, and men ready to prostrate themselves before those false gods—Lely and Kneller. Hogarth, who hated them as a clique favouring the "black masters," stigmatizes them as a body of coach-painters, scene-painters, drapery-painters, picture-dealers, picture-cleaners and frame-makers, and says that they "thrust the canvas between the student and the sky, and tradition between him and his God;" for which latter it would be more true to read *nature.* Here "hail fellow well met," they praised all art that was according to their rules, and despised all innovators. Among them, no doubt, was Ellis, the pupil of Kneller, who expressed his contempt of Reynolds's portraits when they were shown on his return from Rome, saying, "This will never answer; why, you don't paint in the least like Sir Godfrey!" and on the painter's attempting to reason with him on the subject, contemptuously finished the conversation by exclaiming, "Shakespeare in poetry, and Kneller in painting, damme!" and stalked pompously out of the room.

The artists of that day led a life of careless independence, living from hand to mouth, a jovial improvident set, spending their days at the easel, their nights at the club or the tavern. Art to them was but a trade, and provided they fulfilled the orders of their customers, they were little solicitous about its improvement—it was compounded by recipe and on the conventional rules of the past, the same artistic properties, the same shop stock of postures and attitudes, as may be inferred from the oft-repeated tale of the portrait painted for the innovating sitter, who, desiring to wear his hat on his head, had another as usual placed under the arm—the very studio was a workshop in the commonest sense of the term ; one painted the head, another the hands, if hands were included in the price, while a third fitted on the coat and the ruffles. In such a school, and from such companions, Gainsborough could acquire little that would forward him in his art except mere drawing power, which having obtained he wisely left this knot of incapables, and quitting London, returned to his native place, after an absence of three years. Here he entered upon the battle of life as a portrait painter, occasionally producing also small studies of landscape scenery, for which, we learn, his price was from three to four guineas.

We are not told that Gainsborough ever left this country. He, therefore, had no opportunity like Reynolds and Wilson, of profiting by foreign art, except such as was to be found, and to which he could gain access, in his own land.

We cannot at the present day, with our annual exhibitions of the works of the "Old Masters," realize the position of a youth entering upon the pursuit of art, almost wholly deprived of the means of studying past or contemporary works—for Gainsborough studied long before the foundation of the National Gallery, and was thus obliged to start from the very beginning, and to achieve for himself every new step on the road to excellence.

Of what opportunities there were, however, Gainsborough was not slow to avail himself. There are at Hampton Court two copies by him from Rembrandt, which show that he was quite ready to study, by means of copying, where any benefit to his art was likely to arise. It is quite evident that he dwelt much upon the works of Vandyck, whose influence pervades the style of Gainsborough, giving it that tendency to silvery freshness which contrasts so strongly with the warmer and more golden tones of Reynolds. But the early age at which he began to practise his profession, the fact that he was never warped by foreign study, and the independent bent of his own character, kept him from following any of the old methods, and left him free to adopt a style and manner entirely his own. Sir Joshua says that "his handling or the manner of leaving the colours, or, in other words, the methods he used for producing the effect, had very much the appearance of an artist who had never learned from others the usual and regular practice belonging to the arts; but still a man of strong instinctive perception of what was required, he found out a way of his own to accomplish his purpose." Yet Sir Joshua had already told us that the painter had studied and even copied the works of the great Flemings, and those after Rembrandt are imitative of the master, and free from Gainsborough's own peculiarities of handling. That he was quite capable to paint decidedly if he pleased, many of his portraits give evidence; among others, the fine head of Gainsborough Dupont, now in the possession of Mr. G. Richmond, R.A., a work of rare executive beauty. But there is no doubt that the mind of a man of genius is as much shown in his executive handling as in the treatment of his subject, and that it is a part of his individuality. That Gainsborough adopted his peculiar manner advisedly, we cannot doubt from a letter which he wrote to one of his sitters, a lawyer, who, perhaps, thought he had not finish enough for his money. "I don't think," he says, "it would be more ridiculous for a person to put his nose close to the canvas, and say the colours smelt offensive, than to say how rough the paint lies— for one is just as material as the other, with regard to hurting the effect and drawing of a picture. Sir G. Kneller used to say that pictures were not made to smell of."

That the manner he adopted is agreeable from the felicitous ease of execution which is its characteristic, we are sufficiently able to judge, and the President himself allows that "all these odd scratches and marks which, on a close examination, are so observable in Gainsborough's pictures; this chaos, this uncouth and shapeless appearance, by a kind of magic, at a certain distance, assumes form, and all the parts seem to drop into their proper places;" and he afterwards adds, that this "hatching manner" greatly contributed to the lightness of effect which is so eminent a beauty in his pictures, and "contributed even to that striking resemblance for which his portraits are so remarkable."

But are his pictures a chaos of uncouth and shapeless appearances? Is his handling so hatched and scratchy as the President would infer? On the contrary, many of his pictures are painted with extreme firmness and precision; nay, the truth is, however paradoxical the statement may appear, that Gainsborough had more executive power than his critic. Whatever may be the case with respect to his landscapes—which are not painted in face of nature, but from drawings and from memory—in his portraits, when he had his sitters before his eyes, his work was done at once without hesitation and without repetition. Many of his portraits, indeed, seem as if painted at one sitting.

In her Majesty's collection at Windsor there are seventeen life-size heads of the sons and daughters of King George III. It is hardly possible to speak too highly of the ease and freedom, yet the firmness of execution of these works—they are of great purity in colour and of a sweetness and loveliness of expression most captivating; it is true that the painting is thin and sketchlike, as it mostly is in the works of Gainsborough, but there is not the slightest appearance of indecision or repetition. Of the extreme rapidity of his execution these seventeen works are a curious evidence; they are all dated on the back in the same month, and seem to have been done during a stay of that time at the Castle. Now we know that Reynolds repeated his painting again and again. Yet the refined taste of Gainsborough, who did not repeat, who can gainsay? Examine carefully the expressive portrait of Mrs. Siddons, now in the National Gallery, and it will be found that the *handling* is as easy and light as the expression and drawing are refined; added to which, the discriminative texture and the broad realization of the striped silk dress, given without any sign of labour, is such that it will be hard to understand what is meant by the "odd scratches and marks" of his execution. When accessories are introduced into his pictures, they are often painted with such truth as to delight us, while we at the same time enjoy the ease with which the painter has achieved them. The fiddle on the chair beside Dr. Fischer, in the portrait at Hampton Court, is a notable example—a connoisseur in the instrument would at once name the builder.

Further to compare Gainsborough with Reynolds. It hardly seemed possible with the latter to paint less than life-size, or to achieve the greater refinement of execution necessary for small works. What does remain of this nature is very clumsy in execution. Gainsborough could work minutely as well as in life-size, and that not in landscape only, where he is at times minute in his handling, but also in heads and figures—as in the "Cottage Children" in the Vernon collection, where the heads are miniature size and delicately wrought. Reynolds seems to have felt Gainsborough's executive facility as a great beauty, by which the painter gave freshness and vivacity to his works; but to have considered that he used it too freely, or exaggerated it beyond proper limits; if so, however, time has chastened down the peculiarity, as we know it has done in Constable's works, in the best of which it is hardly possible to understand now what could have been called "Constable's snow;" and time has, in some degree, also tamed into their proper subordination the hatchings of Gainsborough's portraits.

Gainsborough's facile and rapid execution has had one fortunate result, both for himself and posterity, in which he contrasts finely with Sir Joshua ; his pictures have come down to us in a pure state, his portraits are rarely cracked, even in the darks.   It results from rapid handling without repetition, that even with an imperfect medium the pictures do not suffer.

It is said that Sir Joshua at an Academy dinner gave "the health of Mr. Gainsborough, the greatest landscape painter of the day," to which Wilson, in his blunt, grumbling way, retorted, "Ay, and the greatest portrait painter, too." In Gainsborough's own time, the world of art patrons seem to have employed his talents as a portrait painter, but to have disregarded his landscape art, after his death, however, and the eulogium Reynolds had pronounced on his landscapes and rustic children, these came to be considered his finest works.   But it is more than doubtful whether Wilson did not judge more truly of his talent than Sir Joshua ; and it is certain that Gainsborough, in his finest portraits, formed a style equally original, and produced works that are in every way worthy to take rank with those of the great President.   They contrast with the latter in being more silvery and pure, and in the absence of that impasto and richness in which Reynolds indulged, but his figures are surrounded by air and light, and his portraits generally are easy and graceful without affectation.

Reynolds's out-of-door portraits have more of the light and dark of the studio than Gainsborough's indoor ones, which is due, in the works of the latter, to the cool colour of the flesh and the cool shadows, and partly to the greys on the retiring sides of the figure.

As to his practice, we are told that Gainsborough got far from his canvas while painting his portraits, and that he used brushes with very long handles.   There is no doubt that he so placed the canvas and the sitter that, by retiring, he could view both at an equal distance, and then, by means of the long-handled tools, he was enabled to give the general truth of tint and form without descending into minute details.   Of his rapidity we have already spoken, and of the power of doing his work at once and without repetition.   It has been said that a painter's execution and handling is a part of his individuality, and how truly does this agree with the character of Gainsborough.   We have but few details of his private life, but what do remain show him to have been a man of child-like nature, prone to anger, impulsive, yet simple to excess.   Thus he indulged in his extreme love for music as heartily as a child.   He could listen, with streaming eyes, to Colonel Hamilton playing on the violin, and, to induce him to proceed with his strain, give him, unreservedly, his picture of the "Boy at the Stile."   He was surrounded with musical instruments of all kinds—his toys, with which he recreated his leisure, and too often spent time that should not have been leisure.

Did he hear a new viol or hautboy, a new lute or theorbo, he must at once purchase it, purchase the lesson-book for it, and pay the professor to immediately come with him to instruct him how to play it. Like children, he was hasty and impetuous, easily roused and easily pleased, going from moods of sadness suddenly into gaiety and hilarity. What curious *naïvet* and simplicity is shown in his letter to the lawyer before quoted, which, alluding to some prior conversation with a friend, he thus finishes :—" I little thought you were a lawyer when I said, not one in ten were worth hanging. I told Clubb of that, and he seemed to think me lucky that I did not say one in a hundred. It is too late to ask your pardon now, but really, sir, I never saw one of your profession look so honest, and that's the reason I concluded you were in the wool trade." This simplicity, frankness, and quickness of feeling is characteristic of his works, and of the executive treatment both of his portraits and landscapes, on which we must now make a few remarks.

Gainsborough's fancy pictures of rustics and rustic children form a connecting link between his landscape and his portrait art ; some are truly figure-subjects, as the " Girl Feeding Pigs," the " Girl and Pitcher," while in others the landscape predominates, or the size and treatment of the figures is that of the landscape painter. In these works his good taste is as apparent as in his portraits. He took the children of the soil as he found them, even to their poverty and rags, and neither sought to give them sentiment nor prettiness, yet they charm us by their simple truth.

Reynolds says, " It is difficult to determine whether Gainsborough's portraits were most admirable for exact truth of resemblance, or his landscapes for a portrait-like representation of Nature,"—a strange judgment, written more with a view to a well-rounded period than to any true criticism on his rival's landscape art, which was anything but portrait-like. It would puzzle a critic to say what his trees really are, and to point out in his landscapes the distinctive differences between oak and beech, and elm. The weeds, too, in his foregrounds, have neither form nor species, his rocks are not geologically correct, he is said to have studied them in his painting-room from broken stones and bits of coal. The truth is, however, that he gave us more of Nature than any merely imitative rendering could do. As the great portrait painter looks beyond the features of his sitter to give the mind and character of the man, often thereby laying himself open to complaint as to his mere *likeness* painting ; so the great landscape painter will at all times sink individual imitation in seeking to fill us with the greater truths of his art.

In the history of British art, the great merit of Gainsborough is, to have broken us entirely loose from old conventions. Wilson had turned aside from Dutch art to ennoble landscape by selecting from the higher qualities of Italian art; but Gainsborough early discarded all he had learned from the bygone schools, and gave himself up wholly to Nature; he was capable of delicate handling and minute execution, but he resolutely cast them aside lest any idol should interfere between him and his new religion. There may be traced a lingering likeness in his landscapes to those of Rubens; but this arose more from his generalization of details, his sinking the parts in the whole, than to any imitation of the great Fleming.

The pictures of Gainsborough, on the whole, stand better far than those by Reynolds, but in examining the landscapes of this painter, much must be allowed for the present state of some of his works. Many are covered with a dark-brown varnish, obscuring the silvery freshness of their first state. This has cracked up in the darks and quite changed them. The "Market Cart" and the "Watering-place," as well as others in the national collection, are in a very different condition to that in which they left the easel. The world, however, has become so conservative, and has such belief in the picture-vamper's "golden tones," that so they must remain.

Gainsborough's contemporaries speak of him as fickle in character, lively and witty in society, but uncertain in his friendships. He was one of the foundation members of the Royal Academy, but he took little interest in that institution, or share in its management; nor did he associate with his colleagues. From 1758 to 1774, he lived at Bath, where he practised as a portrait painter, and then coming to London, he occupied a part of Schomberg House, in Pall Mall. His estrangement from the Academy is attributed to the discussion which arose on his expressed wishes relative to the mode of hanging a picture sent by him for exhibition in 1784. The fate of this picture, which must have been one of his finest works, is lamentable. It was a group of the three princesses—the Princess Royal, the Princess Augusta, and the Princess Elizabeth. In sending it, Gainsborough acknowledges he is aware that by the laws of the Academy it must be hung above the line; but he adds, that while this law does very well for pictures of strong effect, "he cannot possibly consent to have it placed higher than eight and a half feet, because the likenesses and the work of the picture will not be seen higher." Finding the work had not been hung as he desired, it was, on his request, returned to him, and he never afterwards exhibited at the Academy. In after years some officer of the palace, in charge of the furniture, had the picture cut down to form a *supra-porte* in one of the rooms; and then finding, or fearing, that he had committed a very unwarrantable act, he burnt or destroyed the part which had been cut off, so that the portrait now exists as a dwarfed half-length. What remains is exceedingly beautiful, and the work, by a cruel fate, has been reduced to a size which would have allowed its exhibition below the line, as the painter had originally desired.

Northcote says, " Gainsborough was a natural gentleman, and with all his simplicity he had wit too." He died at his house in Pall Mall in 1788. On his death-bed he was visited by Reynolds, with whom some coolness had existed, and the dying man, thinking to the last of his art, said to his brother painter—" We are all going to heaven, and Vandyck is of the party."

F

CHAPTER VII.

In the preceding chapters an attempt has been made to show the state of art and artists at the death of Hogarth, and coincident with the efforts successfully made to found the Royal Academy. From the date of this last event, and, no doubt, arising principally from the opportunity which its periodic and well-attended exhibitions gave to artists to make known their works to the public, both pictures and painters began largely to increase. But, as we look down the annual list of exhibitors, ranging over the long period of more than one hundred years, how few do we find whose lives and labours have been thought worthy of any record; how still smaller the number of those who have had a marked influence on art, and whose names have become household words. Many of those, moreover, whose names in their own day were in men's mouths, and who waxed rich through Court favour, ignorant patronage, fashion, or caprice, have fallen from their first estate; while some who in their life-time were despised or little appreciated, have at last obtained their due meed of honour. Our task is to treat of those few who have done honour to our school or who have influenced its progress, and to try to explain their merits and the causes of their success.

Nor will this prove any limited labour, since it is characteristic of Englishmen that they are a people of marked individuality and independent thought, and this is characteristic of their art also; in the British school, although there is a marked national style, yet the manner is as varied, as the men of note it includes. Nor is it to be supposed that at this period England was wholly unvisited by foreign artists; some such will be found in the list of the first members of the Academy; and as it may be thought they exerted some influence on the rising school, it will be proper to examine, in this chapter, how far this was the case; of these painters the following deserve an especial notice :—Giovanni Batista Cipriani, Angelica Kauffman, and Johann Zoffany, among the figure painters; Francesco Zuccarelli and Philip de Loutherbourg among the landscape painters. These alone possessed that distinction and attained that eminence which would lead us to infer any durable impress on the character of our art.

Giovanni B. Cipriani, R.A. (B. 1727, D. 1785), was a Florentine, descended from an ancient Tuscan family. He became acquainted with Sir W. Chambers in Rome, and on his return in 1755 accompanied him to London. Here he married an English lady with a moderate fortune, and actively pursued his profession for nearly thirty years in close fellowship with our artists. He was one of the two teachers appointed for the Duke of Richmond's gallery; and the English school is, perhaps, indebted to him for some of the grace that tempered the rude vigour of its first founders, and for that attention to the figure which led to greater refinement in drawing. In his day he was esteemed the first historical painter, outrivalling the jovial Frank Hayman, yet he painted few pictures in oil. His attempts at high art were weak, and his pictures exhibit the perfection of inane generalization; he treated his subject with an insipid elegance which took away all individuality. It has been shown that English art derived little from the Flemish painters who had practised among us; and it cannot be said that Cipriani's art—the worn-out and effete art of modern Italy—added much to the rough and rising school which had Hogarth, Gainsborough, Reynolds, and Wilson for its founders. His reputation is a proof of the low state of public taste when it was achieved; his feeling for colour was gay, even gaudy; and his chiaroscuro had still less merit. It is by his drawings that he is best known, chiefly in pen and ink, but sometimes coloured; they are full of forced elegance and pretty fancies; his females and children, models of unmeaning prettiness in art and taste. The influence of his works on the public mind is seen by their wide diffusion in the engravings of his friend and countryman Bartolozzi (also a member of the Royal Academy), through whose labours their reputation has extended even to our own time.

Angelica Kauffman, R.A. (B. 1740, D. 1807), the next on our list of foreigners, arrived in this country just before the foundation of the Academy. "The fair Angelica," as the artists gallantly called her, was a native of Schwarzenberg, a village in the Bregenzer Wald, Tyrol. She showed a very precocious taste for drawing, and, after travelling for her improvement through the chief Italian cities, came to London to seek her maiden fortunes in 1765, heralded by a brilliant reputation. Clever and amiable she at once found a kind patron and protectress in the young Queen Charlotte, and was admitted to a high place in the ranks of art. She is said to have looked with tenderness upon Reynolds, as to whose sensibility gossip has been dumb; but another painter, Nathaniel

Dance, led by her charms, wandered hopelessly through Italy in her train. A dramatic interest attaches to her unhappy marriage. Mistress of the German, French, Italian, and English languages; excelling in music, both vocal and instrumental, she added to learning, art, and to all, refined, amiable and affectionate manners, and was not only famed but wealthy; yet she was deceived into marriage in 1769 by the servant of a Swedish nobleman who passed himself off for his master. Separated from this impostor, and the object both of sympathy and scandal, she continued in the practice of her profession till his death in 1782, when, at the age of forty-two, with but little more prudence, she married Zucchi, a Venetian artist, and retaining her own maiden name, retired to Rome. There, after twenty-five years passed with undiminished reputation, she died and was buried with unusual pomp—above one hundred ecclesiastics in the habits of their different orders, the members of the literary societies in Rome, and many of the nobility walking in the procession, the pall supported by young females dressed in white, and two of her best pictures being carried immediately after her corpse.

But we have digressed—led aside, like the many eulogists of her day, by her charms and her talents. Her works were gay and pleasing in colour, yet weak and faulty in drawing, her male figures particularly wanting bone and individuality. Her influence is reflected in our day by the numerous engravings from her works. Six classical subjects, with several others, were engraved by Ryland; Schiavonetti engraved a number in the dot manner; Bartolozzi also; and it is a proof of her great popularity that Boydell published above sixty plates from her works. The ceiling of the Council-room of the Royal Academy is by her hand. In the present day her works are of small value, inferior even to the later pictures of West. They seem to contain but the creatures of her own brain,—beings which evidence a common parentage and family likeness, whether representing the gods and goddesses of antiquity, or those deities who in her day ruled the world of fashion. If any progress were to be made in art the British school did well to forget her.

The third foreigner whom we have named is *Johann Zoffany, R.A.,* descended from a Bohemian family, but a native of Frankfort, where he was born in 1733 or 1735. He came to England when about thirty years of age, and it is said at first found little encouragement, and was reduced to great distress. On the foundation of the Royal Academy, however, in 1768, which, if the above dates are correct, must have been within three or four years of his arrival, we find him enrolled among the forty original members by direction of their patron George III., so that he had already obtained royal notice and favour. His early works, judging from some small whole-lengths in the royal collection, were cold and slaty, heavily painted, and with no impasto or textural variety in execution, but during his stay in England he improved almost into a colourist. He adopted a small scale for his figures, and usually painted subjects which necessitated a careful study of individual nature, such as theatrical groups with portraits of the leading actors, &c., and he consequently followed the direction of the rising school ; it is great praise to say that he was not led into a stilted manner, but that his portraits have the truthful air of nature. In his large compositions, such as the group of " The Members of the Royal Academy," or " The Tribune at Florence," with portraits of distinguished connoisseurs inspecting the works, there is a little want of keeping and relief ; but the execution is excellent and the finish careful without littleness, while the general colour of the work is agreeable and the likenesses truthful. When he painted life-size he was apt to be wooden, and such works have the appearance of being beyond his power.

In 1781 he left England to push his fortunes in India, and during some years' residence at Lucknow continued to practise his art on the same class of subjects that had occupied his pencil in England, combining incident and portraiture, such as " The Cock-fight," " An Indian Tiger Hunt," &c. He returned to London about 1796 with a competent fortune, and continued to practise his art, but, whether weakened by the effect of climate or by advancing age, his later works are of less interest than those of his early years. He died in 1810. It is probable that his careful manner of painting, his attention to accurate costume, the individuality of his heads, and the general truthfulness of his backgrounds, had some influence on the young artists who, in the next century, were to give a strong impress to the English school ; but there is little doubt that the best qualities of his art were obtained in this country, and that he gained here as much as he gave to the fellow-artists of his adopted land.

We have already described the art of Gainsborough and Wilson ; the freshness and novelty of the one, the breadth and grandeur of the other. While these great men were laying the foundation of a better future for English landscape art than the Claude-like imitations of the Smiths and others, two foreigners were also practising their art in England with a pecuniary success not accorded to our great native painters. One of these, *Francesco Zuccarelli, R.A.*, was born in Tuscany in 1702, and had already obtained an European reputation before his arrival in London in 1752. It is greatly to the credit of his discernment as well as of his generous feelings that he appreciated the talent of Wilson when in Venice, and advised him to leave portraiture for landscape. Nor is he to be blamed if the public and the artists of his day, lacking his own discernment, sought his works in preference to those of their countryman. Zuccarelli soon became fashionable in England, and led the taste both of the artists and of the public, while Wilson was left in want of bread.

Zuccarelli was one of the original members of the Royal Academy (founded six years after his arrival in London). His landscapes are marked only by a pretty insipidity and a continual re-combination of stale thoughts and used-up compositions. Zuccarelli died in Florence in 1788.

Philip de Loutherbourg, R.A., was another foreigner who practised in England as a landscape painter while her own sons were struggling to form a school and to obtain a name. He was born at Strasbourg in 1740, and came to England in 1771, having previously arrived at fame in Paris, where he had been elected a member of the French Academy. He was a landscape painter of great power, although his art was very conventional, and his works have little *finesse* of execution or of truth to nature. On his arrival in England he was engaged by Garrick to design scenes for Drury Lane Theatre at a salary of 500*l.* a year. His ready and facile execution and his power of artificial composition suited this branch of art; but such facility is rather a curse than a benefit, and the scene painter always predominated over the artist. Trusting to his ready memory he needed or sought little reference to the great teacher Nature; hence, though his drawing is good, his colouring is often unpleasant—hot skies contrasted with cold slaty greys and greens. Thus Peter Pindar writes—

> " And Loutherbourg, when Heaven wills,
> To make brass skies and golden hills,
> With marble bullocks in glass pastures grazing,
> Thy reputation, too, will rise,
> And people gazing with surprise,
> Cry, ' Monsieur Loutherbourg is most amazing.' "

Though mannered and conventional, his art was never feeble; it is impossible to overlook the vigour with which he wrought, the motion and action of his figures, and the skill with which they are placed in his landscapes. In his picture of " The Victory of the First of June under Lord Howe," which has been finely engraved by Woollett, we have the various incidents of a battle scene given with fire and animation.

De Loutherbourg was elected an associate in 1780, and a full member of the Royal Academy in 1781. There is no question that his facile execution and the great vigour with which he painted, had many charms for his brother artists, and influenced for a time the practice of the school; but they soon passed away when the habit of referring to nature as the fountain of freshness in art obtained a hold on those who practised it. He contributed greatly to the improvement of scene painting, for which his art and genius were peculiarly suited; and when, on an attempt to reduce his salary, he left the theatre, and planned his "Eidophusicon," all the world went to Spring Gardens to see and admire his moving picture, and his shifting effects of calm and storm. Late in life he became a disciple of the notorious Brothers. Like him he professed the gift of prophecy, and the power to heal diseases; but this proved too much for his skill, and the deluded mob broke his windows. He died in 1812, and found a quiet rest near the great Hogarth in Chiswick churchyard.

In the succeeding chapters we purpose to examine the state of historical and portrait painting, landscape and animal painting, at this transitional period when the influence of the new Academy could only be felt in its exhibitions, and the fruits of its teaching were as yet but ripening. So much has been said of the evil of exhibitions, that perhaps the good they do by leading young men to see their faults and weigh their powers, has hardly been enough insisted on.

CHAPTER VIII.

CONTEMPORARY fame gave to the historical works of Frank Hayman, in the existing dearth, a rank which was not afterwards assigned to them, or to the higher merits of Sir James Thornhill's decorative paintings; and the claim to have possessed a painter of history in the English school was deferred for nearly two generations.

We have already said that Sir Joshua Reynolds painted several historical pictures, as his "Ugolino," "Macbeth," "Infant Hercules," and some others. But such hours as he could spare from his sitters, he loved much more to devote to fancy subjects; and he told his pupil, Northcote, that "history cost him too dear." Other and younger men, however, stimulated by the love of fame, were anxious to occupy the field which the successful portrait painter had abandoned. Three of these, West, Barry, and Copley, young men of nearly the same age, within a year or two of thirty when the first exhibition at the Royal Academy took place, deserve especial notice from their continuous and lifelong efforts to produce works of high aim.

They were not academically educated, so that neither their faults nor their excellences can be considered the result of the Academy system; nor were they taught in the *atelier* of any great artist, but each learnt his art individually and alone. Three artists instructed more variously and from their early associations, more separated from art influences while obtaining their elementary knowledge, can hardly be found. One advantage they had in common. In early life, soon after entering upon the practice of their art, and when their elementary training may be supposed to have been completed, each visited Italy, making a more or less prolonged stay. West went there when twenty-two years of age, and was three years in the various capitals of that country; Barry in his twenty-fifth year, and remained nearly four years; but Copley was in his thirty-seventh year, and stayed only one year in the land of art. What influence had these visits on their future art and practice ? Barry and West, who went when young, and made the longest stay in Italy, will be found most imbued with the desire to excel in the highest walk of art, they were also most scholastic in their treatment of it ; Copley was the freshest and most original. Barry, who, from his religious opinions and influences, and the great admiration he expressed of Raphael and Michael Angelo, might have been expected to apply himself to religious art, was led away by classic influences while abroad, and at home by the only opportunity afforded him of exhibiting his powers. He devoted his life to a work on social culture, of which the heathen myths and sports are made to form the principal groundwork, and a half-classic Elysium the object and end. He, no doubt, owed his enthusiasm and devotion to art to the noble works of the master minds of Italy ; and he toiled on, under good and evil report, at a work, which, if too high for his art-power or mental culture, was yet treated in a manner of his own, and with little obligation to the inventions of the great painters whom he reverenced ; he thus completed an epic in art, unique of its kind, the first, and, so far, the last which his country has produced. West was of a religious faith, which rejects material aids to worship and rests wholly on spirituality, which eschews the use of arms, and which objects to the warrior caste. In obedience to the claims upon his talents he passed his life in alternately painting religious and heroic subjects, cherished, how-ever, with the substantial consolation of his sovereign's favour and having 1,500*l.* a year to enable him to devote his heart and soul to his labours.

Both these men seem to have received their art inspiration from the Florentine school, but from Raphael rather than from Michael Angelo, yet it is singular how little they obtained beyond the conventionalities of art, such as composition, grouping, &c.

Both visited Venice, but how little did they, or, perhaps, could they, profit by the noble works of that school ! West seems almost insensible to colour ; and Barry to have mistaken the brown tone of time and varnish, for the glories they did but entomb. West only attained to an imitative facility and a barren power that enabled him, during a long life, to cover acres of canvas with much that is insipid and mediocre, leaving him no time to produce one work, hardly one figure evidencing intense feeling or keen perception. This very facility led him to a painty and mechanical execution which repels the spectator, makes him long for less respectability and more vigour, and, if at the cost of a little coarseness, for something to find fault with or something to praise. West drew well, cast his draperies well, painted his picture satisfactorily throughout ; but no part excites us to admiration or enthusiasm, or invites our special attention.

Barry, while in Rome, seems to have made the proportions of the classic figure his study, rather than that consideration of its structure which would have given him power to impart life and motion to his figures. We are told that his mode of work was singular, that "in drawing from the antique he always employed an instrument called a delineator, not aiming to make academic drawings, but a sort of diagram on which a scale of proportions was established, to which he might at all times refer as a guide and authority." On his return he seems to have adopted a proportion, which, from the smallness of the heads and extremities, and the largeness of the limbs and trunk, he supposed would give his figures grandeur and power. They are apt, on the contrary, to look clumsy and ponderous; and, from the mode of study described, there is no clearness of form and contour, none of the appearance of breed and training in his figures, which, at the least, we should look for in the athletæ of the Olympian Games; but rather the sense of stuffed roundness, as of the limbs of lay figures. The muscles are rarely in true action, but a posed equality throughout his figures gives them an appearance of unreality, inconsistent with the action they are intended to represent.

Singleton Copley began *his* life as a portrait painter, and was in mature years and the full practice of his art when he visited Italy and finally settled in England. He continued here to devote himself to portraiture, and even his historical works are allied to his early practice; of this "The Death of Chatham" is an extreme example. In his historical works Copley was, as has been inferred, but little influenced by his visit to Italy; though educated in art in a land where the means and appliances were few, he was a good and intelligent draughtsman, treated his subjects simply and naturally and with sufficient individuality to carry us into the scene represented.

Having premised thus far as to the education of these three distinguished painters, we will add such a brief account of the life and works of each as will bear upon the practice of his art and its influence upon our rising school.

Benjamin West, P.R.A., the descendant of English Quaker ancestors, was born in Pennsylvania in 1738. He seems to have been born an artist. From the Indians he obtained his first pigments—red and yellow, to which, from his mother's stores, he added indigo, thus possessing the primary colours. His brush he made from hairs cut from the cat's back. He had already, when in his seventh year, drawn a likeness of his sister, whose cradle he was set to watch, which earned for him the fond kisses of his surprised mother. Showing much of the resolution of the old race from which he sprang, and proudly determined to follow art, he declared that a painter was the companion of kings and emperors. At sixteen, his Quaker relatives, impressed with his intelligence and the genius with which they believed him especially gifted, allowed him, after much discussion, to follow a profession which, according to their peculiar tenets, was at least doubtful. It is said that when this discussion was ended the women rose and kissed the young artist, and the men one by one laid their hands on his head, and from that time the painter felt himself dedicated, like Samuel of old, to high and holy subjects for his art.

West nevertheless began with painting portraits—first in his native city, and then in New York, where, meeting with encouragement and friends, he was enabled to travel to Europe, deeply impressed with the greatness of his art mission. Arrived at Rome, the young American was the object of much curiosity, and Cardinal Albani, who was blind, asked, when introduced to him, whether he was black or white. The *virtuosi* crowded about him to note his sensations on first seeing the great works of the capitol, and to watch their effect on the virgin mind of the genius from the new world. Dazzled by his reception, more and more impressed with the passion for elevated art, he visited Florence and Bologna, and, as we have already said, remained in Italy during three years.

He arrived in London in the summer of 1763, provided with good introductions, and preceded by a somewhat exaggerated reputation. In 1766 we find him exhibiting his picture of "Orestes and Pylades," which is now in the National Gallery. This picture was immensely admired, and led to an introduction to George III., which was the beginning of a royal patronage extending over thirty-three years.

On the formation of the Royal Academy in 1768, West was one of the foundation members, and year after year contributed three or four works to the exhibition. On the death of Sir Joshua Reynolds in 1792, he was elected president, and delivered an inaugural address, which was much applauded, but which his biographer tells us "must have cost him little thought, as it dwelt but on two topics—the excellence of British art, and the gracious benevolence of his Majesty." On this occasion, firm to his religious opinions, he declined the honour of knighthood. When his royal patron fell permanently under the illness which ended in his death, West's labours for the Crown terminated, but he afterwards painted many religious subjects, some of them among his best works, such as "Christ Healing the Sick," now in the National Gallery; "Christ Rejected," exhibited in 1814; and "Death on the Pale Horse," in 1817. He died on the 11th March, 1820, in his eighty-second year.

West's compositions were more studied than natural, the action often conventional and dramatic, the draperies, although learned, heavy and without truth. His colour often wants freshness and variety of tint, and is hot and foxy. His courage in undertaking works of deep importance and magnitude far exceeded his powers, and he could not identify himself with the place and time, and the *dramatis personæ* represented.

From this want of individuality, his heads are all of one mould, and have little savour of humanity in them, and therefore do not interest us. It is true he used the model for his works, but it was rarely well chosen, and the same models played many parts in the same picture, changed and modified by the painter, until, with all individuality taken out of them, they are vapid and characterless. His back-grounds are very tame, and there is a great want of contrasts in his pictures, which are pervaded by a level mediocrity too good to be passed over, and too weak to excite much emotion. The hands have been said to be second only to the face as vehicles of expression. West made great use of them for this purpose, but the actions he chooses are generally stale and conventional.

How then shall we account for the great reputation he enjoyed—if we attribute it to Court patronage, and the kindness of his Royal patron, we are at a loss to explain the opinions of his brother artists—what can we say to the opinion of Sir Thomas Lawrence, that " his compositions were profoundly studied and executed with the most facile power, and not only superior to any former productions of English art, but far sur-passing contemporary merit on the Continent, and unequalled at any period below the schools of the Carracci"? Later, Sir Martin Shee, P.R.A., speaks of him in 1836, in almost the same terms. Yet was one at least among West's contemporaries who dissented from such opinions, for we are told that on West's re-election to the president's chair, after his temporary secession in 1803, the votes were unanimous except one—only one—which was in favour of Mrs. Lloyd, then an academician, and that Fuseli, when taxed with giving this vote, said, "Well, if I did, she is eligible, and is not one old woman as good as another?" West's pictures fetched high prices, but now his works have almost ceased to have a market value with collectors, and would only command furniture prices.

But West, too highly rated in his day, has been perhaps too much depreciated in ours; we must recur to the state of art prior to his time, in order to understand the judgment of his contemporaries. After Verrio and Laguerre (the latter no mean artist, as his wall-paintings at Marl-borough House will show) came Thornhill and Hayman, and it may well be supposed, that compared with their works, West's pictures show a great advance.

The English school certainly owed to West the abandonment of classic costume in the treatment of the heroic subjects of our own time ; and perhaps also his gentle and dignified life served to set the taste for more refined manners in his brother artists. Since then we have fewer of the roystering school, who mistake debauchery and wildness for genius ; and the artist has risen in the social scale. Otherwise, West's art, his position in the Academy as its president, and his continued employment by the King, left little or no trace on our school.

What West undertook in religious and historical art, *James Barry, R.A.*, attempted for classic or heroic art, and in some respects more successfully, because with greater originality. He was a native of Cork, born in 1741, the son of a coasting trader who kept a small public-house. Determined from boyhood to be a painter, and disgusted with the sea after two or three coasting trips, he secretly followed the strong bent of his genius, and made rude attempts in chalk upon any smooth surface within his reach. After such small help as he could get in his native city, he made his way to Dublin, and there found sudden distinction by a picture which he painted and exhibited—" The Conversion and Baptism of an Irish Prince by St. Patrick." Here the youth and his work attracted the notice of Edmund Burke, who advised and befriended him. Then after a short continuance of his studies in Dublin, he went to London under the guidance of Burke, in 1764, in his twenty-third year. For some time he subsisted by copying in oil the drawings of Mr. Stuart, better known as "Athenian Stuart," who was Hogarth's successor as Serjeant-painter, and by whose works there is no doubt his classic taste was strengthened. In the latter end of the year 1765, Burke and his brother provided Barry with the means of visiting Rome. Here his careful and frugal habits enabled him to subsist and study for the greatest part of five years ; his rugged independence and hatred of the *virtuosi* and their jobs, having shut him out from the many ways of increasing a small income, which fall to the share of artists residing in that capital.

On his way out he stayed some months at Paris, occupied in sketching and studying the works there. Arrived in Rome, his chief study seems to have been directed to the antique statues and marbles, and the great frescoes of Michael Angelo ; though from many passages in his letters it is clear that Titian stood very high in his estimation—higher, it would appear, than the two great Florentines. Thus in one of his letters from Venice, he afterwards writes :—" I have said formerly, that I find Titian is the only modern who fills up an idea of perfection in any one part of the art. There is no example of anything that goes beyond his colouring, whereas the parts of the art in which Michael Angelo and Raphael excelled, are almost annihilated by the superiority of the antiques." While at Rome he began his picture of "Adam and Eve," and did not seem to fear to compare it with that by Raphael.

On his way back to England he lingered in some of the great North Italian cities, studying Correggio at Parma, and the Bolognese school, which he commended, in the city of its birth ; while here his funds ran out, and he was beset with difficulties, partly arising from missing a small letter of credit, but showing the low state of his finances. As he approached home his spirits seem to have sunk at his prospects. The battle of life must now be fought; he could no longer depend upon the kind aid of his patron, but it would be necessary to be self-reliant.

He returned to London in 1771, and in the same year exhibited his "Adam and Eve," which as we have seen he painted during his stay in Italy. To our eyes, as possibly to those of his contemporaries, the picture (though unpretending and agreeable in tone) evinces no feeling for colour, and even the forms are inelegant, unduly round, and without interior markings, their pose somewhat stiff, and the action not easy. He hints even, that he was aware the Burkes were not quite satisfied with his work. But undismayed by imperfect success, he resumed his labour, choosing a subject which required the highest feeling for form and colour, and entering upon a rivalry with the greatest masters. This picture, "Venus Rising from the Sea," was exhibited in 1772, and resulted in his election as an associate of the Royal Academy in the autumn of that year, and as an R.A. in 1773.

Barry had now reached a distinguished place in art, and the right to come before the public, educated and uneducated, to receive or to influence its judgment; but while in Rome his headstrong, violent, and obstinate temper had made him many enemies, and within three years of his return he endeavoured to quarrel with his long-tried friend Burke, on a mere point of ceremony. His was of a temper that never yielded; adverse criticism only produced in him a state of obstinate opposition; nevertheless, we from a distance cannot but admire the man who, in pursuit of what he considered the true end of art, devoted himself to a life of lonely poverty, that he might work out this great aim.

He was foremost among those who at this time offered to decorate the interior of St. Paul's, and when, in 1774, on the failure of this proposal, the Society of Arts, through Mr. Valentine Green, the engraver, offered their room for decoration, Barry entered warmly into the scheme, and in 1777, after some previous negotiation with the newly-founded society, agreed to paint on the walls of their meeting-room in the Adelphi, a series of works illustrating human culture. All he asked was, that the society should provide him with materials and models; and this being arranged to his satisfaction, he commenced his gratuitous labours, and for seven long years perseveringly occupied himself with the execution of these works, which are at least his best monument. Some have said that he literally starved during the time he was so occupied. He tells us himself, that at the time of undertaking them he had only sixteen shillings in his pocket, and that in the prosecution of his labour, he had often, after painting all day, to sketch or engrave at night some design

for the booksellers, which was to supply him with the means of his frugal
subsistence ; but the society allowed him a small sum, and there is good
evidence that his economy, and his long acquaintance with simple and
hard fare, kept him above actual want.

Barry's work in the Adelphi claims especial notice in the history of
art. His pictures propose to illustrate the great truth, " that the attainment of happiness, individual as well as public, depends on the development, proper cultivation and perfection of the human faculties, physical
and moral ; " and in their story, treatment, and accessories are appropriate to the society whose meeting-room they ornament. They consist
of six separate paintings—four, each 15 ft. 2 in. long ; two, each occupying the whole length of the chamber, 42 ft. long, and all 11 ft. 10 in.
high. The first of the series represents the story of Orpheus reclaiming
mankind from the savage state. This, probably the first executed, is the
weakest. With good expression both of face and figure, the action of the
Orpheus is constrained, the group before him huddled and confused ;
but the landscape and the incidents in which it abounds are good accessories to the subject.

The second picture is a Grecian harvest-home or thanksgiving to Ceres
and Bacchus : A classic group of young men and girls are dancing in
the foreground ; the landscape is rich in colour and filled with incidents
showing the abundance of the earth under due cultivation : in the
distance are seen rural sports, a wedding procession, and all that is
associated with a happy rural life, but the dancing figures are poised and
not moving.

The third picture, the first of the two larger ones of the series, represents " The Victors of Olympia." It is grandly conceived and executed
in a large and simple manner, and having but little of positive colour,
it inclines to a composition of tone, and an arrangement of greys and
browns. This is on the whole satisfactory and suits well with the subject,
giving it a grave and heroic character, yet somewhat at the expense of
its appeal to the eye, and rather indicating a sense of timidity in the
painter as a colourist. The light and shade are well considered, giving
due prominence to the principal figures, and, as in the other pictures, the
background and incidents are strictly appropriate. The heroic dignity
of man, the training of the body to endurance and the limbs to action, the
subjugation of strength to will, are the painter's theme. No less than
thirty-five principal figures occupy the canvas, while in the left-hand
corner Barry's own likeness finds an appropriate place.

The forms in this picture are particularly amenable to the remarks
already made upon Barry as a draughtsman ; in them he has adopted
proportions which fail to give grandeur, and a manner which does
not approach to style. The "terrible way" of Michael Angelo,

the classical air of Mantegna, the developed and rounded proportions of Rubens, produce a style felt even in the diluted efforts of their imitators. The sculptors of antiquity were so studious of characteristic form, that a mere fragment of the finest period of Greek art would enable us to distinguish the heroic from the god-like form, the trained athlete, from the youthful follower of Bacchus or Venus. But Barry's figures, intended to represent the heroes of the foot-race, the wrestlers and boxers, who had long had the body in training "to bring it into subjection," striving for the mastery, that they might obtain the much prized crown, look big and boneless, mere sacks of flesh. As boxers they might conquer by weight, by brute force, but not by trained skill. Yet Barry's work is beyond any work of his contemporaries, and is a monument to be spoken of with great respect.

It is curious that the subject of mental culture ends here; the next picture gives rather the triumph of navigation than its culture. It is called "Navigation, or the Triumph of the Thames," and is a glorification of navigation and commerce, perhaps indicating their value in bringing together the nations of the earth though the intention is obscure. Our great river is typified by an imposing but somewhat heavy male figure borne in a car upon its waters; around the car float the navigators Drake, Raleigh, Cabot, and Cook in full costume, and Dr. Burney, introduced to typify music, in coat and wig of the time, all intermingled with Naiads and Nereids sporting with them amid the waves. Strangely incongruous, and not very clear as to its subject, it fails to interest us except for its oddity.

The fifth subject, depicting "The Distribution of the Society's Rewards," and the sixth, "Elysium and Tartarus, or the State of Final Retribution," are contrasted pictures. In the fifth, princes and judges are distributing earthly rewards to all orders of people for all sorts of works; in the last—perhaps, on the whole, the finest of the series—the wise and the good are entering upon their heavenly reward. It is honourable to Barry's liberality that his Paradise contains men of all ages, all countries, and all religions. Homer, Milton, and Shakespeare are side by side on the Olympian height; Raphael and Titian have their easels on its slopes. Popes and cardinals are there, with Bishop Butler among them, whose *Analogy* is said to have made much impression on the mind of the painter. The "Elysium" is an impressive work, grandly conceived, and certainly has this great merit, that it differs essentially from the treatment which the subject of final retribution has received at the hands of others. We have pointed out the defects and shortcomings of this painted epic in no spirit of depreciation; no other work of the English school, even down to our own day, aspires to so high a rank in a region of art, in which even to be short of perfection is not to be disgraced.

Barry finished this great work in 1784, and in itself it almost represents the labour of his life in art. The society, according to agreement, gave him the proceeds of the exhibition of his pictures, and added a gift of 200*l.* He etched the series on a large scale, and the sale of these etchings was henceforth the principal source of his income. It were well, if possible, to pass over the dissensions with his brother artists, arising from his irritable and pugnacious disposition, which separated him from those who wished to be his friends, and embittered his own life. Among his other troubles, some thief broke into his comfortless lodgings and stole 400*l.*, which, amid all his poverty, his saving habits had enabled him to accumulate; the next morning he is said to have placarded his doors with a notice that the burglary was committed by the thirty-nine academicians.

He violated, in his lectures, the established rule, that no allusion should be made to the works of contemporaries, and he taunted Reynolds with " the poor mistaken stuff of his discourses." But want of sympathy and success had soured a disposition never very amiable, and while it were to be wished that in the best interests of art such petty insults had been overlooked, it was hard to hear their constant repetition. He was first removed from his professorship of painting—to which he had been elected in 1772—and, finally, in 1799, by a vote of the general assembly, approved by the King, he was dismissed from his membership.

From his unceiled room, which had been a carpenter's shop, not even impervious to the weather, uncleaned, unfurnished, with scarcely a bed, Barry had been, in the early days of 1806, to the house where he usually dined : when about to return, he was seized with a pleuritic fever ; after some cordial had been administered to him, he was taken in a coach to the door of his lonely home. Alas ! he either had neighbouring enemies, or some mischievous boys had stuffed the key-hole with dirt and stones ; the door could not be opened, and the poor painter, shivering with cold and disease, was obliged to resort to the temporary shelter which a companion found for him, and then left him sick and alone. He unfortunately remained two days without medical aid ; delirium and severe inflammation ensued, and although he rallied so much as unadvisedly to go forth to the house of his friend Bonomi, he lingered but a few days, and died on the 22nd of February, 1806.

His body lay in state in the rooms of the Adelphi, in the presence of his great work, and he was buried in St. Paul's, where he rests, side by side with the great ones of his profession.

The third painter, whose works are the subject of comment in this chapter, is *John Singleton Copley, R.A.* Less lofty in the subjects he chose for illustration than West and Barry, and finding his inspiration in the exalted deeds of his own time rather than in sacred or classic lore,

G

his works naturally appealed to popular enthusiasm. Born 3rd July, 1737, of Irish parents, immediately upon their arrival in America, at Boston, then a British colony, he was led early in life by his own tastes to drawing, and, out of the reach of academies and masters, he was left unobtrusively to make his own way. He began with portraits and domestic groups, for which he found the backgrounds in the wild-wood scenery around him. In 1760, and yearly till 1767, he sent pictures to London for exhibition, where these works attracted notice, and raised expectations of his future career. He was making a good income at Boston by his portraits, but he looked forward with a longing desire to see the great works of art in the old country, and for this he husbanded his gains. In 1774 he was enabled to start for Europe with the intention of making a three years' tour. He took London on his way, and from thence went on direct to Rome, but in the following year he visited the chief seats of art in the cities of Italy, Germany, and the Low Countries, and after a short stay in Paris, returned to London at the end of the year 1775, and decided to settle here.

In 1776 he exhibited at the Royal Academy a work called, in the phraseology of that day, "A Conversation," that is, a group of portraits, either small or of life-size, engaged or grouped in some simple manner; and in the same year he was elected an associate of the newly-formed body. Shortly after Copley had exhibited his first work in the Royal Academy, an event occurred of great national importance, which must also, from the circumstances of his birth and parentage, have had a peculiar interest for the painter. In the spring of the year 1778, William Pitt, the celebrated Earl of Chatham, who had ever opposed the taxation of our American possessions, and held the opinion "that this kingdom has no right to levy a tax upon her colonies," came down to the House of Lords, while still suffering from a severe attack of the gout, to take part in a discussion on American affairs. He had already spoken at some length, but got up again to reply to some observations of the Duke of Richmond, when he suddenly fell fainting and insensible into the arms of the surrounding peers. This was on the 7th of April. He was removed at once to his house at Hayes in Kent, where he lingered for a short time, and died on the 11th of the succeeding month. This incident furnished a noble subject for the painter, and one for which Copley was peculiarly well qualified. He commenced the large picture of "The Death of the Earl of Chatham," now in our National Gallery, painting distinct portraits of the various peers holding office, or otherwise present on that occasion.

Altogether the work is a fine composition : the principal incident and group well supported by the secondary ones ; the difficulties on the whole successfully surmounted, and the story solemnly and touchingly told ;

while as a group of portraits of the great men of that age, it will grow in interest with the natives of our own land, as well as with those for which the great orator laboured with his last breath. The picture was engraved by Bartolozzi, who made some beautiful drawings from the principal heads, and produced a work so highly popular, that we are told 2,500 copies were sold in the course of a few weeks.

It has been said that the painter, on his first arrival in England, took the house, No. 25, George Street, Hanover Square, in which he lived until his death, and in which his distinguished son resided during a long life and also died. But from the original proposals, issued in March, 1780, for publishing a print from "The Death of Chatham," we find it stated that, "subscriptions are received by Mr. Copley, at his house No. 12, in Leicester Fields," so that it must have been somewhat later that he removed to George Street.

In 1779, Copley was elected a full member of the Royal Academy. He had now the difficult task of supporting the reputation he had gained, but he was equally fortunate in the subject he chose for his next important picture. "A body of French troops having invaded the island of Jersey in the year 1781, possessed themselves of the town of St. Helier's, and taking the Lieutenant-Governor prisoner, obliged him, in that situation, to sign a capitulation to surrender the island. Major Pierson, a gallant young officer, less than twenty-four years of age, sensible of the invalidity of the capitulation made by the Lieutenant-Governor whilst he was a prisoner, with great valour and prudence attacked and totally defeated the French troops, and thereby rescued the island, and gloriously maintained the honour of the British army. Unfortunately this brave officer fell in the moment of victory; not by a chance shot, but by a ball levelled at him, with the design, by his death, to check the ardour of the British troops. The major's death was instantly retaliated by his black servant on the man who shot the major."

The background of the picture is an exact view of the spot where the battle was fought; introduced in the central group are the portraits of twelve persons, officers of the 95th Regiment and others, including the faithful black who avenged his master's death.

There is but little of conventionality, and great sense of truth and naturalness, in the way in which the painter has treated the incident. It appears as if the event must have happened as it is represented. Indeed, an authority on battles, the great Duke of Wellington himself, when seated before it at dinner, is said on more than one occasion to have expressed his admiration of the picture, and to have affirmed that it was the best representation of a battle he had ever seen.

The colour of the picture is agreeable, fresh, and pure—the handling very vigorous; and it remains to this day one of the first pictures of its class in the English school ; less talked of, perhaps, because less known than West's "Death of Wolfe," but a work of far higher merit. It was painted for Alderman Boydell, but it is now in the National Gallery.

Copley next proceeded to carry out a work of which the composition and design had been prepared for some years : " Charles I. demanding, in the House of Commons, the Five Impeached Members."

The City of London now gave him a commission to paint for their Guildhall a large picture of " The Repulse and Defeat of the Spanish Floating Batteries at Gibraltar by Lord Heathfield." It is said that the painter went to Gibraltar to prepare sketches of various officers of the garrison, and to study the locality for this work, which is quite in keeping with his known desire to treat his incidents in strict accordance with the locality. Many of the drawings of groups for the picture remain, which serve to illustrate his readiness as a draughtsman, and the manner in which he conducted his work. The groups were carefully arranged, and spiritedly drawn from nature, on a small scale in black and white chalk on grey paper. These drawings were evidently enlarged by squaring on to the canvas, and the work was painted at once. The picture itself is finely composed, and painted in the same simple and vigorous manner as Copley's other works—a manner which, if it pre-cludes the refinements of colour, stands well because the work was done at once. It has the same freshness of colour and look of out-of-doors daylight which is characteristic of his art. It is boldly conceived, uniting an action on the sea with one on shore, the difficulty of the two planes being well overcome by placing the military on the raised platform of the fort. The sailors are thus sufficiently removed into the distance, although close to the bottom line of the picture, and the figures in the naval action are reduced to about half life-size. The portraits of the fifteen principal personages engaged in the conflict are introduced into the work. No doubt naval critics may find fault with the accessories, but to the artist or to the general spectator the bustle and animation of the scene are well given. The picture, when exhibited, was so popular that it is said to have been visited by 60,000 people, and that the net profits arising from the exhibition of that work and the " Death of Chatham," amounted together to 5,000*l.*

Copley continued in the practice of his profession, painting both portraits and historical pictures until his death at the advanced age of seventy-eight, on the 9th December, 1815. He was very fortunate in the line of art he adopted ; he appealed to national taste in his subjects, and to the national love of portraiture in his mode of illustrating them. When he turned to sacred themes, of which he left behind him a few small pictures, he was far less successful, because less original. We can trace the adoption of figures and attitudes from the greater masters who had occupied that field, and we feel how wise he was to continue in the walk he had chosen for himself.

Many have since his day undertaken groups of portraiture connected with some historical event, but few have treated such subjects so satisfactorily as John Singleton Copley. His manner, we are told by several authorities, was laboriously slow, though we should not have judged so from his works. Mr. Serjeant, an American painter, says :— " He painted a very beautiful head of my mother, who told me that she sat to him fifteen or sixteen times, six hours at a time ; and that once she had been sitting to him for many hours, when he left the room for a few minutes, but requested she would not move from her seat during his absence. She had the curiosity, however, to peep at the picture, and to her astonishment she found it all rubbed out." " When painting a portrait Copley used to match with his palette-knife a tint for every part of the face, whether in light, shadow, or reflection. This occupied himself and the sitter a long time before he touched the canvas. One of the most beautiful of his portrait-compositions is at Windsor Castle, and represents a group of the royal children playing in a garden with dogs and parrots. It was painted at Windsor, and during the operation, the children, the dogs, and the parrots became equally wearied. The persons who were obliged to attend them while sitting, complained to the Queen ; the Queen complained to the King ; and the King to Mr. West, who had obtained the commission for Copley. Mr. West satisfied his Majesty that Mr. Copley must be allowed to proceed in his own way, and that any attempt to hurry him might be injurious to the picture, which would be a very fine one when done." The tedious preparatory practice for this picture (which is now at Buckingham Palace) is, however, not inconsistent with rapid execution when the work was actually begun.

CHAPTER IX.

GEORGE ROMNEY AND JOSEPH WRIGHT (OF DERBY).

WHILE Barry, West, and Copley were devoting themselves principally to historic art, there were other English painters, their contemporaries, who endeavoured to uphold and continue the fame of English portraiture, even during the lifetime of Reynolds and Gainsborough. Of these George Romney and Joseph Wright, known as Wright of Derby, demand our notice; but while making them the joint subjects of this chapter, they have no other connexion either in their art or their lives, than may be assigned to them as contemporaries holding rank in the same profession, of whose art it is convenient to treat together.

It has been objected to Reynolds that he spent much of his life and wasted his fine powers in experiments on colouring. The same cannot be said of either Copley or West; one method seems to characterize all their works, which evince great readiness, and in Copley's case great apparent power of painting at once, great decision of handling; but both had little feeling as *painters*.

There is no doubt that much of the *common* appearance of the works of both Copley and West resulted from a poor executive; even in the disrupted and cracked surface of Reynolds there is ever a noble quality seen beneath, and the very texture of decay is less offensive in him than the uniform hard surface and dry juiceless cracks in their pictures—for even their works have cracked—but without that luscious richness as of an over-ripe fruit, which characterizes the work of Reynolds.

West, Copley, F. Cotes, R.A. (B. 1726, D. 1770), N. Dance, R.A. (B. 1730, D. 1811), and, in his early portraits, Wright of Derby, painted solidly and at once, and cared very little if at all for the ground; and in this they followed the executive methods of the old school. They showed great dexterity, but at the same time great sameness of handling, and a dry unvaried surface that gets hair-cracked, and may rise from the ground and scale off, but rarely draws together, and never gives signs of flowing in the darks.

A curious portrait on one of the staircases at Hatfield will illustrate both this indifference to the ground on which they painted, and the solid execution of the period. It is a whole-length of one of the noble house of Cecil, in the flowing wig and costume of the early half of the eighteenth century. Having on some occasion been placed in the hands of a picture-cleaner, the curls of the wig were wiped away, and a portrait of the Duke of Monmouth in armour began to emerge to the light of day. No doubt the painter had taken a portrait of the disgraced duke, and used the canvas for another sitter without further preparation, solidly painting the head of his new sitter over the old one. By the followers of such a method, the only advance possible is in the direction of rapid and dexterous execution, and this it has been shown that the painters we have been adverting to achieved. Northcote, Opie, Hoppner, and others of the succeeding race, of whom we shall presently speak, followed, on the contrary, or attempted to follow, the methods of Reynolds. They adopted and used his pigments with all their faults, realizing few of the beauties he achieved with them ; they sought to arrive at his impasto, but rather by the loading of successive repetitions than by the proper preparation of a ground on which to place their finishing paintings ; and the result was, and is, that their works, like his, have made rapid progress in decay—a decay that is unaccompanied with the richness and beauty that lingers even in the perishing works of Reynolds. Still the method, although ill-appreciated and faultily adopted, was one that permitted progress and encouraged experiments, and the English school, after floundering awhile with perishing materials, falsely used, and methods of painting ill-understood, is at last again making sound advances, and has maintained a reputation as a school of colour which could never have resulted from the methods of West, Copley, and their predecessors.

George Romney was born on the 26th December, 1734, at Dalton-le-Furness, Lancashire, and Hayley, his biographer, tells us he was the son of a man of many occupations, builder, merchant, and farmer, and was apprenticed to a cabinetmaker, with whom he acquired some skill at his trade. His first indication of talent for the art in which he became celebrated, was shown in sketching from memory the features of a casual visitor at the parish church of his native village, and he was stimulated to improve himself by a friend of the name of Williamson, an eccentric man devoted to chemistry and alchemy. Romney afterwards studied under a Cumberland artist of the name of Steel, to whom he was apprenticed by his father. His master, who seems to have been a rollicking blade, and was known by the cognomen of Count Steel, was but little older than the pupil, and being engaged in a love-affair with a neighbouring lady, employed his apprentice to assist him in carrying on a clandestine correspondence with her, which ended in Steel's eloping with the lady to Scotland, and leaving his pupil behind in a fit of fever and sickness arising from "his exertions in assisting the escape of the bride." Romney was nursed in his sickness by a compassionate young girl, and her attention and his gratitude resulted in a precipitate marriage in 1756, when the painter was barely twenty-two years of age. The painter's son speaks of his mother as of the same rank in life as his father.

The after-conduct of Romney towards his wife and children seems to evidence tenderness for himself, love of his own ease and advancement, but little for those whom it was his first duty to cherish and protect. He resolved, instead of settling, "to wander forth alone in quest of professional adventures." Rambling over the north, painting heads life-size at two guineas, and small whole-lengths for six guineas, he contrived to save nearly 100*l.*, when, taking 30*l.* of this sum for his own expenses, he gave the rest to his dutiful and unoffending wife, now burdened with two children, and left the north and his family to seek his fortune in the great metropolis.

He arrived in London in the year 1762, and his first success was attained in historical painting. For a picture of the "Death of General Wolfe," he obtained from the infant Society of Arts a donation of 25*l.* In 1764, Romney left London for the Continent, for a short visit to Paris, where he carefully examined the works of art. On his return he removed into Gray's Inn, and was soon engaged in painting the members of the legal profession. In 1765 he exhibited a picture of the death of "King Edward," and now received from the Society of Arts its second prize of fifty guineas. He then removed to Newport Street, Long Acre, and was, we are told by one of his pupils, in the receipt of 1,200*l.* a year from his profession, when he boldly resolved to quit present affluence and reputation, and with a view to improvement, to make a long visit to Italy. In March, 1773, in company with Ozias Humphrey, a brother artist, he took his way to the Continent for the second time; after a short stay at Paris, the two companions proceeded slowly, making their journey somewhat of a tour of pleasure. During their passage from Genoa to Ostia, they were in great danger from a storm, and, when Romney's companion rallied him on his consternation and gravity, he was assured that "it did not arise from personal fear, but from tender concern at the prospect of being suddenly separated for ever from his friends and relations;" relations whom, in his now affluent condition, he left in separate loneliness in the far north, nor sought to share with them the advantages arising from his gratified ambition. The travellers arrived in Rome on the 18th of June, and here from a singular mental infirmity—a perpetual dread of enemies—Romney avoided all further intercourse with his fellow-traveller, and with all his countrymen then studying in Rome. What the nature of his labours was, it is not possible at this distance of time to determine : he made a few studies, and at least one copy from Raphael, and after some months returned to England, by way of Venice and Parma (making a stay at both places), in the beginning of July, 1775 ; and at Christmas of the same year, finally settled himself in Cavendish Square, in the house where Cotes had lived before him, and which was afterwards occupied by Sir Martin A. Shee.

The time had now arrived when we should expect that Romney would send for his wife and children, who, during the many long years he had been struggling upwards, had been left to lead a life of lonely separation in Lancashire. He was master of his time, in full practice, established in reputation, settled in a noble mansion, where a wife's help might indeed be useful, and her society, with that of his two children, have tended to drive away the moody demon that seemed to be his continual companion. But, though his poet-biographer, Hayley, induced Romney to spend a few weeks with him at Earlham every season for twenty years, during the whole of this time he paid only two visits to his wife and children.

Settled in Cavendish Square, Romney began by charging fifteen guineas for a head life-size, and proportionately for half- and whole-lengths. With such time as a constant influx of sitters left at his command, he was now ambitious of higher and nobler attempts and wished to return to historic art ; thus many subject-pictures were begun. But the painter's invention was more fervid than deep ; easily excited, but soon satiated.

Moreover, Romney had never had a proper education in art, he was no anatomist, and as a work approached completion, partly from imperfect knowledge, and partly from not having carefully considered it as a whole before commencing, he found his difficulties increase upon him, and no doubt was tempted to lay the canvas aside in hopes of an easier conquest. He loved sketching, he loved portrait painting, which required little more thought, as *he* painted, than to follow the leadings of his model. He loved to paint from the fair Emma, as Hayley calls Lady Hamilton, the person raised from a painter's model to be an ambassador's wife and the intimate of queens and princesses,—to paint the fair Emma as Contemplation or Innocence, or any other abstraction ; but he did not love the dry labour of thought, the painful toil of completion when the first fervour of the imagination is jaded ; he disliked that mere executive which is the body to the spirit, the necessary clog that holds the painter to the earth when he would desire to soar aloft into the heaven of invention. Hence the number of his portraits and sketches, the number of commencements of pictures—cartloads it is said, which were removed from Hampstead after his death—and hence the incompleteness of even those works which Romney himself deemed finished.

Nevertheless in portraiture, having adopted a broad and general manner, and being ready in execution to the extent which he carried his art, his pencil was in continual occupation.

We find that in 1783 his portraits had risen so high in the public estimation that he was regarded as the rival of Reynolds. Lord Thurlow, who was among the number of his sitters, alluding to the rivalry between the two painters, said, "Reynolds and Romney divide the town, I am of the Romney faction." Even Northcote allows that "Reynolds was not much employed as a portrait painter after Romney grew into fashion." With increase of sitters our painter from time to time increased his prices, and during the latter years of his practice his annual income from portraits alone was nearly four thousand pounds.

In this full tide of fame and practice we might have expected that Romney would seek to become a member of the Royal Academy. There is no doubt that his talent would have claimed a ready entrance, and that among the members generally he would have found a welcome; but there were many reasons why he was disinclined to this step. To the original forty members had now been added the body of associates, and though, in his own opinion, and in the eyes of his immediate friends, equal to the best, he must have gone through the prescribed form, and entered in the junior rank, waiting a longer or shorter time for his translation to the higher honours. Besides, it would appear that at that time some canvassing was expected (a thing positively unknown in the last quarter of a century), and to this he could not stoop.

We are told elsewhere that he avoided the company of his brother artists, yet continually complained that they neglected and shunned him; and that professional rivalry with Sir Joshua made him beyond measure jealous, yet fearful to place his works side by side with those of the President on the walls of a public exhibition. They would certainly have shown to disadvantage so contrasted, which Romney avoided by their being only seen in his domestic gallery. Dr. Johnson said of Reynolds, "that he was one of the most invulnerable of men," yet he felt annoyed by this rivalry of fashion rather than of art, and could speak disparagingly of "the man in Cavendish Square," while there hardly existed one whose sensitiveness it was more easy to wound than Romney; and he, notwithstanding his success, was but too well aware

that the world of art was with Reynolds, if for a time the world of fashion
had left the President's door to throng to his own.

While in full practice as a portrait painter, and in the intervals of his
sitters, giving reins to his imagination in multitudes of sketches for
subjects never completed, he occasionally finished what may be called a
fancy picture. In 1786, when Alderman Boydell first broached his
scheme of a gallery of subjects from Shakespeare's plays, Romney entered
into the project with his usual ardour. He immediately begun a
picture of "The Shipwreck" from the *Tempest*, and working at it more
perseveringly than was usual with him, finished it early in the spring of
1790.

When this work was completed, his great rival Reynolds had ceased
to paint, and Romney was left supreme in portraiture. But the demon
of melancholy that had haunted him in his lonely home from the very
days of his youth upward, was not to be driven forth by prosperity or
by fame. The painter, to shun it, might fly from London and from his
sitters to Earlham or Felpham, he might muster his sketches and propose
to himself the happiness of new labours, but it followed him and dogged
his path. London was, or was supposed to be, unhealthy, and the
painter took to sleeping at Hampstead, first riding, afterwards walking
in the morning to his town studio. For a while he flattered himself
that his evil spirit had left him. He bought land and erected a house
after his own heart, and to his own plans in that healthful suburb. He
had a large gallery for his works, a chamber where, as he lay, a magnificent view of the far-away city was before his eyes—an intervening
country, not as now, covered with a tangled net of railways, where
houses seem daily to grow out of the ground, but where sweet pastures
and bright meadows sloped away to the quiet outskirts. Here again he
dreamt of finishing his many subjects; but alas! the time was gone by,
the power of his hand—the cunning of his art had fled. He thought of
those he had left in the north, and in 1798 he paid them at last a visit.
No more the ambitious youth who had left wife and children in search
of wealth and fame, but a poor broken-down hypochondriac. It is true
that he came back awhile to find his house at Hampstead, his gallery, and
his studio, in every respect complete—to pay one more visit to Felpham
and Hayley, but no less to find his utter inability to paint. His dream
of ambition was at an end. He sold his house in Cavendish Square to
Shee, and soon after quitted London, and saw it no more.

Hayley's influence over Romney seems, on the whole, to have been
unpropitious, since he nursed the painter's maudlin sensibility, encouraged him in the idle habit of mere sketching, and flattered many of
his foibles and weaknesses.

How did his long-neglected wife receive the man who had only come back to her when the pleasures of life had passed away ; the man who had deserted the mother of his children in her young days, and had selfishly passed all his best years apart from her, nor had allowed her to share his hopes, his fame, or the society that wealth had gathered around him ? O wonder of woman's loving patient endurance during thirty years of cruel absence ! She received him on his return without upbraiding ; and "he had the comfort of finding an attentive, affectionate nurse in a most exemplary wife, who had never been irritated to an act of unkindness or an expression of reproach by his years of absence and neglect."

Romney's character was a strange anomaly. He could be sentimentally eloquent, no doubt, and speak tenderly, though his life was a long act of cruelty. A year before his own malady drove him to his long-shunned home he wrote thus of the widow of poor Hodges :—" I shall never forget when I found her at breakfast with her little children, her voice, her face, more enchanting than I ever thought them before : for the gratification of the same looks and voice, I think I could travel a hundred miles." Did he think of his own wife at Kendal ? of his own children, whose youthful love he had never known ? Now he lingered awhile at Kendal, acknowledging, in his letters to his London friends, the tender solicitude of his wife ; longed earnestly for the return of his brother, who had risen to be a general in the Indian army, and who came just in time to see, and to be doubtfully recognized by Romney, ere, as Cumberland says, in his memoir of the painter, he sank into an inglorious grave in November, 1802.

When we endeavour to form an estimate of Romney as an artist, we are inclined to wonder at the position he held in his own day, and while Gainsborough and Reynolds were yet living ; for whatever merit we may allow to Romney as a painter, and he had great merit, yet we cannot compare him with either of these his contemporaries. He was enthusiastic and energetic, and full of a certain nervous sensibility that is akin to poetic genius. His imagination was more active than his perseverance, and he was easily excited to begin, and as easily tempted to lay aside, his work ; as far as observation went he endeavoured to overcome the imperfection of his early training, but downright labour to that end was easily laid aside. Could art come by mere impulse, he would have been a great artist. His sojourn in Italy led him to love and follow Correggio rather than the Venetians, and from him Romney derived a certain breadth and simplicity of manner that was apt to degenerate into generality and emptiness. His manner once fixed, we see none of the varied modes of execution, and of the preparation of the work that are so evident even from the very failures of Reynolds. We are told by his pupil, Robinson, that latterly he glazed his pictures much, and missed the pure tints of his earlier works ; but by glazing he must have meant "toning," since Romney's works are very solidly painted. He had little of the power of adding individuality to beauty. His colouring is void of variety of tint, and tends to red and brown, his flesh is apt to be rather bricky, and to want that luminous and golden glow which hardly any but Reynolds and the great Venetians have achieved, while his forms are unmodelled and devoid of bones. There is a pleasing breadth almost amounting to grandeur in some of his works, but it ever seems as if he had the power to carry them up to a certain point only, and could not complete them. If they have a flavour of Correggio, it is without his rich completing glazings, and rather as the works of that great artist appear after they have been, by the *skill* of the picture-cleaner, divested entirely of their richness of surface.

Romney's art was rather largely represented at the autumn exhibition of the British Institution, in 1863, twenty-one of his works being hung in juxtaposition with some of those of his great rivals, Gainsborough and Reynolds. Among these works were, of course, three or four Lady Hamiltons, with Serenas, Hebes, &c., most likely inspired by the same enchantress. Here was also the historical picture of " Newton Showing the Effects of the Prism," painted as a companion to " Milton Dictating to his Daughters." The drawing is poor and without much character, the flesh dirty and hot, and the treatment of action and expression weak and common-place; there is little of dignity either in the personages represented or in the painter's art.

One or two of his portraits here were finely and solidly painted and beautifully handled, and certainly better than many by Lawrence. Others in the collection, however, were as bad as these were good, and it was singular to feel how weak and tame were his portraits of children. A portrait of Lord Stanley and his sister in their childhood—but beyond that infantile period to which we allude—is, however, a good specimen of the painter, the boy's head really good. But we may sum up all that is to be said of Romney in this, that whatever he did Reynolds had done far better; that his art did not advance the taste of the age, or the reputation of the school, and that it is quite clear, however fashion or faction may have upheld him in his own day, the succeeding race of painters owed little or nothing to his teaching.

Joseph Wright, called Wright of Derby, like Romney, was among the painters who were established in full practice before the foundation of the Royal Academy. He was born in Derby, 3rd September, 1734 and was the son of an attorney of that midland town. His first bent was towards mechanical contrivance. He afterwards showed a liking for art, which his father encouraged, sending him to London in 1751, and placing him under Hudson, then in the height of fashionable employment. After studying two years with the master of Reynolds, young Wright returned to Derby, and there practised his profession with some success, but subsequently feeling his deficient art-knowledge, the young painter revisited the metropolis and the studio of his old master, remaining with him on the second occasion for fifteen months, after which he settled in his native town. Here he obtained the patronage of the neighbouring gentry, and painted many portraits, and also subject-pictures, such as "The Orrery," "The Iron Forge," and "An Experiment with the Air Pump." In all these the painter has sought to give the effect of artificial light, a walk of art which he eventually made almost his own, treating both subject-pictures, and afterwards landscapes and marine pictures, as lighted by fire-light, by conflagrations, or by moonlight, and rendering such treatments with much fidelity and truth. He continued to reside in Derby until 1773, and many of his best pictures, including those named above, were painted in this period.

In 1773 he married, and took that opportunity to visit Italy, where he remained two years, studying, it is said, the works of the great masters, especially those of Michael Angelo, from which he made many copies on a large scale. But however much the works in the Sistine Chapel may have impressed him at the time, they had little influence on his subsequent practice. During his residence in Italy, he made many landscape-sketches, and collected a large amount of material, which enabled him on his return to practise this branch of art largely, treating it also under his favourite effects of artificial light. While at Naples he was fortunate in seeing a memorable eruption of Vesuvius, when he carefully noted the effect of the flames on the noble scenery of the city and the bay. He also visited the caves at Capri, and the Grotto of Posilipo, and on his return painted these subjects frequently, varying the effects and the accessories. Thus in the list of his pictures, "Vesuvius," and "Conflagrations of Vesuvius," often recur, together with "Cottages on Fire," "Moonlights," "Cavern-scenes," "Sunsets," &c. Wilson, who admired Wright's artifice, used to say:—" Give me your firelight, and I will give you my daylight." But Wright had no need to exchange, since he was well patronized in his day, and in a list of 164 of his works published after his death, there are only about twenty-five which have not the name of the proprietor to whom they belong or for whom they were painted.

When Wright returned to England in 1775, he went to live at Bath. Gainsborough had just left, and he hoped to find a good opening for himself as a portrait painter. But he met with no encouragement, and after about two years he returned to Derby, where he finally settled. In the midst of his relations, honoured by his townsmen, with ample professional employment, he had little inducement to leave it for the great metropolis, although often urged to do so.   Here he continued to reside until 1797, when a lingering illness terminated his life on the 29th of August.   There is a painful solidity of execution, a want of quality and texture both in the flesh and the draperies of his portraits, so that when placed beside the works of Reynolds or Gainsborough, they remind us of the labours of the house-painter ; they show little variety of handling —flesh, drapery, sky, and trees, being all executed in the same painty manner.   He adopted a shadow colour, with a purplish hue, such as would result from Indian red and blue-black, which prevails throughout his portraits, and gives them a heavy look, and has an unpleasant effect both in the shadows and half-tints.   The colour in these works is defective, but in his subjects treated with artificial light, since tone rather than colour is sought, his defect as a colourist is less seen.   His landscapes are large and simple in manner, but heavy and empty.

Some of them have sadly failed from the pigments and vehicle used in them, while others remain perfectly sound—those on which, in order to obtain an artificial effect, he had often to repeat his painting, are the most injured, such as his " Eruptions of Vesuvius ;" while the simpler treatments, as the " Windermere " and other lake scenery, painted after his visit to Westmoreland in 1793, are in good condition, as are also most of his portraits.

Wright's intercourse with his brother-artists was limited to sending an occasional picture to the Exhibition of the Incorporated Society.   When the Academy was formed, although he was at that time producing some of his best pictures—pictures which fully entitled him to a place among the forty—his name was not included in the first list.   On his return from Rome in 1775—perhaps for the sake of keeping up his practice while in London—he entered as a student in the Royal Academy, and in November, 1781, was elected an associate of the body.   It has often been a cause of complaint and animadversion that he was never elected a full member, and he is said to have thrown up his diploma of associate in disgust.   In a sketch of his life, written the year he died, we are told that " he felt a repugnance to send his works to an exhibition where he had too much cause to complain of their being improperly placed, and sometimes even upon the ground, that, if possible, they might escape the public eye.   This narrow jealousy, added to the circumstance of his being rejected as an R.A. at the time Mr. Garvey was a successful candidate, did not tend to increase his opinion of the liberality of his brethren of the profession.   The Academy, however, being afterwards aware of the impropriety of thus insulting a man of his abilities, deputed their secretary, Newton, to go to Derby to *solicit his acceptance* of a diploma, which he indignantly rejected."

We find from the Academy records, though, that Wright was elected a full member in February, 1784, but he then refused to comply with the law of the Academy, which requires a member to present one of his works to the Academy before receiving his diploma, and ordered his name to be removed from the list of associates.

All we know of Wright proves him to have been a man of a shy, nervous, melancholic temper, always ailing, and not suffering the less if his ills were only fancies. His portrait alone is a sufficient confirmation of this, but all accounts confirm it. Dr. Darwin, who was his friend, and was often consulted upon his imaginary complaints, once told him "he had but one thing more to recommend. He thought that it would do him good to be engaged in a vexatious lawsuit"—anything to divert the hypochondriac from dwelling upon himself.

Wright had never been more than an occasional exhibitor at the Royal Academy—indeed the account he gives of his own health would preclude us from looking for him as a constant contributor. After his refusal of the Academy honours in 1784 we are not surprised to miss his name for two or three seasons, but in 1788 he reappears as the exhibitor of five landscapes. In 1794, his name appears for the last time, his works being "An Eruption of Vesuvius," and "A Village on Fire."

Having made a journey into the county expressly to see some of the works of this Derbyshire artist, we were shown many, both portraits, landscapes, and figure-subjects, reported to be amongst his best, but always disappointing to our expectations. It was, therefore, a source of real satisfaction when Mr. Edward Tyrrell presented to the National Gallery the picture we have mentioned—"An Experiment with the Air Pump." It is a very clever and vigorous work, with the figures life-size. The air pump is on the table in the centre of a group, and the light placed within the machine radiates out on the surrounding faces of children, young men and maidens, and more aged spectators. The drawing and composition is satisfactory, and there is a great contrast in the character, expression, and the very varied attitudes of the several heads. The flesh of the faces is good in colour and most carefully modelled; indeed, the young woman on the right, in blue, and the lad drawing down a curtain to shut out the moonlight on the left, are worth especial observation for this quality. The draperies are all carefully painted from Nature, a merit apparent also in most of Wright's portraits. There is a pretty little incident, rendered with feeling and true expression, in the group of two young girls, touched with childish sorrow and dread of what they are told is to be the result of "the experiment"—the death of the bird confined in the glass receiver of the machine.

The colour of the whole is pleasant, the execution firm and solid, and the brown shadows, although dark, are sufficiently rich and luminous, the picture very agreeable in general tone. It is satisfactory to find this work so sound, and to have such a representation of this painter's art; yet on the whole it cannot be said that Wright's pictures have added much to the reputation of the British school, and as a portrait painter, he is only in the second rank.

H

CHAPTER X.

PROGRESS OF HISTORIC ART.

VERY soon after the foundation of the Royal Academy a great movement took place in art. Our artists were emulous to distinguish themselves; and, as a body, were desirous of engaging in works which should cultivate the taste of their countrymen for pictorial design. The members of the Academy led the way, and offered to decorate St. Paul's Cathedral at their own expense, with appropriate paintings from Scripture subjects. They selected Reynolds, their president, West, Barry, Cipriani, Dance, and Angelica Kauffman, for this undertaking, and made this generous proposal in 1773, to the Dean and Chapter, in such terms as they hoped would insure its acceptance and success—offering to receive the suggestions of the Dean and Chapter for alterations or amendments of their works when completed, and to remove them if not finally approved. This noble offer was accepted by the Dean, who readily obtained the sanction of the King; but the Archbishop of Canterbury and the Bishop of London, who are the trustees of the cathedral, disapproved; and the latter (Bishop Terrick) strenuously opposed it as an artful intrusion of Popery, and the whole plan fell to the ground, and the ardent desire of the body of artists ended only in disappointment.

Looking back from our present position, and with our advanced knowledge on the subject, we feel confident that this disappointment was on the whole for the advantage of art. The subject of mural decoration at that time had not received the consideration it has since obtained throughout Europe. The principles of pictorial art as an adjunct to architecture had not been in the least studied, and mere pictorial treatment would have undoubtedly prevailed. The vehicle in which the works would have been executed would most likely have been oil; and oil, with all the faulty and insecure pigments then and for a long time after in use. Had the proposal been carried out we might now be contemplating an incomplete series of works far advanced in ruin and decay, unsuited to their situation, incongruous with one another from lacking the direction of a leading mind, and altogether affording an argument against rather than in favour of further attempts.

A few years later the members of the Academy warmly supported the plan of a "Shakspeare Gallery," which originated with Alderman Boydell. When a young man, John Boydell had been struck by an indifferent engraving, the work of Mr. Toms, probably from its accurate delineation of a scene familiar to him ; and at the age of twenty-one, and in spite of the wishes of his family, he walked up to London from Derbyshire, and apprenticed himself to the engraver by whose work he had been so suddenly impressed. Although his assiduity led to no eminence in his adopted art, by his enterprise and generous dealing he was enabled to found and foster a great school of engraving in England, and rose himself to opulence and distinction. Then he desired to accomplish for the painters' art what he had done for the engravers'. His great scheme of the Shakspeare Gallery arose in a conversation over the dinner-table, in November, 1786, when he entertained West, Romney, and Paul Sandby, with some other eminent men. Boydell expressed his desire, "old as he was, to wipe away the stigma that we had no genius for historical painting ;" and in the discussion which arose the name of Shakspeare was mentioned by Nicol, the well-known printer, who was one of the guests ; and the idea of the Shakspeare Gallery, which then took a form, was so steadily pursued, that early in 1789 the gallery (later occupied by the British Institution in Pall Mall) was finished, several of the paintings were completed, and the whole undertaking far advanced.

All the first artists were invited to assist, and received liberal commissions.

The collected works were exhibited to the public in the gallery built for them ; and, as a part of the original scheme, were engraved and circulated throughout the country and on the Continent. They were of very mixed merit, but the magnitude of the scheme, and the renown by which it was attended, no doubt assisted to create a public appetite for pictorial art ; while it is equally certain that generally the weakness of drawing, the want of power in the artists to enter into the manners and habits of the time and the characters represented, would hardly be tolerated now, and justifies the neglect into which the greater part of the works have fallen. Need we tell the painful end of Boydell's great enterprise, undoubtedly begun with higher motives than the mere love of gain. In sixty years of active life he had accumulated a capital of 350,000*l.*, which he sunk to found a school of engraving and of historic painting. He had purposed to leave to the nation the gallery

H 2

he had erected, and the works painted to illustrate his country's great dramatic poet ; but the disturbance of all his commercial relations with the Continent by the breaking out of the French Revolution, paralyzed his extensive trade, and at the age of eighty-five he sought of Parliament the power to sell by lottery his galleries, pictures, drawings, and stock, that " he might be able to pay all that he owed in the world," and he was taken from the world just as this last request had been granted.

Henry Fuseli, R.A., was the promoter of a scheme like Boydell's. He was the most poetical, as also the most original of the group of painters on which we are now entering. Born at Zurich on the 7th of February, 1741, he was the second son of John Casper Füessli, himself a painter of portraits and landscapes—a man otherwise endowed with learning and talents, and the intimate associate of men of varied acquirements, whose names are still held in honour. The elder Füessli did not wish his son to be an artist, but intended him for the clerical profession. We are told that his dislike to his son's being a painter might partly have arisen from the boy's awkwardness, and want of manual dexterity, which was so great as to have resulted in a family saying : " Take care of that boy, for he destroys or spoils whatever he touches ;" a defect which in after life was seen in the great want of executive power apparent in his pictures. But Fuseli's love of art was not to be checked, and he followed secretly what it was denied him to work at openly. The hours of night, when the family were at rest, were devoted to his pursuit of art, and even thus early his efforts were marked with a tendency to the extravagant, either on the side of the burlesque or of the terrible. In order to prepare the lad for his future duties, he was put in charge of a tutor, who read aloud to him the works of those theologians which formed part of his course of study. But while the tutor read, the pupil drew, and the better to escape observation, learnt to use his left hand, which was attended with this advantage, that he was enabled to use either hand freely during his after life. Removed to the country for the benefit of better air, he seems to have enjoyed with great zest the new scenes and new objects brought within his observation. But his father was not a man to change the determination he had made, and when he had reached a proper age, the future painter, returning to Zurich, entered the Caroline college in that city, and finally obtained the degree of Master of Arts. While at college, he had for fellow-students many very remarkable companions, among others the well-known Lavater, with whom he afterwards kept up a constant intercourse, and whose mind, innately sympathizing with the mysteries of spiritualism and demoniacal possession, must have had some influence on one, in many respects, so like-minded as Fuseli. While at college, Fuseli made himself acquainted with various modern languages, and among others perfected himself in English : learning to read and enjoy the works of Milton, Shakspeare, and the painter Richardson, in their native tongue.

It is told of him that at college he was very satirical, and students at the Royal Academy during his keepership will remember that this satirical temper never left him. After passing the prescribed time at college, Fuseli fulfilled the wishes of his father, and in 1761, together with his friend Lavater, entered into holy orders, and he preached his first sermon before the *literati* of Zurich, from the query of the philosophers of Athens when Paul preached in the Areopagus :—" What will this babbler say ? " We are told that his discourses, though appreciated by the learned, were caviare to the multitude. He might, however, have continued in the duties of the holy office, and been lost to the world of art, had not his strong sense of justice united him with Lavater in exposing the land-bailiff, or ruling magistrate of the canton, who had been guilty of peculation and injustice. For a time the two friends triumphantly succeeded, but in the end, the powerful family connexions of the magistrate made Zurich too hot for the young divine, and in 1763 he was advised, for a while at least, to quit the town. He spent some time in visiting various German cities, and at Berlin began his art career, but was eventually induced to visit England with a view of establishing a channel of literary communication between Germany, Switzerland, and our own country. He left Berlin for London in 1765, with the British Minister, Sir Andrew Mitchell, who introduced him here to several persons, among others, to Mr. Coutts, for whom he afterwards painted several pictures, and whose friendship he maintained through life.

At first he was employed in literary labour—translating works from the French, German, and Italian ; occasionally varying this drudgery by designing book-illustrations for novels. At the end of 1766, an offer, too advantageous to be rejected, was made to Fuseli to travel as tutor to Viscount Chewton, son of the Earl of Waldegrave, an office for which his independent manner and irritable temper particularly disqualified him. We cannot therefore wonder that, having accepted it, he managed to quarrel with, and even to strike, his pupil, whom he left in France, " determining," as he said, " to be a bear-leader no longer." On his return to England in 1767 he sought an introduction to Sir Joshua Reynolds, in order to obtain his advice in the prosecution of his plan of making the fine arts his future profession.

The great portrait painter received Fuseli with his usual urbanity, and seemed much struck with the originality and style of the designs he exhibited to him. Reynolds further encouraged him on seeing his first work—" Joseph Interpreting the Dreams of Pharaoh's Chief Butler and Chief Baker "—by saying that " he might, if he would, be a colourist as well as a draughtsman." Looking at the quality of tone, and disposition of colour in many of his works, there seems to have been some ground for the president's judgment : but Fuseli had had no proper education in art ; he was too impatient to go through the trials of processes and modes of execution, which Reynolds himself was continually making ; he was satisfied by *feeling out* what he wanted in colour and effect by the easiest means that would give him present satisfaction ; and this resulted not only in his *not* attaining to the rank of a colourist, but in the early and total destruction of many of his pictures. His biographer, Knowles, tells us that " until he was twenty-five years of age, he had never used oil-colours, and he was so inattentive to these materials that during his life he took no pains in their choice or manipulation. To set a palette, as artists usually do, was with him out of the question ; he used many of his colours in a dry powdered state, and rubbed them up with his *pencil* only, sometimes in oil alone, which he used largely, at others with an addition of a little spirit of turpentine, and not unfrequently in gold size." How could such carelessness result in anything but premature decay ?

Having determined at last to adopt painting as a profession, Fuseli, now nearly twenty-nine years of age, turned his thoughts towards Italy. He was at this time neither a draughtsman nor a painter, and had attained an age, when it is difficult to sit down to that dry elementary study, which is so necessary in order to obtain executive power. He arrived in Rome early in the spring of 1770, and shortly afterwards changed the spelling of his name from Füessli to Fuseli, to accommodate it to the Italian pronunciation. While in Italy he seems to have made earnest study of the antique and the works of Michael Angelo. We do not hear that he drew much ; we are told that he made no copies, and that while he sometimes attended in the school of the living model, he was averse to dissecting.

Thus Fuseli never had the advantage of academic training ; and though he appears to have been absorbed in the works of Michael Angelo, he much needed that elementary training which had led Michael Angelo into the full power of expressing his noble thoughts. Grand in invention, revelling in the mystic and terrible, and with a wild energy of action that defies the charge of being theatrical, bordering as it does on the fearful ; having indeed a formed and marked style, he yet entirely fails to satisfy us. He has no refinement nor accuracy of drawing, many of his attitudes are impossible ; his females are somewhat more than masculine, they are absolutely coarse and at times disgusting ; while, as has already been said, his entire want of knowledge of the elementary laws of colouring and processes of painting, not only hindered him from developing his innate sense of colour, but from the imperfect methods he resorted to, have left us too often to contemplate fading ghosts and moribund canvases. The only thing that can be said on the other side is, would not a sound elementary education have tamed down his originality and poetic feeling, while giving him the language in which to express it?

Fuseli remained in Italy until the autumn of 1778, having passed more than eight years in Rome and the other Italian cities. During his stay he had sent two pictures to the Royal Academy, but of his other labours we are less informed. If he was unable to profit by the purity and refinement of Raphael, of whom Fuseli himself said that "propriety rocked his cradle," he imbibed so much of the feeling and power of Buonarotti, that we may boldly say no painter, before or since, has entered in the same degree into the spirit of that master. On his way back to this country, he made a stay of some months in his native city, painting various pictures, among others, "The Confederacy of the Founders of Helvetian Liberty," which he gave to the senate-house at Zurich, where it is still preserved. His father had at this time an opportunity of seeing the works of his painter son, and was able to estimate, and take delight in, the talents which were shortly to place him high in the rank of modern artists.

On Fuseli's arrival in London, he took a part of the house of Cartwright, a painter, whom he had known in Rome, and who now resided in St. Martin's Lane, and began to labour diligently on poetic subjects; sending three pictures to the exhibition in 1780; and in 1782, a work called "The Nightmare," which by repetitions and engravings soon became very popular, and was engraved for and published by J. R. Smith, who allowed that he made a profit of 500*l.* by the speculation, Fuseli himself having only received 20*l.* for the picture.

In 1786, Alderman Boydell's scheme for obtaining a series of pictures from the plays of Shakspeare, to be engraved for publication, was set on foot, and Fuseli was one of those whose assistance was considered of the first importance. He entered zealously into the project. He painted eight large, and one small picture for this series; among them some of his finest works.

While these pictures were in hand, and Fuseli's pencil in full operation, he married Miss Rawlins of Bath Easton, and it is said that prudential motives, viz., the certainty in case of his death of a small provision for his widow, induced him to overcome his objections to such institutions, and to become a candidate for membership in the Royal Academy. Whether this was really the cause, or whether, as we believe, he had worthier and better motives, he put down his name and was elected an associate in the autumn of 1788, and in 1790, a full member of the Royal Academy. On the occasion of his election a disagreement arose, which resulted in the temporary resignation of the presidentship by Sir Joshua Reynolds, and had nearly ended in his final retirement.

Shortly after, on the completion of the Boydell pictures, Fuseli was led to project a work of his own. When his scheme was matured it took the shape of a gallery of illustrations of Milton. He determined to paint a series of pictures from our great epic poet, and to exhibit them together for his own benefit. He had saved a little money from the completion of his engagements with Boydell, which gave him the means of proceeding some length with the task he undertook; and when this was exhausted, six of his friends came forward liberally to assist him by advancing money for his support until the pictures he purposed to paint for his exhibition were completed; besides which, one or two of them made him handsome donations in aid of his attempt.

Forty pictures of the most lofty range as to subject, and some of them on canvases of the grandest scale, were opened to the public in the rooms in Pall Mall previously occupied by the Royal Academy. The exhibition, alas! in the first season did not pay its expenses. Still hoping against hope, the persevering painter completed during the recess six additional works, and reopened in the spring of 1800 with forty-six pictures, the Academy leading off with a public dinner in the room, to endeavour to awaken attention to this great effort of genius. The painter tells us he "had much mouth-honour" on the occasion, but the public did not respond; this season was as unproductive as the former one had been, and at the end of four months Fuseli closed the exhibition, rather than carry it on at a loss.

It is sad to have to record the utter failure of a scheme that had so long occupied the mind and hand of a man of true genius; but Fuseli's pictures were not of a nature to appeal to the eye, but to the mind of the public; and mind is much wanted in common sight-seers. This Fuseli found when questioned by one of the visitors to his gallery who did not know him. "Pray, sir, what is that picture?" "It is the bridging of Chaos; the subject from Milton." "No wonder," said the questioner, "I did not know it, for I never read Milton, but I will." "I advise you not," said Fuseli; "for you will find it a d—d tough job."

Meanwhile, Fuseli had been elected professor of painting, for which his knowledge and classical attainments so well fitted him, and in 1801 he delivered his first course of lectures to the students of the Royal Academy. In 1804, on the death of Wilton, he was appointed to the keepership, and resigned the lectureship, which Opie, and, on his death, Tresham, was elected to fill: but Tresham in the end declined on the plea of indisposition, and Fuseli was re-elected, and held the keepership, with the office of professor of painting, during the remainder of his life. For

more than twenty years he filled these offices, with satisfaction to himself
and credit to the institution. When we recollect the great men who
were formed wholly or partly during his keepership, we may estimate the
influence he had on those around him. Among these, Hilton, Wilkie,
Etty, Mulready, Haydon, Leslie, Jackson, Ross, Landseer, and Eastlake,
are sure evidence of the sound training obtained in the Royal Academy
while Fuseli was the keeper. He continued to paint, if with less ardour
than formerly, until the last days of his life. Just before his final illness
he had sent two pictures to the Academy for exhibition, one of them in
an unfinished state, hoping to have time to glaze and tone it during the
varnishing days; and he was employed just previous to his death on a
scene from *King John*, which was nearly completed when he died. He was
seized with his last illness while on a visit at the house of the Countess
of Guildford, at Putney, and he died there on the 16th of April, 1825.

Fuseli certainly derived more from Michael Angelo than others of our
British painters who have made the Sistine Chapel their study—more of
the terrible and grand, more of that largeness of treatment and noble
simplicity that lifts us out of and above common nature. His figures
are never tame, indeed, they are too apt to err on the side of violent
and overstrained action. Such actions, however, rarely offend us; rarely
give the feeling of being vulgar or theatrical, and sometimes they are
truly grand.

With much that is noble and dignified in *style*, Fuseli adopted from the
great Florentine much that is mere manner—much that is conventional
and untrue. Such as forced muscularity both in his male and female figures,
disproportionate extremities, limbs far beyond Nature's length, and draperies, that are no draperies, fitted tight to display the form. In some of his
figures Michael Angelo bent the hand unnaturally at the wrist, with a strong
action of the index finger. Fuseli adopted this, and used it so frequently,
that it is one of the characteristics of his figures. Fuseli's figures too
whether classic, Scandinavian, or mediæval, are ever of the same race,—
have the same individuality, and, from his seldom having recourse to
Nature, the heads have a likeness and character in common. But then
the painter is never commonplace; he always carries us away with him
into a poetic region of his own—a region apart from the everyday world
we live in; and if we cannot agree that it is the same that Shakspeare
or Milton would picture to us, it is at least a dream-land in which we
awaken to sublime thoughts and curious pleasures too often wanting in
the works of those who are more literal or more faithful to their text.

Fuseli was quite indifferent to propriety of costume, treating ages and
countries far separated in the same draperies, classic and modern alike.
Partly from the failure of his works—many of which have gone wholly
to decay—and partly from their large size, which has confined them to

the walls they originally occupied, Fuseli is better known in the present day by engravings from his pictures, than by the pictures themselves. Turning over the pages of Boydell, he stands apart from all the other illustrators. His bold energetic style—the wildness and originality of his inventions, were fitted to take great hold of the imagination of the young, and there is no doubt that he had great influence over the minds of the students of his day. They liked the man; and even the sharp bitter sarcasms with which he at times reproved them were forgotten as soon as uttered, since at heart he was kindly, and wished them well, and treated their wild pranks as the boisterous fun of boys, which it is better should find vent than be repressed.

CHAPTER XI.

THE first successor to Reynolds in priority of date was *Nathaniel Dance, R.A.*, who is best known in art by this name, though he afterwards became Sir Nathaniel Holland, Bart. He was the son of the city surveyor, and was born in London in 1734. He began the study of art under Frank Hayman, and sought to improve himself in Italy. Here he remained eight or nine years, and travelled with the fair paintress, Angelica Kauffman, with whom gossip said he was hopelessly in love. On his return to England he distinguished himself by his portraits and as a history-painter, exhibiting a "Death of Virginia" with the Society of Artists in 1761. Among his paintings may be mentioned "Garrick as Richard III.," "Timon of Athens," in the Royal Collection, "Captain Cook," at Greenwich Hospital, and at Up-Park, Sussex, fine full-lengths of George III. and his young Queen. Dance's portraits were carefully and solidly painted, well drawn, and passable in colour. Northcote says, "He drew the figure well, gave a strong likeness and certain studied air to all his portraits; yet they were so stiff and forced that they seemed as if just out of a vice." His works, however, held a place in art which entitles them at least to brief mention. He was one of the original members of the Royal Academy, and resigned his diploma in 1790, on his marriage with a widow lady of large property. He afterwards took the name of Holland, was created a baronet in 1800, and for many years represented the borough of East Grinstead in Parliament. He virtually quitted his profession when he left the Academy, but he afterwards exhibited some landscapes which showed great ability.

James Northcote, R.A., fills a much larger space in the history of art. He was the son of a watchmaker at Plymouth, where he was born October 22, 1746, and though he showed an early attachment to art, was, by his prudent father, bound his apprentice and learnt his trade. During the long seven years of his apprenticeship he gave his spare time to drawing, and, on their termination, devoted himself wholly to art. He began by portrait painting, and contrived so far to make his art known in Plymouth as to gain the notice of Dr. John Mudge, and, through him, an introduction to Sir Joshua Reynolds. This was, probably, the turning-point in his fortunes. He became the pupil of Reynolds, was admitted not only to his studio, but into his house, and was fortunate in gaining the friendship of the painter whom he reverenced. During a second apprenticeship of five years as the pupil of Reynolds, he had full opportunity of acquiring the technical knowledge he must have so greatly needed. He stood beside Reynolds before his easel; he enjoyed free converse with him; he saw his works in all stages; he assisted in their progress, laying in draperies, painting backgrounds and accessories, and forwarding the numerous duplicates and copies required of such a master, and he shared the usual means of advancement and study enjoyed by Reynolds's pupils; at the same time he did not neglect the essential study of the figure at the Royal Academy. In 1775 he had completed his engagement. He was in his twenty-ninth year, and thought the time had arrived when his pupilage should finish, and so did Reynolds. They parted with mutual regret, and Northcote returned to Devonshire, where, by portrait painting, he soon made a little purse, and resolved to visit Italy for his further improvement.

In March, 1777, he set out alone, and, as he tells us, travelled from Lyons to Genoa, from Genoa to Rome, without speaking a word of the language. With his incentives to work, we cannot doubt that he made good use of his time. He spent three years in Italy, visiting the cities distinguished as the seats of art, but passing the greater part of the time at Rome. Following the teaching of Reynolds, he studied Michael Angelo, Raphael, and especially Titian. His powers were recognized by his election into the Academies of Florence, Cortona, and Rome, and with this prestige he returned homeward, studying the great Dutch and Flemish collections in his way, and arrived in London in May, 1780.

Northcote's first resource on his return was portraiture. He visited his native county, where his reputation or his connexions attracted some sitters, and finally settled in London. In 1781 we find him at No. 2, Old Bond Street, and contributing two portraits of "Naval Officers" to the Royal Academy.

In 1783, for the first time, he exhibited subject-pictures, homely and not of a very elevated class, such as "Beggars and Dancing Dogs," "Hobnelia, from Gay's Shepherd's Week," and "The Village Doctress," &c. They do not afford much promise. With some character, and in his females some beauty, there was an absence of grace and taste; a pervading commonness, the drawing stiff, and the figures without a sense of motion. Meanwhile he had many sitters, and was making a little harvest in portraiture.

Northcote was ambitious—his aim was, from the first, historic art ; but it seems at least doubtful whether he would have reached his ideal goal, had he not been opportunely favoured by fortune, for he was settling into a painter of domestic scenes, when Alderman Boydell broached his great scheme of the Shakspeare Gallery. Here was the opportunity Northcote wanted. He engaged earnestly in the work, and finding a higher impulse with the higher aim, he was stimulated to excel. Taking them in the order of exhibition, his first truly historic work was in 1786. "King Edward V., and his Brother Richard, Duke of York, Murdered in the Tower by Order of Richard III." (From Shakspeare's *Richard III.*, act iv., scene 3.) In his picture the children are truly babes of six or seven years old ; the Duke of York having far more the appearance of a girl than of a boy. The painter had not yet got quite clear of pretty and domestic art, and the children seem rather the petted darlings of the day than the sad youths who had wept together, parted from mother and sister within a prison's walls. The painter seems to have learnt his error as to the age of the princes, for in the subsequent picture of "The Burial," the bodies that are being let down into the hole at the stair-foot are full ten years older than those who were slain. Judging from the engraving, there is far too strong an expression of hate in the armed ruffian, who is about to blot out the life of the princes, as though they were some personal enemies or disgusting reptiles, while no doubt he was only fulfilling his mission for mere gold or gain.

The work, however, must have been successful in the eyes of his brother artists, since we find that in 1787 Northcote is entered in the Royal Academy catalogue as R.A. elect. He must, therefore, have been chosen an associate in November, 1786, and an academician in February, 1787. He justified the choice of the members by exhibiting his great work of the death of Wat Tyler. It is a picture of much merit, though, as is not unfrequent in his works, it is built on the composition of another. In this case, the motive has been one of the "Conversions of St. Paul " by Rubens, in which a rearing horse throwing his smitten rider is recalled to us by that of "Wat Tyler," while the horse of his assailant, also rearing, is like the horse of Rubens's standard-bearer.

In the year that Northcote exhibited this picture Opie exhibited his large, and, in many respects, most important picture of "The Assassination of David Rizzio." There are some curious coincidences relating to these works of the two painters. Northcote, as we have just said, had this year attained the full honours of the R.A., obtaining both steps within a year. The same had been the case with Opie, who steps at once from plain John Opie, of last year's catalogue, to John Opie, R.A., in this.

The two pictures were painted, no doubt, in rivalry for these honours, exhibited in the same exhibition, and have found a final resting-place together.   They both belong to the same great Corporation, and hang in the same room of their Guildhall in London.

In the following years he only occasionally exhibited at the Royal Academy, and mostly portraits.   He was diligently at work for Boydell's Gallery, for which he painted in all nine pictures : " Meeting of the Young Princes " (*Richard III.*, act iii., scene 1), then " Romeo and Juliet," " The Death of Mortimer," " The Burial of the Princes in the Tower," &c.

The faults of Northcote in these pictures are equally the faults of the other artists of his day.   The first thing that strikes us is the want of proper consideration of his subject.   We are told by one of his contemporaries, that of studies prior to commencing his pictures he made few or none—that the scheme of his work was little considered ere he began on his canvas.   This he may have learnt from Reynolds, whose habit, we know from many incidents, it also was.   Hence in some works, figures have no ground plane on which they can stand ; in others the space is empty, or unmeaning figures have been added unnecessarily to fill up the canvas.   Character he studied but little, and seems to have given as little attention to obtaining suitable models for his work, the same head doing service on many figures in the same picture ; nor does the work ever carry us back into the period it represents.   The light and shade is generally extremely conventional and often untrue.   To show that he could paint flesh, he gives us too many bare arms and legs in his costume pictures ; thus one of the figures lowering the young princes into their untimely grave, has his head, body, and upper limbs in full armour, while his legs are bare and his feet completely naked. This want of due consideration before commencing the work, also causes much of the wretched *executive* of the pictures of the time.   Instead of that careful preparation of the ground—that washing and minute grinding of each separate pigment under the eye of the master—that attention to dead colouring, with a view to second colouring and glazing, to the purity and fitness of the vehicle, and its complete admixture with the whole of the pigments of the palette, which was not only a tradition of the studios of the old masters, but a faith handed down from each to his successors, resulting in a practice which gave even bad pictures of their schools a preciousness of workmanship and translucent beauty.   The artists after Reynolds were like flies in a honey-pot, entangled with viscid and sticky paint, plastering it on to the canvas to endeavour to reach at once what was before them ; some portions of the pigment as it came from the bladder, some fluent with an overdose of magylph or asphaltum ; losing their ground, and careless of renewing it, painting in and painting out with the most perfect indifference, the result being that such pictures have perished almost in the painting, and are now sad wrecks indeed—or if otherwise have none of the qualities described above, which are to be found even in the poorest pictures of a past age. Frequent instances of the faulty indifference to processes of painting have been given in our work, and we feel that they cannot be too often repeated if the works of our day are to remain to show posterity the talent of their predecessors, instead of needing an apology almost before leaving the easel.

It is curious, in looking over the series of pictures painted at this period and published by Boydell, to note, not the inaccuracies, so much as the glaring inconsistencies of costume which pervade them all. As the landscape painters of those days enjoyed a painter's tree, that flourished in all landscapes and for all foliage, so the figure painters seem to have had a costume equally applicable to all persons, all periods, and all countries; the nobles of Bohemia being dressed in trunk-hose, and armed like the men of Britain with the patched armour of the kingdom and the commonwealth. Another peculiarity is that in the hands of some of the Shakspeare illustrators, the armour fits like the most pliant leather, and bends where there are no joints, to suit the artist's drawing; while in others, as in Opie's " Winter's Tale," it is so extra rigid that the figure looks as if motion were impossible. In some of the pictures it is evident that the painter could never have read the passage he has illustrated.

We must recollect, however, that paintings, up to this time, abounded in anachronisms, and that Rubens, in some sense the father of our school, was guilty of equally flagrant absurdities. Nor had there been any attention given at the theatre to proprieties of scenery or costume, while works of reference or authority on such matters were rare, and the opportunity of consulting them very limited. After all, there may be question how far the effort after exact costume is to be carried, since it may be made to cramp and confine the genius of the artist, and lead him to sacrifice the highest qualities of his art, to become a mere " property man." No doubt it greatly depends on the nature of the subject, and the implied intention of the work. When Reynolds paints three ladies in a semi-exact costume of his own time as the " Graces sacrificing to Hymen," and weaving wreaths of roses round a classic term, we accept it with pleasure, as we do the royal shepherds and shepherdesses in Watteau's Pastorals, as a pleasing masque or fancy tableau; but we can far less tolerate history dressed in the false millinery of Peters or Tresham. Again, in the noble idylls of Michael Angelo, we are satisfied with portions of dress that fit as though they were the skin without folds, and serve to remove the sense of nudity in ideal beings. But the same treatment is more questionable in Fuseli or Westall, when dealing with the nearer realities of Macbeth or Hotspur.

But to return to Northcote, his pencil in these days was tolerably prolific; while engaged on the Boydell pictures he found time to attempt another series, in which the artist was to invent the story as well as to paint it. The subjects are of a lower class than those we have described, but in addition to his pecuniary interest he intended them to aid the cause of morality. He painted ten pictures to contrast the progress of the diligent and the dissipated, by the example, as he describes, "of two female servants who are supposed to live in the house of a young unmarried man of fortune. One acts uniformly from motives of prudence, delicacy, and virtue; the other is careless, dissipated, and inclined to immoral gratifications."

Northcote was successful as a painter of animals, and introduced them skilfully into his pictures, though they are rather too melodramatic; this fault is apparent in his "Angel opposing Balaam," painted for Macklin's Bible. Of this picture, Fuseli said, bearing testimony to the delineation of the animal:—"Northcote, you are an angel at an ass; but an ass at an angel;" and truly his angel is a fine broad-shouldered corporeal reality.

Admitted at the commencement of his career to the home and intimacy of Reynolds, Northcote became at its latter end the depository of the art-lore of nearly two generations; and, without any pretensions to authorship on the score of education, a writer on art. But like his great master, his writings have been so largely attributed to the assistance of others, that their true merits have, we think unjustly, been denied to him. He was unquestionably a man of marked natural abilities—observant in all that related to his art—reflective by habit—and competent to express his ideas clearly, whether orally or with his pen.

With some other papers of less importance, he also contributed *The History of a Slighted Beauty,* under which name he allegorically describes the birth of the fine arts, their progress through Europe, and arrival in this country; an ingenious conceit very well and amusingly written, and extending into three numbers of *The Artist.* In 1813, Northcote published his *Life of Sir Joshua Reynolds.* He says in his preface, "It is my fixed opinion that if ever there should appear in the world a memoir of an artist well given, it will be the production of an artist;" a remark which to a great extent is borne out by his own work, for its merits are precisely those which his professional knowledge of art has given to it. His *Fables* (original and selected) were partly written by himself, his own being distinguished by his initials, which, we believe, are confined to the prose fables. Though without claim to much originality, they are tersely and well written.

It was Northcote's habit to take an early walk, then to breakfast, and afterwards to enter his studio. He was distinguished for his conversational powers ; and it was his practice to admit his visitors to his painting-room, so that about eleven o'clock in the forenoon, unless he had a sitter, a sort of *levée* commenced, and it seldom happened that he remained long alone—he talked over his work till his dinner-hour, freely discussing any subject which arose with great sagacity, acuteness, and information, always maintaining his opinions.

We learn from all accounts of him that Northcote had the character of independent self-assertion, and that he did not abstain from cynical remarks. He says of himself, "I am sometimes thought cold and cynical." We add a personal description of Northcote, who is thus painted by Leslie, R.A., in 1821 :—"It is the etiquette for a newly-elected member to call immediately on all the academicians, and I did not omit paying my respects to Northcote among the rest, although I knew he was not on good terms with the Academy. I was shown upstairs into a large front room, filled with pictures, many of the larger ones resting against each other, and all of them dim with dust. I had not waited long when a door opened, which communicated with his painting-room, and the old gentleman appeared, but did not advance beyond it. His diminutive figure was enveloped in a chintz dressing-gown, below which his trousers, which looked as if made for a much taller man, hung in loose folds over an immense pair of shoes, into which his legs seemed to have shrunk down. His head was covered with a blue silk nightcap, and from under that and his projecting brows, his sharp black eyes peered at me with a whimsical expression of inquiry. There he stood, with his palette and brushes in one hand, and a mahl-stick twice as long as himself in the other ; his attitude and look saying, for he did not speak, 'What do you want ?'"

From what is known of the character of Northcote we are far from deeming him the heartless cynic which he has been represented. He was benevolent to those who applied to him for assistance, and courteous to the young artist who sought his advice. He was temperate and just, and his prudence enabled him to secure independence. Northcote never married. His long life was entirely devoted to the enthusiastic pursuit of his profession, and was quietly terminated the 13th July, 1831, in his eighty-sixth year.

James Opie, R.A. (never Oppy, as has been said), was in his art-relations the twin brother of Northcote, occupying the same place both in portrait and history. He was born at St. Agnes, near Truro, in May, 1761 ; the son and grandson of the village carpenter, respectable men, who intended that he should succeed to the family trade, but his genius led him in another course. He was early remarkable for the strength of

ɪ

his understanding and the readiness with which he acquired all that the village school could offer. At ten years of age he was not only able to solve many difficult problems of Euclid, but was thought capable of instructing others ; and at twelve he set up an evening-school, where he taught scholars of twice his own age. He early showed an attachment to drawing, and gave evidences of his inclination, which his mother secretly encouraged. His father checked such attempts, since they led him aside from the trade he had chosen for him ; but gradually the boy's strong inclination prevailed, and he was left to practise openly the pursuit he had secretly followed. He had already made sufficient progress to get some country employment in portrait painting, and had been commissioned by Lord Bateman to paint some rustic subjects, when he fell under the notice of Dr. Wolcot, known as Peter Pindar, who was then trying to establish himself in practice at Truro.

The painter and the doctor later on entered into a sort of partnership, though we find that Opie did not come to London until 1780, and that he dissolved the unsatisfactory connection within a year. Wolcot's trumpet though must have been blown to announce his expected arrival, and had evidently made an impression on the painters, whatever it did on the public. Northcote was absent in Italy when Opie arrived in London ; he returned in May, 1780, and, as Leslie relates, called on Reynolds immediately, who said to him, "Ah, my dear sir, you may go back ; there is a wondrous Cornishman who is carrying all before him." "What is he like ?" said Northcote, eagerly. "Like ? why like Caravaggio and Velasquez in one." Poor Northcote was alarmed at the prospect of such a rival ; but he thought it best to strike up a friendship with him at once, and friends they were, said Leslie, as long as Opie lived : such great friends, apparently, that Lonsdale, the painter, feared to announce Opie's death to Northcote, lest the shock should be too much for him. When he did tell him, however, Northcote said, "Well, well, it's a very sad event ; but I must confess it takes a great stumbling-block out of my way, for I never could succeed where Opie did."

Notwithstanding this little touch of worldliness, and the fashion to represent the rivalry of the two men as extreme, we do not believe that it was any bar to their friendship, or exceeded that natural feeling which would exist between those advancing by the same path, where each must strive to be first. We do not find the least trace of bitterness in Amelia Opie's letters, where, if any existed, it would surely have found expression ; but we see, on the contrary, that Northcote, of whom she speaks "as this queer little being" and "the little man," was evidently on terms of familiar intimacy with her and her husband. If any such feelings had a momentary expression, as might be assumed from Northcote's words, it was surely not deep-seated.

Soon after Opie's arrival in London, he married his first wife, who was reputed to have possessed some property, but about whom little is known. The union was not a happy one, and was dissolved by the lady's misconduct in 1795. His second wife tells us that "passing St. Giles's Church in company with a gentleman of avowedly sceptical opinions, Mr. Opie said, 'I was married in that church' (alluding to his first marriage) ; 'And I,' replied his companion, 'was christened there.' 'Indeed,' answered Opie. 'It seems they do not do their work well there, for it does not hold.'"

Opie had for a time sufficient employment as a portrait painter, varied occasionally by single figures—pictures midway between subjects and portraiture. The first time his name appears as an exhibitor at the Royal Academy is in 1782 ; his contributions being "An Old Man's Head," and "An Old Woman." In 1783 he exhibited two fancy subjects, together with three portraits. In 1786 he sent seven pictures to the Royal Academy, one of them "James I. of Scotland Assassinated by Graham at the Instigation of his Uncle, the Duke of Athol," together with "A Sleeping Nymph," "Cupid Stealing a Kiss," and five portraits. These were followed in 1787 by "The Assassination of David Rizzio," which won the painter his election, not only as an associate, but in the following spring as a full member of the Royal Academy, as we have related in our account of Northcote.

This shows a rapid advance in the short space of five years, for one whose education in art must have been carried on apart from the companionship of artists, and with the very limited opportunities that so distant a county as Cornwall could in that age supply. It is true that his methods are rude, and his execution the most common and unsatisfactory possible ; but the feeling of vigour and power they display makes us overlook many of their defects, and we tolerate his works when not brought under too close inspection ; but when weighed as to their real merits and defects, they are at times sadly wanting in many qualities.

"The Murder of Rizzio" is an example of Opie's coarse and slovenly execution ; it is in a sad state of dilapidation from the painter's want of knowledge, or his carelessness and indifference to means and method ; but it may be referred to as a proof of Opie's power in the real qualities of art. It is a vigorous work, and shows how little he was disposed to shirk difficulties in his practice. The composition is rudely energetic, the figures in violent action. Rizzio, the principal figure, falling backwards out of the picture, smitten down by the sword of the ruthless Ruthven, is a strong example of a difficulty overcome, and so is the queen, rushing forward to interpose herself between the assassin and his victim, but restrained by the fierce grasp of Douglas : a group which perhaps suggested Fuseli's "Hamlet Held Back by Horatio from Following his Father's Ghost." The light and dark of the picture is too pronounced, probably from the failure of the darks, which have become black, and this shows as a great defect, bringing lines into prominence which no doubt were more subdued when the picture left the painter's studio.

Shee, writing in 1789, thus describes our painter :—"I have been introduced to Mr. Opie, who is in manners and appearance as great a clown and as stupid a looking fellow as ever I set my eyes on. Nothing but incontrovertible proof of the fact would force me to think him capable of anything above the sphere of a journeyman carpenter, so little, in this instance, has Nature proportioned exterior grace to inward worth. I intend calling upon him occasionally ; for I know him to be a good painter, and though appearances are so much against him, he is, I am told, a most sensible and learned man."

This description, however, though no doubt Shee's honest impression of the man, differs totally from Opie's fine portrait painted by himself, now in the Royal Academy, in which there is a look of self-dependence, of decision and intellect curiously agreeing with the square vigorous handling of the work, and far removed from clownish stupidity, or even from the inspiration of a mere peasant. Indeed, however obtained, his knowledge seems to have greatly impressed literary men well qualified to judge. Horne Tooke, who sat to Opie, said of him, "Mr. Opie crowds more wisdom into a few words than almost any man I ever knew, he speaks as it were in axioms, and what he observes is worthy to be remembered ;" and Sir James Macintosh remarked, that "had Mr. Opie turned his mind to the study of philosophy, he would have been one of the first philosophers of the age," adding, "had he written on the subject, he would have thrown more light on the philosophy of his art, than any man living."

Soon after Opie's election to the Academy, he was engaged by Boydell to take part in his great series of Shakspeare Illustrations, for which he painted five pictures. There is a marked advance as Opie progresses in these works ; the first is an inferior picture to the "Rizzio," the composition is scattered and ill-arranged, the story not well told, the figures want individual character, and do not seem as if painted from the life. The draperies not only have no character of antiquity and are wholly incorrect, but they are arranged and thrown without taste, and look as if hung on a peg or a lay figure, but each succeeding picture is an improvement. They impress us with a sense of rude power and genius, and contrast finely with the feeble inanities of many of his contemporaries engaged on the same series.

When Boydell's work was ended, Opie had to recur to portraiture as his chief means of support, occasionally painting and exhibiting subject pictures. His sitters introduced him into society at Norwich, and on the occasion of an evening party he saw for the first time Miss Alderson, the daughter of a physician in that city, who afterwards became the second Mrs. Opie. Their meeting has been described by Miss Bright-well, her biographer, who tells us that Opie, being at a party where Miss Alderson was expected as one of the guests, she did not make her appearance until a late hour. At length the door was flung open, and the lady entered in a garb far different to that she assumed later in life. "She was dressed in a robe of blue, her neck and arms bare, and on her head a small bonnet, placed in a somewhat coquettish style, sideways, and surmounted by a plume of three white feathers. Her beautiful hair hung in rich waving tresses over her shoulders ; her face kindling with pleasure at the sight of her old friends ; and her whole appearance animated and glowing." Opie was at the time in conversation with the host who had been anxiously expecting her ; and suddenly interrupted it by the exclamation, "Who is that ? who is she ?" and hastily rising, pressed forward to be introduced. He was evidently smitten, charmed —as was characteristic of his impulsive nature—at the first sight. Mrs. Opie said of this meeting :—"Almost from my first arrival, Mr. Opie became my avowed lover." She vowed that his chances of success were but one in a thousand ; but he persevered. He knew his own mind, and persuaded her at length, during a stay in London, that he had read her heart. So she went home again to Norwich, to think of the future, and to prepare for it. They were married in 1798, and his wife said that "he found it necessary to make himself popular as a portrait painter, and that in the productive and difficult branch of female portraiture." For this we should have thought his art, from its rude strength, particularly unfitted him ; yet on examining the catalogues, we find that nearly half of his sitters were ladies.

We find from his wife's memoirs of him that the first years of their married life were not without anxieties. She says that his "picture in the Exhibition of 1801 was universally admired, and was purchased ; yet he saw himself at the end of that year and the beginning of the next, almost wholly without employment." . . . . "Gloomy and painful indeed," she adds, "were those three alarming months ; and I consider them as the severest trial that I experienced during my married life." And she bears this affectionate testimony to his perseverance :—"His love of his profession was intense, and his unremitting industry in the pursuit of it, drew from Mr. Northcote the observation, 'that while other artists painted to live, he lived to paint.'" In 1806—we quote her words with pleasure—she notes, "that prosperity had reached them, and that Mr. Opie was rewarded for his perseverance and disappoint-ments by success and fame." But he was stimulated to too high efforts, and we find from his letters, that " he laboured so intently the latter end of 1806, and the beginning of 1807, that he allowed his mind no rest, hardly indulging in the relaxation of a walk." A disease of the spinal marrow, affecting the brain, had commenced. He strove hard to finish his works for the Academy Exhibition ; but delirium ensued, and in this state, the mind wandering upon his art, he gradually sank, and died 9th of April, 1807, in his forty-seventh year. He was buried with some pomp in St. Paul's.

In his last hours he was anxious to finish a picture for the Royal Academy, which was nearly ready, and his pupil Thomson, who afterwards became a member and the keeper of the Royal Academy, volunteered to work on it for Opie. Delirium had set in, but when the picture, in one of his lucid intervals, was brought for him to see, he was clear enough on the subject of art to say, "I think there is not colour enough in the background." Thomson was struck with the justice of the remark, and having added more colour, again brought it into the room. "It will do now," said the dying painter with a smile ; "take it away ; indeed, if you can't do it, nobody can." " And his countenance," says his wife, who relates the anecdote, "gave us the consolation of knowing that his feelings were comfortable ones, and that he was conscious of neither our misery nor of his own situation."

Reynolds, as we have seen, said Opie's art was like Caravaggio's and Velasquez's. Dayes, no mean critic, thought it approximated to Rembrandt. All these three artists are distinguished by their power and breadth, qualities which Opie possessed. His colour, however, was deficient in purity ; his lights are often heavy and cold ; his execution was broad and spirited, but very coarse ; his conception of his subject real and vigorous, full of action, but showing those defects which the neglect of early training render inevitable. He had, however, great claims to merit as a portrait painter.

Opie also made himself known as a writer. His first work was the *Life of Reynolds* for Dr. Wolcot's edition of Pilkington. He next printed *A Letter on the Cultivation of the Fine Arts in England,* in which he recommended the formation of a National Gallery. He delivered four lectures on art at the Royal Institution ; and on his election as Professor of Painting at the Royal Academy, in 1805, he delivered four lectures : on " Design," " Invention," " Chiaroscuro," and " Colour." These four lectures were published after his death, with a memoir by his widow, who enjoyed a high literary reputation.

Sir William Beechey, R.A., Knt., is the last painter of the time who merits notice in this chapter. He has not found a biographer ; not even a memoir of him, that we are aware of, appears in print, and we are surprised to find that the recollections of an artist, who filled some space in his time, have so speedily passed away, leaving no trace behind. Dayes, who was an early contemporary of Beechey, tells of him, in his account of the painters who then flourished, that he was originally a house-painter and for many years struggled with fortune. In a brief notice of him, which, at the time of his death, appeared in the *Gentleman's Magazine*, no mention is made of this, but he is stated to have been born at Burford, in Oxfordshire, December 12, 1753, and to have been articled to a conveyancer at Stow in Gloucestershire, but that being tired of the monotony of a provincial lawyer's office, he came to London and continued under his articles with a Mr. Owen of Tooke's Court. This is certainly explicit enough, but the two accounts are hardly consistent with each other. In London, Beechey became acquainted with some students of the Royal Academy; delighted by their pursuits and enamoured with art, he prevailed upon his master to release him from the law, and in 1772 he gained admission to the schools of the Academy, and thenceforth devoted himself to his new profession.

He began the practice of art as a portrait painter and met with some encouragement in London; and then, in 1781, an opening at Norwich induced him to try his fortune in that city, where he painted some conversation pieces of the character introduced by Hogarth, and tried his hand on one or two subject pictures. At the end of four or five years he returned and settled in the metropolis, where he soon gained practice and celebrity. Dawe, in his *Life of George Morland* (1804), tells how Beechey was introduced to the notice of George III. The portrait of a nobleman, painted by him, being returned by the Hanging Committee of the Royal Academy, so incensed the peer, that he had the picture sent for to Buckingham Palace to be inspected by the King and the royal family, who all, in consequence, became sitters to the painter. This was the beginning of his fortunes. In 1793 he painted a whole-length portrait of the Queen, who appointed him her portrait painter, and the same year he was elected an associate of the Royal Academy. Increased commissions followed the royal patronage. Dawe says, " Beechey may justly be considered the only original portrait painter we have, all the rest being more or less the imitators of Sir Joshua." But we do not think that the large portrait group which he completed in 1798 would ever have been painted had not Reynolds preceded him.

This equestrian group of George III., with the Prince of Wales and the Duke of York, reviewing the 10th Hussars and the 3rd Dragoons, is now at Hampton Court (No. 166). Although a clever and somewhat showy group of portraits, it has little of real nature, but is full of painter's artifices. It attracted, however, much attention at the time, and the same year (1798) Beechey was knighted and gained his election as a member of the Royal Academy.

Beechey had obtained his introduction to the Court by accident, and so it happened to his pupil, Sharpe—known afterwards, from a picture he had painted, as "Bees-wing Sharpe." Sharpe was so pertinacious in his request to be present at a sitting of royalty that at last Beechey consented, on the express stipulation that he should be quite silent, keep out of the way, and merely set, and from time to time hand him, a fresh palette. Under these conditions, he accompanied Sir William to the palace. They had hardly reached the apartment where the sitting was to take place when the door was thrown open and the astonished pupil heard the cry of Sharp!—simply a warning to be on the *qui vive* for royalty. Nervously impulsive, he thought that he was called, and rushed forward, to hear from the domestics in the suite of rooms he traversed the same cry of "Sharp! Sharp!" This only increased his confusion, until, at length, in passing through one of the doors, he ran right into the arms of some one. "Hallo! hallo! what's this, what's this? Who are you?" were uttered in quick succession. "Who are you?" "Sharpe, your Majesty," said the young painter, who, though dreadfully alarmed, saw at once that it was the King. "Sharpe, Sharpe," said the King; "what, son of the hautboy player of Norwich?" Now it so happened that the King had hit upon the right person, and when the youth acknowledged that Sharpe of Norwich was his father, the King at once was gracious. "Well, Sharpe," said he, "you had almost knocked royalty down, but it is well it is no worse. What brought you here?" Sharpe explained that he was Sir William's pupil, had come to aid him in the sitting, &c. The story amused the King as much as it annoyed Beechey, and the accident led to a commission to Sharpe to paint the Princess Amelia and others of the royal family.

Sharpe is said to have lost favour as oddly as he gained it. He became a great favourite with the pages, and one day exercised his skill in painting a pair of scissors hanging on a nail in their room. The King, on some occasion, coming into the pages' apartments, attempted to take the scissors off the nail, at which there was the faintest of titters, and, offended at the deception which had taken him in as well as others, he inquired who was the delinquent, and Sharpe, being pointed out, fell as rapidly as he had risen in royal favour.

Unlike his contemporaries, Beechey was not led aside by attempts at history painting. If he has left little for posterity, he was fortunate in his own day. He painted for the King the full-length portraits of all the royal family, and for the Prince of Wales the portraits of the princesses, his sisters. For the Queen, an exceptional work, he painted the entire decorations of a room in the royal lodge at Frogmore. The chief persons of fashion and distinction in his day were his sitters. His colouring was pleasing. He excelled in his females and children; but his males wanted power. His portraits generally were deficient in grace, his draperies poor and ill-cast, and he showed no ability to overcome the graceless stiffness which then prevailed in dress. Yet he possessed much merit, and his portraits have maintained a respectable second rank. He enjoyed a long career in portrait art, but Lawrence and others had for many years succeeded to the monopoly of fashion and reputation before Beechey finally retired. He sold his pictures, studies, engravings, and materials by auction in 1836, and removed to Hampstead, where he died 28th January, 1839, at the age of eighty-six. The gossip of art has left little to tell of Beechey, but we learn he was of the old school, who did not abstain from the thoughtless use of un-meaning oaths. Calling on Constable, the landscape painter, he ad-dressed him, " Why, d—n it, Constable, what a d—d fine picture you are making ; but you look d—d ill, and have got a d—d bad cold." It is said that in his latter years he complained of the increasing sobriety and decreasing conviviality of both artists and patrons of art. At one of the annual dinners of the Academy he remarked that it was confoundedly slow to what was the wont in his younger days, when the company did not separate until a duke and a painter were both put under the table from the effects of the bottle.

CHAPTER XII.

THE ANIMAL PAINTERS OF THE EIGHTEENTH CENTURY.

OUR countrymen have ever been lovers of the chase and of the race-course, and, such being the case, it is natural that after the portraits of the squire and his dame, and the goodly array of sons and daughters who served to uphold the family name, the portraits of their most famous hunters and racers would be objects of desire to our country gentlemen. Hence it is that while in the dining-room and staircase gallery of the country mansions of our old landed proprietors we are often introduced to their interminable ancestry, be-wigged and be-powdered, or to the toasts and beauties that fired them to feats of noble horsemanship, the hall itself is surrounded with portraits of the animals that carried them in the field, or filled or emptied their pockets on the racecourse, each horse led, as it might be, by the favourite groom or the successful jockey of the day.

The love for this art at the time we are describing was gratified by *John Wootton*, an animal and landscape painter of merit, who was a pupil of John Wyck the younger, and imbibed the traditions of the Flemish school of painters. He furnished the halls and galleries of our old family mansions with views of the estate, and portraits of the class we have described, of the favourite horses and dogs. Frequenting Newmarket, he made himself known as an animal painter. He drew with great spirit. He painted hunting-pieces, which were much esteemed, and were engraved, and he received as much as forty guineas for the portrait of a single horse. Later, he applied himself to landscape, imitating, but at a long distance, the manner of Claude and then of Poussin. Looking at him, however, only as a horse painter, we are inclined to think better of him. His works may be seen in the royal collection, and at Blenheim, Longleat, Althorp, Ditchley, and other mansions, but their merits are obscured by the blackness which has come over them.

It cannot be said that patronage of the kind alluded to did, or was likely to do, much for art, but Wootton made some property by it and built himself a house in Cavendish Square, which he decorated with his paintings, and here he died in January, 1765.

During Wootton's career, *James Seymour* was also celebrated as a horse painter. He was born in 1702, the son of a banker, who was the friend of Lely, and fond of art. Possessing great power of drawing, he drew the horse with the pen with much spirit and character: but he was too idle to study; and his attempt to give more finish to his work, and his bad style of colour, showed his defects. It is told that the Duke of Somerset employed him to paint his stud at his seat in Sussex; and that having admitted the artist to his table, he drank to him as "cousin Seymour;" and took offence when the artist expressed his belief that he really was of the same race. The "proud Duke" left the table, and ordered his steward to pay and dismiss his quondam cousin, but finding afterwards the impossibility of getting an artist to complete the work, he sent again for Seymour, who retorted, "My lord, I will now prove that I am of your grace's family, for I won't come." It is probable that Seymour's finished works are few, for we find little mention of them. He died in 1752. He is best known by his drawings; we are unable now to point to a painting by him.

George Stubbs, A.R.A., who succeeded Wootton as an animal painter, was born in 1724, at Liverpool, where his father practised as a surgeon. It is probable that his attention was thus especially directed to anatomy, and that he continued the study of it after he had finally elected the profession of painting. Little is known of his early life, or even whether his original bent was to the arts; but we learn that when about thirty years of age he paid a visit to Italy, extending his journey as far as Rome, and that on his return he settled in London, and soon became known for his talents both as a painter and an anatomist. In 1776 he published *The Anatomy of the Horse*, with eighteen plates drawn from nature, and engraved by his own hands. In the title-page he styles himself "painter."

Stubbs soon became the fashionable horse painter of the day, and was patronized by all who delighted in the art; but his anatomical knowledge fitted him for something better than the mere lay-figure treatment of the animal which satisfied the friends of his equine *sitters*. He aspired to be ranked as an artist, and to treat the horse as a heroic animal, instead of the tame prosaic steed that was led forth from the stable to show its points and breeding by its mere bony and muscular development, rather than by expression and energy of action and motion. He aimed to show his skill in designing this noble animal in its wonderful variety of form; in motion, and under the influence of artistic foreshortenings, as well as grouped in combination with others of the higher animals of the chase. Barry, who seems to have attentively watched his progress, praises his works warmly ; he says, "His 'Lion Killing a Horse ;' a 'Tiger Lying in his Den,' as large as life, appearing as it were disturbed, and listening, which were in the last year's exhibition, are pictures that must rouse and agitate the most inattentive ; he is now painting a lion, panting and out of breath, lying with his paws over a stag he has run down : it is inimitable."

In 1780 the Royal Academy acknowledged Stubbs's talents by electing him an associate of the body, and in the following year a full member. But on his election, like Wright of Derby, he declined to present one of his own works to the Academy, and the diploma was withheld, Stubbs choosing rather to remain an associate, in which rank he continued during the remainder of his life. It has been said that the painter's fortune was greater than his merit, in that his works were engraved by such eminent artists as Woollett, Earlom, and Green, and there is no doubt that the celebrity of Woollett's graver would have given reputation to works of far less excellence than those of Stubbs. But these very engravings are a testimony to the painter's popularity, and it is doubtful, even in our own day, if the taste of the general public is not satisfied with subjects of far less merit as works of art, than the four well-known "sporting pictures" engraved by Woollett : or "The Horse Frightened at a Lion," "The Farmer's Wife and the Raven," or "The Tigers at Play." Stubbs's name, however, is more frequently associated with his picure of "The Fall of Phaeton," which he is said to have repeated four times. As lately seen, it hardly sustains its reputation ; although the horses are well and spiritedly designed, the whole is scattered and disjointed in effect, and wanting in the ideal treatment which such a subject requires.

Stubbs was ardent in the pursuit of his art, an indefatigable dissector, fearing none of the attendant dangers. It is told of him that he was of great muscular strength, in so much that on one occasion he carried a dead horse on his back up a narrow staircase to his dissecting-room, a feat which, unless the animal was of the smallest of the equine race, does not admit of our belief. For the latter part of his life he was very abstemious in his food, and a strict water-drinker. Yet he lived to enjoy eighty-two years of vigorous life, dying on the 10th of July, 1806. On the whole, the art made a great advance under Stubbs.

Sawrey Gilpin, R.A., was another artist of the eighteenth century, who earned distinction as an animal painter. He was born at Carlisle, in 1733, of an old Cumberland family, and when fourteen was sent to London, where it was intended he should be brought up to some business. But his desire to pursue art led to his being placed with

Samuel Scott, the marine painter. His affections turned to cattle rather than to ships, and he soon attained much power as a draughtsman. At Newmarket he gained the favour of the Duke of Cumberland, then ranger of Windsor Park, who gave him apartments, and many facilities for his improvement. He excelled greatly in his portraits of horses, and was fully employed. He painted wild animals with equal success, and tried some subjects in history; among them of course the "Story of Phaeton." He exhibited at Spring Gardens, in 1770, a sketch in oil of "Darius Obtaining the Persian Empire by the Neighing of his Horse;" and in the following year, "Gulliver Taking Leave of the Houyhnhnms," both of them works which attracted much notice. He painted both in oil and water colour; all his works were marked by great spirit, but his colouring was poor, and his pictures failed from the absence of higher technical qualities. He was elected A.R.A., 1795, R.A., 1797. He died in 1807. The Rev. W. Gilpin, who wrote several works on picturesque beauty, was his brother.

In treating of the animal painters, it will be desirable next in order to class *George Morland.* Although his art was of such a mixed character that it comprised both landscapes, rustic figures, and animals, still it is as an animal painter—as a painter of pigs and sheep and asses —that he is principally known. These, in combination with rustic figures, formed the subject of his pictures, while the landscape part of his art was never much more than a background for them.

George Morland was born in 1763, just at the time when the artists of this country awoke to a sense of their own strength, and found a new aid to progress in the establishment of public exhibitions of their works. Henry Morland, the father of George, was himself a crayon draughtsman, painter, and engraver, and a man of some reputation in his day. He was already advanced in life, being fifty-one years of age, when his son was born. Respectable and respected both for his art and his manner of life, he passed for a well-educated man, and brought up his family with more than ordinary strictness and regularity.

Of this family George was the eldest and favourite child, and early displayed a talent for art, combining with an active restless disposition, great drollery and love of fun, with occasional fits of melancholy. These, the sure accompaniment of an artistic temperament, were in-creased, perhaps, in his case, by his being debarred from associating with boys of his own age, and subjected to the discipline of a parent who had long passed the period of youth. Young Morland had made some progress in art when only seven years of age, and at ten exhibited drawings at the Royal Academy, which it is evident must have had some merit. The very precocity of his art was perhaps the first misfortune of his life, since at fourteen years of age he was articled to his father, and his days henceforth devoted to continuous and steady application. His father seemed to consider every hour not spent at his easel as wasted,— a discipline so opposed to the natural temperament of the boy, as to make labour hateful to the young artist.   Under his father, however, he attained great power of hand and correctness of eye, and learnt to paint by copying the works of the Dutch and Flemish schools.   Although the schools of the Royal Academy were now open to the rising artists of the metropolis, young Morland was not allowed to study there, since his father—over anxious about his morals—did not like his mingling with the students who resorted to them for instruction, and he conducted his education principally himself.   Morland is sometimes looked upon as an untaught genius, who obtained his knowledge without the aid of schools ; but on the contrary, no teaching could be more direct and continuous than that he received from his anxious parent.

After some time passed in preliminary study, he attempted original sketches from the poets, and made many illustrations from Spenser's "Faery Queen" as well as from ballads, such as "Robin Grey," "Margaret's Ghost," &c.   These were bought and engraved and found a ready sale.   Occasionally, also, he tried his powers in caricature, and soon showed, if not a refined, yet a sufficiently fertile invention.   At this time he rarely sketched from Nature on the spot, but stored his mind with the broad characteristics of his subject to reproduce them from memory at home, and it is from this cause that there is little of individual imitation in his pictures, but rather that general aspect of the scene or subject which often appeals to the mind more than the most literal truth.

As he grew in years and became conscious of his own powers, young Morland rebelled against the restraint imposed upon him at home, and the severe and continuous labour exacted from him.   When about nineteen he first began to evade this discipline, from which he shortly afterward broke entirely loose, following a dissolute course, and justifying himself without shame and without self-reproach.   His innate dislike to labour was soon apparent ; he avoided all regular study or occupation, and gave himself up to extravagance, debauchery, and folly.

Means of subsistence, however, must be gained, and his abilities and necessities soon attracted those who live by preying upon others ; he became the debtor and slave of a picture dealer, who tempted him to lodge in his house, and while he pandered cheaply to his vices and follies, kept him in a state of bondage.   "His meals were carried up to him by his employer's boy, and when his dinner was brought—which usually consisted of sixpenny-worth of meat from a cook-shop, with a pint of beer—he would sometimes venture to ask if he might not have a pennyworth of pudding.   Yet even under this treatment he contributed so much to the profits of his employer as to paint a sufficient number of pictures to fill a room to which the price of admittance was half-a-crown." From this condition he escaped, and was assisted at Margate by a lady who found profitable employment for him in taking miniature portraits ; with her he went to France, where he might also have obtained employment of the same kind, but his restless nature prevented him, at this important crisis, from settling to any steady labour, and he resumed his former reckless habits. He went to lodge with Mr. William Ward, the mezzotint engraver, and while with him seems for a time to have pursued his painting with some steadiness and in a manner tending to his improvement, possibly influenced by a growing attachment to Miss Ward. He painted "The Idle and Industrious Mechanic," a pair of small pictures, "The Idle Laundress and Industrious Cottager," and "Letitia, or Seduction," a series of six pictures depicting the fall of a young country girl. Morland is said to have studied every part of these works from Nature, even to the minutest details ; the figures are well drawn and the whole executed with considerable skill.

In July, 1786, the painter married the sister of his friend Ward, who followed his example by marrying a month after one of the Miss Morlands. But marriage produced no reform in Morland's reckless and irregular habits ; he soon quarrelled with his brother-in-law, and gave himself up to the company of low associates and to habits of intemperance and dissipation, from which he never after was able to disentangle himself. He painted rapidly, and sold his pictures for anything he could get, yet his genius made him popular notwithstanding, and his productions were eagerly sought after. His boon companions also acted as his agents, and sometimes got as much as five guineas for what he had formerly been paid only five shillings. Such was the request for the painter's works that he might have demanded large prices ; numbers of purchasers resorted to him ; yet by his absurd and useless extravagance Morland had incurred debts in eighteen months to the amount of nearly 4,000*l.*, and was compelled to abscond for a while, until his friends could attempt some arrangement of his affairs. For a time he continued to improve in his art ; he overcame the somewhat laboured finish of his first manner, and the ease that was induced by the rapid pencil required to meet his urgent wants, had not yet resulted in his using up the stores of his memory.

About 1790 Morland arrived at the meridian of his art, but maintained his elevation only a short time, and soon began rapidly to decline. "The Gipsies," 1792, is a good example of this period. The size of that work is larger than usual with Morland ; it is painted with a full pencil and evidently with great ease and rapidity.

As his difficulties made no change in his habits, his debts continued to increase, notwithstanding the rapid means at his command for satisfying them. He was continually making compositions with his creditors to pay 12o*l.* per month, 100*l.*, 50*l.*, 10*l.*, and was earnest to do so, but after one or two payments constantly neglected to fulfil his engagements. Hunted from house to house by noisy creditors, always compounding for his debts, but never keeping any engagement he had entered into, he lived in constant dread of a prison; the resources of his memory once worked out, how was an artist, plunged into such hopeless degradation, and beset with such terrors, to realize any more of the true freshness of that rural life in which lay the subjects for his pencil; he could not leave home from dread of the bailiffs who were continually on the watch for him, and the country with its pigs and its sheep must be sought within his own walls. While living in perpetual dread of his creditors his excesses not only continued but increased; his naturally fine constitution was undermined by them. He now seldom left his painting-room : "he even took his meals in it, though never at any regular periods, but would sometimes at seven in the morning have beefsteaks and onions, with purl and gin or a pot of porter for breakfast. His dinner he would take at eleven, twelve, one, or three o'clock, according as his appetite served. He seldom ate his meals with his wife, and though he kept several servants, would cook his own food and eat it off a chair by the side of his easel; while in the same apartment were to be seen dogs of various kinds, pigeons flying, and pigs running about. During the whole day he swallowed all kinds of strong liquors; tea he could not drink, but when invited to partake of this refreshment he would shake his head and say it was very pernicious and made his hand shake." We remember having seen, in the possession of an old friend, a pair of small pictures painted about the latter end of Morland's life, and we were told by their possessor that he sat beside the painter's easel while he completed them, and having paid for them, he took them away with him wet; the only way to secure an original work of such a master.

In November, 1799, Morland was arrested, and, obtaining the rules, took a house in Lambeth, which was a rendezvous for all the profligates of the prison. He was daily intoxicated, and generally lay the whole night on the floor. The ruin of his health and character were soon completed. He was released under the Insolvent Act in 1802, but was now broken-hearted and downcast, harassed by diseased fears and fancies, his intellect and sight also impaired. He was again arrested for a publican's score, and overwhelmed with misfortune, neglect, and self-reproach, he drank, in a state of desperation, great quantities of spirits, and after eight days of delirious fever, died in a spunging house on the 29th October, 1804, in his forty-second year. His wife, to whom—it is hard to believe—as stated by his biographer, he was sincerely attached, fell into convulsive fits on learning his death, and finished a life, which must have been one of hopeless misery, on the 2nd of November, in her thirty-seventh year, and both were interred together. He had shortly before written his own epitaph—alas! too truly—" Here lies a drunken dog."

Any one who will read with attention a more extended life of the painter, will be aware that his reputation in his own day was partly accidental, and largely arose out of the very irregularities which we must condemn. Many were eager to possess works which were only to be obtained as it were by lottery, and which all hoped would turn up prizes either then or in the future.

We have passed over most of the stories of wild riot and excess that marked the short life of the painter, but we are not prepared to say that his freaks and follies were entirely hindrances, or that they did not in many cases prove of assistance to him in that low walk of art which he had made his own. He was quick of observation, and gathered hints readily from the society into which he was thrown. Thus one of his first follies, related by Dawe, his biographer, as taking place when Morland had not yet completed his apprenticeship, shows this readiness of perception in the painter. He had been spending the evening with a roystering company at a favourite tavern, the "Cheshire Cheese," and on leaving about ten o'clock, took it into his head to start by the hoy to Gravesend. He arrived there a perfect stranger, about two o'clock in the morning, and in company with two strollers, took the road in the dark to Chatham, and ended by joining one of them in a short sea-voyage in which he was nearly wrecked. Returning almost penniless to the "congress" at his tavern, we are told he brought out such a fund of information on nautical matters, as to perfectly astonish the company. It is quite evident that he had gained more by his wild adventure than if he had remained at home pinned to his easel.

Again his boon companions were his models, sitting and posing for him. In "The Sportsman's Return," "Dirty Brooks" the cobbler, one of his pot companions and agents, is represented leaning out of his own stall. When surrounded by companions that would have entirely impeded the progress of other men, "Morland might be said to be in an academy in the midst of models—he would get one to stand for a hand, another for a foot, another for a head, an attitude, or a figure"—nay, he often regulated his compositions, and that in some of his best works, entirely by the chance presence of some choice spirit whom he could use as a model. He would set the low associates, who surrounded him while painting, to watch for passers-by, suitable to paint into his pictures, and despatch them to induce these wayfarers to come and be painted, treating his sitters liberally with beer, spirits, and food, and making

K

them satisfied and delighted by his good fellowship. He once took it into his head to serve the office of parish constable, and although it was a freak of which he was soon heartily tired, yet it will be seen that even this he managed to turn to his professional advantage. Dawe tells us that, " Just as Morland was about to begin his four pictures of ' The Deserter,' a sergeant, drummer, and soldier, on their way to Dover in pursuit of a deserter, came in for a billet. Seeing that these men would answer his purpose, he accompanied them to the ' Britannia,' and treated them plentifully, while he was earnestly questioning them on the modes of recruiting, with every particular attendant on the trial of deserters by court-martial, and their punishments." When, flying from the pursuit of his creditors, he sought refuge in the country, he visited the cottages of the peasantry, made himself at home with them, and with the habits of their household, and children. We are also told that in company with Brooks, he at times associated with the gipsies, remaining with them several days together, adopting their mode of life, and sleeping with them in barns at night.

Morland's name as a painter stands out prominently before that of many of his contemporaries of far higher merit; it was spread by the vast number of works his facile hand produced, and by their still wider dispersion by means of engraving. We have from good authority a fact which closely relates to the great number of the works, many of them very indifferent ones, attributed to Morland. He was for some years (commencing about 1794) under articles to Mr. B———, a picture dealer, who employed him in painting original pictures at his own house; his daily service beginning early, and concluding at dinner time, probably twelve o'clock. Immediately Morland had left, expert copyists were employed in making accurate and elaborate repetitions of his day's work, which were carefully *concealed.* Returning to his own work on the following morning, any changes, which, upon reconsideration, Morland might think well to make in his picture, were in the afternoon transferred to each copy in progress under the hands of his treacherous copyists. Thus at least four or five pictures were carried on *together* to completion, the painter never suspecting the trick that was played; each of these counterfeits bearing those marks of changes in design and alterations of effect that would seem to give proof of its genuineness.

We cannot place Morland in the first rank of English art, but his works had this influence on its progress: they showed that there was a store of subjects in our own scenery, and a public to appreciate them; that, without seeking inspiration in Italy or Greece, an artist might succeed and be original. Henceforth "compositions," such as had pleased the town, from the pencil of Zuccarelli, had as rivals, and as successful rivals, these works, the simple pictures of our own picturesque land.

Gainsborough had, in this respect, in some degree anticipated Morland ; but even he clung a little to the best art of the Dutch. Morland threw aside all he had learnt from their school, and made an art of his own.

We have classed him here as an animal painter, which, it has been shown, comprises only a part of his art ; but as an animal painter, he was not like his predecessors, a portrait painter of animals ; for this he was unfitted, and too vulgarly independent. He was ill-grounded in anatomy, and consequently he succeeded best in portraying those animals whose forms were most hidden by their covering, such as sheep, pigs, rabbits, &c., and when he chose the horse, it was generally an aged one, not so much on account of its picturesqueness, as for the strong character of its form.

CHAPTER XIII.

THE great artists who contributed to the foundation of the Royal Academy, and by their talents and reputation had set it fairly afloat in public opinion, had hardly passed from the scene of their labours, when a new art, or what may well be called such, began to rise into importance. The art of painting in water-colours is so peculiarly English, that it may be designated as a national art; and growing up from this time side by side with oil painting, it has singularly influenced that branch of art, which has, in its turn, beneficially reacted upon it.

Although water-colour painting had been practised, both in this country and abroad, long previous to oil painting, and was thus the older art, and had, by our great miniaturists of the age of the Tudors and the Stuarts, been carried to the highest degree of perfection, it was, as in its original use, practised differently from the art of our own times. It was indeed but a species of tempera-painting, wherein the ground was obscured and hidden, and the colours used opaquely as in the ancient missal-paintings.

But though the miniaturists and " painters in little " began with using opaque colours, their practice gradually changed to the use of transparent pigments, and the preservation of the white ground on which they painted. At first such works were wrought on vellum or thin card-board, and we have no precise date when sheets of ivory were substituted, probably about the middle of the seventeenth century. A pocket-book, said to have belonged to Samuel Cooper, whom writers of his own time call "the prince of limners," has come down to us, containing fifteen portraits in various stages of completion. These portraits are all on card, some being left as at the first sitting, whilst one or two are completely finished. The following seems to have been the process of painting, and whether the work of Cooper, or, as is more probable, that of Flatman, gives us an insight into the mode of painting at that period. The outline was suggestively sketched, and then the smooth surface of the card, under the flesh, was covered with a thin wash of opaque white, which, as he used it, must have been an excellent pigment, as it has not changed in any instance. Then with a brownish lake tint the features have been most delicately and beautifully drawn in, and the broad shades under the eyebrows, the nose, and the chin, washed in flatly with the same tint. This seems to have completed the first sitting. In the next, the painter put in the local colour of the hair, washing in at the same time its points of relief or union with the background, in many cases adding a little white to his transparent colour to make the hue absorbent, and to give it a slight solidity. The shadows of the hair were then hatched in, and the features and face in succeeding sittings were hatched or stippled into roundness. Finally, the colours of the dress were washed in, in some cases transparently, in others with a slight admixture of white, the shadows of the dress being given with the local colour of the shadows.

Some of the works of this period were, however, painted wholly in transparent colours, and it must not be overlooked that highly-finished water-colour drawings, wrought with transparent colours, had been produced in the Dutch school, particularly by Ostade (1617-1671), Backhuysen (1631-1709), and Dusart (1665-1704).

Thus we find the various methods of our modern painters in water-colours were well known to their predecessors of the seventeenth and eighteenth centuries—the practice of using transparent colours, of mingling transparent with opaque colour, of imitating the local colour of objects in shade, of hatching and stippling—most indeed of the resources of the art—applied, it is true, rather to the human figure than to landscapes.

But water-colour art, as now practised, neither grew out of the early method of the missal-painters and illuminators, who were followed by the miniaturists, nor from the tempera-painting of the scene painter, but evidently from the humbler art of the topographer, from which its origin may be distinctly and clearly traced. It began with the tinted representations of antiquarian remains and ancient buildings, and was chiefly the offspring of the spirit of antiquarianism of the latter part of the last century. The artist painted on the inspiration of the antiquary and for the illustration of his books. He was frequently at the same time both the draughtsman and the engraver; and though the names and works of those so employed are known, they have little claim to any record on the ground of their art-merits. The outline being of the first consequence was carefully and firmly drawn, and was often completed with the pen, with the light and shade simply added in black or grey. Afterwards such works advanced a step, and were slightly tinted with transparent washes, to indicate the local colour of the objects or scenery, the colour of the sky being frequently the most positive tint used. The careful delineation of the many fine remains of abbeys, cathedrals, churches, castles, and mansions, was thus the aim of the early water-colour draughtsman. Such subjects employed the pencils of Sandby, the two Rookers, Hearne, Webber, Alexander, Malton, Dayes, Byrne, and some others who were the true founders of the art.

Although most of the men we have just named were essentially topographers, the natural course of their professional practice led some of them into new scenes and foreign climes, extending their knowledge and observation of nature. *John Webber, R.A.* (B. 1752, D. 1793), accompanied Captain Cook, in 1776, on his last voyage, and brought home many drawings of the scenes and localities he had visited ; some of these will be found in the collection at South Kensington. *William Alexander* (B. 1767, D. 1816) was draughtsman to Lord Macartney's embassy to China in 1792, and some of his drawings, swarming with groups of Chinese, sparkle with life and colour. The direct reference to nature, both at home and abroad, which was the essence of the art of these men, was beginning to work a change, and was in itself a source of steady progress towards true art. It was impossible for men who as topographers were brought face to face with nature, though at first attending only to the most obvious facts and details which were their chief aim, not to observe also nature's more varied moods and changes ; and it only required a man of genius to arise, who, pursuing the same course, should be able to give life and vitality to the meagre truthfulness of the topographer, to place the art on a wholly different footing. In such hands, and with the new materials, there were no traditions of the "black masters" to stand in the way of progress—to prevent a man from using his own eyes, and seeing nature as she really is. It was soon found that nature did not attitudinize into set compositions ; that it was not necessary to be brown to be like her ; that she did not insist upon dark foregrounds ; and, in fine, that the imitation of nature's great truths was not inconsistent with the utmost variety ; with selection of subject, and the choice of what is beautiful. But men were already training who were to effect a change, though the advance was necessarily slow, and it may be desirable to trace their progress step by step.

Previously, however, to doing so, it is necessary to say a few words on the materials and pigments used, as in a degree regulating the new art, and of themselves obviating some of the defects of a moribund school. At first, no doubt, the topographer having made accurate sketches in outline on the spot, completed the drawing more at leisure in his own home ; but the very portability of the new materials, the facility of execution in their first simple use, and the rapidity with which they dry, rendered painting in water colours direct from nature easy and agreeable, and led to its practice.

A general description of the methods of executing "stained," "washed," or "tinted" drawings, as such are called in the early catalogues of the Royal Academy, has already been given, but the more precise directions of Edward Dayes in his *Instructions for Drawing and Colouring Landscapes*, published in 1808, may suitably precede an account of those changes which have led to the great excellence of the water-colour school. He tells us that his work is particularly intended to treat of the use of *transparent colours*, and he does not confine himself to the old method alone, but gives those improvements upon it which had made such progress at the date of his publication. Supposing the outline complete, he says, "The first and most easy way is to make all the shadows and middle tints with Prussian blue and a brown Indian ink ; the clouds being sketched in, and as light as possible, the student begins with the elementary part of the sky, laying it in with Prussian blue, rather tender, so as to leave himself the power of going over it once or twice afterwards, or as often as may be necessary ; then, with the blue and a little Indian ink, lay in the lightest shades of the clouds, then the distance, if remote, with the same colour, rather stronger. Next proceed to the middle ground, leaving out the blue in coming forward, and lastly work up the foreground with brown Indian ink only. This operation may be repeated until the whole is sufficiently strong, marking the dark parts of the foreground as dark as the ink will make it—that is to say, the touches of the shadow in shade. Great care must be taken to leave out the blue gradually as the objects come forward, otherwise it will have a bad effect. Attention must also be given to the middle tints, that they are not marked too strong, which would make it, when coloured, look hard. The same grey colour, or aërial tint, may be first washed over every terrestrial part of the drawing required to be kept down—that is, before colouring—as colour laid over the grey will, of course, not be so light as when the paper is without it. The shadows and middle tints being worked up to a sufficient degree of power, colouring will be the next operation. This must be done by beginning in the distant parts, coming on stronger and stronger, colouring light and middle tint to the foreground, and lastly retouch the darker parts of the foreground with Vandyck brown. Great caution will be required not to disturb the shadows with colour, otherwise the harmony of the whole will be destroyed, or, at any rate, not to do more than gently to colour the reflections." Such was the older method, the method in which the works of Webber, Sandby, and Cozens were wrought, but which was afterwards changed by Dayes, Girtin his pupil, and Turner, the rising genius who was to go beyond all who had preceded him in the practice of this delightful art.

The first to break away from the trammels of topography, and to raise landscape painting in water colours to a branch of fine art, was Cozens. The materials for his life are very scanty, and we gather much of the following from Leslie's *Hand book*, his information being obtained from family connections of the painter. *John Cozens* was the son of Alexander Cozens, who was born in Russia, the natural son of Peter the Great by an Englishwoman whom the Czar took home with him from Deptford, and by whom he had another son, who became a general in the Russian service. The Emperor sent Alexander Cozens to Italy to study painting, from whence he came to England in 1746, where his son John was born in 1752. "I have seen," says Leslie, "a very small pen-drawing of three figures on which is written 'Done by J. Cozens, 1761, when nine years old.' I have also seen a book of views in Italy, drawn in pencil, some finished with a pen, and others half finished in the manner of line engraving, on which is pasted the following memorandum :—'Alexander Cozens, in London, author of these drawings, lost them, and many more, in Germany, by their dropping from his saddle when he was riding on his way from Rome to England in the year 1746. John Cozens, his son, being in Florence in the year 1776, purchased them. When he returned to London, in the year 1779, he delivered the drawings to his father.'" This was probably while the son was travelling in Italy with Mr. Beckford, for whom he wrought many of his best pictures. About two years previous to his death, which Dayes tells us happened about 1796, John Cozens became a lunatic, and was supported by the generous humanity of Sir George Beaumont. Pilkington places his death in 1799.

His works go little beyond light and shade and the suggestion of colour, but they are full of poetry; there is a solemn grandeur in his Alpine views; a sense of vastness, and a tender tranquillity in his pictures that stamp him as a true artist; a master of atmospheric effects, he seems to have fully appreciated the value of mystery, leaving parts in his picture for the imagination of the spectator to dwell on and search into. Leslie well says that "pensive tenderness forms the charm of his evening scenes," that "he had an eye equally adapted to the grandeur, the elegance and the simplicity of nature, but loved best her gentlest, most silent eloquence." We learn also from him that Cozens's art made such an impression on Constable that, in a moment of enthusiastic admiration, he pronounced John Cozens to be "the greatest genius that ever touched landscape."

Cozens was one of our first water-colour painters who visited Italy, and he seemed thoroughly to have entered into the grander features of the country; he is best known by his Italian views; but there are some fine studies from trees in Windsor Forest painted by him. While he departed but slightly from the earlier method of tinted drawing, he made the first move in the right direction. The pigments he used were different from those named by Dayes; he compounded his cloud tints, and those of his distant mountains, of Indian red, a small portion of lake, indigo, and yellow ochre; in his middle distance, he blended a tint of black and burnt umber. His distant trees were tinted with the warm washes used for the sky, and those nearer with yellow ochre and indigo, enriched with burnt sienna; in the immediate foreground trees and shrubs, the same pigments are used with greater power. With such simple means he produced works which were thought worthy of being copied by Girtin and Turner, his great successors in the art—nor is this advance from topography to true poetry, from tinted drawings to the suggestion of local colour from the first *laying-in* of his drawings, all that Cozens achieved in advance of his predecessors. His works show that he was acquainted with the use of gentle washings, of abrasion of the surface to give atmosphere and distance, or to indicate sun-rays through intercepting clouds; and prove no less that he was a true master of light and shade, and of the use of *accident* in painting.

We have searched the catalogues of the Royal Academy with great care, and find that John Cozens only exhibited there on one occasion. In 1776, when he was about twenty-four years of age, he sent "A Landscape, with Hannibal, in his March over the Alps, Showing to his Army the Fertile Plains of Italy." This is surmised to have been painted in oil, and must have been a work of rare excellence, since it is reported that Turner said he had learned more from it than anything he had seen. Where is the picture now? It is hardly to be wondered at that Cozens, who refrained from exhibiting, worked so largely for one patron, and was almost continually abroad, was so little known as an artist. How should the general public know anything of his works?

Another artist, who flourished in the latter half of the eighteenth century, was *Paul Sandby, R.A.* Born at Nottingham in 1725, he lived into the succeeding century, and died in 1809. He has been called the father of water-colour art, and certainly as contemporary with Taverner, an amateur, and Lambert, whom we have already mentioned; and as preceding Hearne, Rooker, Malton, Byrne, and Webber, by more than twenty years, he may claim that title by priority. As contrasted with Cozens, he was a man of ripe years when Cozens was an infant, yet he was essentially a topographic artist, and when in his later works his art seemed to touch the confines of poetry, the influence of Cozens may be traced. He was for many years drawing-master to the Royal Military Academy at Woolwich, and on the foundation of the Royal Academy was one of the original members. George III. employed him to give instruction in drawing to the royal children, and perhaps from this cause a large number of his works are scenes in the neighbourhood of Windsor

and Eton. He painted both in body-colour, or, as works in this manner
were then called, " water-colour," and made " tinted drawings." A fine
specimen of the former will be found in the collection at South Kensington, No. 383, with many specimens of the latter ; while there are a
large number of his tinted drawings in the royal collections at Windsor.
These drawings are simple in their general treatment of light and shade,
and weak in colour; for Sandby seems never to have given up the early
methods. They are more valuable for their accurate rendering of the
various scenes than as works of art.

William Payne, of whose history but little is at present known, is
another artist of the period, and one to whom but scant justice has yet
been done. He seems to have been a native of Plymouth, as we find
him in 1786 residing at Plymouth Dock, and, for the first time, contributing to the Royal Academy Exhibition five views of Plymouth and
its neighbourhood. He continued to reside there during the years
1787–9, still contributing to the exhibition tinted drawings of Devonshire scenery. In 1790 Payne seems to have removed to London, and
resided in Thornhaugh Street, Bedford Square. We find him this year
again sending four Devonshire scenes to the exhibition, after which date
his name entirely disappears from the catalogue. Reynolds is said to
have expressed great admiration for some of Payne's Devonshire
drawings, particularly a representation of the slate quarries at his native
Plympton. Even these transcripts from nature were said to be entirely
novel in their excellent treatment.

Payne adopted many peculiarities in his methods of execution, some
of which are valuable additions to the art. He abandoned the use of outline with the pen. His general process was very simple. Having invented
a grey tint (still known by the colourmen as Payne's grey), he used it
for all the varied gradations of his middle distance, treating the extreme
distance, as also the clouds and sky, with blue. For the shadow, in his
foreground, he used Indian ink or lamp-black, breaking these colours
into the distance by the admixture of grey. In this he but slightly
differed from the other artists of his time, but his methods of handling
were more peculiarly his own. These consisted in splitting the brush to
give the forms of foliage, dragging the tints to give texture to his foregrounds, and taking out the forms of lights by wetting the surface and
rubbing with bread or rag. He seems to have been among the first
who used this practice, which, in the hands of Turner, became such a
powerful aid to effect, and enabled the early painters in water-colour to
refrain from using white or solid pigments in the lights.

Having thus prepared a vigorous light and shade, Payne tinted his
distance, middle distance, and foreground with colour, retouching and
deepening the shadows in front to give power to his work, and even

loading his colour and using gum plentifully. He sought to enrich scenes wherein he had attempted effects of sunset or sunrise, by passing a full wash of gamboge and lake over the completed drawing. He abandoned mere topography for a more poetical treatment of landscape scenery, and although he has none of the delicacy of Cozens, and rarely touches our sympathies, he set an example of what might be done, even in the simpler practice of "tinting," by accidental effects, by selection of forms, by sun-rays piercing through clouds which, like Cozens, he obtained by washing out, by mists and vapours, introducing such treatments into the practice of the art. Many of his works are of large size, and although occasionally very vacant and empty, and too often displaying great mannerism in handling, and little reference to nature, they yet served to lead the way for the abler men who followed. Time has acted unfavourably on his pictures; they have darkened considerably, partly from the foxy-brown to which the general wash has changed, and partly from the too great strength of the black in the foregrounds.

"Unfortunately for the reputation of the artist, '*Payne's style*' became corrupt merely from its becoming too common, being so rendered from the folly of fashion; for so obviously simple and easily comprehensible was his process, that all the mammas in the land were eager to obtain him as the instructor of their daughters." Mr. Payne for some years derived a large income from teaching, but failing to refill and refresh his mind by studying from nature, he degenerated into the merest mannerist, and while the art was advancing on every side, he not only stood still, but sank into weakness and inanity.

Another artist who aided in laying the foundation of our school of water-colour painting is *John Smith*. Born in 1749, we have but little record of his life and history, and have to trace his progress by his works. These, as they are mostly dated, enable us to compare him with his fellow-artists, and to see how much or how little he contributed to the general progress. Byron describes the difficulty fame finds in registering the deeds of men who rejoice in like names with that of our artist:

> "Men of pith,
> Sixteen named Thompson, and nineteen named Smith."

And he that would follow the course of Smith's art in the catalogues and records of the day, will find it difficult to make choice of the right man. Smith is said to have travelled in Italy with or for the Earl of Warwick, and thus to have acquired the cognomen of "Warwick" Smith.

His contemporaries said that he tinted his works almost to the force of oil-painting; and Gainsborough is related to have remarked that "he was the first water-colour painter who carried his intention through;'

high praise from one so capable of judging, and made upon a larger view of his works than has fallen to our share. A writer in 1808, in the *Review of Publications of Fine Art*, says of him, that " he is the father of the system of colouring on paper, which at present prevails almost universally ; " and adds, " we have heard, and indeed there are those among us who know, that Mr. John Smith first discovered and taught the junior artists the *rationale* of tempering their positive colours with the neutral grey formed by the mixture of red, blue and yellow : that this grey, constituted of all the primary colours, would harmonize with any, and form a common bond of concord with all, and that, tempered with a little more or less of warm or cool colours, as time, or climate, or season might require, it became the air tint, or negative colour of the atmosphere which intervened between the eye and the several objects of the landscape." He died in 1831.

We have traced thus far the progress of water-colour painting from its topographic founders, through the changes they introduced into their practice, until, in the hands of Smith, Payne, and Cozens, it rose into a truly poetical art.

Thomas Girtin was the first to give a full idea of the *power* of water-colour painting ; the first wholly to change the practice of the art, to achieve in this medium richness and depth of colour, with perfect clearness and transparency, and the utmost boldness and facility of execution ; the first who followed out a procedure the reverse of that which had hitherto prevailed—laying in the whole of his work with the true local colour of the various parts, and afterwards adding the shadows with their own local and individual tints. Girtin was born in Southwark, on the 18th of February, 1773. Like most other children, he early showed a great predilection for drawing, and covered every scrap of paper that came to hand with his boyish fancies; but as he himself said that "other boys of his own age, ten or twelve, who amused themselves or idled in the same way, drew as well as himself," we may be assured that there was nothing very marked in these childish efforts. We do not learn how or when he became acquainted with Dr. Munro, but to this acquaintance he was indebted for good examples to study, for companionship with some of the rising youths of the day, and for sound advice as to the practice of the art he soon resolved to follow.

Dr. Munro, who then lived in the Adelphi Terrace, inherited from his father a valuable and extensive collection of drawings by Marlowe, Gainsborough, Hearne, Sandby, Rooker, Cozens, and others, and being himself a sincere lover of art, who had known most of these painters in his youth, he had greatly added to his inherited collection. Towards the end of the last century, he opened his house and his well-filled folios to the young artists of the day. Girtin, Turner, Francia, Varley, Edridge

Linnell, and others gladly availing themselves of this privilege, attended at his house on stated evenings, to make copies and studies of the choice works he possessed, aided by the remarks of the doctor, who from his intimacy with the older artists, was well able to speak as to the methods they employed, their various pigments, and the modes of using them.

Dr. Munro also encouraged the young artists to sketch from nature, and to bring their sketches and to work them into pictures at these evening meetings. Studies for their pencils abounded everywhere on the shores of the river overlooked by his house. Among others, the ruins of the old Savoy Palace furnished many subjects for them ; and Girtin said that a study he made of the old steps of this ruined palace, was a lesson from which he dated all the future knowledge which he displayed in the pictorial representation of ruined masonry. Here he studied detail carefully, in order to treat it afterwards with breadth. Girtin and Turner were well aware that the labour of the mind is higher than that of the hand, and that "it is not in the scene itself, however great, or however beautiful, that the merit of a picture consists ; it is in the manner of treating it." This axiom was a new one in water-colour art, which had begun in exact delineation, ignoring any particular mode of viewing scenery.

Girtin, in his young days, had taken drawing lessons from one Fisher, of Aldersgate Street ; later in life he was placed for a time to study art under Edward Dayes, partly a topographer, partly an engraver—a man who knew well the general principles of art, and drew the figure passably well, but had little of the genius of his pupil, whose rapid progress made the teacher jealous and unwilling to admire works so different and so superior to his own. Girtin visited many towns and cathedrals in order to sketch them, and the lakes of Cumberland and Westmoreland. He also made excursions into Scotland and Wales, both north and south, and soon began to treat mountain and lake scenery in a manner very different to that of his predecessors. One of the writers of the day tells us that "Girtin usually finished the greater part of his drawing on the spot." We have no doubt that his less important works and his studies were wrought in this way; but that his finest works should be, is inconsistent with the daring effects of cloud and storm, of gloom and the solemn massing of objects, embodied in his best pictures. Where, but in his own studio, after deep observation on the spot, could such works have been produced? One who had frequently watched his progress, tells us that "his finely coloured compositions were wrought with much study, and proportionate manual exertion;" and that though he did not hesitate, nor undo what he had once done, for he worked on principle, yet he reiterated his tints to produce "splendour and richness, and repeated his depths to secure transparency of tones. He resolutely suppressed details, seeking for breadth and largeness of parts, qualities difficult to achieve in the presence of Nature."

When fully settled in the practice of his art we find him drawing chiefly on cartridge-paper of a rough surface and low tone of colour, choosing this material to work on for the scope it gave to his largeness of manner and omission of details, as well as for its low tone which accorded with the phase of nature he most loved to delineate. It has been well remarked that associating with Turner, working much with him at Dr. Munro's house, and ever in emulous but friendly rivalry, it is curious how markedly unlike are the works of the two painters; the direction of Turner's art in water-colours was rather towards light, and the effects of light and atmosphere; that of Girtin to largeness of parts, generalization, and gloomy grandeur.

Girtin was fond of contrasting cool shadows with warm and brilliant lights spread over the picturesque ruins in which he delighted, giving by these means an appearance of sunshine and a splendour of effect, startling to those who had been accustomed to the tamer manner of the topographers, or even to the poetical tenderness of the works of Cozens.

Girtin washed-in his skies with a mixture of indigo and lake, and the shadows of his clouds with light red and indigo, or Indian red and indigo. The warm tone of the cartridge-paper served for the lights, and was enhanced by being opposed to the azure, and to the cool tints of the clouds. It is said that the wire-marked cartridge he loved to work on was only to be obtained at a stationer's at Charing Cross, and was folded in quires. As the half sheet was not large enough for his purpose he had to spread out the sheet, and the crease of the folding, being at times more absorbent than the other parts of the paper, a dark blot was caused across the sky, and indeed across the whole picture in many of his works. This defect was at first tolerated on account of the great originality and merit of his works, and gradually it gave a higher value to those in which it occurred, being considered a proof of their originality. For his light stone-tints, Girtin used thin washes of Roman ochre, laid on tolerably wet, adding light red ochre and lake to vary the effect; for brick buildings he used burnt sienna, madder brown, and lake with the ochres, at times contrasting these warm tints with indigo and even with pure ultramarine.

For finishing the foreground when the local colour was to be represented with the fullest force, Girtin used Vandyck brown and Cologne earth. His greens, which were mostly very negative, were composed of gamboge, indigo, and burnt sienna, the two latter predominating. Occasionally he gave the fullest richness, by yellow-lake, brown-pink and Prussian blue, shading the trees with indigo and burnt sienna, and adding, in the most neutral parts, a beautiful and harmonious shadow tint, composed of grey and madder brown, which, mingling at times with the indigo and burnt sienna, gave great harmony, and kept up that feeling of "tone" which is so marked a quality in his pictures. Girtin made his greys sometimes with Venetian red and indigo, or Indian red and indigo, and a series of harmonious warm and cool greys with Roman ochre, indigo, and lake, mixed in varied degrees.

He had but one manner, and that he had nearly perfected when he died ; and it is just possible that had he lived to be popular he might have become somewhat of a *chiqueur ;* indeed his use of cartridge, and more especially his indifference to, nay, even affectation in parading, what was really a blot upon his work, shows the spirit of a mannerist, a spirit very likely to grow upon a man when he finds even his faults magnified into beauties.

Girtin's success, the bold and vigorous manner in which he wrought, the unrivalled ease and mastery of his touch, made a great impression on the public. His instruction was much sought after, and reams of paper were covered with splashes of Vandyck brown, Roman ochre, and indigo blue. The artists of the day also sought to imitate his style. We are even told that Francia produced many spurious Girtins ; and others far less able than Francia made coarse compositions, opposing hot and cold colours with a crudity and harshness that rendered the school and the style for a time distasteful.

Dayes and other writers speak of Girtin's intemperance and irregularities, and we fear there must be some cause for censure. Yet there are those who treat the matter more lightly, telling us that he was shy, and rather sought the company of his inferiors than of the cultivated and well-bred ; and this not, as in Morland's case, because he loved low society, but because he felt more at his ease, and could indulge his leisure in idleness. Thus, in travelling to the north, he would take his passage in a collier, and delight to live in common with the crew, eating salt-beef, smoking, and drinking grog with them, enjoying their rough jokes and noisy songs. And in his country journeys, the kitchen of the little roadside inn was sought by him in preference, where he found subjects and characters suited to his feeling of the picturesque. Latterly, his evenings were frequently passed at the house of one Harris, a frame-maker, in Gerrard Street, Soho, where Morland also frequently resorted. This Harris was a dealer in drawings, and knew well his advantage in having two such men in his keeping, as he made much money by both of them ; for Girtin, like his companion, rather inclined to sell his works through a dealer than to those who wished to possess them. He is said to have been of a kind and friendly disposition—known as honest

Tom Girtin amongst his associates, and quite ready to tell whatever he knew in art to whoever sought his assistance and advice. For two or three winters before his death he belonged to a "Sketching Society;" probably the precursor of the one that existed almost to our own day, and having rules nearly similar. No society could have been more respectable; and it would seem to show that if his habits *had* been loose and intemperate, he was in a fair way to improvement.

In his twenty-third year he painted a panorama of London, as seen from the roof of the Albion flour-mills, which is said to have been much admired; though Leslie laments that any portion of so short and valuable a life as Girtin's should have been wasted on so transient a work. After Girtin's death the panorama was sold to a Russian nobleman, who took it to his own country. Girtin's health broke down, we know not from what cause, and at the short peace in 1802 he was advised to visit Paris with a view to its restoration; his complaint was on the lungs—asthma, or consumption, for accounts differ. Feeling lonely while in Paris, he occupied himself by making above twenty sketches of buildings and views in that city; these on his return he etched on soft ground, and had the effect laid in from his drawings in aquatint. He also painted two scenes from his Paris views for Covent Garden Theatre. Thus striving against illness, and energetic to the last, we find this man, charged with intemperate habits, doing enough to wear out one of sound health; but whether paying the penalty of past errors, or of overwrought strength, his disease became hopeless, and he died at his lodgings in the Strand, at one Norman's, a frame-maker.

He was buried in the churchyard of St. Paul's, Covent Garden, where a stone was shortly after erected—"To the memory of Thomas Girtin, artist, who departed this life November 1, 1802." Before Girtin's early death he had married, and had one son, afterwards a surgeon at Islington, and a diligent collector of all his father's works that came within his means. Several fine drawings from his collection were shown in the International Exhibition of 1862. The original drawings Girtin made were in the possession of the Earl of Essex.

Thus we have seen that to the poetry of the art, as practised by Cozens, Girtin added power—power of effect, power of colour and tone, and power of execution. "Sobered tints of exquisite truth and broad chiaroscuro," says Leslie, "are his prevailing characteristics;" but as we have remarked, his strength wanted refinement and delicacy—wanted range and variety, qualities which it was left to his friend and companion Turner to supply. Girtin died just as he was rising into eminence—just as he was about to prove whether he had or had not resources beyond those he had already exhibited. Turner was destined to live and to become a landscape painter, both in water-colour and oil, such as the world had hardly yet seen ; as such we shall have a long chapter to devote to him in the history of art, and it is only to show his relation to the progress of painting in water-colours that we give him space in this.

We are told that during Girtin's short career his works were astonishingly numerous, yet we are unacquainted with any treasury of his sketches such as we possess of only the early days of Turner.

Turner, early in his water-colour practice, realized a new and a great truth in art, and this he afterwards carried out in his oil pictures also. Others had tried to give the true effect of light by sacrificing the shadows, hence the heavy forced shadows of even the otherwise truthful Dutchmen, and the rule, adopted almost as a law, of making the foregrounds dark. Turner on the contrary sought to give the true colour of shadows, and of objects in shadow, and as we have but a confined range between the pigments representing light and dark, he had necessarily in a degree to sacrifice his lights ; and was continually endeavouring to increase their brightness and breadth, and by this means to make his gradations as infinitesimal as possible. In the oil paintings of his middle and last periods this is especially seen ; in his water-colours, after he had once obtained the mastery of his means, it is always evident.

Thus though somewhat younger than Girtin, Turner was really ahead of him in art, an opinion which was held by his contemporaries also ; for before Girtin died, Turner had already been elected both an associate and an academician, and must have owed the former distinction at least to his works in water-colours.

In his sketches, properly studied, we may trace not only Turner's progress, but Turner's processes and his art-principles. With Girtin and others, we find him assiduously copying the works of Hearne, Cozens, and Sandby, in those evening meetings at Dr. Munro's. Under Malton, himself a clever topographic artist, Turner studied perspective, and studied it thoroughly ; we know that Malton was well qualified to teach even such a pupil as Turner, and this teaching perhaps led the pupil in after life to accept the professorship of perspective at the Royal Academy. As soon, however, as Turner had passed his pupilage, as soon as he began to see and study nature for himself, he not only gave up the tinting method which he had thus learned, and adopted the practice of laying in his pictures with the local colour first, but he adopted it in a manner wholly his own —a manner whose gradual development, until it arrived at full perfection, is to be studied in his sketches, better even than in his finished pictures.

His practice seems to have been to lay in his warm and cool colours opposed to each other in general masses ; beginning with delicate and transparent washes, repeating them with slight variations of the local colour, as seen in light or in shade, to break up the masses and give

L

variety and texture, yet still preserving great transparency in his early painting, and paying attention to little more than the merest generalities of form. Sometimes, when the masses of light and cool colour had been somewhat advanced, he washed, or otherwise abraded the surface of his paper, and then wrought out the details of form on this surface by luminous shadows varied according to the general hue of the mass, as light or dark, warm or cold; gradually feeling out by such means, with extreme delicacy, the minor forms and details, until these were sufficiently pronounced for their position, either as distance, mid-distance, or foreground. By such means, while he kept up the transparency of his work, he achieved endless variety, delicate gradations, great breadth, and great atmosphere in his pictures; and in all stages of their progress, the general effect was at the same time maintained.

Of course this power was not obtained at once. We see in his early works a gradual transition from tinted drawings to local colouring, and thence, by gradual advances, to the method above described. As Turner arrived at perfect knowledge and perfect mastery he adopted or invented new means to perfect his surfaces and give quality and texture; such as damping the masses of colour, and cleansing them of irregularities by picking or blotting-out portions of the tint, or sharpening the edges of light and giving forms of foliage, buildings or figures, by taking out lights with bread, or damp rag. Again by wetting dark masses of tint, and when in a wet state, by scraping out lights with a bluntish knife; cutting out sharp lights from the surface of the paper, to give broad high lights on white drapery, buildings, or animals, or the glistening and sun-lighted edges of leaves; stippling to flatten and give breadth to skies and distances; or to neutralize and harmonize colour by juxtaposition of hues and tints. Turner used no white or opaque pigments in his pictures: yet no one knew better than he did the value and use of white, for he used it freely in sketching from nature, and in studying his pictures, either on a very delicate greyish tint, on a darker greyish blue paper, on cartridge paper, or even on white paper, of which there are numerous examples at South Kensington. Many of his fine studies of skies are so treated, and whenever he sought great rapidity, he freely used white; but in his finished pictures he purposely avoided it, even to the end of his career.

At a meeting where many water-colour painters were present, Mr. Horsley, R.A., was exclaiming against the injurious practice of Harding and others, who, by the use of white and opaque pigments, were bringing about a total change in a beautiful art. He was joined by the late Mr. Munro of Novar, who, having accidentally overheard him, supported his remarks by saying:—"I am glad to hear your remarks, Mr. Horsley. Turner himself was of the same opinion; he declared to me that water-colour painting would be totally ruined, and lose all its individuality and beauty by the bad practice of mingling opaque with transparent colour." This anecdote supports the conclusion we have arrived at from the examination of his works, and shows that on principle he avoided the use of solid pigments. By the removal of the surface of his paper Turner obtained all the advantages arising from the use of white, without the danger of losing the transparency and harmony of tone supplied by the creamy colour of the paper, and which is sometimes lost by the careless or improper use of white.

Landscape and figure painting in tempera or body colour were practised both by our own countrymen and foreigners side by side with tinted drawings, yet no one seems to have thought of mingling the two methods, or for some time of the possibility, in transparent colours, of laying in the local tints first, and afterwards defining the lights and shadows, as did the tempera painters. The tempera painter continued to the end to ignore his white ground (the paper), and to lay in his work solidly, even to the sky, overlooking the possibility of mingling the two, as is done so effectively in the present day.

It will be perceived that we estimate Turner's influence on the progress of water-colour painting as far greater than Girtin's, or of any of his predecessors ; yet while we give Turner the highest place, both for art and execution, we cannot credit even him with the invention or first use of all the processes which he so successfully adopted in landscape painting, and which have so greatly added to the resources of the rising school. We opened this chapter with some account of the methods of working of the miniature painters, derived from a long ancestry. In their practice we have seen that many, if not all, those executive means had been long in use ; among others, even that which produced the great change in the art from tinting to water-colour painting, namely, the laying in the subject from the first with its local colours.

This branch of art, at the time Girtin and Turner were progressing together in landscape, numbered many clever men—such as Hamilton, Shelley, Westall, and others ; men who did not practise merely miniature painting in water-colours, but painted subjects from history or poetry consisting of single figures or groups, wherein the use of the local colour from the first—washing, stippling, and even the addition of white or body colour—were part of the method employed. A figure of Eve, in the South Kensington Museum, by Hamilton, R.A., who died in 1801, is rich and full of colour, the shadows being hatched in over the local colour of the flesh. Again, R. Westall, R.A., born in 1765, was ten years older than either Turner or Girtin, and had practised as a miniature and figure painter for many years before they effected the change of manner in landscape art. His works also were rich and full in colour, and of great beauty of execution, as we learn by the following anecdote. We are told that he took some of them to Northcote to ask his advice, and that, after attentively examining them, Northcote exclaimed, "Why, this is something new in art. How do'ee do it? I did not believe that water-colour could be brought to this perfection. Why, young man, these are the most beautiful specimens of the art I have seen. I would give the world to do such things." From which we may infer that it was the rich quality of the works, joined to delicacy of execution, that pleased the pupil of Sir Joshua.

Moreover, many of the oil painters wrought in water-colours certainly with more richness and colour than the topographers. We have heard of, but not seen, works in this medium, by Wright of Derby; some by Gainsborough, which we have seen, were far in advance of the tinted drawings of the day, and may have lent suggestions towards the change of practice. Thus we have traced painting in water-colours from mere topography, until it took its true rank as a fine art. In a future chapter we shall enter upon the history of the art, when its professors became numerous, and when its rivalry with oil led to combinations among those who practised it, in order to secure for the new art its fair representation before the public.

CHAPTER XIV.

THE SCHOOL OF MINIATURE PAINTERS.

IN describing, in the first chapter, the rise of art in England, we pointed to our miniature painters as the first native artists who attained eminence, and instanced Nicholas Hilliard, in the reign of Elizabeth, followed by Isaac and Peter Oliver, John Hoskyns, and, later, Samuel Cooper, as highly distinguished in this favourite art ; and we have in the preceding chapter described the processes of the early miniaturists in relation to the origin of water-colour painting. English art, in fact, began in portraiture. We trace, in its earliest efforts, the desire which has always existed to possess such remembrances as art could supply to gratify love and affection, or to retain the memory of great and distinguished men.

Miniature, perhaps, lends itself more to the affections than any other class of art. Cultivated since the days of Elizabeth no other has, to our time, found such steady encouragement. Its intrinsic beauty and elaborate finish are charms which address themselves at once to all, and all can comprehend and esteem its merits.

It is not our purpose to include here as miniaturists those artists, briefly mentioned in the following chapter, who in early times drew highly-finished heads of a small size in pencil, or with the pen, and slightly washed them in with Indian ink, usually on vellum ; but to consider the term miniature as strictly applying to portraits executed in water-colours on ivory, or in enamel on copper, in some few instances on silver or gold ; these materials fixing an absolute limit to the size of the work, and being those solely used by artists to whom the term miniaturist may be most correctly applied. We have said " fixing absolutely," for, though the diameter of the tooth determines the surface of ivory which can be obtained from it, attempts have been made to unite the pieces without apparent joint, or to turn, and afterwards flatten, a plate from the circumference of the tooth, so as to form large surfaces ; and also in enamelling, experiments have been tried to vitrify large plates; yet the success has been doubtful, and even if obtained would destroy the peculiar character of miniature art.

Miniature painting on ivory is practised with the ordinary transparent water-colours with occasionally a little opaque colour for the high lights. Some few expedients are used in practice; but the art is simple. Enamel painting is a more complicated process, attended with many difficulties, and each artist who has excelled in it has usually adopted some expedients of his own which may be deemed his secrets. The risk of failure attends every process; the design must be traced in the first instance, and cannot be altered or amended. Success is only ensured by the utmost care and attention, assisted by that skill which long experience alone can give. Yet in the enduring brilliancy of his delicate work the artist has his reward. *Jean Petitot,* born at Geneva 1607, died 1691, was not the first who applied this art to portraiture; for it had been extensively practised by the Limoges enamellers; and their large plaques with portraits of the families of Guise and Navarre show their mastery of the means and their artistic skill as painters. Petitot, however, was the first who brought the art into perfect competition with miniatures on ivory, a perfection which has hardly been surpassed in the art of miniature painting in enamel. Though not to be classed with the English school, Petitot practised in England for some time in the reign of Charles I., and was greatly assisted in his experiments in the processes of vitrification, and in the choice of colours which will stand the furnace, by the chemical knowledge of Sir Theodore Mayerne, the Court physician.

In our first chapter we mentioned the great merits of the early miniature painters in this country. Holbein's miniatures are marked by a wonderful power of drawing and character, but a true work by him is rare. Hilliard's miniatures are well drawn, not wanting in character, beautiful in their delicate finish, the dresses and ornaments enriched by the use of gold, but they are only weakly and faintly coloured, and the faces are wanting in roundness and power. The Olivers showed an advance in art-qualities and in power, yet wanted the delicacy and refinement of Hilliard; and the same may be said of their contemporary, Hoskins. In Samuel Cooper, who succeeded them, miniature art culminated. His works have known many clever copyists, and have suffered greatly by repairs, but a fine work by him in a good condition, is indeed a treasure. Well drawn, full of character and expression, graceful in truthful simplicity of manner, the hair of his females charmingly treated, quiet and sweet in colour, we feel assured that the mind and very image of those who were distinguished and beautiful are before us, though two whole centuries intervene. We know nothing—even in the works of the most distinguished artists of our own times—which can compare with those of Cooper. It has been said that he could only draw the face, but this is a mistake : he was assuredly a correct and powerful draughtsman.

Following these distinguished miniaturists, we find *Thomas Flatman* (1633–1688). He was of New College, Oxford, and was called to the bar ; but he did not succeed, and he left the law for the arts. He arrived at much excellence in his miniature portraits, and his works were highly esteemed. They were on rather a larger scale than those of his predecessors, more largely painted in body colour, and though not wanting in character, were less refined in their drawing and manner. Flatman is also known as a poet, and his *Songs and Poems*, published in 1674, reached a third edition within ten years. *Alexander Browne*, a miniaturist of the same period, painted Charles II., the Countess Stuart, the Prince of Orange, and other notables, and was also a writer. He published, in 1669, *The Art of Painting, Limning, and Etching*. In Queen Anne's reign, *Lewis Crosse* excelled in miniature, and in miniature copies of the Italian masters, and had many of the nobility for his sitters. He possessed a fine collection of miniatures, which he sold in 1722. He died in 1724. *Charles Boit* was of the same period. Born in Sweden, the son of a Frenchman, he came early to England, and his art was English. He was a jeweller, and not being successful here in that trade, he tried to gain a livelihood by teaching drawing. Walpole says that he had inveigled one of his pupils, the daughter of a general officer, into a promise of marriage, and that the affair being discovered, Boit was thrown into prison, where, during two years' confinement, he studied enamel painting. He practised the art in London with very great success, and received extravagant prices for his work. His colour was frequently crude and disagreeable. The difficulties of his art are shown in his attempt to execute an unusually large plate for the Queen, representing her Majesty, Prince George of Denmark, and the chief officers of her Court. He received very considerable advances for this work ; but though he built a furnace for the purpose, he was unable to lay an enamel ground over the large surface of his plate, and failed after many experiments. The Queen had died in the meanwhile. Boit ran into debt, and fled to France, where he was well received, and where his works were greatly admired. He died suddenly at Paris about 1726. *Bernard Lens*, born in London, 1680, died 1740, was distinguished in miniature, and was appointed miniature painter and enameller to George II. He was also much esteemed for his miniature copies after Rubens and Vandyck. He left two sons who followed his profession, as did also his nephew, *Lewis Goupy*.

These artists were Englishmen, with the exception of Boit ; who, however, belongs to our school. We have only an exceptional knowledge of their art, which, from its character, is not easily identified. Yet we cannot doubt from what is known, that their reputation in their own day may be taken as a test of their merits. Approaching the time when the memories of artists and their works were more regarded, we find many notices of *Christian Frederick Zincke,* and in the British Museum, the genial portrait of the old man seated at his work—no doubt as true as a photograph—with all the accessories of his art. He was born at Dresden, in 1684, came to England in his twenty-second year, and became the pupil of Boit. He pursued enamel painting with great success. His drawing was graceful; his works simple and refined in expression; his colour pleasing. He soon equalled, and then excelled his master, almost rivalling Petitot. He met with such great encouragement that his industry could hardly keep pace with his sitters; and he was especially patronized by George II. and his queen. His eyesight failing in 1746, he retired from his profession, and died in South Lambeth in 1767. His enamels are well known; several are in the royal collection, and though his works are numerous, their merit has always secured for them a high price. *James Deacon,* a young English artist, on Zincke's retirement, took his house in Tavistock Street, Covent Garden. Deacon's miniatures are full of character and expression, and though elaborately careful, are in a very masterly style. But he had scarcely begun his career, which was one of much promise, when, attending as a witness at the Old Bailey, he caught the gaol fever, and died in 1750. At this time *Jarvis Spencer* became celebrated for his miniatures. He had been a gentleman's servant, and having a natural talent for art, he gained by his own perseverance many eminent sitters, and became the fashionable painter of his day. His enamel portraits were collected and exhibited in 1762, and he died in the following year.

The delicate art of the enameller connects itself closely with the craft of the jeweller and the gold-chaser in their highest branches. To these trades—we would rather call them arts—the great enamellers Petitot and Boit were bred; and in *Michael Moser, R.A.,* we have another enameller who was led to art by the same road. He was, in the true sense of the word, an ornamentist. Eminent as a painter, modeller, sculptor, and teacher, he is particularly distinguished by his medals and enamels. He was born at Schaffhausen in 1704, and came to England when young. As manager of the St. Martin's Lane Schools, and one of the foundation members, and the first keeper of the Royal Academy, the arts of this country owe too much to him to permit his exclusion from any connected account of their progress. His chief works will be found on the trinkets of the day, which, according to the prevailing fashion, were ornamented by his beautiful and tasteful enamels, and we are told that he was paid a high price for two fine portraits of the young

Prince of Wales and the Duke of York, which he painted in enamel on a watch-case for George III., for whom he also executed the Great Seal of England. He died in 1783. His only daughter, *Mary Moser*, an admirable flower painter, was one of the original members of the Royal Academy. She was an amiable, lively, clever woman, and was reputed to have formed an unrequited passion for Fuseli. Her letters prove her desire to establish a literary flirtation with him. Perhaps this was the extent of her weakness, for she married a Captain Lloyd, a military officer, and afterwards only practised art as an amusement. She died in 1819.

The artist, however, who, though a long way behind him, ranked first in miniature art after Zincke, was *Nathaniel Hone, R.A.* He was the son of a merchant in Dublin, and was born there about 1718. He had a natural love of painting, and was a self-taught genius; he soon made his way to England and practised portrait painting in several parts of the country, more especially at York, where he married a lady of some property, and shortly afterwards came to London and settled. Here he was the fashionable miniature painter, particularly on enamel, and he became one of the foundation members of the Royal Academy. We do not know on what provocation, but he had the temerity to lampoon the President in a picture which he sent for exhibition, and also the gentle Kauffman. This brought upon him the anger of the Academy. They rejected these objectionable works, and he then made an exhibition of them with between sixty and seventy of his other works in 1775, but does not appear, like poor Barry, to have met with expulsion for his contumacy. Hone was a clever artist; he painted in oil, scraped some good mezzotints, and is known as an etcher and as the collector of some good pictures. His miniatures were hot in colour, and wanting generally in refinement of execution and beauty of finish, but they are by no means without merit. He died in 1784.

At the same time flourished *Jeremiah Meyer, R.A.*, born in Wurtemberg in 1735. He came to this country at the age of fourteen, and was reputed to have been a pupil of Zincke, though M. Rouquet says Zincke never had a pupil. He was an industrious student in the St. Martin's Lane Academy, and proved himself a good draughtsman. He was appointed enamel painter to George III., and miniature painter to the Queen, and arrived at great excellence. He gave power and elegance to his work by the study of his contemporary Reynolds, and his miniatures please by their life-like truth and expression, added to a quiet refinement of colour. He was one of the original members of the Royal Academy, and died in 1789. Hayley thus complimented his art,—

> " Though small its field, thy pencil may presume
> To ask a wreath, where flowers eternal bloom."

Richard Collins, born in 1755, was the pupil of Meyer. He practised miniature and enamel for some time among the fashionable world at Bath, and for a while in Dublin.   He was appointed miniature painter to George III., and painted some fine portraits of the King and the royal family.   He was largely patronized, and his works were looked upon as the gems of the Academy exhibitions.   He retired from his profession with a comfortable competence about 1811, and died about 1831, aged seventy-seven years. With him *Samuel Shelley* (and Cosway, of whom we shall presently speak more at large,) divided the fashionable patronage of the day.   Shelley was born in Whitechapel, and had little instruction in art.   He copied Reynolds, founded his style upon him, and became a rich and harmonious colourist.   He was distinguished for his miniature portraits, and for his treatment of historical subjects in miniature. He was one of the founders of the Water-colour Society, and died in 1808.   We must not omit also *James Nixon, A.R.A.,* born about 1741, died 1812, who was appointed limner to the Prince Regent, and miniature painter to the Duchess of York ; or *Charles Shrriff,* a deaf and dumb painter of the same period, who practised at Bath about the last quarter of the last century.   Both artists took a first place among miniature painters.

Ozias Humphrey, R.A., born at Honiton 1742, was another distinguished miniaturist.   His passion for drawing induced his parents to send him to London, where he became a student in the St. Martin's Lane School.   He afterwards practised for some time at Bath, and then, invited by Reynolds, returned to London.   In 1766 he exhibited a miniature at the Spring Gardens Exhibition, which was greatly extolled, and was purchased by the King, who presented him with 100 guineas, and gave him commissions to paint the Queen and other members of the royal family.   He continued to practise his art with increasing success till 1772, when an accident caused so severe an injury that he travelled in Italy for his recovery, and made, during five years, a study of the great works there.   Returning in 1777, he wished to try historic art ; but neither in that, nor in his portraits in oil, did he meet with the success secured by his early miniatures.   He was elected an A.R.A. in 1779. He embarked for India in 1785 ; and visiting the different provinces, painted the distinguished native princes, nabobs, and others. Compelled to return in 1788 by failing health, he resumed miniature painting in London. He again found plenty of employment, and in 1791 was elected an R.A. ; but his health was exhausted, his eyesight impaired, and, though after some rest, he was enabled to resume his profession in the less minute manner of crayon drawings, which he followed very successfully till 1797, his eyesight then suddenly and finally failed. His miniatures, before those of any other, remind us of the excellences and graces of Reynolds. He excelled in sweetness of colour and in expression, and both in miniature and crayons he displayed the greatest taste, and was deemed the head of his profession for many years. He died in 1810.

Richard Cosway, R.A., was a hero of another class, a genius of another feather. Gossip of him is still rife, and the maccaroni miniature painter, quack, charlatan, or by whatever epithet he has been assailed by jealous caricaturists or envious rivals, has never been denied the title of an artist of the first rank. He was born in 1740, at Tiverton, where his father was master of the public school; and showing a fixed attachment to drawing, he was sent to London, and became the pupil of Hudson. He was at the same time a student at the St. Martin's Lane School, and afterwards at the Royal Academy. His abilities soon gained him notice. He had formed his taste by a careful study of the antique, and drew with freedom and elegance. He began life as a teacher in Parr's Drawing School, and drew heads for the shops, and fancy miniatures, not always of the most chaste class, for snuff-boxes; but his prominent abilities soon found him higher employment, and he rose rapidly to be the miniaturist of his day—his works not fashionable merely but the fashion itself. He was celebrated for his small whole-lengths; the figure tastefully drawn in pencil, in a manner entirely original, and in a sketchy style of easy elegance, the face carefully and usually highly finished in colour. Thus he drew all the beauties of the day, and, it is said, all the affianced brides. His miniatures on ivory were exquisitely wrought; they excel in finish, grace, colour and, above all, in expression; they never fail to charm, and are still as deservedly prized as by their first possessors. But his ideal went beyond his sitter, and he added a beauty and grace of his own, which, while it detracted from the accuracy of his likeness, was, nevertheless, an error on the right side—a fault which was readily overlooked or forgiven. His talent and great reputation gained him an early admission to the Academy. He was elected an A.R.A. in 1770 and an R.A. in 1771.

In person, Cosway was not only little, but mean. He assumed great airs, and his vanity tempted him to deck himself in portraits *ipse pinxit,* in the most ludicrously gorgeous costume. Aiming also at a luxurious manner of life, his house, and especially his studio, was filled with costly works of art, jewels, china, silks, gems, and gewgaws of every description, and was the resort of idle fashion and rank, including the Prince Regent himself, whose favourite beauties Cosway had painted and flattered, and of whose favour and intimacy he boasted. His wife was a congenial helpmate, and by her talents, beauty, and great musical abilities she added *éclat* to the splendour of his crowded parties.

Maria Cosway was the daughter of an English hotel-keeper at

Florence, and claims our notice on her own merits as a miniaturist and a painter. Nagler, who gives a long description in the most stilted language of her personal charms, her talents, and her paintings, says, "the English galleries are full of her exquisite works," and then turns to Richard Cosway as "husband of the foregoing!" Without joining in such high-flown opinions, we must admit that she was certainly a clever artist; she painted miniatures well, but not professionally; she also painted both for Boydell's *Shakspeare* and Macklin's *Poets*, and exhibited several compositions, which were of much merit, and were well engraved; of her character it is more difficult now to speak. She has been called a splendid specimen of humanity, and is said to have run away from her husband. She certainly joined in all her husband's vain extravagance, and the pair were the wonder and whisper of the town. For a time she resided in Paris in much gay luxury, and finally abandoned her husband in 1804, to become the superior of a religious house at Lyons, and only returned to England after the lapse of many years, in time to erect a monument to his memory. Of him we have only to add that, with age, his eccentricities and vanities increased. He believed in Swedenborg, and in animal magnetism. He held conversations with more than one person of the Trinity, and conversed with his wife, who was absent in Mantua, through some peculiar medium or additional sense. Whether he acted the charlatan in all this, or believed himself inspired—most probably the former—he at last professed to be able to raise the dead; and he asserted to his niece, the daughter of Dr. Syntax Coombe, that the Virgin Mary had sat to him several times, for a half-length figure, which he had just finished. He died in 1821, at a very advanced age, having for some years been prevented by sickness from following his profession.

Some of our eminent miniaturists have practised their art both in enamel and on ivory; others have painted exclusively on one only of these materials. Cosway was of the latter class, his practice, if we except his drawings, was confined to ivory. *Henry Bone, R.A.*, was an enamellist, who attained great celebrity in that art alone ; and, as seems to be peculiar to the painters whose pigments are fluxed on metal, he had, in his early career, been engaged in processes where the furnace was used. He was born at Truro, in 1755, and was apprenticed to a china-manufacturer at Plymouth. Commencing life as a painter of flowers and landscapes on china, in the processes connected with that manufacture, he obtained the knowledge which led him on to the higher practice on metal. He removed with the manufacturer to whom he was apprenticed to Bristol, and, on the termination of his apprenticeship in 1778, he came to London, and found employment as an enameller of watches and trinkets, occasionally painting a miniature in water-colour.

The fashion of enamelling devices on jewellery then changing, he determined to try for employment in works of a higher class, and after much study of his colours and the required fluxes, he painted the "Sleeping Girl" after Reynolds, and then a portrait of his wife, which he exhibited at the Royal Academy in 1780, and which at once attracted public notice. He continued to execute such device-painting as was offered him, and, pursuing his studies meanwhile, was able to produce from his own design "A Muse and Cupid" of a size far exceeding anything hitherto finished in enamel.

His works were now held in general estimation. He was noticed by the Prince of Wales (who for several years purchased his best pictures), and was largely employed; he was elected an A.R.A. in 1801, an R.A. in 1811, and was appointed enamel painter successively to George III., George IV., and William IV. He executed in enamel many portraits from his own sitters, but his most valued works were those after Reynolds, Titian, Raphael, and Murillo. He also executed a series of portraits of the Russell family from the time of Henry VII. and of the Royalists distinguished during the Civil War ; and from the royal and other collections eighty-five portraits of the great men of Queen Elizabeth's reign. These works were of course all copies, and it seems a peculiarity of the enameller's art, arising perhaps from its uncertain, difficult, and laborious processes, that the artist is tempted aside from original effort to seek, though it places him in the second rank, reputation and profit as a copyist of the celebrated or favourite works of the great masters. Of this class was his "Bacchus and Ariadne," after Titian, which he sold for 2,200 guineas. His eyesight failing, and no wonder after such trying labours, he retired to Somers Town. He had brought up and educated a large family, and was reluctantly compelled to receive the Royal Academy pension. He died in his seventy-eighth year, in 1834, complaining in his old age that his artist friends had forgotten him. His works were sold after his death, greatly beneath their value, and his collection of Elizabethan portraits, of which he left the refusal to the Government for 5,000*l.*, was dispersed.

Founding his manner somewhat on the pencilled portraits of Cosway, *Henry Edridge, A.R.A.*, rose to a well-earned distinction as a miniature painter. He was the son of a tradesman in St. James's, Westminster, and was born in Paddington in 1768, being one of five children left dependent upon a young widowed mother with only a scant provision. By her he was chiefly educated, and, showing an early predilection for art, was, at the age of fourteen, apprenticed to William Pether (the cousin of old Pether) who was a portrait and miniature painter, and distinguished by his mezzotint engraving. At sixteen Edridge was admitted as a student to the Royal Academy, and in 1786 gained the

Academy silver medal and with it the notice of the President, Reynolds, of whose portraits he was permitted to make miniature copies for his own improvement. After a time he laid aside engraving and, continuing the study of miniature, established himself as a portrait painter. His earliest works were on ivory, but afterwards his portraits were executed with much spirit on paper with the black lead pencil or with washes of Indian ink. This manner, however, after several years, he discontinued and worked in water-colours, touching in the figure in a slight, graceful manner, but finishing the head. In such works his finish was remarkable for its brilliancy and truth, uniting richness with freedom and freshness, perhaps acquired by his study of Reynolds. He had also a great taste for landscape art, which he had cultivated in his intimacy with Hearne ; and, in 1817, and again in 1819, he visited France and found many subjects for his pencil in the picturesque beauties of Paris and the fine Gothic edifices of Normandy. These he drew chiefly with the pencil, but he also made finished water-colour landscape drawings which possess great merit. In 1820 he was elected an associate of the Royal Academy. He was then in ill-health and in a desponding state ; he had lost his daughter in her seventeenth year, followed by his only remaining child, a son of the same age, and his constitution sank under the last blow. He died of an attack of asthma in 1821, and was buried in Bushey churchyard by his friend Dr. Munro, whose name is so well known in art.

Early in the present century, *Andrew Robertson* rose to eminence as a miniature painter, and came to be regarded in his day as the father of his art. He was born at Aberdeen about 1777 and was the son of a cabinetmaker. In 1800 he walked up to London to seek his fortune. He was noticed by President West who sat to him for his portrait. His miniatures are correct in drawing, and well finished, though sometimes crude in colour, and have the appearance of being correct likenesses with good expression. They possessed such merit as to attract great patronage ; but they wanted those perfections which are indicative of that true genius given only to the few. He enjoyed a considerable reputation for above thirty years, and on retiring from his profession in 1844, the most distinguished miniature painters presented him with a piece of plate in testimony of his merits. It has been said that he might have risen to higher eminence if his love of art had been undivided ; but he was greatly attached to music, and was renowned for his skill on the violin. He was also a contributor of articles on art to the *Literary Gazette*, and gave much of his time to the promotion of charitable institutions. He was a member of the Associated Artists in Water-Colours. He died at Hampstead, December 6, 1845.

Coming nearer to our own times and to our own personal recollections and friendships, we have to speak of *Alfred Edward Chalon, R.A.*, who for one generation at least held a distinguished rank as the fashionable portrait painter in water-colours. He came of an ancient French family which had left France at the revocation of the Edict of Nantes, and had been long settled in Geneva. His grandfather was wounded at the battle of the Boyne, where he served as a volunteer in a French Protestant regiment under William the Third (whose military pass the family possessed). His father, to whom some property had descended, left Geneva on the troubles which followed the breaking out of the French Revolution, and with his young family settled in England. He was appointed Professor of the French Language and Literature at the Royal Military College, Sandhurst, and afterwards, coming nearer to London, lived for many years in Kensington Square, with his wife, two sons, and a daughter. Alfred Chalon, the younger of the two boys, was born at Geneva in 1780, and with his brother was first placed in a large mercantile house, but the drudgery was equally distasteful to both ; they had a desire to be artists, for which their talents eminently fitted them, and with the consent of their father they both studied art. Alfred became a student of the Royal Academy in 1797. He was gifted with great taste and power, and soon acquired a bold vigorous style of drawing. He devoted himself chiefly to portraiture in water-colours, and became distinguished by his genius, fancy, and great feeling for brilliant colour. His full-length portraits in this manner, usually about ten inches high, as well as his miniatures on ivory, were full of character, were painted with a dashing facile grace, and were never common-place. His draperies and accessories were drawn with spirit and elegance, imitating all the vagaries fashion can commit in lace and silk, and though he was not a mannerist, he had a style peculiarly his own.

Alfred Chalon was one of the members of the Associated Artists in Water-Colours, a short-lived society founded in 1808, and in the same year he and his brother, with a few friends, established " The Sketching Club," of which we shall speak hereafter. In 1810 he exhibited his first picture at the Royal Academy. In 1812 he was elected an A.R.A. ; in 1816 an R.A. His genius was not restricted to the limits prescribed by the use of water-colours. He exhibited many excellent works in oil, powerfully painted and treated with all the skilled manner of a master in that medium.

We have had a difficulty in speaking separately of the two Brothers Chalon, and the plan of our work seems wrong, in that it places even the art of the two in different chapters. Unmarried, they had passed a long life together. They lived many years in Great Marlborough Street, then in Wimpole Street, and finally removed to a part of the old house on Campden Hill, Kensington, which Alfred Chalon, full of pretty conceits, named " El buen Retiro ; " but his brother's paralytic attack following soon after, his friends noticed that these words were removed from the gate, and repainted with the omission of the adjective, from a feeling of too presumptuous hopes, or possibly a presentiment of approaching sorrow. Alfred Chalon was a true Englishman in heart, though his manner was French. He was an accomplished musician, witty, with a keen sense of satire, which, if provoked, found only a momentary expression ; and full of the anecdotes and the gossip of his profession. As a host, he was active to the last in providing for the enjoyment of his friends, and full of expedients for their amusement. Many would join in the expression of Leslie, that he counted his intimacy with the Chalons among the best things of his life.

He had been for some time unwell—but hardly appeared less gay in society—when his friends learnt that after a sudden attack of severe sickness, he had died on the 3rd October, 1860, aged eighty years. He was laid in the same grave with his brother in the Highgate Cemetery. He had a large collection of pictures, drawings and sketches by himself and his brother, with many hoarded family reminiscences. This collection he proposed in 1859 to give to the inhabitants of Hampstead, with some endowment for its maintenance, but they were unable to provide a suitable building for its exhibition ; and he then offered the collection to the Government, but no satisfactory arrangement was arrived at when he died. A will which was found, was informally executed, his property came to his heirs-at-law—some distant relatives at Geneva—and his treasured collection was sold by auction.

Sir William Charles Ross, R.A., who both on the male and female side was descended from a clever race, was born on the 3rd June, 1794. At an age when most children seek their toys, he found his amusement in drawing the likenesses of his family ; and debarred by a weakly constitution from sharing in the robust exercises of boyhood, he was led to the more close application to drawing, and was an earnest and precocious student. In his boyish days he had gained several of the Society of Arts medals, and no less than five silver medals were the prizes of his student career at the Royal Academy. At the age of twenty he was engaged by Mr. Andrew Robertson, as his assistant, and under this eminent miniaturist, he enjoyed great means of improvement. His ambition led him to devote his spare hours to the study of historic art. One of the Society of Arts prizes which he had gained was a gold medal for an oil painting, " The Judgment of Brutus," and following the same bent in 1825, he exhibited at the Royal Academy a large work in oil, the figures life-size, " Christ Casting Out the Devils from the Maniacs of the Tombs," but his art, if not his inclinations, lay in another direction, and he soon established a high reputation as a miniature painter.

In 1837 he was commissioned by the Queen to paint her Majesty's own miniature, and also the miniatures of the royal family.   In 1838 he was elected associate, and in 1839, a full member of the Royal Academy ; and in the same year he received the honour of knighthood. Then he was surrounded with distinguished sitters.   He confined his work to ivory ; we know of no attempts by him in enamel.   In his style we see more indications of his study of Reynolds than of any other master.   He possessed the great power of combining a faithful resemblance and individuality of character and expression, with art of a high class.   His drawing was refined and accurate, his composition and grouping agreeable, his colouring of the complexion, hands, and arms of his female sitters admirable, and the draperies, accessories and backgrounds, painted and arranged with great taste and skill.   We should add that, amid all his engagements, his dormant passion was revived by the cartoon competition in 1843 ; and that for his " Angel Raphael discoursing with Adam and Eve," which he sent in anonymously, he was awarded one of the extra premiums of 100*l.*   Sir William Ross was of amiable and simple manners, true to all, without offence, always showing the most loyal attachment to art and its professors.   As a bachelor, he passed a quiet, uneventful, and successful life ; ready at all times to do any act of charity, or to assist in any good work.   About the beginning of 1858 he was overcome by a gradual attack of paralysis, from which he partially rallied, but after a relapse he died on the 20th January, 1860, in his 66th year.   He rests in the cemetery at Highgate.

Our chapter must conclude with *Robert Thorburn, A.R.A.*, who, less fortunate than his predecessors, lived to see miniature art nearly extinct. Ross on his death-bed bewailed the fact " that it was all up with miniature painting," being in this wiser than Alfred Chalon, who is said to have replied to the Queen when she remarked to him that photography would ruin his profession, " Ah, non, Madame, photographie can't flattère." There can be no doubt however that photography has for the present superseded miniature painting in this country.   Thorburn was born in 1818 at Dumfries, and studied his art first in Edinburgh and then in the Royal Academy Schools.   His miniatures are often on a large scale, and he frequently painted portrait groups.   His colouring though fresh was a little inclined to be heavy, but his execution was refined and his compositions were graceful and dignified.   He took care to adapt his background to his sitters, and to place them in appropriate attitudes. His work was much admired in Paris, where he gained a gold medal at the Universal Exhibition of 1855.   He was elected an associate of the Academy in 1848, and resigned his membership in 1885, dying the 3rd of November of that same year at Tunbridge Wells.

M

CHAPTER XV.

BOOK ILLUSTRATORS AND DESIGNERS.

THE painter's art in its early dissemination received powerful aid from that of the engraver; and the painter and engraver stood in nearly the same relation towards each other as the poet and the painter, for Raphael and Rubens may be said to owe as much of their wide-spread fame to the one, as Dante and Milton to the other. Painting and engraving have also been frequently practised with success by the same individual, both on the first dawning of art here, and down to our own day. The most renowned painters also have practised etching—so peculiarly a painter's art—and dating from the discovery of mezzotint, we are repeatedly told of our painters, in the language of the last century, that "they scraped a bit."

Some of the earliest books printed were of a religious character, and, following the missal style, some of the first illustrations of printed books were repetitions on wood of the early illuminators' art, occasionally tinted with colour. Such were soon followed by portrait-frontispieces, sometimes surrounded by allegories. *William Faithorne* (B. 1616, D. 1691) drew from the life some of the many interesting portraits which we owe to his graver; so did also *David Loggan* (B. 1630, D. 1693), of whom Dryden, in his satire on a would-be poet, said,—

> " And at the front of all his senseless plays
> Makes David Loggan crown his head with bays."

Robert White (B. 1645, D. 1704) was the pupil of Loggan, and a notable example of the union of the painters' with the gravers' art, in works deemed of great merit in his day, which have not lost favour in ours. These men, and their less known contemporaries, produced portraits on copper, frequently most carefully and elaborately finished with the etching point, and as is recorded upon them "*ad vivum,*" which have been carefully sought out in succeeding generations by the enthusiastic art-collector and antiquary, till rare frontispieces torn from valueless books have found greedy purchasers at prices which might have stirred the artists in the graves where they have so long lain.

Coëval with the portrait-frontispiece, though commencing at a later period, were the topographical views, and other subjects, chiefly stimulated by antiquarian research, and usually both drawn and engraved by the same artist, but rarely with much merit : objects of natural history followed, botanical specimens, insects, birds and beasts. These were mere accessories necessary to the elucidation of the subjects to which they related, not art-illustrations of the thoughts of the poet, the inventions of the novelist, or the great events of the historian. Hogarth, having executed some small commissions for booksellers, which did not go much beyond diagrams, completed, in 1726, a set of small designs for an edition of *Hudibras*, which, so far as we can discover, were the first book illustrations of story and character, and the beginning of a new art. His example was soon followed by his genial friend *Frank Hayman*, who enjoyed the reputation of being our best history painter, and of having established the practice of book illustration. He made designs for Moore's *Fables*, Congreve's *Plays*, Newton's edition of *Milton*, Hanmer's *Shakspeare*, and Smollett's *Don Quixote*, and in conjunction with *Nicholas Blakey*, with whom he was also associated in some other undertakings, for Pope's works. Hayman's designs had much merit. They showed humour and character, and were well composed, though they were slight and sketchy, and smacked of a French origin.

Samuel Wale, R.A. (D. 1786) was a follower and imitator of Hayman. He found employment chiefly as a book illustrator, and is only remembered by such designs. *Henri Gravelot*, educated in Paris, a designer by profession, an engraver of necessity, was a book illustrator, and a caricaturist to boot, who worked hard while here, and returned to France with a fortune. *John Vanderbanck*, who was born and bred in England, engaged in the same pursuit, and designed among other works for Lord Carteret's translation of *Don Quixote*. To these we must add *Joseph Highmore* (B. 1692, D. 1780), who illustrated his friend Richardson's *Pamela*, and painted his portrait, which hangs, or did so until lately, in Stationers' Hall.

Bell's well-known edition of the British poets, which extended to one hundred and nine duodecimo volumes, was begun in 1778, and was followed by his *British Theatre*, and his *Shakspeare ;* of these works the miniature illustrations were a prominent feature, and no doubt contributed to their success. The art of the designer became a fashion. *Cipriani, R.A.*, and *Angelica Kauffman, R.A.*, of whom we have already spoken, were mainly employed by the publishers, and their

M 2

works lent some taste and elegance to design. *William Hamilton, R.A.* (B. 1751, D. 1801), was also extensively employed by Boydell, Macklin, and Bowyer. His best works were designed for their publications. With him we may also class *Francis Wheatley, R.A.* (B. 1747, D. 1801). His forte lay in landscape with rustic figures, treated with taste, but marked by an over-refined prettiness.

William Blake, engraver, painter, poet, and we might add, printer, was the son of a respectable hosier. He was born in London in 1757, and died in 1827, finding his resting-place in an unknown common grave in the great Bunhill-Fields burial ground. He was at first intended for his father's business, but as a child he gave signs of a restless genius. At an early age he attempted both poetry and designing, and, that an attachment to such pursuits might not be altogether thwarted, he was apprenticed to Basire, the engraver, second of the name. His love of poetry did not lead him astray; he was careful to attain a mastery of the engraver's art, though he repudiated the love of money and declared that his business was "not to gather gold, but to make glorious shapes, expressing god-like sentiments," and to this he surely devoted himself. By his labour during the day with his graver he gained a bare subsistence, while his nights were given to the realization of his dreams with his pen and his pencil. At the age of twenty-six he married, and the necessity arose for the greater use of his graver. In his engravings he was minute and painstaking; his drawing good, his line pure and true. His works are sometimes marked by minute finish, at others left in a state of unfinish, apparently from caprice, or as though he did not care to go further than the realization of his idea. From the termination of his apprenticeship till 1782, and occasionally afterwards, he was employed in engraving for book illustrations, chiefly from some of Stothard's earliest designs, but in some instances from his own. It is as a designer and painter, however, not as an engraver, that William Blake falls within the scope of our work. In 1791, six plates designed and also engraved by him, were published as illustrations of Mary Wollstonecroft's *Tales for Children;* and in 1793, nine plates for an expensive edition of *Gay's Fables*, published by Stockdale. These designs have a natural air of original simplicity, with sometimes a peculiar touch of wildness, as in the "Father Beside his Dead Children in Jail" in the *Tales for Children*, upon whose youthful minds we are told it left an impression of pained dreamy fear.

At this time Blake, following the wild promptings of his own imagination, began those mysterious compositions of which he was at once the poet, painter, and engraver. Taught by necessity, he invented a process of his own, though he alleged it was revealed to him in a vision. By drawing on copper with a medium which resisted acid, he obtained a raised design. From this he was enabled to print both the design and his closely written poetry, which covers some entire pages, and in others, crowds round his figured imaginings, filling every cranny upon his copper. These works, aided by his wife, he pulled off at a common printing press and then tinted. His colouring is produced with the commonest pigments, probably prepared by himself,—Dutch pink, ochre and gamboge, blue, red, and green. Sometimes he has neglected to reverse part of the lettering on his plates, and it prints backwards: occasionally a principal figure has been printed both ways by transferring, and with a dark or light background is made to serve for two designs. The engravings themselves produced by this process were rude in character, and the outlines thick and crude, nevertheless the effect is singularly pictorial. In this manner he completed his *Songs of Innocence*, and *Songs of Experience*, which contain some most beautiful ideas both in design and poetry; and the plates for which are very refined and lovely in colour. These were followed by his *America, a Prophecy.* Unbalanced minds are always disturbed by great events, and this latter work arose out of the excitement which attended the breaking out of the American Revolution; as a rhapsody, it is altogether incomprehensible, and it would be impossible to look at it as the production of a sound intellect. His *Europe, a Prophecy* followed in 1794, full of diseased horrors, from the grand wreathed serpent, which forms the title, to the illustration of "Famine,"—a father and mother preparing the cauldron to cook their dead child, which lies stretched out at their feet.

Blake's most mad, most strange imaginings, were published in 1804, *Jerusalem, the Emanation of the Giant Albion*, dated South Molton Street—Bedlam might have been more appropriate. This poem, with occasional illustrations, runs over one hundred pages, closely engraved in a small script hand. Blake says of it, "To the public, after my three years' slumber on the banks of the ocean, I again display my giant forms to the public; my former giants and fairies having received the highest reward possible. . . . I cannot doubt that this more consolidated and extended work will be as kindly received. . . . I also hope that the reader will be with me, wholly one in Jesus our Lord," and then he concludes with these obscure lines,—

> " Even from the depths of hell, his voice I hear
> Within the unfathomed caverns of my ear ;
> Therefore I print, nor vain my types shall be,
> Heaven, earth, and hell, henceforth shall live in harmony."

It seems that Blake's most disordered dreams found their expression in the process he had invented, and he probably flew to this process when in his excited moods, as the means of rapidly embodying his heated ideas. Certainly he thus traced his wildest and most incomprehensible forms, in extravagant and often impossible action—a map of muscular development. On the other hand, his best thoughts are represented with his graver—perhaps the early associations connected with the toil of his 'prentice years, and the process of patient labour which its use involves, may have assisted to temper the artist's impetuous fancy—and we would rather speak of his genius in reference to the works he engraved in a pure manner; they are also the best known : the Young's *Night Thoughts*, an uncompleted work commenced in 1797, of which every page was a design, the type forming the centre; and Blair's *Grave*, published 1804-5. The daring fertility of Blake's invention will be shown by his own description of the subjects in the former poem. What other artist has attempted such a theme as " The Universal Empire of Death characterized by his plucking the Sun from his sphere "—a striding figure of death, trampling under each gristly foot a crowned head, and, with one hand impetuously seizing the sun, represented as a shaded globe giving light, and the other hand grasping his dart?; or "A Personification of Thunder, directing the adoration of the Poet to the Almighty in Heaven"? Here the head and hand only of a fearful figure in human form are seen surrounded by lightning, and on a corner of earth, the poet. We quote only one more, where all are of the same character, "A Personification of Truth, as she is represented by the Poet, bursting on the last moments of the sinner in thunder and in flames."

Blake's inventions were hardly of this world. The Creator frequently occupies the centre of his subject; spirits and angels, good and evil, crowd his compositions; monsters, and distorted forms of another creation, fill up ideal space. His illustrations of the *Book of Job*, the labour of his last and ripest years, are of these, mingled with much of the sweetest and most impressive humanity. The work was published in 1825, and comprises twenty-one plates minutely drawn and carefully engraved. Impressed with Blake's ungovernable imagination, they are yet full of passages of great tenderness and feeling. "Thus did Job continually" represents Job, his family and friends, returning thanks to God, and is a composition teeming with poetry. An expression of dignified passionate grief fills "Let the day perish wherein I was born,"—the upraised hands of the prophet, the utter despair of the prostrate family, and the gloomy character of the background, all combine in the same sentiment. "The just, upright man is laughed to scorn," is of the same high conception ; while "When the morning stars sang together and all the Sons of God shouted for joy," is marked by a combination of grace, sweetness, and poetry ; qualities which are also united in "There were not foun women so fair as the daughters of Job," and in the concluding subject, "So the Lord blessed the latter end of Job more than the beginning." These were the works of a great and noble mind. They impress us with Blake's genius. His art was too original to breed imitators, though it was not without its influence even in that day, and we find traces of it in the designs of the period. This influence has grown from the effect it produced on the minds of younger men, such as Palmer, Richmond, Calvert, and Rossetti, who all alike acknowledged their indebtedness to him, and praised his rare talent.

A few words more on Blake's character. He was contentedly poor. His industry must have been unwearied, and we do not doubt that though neglected, he was happy when laboriously engaged in realizing the creations of his fruitful genius. His designs alone would indicate a nervously sensitive, irascible temperament, of which proof is not wanting. His friend, Hayley, the poet, who tempted Blake to live near him for a time in a small village on the Sussex coast, calls him the "gentle, visionary Blake." Yet when irritated, and Blake was not without many real causes of irritation, he took no care to conceal his passion, and was not mealy-mouthed either in word or in print, nevertheless he loved little children, and was a most affectionate friend. We know too that his love for a tender wife was as enduring as his love for art.

Gilchrist's *Life of Blake*, to which we are indebted for many facts concerning him, should be studied for a more detailed account of this wayward genius; the biography is one which brings before us with great distinctness the episodes of his strange career and presents us with a true picture of his character.

It is pleasant to write of *Thomas Stothard, R.A.*, with whose works so many sweet memories are associated. He was born in London, 1755, and being a delicate child, was sent to Acomb, in Yorkshire, his father's native county, and placed in the charge of the widowed mistress of the little village school. Of a gentle, retiring disposition, he found a solitary amusement in drawing. He was afterwards removed to a school at Tadcaster, and at the age of thirteen returned to his parents in London, and was sent to a boys' school at Ilford. In 1770 his father died, leaving him 1,200*l*. in the funds. He began life as an apprentice to a pattern-draughtsman for brocaded silks in Spitalfields, and occupied his spare hours in designs from the poets. Some of these by chance falling under the notice of the publisher of the *Novelists' Magazine*, he engaged him to make a few designs, and though at the time he did not receive further employment, his attention was thus directed to book illustration. He had fallen upon his right path, and he abandoned pattern-drawing.

Stothard's first designs were engraved for an edition of *Ossian*, and for Bell's *Poets*. The subjects were congenial, and his talents were conspicuous. But he showed a higher excellence in the series of illustrations which he now commenced for the *Novelists' Magazine.* The subjects which this publication offered were peculiarly suited to his pencil. His tender and gentle nature led him to delineate the affections rather than the passions—beauty and grace rather than the higher emotions. His sympathies found little pleasure in the heroic—less in the tragic. He delighted in such incidents of every-day life as the novel afforded, and he treated them in the costume of the time with great character, truth, and grace. He has left us graceful little mementoes of court balls and birthday suppers, and we trace his all-pervading taste in every variety of design—slight sketches of popular performers, tickets for concerts, headings for charitable announcements, and drawings for goldsmiths' work, of which last his " Wellington Shield " is a renowned example.

Early in life Stothard married, and a wife, soon followed by a large young family, proved indeed hostages to fortune. The circumstances of his wedding bring home to us the artless simplicity of the man, which all his works testify. He took his bride home from the church, and then quietly betook himself to his studies at the Royal Academy ; and when at 3 P.M., the schools closed, he said to a friend, who as fellow-student had sat by his side all the morning :—" I am now going home to meet a family party. Do come with me, for I have this day taken to myself a wife." If trials were necessary to such a disposition, they did not fail him. One son, a lad of thirteen, was suddenly shot dead by a companion ; another in his thirty-fourth year, was found dead, having fallen on the floor of a church, where he was engaged in making a drawing for his work illustrating the " Magua Britannia."

Stothard's amiable biographer, Mrs. Bray, the widow of his son, speaks of him "as the greatest historical painter this country ever produced." While not yielding to the highest appreciation of Stothard's genius, we cannot concur in this eulogium. The bent of Stothard's own mind would not have led him to sacred, or even to historical subjects ; his conceptions were not of the severe character such require, and his works of this class are wanting both in expression, and in elevation of character. Again he wanted individuality, particularly in his women. His beauty, perfect as it is, is of one conventional type.

The Royal Academy was not slow to recognize Stothard's talents. He was elected associate 1791 and full member 1794. His habit of study did not lead him to make elaborate drawings from the figure ; he chose rather to make slight sketches of the model from several points of view. He was a close observer of nature, but felt cramped by the stiffness of the posed model, and strove rather to attain motion and grace, relying upon the truth of the first impression. He had a catholic love of art, and as recollections of Raphael, Rubens, Watteau, and other artists possessed his mind, we may trace the reflex of their influence on his work, but without loss of his originality. His larger works in oil do not equal his drawings. His designs have been estimated to amount to 4,000. Stothard died in 1834, and the venerable artist has left an additional picture in our minds, when in his last years, deaf and feeble, he was occupied in his evening duties as librarian at the Royal Academy. There bending over some book of prints, with many unconscious sighs and moans, his unsteady hand was unable to pour out the cup of tea in which he found a solace, yet even then, retiring into the recess of the window, he would, from time to time, occupy his pencil for a few moments, in the realization of some thought, in a slight but still elegant and graceful sketch.

Among the contemporaries of Stothard, pursuing the same walk in art, we must notice *John Hamilton Mortimer, A.R.A.*, if only for the great reputation which he enjoyed at the commencement of his career. He was born at Eastbourne in 1741, and, coming to London to study, acquired a knowledge of the figure and became a good draughtsman. He painted three or four large historical compositions which attracted great notice, and in competition with Romney, in 1764, he gained the Society of Arts premium of one hundred guineas. He was looked upon as of much promise. Of a strong frame and handsome person, he affected a style of dress beyond his station, made acquaintance with some of the so-called wits upon the town, and, falling into glaring irregularities, ruined his health and neglected his art. His works in oil were badly painted, heavy and disagreeable in colour, and he abused the hours which should have been devoted to his improvement. His best works were his drawings; they could be sketched off with less study, and did not much vary in subject; his favourite imaginings were strained imitations of Salvator Rosa—banditti, monsters, and such like.

Mortimer is an example of talents abused and good intentions adopted too late. He had married a clever, respectable young girl, to whom he had been long attached; he was beginning to lead a new life, devoting himself to his art; and had just gained his election as an associate of the Royal Academy in November, 1778, when shortly after he was seized with fever, under which his broken-down constitution succumbed, and he died in February, 1779, leaving little more than a name to the art of his country.

Of the painters to whom the new taste for book designs gave employment, while their works added a character to the publications of the time, we must distinguish two or three other artists. *Thomas Kirk*, who gained an early reputation as designer, miniature painter, and engraver, produced a few pastoral designs, and was noted for the elegance of his female figures. His chief works were for Cook's *Poets*, but his career in art was short yet of much promise. He died of consumption in November, 1797. *Richard Westall, R.A.* (B. 1765, D. 1836) has already been mentioned as a water-colour painter. He made many designs for books, and has been characterized as "great in little things." In such, his art seems truly to have found its best development. His illustrations for the Bible and the Prayer-Book were greatly admired, and so far suited the public taste as to become very popular, and he made money, though he afterwards lost his savings by traffic in the works of the old masters. His female ideal, with great sameness, had great prettiness ; his males partook too much of the same character ; they sadly lacked the manliness of the heroes they represented, and in both sexes the mannerism of the artist was always apparent. His brother, *William Westall, A.R.A.*, who died in 1850, also found employment as a designer, chiefly in landscape, which he rendered with great fidelity and skill. *Robert Smirke, R.A.* (B. 1752, D. 1845) is better known as a designer than as a painter, for though he painted many works from the poets and dramatists, they were designed with a view to engraving, and were most of them engraved ; he also made many book designs. His best works possess a quiet refinement of original humour.

Thomas Uwins, R.A., born in 1782, was apprenticed to an engraver, but quitting the graver on the end of his apprenticeship, he entered the Royal Academy as a student and became a designer for books, occasionally painting portraits. His works had been mostly in water-colour, and in 1808, he was elected an associate of the Water-Colour Society, and in the following year a full member. The drawings he exhibited at the society were frames of designs suitable for book illustration, and rustic figures. His contributions to the Royal Academy were of the same class, together with portraits. His employments, not his own will, seem to have shaped his career, and his works are conspicuous in the book illustrations of this time. In 1818 he suddenly resigned his membership and his office of secretary in the Water-Colour Society. An officer of the Society of Arts for whom Uwins was security became a defaulter, and greatly to the hindrance of his professional advancement, he devoted himself to the drudgery of his art till he had honourably fulfilled his obligations. He visited Edinburgh and was successful in portraiture, chiefly in the chalk manner. In 1824 he went to Italy, where he remained till 1831, gathering the materials for his future new career.

Up to this time, as we have shown, Uwins was a book-illustrator, and painted portraits when sitters offered. He did not seek re-admission to the Water-Colour Society, and its exhibitions are closed to the works of non-members. For seven years his labours had not been seen in our exhibitions, and now, when approaching his fiftieth year, he began to exhibit on the walls of the Royal Academy a series of pictures, whose inspirations were all of Italy, and at once established his reputation as a painter, emancipating his art from the toils of his early life. His merits were at once acknowledged, he was elected an associate of the Royal Academy in 1833 and an academician in 1838. Further honours were in store for him. The Queen appointed him surveyor of her Majesty's pictures in 1845, and the national pictures were added to his charge in 1847. He died at Staines, where he had sought a quiet retirement, in 1857.

But we must retrace our steps to describe a new school of book illustration which arose from the genius of one man, far from the metropolis and its art influences, and gave a great impetus to the embellishment of books, both by the original freshness of its art and the greater facilities of its process. The first book designs of our artists were engraved on copper and printed separately—the printing of the type and the designs by which it was to be illustrated being necessarily two distinct and separate processes ; this enhanced the cost, which was somewhat further increased in the stitching or binding by the mode of securing the engraving, so that the introduction of engravings entailed additional expense in the mere mechanical processes.

Thomas Bewick, born near Newcastle-on-Tyne in 1753, is said to have re-discovered the lost art of wood-engraving, and though we cannot assume that the art was lost, or that he preceded a French artist in its modern use, we may well attribute to Bewick the merit of having given to wood-engraving, by the impress of his own talent, a development it had never before known in England, and of having employed it in the illustration of books, printing his blocks at the same time and by the same process as the metal type, and thus greatly economizing and facilitating book illustration. Apprenticed to an engraver in metal at Newcastle, who undertook every description of work, Bewick was after a time specially attracted to wood-engraving, which he made his peculiar study. On the completion of his apprenticeship he came to London, but he disliked the metropolis, and within about twelve months we find him again settled in Newcastle, and soon after in partnership with his old master ; and there he passed the remainder of his life.

After nearly five years' labour Bewick published in 1790 his *General History of Quadrupeds*, and such was its success, that in each of the two succeeding years it was followed by another edition. This work was also embellished with a number of small tail-pieces full of humorous idea and graphic satire. Then gratified by the popularity of this work, he began, 1791, the designs and cuts for the *History of British Birds*, and in 1797 issued the first volume, comprising the land birds. His reputation both as a designer and engraver was spread far and wide, and in

1804 the water birds followed, completing the work. In these works Bewick carried the art to a higher pitch of excellence than it had ever before attained. His designs were the work of a naturalist and close observer, true to the habits as well as the forms of the animals he represented; his engravings are unsurpassed, both in the variety and truth of his feathery and furry textures as well as in the general finish of his background and accessories. But we must not say, as others have, that all was by his own hand. He was ably assisted by his brother John, and had the merit of establishing by his talented pupils a school of wood-engravers. Of these Robert Johnson, who unhappily died in his twenty-sixth year in 1796, designed many of the tail-pieces in the *Birds*, and the greater number of the illustrations of the *Fables*, which were not published till 1818; and Luke Clennell, an artist of great powers, who died in 1840 after a long loss of intellect, engraved many of the illustrations to the *Birds*, and the majority of the tail-pieces in the second volume. Bewick died near Gateshead, in 1828.

Book illustration had fairly taken hold of the public mind, and the publishers did their best to pander to the public taste. In 1823, Akermann commenced an annual gift-book, *The Forget-me-not*,—a German notion, a series of pictures and tales. This was followed by a rival, *The Friendship's Offering*, and then a whole brood, *The Literary Souvenir*, *The Keepsake*, *The Amulet*, and in landscape art, *The Picturesque Annual*, *The Continental Annual*, *The Landscape Annual*, *Prout's Annual*, *Turner's Annual Tour*, till the number issued was above twenty, and found its climax in *The Flowers of Loveliness*, and *The Book of Beauty*. In these publications the order of proceeding was inverted; the painter did not embody the thoughts of the writer, but the writer was hired to fit a tale, in verse or prose, to the painter's invention. Art of all descriptions was at the same time seized upon by the publisher : old masters and moderns, countrymen and foreigners, all whose works were within reach; and the engraver and the writer were set to work to make the book. The issue of the "Annuals" was an event, till a sudden collapse fell upon the whole series, and the "Annual" became a thing of the past. We have nothing to say of the literature of these books, and very little of the art. Many really fine paintings were engraved, and some of the most talented engravers were employed; but after all, the art was puerile and meretricious, and it is to be feared that the production of engravings of a higher class was checked, and that art suffered while thus held in durance by fashion.

Shortly after this another attempt was made in book illustration which claims its place in this chapter, the aims and objects of which were entirely different—art, not gain, was the sole stimulus. Some young friends, studying side by side, seeking no further than to promote art and the love of etching, formed themselves in 1838 into a society, whose numbers have averaged twelve members, which they called the *Etching Club.* They framed a few simple rules, binding themselves to complete etchings at stated periods, and to meet at each other's studios in rotation. Their meetings were of a social character: a cup of tea, and then business. Works for illustration were next discussed, subjects selected, etchings criticized, and the evening concluded with a simple supper. Their first work, the *Deserted Village,* when published, secured great and honourable distinction. Her Majesty and the Prince Consort graciously proffered their patronage and their subscriptions, and Thomas Hood wrote a laudatory article on the club in *Blackwood's Magazine* for January, 1842.

The club has since published several works, and in addition to many living members of distinction, has had among its contributors who have passed away, Webster, Palmer, Ansdell and Taylor. The example, not the pecuniary success of the club, led to the formation of a Junior Etching Club, which published illustrations of Thomas Hood's *Poems,* containing some excellent etchings.

The English school can still honestly boast of its great living engravers. Our work is confined to painting, so we must not mention the great school of engravers which grew up in England in the latter half of the eighteenth century, or go into the impetus which that art has received in our own day. We have only spoken of the two etching clubs, because their members were all painters, but perhaps it is hardly fair as we have written a few words on book illustrations to pass over the names of one or two artists who have created, as it were, a new art by their talents. We would mention George Cruikshank (B. 1792, D. 1878), Hablot K. Browne, (B. 1815, D. 1882), better known as "Phiz," Richard Doyle (B. 1826, D. 1883), and John Leech (B. 1817, D. 1864), who for twenty years drew for *Punch,* and delighted every one not only by the humour of his designs and the truth of his figure drawing, but also by the charm of his landscape backgrounds given with a few dashes of the pencil; nor must we pass over Randolph Caldecott (B. 1846, D. 1886), painter and designer, principally known by his quaint and original illustrations for children's books. The progress which this branch of art has made during the last forty years is perhaps one of the best examples of the real advance which sound draughtsmanship and appreciation of what is beautiful in the minor processes of art, has made in our English school.

CHAPTER XVI.

THE BRITISH INSTITUTION AND THE WATER-COLOUR SOCIETIES.

THE impulse to promote art which followed the establishment of the Royal Academy was manifested in many ways, leading to one important result in the foundation of the British Institution in 1805. Its defined objects were " to open a public exhibition for the sale of the productions of British artists, to excite the emulation and exertion of younger artists by premiums, and to endeavour to form a public gallery of the works of British artists, with a few select specimens of each of the great schools." That these laudable aspirations were not fulfilled may have partly arisen from the entire absence of any man on the committee—composed solely of great people and art patrons—who was capable of giving professional advice on art subjects. The directors opened exhibitions and awarded premiums to which they generously devoted large sums, but their awards did not always please at the time of competition, and have not always been endorsed by the judgment of posterity. Perhaps their greatest failure was in commissioning *James Ward, R.A.*, who had competed with others in sending in a sketch to illustrate " The Successes of the British Army in the Peninsular War," to paint this sketch in a large size, namely " The Battle of Waterloo, an allegory," for 1,000*l*. Ward was highly distinguished as an animal painter. He had great power of execution, and we have no doubt that his sketch was a vigorous bit of painting, and as such would be likely to allure a judgment not tempered by professional knowledge. But the subject was not suited to a great work, which would have been, from its allegorical treatment, a trial and a task to Rubens himself. The result was fatal to the judgment of the directors. This great allegory when completed was never exhibited. The directors presented it to the Royal Hospital at Chelsea. Like the Vicar of Wakefield's family group, " it was so very large they had no place in the house to fix it," and it is stowed away on a roller in an oblivion which is perhaps happy for its really talented painter.

But James Ward's powers as an artist should not be estimated by our opinions on the ambitious work which, on the mistaken commission of the directors of the British Institution, he was induced to attempt. He came of an art family. George Morland married his sister. Bred a mezzotint engraver, he early distinguished himself, his engravings possessing very great merits, from their truly artistic character. He became no less distinguished as a painter of landscape with figures, and of animals; particularly the latter. His great work of "The Bull" has found its proper place in the National Gallery. He had a strong, but peculiar feeling for colour. His style of drawing was vigorous, though imbued with an evident desire to exhibit his knowledge. He was elected an associate of the Academy in 1807, and a full member in 1811; and living to the age of ninety-one years, he died on the 17th November, 1859.

In 1842 the directors of the British Institution ceased the giving of premiums, as "their effect had not been commensurate with their expectations."

They were more fortunate in their exhibitions of "Works of the Old Masters," which, notwithstanding adverse criticisms, were much enjoyed both by the public and the artists. They likewise exhibited the works of Reynolds after his death, also those of the chief British artists of a former generation, and of many other deceased members of the English school. Their example has been since followed with great success both by the Royal Academy and by the directors of the Grosvenor Gallery. The spring exhibition of the works of living painters at the British Institution gradually declined, being much pressed upon by the Society of British artists, and by the fact that the painters naturally sent their best works to the Royal Academy exhibitions. The purchases of modern and ancient pictures made by the directors were few in number, and were presented by them to Greenwich Hospital, to several London churches, and on its formation to the National Gallery.

For some time after the winding up of the British Institution, the Royal Academy and the Society of British Artists were the only general exhibitions opened in London. Now what a number of both public and private exhibitions have been started! The Grosvenor Gallery, opened by Sir Coutts Lindsay, exhibits every spring the works of specially invited artists, and the New Gallery has just opened another annual exhibition with great and encouraging success. Meanwhile numerous dealers' exhibitions compete with one another every spring and autumn for the suffrages of the public.

But we have strayed far away from our subject, and must now recur to the practice of water-colour painting, and resume our account of the progress of this truly English art.

Year after year the works of its professors had increased on the walls of the Royal Academy, up to that time the only public exhibition; but though their art grew in public estimation, it had only one small room devoted to it at the Academy, where water-colours were placed at a great disadvantage in point of light. A certain number of water-colour painters resolved to establish a new society wholly devoted to their own art. The originators and promoters were Hills, Pyne, Shelley, and Wells, who were afterwards joined by John Varley and Glover; and after some preliminary meetings at Shelley's house, in George Street, Hanover Square, at which the outline of the society was determined, a meeting was called; William S. Gilpin, who was invited to attend, took the chair; and the "Water-Colour Society" was founded on the 30th November, 1804, the main features of which were the annual exhibition of original subjects in water-colours, exclusively the works of the members, who were limited to twenty-four; the management to be vested in officers elected annually, but eligible for re-election. Subsequent meetings were held; the adhesion of others of the profession was gained, and the society, when constituted, consisted of sixteen members; all of whom at the time enjoyed distinction as painters in water-colours.

Their first exhibition was opened on the 22nd of April, 1805, with a collection of two hundred and seventy-five drawings, in the large room built by Vandergucht, the engraver, in Lower Brook Street; the catalogue containing the announcement that, if successful, it was intended to be annual. The following year the exhibition was held in the same room, and the members then stated that the very flattering reception of their first exhibition had encouraged them to open their second, and that their third would be held in the old Royal Academy Rooms in Pall Mall. Before their second exhibition, they had strengthened themselves by adding to their body eight "fellow exhibitors," the number of this rank being limited to twelve, who were to enjoy all the rights and privileges of the original founders. Gilpin, who had presided at the foundation meeting, was elected the first president, but he resigned in 1806; he had formed an extensive connexion as a teacher, and enjoyed a meretricious reputation which he could not sustain.

The exhibitions of the society at first proved a great success. Several artists, by works of great merit, had first made themselves known, gaining much distinction, and the new exhibition and the new art were the talk of the town.

The profits of the exhibitions belonged to the members, and were apportioned among them *pro rata*, according to the selling prices, which each was allowed to affix to the works he exhibited, and which were not, therefore, so far, without some check.

The new society was not long without rivalry. Its success had given a sudden impetus to water-colour art, and many talented men who were left outside, were by this exclusion placed at much disadvantage; they had only the condemned walls of the Royal Academy on which to compete with the advantages enjoyed by the members of the society. This led in 1808 to the formation of "The Associated Artists in Water-Colours." We cannot now learn much of the society's proceedings, but we know that though it was not exclusive, it was very short-lived.

While the members of the Associated Society found themselves without support, the original society saw its interest rapidly declining. The exhibition was much more varied and interesting than it had ever been before; but the novelty was gone by, it had ceased to be fashionable. The doors were no longer crowded with carriages; and the works of the artists remained on the walls unsold. Spoiled with success, and panic-struck at this reverse of fortune, the members called a general meeting, at which it was agreed to dissolve the society. Twelve men more courageous than the rest, immediately united. These were Barret, Cristall, Fielding, Glover, Havell, Holworthy, Nicholson, Smith, William Turner, Uwins, Cornelius Varley, and John Varley. These artists then added to their number David Cox, Miss Gouldsmith, Holmes, Linnell, Mackenzie, and Richter; and the exhibition was continued for two or three years with indifferent success. The seceding members opened in 1814 "An Exhibition of Paintings in Water-Colours" in New Bond Street, to which they invited the contributions of the artists of the United Kingdom, who were unconnected with any other society; but, so far as we can learn, this exhibition did not extend to a second year.

It is now difficult, when considering the very distinguished artists who were at that time members of the original society, and the fine works they were then producing, to account for its failure. The public were, we fear, unable to appreciate the high merit of their works, and they were patronized for a time as fashionable novelties, only to be neglected when fashion was tired of them. It is well that art now rests on a broader basis, though by fashion, or more frequently the speculations of dealers, artists occasionally obtain a false and ill-earned temporary reputation.

The old society was reformed in 1821, and shortly afterwards, Mr. Robson, one of the most zealous members, taking advantage of the alterations at Charing Cross, secured, on his own responsibility, the convenient premises the society now occupies in Pall Mall East. The first exhibition was opened there in 1823, and from that time there has, we believe, been no interruption to the continued and well-merited

N

prosperity of the society. Its peculiar charm has always been the select character of its exhibitions, arising from their exclusiveness.

The society, which is now styled The Royal Society of Painters in Water-Colours, by its elections has always wisely endeavoured to include men whose practice of the art is varied. Landscape painters, animal painters, figure and subject painters are among its members. By its judicious selection it has, since it moved into its present home, gone on in an uninterrupted course of prosperity, its exhibitions always attractive, the sale of the works constant. The only change being the gradual loss of its old members by death, and the rising of a new race, differing from the old in their views of art, in their methods of execution, their choice of subjects, as well as in their modes of imitating nature. We who live in remembrance of some of the glories of the early exhibitions, may at times feel a lingering regret at the change ; but a candid consideration of the present state of the art leads us to the conclusion that, though changed, the talent of the living painters quite supports the reputation achieved for the society by those who have passed away.

It has always been the policy of the society to absorb the rising talent of the water-colour school, and by this means to maintain its general superiority : as any new genius arose, he was at the first opportunity elected an associate exhibitor, and finally, a member of the society. But it was also found advisable to limit the number of members ; and as the time arrived when the spread of art rendered it impossible, under this condition, to admit many men whose talent could not be questioned, a powerful body remained outside. This led in 1831 to the foundation of "The New Society of Painters in Water-Colours," which in 1833 took the name of "The Associated Painters in Water-Colours," and which after several changes in its constitution is now amalgamated with a body of painters who exhibited at the Dudley Gallery; its name being now the Royal Institute of Painters in Water-Colours. It differs from the other society as it wisely admits outsiders to the benefits of its exhibitions. It is located in Prince's Hall, Piccadilly.

Some account of "*The Sketching Society*" cannot be omitted, and it connects itself most appropriately with the subject of this chapter. Its professed object was the study of epic and pastoral design, with which, in practice, good-fellowship and the love of art-gossip were largely associated. The idea arose with the two brothers Chalon and Francis Stevens. The society was founded on the 6th January (Twelfth day), 1808. The rules were simple : the number of members was limited to eight, and the president had the privilege of introducing one visitor. They met at each other's houses in rotation weekly, during the season, the host of the evening being the president, and privileged to name the subject, which, after a cup of tea or coffee, he announced, and at eight o'clock the members began their impromptu designs. Then, after two hours so employed, at ten o'clock the members sat down to supper—at first a very simple repast, but, as in all like cases, by degrees so luxurious that attempts were made to restrain it by sumptuary laws. After supper, the president submitted each member's sketch for criticism and judgment. The first members were (in the order of precedence determined by lot) William Turner of Oxford, Alfred Edward Chalon, Thomas Webster (the author of *Elements of Science and Art*), Michael Sharp, Francis Stevens, Cornelius Varley, John James Chalon, with Henry P. Bone, added at the second meeting.

The subjects selected were of the most varied character; above one hundred were from the Bible. On two occasions the Queen, who felt great interest in the works of the society, sent them sealed subjects, " Desire" and " Elevation." After supper came the criticism of the works, which occasioned many merry quips and jokes in which truths were told, and many grave meanings and true art-judgments were given. The society, in its fortieth year, quietly ceased to exist in 1848. The sketches made at the house of each member in succession became his property, and it was contrary to the rules of the society to alienate them in any way; but in the last few years they have found their way into the auction-room and the shops of the dealers, where some have realized large prices.

CHAPTER XVII.

THIS chapter we purpose to devote exclusively to the distinguished men who were the founders of the Water-Colour Society. They all began and ended their career as painters in water-colour, and whether as painters of landscape, landscape and figures, or as animal painters, each established a manner peculiarly original, and his own; each was as unlike the other, and as distinct in his treatment of nature, as in his modes of execution. We do not know how to assign a due precedence, and have therefore spoken of them in chronological order.

George Barret was the son of the landscape painter of the same name, who was distinguished in his day, and who was a foundation member of the Royal Academy. Notwithstanding the large income the father made by his art, on his death in 1784, he left a large family in great difficulties, and dependent upon the charitable funds of the Academy. The son must have been very young when his father died. We can find no trace of the date of his birth, or of his first beginnings in art, but he did not exhibit till 1795, eleven years after his father's death. His first pictures were a view of a gentleman's seat in Yorkshire, and a scene on Loch Lomond, followed next year (1796) by a view of Lord Grantley's seat, the horses by Sawry Gilpin, and a scene in the Highlands, the portraits by Reinagle, the horses again by Gilpin.

The young painter evidently began life surrounded with troubles, but he continued to labour with patient exertion—and to exhibit one or two works yearly at the Royal Academy up to 1803; but in that and the two following years we miss his name in the catalogue. In 1805 he joined the Society of Painters in Water-Colours on its formation, and from that time his chief works appear on the walls of the society, though he occasionally sent a picture, sometimes a painting in oil, to the Royal Academy. He was of frugal and industrious habits, and though poor, he aimed more at excellence in his art than at gain. Though an unremitting exhibitor at the Water-Colour Society during thirty-eight years, his pictures did not average fifteen yearly. These were mostly effects of light, sunset, evening, the mists of sunrise, moonlight, and twilight; many of which subjects were sought on the Thames, and in the picturesque environs of the metropolis. He painted a few, but very few scenes in Wales, and on the Sussex coast; but born in Paddington, he lived all his days there, and seldom wandered far to find his subjects, or to seek his inspirations in art.

In 1830, and again in 1831, he painted a subject in conjunction with Cristall, and in 1834-35 and 1836 several pictures with Mr. F. Tayler. His works were classic in feeling, and poetic in their treatment. Even the "views" by his hand are so subjected to the *treatment* adopted— the hour and the time, the flood of sunlight, the mists of morn or dewy eve, as to render that subject ideal, which in other hands would be merely prosaic and commonplace. Latterly his pictures were mostly "compositions," in which, if we trace the influence of Claude and Poussin, it is so subjected to the painter's own feeling, as not to deprive his works of their originality. Extended landscapes, with ruins and rocks, wood and water, a few goats in the foreground tended by a goatherd, the whole bathed in the hazy atmosphere of the declining sun; or groves of massive trees, their dark stems and the deep shadows on the grassy floor beneath them, contrasted with the sunny glade beyond, figures seated in the broad shade, and partaking of the hue of the pervading gloom —such were the themes he latterly delighted in. A certain solemn monotony of colour pervaded his pictures, necessitated by the effect he sought to produce, and this removed the subjects quite out of the region of the imitative or the meretricious. His works require careful conservation, as they are inclined to fade if too much exposed, but they will always be esteemed since they occupy a field the painter made his own.

Barret was of a liberal nature, and, struggling with difficulties himself, endeavoured to clear them from the path of others. We well remember in our student days, his being questioned by a group of young artists, in what was then called the Angerstein Gallery where he was copying a picture, as to his mode of painting. He willingly explained to them his practice, and declared that no good painter ought to have "secrets." "Every thing is in the painter's feeling," said he; "without feeling, all the secrets in the world are worthless."

He died in 1842, some time before May, we gather, but no particulars of his private and professional life were made known; a long illness, the loss of his eldest son just growing into manhood, added to pecuniary embarrassments, we fear, hastened his death, and probably the dark shadows by which his latter days were surrounded, prevented any published notice of his life.

John Varley, also one of the original founders of the Society, was born in London on the 17th August, 1778, in the neighbourhood of Hackney. His father objected to the lad's taking up art as a profession; he thought it a bad business, and declared none of his children should follow it. But the stars ordained otherwise. John was sent on *liking* to a silversmith, with the intention to bind him apprentice to that trade. But the father's death intervening, he managed to free himself from the engagement, and was able to obtain some employment—we hardly know what it could be—with a portrait painter. As he advanced in years he grew a strong and resolute youth, able to endure much fatigue of body and mind, and went to work when about sixteen with an architectural draughtsman. Young Varley had to be at the office at eight o'clock every morning, and the work of the day was very trying; yet such was his enthusiasm for art, and his desire to improve himself, that when daylight permitted, he always had two hours' sketching in the morning before proceeding to his office, the carts and barrows in the streets, and the characteristic figures with which at that early hour they are peopled, forming subjects for his pencil. With his master he made a journey to sketch the principal buildings in the towns they visited, and gained some credit for a view of Peterborough Cathedral. This he exhibited at the Royal Academy in 1798, which is the first time his name occurs in the catalogue.

He was one of the class of young painters that met continually at the house of Dr. Munro in the Adelphi, and was consequently early thrown into the company of the two rising water-colour painters, Turner and Girtin, the latter of whom Varley took for his model; and the impression Girtin made upon him lasted through life, rather leading Varley to disparage the art of his other companion Turner. In 1799, Varley made a sketching tour in North Wales, in company with George Arnold, the landscape painter, who afterwards became an associate of the Academy. Here Varley had found the true field for the exercise of his art. He made numerous sketches and studies of the mountain scenery, revisited Wales in 1800, and again in 1802, and afterwards, Northumberland, Yorkshire, and other parts of England.

In 1803 John Varley married one of three sisters who all became the wives of men of reputation. One married Muzio Clementi of musical celebrity, and the founder of a large pianoforte manufactory; the other, Copley Fielding, the president of the Water-Colour Society. Varley exhibited at the Royal Academy, in 1804, the last time for a long term of years. On the foundation of the Society of Painters in Water-Colours, he joined them, and to their first exhibition, in 1805, he sent forty-two paintings, mostly Welsh subjects, except four or five, which were York-shire views. In the following year he contributed many works, some of them styled compositions, many, no doubt, hasty works done as lessons before pupils. He sent in all, no less than 344 works in eight years, showing rapidity and application, but leading to sad repetitions of manner and subject. What wonder that there are so many inferior works by his hand, and that he became insipid and commonplace! He searched the prints and etchings of the old masters for portions to introduce into his compositions, and repeated his sketches with varied stock-foregrounds. Nevertheless, when he laid himself out to do his best, and when he studied his subjects on the spot, his pictures have qualities that we find in no other painters,—freshness, clearness, largeness of manner, and a classical air, even in the most common and matter-of-fact subjects.

In 1813 a change was made in the constitution of the Water-Colour Society, and several of the old members seceded ; but Varley was not of these. He clung to the society through all its vicissitudes and changes. From the opening of the Water-Colour Gallery, Varley ceased to exhibit at the Royal Academy, and up to 1825 no work of his appeared on the Academy walls. In that year he is again an exhibitor, and with the exception of three years only, he was a regular contributor to the time of his death. One or two of his works were, we believe, in oil. His last work was a drawing from the well-known cedar-trees in the Botanical Gardens at Chelsea, which are seen from the Thames in all their funereal grandeur. He had suffered from an affection of the kidneys, and probably allured by a remembrance of the old trees, he sat down to sketch them and had a relapse. He was unable to reach home, and died in a friend's house on the 17th November, 1842.

Varley was a great enthusiast in all he undertook, and, like all enthusiasts, communicated the feeling to those around him : many stories are told in illustration of this ; among others, that being engaged to teach in Bedford Square, not only his pupils, but even the very servants took brush and paper to try their skill at landscape painting. Varley, knocking at the door on one occasion, was delayed a minute or two, and when the servant opened it, the painter found that the delay had been occasioned by John's being engaged, at the moment, washing in a sky at the hall table ; the work did not please Varley, so he stopped on his way to the parlour, seized the brush, and immediately began to exemplify the necessary changes in the work before him.

He was very kind to young artists, often giving them gratuitous instruction ; lending and even giving them drawings and sketches. Of the value of this instruction, we have the best evidence in the artists he formed. W. H. Hunt and William Turner of Oxford, together with John Linnell and Oliver Finch, were his pupils ; the two former—if not the latter—having been apprenticed to him. A man who could turn out two such pupils as W. Hunt and J. Linnell must have had something to teach as well as a good method of imparting knowledge.

From his pictures we should say that Varley was a perfect master of the rules of composition, and applied them in his best works with great genius—perhaps relying too much on them in his mere stock-in-trade drawings. Many pithy sayings remembered by his pupils, clearly inculcate art truths. Thus his remark that " nature wants cooking," no doubt implies in a terse way that the painter must not take nature merely as he finds her, but, by selection and arrangement, must make her palatable. Again, he would say, " Every picture ought to have a look-there !" a point of interest to which the eye should at once be carried—something that having impressed itself upon the painter's mind, it was his business to impress also upon the spectator. He used jokingly to say that every landscape ought to compose in the form of a cross ; perhaps implying the predominance of some object in the foreground on one side of the picture, over every object on the other side. Some one, taking him too literally, objected that there were subjects in nature in which this was an impossibility, and made a rude sketch of Waterloo Bridge with the shot tower rising high above it, remarking triumphantly, " Where is the cross in this composition ? " "Ah," said Varley, quietly, " you have forgotten the reflection in the water," and taking the pencil, he dashed in the dark under the tower, and the cross was complete. He likened the deliberate progression of oil painting to philosophy, while water-colour painting was, he said, to be assimilated to wit, which loses more by deliberation than is gained in truth.

Varley was a man of large, liberal, and genial character, full of conversation on many topics, brilliant on all, witty in his command of apt analogies. One who was his pupil writes, " I scarcely remember any man upon whom we might make a call with more certainty of half an hour's refined amusement and instruction ; " and his wife adds, " he was very kind to children, taking great interest in their childish attempts. I remember him with his laughing, rosy, good-natured face, telling his stories to my father and to the delighted wonderment of his children." In the latter part of his life, he fell into difficulties arising from the bad management of his household, and not in any way from extravagance, self-indulgence, or indolence on his part, for he was ever temperate, energetic, and a hard-worker. " Sometimes that he might get on with his work," says a friend, " his dinner was sent into his study. There lay together in a pleasant confusion, 'curious books,' deep twilights, and fruit pie ; a bit snatched now and then in the intervals of very solemn talk about tolling curfews, setting moons, or Macbeth's castle in its *inspissated gloom.*"

Varley said his domestic difficulties, which would have worried any other man into his grave, were beneficial to him, as just preventing him from being *too* happy. The Vicar of Wakefield had a pleasant way of getting rid of troublesome poor relations, by lending them a great-coat or an umbrella, which the vicar knew would secure their absence for the future. Varley had an equally original way of getting paid by rich, but forgetful debtors,—a way he used to say which saved the unpleasantness of law. "I send in a new bill," said the painter, "making a mistake in the amount of a guinea or two *against myself*, and the money comes in directly." Every one who has heard anything of Varley has heard of his enthusiasm for astrology; there is no doubt he was shrewd enough to see, as indeed he was candid enough to own, that his astrology was one of the great causes of his popularity as a drawing-master. "Ladies come to take drawing lessons," said he, "that they may get their nativities cast," but there is no doubt also that he was to a certain point sincere in his belief of his astrological powers, and many curious coincidences between his predictions and the event are related by his friends and pupils. We have told how he predicted the marriage of Sir Augustus Callcott, and he seems also to have cast the nativity of Cotman : who, by the way, was as eccentric as Varley, and a man of genius also. Varley calling one day to inquire about his friend, who was very ill, learnt that the doctor had given him over and that he was dying; to which he replied, "Nonsense, he won't die these ten years," and, being taken into the sick man's room, he addressed him : "Why, Cotman, you are not such a fool as to think you are dying? No such thing, the stars tell another story," and his friend recovered. Mr. Linnell mentions that one day the stars revealing to Varley that he was in danger from *water*, he would not go out, thinking it safest to remain in the house ; but, towards evening, he fulfilled the prediction by falling over a pail of water and wounding his leg. A friend introduced a young artist to Varley—an utter stranger—and the painter at once proceeded to cast his nativity: "Some very unpleasant affair must just have happened to you, some disagreement with a man of florid complexion, light sandy hair, &c.," and the stranger looked utterly astonished, for he owned that Varley was accurately describing a man with whom he had just quarrelled.

It is said that he was thrice burnt out of his house, and that on one of these occasions, instead of exerting himself to remove his goods, he merely remarked, "The fire is not *destined* to go beyond the study which it is now consuming." All this serves to mark the character of the man, but it distracted his attention from the proper pursuit of his profession.

Varley wrote a *Treatise on Zodiacal Physiognomy*, besides works really relating to his profession, such as *Observations on Colouring and Sketching from Nature* in 1830, and *A Practical Treatise on Perspective.*

Varley's compositions have few parts; the details are passed over, and great breadth and simplicity is the result. Varley's tints are beautifully laid, with a full and free pencil, and stippling is not resorted to, to flatten the masses; but he said that he got very fine qualities and suggestions in his skies by pumping vigorously upon them; yet the washing is not apparent, the tints of clouds being generally very sharply defined, and this is the case also with his foliage, which is massive and large, rather than imitative; he oftentimes resorted to taking out the light in his foliage with bread, but did not use body colour in his best works. He usually painted ordinary sun-light, and summer foliage rather than autumnal tints, seldom treating sunsets, or what are called effects. He was very happy in the introduction of figures to his landscapes, so as to lead the eye to the interesting point, the "look there" of his picture. He loved to have children around him when sketching from nature, and often encouraged their gambols by cakes and scrambles for half-pence. Thus he never wanted models, and was able to see them at all points of his subject, and to determine where they could most appropriately be introduced into the picture. In his latter years he practised a new mode of execution, which seemed to produce great richness and power, but wanted the freshness and purity of his works in the earlier manner. This new mode consisted in laying down a sheet of whitey-brown over hard white paper, painting the subject richly on the low-toned surface paper, and then rubbing away for the high lights down to the pure white paper; thus he gained great tone, combined with brilliancy, but it was meretricious and was a bad exchange for his earlier and simpler manner. His art has influenced his pupils throughout life, and it may justly be said that in their practice linger most of those great truths that have been acknowledged by all the best painters; and which, if they are ignored for a time for mere imitative art, will have to be revived, and again become dogmas if we are to again have great artists in our school.

William Henry Pyne, another of the foundation members of the Water-Colour Society, is better known by his art publications than by his paintings. He was the son of a tradesman in Holborn, where young Pyne was born in 1769. He practised various branches of art in watercolours, and was by turns a portrait, a landscape, and a figure painter. In 1803, two years before the formation of the society, Pyne published a work which he called *A Microcosm, or Picturesque Delineation of the Arts, Agriculture, Manufactures, &c., of Great Britain.* It is an oblong folio, containing many hundred groups, and rustic figures, utensils, &c.,

etched and aqua-tinted—a kind of store-house for amateur painters to glean aid from in making up their pictures.   Pyne was a great lover of society, and associating much with his brother artists, was full of anecdotes of them and of their art.   His publications and the connection they brought him into with publishers, led him to forsake art for authorship.   He was the author of a series of chatty and agreeable papers, which he named *Wine and Walnuts,* and he afterwards projected and edited a clever gossiping serial, *The Somerset House Gazette,* to which we have been occasionally indebted, and which deserved a longer existence than it was fated to obtain.   It was only continued for two years, when it was merged into the *Literary Chronicle.*   Two of Pyne's sons followed the arts.   One of them married a daughter of John Varley. Pyne himself died in 1843.

In considering an artist's works it is always desirable to know what were the causes that led him to adopt art as his profession.   Hence, his birthplace and parentage, the influences that surrounded him in his youth, the master who taught him and the intimates and associates who formed his taste, all his local surroundings have an interest.   Strange to say, though so short a time has elapsed since many of the founders of our water-colour school have passed from us, the facts of their early life which may now be collected, are, in most cases, very meagre, while all that relates to them is too often entirely forgotten.   Thus it is with *Robert Hills,* the animal painter, of whom we merely know that he was born at Islington on the 26th of June, 1769, and that at school he received some instruction in art from John Gresse, noted for his corpulency.   This John or "Jack Grease," as he was called by his brother artists, was a drawing-master of fashionable repute, who taught, among others, the princesses, daughters of George III., and often had the honour of a gossip with his Majesty.   We know nothing of the profit derived from his instruction by young Hills, who must have commenced art early in life, since, in 1791, when only twenty-one years of age, we find him contributing to the exhibition of the Royal Academy, " A Wood Scene with Gipsies," and, in 1792, "A Landscape."   No doubt, with other artists, he was dissatisfied with the treatment water-colour art necessarily received then, as after this he ceased to be an exhibitor ; and we find his name among the six painters who met at Shelley's rooms to form the Water-Colour Society.   He was one of the first members, and was for many years their secretary.   To their exhibition he was a constant contributor until 1818, when, from some cause, he ceased to contribute until 1823.

Hills died at No. 17 Golden Square, on the 14th of May, 1844, when he had nearly attained his seventy-fifth year.   He was buried at Kensal Green.

He was a diligent student of nature and untiring in collecting materials for his art; his studies of animals amount to several hundreds. Many of these he etched with great skill, and between 1798 and 1835 he published etchings of nearly 800 animals and groups of animals in every variety of action and fore-shortening, treated with great delicacy of outline and careful definition of form. A bronze statue of a red deer modelled by Hills in terra-cotta in 1817, and afterwards wrought by him in bronze, was to be seen in the great Exhibition of 1862, and is a proof how easily the artist who has obtained a thorough knowledge of his subject can overcome the difficulty of expressing it in a material foreign to his usual practice.

Hills's handling and mode of execution were totally unlike the felicitous ease of Landseer, or the dashing freedom of Frederick Tayler. His art is patiently elaborated—the labour bestowed evident and undisguised. He never seems to have worked direct from nature, but from his various studies, these being mostly drawings. Thus that clear, truthful touch that is obtained by working with nature before us, is wholly wanting; in some of his earlier works the handling is less laboured; in all his latter works the animals—nay, even the backgrounds—have a woolly texture that is very disagreeable. Again, painting from drawings has prevented that attention to the accidents of relief so observable in objects seen out of doors or in sunlight, and we miss those subtle interchanges of light and dark, of form lost and found, that may be stored from repeated observations, but are apt to escape us when working apart from nature. Hills generally gives the characteristic actions of the animals with great truth—particularly of his deer; these he evidently loved to paint more than any other animal. He often worked in conjunction with Barret and with Robson.

The professors of the new art of water-colour painting were mostly landscape painters, but the society was fortunate in numbering among its founders *Joshua Cristall*, a figure and a landscape painter, whose works served to give diversity and contrast to their exhibitions. He was the son of Alexander Cristall, the master of a small vessel trading to the ports of the Mediterranean, and was born at Camborne in Cornwall, in 1767.

His mother was well educated, a lady of enthusiastic temperament, full of love for poetry, and for the mythic lore of classic antiquity. She devoted herself to the education of her son, and from her he early imbibed that classical taste which throughout life characterized his works. A friend of his father's offered to adopt young Cristall, and to take him into his business, promising to leave the boy all his wealth. But Cristall hated trade, and had early resolved to be an artist. This his father opposed, and denied him the use of paper and pencils in order to overcome his propensity for drawing and painting. But Joshua found means to pursue his favourite studies ; with his scanty pocket-money he purchased Spanish liquorice, dissolved it in water, and with this colour covered the white-washed walls of his bedroom with designs and drawings, some of which are said to have been very bold and spirited, and to have indicated his future excellence. The elder Cristall removed to Rotherhithe, and engaged in business as a sail- and mast-maker, in which he was assisted and finally succeeded by a younger brother of the painter. Joshua meanwhile was apprenticed by his father to a china dealer in the Minories, but the business was so hateful to him that he quitted his apprenticeship before his term was completed. This led also to his being obliged to leave his home and to enter upon a life of great hardship. A friend recommended him to Wedgwood for employment as a china-painter, and for a time he worked in the potteries. But the mechanical repetition and reproduction required at that time by the manufacturer, was irksome to Cristall, and afforded no scope for his art or his imagination ; he returned to London, living as best he could with secret assistance from his devoted mother. During this time it is related that he seriously injured his health by endeavouring to live solely on potatoes and water, an attempt he persevered in for nearly a year. One of his sisters determined to live with him and to share his difficulties. She got work from an engraver, and by various means they endeavoured to live while he studied his art. He obtained his admittance as a student of the Royal Academy, and not only rapidly improved in his profession, but learned from his brother students many little ways of adding to his stinted income.

In the schools of the Royal Academy he must have diligently studied the antique, and entered fully into its spirit. It entirely delivered him from that tendency to littleness and prettiness which is almost inherent in water-colour art, and formed in him the large, square, and simple style which he retained through life, and which gave grandeur even to common forms and rustic figures. At this period he was one of those who frequented the house of Dr. Munro—the practising academy in which so many of our best water-colour artists were formed. Cristall's diligence and love of his art overcame all obstacles to his progress, and gradually won for him reputation and success. He was one of the six original members of the Water-Colour Society. Though he had studied the figure, and loved figure subjects, he also painted landscapes, marine subjects, and occasionally portraits, so that he sent a great variety of works to the new exhibition.

His works were not numerous : between 1805 and 1821 he exhibited 223 pictures, or on an average about thirteen per annum. In 1821 we find him invested with the office of president; this he held until 1831, when he was succeeded by Copley Fielding. Whilst living at Maida Hill, the painter, about the year 1812, became acquainted with Miss Cozens. She had been left an orphan, and brought up by her aunt, a lady who kept a large school at the Old Manor House, Paddington Green, then a quaint and rural suburb. The aunt sent her niece to France, in exchange for the daughter of a French nobleman, by whose family Miss Cozens was much beloved and treated as a second daughter. At the breaking out of the French Revolution, the château where they resided was attacked by a revolutionary mob, and the family made prisoners, the ladies being sent to Paris, and Miss Cozens with them. After a time she had the good fortune to escape as an American, and, passing through Germany, joined her aunt in England, and eventually succeeded her in the school. This lady Cristall married in 1813 ; her cultivated mind and lively French manners, together with his talents, made their society much sought after, and their house became the resort of the musicians, authors, and artists of the day.

Mrs. Cristall, who thought her husband's works not sufficiently finished, urged upon him greater completion, and also tried to induce him to recommence portraits. Her influence prevailed for a time, but he afterwards returned to his own special subjects and broad manner of treating them. About the year 1821, Cristall's health failing, his wife proposed a country residence ; and by the advice of their friend, Mr. Meyrick of Goodrich Castle, they bought a cottage in that lovely neighbourhood, to which they removed some time in 1822. There the painter passed many happy years, closed at last by the lingering illness of his wife, whose death made Goodrich distasteful to him. He was childless, and in 1840 he again returned to London, and took up his abode in Robert Street, Hampstead Road, and sought to renew his intimacy with his brother artists and old associates. He had continued the practice of his art, and, with the exception of the year 1832, his annual contributions to the water-colour exhibition. On his return to London he found the art-world astir, and artists of all ages entering vigorously into the competition proposed by the Government for the decoration of the Houses of Parliament. Notwithstanding his advanced age, Cristall prepared to join in the struggle for honours and rewards ; but leaving a party at the house of Mr. Rogers, he was knocked down by the carelessness of a cab-driver, in crossing one of the crowded streets of his own neighbourhood. Although he recovered from the accident it incapacitated him from labouring on a large cartoon, and he abandoned the competition. He removed to Circus Road, St. John's Wood, where he died, 18th of October, 1847. One of his Herefordshire friends, who happened to be in London, watched by his bedside the last three days and nights of his illness ; and at his own request, Cristall was buried near his wife at

Goodrich. What little property he had was left to two very faithful servants, who had lived many years with him and his wife.

We have already said that Cristall was a good draughtsman, and that his style served to give dignity to the practice of water-colour painting. If we cannot wholly free him from the charge of mannerism, it was of a nature to give his work a separate and distinct character. His art was large and simple, and entirely free from prettiness and insipidity. In his execution he made but little use of the new processes by which finesse of execution is sought and obtained. He used his brush with freedom, and laid on flat and clear tints, not resorting much to stippling or washing ; taking out his lights broadly, but carefully avoiding the use of body colours. Thus his pictures are wholly transparent, like those of all the best painters of his day. He was, when resident in London, a member of the Sketching Society, of which mention has been made.

John Glover, whose art forms a link between the early practice of water-colour painting, and that which obtains in our day, was the son of poor parents. He was born at Houghton-on the-Hill in Leicestershire, on the 18th February, 1767. Brought up in a small village in the midland counties, there seemed little to lead him to the pursuit of art. He received a plain education, suitable to his station, of which art-teaching formed no part. Yet we are told that, as a mere child, drawing was his delight, and that every scrap of paper he could obtain was filled with his designs. He seemed to have made good use of his school teaching, nevertheless, for in 1786 he was elected master of the Free School at Appleby, and in his leisure hours not only studied art, but cultivated music with some success. His mind, however, ran too much upon art for him to be contented with general teaching, and about 1794 he removed to Lichfield, and gave up all his time to art, and to art-instruction. Up to this period he had painted only in water-colours, but now he began to work in oil, in which he afterwards met with great success. We are told also that he produced some etched plates ; but these have not come under our notice. Glover's practice in water-colours was founded on that of William Payne of Plymouth. Many of his early works are laid in with Payne's grey, and the colour is tinted over this preparation. Like Payne, he was tricky in his execution ; his foliage was wrought by splitting the hairs of his brush, which gives a clever lightness and facility of handling, and a sense of ease in execution, but is apt to result in a great sameness throughout the foliage. This manner he continued to practise after the art had advanced to newer methods in the hands of other painters. Like Payne, he delighted in startling accidental effects, and was very clever in introducing into his pictures sun-rays bursting through clouds or through foliage.

His style seems to have pleased the public, who are soon attracted by any peculiarity or novelty. His works became widely known, and his reputation as an artist was established. So much so, that at the foundation of the Society of Painters in Water-Colours, of which he was one of the promoters, he sent nineteen pictures to the first exhibition in 1805.

On the restoration of the Bourbon family he visited Paris, extending his journey to Switzerland and Italy, and gathering studies for future subjects. He now almost wholly abandoned water-colour painting, and spread large canvases for pictures in oil, for which he was enabled to obtain what at that time was thought very large prices. His terms as a teacher are said to have been very exorbitant. The world, as usual, thought his peculiar manner was a secret, that, once obtained, the possessor could exercise with equal effect. It was Glover's practice to spend the entire day with his pupil, executing a small work in his presence, which was left for a time for the student to repeat, but was afterwards a further source of profit to the painter.

He emigrated to Tasmania in March, 1831, and set up his easel amid scenery wholly different from that he had left ; some few of his works were purchased in the colony and others he sent to England, where it was expected that the novelty of the scenery would prove a charm ; but topography is widely separated from art : it is not the scenery, but the mode of realizing it to the spectator, the mode of presenting it with all the force of the artist's mind, that makes the picture a work of art. Glover's *manner* had become somewhat stale before he left England, and no adaptation of worked-up effects to new scenes, could revive its interest. His works excited no attention, and found no purchasers in England. For several of the latter years of his life he painted but little, passing his time in peace and tranquillity among his children and grandchildren. He died on the 9th December, 1849, aged eighty-two years. The impression he made in his day was more that of successful novelty than of art-excellence, and art was but little advanced by him.

William Havell has well sustained the reputation to which his knowledge of art and his early works justly entitle him. He was the third son in a family of eight boys and six girls, and was born at Reading on the 9th February, 1782. His father was a drawing-master, but the pressure of a large family made it necessary to seek some addition to his small professional earnings, and he engaged in a retail business in the town. William Havell was sent early in life to the grammar-school at Reading, of which Dr. Valpy was then the head master. His father was the drawing-master at the school. His son continued there several years, and gained a good classical education which fitted him for a better position than his birth and family prospects promised him.

Dwelling in a country town with many sons to provide for and little means of placing them out in life, his father—when young Havell left school—wished him to follow his business rather than to adopt his art. He had felt, as who engaged in teaching has not, the incessant toil, the exposure to all weathers, the uncertainty of engagements, and the small remuneration of a country teacher, and he thought the certainty of trade afforded a better prospect; but the youth thought otherwise, and sought every opportunity secretly to improve himself in drawing. Being surprised by his father, on one occasion while finishing a sketch, the latter was so much struck with the artistic feeling it displayed that he saw it would be no longer right to oppose his son's decided inclination. Henceforth he was permitted to study openly. He received every help from his father, and was aided to make a journey to Wales in pursuit of his art. He returned with a large number of sketches, and with deep and vivid impressions of the marvellous effects of cloud and air in mountain scenery. We first trace young Havell as exhibitor in the catalogues of the Royal Academy in 1804 and 1805, after this he became a member of the Society of Painters in Water-Colours.

His sister Lucy, in a short biography of her brother, tells us that in 1807 Havell went to Westmoreland, and that in order to study the scenery thoroughly, he took a cottage at Ambleside, and remained more than twelve months. In this time he painted many of his finest water-colour works. She says that " from this date until he left for China in 1816, he was in the height of his prosperity." Meanwhile he had lived occasionally with a married sister at Hastings, and in 1810-11 came to Reading to assist his father, whose declining health prevented him from continuing his professional teaching in that neighbourhood.

When changes took place in the Water-Colour Society in 1813, Havell seceded from it, although he annually sent one or two pictures for exhibition until he left England. When the embassy to China, under Lord Amherst, was determined on, Havell was appointed to accompany it as an artist, and sailed in the *Alceste* on the 9th July, 1816. His journal, full of descriptions of character and scenery, is still in the possession of his sister. Unfortunately, Havell did not agree with the officers with whom he messed, and having gravely offended one of them and refused him the satisfaction demanded, his position was rendered exceedingly unpleasant, and Sir Murray Maxwell being detached with his ship to India, Havell was glad to accept his offer of a passage there, and left the embassy at Macao. He spent a fortnight at Manilla and landed at Penang, the scenery of which struck him from its extreme richness. Here he was invited to remain, and would have had full employment for his talents, but fearing to lose the good introductions he had obtained for Calcutta, he determined to proceed, and reached that Presidency on the 4th April, 1817. In a letter written shortly after, he appears to have been highly satisfied with his prospects; he was in full employment, chiefly painting small portraits in water-colours, and hoping to realize a purse for his return. He remained in India until 1825, but soon found that if there was ample employment the terms were inadequate to pay the expenses of travelling from place to place, and to maintain an establishment suitable to his position and the costly style of living. An attack of fever following cholera determined him to return to his native country. Though without the fortune he had expected in the sanguine days of his arrival, he had realized a small sum as a provision for the future.

In 1827, he re-entered the Water-Colour Society, and the same year he visited Florence, Rome, and Naples. For two years he continued to exhibit works in water colour, but he had begun to devote himself to oil, and after 1828 his pictures are no longer in the society's catalogue; and in 1830 his name disappears from the list of members, to re-appear in the list of exhibitors of the Royal Academy as a contributor of works in oil, mostly from Italian sources. He continued to exhibit there until 1857, the year of his death.

After his return from abroad Havell lived at 16 Bayswater Terrace, where his sister kept house for him until her death in 1853. This was a sad shock to him. He had lost most of his early friends by death and absence, and his future prospects, owing to money losses, were far from encouraging. To add to his troubles, his house was robbed, and among other valuables a number of his drawings and unsold works were stolen from the walls. On this occasion the aid of the police was sought, and a knowing detective, who, however, had not added connoisseurship to his other attainments, supplied with one of Havell's drawings as an example, was sent round to pawnbrokers and dealers in search of the lost works. Entering a shop of this kind in Wardour Street, he asked, "Have you purchased any pictures like this lately?" The dealer, struck by the work exhibited, exclaimed at once, "Ah, a fine Havell! a very fine Havell!" The detective, whose suspicions were aroused by the recognition, replied, "Ah, yes, a Havell true enough; but how the devil came you to know that it is a Havell?" Eventually the drawings were discovered at a pawnbroker's at Paddington, and the artist was more hurt by the fact that only two or three shillings had been obtained upon his best works, than he had been by their loss, notwithstanding its importance to him.

His health declined, and having gone to his native place for a change of air too late in the season, be returned in a weakened state, and gradually became worse. On his death-bed he made a gift of what little remained of his property, to two of his remaining sisters, and died 16th December, 1857. He was buried at Kensal Green, where a simple stone has been erected to his memory.

It is for his early connection with water-colour art that we have introduced in our work a memoir of Havell. He aided to lift the art out of the littleness of the topographic school. His early manner was large and massive, suppressing unimportant details, and treating the picture for its general effect. His oil pictures have much excellence, for though rather yellow in hue, and somewhat monotonous, the effect of sunshine is admirably given ; the picture is usually well composed and arranged, while these works are at least marked by a distinct and characteristic style.

To complete this chapter we must notice *Francis Nicholson,* born at Pickering in Yorkshire on 14th November, 1753, of a family well known as the possessors of a small property in that neighbourhood. After two visits to London, he settled at Whitby, where he continued nearly ten years. He then resided for a time at Knaresborough, and subsequently at Ripon, and afterwards came to London and established himself as an artist. We find no information as to how or when he began art, and can only trace that he first exhibited at the Royal Academy in 1789, "A View of Castle Howard."

His practice was in water-colours, and he must have made good progress in 1804, to have then been accepted as one of the members of the Water-Colour Society. But his art, though highly respectable, and showing much power, never attained excellence. He published *The Practice of Drawing and Painting Landscapes from Nature.* He devoted much time to the advancement of lithography, giving up the practice of his own art, and having acquired a competency, only worked for his pleasure, amusing himself with experiments in painting, and the use of different vehicles, and at the advanced age of ninety-one years, died in Charlotte Street, Portland Place, on the 4th March, 1844.

CHAPTER XVIII.

SIR THOMAS LAWRENCE, P.R.A.

THOMAS LAWRENCE, afterwards Sir Thomas, and the fourth president of the Royal Academy, was born at Bristol on the 4th of May, 1769. His father was the son of a clergyman, and although originally bred to the law, was at the time of his son's birth, the landlord of the White Lion Inn, in that city; his mother was a daughter of the vicar of Tenbury. The marriage of the parents of the painter had been somewhat clandestine, and Mrs. Lawrence was disowned by her family on that account; she seems to have been a woman of much refinement and sweetness of disposition, and was hardly fitted for the hostess of an inn. In 1772, when young Lawrence was about three years of age, the father having failed in his business in Bristol, removed to Devizes, and was aided by his friends to take the Black Bear Inn, in that town. These were the days when all travelling was comparatively slow, and when all the better class travelled post; and as Devizes was on the high road to Bath, then the great centre of fashionable resort when the London season was over, the Black Bear, the principal inn, was the resting-place of most of the visitors to that city of waters.

Young Lawrence, as a child, was eminently beautiful; by his father's zealous teaching he had committed many fine passages from our poets to memory, and was able to repeat them with much taste and innate feeling; added to this he early developed a power of sketching likenesses, and would readily pencil either the profile or full face of those who sat to him. The father was very proud of his child's beauty and precocity, and would often introduce him to his guests to exhibit his talents.

Lawrence's biographer tells us that in 1775, Mr., subsequently Lord Kenyon, arrived with his lady late in the evening at Devizes. After the fatigues of travelling—slow enough in those days—they were not in the best possible humour when the innkeeper entered their sitting-room, and proposed to show them his wonderful child; he told them his boy was only five years old and could take their likeness or repeat to them any speech in Milton's "Pandemonium." To that place the offended guests were on the eve of commending their host, when the child rushed in ; and as Lady Kenyon used to relate, her vexation and anger were suddenly changed into admiration. He was riding on a stick, and went round and round the room in the height of infantile joyousness. Mrs. Kenyon, as soon as she could get him to stand, asked the child if he could take the likeness of that gentleman, pointing to her husband. "That I can," said the little Lawrence, "and very like too." A high chair was placed on the table, pencils and paper were brought, and the infant artist soon produced an astonishingly-striking likeness. Mr. Kenyon now coaxed the child, who had got tired by the half-hour's labour, and asked him if he could take the likeness of the lady. "Yes, that I can," was his reply once more, "if she will turn her side to me, for her face is not straight"—an indication of his early sense of correct form, which produced a laugh, as it happened to be true. He accordingly took a side likeness of Mrs. Kenyon, of which it is said, that twenty-five years afterwards the likeness could still be recognized. This drawing seems to have been nearly half life-size, and delicately shaded.

Soon after this, at the age of six, young Lawrence was sent to school at Bristol for two years, at the end of which time his father's increasing difficulties occasioned his recall. These two years were all young Lawrence was allowed to devote to his education ; he not only went no more to school, but it will be found as we proceed, that he had to employ the years mostly set apart for education in making drawings and portraits. A few lessons in French, which enabled him to translate with difficulty, and the desultory instruction of his father, mostly turned towards reading and recitation, forming the only exception. The painter's education was, indeed, rather carried on by conversation with the many distinguished and cultivated persons who sat to him, or sought his society as he advanced from childhood to early manhood. Even instruction in his art was denied to him. It is said that a Devonshire baronet took such a liking to the boy that he offered to send him to Rome to study, even at the cost of a thousand pounds, but Lawrence, the father, declined, saying that "his son's talents required no cultivation." In 1779, the elder Lawrence was obliged to leave Devizes with his family ; they repaired first to Oxford, where the youth, whose fame had preceded him, found many sitters. The college dignitaries, on their way to Bath, had travelled by Devizes, and many, no doubt, had witnessed the performances of the boy-painter.

From Oxford, after a short stay at Weymouth, the Lawrence family went to Bath, where the eldest brother of the painter, who was a clergyman, had obtained the lectureship of St. Michael's, and the studio of the younger quickly became the resort of the idleness and fashion of that pleasure-town. His first works were in crayons—his charges one guinea, and one guinea and a half for heads in ovals. At Bath he became acquainted with Mr. Hoare, R.A., who was eminent in this walk of art, and highly esteemed for his crayon portraits, and Lawrence acknowledges having received much advice and assistance from him. The collection of the Hon. Mr. Hamilton, of Lansdowne Hill, afforded him the means of studying—it would appear at second hand—some of the works of the Italian painters. Lawrence made crayon copies of the "Transfiguration" of Raphael, the "Aurora" of Guido, and the "Descent from the Cross" of Daniel de Volterra. For the first of these works, done in 1783, when Lawrence was only thirteen years of age, he obtained, two years later, the silver palette of the Society of Arts. The council would have awarded the work their gold medal had the rules permitted, but this was not possible. To mark their sense of the merits of the work, however, they had the palette "gilded all over," a good omen for the young painter. Meanwhile his sitters increased, as did his prices; and he was in the habit of completing three or four portraits in each week at two or three guineas each. The beautiful Duchess of Devonshire and Mrs. Siddons were among his sitters; a portrait of the latter as Aspasia in the *Grecian Daughter* was engraved, and proved highly remunerative.

In 1787, the elder Lawrence removed with his son to London, and on the 13th of September, the young painter, then in his eighteenth year, was admitted a student of the Royal Academy. Mr. Howard, the secretary, said, "His proficiency in drawing, even at that time, was such as to leave all his competitors in the antique school far behind him. His personal attractions were as remarkable as his talent; altogether he excited a great sensation, and seemed to the admiring students as nothing less than a young Raphael suddenly dropt among them. He was very handsome, and his chestnut locks flowing on his shoulders gave him a romantic appearance." Lawrence soon after obtained his wished-for introduction to Sir Joshua Reynolds; he took with him a portrait of himself which he had painted at Bath, but with all his self-confidence he trembled as he awaited the judgment of the great president. Sir Joshua was at the moment engaged with another aspirant for fame, whom he dismissed with but negative encouragement. Young Lawrence's work, however, he regarded some time, and with great attention, then turning to him said, "Stop, young man—I must have some talk with you—I suppose, now, you think this is very fine, and this colouring very natural : hey—hey !" and then began to criticise the work and to point out its various faults. After a time he took the picture away into another room, probably to examine it more at leisure and freer from the observation of the young painter; on his return, he advised Lawrence to study nature diligently rather than the old masters, and with a general but impressive invitation to visit him often, dismissed him. Lawrence, who at once took advantage of this opening to Reynolds's house, soon became a frequent visitor, and had no occasion to feel that he trespassed on the welcome given him.

Lawrence at this time had made but few painted copies from the old masters—and had but little practical study of his art ; being warned by Reynolds of the danger of various experiments the method he adopted was very simple, and he continued to practise it in all his future work. Mr. Shee, afterwards P.R.A., writes of Lawrence in 1789 :—" He is a very genteel, handsome young man, but rather effeminate in his manner. A newspaper that puffs him here (in London) very much, says he is not yet one-and-twenty ; but I am told by the students, who knew him in Bath, that he is three-and-twenty. . . . . . He is wonderfully laborious in his manner of painting, and has the most uncommon patience and perseverance. As yet he has had the advantage of me in length of practice and opportunities of improvement. This is his fifth year of exhibiting in London. His price is ten guineas a head, and I hear he intends raising it. There is no young artist in London bids so fair to arrive at excellence, and I have no doubt that he will, if he is careful, soon make a fortune."

Lawrence's career as a *student* of the Royal Academy was a very short one ; the Queen and King were both interested in what they had heard of the provincial prodigy. The painter became an aspirant for higher honours than studentship, although much below the academic age. In November, 1790, being then little more than twenty-one, he came on the ballot at the election for associates, and received three votes against sixteen, with which his opponent Wheatley was successful.

It is probable that West, who owed so much to royal patronage, and most likely felt satisfied with the superior talent of the candidate, may have used his influence in Lawrence's favour, and have been one of the three voters. However this may be, at the election of the ensuing year, 1791, Lawrence was successful in obtaining his associateship. Honours came thick upon him. Sir Joshua died in February, 1792, and ere the month was out the King had directed that Lawrence, then not twenty-three years of age, and not yet a full member of the Academy, should be appointed his successor as painter in ordinary. The Dilettante Society also, setting aside one of its important rules in his favour, elected him a member of their body, and their painter at the same time. Never, perhaps, in this country, had a man so young, so uneducated, and so untried in his art, advanced as it were *per saltum* to the honours and emoluments of the profession.

In February, 1794, Lawrence, then nearly twenty-five years of age, was admitted to the full honours of the academic body. How rapidly he obtained employment in the metropolis is shown by a reference to the early catalogues of the Academy. He had not ventured to exhibit there before 1787, in which year there were seven pictures by him on the walls; following out his career until 1793, when he sent six pictures, we find he had up to this period exhibited sixty-five works, with but one or two exceptions, portraits, including those of the King, the Queen, the royal children, and many of the most distinguished personages of the age; a pretty good catalogue of seven years' labours. But henceforth, instead of the second, Lawrence was to take the first rank in his profession, and was to have a great influence on the school to which he belonged. The modes of execution adopted by Reynolds, Gainsborough, and Romney, were to give place to one less painter-like in quality, one of less richness and impasto, more facile, and wherein drawing was placed before painting, and purity more esteemed than tone. Lawrence began with some slight attempts to follow in the footsteps of Reynolds. The head presented to the Academy on his election has a meretricious appearance from glazing and forced colouring, and shows that the attempt was ill-judged, and not in harmony with his powers. After Reynolds and Gainsborough, Lawrence looks pretty and painty; there is none of that power of uniting the figure with the ground—that melting of the flesh into the surrounding light which is seen in the pictures of the first president— Lawrence's work seems more on the surface—indeed only surface—while his flesh-tints have none of the natural purity of those by his two predecessors; we think them pretty in Lawrence, but we forget paint and painting in looking at a face by Reynolds or Gainsborough. How vastly superior, too, in painting children, Sir Joshua was to his successor, who had no apparent admission into the inner heart of childhood. His inferiority in this respect—and how much his children depended on mere prettiness and fashion for their charm—will be felt on looking at such pictures as "Lady Grey and Child," or "The Daughter of Lady Augusta Murray," or "Young Lambton."

Lawrence's heads are well drawn, and at times passably well modelled; but the flesh is flesh colour and not flesh, having the appearance of being painted on a hard ground, such as china, and have a thin and somewhat starved appearance as compared with the works of his predecessors. This poverty and thinness was less seen in his early works than afterwards, when the pressure upon him for portraits became great, and he was obliged to use the most facile means of rapid completion.

The portrait of Lady Cremorne, a whole-length painted shortly after Lawrence's arrival in London, which was exhibited in the British Institution in 1864, is an excellent specimen of his art at that period, and we cannot but feel that if he had continued to paint such pictures he would have enjoyed a far higher reputation than can now be accorded to him. It appears to be a faithful, and it is certainly a characteristic likeness ; much more powerful in contrast than are his latter works, and of a far richer tone. The flesh and white drapery are clear and sparkling, without that look of being lately washed which is peculiar to the flesh of his later portraits. Lady Cremorne is dressed in black, with the enormous mob-cap of white cambric (trimmed with black ribbons) characteristic of the period, and assisting to increase the principal light. The action is most simple ; there is no affectation of making the portrait more beautiful than the original, and the robes are exceedingly well introduced behind the figure as part of the back-ground. For this work we are told that he received only forty guineas. When fashion and beauty flocked to his doors and begged to be painted at prices increased twenty-fold, it is no wonder that he was obliged to use every artifice to lighten his labours.

We are aware that his contemporaries had a far higher opinion of Lawrence's powers than we have expressed. Fuseli said, " The portraits of Lawrence are as well if not better drawn, and the women in a finer taste than the *best* of Vandyck's : and he is so far above the competition of any painter in this way in Europe, that he should put over his study, to deter others who practise the art from entering, the well-known line— You who enter here leave hope behind." We have, however, spoken upon our own convictions, not hastily formed.

In the year 1793, Lawrence made an attempt at poetic art ; he painted and exhibited a picture from the *Tempest*—" Prospero Raising the Storm." What its merits were we are unable now to ascertain, as the picture is destroyed, and no reminiscences of it remain.

Walter Scott writing to Wilkie at the time of Lawrence's death, says of him, " I used to think it a great pity that he never painted historical subjects ; " and then goes on to remark that, like Sir Joshua, Lawrence often approached the confines of history in his portraits. How far this latter is the case may be estimated by those who remember his "Cato" (1812), or " Coriolanus " (1798) ; or will take the trouble to look at his "Hamlet" (1801), in the National Gallery, and to compare either with Reynolds's " Mrs. Siddons as the Tragic Muse," at Dulwich. But his powers as an historical painter may be judged of by the "Satan Calling up his Legions," which was exhibited in 1797, and after being for some years in the possession of the Duke of Norfolk, is at present the property of the Academy. Satan is lanky and ill-drawn ; the action of the figure is stagey, the disposition of the limbs all abroad, and the colour of the flesh tough and leather-like. There is a great want of style in the drawing of the figure, which seems to be a mixture between the living model and the Apollo. It is a large canvas covered with a subject which the artist has failed to make interesting.

Nevertheless, Lawrence himself, from some passages in his letters, thought he had achieved success. He says, apparently in allusion to his "Satan," "I have gained fame, not more than my wishes, but more than my expectations."

Knowles, in his life of Fuseli, speaks of it as "the splendid picture which for a long period was a prominent feature in the collection of the Duke of Norfolk, and which by the style of drawing as well as its tone of colour abundantly proves that this artist would have been equally distinguished for his powers in treating epic subjects as in portraits, if he had employed his pencil exclusively thereon." But this is said rather as an apology for Fuseli's having declined the offer of a place in the Milton Gallery to this great work. And we know that, on another occasion, Fuseli described the Satan "as a d——d thing, certainly, but not the devil." Mr. John Bernard, in his *Retrospections of the Stage*, tells us that the boy Lawrence had a great desire to recite " Satan's Address to the Sun," which, however, his father had interdicted. Once when in company he was urged to give it, but on opening the forbidden page a slip of paper dropped out ; this was picked up by one of the company and read aloud—"Tom, mind you don't touch Satan." It would have been well, perhaps, when he spread his canvas for his great work, that he had remembered his father's inhibition, "Mind you don't touch Satan."

Lawrence's practice continued to increase, and he steadily advanced beyond his numerous competitors. Hoppner alone, sustained by his appointment as painter to the Prince of Wales—a prince who, at that time, led the fashion in matters of taste, was able to rival Lawrence in the extent of his practice and in the beauty and fashion of his sitters. From time to time, as already noticed, Lawrence painted what he calls "half-history," but which we should call costume portraits ; such as his Kemble in *Coriolanus*, and the same great actor as Hamlet. Perhaps the costume portraits painted from the actor may have led Lawrence into theatrical action and forced expression from studying the character on the stage as well as in the studio.

Even if it were our province to enter minutely into the lives of the artists who come under notice in this work, there would be little of incident in that of Lawrence. A yearly catalogue of his sitters affords us almost the only subject for comment ; an occasional notice of more or less successful works—of some portrait of a distinguished sitter, or a noted beauty—is all that can be told of most portrait painters. As to Lawrence this is more particularly the case, since his style once adopted he changed but little—he tried no experiments in pigments—he sought no new methods of execution. He did not travel abroad to examine the pictures of other masters, or to study art for his improvement. Having obtained a good position in the profession, and plenty of occupation for his pencil, his life henceforth had somewhat of routine in the fulfilment of his various engagements. The death of Reynolds, followed in a few years by the retirement of Romney, left a great opening to him, yet he had at first many competitors. Opie was in full practice till his death in 1807 ; though his coarse strength of manner in a degree unfitted him for the first rank in female portraiture, yet in his male portraits he held his own against the future president. Hoppner lived until 1810, patronized by all who loved the school of Reynolds and worshipped the rising sun. While as to court patronage, even the King, who had hastened to grace Lawrence with the office of Sergeant Painter, left vacant by Reynolds, sat to Beechey for those portraits which seemed to belong almost of right to the Painter in Ordinary.

In 1801 an incident occurred which is here alluded to as having had an indirect influence on Lawrence's practice. He was required to attend at Blackheath to paint a portrait of the unfortunate Princess of Wales and her daughter, and in order that he might lose no time in journeys to and fro, he asked permission during the progress of his work to sleep at Montague House, a convenience that, on a like occasion, had been accorded to Beechey. His agreeable manner, pleasant conversation, and fine taste in reading poetry, together with his intimacy with the Angersteins and other families in the neighbourhood who visited her Royal Highness, introduced him occasionally to a seat at the dinner-table—and on one or two occasions when the Princess was alone with her ladies, he was admitted to read aloud to her, and even to amuse her at the chess-table. The painter, it must be remembered, was young and handsome, as well as talented and agreeable, and the circumstance was seized upon as a source of scandal, which was inquired into by the commissioners who sat in 1806 on what is called "The Delicate Investigation." Though the commissioners, in their report to his Majesty George III., attach to the Princess a levity of conduct with Captain Manby, they make no such allusion to Lawrence ; yet it would appear that for some time his female sitters, those whom his art most suited, fell off. Thus in the next seven years, we find the proportion of male portraits to females was twenty-four to seven ; after 1810 this feeling passed away, and in 1815, the Prince Regent, who had hitherto avoided Lawrence's studio, sat to him, and, pleased with his agreeable manners, as well as with the art which Lawrence certainly possessed of making his sitters ladies and gentlemen—at once gave him full employment in Court orders.

In 1814, as soon as the Continent was open to travellers, Lawrence hastened to Paris to see the wonderful collection in the Louvre, before it was dispersed. Writing to his friend, Miss Crofts, he says:—"Had I delayed my journey one day longer, I should have lost the view of some of the finest works of this gallery, the noblest assemblage of the efforts of human genius that was ever presented to the world." His stay, however, on this occasion, was but a short one ; he was recalled home by order of the Prince Regent on important business. The Prince was desirous that the kingly personages, the statesmen, and military officers who had aided in the restoration of the Bourbon dynasty should sit for their portraits, to form a commemorative gallery—and that the opportunity of their expected visit to London should be taken advantage of for this purpose. Such a commission was highly honourable to Lawrence ; it raised him to the summit of his fortunes, and if satisfactorily accomplished, was likely to give him a European reputation. His whole time on his return was taken up in watching for the short irregular sittings which he could obtain, during the intervals of leisure from feast and festival, from the Emperor of Russia, the King of Prussia, Prince Blucher, and the Hetman of the Cossacks ; but the length of their visit did not admit of the scheme being fully carried out on this occasion, and shortly afterwards the country was again plunged into war by the flight of Napoleon from Elba.

In the April of 1815, the Regent, pleased with the present success, conferred on Lawrence the honour of knighthood. The Prince had now fully accepted Lawrence as the Court painter, and although some time intervened before the full execution of his project, it was not forgotten, but simply postponed to a more fitting opportunity. Meanwhile, the most distinguished persons of the time, the court beauties, and the military officers who had taken part in the crowning victory of Waterloo, sat to the painter—among them the Duke of Wellington, in the dress he wore and on the horse he rode, on that great day—almost the only equestrian portrait by Lawrence's hand. Honours flowed in upon him. Foreign academies sent him diplomas of membership, America vying with Florence, Vienna, and Rome, while the French King, Charles XII., made him a Chevalier of the Legion of Honour, and our own King relaxed the iron law as respects civilians to whom this honour has been given, and allowed the painter to wear it.

The stay of the allied sovereigns in London in 1815 had been far too short to enable the Regent to carry out his favourite scheme. He felt that the one great act of his government was the pacification of Europe, and the settlement of its divisions after the great war ; and he would not allow his intention of collecting the portraits of those great warriors and able statesmen who had co-operated in bringing about the event, to be frustrated. In 1818, the allied sovereigns, their ministers and councillors, assembled at Aix-la-Chapelle, to lay out the new map of Europe, and it was thought a fitting opportunity for obtaining sittings from the principa' actors, in their intervals of leisure from the active duties of congress. In selecting Lawrence for this honourable mission, besides the influence of his suave and gentlemanly manners, it was felt that the best of living portrait painters would be employed to do justice to the theme. The terms were not especially liberal, but the fame and honour to be achieved were great. The magistrates of the city fitted up for him the large gallery of the Hôtel de Ville, a painting-room which he found very suitable and convenient for his purpose. In this room, Lawrence had as sitters the great arbiters of the fate of kingdoms, and received from them such courtesies as the great masters received from the kings and princes they served. He tells us how the Emperor of Russia condescended to put the pegs into his easel, and to help him to lift his portrait on to them, and compares it with the well-known incident of Charles V.'s stooping to take up Titian's pencil for him. But more substantial honours were the presents of snuff-boxes and diamond rings, and the many orders for copies of his portraits from princes and ministers, insomuch that it was said at the time that his year's labours were worth to him more than 20,000*l*.

While at Aix-la-Chapelle, the Prince Regent sent his further commands to Lawrence to proceed to Rome to paint for him the Cardinal Gonsalvi and the Pope. Lawrence would have wished to defer this visit to another year, but the Prince was anxious for the full accomplishment of his scheme, and the painter could but obey. From Aix-la-Chapelle he travelled to Vienna, to paint another portrait of the Emperor Francis and Prince Schwartzenberg. His journey from the borders of the Rhine to Vienna was a very different affair to what it is in the present day. He tells us that during eight nights on the road he only slept one out of his carriage. In Vienna new honours and new labours awaited him, and although, as we learn from his letters, the fine paintings he had seen on the Continent had somewhat lowered his self-esteem, the flattering manner in which he was received, and the admiration expressed for his works, were sufficient to elate any man. He reached Vienna early in January, 1819. Notwithstanding excessive labour, he found it impossible to leave before the 10th May. In the interval he had painted four whole-lengths, three half-lengths, and eight three-quarter portraits, besides making twelve chalk drawings. The faces of the paintings were entirely finished, and part of the figures; every figure being accurately drawn in. No wonder that he was worn out with such continued excitement and exertion, and wrote to his niece:—"My mind and spirits are at times so relaxed and worn when professional exertion is over, as to make the act of taking up this little implement (the pen) a hopeless exertion."

When he left Vienna, his journey towards Rome was very rapid. He again slept in his carriage throughout the route, only staying for a few hours at Bologna to renew his aquaintance at the fountain-head with the masters of a school then far more popular in England than at present. On his arrival at Rome he was received with every mark of attention, and lodged in apartments in the Quirinal. He was much pleased with the subjects for his pencil:—the Pope, a gentle and amiable ecclesiastic, with an air of great benevolence; the Cardinal, with a physiognomy full of sagacity and energy. Both were very desirous of giving Lawrence every assistance; and what with his pleasure in the subjects, and his desire to uphold his fame among his countrymen and others at this seat of art, he produced two of the best portraits of the series which was the object of his journey. During his stay he found time to visit the great frescoes of the Vatican, and declares himself deeply impressed with the great superiority of Michael Angelo over his contemporaries. But it is difficult to perceive that these works wrought the slightest change in Lawrence's style or manner.

Before leaving Italy he paid a short visit to Naples, and in the middle of December turned his face homeward. Visiting in his way Florence, Parma, Cremona, Mantua and Venice, he arrived in London on the 30th of March, 1820. He found that many changes had taken place during his absence. The Regent was now King; and West, the president of the Academy, having died on the 10th of the month, the election for the new president took place on the very evening of Lawrence's return. By an almost unanimous vote he was chosen West's successor, and the King, delighted with the manner in which his commission was fulfilled, presented the new president with a medal and chain of gold, inscribed, "From his Majesty, George IV., to the President of the Royal Academy."

Lawrence left England on the 29th of September, 1818, and, as we have just seen, returned to London on the 30th March, 1820; so that he was absent exactly a year and a half. We are unable to ascertain the precise amount of work he completed in the time; for if we knew the number of portraits, the state of completion to which he carried them on the spot is uncertain. As to those executed in Vienna, a statement has just been made, and we know from his letters, that some of his portraits were so far completed that he carried them with him to Rome as specimens of his powers, whilst others were finished and left with those for whom they were painted. We know also that these portraits were executed under circumstances that must have occasioned a great strain upon his powers, and that, compared with the time he exacted and the opportunities given him by visitors to his studio at home, the sittings given him for his foreign portraits were much less numerous and less lengthy.

He says that the Emperor of Austria sat seven times, the Emperor of Russia seven times, the King of Prussia six times, each sitting averaging about two hours. The Pope, we are informed, sat to him nine times ; but even this is far below the time he usually required, especially if we remember that he completed the hands as well as the heads from his foreign sitters. It is no wonder, therefore, that, contemplating the portraits collected together in the Waterloo Gallery at Windsor, these works look somewhat starved and poor, having a tendency to decorative art rather than to take rank with portraits by the great masters, or with those of his predecessor Reynolds. Whatever there was of meretriciousness in his art is here more particularly visible, and although Cardinal Gonsalvi and the Pope are usually spoken of as Lawrence's best works, we do not feel them comparable to such of his male portraits as he was able to carry to full completion in the quiet of his own studio—for instance, Lord Liverpool, or more especially his fine portrait of Lord Eldon.

On his return, Lawrence's studio was soon thronged as before, and what with constant engagements to sitters, his new duties at the Academy, and his endeavours to increase his collection of drawings from the old masters, which had of late become quite a passion with him, his time was more than fully occupied. On the 10th of December, 1820, Lawrence for the first time presented the medals to the successful students of the Royal Academy ; when it is usual for the president to address a short discourse to the assembled schools : it was on such occasions that the celebrated *Discourses* of Reynolds were delivered. This by Lawrence was, we believe, not published ; but his biographer relates to us that the president wore a full-dress court suit—an evidence of his attention to the effect of personal impressions which is very characteristic, but this ceremonial costume has of late years quite fallen into desuetude.

In the year 1823, Lawrence took a deep interest in the purchase, for the nation, of the pictures belonging to his late friend, Mr. Angerstein ; and the arts certainly owe him a debt of gratitude for his earnestness and effective aid in this national object. During the succeeding years, his life and his art quietly progressed. Working more at his leisure, and giving more time to finish his works, they were more conscientiously painted. Some of his best portraits are of this date. His biographer opens the history of the year 1829 with these words :—" It would be difficult to conceive a man more completely happy or at least possessed of all the means and appliances of happiness than Sir Thomas Lawrence at the commencement of the year 1829." Certainly there was no appearance of decay in his powers. He himself says in a letter just after the opening of the Exhibition in 1829, " Perhaps one or two whole-lengths of the Duchess of Richmond and Marchioness of Salisbury, are the best I have painted ; " and in this, the period of our student life, we well recollect the delight with which the young artists of that day, and the public who were visitors to the Exhibition, hailed the works we have enumerated.   On the 10th of December, the anniversary of the foundation of the Academy, Lawrence was as usual in the chair, distributing the prizes, and delivering a short discourse.   He most probably dined with the changing council on the last day of the old year, and, except that he had complained of being overworked, there was no reason to think that the end of his career was at hand.

He had been intending to eat his Christmas dinner with his sister Ann.   On the 17th of December he writes,—"I am grieved to the soul that urgent circumstances keep me at this time from seeing you ; but in the next month I will certainly break away from all engagements to be with you ; " on the 19th he again writes, " Be assured, dear love, dearest sister, that nothing shall detain me from you on the day, and for the days you mention ; " the day after Christmas day he reiterates his pledge. "On the sixth I have sacredly pledged myself to be with you."   He was making great exertions to finish the portrait of Canning, his engagements were pressing ; yet while continually sympathizing with the distressing illness of his sister, which called forth all his tenderness, he seemed quite unaware that an illness of a more alarming character was hanging over himself.   Though unwell, he dined with Sir Robert Peel on the 2nd of January, and the next morning was well enough to invite two or three of his most intimate friends to dine, spending with them one of his usual social evenings.   He was busied during the following day or two in painting on the portrait of his Majesty, but on the 6th he was obliged to have recourse to Dr. Holland ; yet he again painted during the day for more than an hour on the King's portrait.   He found it necessary, however, to write to his sister Ann—the last note from his hand—and even then he only proposed delaying his visit till the morrow : that morrow which was but to precede his last.   " I meant, my dearest Ann," he writes, "to be with you at dinner time to-morrow, and have made exertions to do so, but it may not be !   You must be content to see me at a late simple dinner on Friday."   That evening he was taken much worse, and Dr. Holland being sent for, bled him ; he seemed to rally a little next morning, but as the bleeding was renewed by accident on two separate occasions during the day, he sank rapidly from exhaustion, and died rather suddenly in the arms of his servant, on the evening of Thursday, the 7th of January, 1830.

Lawrence, beautiful in infancy and in boyhood, was, as a man, of handsome presence and elegant manners, to which nature had added a well-toned and persuasive voice ; these natural advantages are said to have told much in his favour with the great personages who sat to him at Aix-la-Chapelle, as no doubt they did in the fortunes of his life. He was very tender in speaking or writing to women. One of his lady apologists says, " It cannot be too strongly stated that his manner was likely to mislead without his intending it ; he could not write a common answer to a dinner invitation, without its assuming the tone of a billet-doux. The very commonest conversation was held in that soft low whisper, and with that tone of deference and interest which are so unusual and so calculated to please." A very dangerous manner from a man with a handsome person, prominent position, and yet unmarried —a manner which led each woman to think that he regarded her with peculiar interest. He certainly loved female society, yet, though on one or two occasions he was too particular in his attentions, and had even entered into engagements, he still lived and died a bachelor.

Lawrence was during all his life in difficulties as to money, although, latterly at least, in the receipt of large sums from his profession. Lord Durham paid him for " Master Lambton," 600 guineas ; yet we find him writing for payment in some instances before his portraits were completed. This improvidence has been much commented upon, and a charge of gambling was entered against him, but we think without foundation. A portion, at least, of his family were for years dependent upon him, and his only extravagance seems to have been in works of art : it was too-well known that a fine drawing by the old masters was a temptation too strong to be resisted, if money could be had, at whatever disadvantage.

All portrait painters are under the necessity of succumbing to the imperious dictates of fashion ; not always the fashion of the dress of the period—perhaps only the fashion of its portraiture, as in the god and goddess school, or the Roman toga period of French art, a costume which we cannot suppose to have been the habit of the time.

Lawrence was not exempt from the general bondage which had trammelled his predecessors, but by the time he had attained the first rank in portraiture, the fashion that had hidden the golden hair and grizzled the flowing locks of his lovely countrywomen had passed away, and, if still imperious in its sway, it clothed their limbs in garments so tight as to impede motion, and altered the graceful proportion and flowing lines of the female form by waists under the arm-pits rather than where nature placed them, it at least left the complexion free from paint and patches, and the amber locks and golden ringlets free from the paste that stiffened them or the powder that changed them into the ashy hue of age. But while we acknowledge the simpler taste introduced with the present century, and praise the fashion as more akin to nature, it is certain there is less of courtly dignity in the works of Lawrence than in those of his predecessors. Under the altered fashion of his day we look back on the beauties of the last century almost as we do to the quaintness of mediæval times, and are apt to think nature, with her unrestrained ringlets, her mottled flesh and simple drapery, somewhat commonplace beside the pompous barbarisms which added many cubits to the stature of the beauties of the previous age.

In making up his pictures, Lawrence was far inferior to his predecessors. There is far less variety in his compositions, far less of art in his arrangements. We miss the happy, rich suggestions of landscape scenery that their works exhibit, and too often instead are treated to repetitions over and over again, with slight re-adjustments of the stale commonplaces of pillar and curtain, or vase and pedestal, which it may be hoped will be banished from true art, since they now form the stock properties of the *carte de visite* and the photographic studio. It has always been said that the portraits of Sir Joshua were not likenesses, yet to us they have a great appearance of individuality. Sir Thomas was subjected to the same remark both from his sitters and from his brother artists. Wilkie says that "with all the latitude allowed to Lawrence in rendering a likeness, still those who knew and could compare the heads he painted with the originals must have been struck with the liberties he would take in changing and refining the features before him." He adds that, "compared with Reynolds, Lawrence was confined and limited in the arrangement of his pictures far more than his powers justified, admitting but small deviations in the placing of the heads, small variety of pictorial composition. The features in nearly all his heads were painted in the same light and in the same position; but they derived from this a perfection of execution never to be equalled." Such was the opinion of Wilkie: *we* should rather have said, a *dexterity* of execution which was quite his own.

Haydon said that "Lawrence was suited to the age, and the age to Lawrence. He flattered its vanities, pampered its weakness, and met its meretricious tastes. His men were all gentlemen with an air of fashion, and the dandyism of high life—his women were delicate but not modest—beautiful but not natural, they appear to look that they may be looked at, and to languish for the sake of sympathy." Opie had made a similar remark, but far more tersely. Lawrence, said he, "made coxcombs of his sitters, and his sitters made a coxcomb of Lawrence." These are hard sayings, and were remembered when death closed the fashionable career of the painter. As much as he had risen above his true rank in art, he then fell below it, and it has taken a quarter of a century to reinstate him—not to the place which he held in his lifetime, but to the true place which as a painter he should occupy among his countrymen. It must be allowed that many of his faults arose from his courteous weakness to his sitters; they lived and moved in the atmosphere of fashionable life, then far more exclusive than at present, and he submitted to their dictation ; hence it was said that " his women look the slaves of fashion, glittering with pearls and ornaments, his children the heirs of coronets and titles, the tools and the pupils of the dancing master." Something also must be attributed to his overtaxed powers, which obliged him to give over much of the making-up of his pictures to his assistants ; backgrounds and even hands were entrusted to them, and the numerous repetitions of public portraits which were called for, were necessarily almost entirely the work of the Simpsons, father and son, Pegler, and others, who were in Lawrence's constant employment. The repetition of Reynolds's portrait of the Duchess of Devonshire and child —attributed to Lawrence, and now in the corridor at Windsor—is said to have been the work of Etty, during the time he was with Lawrence in Bedford Square.

Yet, with every allowance, we can hardly place Lawrence in the first rank as a painter. There remained a sense of the crayon draughtsman to the last, a tinty mode of colouring, assimilating in some degree to the false brilliancy of paste. Even his drawings, though delicate and refined in line, were somewhat effeminate, and showed little of the force of true genius : they never rose beyond the elegant insipidity of artificial life. Lawrence had adopted a system depending on contrasts rather than on harmonies, and the meretricious qualities of his art in this respect certainly left a bad influence, somewhat qualified by the greater attention to precision and drawing which his manner of commencing his pictures initiated. Wilkie, in his remarks on portrait painting, gives us an insight into Lawrence's practice of the art, he says :—" He wished to seize the expression rather than to copy the features. His attainment of likeness was most laborious. One distinguished person, who favoured him with forty sittings for his head alone, declared he was the slowest painter he ever sat to, and he had sat to many. He would draw the portrait in chalk, the size of life, on paper ; this occupied but one sitting, but that sitting lasted nearly one whole day. He next transferred this outline from the paper to the canvas : his picture and his sitter were placed at a distance from the point of view where to see both at a time. He had to traverse all across the room before the conception which the view of his sitter suggested could be proceeded with. In this incessant transit his feet had worn a path through the carpet to the floor, exercising freedom both of body and mind ; each traverse allowing time for invention, while it required an effort of memory between the touch on the canvas and the observation from which it grew."

Thus we see that the happy facility with which, as a boy, he had been able to seize the likeness of individuals had left him ; or his knowledge of the difficulties, and sense of the perfection of art, had induced in him patient effort and continuous repetition. This practice, in important pictures, was carried even into the accessories and subordinate parts. It used to be told that for the legs alone of the small portrait of George IV. seated on a sofa, the King gave Lawrence nearly twenty sittings; but then his Majesty is said to have had very fine legs, and the painter, in his Majesty's opinion, did not do them justice.

Nevertheless, Lawrence had many facile methods of giving the appearance of labour where the work was really slight; thus the texture of his furs was rendered by a dexterous handling of the scrubby hog tool, which often produced the sense of imitation more exactly than the most laboured execution. He was once reproached that he resorted to tricks in painting, and this habit of splitting up his brush was given as an instance; but he retorted with justice that if his method gave as true an imitative appearance of fur as could be obtained by the laborious process of painting it hair by hair, it was equally satisfactory and far more painter-like. It is probable that had Lawrence trusted in his own powers as he did in early days before he had name and fame to lose, he would have been more successful as a painter. He was fettered latterly by his very fastidiousness and desire of surface-finish, as well as by his endeavour to give the most polished aspect of his sitter. Reynolds and Gainsborough, the latter more especially, struck off some of their best portraits at a single sitting, and it is told of Lawrence, that having tried a portrait of Curran, and having after many sittings totally failed, he met the great Irish orator at a party, saw the fire of his eye and the energy of the natural man under the influence of after-dinner freedom, and exclaimed that the portrait he had laboured over was no portrait at all. He asked and obtained another sitting on the only day that intervened before Curran's departure for Ireland, and at that one sitting completed a fine likeness of this extraordinary man.

Lawrence, after his first start, when he made some slight attempt at imitating Reynolds, soon adopted and ever continued to maintain a manner of his own; it had this good influence on the school, that it encouraged more careful drawing, and the study of the head by this means, before beginning painting. It also contributed to restrain awhile the use of bad vehicles and fugitive pigments, and hence also the faulty execution which had arisen from the pranks of Reynolds; but Lawrence's example tended to bring about that prevailing chalkiness of which Wilkie complained on his return from the Continent, and which, after Lawrence's death, he laboured by such fatal means to change. We would conclude our notice by saying, that while we are obliged to allow that Lawrence ranks below his immediate predecessors of the English school, it was hardly possible, at his death, to point to a successor likely to stand beside him in the opinion of posterity.

CHAPTER XIX.

THE CONTEMPORARIES OF LAWRENCE.

WHILE Reynolds, with the single exception of Gainsborough, who in his day was styled a landscape painter, stood alone and far above rivalry in portrait-art, Lawrence had many rivals who, far from yielding the palm, long contested with him the pre-eminence which, assisted by fashion and court-favour, he at last secured. The men and the times had alike changed. Lawrence when at the head of his profession was far from obtaining the unapproachable excellence of Reynolds and Gainsborough, and the ranks of art had also been largely extended since the foundation of the Royal Academy, by distinguished artists chiefly trained in its schools, who became the formidable competitors of Lawrence.

In beginning with *Sir Henry Raeburn, R.A.*, the earliest of these men in point of date, we can hardly designate him as a competitor. A native of Scotland, the most distinguished portrait painter of that country since the days of Jamesone, he was born 4th March, 1756, at Stockbridge, a suburb of Edinburgh, and had there his art training and practice. The son of a respectable manufacturer, and at an early age left an orphan, he was educated at Heriot's Hospital; and at the age of fifteen was apprenticed to an eminent goldsmith at Edinburgh. His love of drawing led him to attempt portraits, and he soon attracted notice by his skill in miniature, so much so that he gained enough employment to enable him to obtain his release from his master. He had had no teaching, it is said, except some hints from David Martin, a portrait painter, who then had the chief practice in the northern metropolis, but his miniatures show such art-treatment as could not have been attained without the means, at least, of studying fine works. As his powers increased he tried full-size portraits in oil, and his success raised the jealousy of his quondam adviser. His sitters increasing, he abandoned miniature, and devoted himself exclusively to oil. He worked in a free spirited manner, and aiming at character succeeded in impressing it on his canvas. He was advancing in his profession by the strength of his own genius, when in his twenty-second year, fortune assisted him in taking a firmer footing, by the help of an estimable wife with whom he acquired some property, and he soon afterwards came to London. His early miniatures showed a knowledge of the works of Reynolds, and his object was to obtain advice from the great painter. We are told that he was cordially received, that Sir Joshua saw his merits, admitted him for two months to his studio, and advised him to visit Rome, offering to assist him with funds. Though this was not needed, Reynolds gave him letters of introduction, and he set out for Italy with his wife.

Here he remained for two years, and then returning, settled in Edinburgh, in 1787, and soon gained full employment as a portrait painter, for years taking the lead in that branch of art. The most distinguished men of the city were numbered among his sitters, and many of them his personal friends. He was fond of architecture, and in 1795 he built a large house in York Place, the basement of which formed his studio, with the required offices, and the upper floor a handsome gallery for his pictures, lighted from the roof, while his family dwelling was at St. Bernard's, Stockbridge. He appeared to have quite taken root in the congenial soil of his native city; both his art and his society were highly esteemed, and he was surrounded by friends. He made no long visits to London, and had few opportunities of knowing the works of his contemporaries in that metropolis; yet he probably longed for a larger sphere, and to measure himself with men whose fame at least must have been well known to him. He was ambitious too of the distinction which admission to the Royal Academy confers on its members, and had placed his name on their list of those who sought election. We are told that late in life he thought of establishing himself in London, but that Sir Thomas Lawrence, whom he consulted, succeeded in dissuading him; and this advice, it is insinuated, arose from the desire to keep him out of the way. Probably this was in 1810, in the May of which year Wilkie records that he "had a call from Raeburn, who told me he had come up to London to look out for a house, and to see if there was any prospect of establishing himself:" and a month later, Wilkie again notes, "Went with Raeburn to the Crown and Anchor to meet the gentlemen of the Royal Academy. I introduced him to Flaxman; after dinner he was asked by Beechey to sit near the president, and great attention was paid to him." He was evidently thought well of by his brother artists in London, and we can find many reasons why Lawrence, without laying himself open to any narrow-minded suspicions, might very conscientiously recommend an artist, in his fifty-fifth year, not to quit a field where, surrounded by tried friends, he had earned and maintained an undisputed pre-eminence in his profession, and thus break away from the companions whose society he loved, and enter into a contest with established rivals on a new field.

Honours, however, at last fell thick upon Raeburn, and in his native city. In 1812 he was elected president of the Society of Artists in Edinburgh ; in 1814 an associate ; and in the following year, a full member of the Royal Academy in London ; and on the King's visit to Scotland in 1822, Raeburn was knighted, and soon after appointed his Majesty's Limner for Scotland. He did not long enjoy these honours. After a very short illness, without any marked symptoms, he died on the 8th July, 1823. His portraits were distinguished by great breadth, both of treatment and character. Commencing with the brush, he aimed to secure at once the individuality of his sitter, rather than to attain a likeness by the studied drawing of the features, and he succeeded in seizing a truthful and characteristic expression.

No doubt, Raeburn in some degree founded his art upon that of Reynolds, though, from the great difference in their execution and handling, we suspect that he studied Reynolds through the fine mezzo-tints of MacArdell and others, rather than direct from his paintings. We find the same value given to breadth of light and shade—so distinctive a quality of the English painter, and very fully given in the prints from his works ; but we find none of the richness, none of the impasto, of Reynolds. The Scotch painter's manner of execution is more like that of Gainsborough in its thinness and once-ness, with a certain appearance of facility which may have made Wilkie, when in Spain, remark that the works of Velasquez reminded him of Raeburn—but the low tone adopted by the Scottish president sometimes gives to his thin execution a some-what impoverished look, and he loses entirely the pearly freshness, so great a charm in Gainsborough.

It is said that Raeburn had a theory that as portraits are intended to be seen at some elevation on the walls of the apartment in which they are hung, so ought the sitter to be viewed from below, and that, acting on this principle, he painted his whole lengths as if level with the feet of the sitter. This obviated any danger of his being included in the "tip-toe school," but it caused the painter's subject to be seen under the least pleasing aspect—namely, looking under the jaw and up the nostrils of the sitter ; the forehead also, the portion of the face which expresses the higher qualities of the cultivated man, becomes foreshortened, the more considerably in proportion as it recedes over prominent brows. It was no doubt from this practice of Raeburn that Sir Walter Scott complained that his portrait made him look clownish and jolter-headed—the animal features of the face, thus viewed, being increased, and the fine but peculiar and conical head of Scott being reduced in height and otherwise seen to disadvantage. Raeburn's art was more suited to male than to female portraiture—he failed in giving the grace and loveliness of his female sitters. He may have owed part of the great reputation which he enjoyed to his somewhat isolated position as the head of his profession in Scotland, and perhaps might not have been able to sustain it to the full, had he removed to London.

John Hoppner, R.A., born in Whitechapel, April 4th, 1758, has been characterized as the most daring plagiarist of Reynolds, and the boldest rival of Lawrence. In the meagre information as to his early days, given by his biographers, mystery and scandal have been attached to his birth. His mother is said to have been one of the German attendants at the royal palace, and George III. so particularly interested in him as to see that he was well-nursed and educated. We think the fact that Hoppner was born above two years before George III. was king, or the occupant of the royal palace, may be accepted rather than the vague undated statements relative to Hoppner's birth, and the scandals which have been founded upon them. So far upon the vexed question of his parentage. There seems, however, none as to his having been at an early age a chorister in the royal chapel, and that, manifesting a strong inclination for art, the King gave him some assistance for its study. This was probably when his voice naturally became unfitted for the choir, and we find that he entered the Royal Academy as a student in 1775, being then in his seventeenth year.

As a student he laboured diligently, and in 1782 gained the gold medal, the great prize of the Academy, for an original painting from *King Lear;* and in the same year he married a daughter of Mrs. Wright, the celebrated modeller in wax. He showed much aptitude for landscape art, but at once adopted the portrait branch of his profession ; then, it may be said, the only one to insure the artist a living. Early in his career he produced a portrait of Mrs. Jordan as the Comic Muse. This picture is at Hampton Court, and was an attempt beyond the young artist's powers. The group consists of two females life-size and whole-length ; the figures have a straddling action, with little taste and without poetic feeling ; the drapery is wooden and without flow, and the colouring disagreeable and heavy. Later in his career (in 1791) Mrs. Jordan again sat to him as Hippolyta.

That he lost no time in entering upon the practice of his profession is evident, since we find his name in 1780, when barely twenty-two years of age, in the catalogue of the Royal Academy. For some years he continued to exhibit portraits of " A Lady," of " A Gentleman," as they were then entered in the catalogue, leaving us in perfect ignorance as to the individuals represented, and rendering their verification hopeless. This absurd practice, by which every one not of the blood royal was vaguely designated in the catalogue, was common to all the portraits it contained, until 1797.

However obtained, it is clear that Hoppner retained some influence in the palace. In 1785, he exhibited three portraits of the Princesses Sophia, Amelia, and Mary, and in 1789 he is styled portrait painter to the Prince of Wales, and is often employed by the Prince and his brothers, the Dukes of York and Clarence, as well as by many of those most distinguished for rank and fashion. His reputation largely increased; he was esteemed by many the first portrait painter since Reynolds; and Lawrence owned him to be a formidable rival; in 1793 he was elected an associate, and in 1795 a full member of the Royal Academy. By this time, Lawrence, much his junior, had rapidly risen into court favour and fashionable distinction. He had been appointed portrait painter to the King, while, as we have seen, Hoppner held the same office under the Prince, and the two artists are represented as of the two factions which then unhappily prevailed. We are amused by the tale of Hoppner having offended the King, who had been his friend, by praising Reynolds; and the tattle of his having used his ready wit and influence in support of Whiggism, whose talents and beauty were the reward and objects of his pencil alone. Art is of no party; and, above all parties, is indifferently sought by all.

Hoppner had to contend with a chronic state of ill-health, arising from a constitution naturally weak; and much of his proverbial irritation, if not produced, was aggravated by the ailments which attend a diseased liver. He must have been often tried by his sitters. He told the critic, Gifford, as an example of his annoyance, how "a wealthy stockbroker drove up to his door, whose carriages emptied into his hall, in Charles Street, a gentleman and lady, with five sons and seven daughters, all samples of *Pa* and *Ma*—as well fed and as city bred a comely family as any within the sound of Bow bells. 'Well, Mr. Painter,' said he, 'here we are, a baker's dozen; how much will you demand for painting the whole *lot* of us; prompt payment for discount?' 'Why,' replied the astonished painter, viewing the questioner, who might be likened to a superannuated elephant, 'why, that will depend upon the dimensions, style, composition, and——' 'Oh, that is all settled,' quoth the enlightened broker; 'we are all to be touched off in one piece as large as life, all seated upon our lawn at Clapham, and all singing *God Save the King.*'"

As we have seen, Hoppner copied Sir Joshua, the attitudes of whose sitters he even adapted to his own compositions; he also followed Gainsborough in his backgrounds. Two or three of his whole-length portraits are at Hampton Court, to which place they have probably been banished from their sad state of dilapidation, arising from the painter's having copied the defective materials of Reynolds as well as his compositions and general arrangement. Those remaining at St. James's, painted after Reynolds's death, are less injured by the use of asphaltum ; but they are devoid of any special originality in art, though highly respectable as portraits. Hoppner's colouring was thought brilliant, and yet mellow, by his contemporaries; but it has changed with time, and is now somewhat heavy and horny. Hoppner was sometimes very happy in his portraits of ladies and children ; his handling was free, his execution unlaboured, but his drawing often faulty. The painter's ill-health shortened his days, and he died on the 23rd of January, 1810, aged fifty-one years : a time of life which might still have left some years of promise, and Lawrence was able to write—" The death of Hoppner leaves me without a rival."

In examining the works of Lawrence's contemporaries, it is remarkable how repeatedly we are reminded of the great influence which the works of Reynolds have had upon our school. The artists to whom this chapter is devoted painted under this influence. They did not exhibit any high or original qualities in art. But though they did not obtain great distinction, or leave us works we may point to with full satisfaction, they yet form not unimportant links in the history of English art, and their portraits of many great personages will long occupy places in our mansions and public edifices.

William Owen, R.A., is no exception to this class. He was born at Ludlow, in Shropshire, in 1769—the more precise date is not recorded —and was the son of a bookseller. He received a fair education in the grammar school of his native place, and gave early indications of genius by sketching the beautiful scenery surrounding the town. In 1786 he came to London, as the pupil of Catton, R.A., and was admitted to the schools of the Royal Academy. He also gained an introduction to Reynolds, who was pleased with his indications of ability, and assisted him with his kindly advice. In 1792 and the following year he appeared on the walls of the Royal Academy as a portrait painter ; but his natural talent appears to have inclined him to subjects of rustic life, elevated both above common life and mere portraiture by some reference to poetry or story. In 1797, he exhibited a portrait of two sisters, by which he gained great credit, one of whom he soon afterwards married ; and his proficiency and his sitters steadily increased. In 1800 he settled with his family in Pimlico, and kept a studio in Leicester Square. He now produced some of his best works. A fine portrait of Mr. Pitt established his reputation, and was followed by successful portraits of Lord Grenville, the Duke of Buccleuch, and a long list of distinguished sitters. He was at the height of his practice, and was elected an associate of the Royal Academy in 1804, and a full member in 1806 ; followed in 1810—on the death of Hoppner—by the appointment of portrait painter to the Prince of Wales. At the summit of his prosperity his income, though it received but little increase by the prince's appointment, now reached 3,000*l.* a year, and in 1818 he removed both his family and his practice to Bruton Street. Here his health soon failed, probably from overwork, and for five years he was confined to his room, and unable to continue his art. In this state he died suddenly on the 11th of February, 1825, from the effect of laudanum wrongly labelled by the chemist who made up his prescriptions.

To the genius and aptitude for art with which Owen was gifted by nature, he added unwearied diligence. His drawing was superficial, but his manner of painting did not want power, and his colour, though with a tendency to be hot and monotonous, was good. His feeling for landscape was shown in the taste displayed in his backgrounds. His subject pictures were pleasing, and enjoyed a high reputation in his day, which has not been maintained in our own.

It seems to require an apology to the memory of *Sir Martin Archer Shee, P.R.A.*, as hardly befitting one distinguished by such varied talents, and who attained the rank of president of the Royal Academy, that we have given him a place only in this chapter; and yet in the plan of our work it is here that he finds his true place as an artist. He was descended from an Irish family of old Connaught lineage, and was born in Dublin, 20th December, 1769. His first attachment was to art, and he was fortunate in being placed under Robert L. West, then the talented master of the school connected with the Dublin Royal Society. He very early commenced portraiture, and soon met with some encouragement and success. In the summer of 1788, he tempted fortune by removing to London.

Here he soon met friends who were well disposed to assist him. He had exhibited two heads in 1789, and he now completed four portraits, which he submitted for exhibition in 1790, but was grievously disappointed that they gained no place on the Academy walls. Made known by an Irish relative to Burke, he was by him favourably introduced to Reynolds as "his little relative," and by the advice of Sir Joshua, he entered the schools of the Royal Academy; though with some hurt to his pride, as he thought he had finished his pupilage in Dublin. In 1791 he exhibited his first whole-length, and struggling on like others have done before him and since, now elated by a good work well placed in the exhibition, now depressed by want of success, he quietly gained a name and a place in art. His earliest works were mainly theatrical portraits; and he tells of an historical attempt exhibited in 1794, which had cost him at intervals, three years' thought and toil, "The Daughter of Jephthah Lamenting with her Companions." In 1798 he exhibited a large equestrian portrait, which added to his reputation; and in the following year he gained his election as associate, and in 1800, as member of the Academy.

Shee's constant occupation in art was portraiture, yet he found time to try his hand at subject-pictures, but he acknowledged that he owed his election into the Academy to his portraits, not to his historical attempts. By portraiture he had established his reputation, and steadily following this art, he found employment, if it did not lead to fortune. But he was not a man of one talent. He was early known as a critic and writer on art. His *Rhymes on Art*, published in 1805, gave him a literary reputation, and he was apostrophized in Byron's satire of *English Bards and Scotch Reviewers* :—

> " And here let Shee and genius find a place,
> Whose pen and pencil yield an equal grace."

In 1809 he published a continuation of his rhymes under the title of *Elements of Art*, and next, among other lesser writings in 1824, *Alasco, a Tragedy*, which was withdrawn from the theatre in consequence of some considerable expurgations absurdly insisted upon by the deputy licenser of plays. He also published anonymously, in 1829, *Old Court*, a novel, which attracted but little attention. He had gained the esteem of his profession. A man of both artistic and literary talent, of sound judgment and good business aptitudes, of gentlemanly breeding and manners, able to express himself well on all occasions, and devoted to the interests of art, he was deemed by his friends a worthy successor to the presidential chair on the death of West. But he himself at once candidly admitted and supported the superior claims of Lawrence, on whose death, in 1830, he was almost unanimously elected to the rank of president, and received the honour of knighthood.

Sir Martin's presidency had fallen on troubled times. The vexed questions connected with the erection of the National Gallery in Trafalgar Square, of which the Royal Academy was to occupy one wing, came at once upon him. He had to maintain the privileged rights the Academy had so long enjoyed without question at Somerset House, and their interests as affected by the proposed removal. He had also to assert the character of the Academy in the face of attacks made by a party in the House of Commons. In all these weighty matters the president acted with promptitude, zeal, and ability, not in the cause of the Royal Academy alone, but in the interests of art in their widest sense; and signally justified the choice of his colleagues, which placed him in a position to render important services to his profession.

We may judge of Shee's early art by the picture of Lewis the comedian in the character of the Marquis, in *The Midnight Hour*, bequeathed by the comedian's son to the National Gallery collection. This was

painted in 1791, and was the first whole-length by him which obtained
a place on the Academy walls. It is an exceedingly clever work, and
not too much like Reynolds,—the common fault of the young painters
of that time. Easy in action and well drawn, it has much individuality
of character, and no doubt was a good likeness, with just a flavour of
the natural affectation of the actor. Like most portraits by young men
(Shee was in his twenty-first year), it is very carefully finished; the flesh
is a little ruddy, and the cheeks have the appearance of rouge, not unsuitable in the portrait of an actor, but a fault apparent in most of Shee's
after works. The handling is sharper, and the touch more square than
in his later works, in which he fell into a method of painting as if with
a thick and somewhat viscid vehicle; the colour, after being laid by the
brush, was softened and smoothed by an extensive use of the "sweetener,"
giving the flesh an unnatural softness, while it is wanting in that interchange of cutting with softened edges, so valuable in aiding relief.
Haydon asserted that portrait painters always painted their full-length
figures standing on the tips of their toes, and he ironically gave linear
rules how to draw the feet properly in perspective. But he was himself ignorant of the cause of the apparent error; which, moreover,
to suit his own purposes, he greatly exaggerated. The feet were mostly
right in perspective, in relation to the objects in the foreground, but the
loose and careless habits of the portrait painters, or their desire after some
effective arrangement of light and shade, often led them into the gross
error of having one horizon for their foreground objects, and a totally
different one for the background. This is seen in Shee's "Portrait of
William IV.," now in the council room of the Royal Academy, although
in a less degree than in many other works. In this picture, the top of
the table on the right, on which the crown rests, is just on a level with
the eye, and the circular lines of the crown are drawn as if in plain
elevation, as an architect would call it; but Windsor Castle on the left,
whose round tower is seen just above the ground plane on which the
King is standing, from the perspective curve of its lines, and as we do *not*
see the top, must have an horizon two feet lower down than the table, so
that we have two horizons in the same picture; and if the feet of the
King are referred to the lower one, he has partially the appearance of
standing on his toes.

We would not, however, credit Shee particularly with this fault:
Lawrence is a frequent and a far greater sinner; and we remember that
when a recent professor of perspective pointed out to an eminent painter
a like fault in a portrait of the Duke of Devonshire, in which Chatsworth was seen in the distance in very false perspective, the painter
justified it by saying that it must be recollected Chatsworth was on a
" devil of a hill," showing a twofold error in his very justification: first,

that anything could justify the eye being supposed to be in two places at once ; and, secondly, his want of knowledge, that if the mansion were on a hill—the higher the hill the higher the horizon would seem to be ; instead of this being a reason for lowering it down to the ground.

Shee's last contributions to the exhibition were in 1845. Age, and the exertions he had undergone, had begun to tell upon him. He had for some time suffered from illness, on the increase of which he resigned his office of president in 1845, but was induced by the affectionate wishes of the Academy to resume it. But though he consented to resume his office, his health gradually declined, and his death, accelerated by the sudden death of his wife, took place at Brighton on the 19th August, 1850, in his eighty-first year.

Thomas Phillips, R.A., another contemporary who passed a long life in the practise of portrait-art, was born of respectable parents at Dudley, in Warwickshire, 18th October, 1770. He was placed by them with Mr. Edgington, the well-known glass-painter, at Birmingham, but fostering higher aims he came to London at the end of 1790 ; and West, P.R.A., is said to have found him employment connected with the execution of his designs for the painted glass windows at Windsor. At first he exhibited subject-pictures, but adopting portraiture as his chief pursuit, he steadily and industriously made his way. In 1804, he was elected an associate, and in 1808, a full member of the Academy. The subject of his presentation picture was " Venus and Adonis." His portraits were faithful, and he found full employment, many persons of distinction sitting to him. In 1824, he was appointed professor of painting to the Royal Academy, and travelled to Rome, the better to fit himself for the office. His lectures were published. He wrote some articles on art subjects for *Rees's Encyclopædia,* and occasionally for other publications. He died, 20th April, 1845, in his seventy-fifth year.

The portraits of Phillips are marked by soberness and propriety, by negative rather than positive qualities ; they are generally good as to likeness, solid and careful in execution, free from meretricious colour, and truthful as to character. He takes no rank as a colourist, but a pleasant tone pervades his works.

John Jackson, R.A., is another example of one possessing many fine qualities in art, yet falling short of excellence. He was the son of the village tailor, at Lastingham, in the North Riding of Yorkshire, where he was born on the 31st of May, 1778. He was apprenticed to his father's trade, but was soon known in this out-of-the-way village by his attempts to draw the portraits of his companions ; by these attempts he attracted the notice of Lord Mulgrave and of Sir George Beaumont, the latter of whom induced him to make a trial at painting in oil, and lent to him, for that purpose, Sir Joshua's portrait of George Colman the dramatist; but in his native village the materials were wanting, and Jackson was indebted to the kindness of a friend, a house-painter, who gave him the use of his workshop, and by whose aid the young artist soon improvised tools and colours sufficient to make a copy that surprised his patron, and satisfied him that Jackson was intended by nature for the pursuit of art.   Sir George is said, after consultation with Jackson's other patron, Lord Mulgrave, to have advised the young painter to go to London, as the best means of enabling him to study for the profession, and to have generously offered him a table at his own expense and £50 a year until he had gained a footing in the great capital.   Under these favourable auspices he came to town, and in 1805 was admitted a student of the Royal Academy.

His attempts, although, as we have seen, he had painted in oil before he left the country, had hitherto been likenesses taken in pencil and slightly tinted with water-colour, and his first portraits in oil did not give much promise.   His water-colour portraits were, however, as he improved, universally admired; the heads were well drawn, the likenesses faithful, and spiritedly though carefully finished.   He did not, indeed, abandon the hope of the higher distinction to be gained by portraiture in oil; and trying the wide-spread canvas of that medium, he soon attained complete success.

In 1816, he was elected an associate of the Royal Academy, and travelled through Holland and Flanders, studying the art of the Dutch and Flemish schools.   In 1818, he became a full member of the Academy, and in the following year he visited the chief cities of Northern Italy and Rome.   Sitters gathered round him.   He wrought with great facility and extraordinary rapidity, and during the last years of his practice his portraits displayed great ability: solidly and powerfully painted, faithful, but wanting elevation of character; in his female portraits simple, without any meretricious attempts at simpering graces or the millinery of dress.   He particularly excelled in the subdued richness of his colour, a quality in which Leslie, R.A., said "Lawrence certainly never approached him," and in another place, "that he stood with Lawrence and Owen, and occasionally before either of them, in the first rank of portraiture."

His portrait of Flaxman was greatly admired by his brother artists, and when exhibited, Sir Thomas Lawrence praised it warmly at the public dinner before the opening of the exhibition, speaking of it as "a great achievement of the English school, and a picture of which Vandyck might have felt proud to own himself the author."   We are well aware that Sir Thomas was rather a politician in praise, but though so many years have passed, we can well recollect our own great pleasure at seeing this portrait on the walls. The execution was different to that of the works of most other painters; it appeared laid in with pure and somewhat crude tints, as he would have laid in his first broad hatchings in water-colours. Over this a thin painting gave the broken and mottled hue of flesh, and put the work into unity; it was then lowered in tone by a slight general glaze. It is related that a French artist of eminence, standing before this picture in the exhibition, was heard to say "fine—very fine—almost as fine as Gerard," and, growing in admiration as he continued to examine it, "quite as fine as Gerard," which, from a Frenchman, was a high proof of his appreciation of its excellence.

Jackson was of the Methodist persuasion, and his connection with that body led to his being usually employed to produce the monthly portrait for their organ, the *Evangelical Magazine*, and thus conduced to a connection, extensive although not lucrative. Unlike sectarians in general, he was liberal in his feelings to the Church, and had such an affection for his native parish of Lastingham, as to copy, on an enlarged scale, the picture of "Christ in the Garden," by Correggio, which he had borrowed for that purpose from the Duke of Wellington, and which he presented as an altar-piece to the village church. He was a man of deep religious feeling, but in the last two years of his life he fell into a desponding, low state of health. He was twice married; his second wife was the daughter of James Ward, R.A. He was a frank and amiable man in private life; his friend Constable wrote thus of him:— "He is a great loss to the Academy and the public. By his friends he will be for ever missed; and he had no enemy. He did a great deal of good, much more, I believe, than is generally known, and he never did any harm to any living creature. My sincere belief is, that he is at this moment in heaven." He died June 1st, 1831.

George Henry Harlow, one of those painters who, it is thought, had he been spared, might have proved a competitor of Lawrence more formidable than any other, had the misfortune to be a posthumous child. His father, who had realized money in the China trade, died some few months before the birth of his only son on the 10th of June, 1787. The mother was left a widow with five daughters and one infant son, who was petted and spoiled, as a matter of course, by the whole family, and grew up to think himself, almost before his boyhood was passed, a man, and a most important personage too. Some excuse may well be made for the women of the family, since young George early gave indications of great talent, and must have been a handsome youth.

So clear was the bent of his genius towards art, that his mother was induced to agree to his following it as a profession; she placed him first with De Cort, afterwards with Drummond, the associate, and finally with Sir Thomas Lawrence, who was paid a sum of money to allow the young man the run of his studio, and to pick up any accidental scraps of information that might fall in his way—seeing Lawrence's pictures in progress, if he did not see him paint, the set of his palette, his vehicles and processes, and occasionally getting a sententious scrap of wisdom from the president, which he might apply or not as he had the ability or wisdom. He did not continue with Lawrence above eighteen months; but he imbibed somewhat his manner. He quarrelled with the mechanical part of the work assigned to him, and did not like the cold graciousness of his master. This, added to his vain appreciation of his own powers, led to mutual separation, not on the best terms. When Harlow left the studio of Lawrence he had to depend upon his own industry and ability for his support. There is no doubt that he had adopted much of the peculiarity of Lawrence's manner and execution; a manner which, in his life-size works, gave them even a greater impression of meretriciousness than is seen in his master's; while in the small portraits of painters and men of eminence, which latterly he sought to paint for his own profit and improvement, the manner induced breadth with refinement, although it appeared empty and poor in the larger heads.

His early training had been that of a spoiled child. When he began to practise his profession as a means of livelihood, he painted, at a low price, portraits of many of the actors of the day, and thus fell into the society of men whose life is seldom the most regular; and being of an easy and careless disposition, he was led into dissipation, and soon became embarrassed in his circumstances. He had ever been noted for his love of dress, and for his great attention to personal appearance— valuable qualities in the young if arising from a sense of neatness, and not the result of vanity; which last, it is to be feared, was the motive with young Harlow. What wonder, with these causes at work, that a young and thoughtless boy, who commenced housekeeping and the practice of his profession at sixteen, should, as Smith tells us, have "had *many* tailors' bills to discharge, without an income to discharge one," and that he soon found himself mixed up with bill-brokers and attorneys, while with the elders of his profession he got a character for extravagance and dissipation.

The first time Harlow exhibited at the Royal Academy was in 1805, when we find No. 125, "A Portrait," and he continued to exhibit until the year of his death, with the exception of the year 1813. He was a competitor for Academy honours, but was unsuccessful; having only one scratch, that of Fuseli, who declared (very properly) that he voted for the painter and not for the man. It must be remembered, also, that Harlow was only thirty-one when he died, and that had he lived to an average age he might have overcome the prejudice arising from his

Q

conceit, and would have had ample time to achieve the highest reputation and honours.   He met with plenty of encouragement as a portrait painter.   In June, 1818, he went to Italy, and stayed some time in Rome, where he received many flattering attentions, and was elected member of several Italian Academies, of which he was justly proud, and not a little vain.   On the 13th January, 1819, he was again in England, his head full of historical pictures, and his art no doubt improved by the study of the works of the great masters ; but, in the full ardour of youth and hope, and with many works just begun, he was attacked by a cold which resulted in a glandular disease of the throat, and ended in his death on the 4th of February, 1819.   He was buried in a vault of St. James's Church.

Harlow's reputation was great in his own day, and the public placed him higher as an artist than a review of his works will allow us to do. It is evident his genius was wholly for portraiture, that he would very probably have failed in historical compositions, and that even in portraiture he had probably done his best ere his early death.   Several of his works were engraved, among others two groups of female heads, the subject of the first being "The Proposal," and of the second, "The Congratulation ;" they were rather of the class pretty and pleasing, but they were extremely popular.

From Knowles we further learn that Harlow's "Trial of Queen Katharine" owed much to the critical remarks of Fuseli, "for when he first saw the picture (chiefly in dead colour), he said, 'I do not disapprove of the general arrangement of your work, and I see you will give it a powerful effect of light and shadow ; but you have here a composition of more than twenty figures, or I should say parts of figures, because you have not shown one leg or foot ; this makes it very defective.   Now, if you do not know how to draw legs and feet, I will show you,' and taking up a crayon, drew two on the wainscot of the room. Harlow profited by these remarks, and the next time we saw the picture, the whole arrangement was changed.   Fuseli then said, 'So far you have done well ; but now you have not introduced a back figure, to throw the eye of the spectator into the picture,' and then pointed out by what means he might improve it in this particular.   Accordingly Harlow introduced the two boys who are taking up the cushion ; the one which shows the back is altogether due to Fuseli, and is certainly the best drawn figure in the picture.   Fuseli afterwards attempted to get him to improve the drawing of the arms of the principal figure (Mrs. Siddons as Queen Katharine), but without much effect ; for, having witnessed many ineffectual attempts of the painter, he desisted from further criticism, remarking, 'It is a pity that you never attended the Antique Academy.'"

Our own opinion of this picture is that it is clever, but *stagey*, with rather too much of the tableau and attitude school ; and, although the painter prided himself upon it as an historical picture, we consider that it has none of the qualities to uphold its claim to that rank.

Sir John Watson Gordon, R.A., was born in Edinburgh, in 1790, being the son of Captain Watson, of Overmans in Berwickshire, a post-captain in the British navy. Through his father's family, young Gordon claimed a Scottish cousinship with Sir Walter Scott, through his mother's relations with Robertson the historian, and Falconer the seaman, who wrote *The Shipwreck*, and afterwards perished in a storm at sea. Young Gordon was educated with a view to the army, and interest was made for him to enter the Royal Military Academy at Woolwich, but being too young for admission he was remitted for a time to the Trustees' School at Edinburgh, to improve himself in drawing. John Graham, who then was head-master, must have been either an exceedingly clever teacher, or particularly fortunate in his pupils, since Wilkie, Allan, and Burnet were among them, besides many others who afterwards attained a higher reputation than their master. Here Gordon remained four years, and whether inspired by the atmosphere of the place, or by the clever companions by whom he was surrounded, he after a time turned his views towards art as a profession. His first efforts, like those of most young men, were in the direction of history painting. Shrewd no less as a youth than as a man, he soon found that his talent might be better employed in portraiture, and succeeding in his efforts, continued true to this branch of art all his life. After Raeburn's death in 1823, Watson Gordon became his successor in his Edinburgh practice, and all the celebrities of the Scottish capital visited his studio. He was one of the earliest members of the Scottish Academy ; and in 1850, on the death of Sir W. Allan, became their president. At the same time, her Majesty gave him the vacant appointment of Queen's limner for Scotland, and conferred on him the honour of knighthood. Watson Gordon had been elected an associate of the Royal Academy of London in 1841, and obtained the full honours of the body in 1851. Loving his profession, he lived in the practice of it, and led a single life in the social circle of his Scottish friends. True to his native city till the last, he died there, rather suddenly, on 1st June, 1864.

His portraits are bold and manly, his figures well placed on the canvas, and he at all times seized happily the best expression of his sitters, giving them character without an approach to caricature—the sagacity and shrewdness of the Scottish character in all its best aspects, when united to intellect and a high cultivation. He had little sense or feeling for colour, and never seemed to wish to escape from the black garments of his male sitters by the introduction of the *furniture*, in which most portrait painters so largely indulge. Frequently in his male portraits the only colour is that of the flesh, with a negative warmth in the background; yet there was a great harmony in the grey tones of his work, which prevents us from feeling so much the absence of colour; and even his female portraits, in which the same scale predominated, did not lose so much from this cause as might have been expected. He was most successful in his male heads of persons advanced in life, which are painted more as completed sketches than as pictures, and gain thereby great force, freshness, and vigour. His works when exhibited in Paris, in 1855, were greatly admired, particularly the portraits of Professor Wilson and the Provost of Peterhead, and won for him a medal on that occasion.

It is not right to close our list of the contemporaries of Lawrence without some notice of *Henry Perronet Briggs, R.A.*, although he can hardly be so designated. Born in 1792, he entered as a student of the Royal Academy in 1811, and beginning life as a subject painter, won his way to honours by pictures which, if not of the highest class of art, have great merit in the construction of the subject, the frequent originality of action in the figures, and the mode of telling his story. His drawing is usually correct, the colouring forced and somewhat rank, and the flesh has often a polished and shining look, very different to the tender and somewhat absorbent nature of its true surface.

After his election as a full member, Briggs almost entirely devoted himself to portraiture, finding himself compelled, from the confined patronage of art at that time and the necessities that followed upon his marriage of providing for the future household, to adopt this more lucrative branch of his profession. Many of the most eminent persons of the day sat to him. His portrait of Lord Eldon is one of his most characteristic works; but, both in his subject-pictures and in his portraits, his colouring was rather strong than true, and his flesh painting hot in the shadows and forced in the lights. His wife, to whom he was much attached, died some years before him; his own death took place on the 18th January, 1844, in his fifty-first year.

CHAPTER XX.

His birthplace and the scenes among which Turner passed his childhood, may be thought not the best fitted to form a landscape-painter, or to fill his youthful mind with images of beauty. Born 23rd April, 1775, the son of a hairdresser of small means, and bred in Maiden Lane, in the heart of this great metropolis, he could enjoy very little of the sight of " fresh fields and pastures new." In the hovels and sheds of the Covent Garden of that day, he might make acquaintance with a few specimens of roots and flowers, and, strolling down to St. James's Park in the summer evenings, get a glimpse of trees and greensward. But even the park was far less foliated than in the present day. Many of the old trees were stagged and dead, and new ones were not yet planted.

But, straying down a set of winding lanes and alleys, young Turner might, and no doubt often did, wander away to the strand of the broad river, a river unequalled in the world for its picturesque variety, and not then spanned by so many bridges, or cumbered with steamboats and steamboat-piers ; not then quite so muddied and thickened with the refuse of the extra million dwellers on its shores. Here his love of rivers and river scenery, no doubt, was fostered. The first drawing he exhibited was a view on its southern bank, as was also the first oil picture—" Moonlight," a study at Millbank, now in the national collection ; and his last days were passed in an obscure dwelling by its side, whence he could see its broad bosom gleaming under the western sun. The quaint picturesqueness and curious relics of architecture in the streets of his own neighbourhood may also account for his love of cities, and of architecture.

It is not very clearly stated by any of his biographers when young Turner began to show a love for art ; but it is most probable that it was developed early, since in 1789, when only fourteen years of age, he was admitted a student in the Royal Academy, and in 1790 he exhibited on its walls for the first time, " A View of the Archbishop's Palace at

Lambeth," and there are some sketches which must be prior to either of these periods.

Turner was from the beginning diligent in the pursuit of his profession, and soon began to turn it to profitable account : it is said that he exhibited his juvenile performances for sale in the windows of his father's shop in Maiden Lane; that he was employed to colour prints for Raphael Smith, the engraver, and to wash in backgrounds for the architects, a practice more resorted to half a century ago than in our own day.   Even at this early time, and under such unpromising circumstances, there was an originality in his work : we are told that he was employed by a Mr. Dobson, an architect, to colour the perspective front of a mansion, and that in putting in the windows, Turner showed the effect of reflected light from the sky, contrasting with the inner dark of the room on the uneven surface of the panes.   This was a new treatment, and his employer objected to it, declaring that the work must be coloured as was usual; that is, the panes an unvarying dark grey, the bars white. "It will spoil my drawing," said the artist. "Rather that than my work," answered the architect: "I must have it done as I wish."   Turner doggedly obeyed, and when he had completed the work, left his employer altogether.   The sequel of the story is curious : some time after, it occurred to the architect to try a drawing on the principle he had disapproved, and remembering Turner's work he coloured it nearly the same.   It was sent to the Royal Academy, and accepted, and was so much admired by Smirke, that he sought the acquaintance of Dobson, which led to a union between the families.   So much for genius in the mere colouring of a window.

It would appear from the un-numbered sketches Turner left behind him, that he thoroughly appreciated and acted up to the maxim of "no day without a line," and that his sketch-book was always in requisition. Smith, it would seem, introduced him to Girtin, and also to Dr. Munro, who employed both Girtin and Turner, as we have already told, to sketch for him, paying them at the rate of half-a-crown an evening, and providing them with a supper after their labours.   We also know that Turner gave lessons ; receiving five shillings and even ten shillings per lesson— a large sum in those days.

Although London and its noble river afforded some of the earliest subjects for his pencil, he soon began to travel, to enlarge his field of study.   He visited when quite young some Bristol relatives, and his early architectural and topographical labours gave him a taste for, and led him to examine, the noble ruins spread over the land.   As a proof of this architectural and topographical feeling, Mr. Wornum tells us that of thirty-two drawings exhibited by Turner from 1790 to 1796, no less than twenty-three are architectural; principally views of the great cathedrals and abbey churches of the kingdom. As evidence of his diligence and promptitude, we learn that Girtin having mentioned, in the presence of Turner, his intention to pay a sketching visit to St. Alban's, but delaying to do so for a few days, he was surprised to meet his friend returning with a book of sketches: Turner having forestalled him and already reaped the harvest, while Girtin was thinking of starting to win it.

From the pictures which he exhibited in 1795, we find that he had been within the previous year to Cambridge, Peterborough, Lincoln, Shrewsbury, Tintern, and Wrexham ; and before he became an associate of the Royal Academy in 1800, his exhibited works range over twenty-six counties of England and Wales, many of which he had apparently visited several times, at a period when travelling was far less easy than in our own day. Turner long continued his topographical labours for the booksellers, which led on to his undertaking, later in life, a series of works illustrating our cities, rivers and coast scenery. For some years prior to 1801, he designed the headings for the *Oxford Almanack*, which were engraved by M. A. Rooker until his death in that year. Wyatt, the frame-maker of Oxford, used to relate a characteristic story of Turner, but whether of this period or later is uncertain. He had employed the painter to make some drawings of Oxford, which obliged him to sit in the public street. The price to be paid for the work was a liberal one, but, as annoyances and hindrances took place from the curiosity of spectators, before Turner began the drawing of Christ Church he made Wyatt obtain for him the loan of an old postchaise, which was so placed in the main street that Turner could work from the window ; and, when the drawing was paid for, the painter insisted on receiving three shillings and sixpence which he had disbursed for the use of the old vehicle.

Turner, we have seen, began his art by sketching from nature, and never omitted any opportunity of enlarging his knowledge by the same means ; continuing the practice to the latest period of a long life, as the following incident, related to have happened within two or three years of his death, will prove :—He had wandered away in the summer months along the coast of Normandy, as he said himself, looking out for storms and shipwrecks : he carried nothing with him but a change of linen and his sketch-book. Arrived at Eu, he found it necessary to have his shoes repaired, and took a lodging in the house of a fisherman. He had not been long there before an officer of the court inquired for him, and told him that Louis Philippe, the King of the French, who was then staying at the Château, hearing that Mr. Turner was in the town, had sent to desire his company to dinner (they had been well known to one another in England). Turner strove to apologize—pleaded his want of dress—but this was overruled ; his usual costume was the dress-coat of the period, and he was assured that he only required a white neckcloth, and that the King must not be denied.   The fisherman's wife easily provided a white neckcloth, by cutting up some of her linen, and Turner declared that he spent one of the pleasantest of evenings in chat with his old Twickenham acquaintance.   On starting for these excursions, he never intimated the route he intended to take, nor the time of his stay or of his return, this being determined by the weather and his success.   The National Gallery alone possesses nearly 1,000 of his sketches, works of high excellence and of the most varied character, which were the fruits of these rambles.

In sketching, Turner used all methods ; but rarely, very rarely, the medium of oil.   And it is this water-colour tendency of his art, and this constant recurrence to nature, that gives the interpreting key to all his after practice.   Passing from the mere outlines, which are rapid pencil sketches of distances and foreground figures, we find colour-sketches reckoned by thousands.   Here we have every variety of subject and every amount of labour.   Sometimes simple flat washes of local tint indicate the whole of a wide extended landscape, sometimes the relation of mountain to sky, or of a bit of foreground to distance, is happily and minutely given ; of mere studies of skies it is said that Turner's are to be reckoned by thousands.   As he advanced in art he made sketches for his pictures, and sketches from nature on grey papers, heightening the lights, or giving the points of expression by white or body colour, but still using the colour of his masses translucently as if on white paper ; some of these sketches, mere broad flat masses of colour, are so truly beautiful and effective, rendering nature so fully to us, that we seem to want no more completion, but are thoroughly satisfied with the result before us.

It has been objected to Turner that he could not draw the figure ; and the ignorant laugh at many of the figures which he has introduced into his landscapes, while others detract from the Academy teaching for the same reason.   But Turner's sketches show that he was a most ready and able draughtsman, while his effort is rather to give the right treatment to his figures—the true effect of light and sun and air, their true keeping in the picture, and the indefinite mystery of sunshine upon them—than to define their forms or to complete their outline.

Mr. Ruskin says :—" The Academy taught Turner nothing, not even the one thing it might have done,—the mechanical process of safe oil-painting, sure vehicles, and permanent colours."   Such assertions as these are easily made, and difficult to disprove ; but this is certain, Turner himself was not ungrateful to the Academy, either as to its teaching or to its friendly membership, as his life-long fellowship with its members clearly proves.   Moreover, his early pictures—when modes of painting learnt in the schools, clung about him—were safely and solidly painted, and show no signs of cracking. Witness his "Crossing the Brook," his "Richmond Hill," and many others of this period. Some notes upon nine or ten pictures of various periods, made on the occasion of Mr. Bicknell's sale in 1863, show that the works of his earlier time were in the soundest state, simply and carefully painted, and without any failure of colour. It was only when his eager pursuit of the effects of sunlight, mist, and extensive distance bathed in air and vapour, led him on to frequent scumblings, and at times to the use of water-colours in his oil paintings, and his impulsive genius carried him away to paint hastily, and to force his works with rapid driers, that the foundations of these failures were laid.

Another cause of failure has also been hinted at,—Turner's known practice of painting largely upon his pictures on the "varnishing days." At these times, such was his love of colour, that any rich tint on a brother painter's palette, so tempted him, that he would jokingly remove a large portion of it to his own, and immediately apply it to his picture, irrespective of the medium with which it was made up. From our own palette he has whisked off, on more occasions than one, a luscious knob of orange vermilion, or ultramarine, tempered with copal, and at once used it on a picture he was at work upon with a mastic magylph. Such a practice, productive of no mischief at the moment, would break up a picture when the harder drier began to act on that which was of a less contractile nature.

Again, as to the pictures left on his own walls for any time,—and this relates to all those now in the national collection, as well as to many others which remained for years in his studio,—the utter neglect and carelessness with which they were treated, would have destroyed pictures of the strongest constitutions, much more the delicate, fragile works which he loved to produce. The scene in his rooms on the occasion of his funeral would have saddened any lover of art, for the works left behind, almost as much as for the genius that had passed away. The gallery seemed as if broom or dusting-brush had never troubled it. The carpet, or matting (its texture was undistinguishable from dirt), was worn and musty; the hangings, which had once been a gay amber colour, showed a dingy yellow hue where the colour was not washed out by the drippings from the ceiling: for the cove and the glass sky-lights were in a most dilapidated state, many panes broken and patched with old newspapers. From these places the wet had run down the walls, and loosened the plaster, so that it had actually fallen behind the canvas of one picture, "The Bay of Baiæ," which, hanging over the bottom of the frame, bagged outwards, with the mass of accumulated mortar and rubbish it upheld. Many of the pictures—"Crossing the Brook" among others—had large pieces chipped or scaled off; while others were so fast going to decay, that the gold first, and then the ground, had perished from the very frames, and the bare fir-wood beneath was exposed. It may well be supposed that in such a damp and mouldy atmosphere any pictures would suffer, much more the fragile works of Turner's last period, irregularly carried out as has been described.

As no lists of the attendance of students were kept at that time, it is impossible to tell how much or how little Turner worked in the schools of the Academy. One thing is certain, that, when elected, his brother members believed in his power not only to draw the figure but to instruct others, since they repeatedly appointed him a visitor in the life school (a duty not usually confided to a landscape painter); and those who studied in the schools during his visitorship have testified to the valuable assistance that he gave the students at those times. When a visitor in the life school he introduced a capital practice, which it is to be regretted has not been continued : he chose for study a model as nearly as possible corresponding in form and character with some fine antique figure, which he placed by the side of the model posed in the same action ; thus, the " Discobulus of Myron " contrasted with one of the best of our trained soldiers : the " Lizard Killer" with a youth in the roundest beauty of adolescence : the " Venus de' Medici " beside a female in the first period of youthful womanhood. The idea was original and very instructive : it showed at once how much the antique sculptors had refined nature ; which, if in parts more beautiful than the *selected* form which is called *ideal*, as a whole looked common and vulgar by its side.

Turner's conversation, his lectures, and his advice were at all times enigmatical, not from want of knowledge, but from want of verbal power. Rare advice it was, if you could unriddle it, but so mysteriously given or expressed that it was hard to comprehend—conveyed sometimes in a few indistinct words, in a wave of the hand, a poke in the side, pointing at the same time to some part of a student's drawing, but saying nothing more than a " Humph !" or " What's that for ? " Yet the fault hinted at, the thing to be altered was there, if you could but find it out; and if, after a deep puzzle, you did succeed in comprehending his meaning, he would congratulate you when he came round again, and would give you some further hint ; if not, he would leave you with another disdainful growl, or perhaps seizing your portecrayon, or with his broad thumb, make you at once sensible of your fault. To a student who was intent on refining the forms before he had got the action of his figure, he would thrust with the point of his thumb at the place of the two nipples and the navel, and—very likely with the nail—draw down the curve of the depression of the sternum and linea alba, to show that pose, action and proportion were to be the first consideration. To another who, painting from the life, was insipidly finishing up a part without proper relation to the whole, he would—taking the brush from his hand, and without a word—vigorously mark in the form of the shadow and the position of the high lights, to indicate that the relations of the whole should be the student's first consideration. The schools were usually better attended during his visitorships than during those of most other members, from which it may be inferred that the students appreciated his teaching. This, however, relates to the middle period of his life, and not to the time now under consideration.

His lectures on perspective, after he was elected to the professorship, were, from his naturally enigmatical and ambiguous style of delivery, almost unintelligible. Half of each lecture was addressed to the attendant behind him, who was constantly busied, under his muttered directions, in selecting from a huge portfolio drawings and diagrams to illustrate his teaching; many of these were truly beautiful, speaking intelligibly enough to the eye, if his language did not to the ear. As illustrations of aërial perspective and the perspective of colour, many of his rarest drawings were at these lectures placed before the students in all the glory of their first unfaded freshness. A rare treat to our eyes they were. Stothard, the librarian to the Royal Academy, who was nearly deaf for some years before his death, was a constant attendant at Turner's lectures. A brother member, who judged of them rather from the known dryness of the subject, and the certainty of what Turner's delivery would be, than from any attendance on his part, asked the librarian why he was so constant. "Sir," said he, "there is much to *see* at Turner's lectures—much that I delight in seeing, though I cannot hear him."

It has already been remarked that the art of water-colour painting had its origin in topography, and that the minute attention to facts and details so necessary in topographical works was a direct and valuable initiation to the careful study of nature. We have seen also that Turner began art as a water-colour painter, labouring at drawings of local scenery. The works which he exhibited at the Royal Academy for the first seven years were all *views*. But Turner's genius was not of a nature to allow him long to continue painting simply representative landscapes, or to treat his subjects merely topographically. In 1793, we note the first indication of an attempt to treat his picture as modified or changed by passing atmospheric effects. For mist and vapour lit by the golden light of morn, or crimsoned with the tints of evening—spread out to veil the distance, or rolled in clouds and storm—are the great characteristics of Turner's art, as contrasted with the mild serenity, the calm unclouded heaven, of Claude. Henceforth, his quotations from the poets are frequent, first from Thomson's *Seasons*, or Milton's

Paradise Lost, but afterwards strange confused stanzas from some mythical manuscript called *The Fallacies of Hope*.

No one knows who was the author of this poem, or whether, indeed, it exists at all; we rather infer that the quotations were manufactured as occasion arose by the painter himself: they are in the strange ambiguous style of his conversation, and his attempts at wit, understood only by himself, and certainly if Turner's pictures had been as unintelligible as his poetry, he would have added little to art.

It has been asserted somewhat unjustly that Turner was underrated and misunderstood by his contemporaries, but the criticisms of the time are favourable to his works, and his election as associate of the Royal Academy at the very earliest period at which, according to the rules, he could be chosen; and, further, his elevation within little more than two years, and when only twenty-six years of age, to full membership, sufficiently prove that his talent and genius were fully appreciated by his brother artists, and received all the honour that their choice could give.

But to return to the period preceding his associateship. Not only did Turner from this time eschew representative landscape and topographical art for that which is far higher and more noble—for a generalized treatment of nature, avoiding minute details, and looking at his subject as a whole, with all the poetry arising from accidents of storm and sunshine, of driving mist, of early morn or dewy eve—but he actually held as a principle that accurate topographical treatment, mere imitative landscapes, painted as they might in our day be photographed from a given point, embracing all that could be seen from that point, and no more, did not represent the place so fully as a far more general treatment would do: a treatment bringing in, it may be, buildings or objects which from that identical spot were not to be seen, being hidden, perhaps, by nearer objects, or out of the field of the picture—but which from their importance, their magnitude, or their singularity, were especial features of the scene. Thus he would say that no one should paint London without St. Paul's, or Oxford without the dome of the Bodleian; and constantly in his pictures he would move a building of importance considerably to the right or left, to bring it into what he considered its best place in the picture. And this is quite consistent with reason, for no one but an artist views a town or any scene from a rigidly fixed point. Again, we may look upon scenery under some aspects, or at one time of day, and see in it neither feature nor beauty: it may even seem essentially commonplace, from those very details which some would delight in giving so imitatively; but the same scene presents itself, perhaps, in the purple gloom of sunset, massed large and solemnly against a luminous golden sky, and we look with surprise and wonder at its beauty. The true mission of the artist, then, is to seize these golden moments, rare and fleeting—unheeded, perhaps, even in their beauty by common minds—and to fix them by his art for ever. What, compared with this, is the merit of building up a tree leaf by leaf and branch by branch; of drawing, as if by the camera, every nameless house and every crumbling stack of chimneys, brick by brick? What is there in such, even if true as truth itself, that affords us delight?

After he began painting in oil, Turner for some time continued in his exhibition-pictures, chiefly to use that medium. We do not find him all at once striking out a new art for himself, but rather walking reverently in the old paths and deferential to old authorities. Many of his earliest works, and of these some of his best, are founded on the Dutch school; Wilson is palpably imitated in many of his pictures, so also are Poussin and Claude. Indeed, Turner evidently felt a strong spirit of rivalry with Claude, and a desire to measure himself, and be measured by the world, in comparison with the great French landscape painter; as he proved by the special bequest of two of his works to hang between two of the best Claudes in the National Gallery, where they have since been placed. Even the figure painters were not beyond his imitative rivalry; as in " The Blacksmith's Shop," painted in 1807.

This picture is specially curious, as showing how ready our painter was to match himself against any aspirant for fame. The year before, 1806, " The Village Politicians," the work of Wilkie, then only in his twenty-second year, was exhibited in the Royal Academy, attracted general attention, and was highly praised. Turner painted " The Blacksmith's Shop," evidently in direct imitation of the manner and characteristics of the young artist who had so suddenly taken rank before the public, and the work was exhibited the same year with " The Blind Fiddler," the second picture that Wilkie painted in the metropolis. This may have been done in a spirit of friendly rivalry, rather than from any envious feeling on Turner's part, still it is alleged that the younger man felt a little sore, and the transaction led to some hostile criticism.

While Turner was painting for the walls of the exhibition those noble works, which *we* at least are inclined to think, with one or two exceptions, his best, and the period during which he produced them (viz., from 1800 to 1820), his best time, he was diligently labouring at the new art of water-colour painting; very rarely exhibiting the works in this medium publicly, but mostly preparing them for the engravers. This practice seems to have led him to a perfectly new view of his art. Water-colour, depending for its lights on the purity and whiteness of its ground, and susceptible of the most infinitesimal gradations of tint and colour by mere dilutions of the pigments with water, has, so far, a wider range than oil is capable of, wherein the tints, when painted solidly—as all the lights must almost of necessity be—are gradated by mixing the coloured pigments with white; this admits of far fewer gradations in scale, and has, moreover, the evil of altering somewhat the nature of the colour by such admixture, making the tint produced in a degree absorbent of light, and far less brilliant than in its transparent state by mere dilution. It is true that by glazing the colour over a light ground, some of the advantages of water-colour are obtained, and some even in a higher degree than in that medium; such as increased depth, brilliancy, and force, far greater from the unctuous richness of oil than in water-colour. But even when thus treated, the gradations are far less delicate, owing to the fluidity of the medium being less; while as there is a sensible colour in all oily media which tinges or tarnishes the delicate tints, the use of oil in this manner is almost precluded.

Turner, in his water-colour art, was led insensibly into these refined gradations; by them he sought detail with great breadth, and managed to give at least the appearance of the multitudinous details of mountain range or extended plain, the effects of air and light, and the mists that are ever floating in our island atmosphere,—a manner that no one had thought of before him, much less had accomplished; and this manner he sought to carry out in his oil pictures also. His water-colour practice led him to the use of the white ground. He soon perceived the far greater luminousness thus to be obtained; that works so treated, when seen in a room, had as it were light in themselves, and appeared as if the spectator were looking forth into the open air, as compared with the solid paintiness of the works of his contemporaries. But how to use his colour in sufficiently delicate gradations to achieve the same result on a light ground in oil, as on the paper ground in water-colours, was one of his first difficulties; and he was led to adopt the use of scumbling, that is to say, of driving very thin films of white, or of colour mixed with white, over a properly prepared ground. By this means he not only obtained infinitely delicate gradations, but he successfuly imitated the effects of air and mist; the brighter tints beneath being rendered greyer and more distant at the same time by the film of white. This enabled him to make the points of the composition—his figures, or other coloured objects in the foreground—stand out in extreme brilliancy, owing to the employment of transparent colour boldly and purely used over the white.

By these means Turner obtained the whole range of the scale, from white—to him the intensest representative of light—to the purest reds, oranges, blues, purples, &c., that the use of the transparent pigments in oil permitted. Or by a black object, such as a black hat, a dog, or a cow, the extreme range of his palette from light to dark. Thus he abandoned the old maxim of art—that a painter should reserve his palette, and always have something to enhance the black, the white, or the colour of his picture—and expended all the force of his pigments so as to realize the utmost brilliancy possible.

This change in Turner's art became manifest about the year 1820. This year was a year of transition; after it we find his execution, as well as the principles on which he wrought, entirely changed from the solid character of his first manner.

Burnet, whose critical remarks on Turner's works are usually sound and well considered, has shown us how contemporary art was affected by this change of principle in Turner. He says (*Turner and his Works*, p. 61), "The light key upon which most of our present landscape painters work, owes its origin to Turner; the presence of his pictures on the walls of the Academy engendered this change from the darker imitations of Wilson and Gainsborough, or the contemplation of the landscapes of the Dutch school; light pictures certainly attract more attention than dark, but the question is, how far this style may be carried with safety; in the opinion of many, the English school are extending this principle to excess. Wilkie used to relate an anecdote, that while he was one of the hangers of the pictures, he carried a copy of 'The Woman taken in Adultery,' by Rembrandt, and put it up amongst the works on the walls of the Academy; there was a general shout of triumph in favour of lights—one cried out 'Away with the black masters!' another said, 'It looks like a hole in the wall;' but after listening to their congratulations in praise of their own style, Wilkie quietly observed, 'If we are on the right road, then the greatest masters of the Italian and British schools have all been wrong.'"

We also know that Wilkie, on his return from Italy, complained that the English works were, to his eyes, painted up in the darks, but left flat in the lights, that is, looking thin and poor. We well remember ourselves the effect of the British pictures when hung in the same building with the works of the French school at the Paris Exhibition, in 1855. They had generally an appearance of chalkiness that had never struck us until we saw them thus juxtaposed, for the French paint lower in tone than we do, even in their landscapes, and always seem to reserve their palette, so as to retain both white and colour more intense than is found in the picture, to enable them to emphasize and give focussing points to their works; while our artists seem lavish of the full power of the palette, and appear to leave nothing beyond for that little more light, which, according to the well-known painter's paradox, may serve to make the picture darker and richer—that brighter pigment which is to neutralize any too-prevailing colour; or that still darker touch which is to take out the dark from a picture, and to give it clearness. Such, however, was no longer the art of Turner in the new manner he adopted, and continued until he ended his labour with his life. Perhaps this style reached its climax in the picture of "Phryne as Venus going to the Baths," painted in 1838.

Soon after this picture, Turner's art began visibly to decline; he pushed his principle of broken tints, of intense light and of confused and commingled forms, to its utmost extreme; and some of the last works, of his hand, while the artist may regard them with wonder, not unmixed with admiration at what they suggest, must ever be but caviare to the multitude.

To us one of Turner's most poetical works is the "Ulysses Deriding Polyphemus," which he exhibited in 1829, and now in the National Gallery. It is impossible to go beyond the power of colour here achieved; it is on the very verge of extravagance, but yet is in no way gaudy. How nearly it is so, is seen in any attempt to copy the picture; such copies are more surely failures than those from any other of the painter's works. The mere handling is a marvel, the ease and freedom of the work, the thick impasto of tints that are heaped on the upper sky, making the lower parts recede in true perspective to the rising sun; the grand way in which the vessel moves over the "watery floor," the dream-like poetry of the whole, make up a picture without a parallel in the world of art. Or, look at his "Shipwreck," 1805, a work whose characteristics are of the Dutch school, but in which the theme is so treated as to speak by its terrible poetry to all, but more especially to English, minds. The heaving and boiling sea, torn by the winds, is mingled with the black heavens all along what might be the horizon: the foam from the crests of the broken waves is driven like a snow-wreath across the dark overhanging thunder-cloud; yonder, almost hidden by the mist and smoky drift of the torn waves, the doomed vessel lies tossed and helpless, the hopeless seamen dropping from hull and bowsprit into the swamping boats. In the foreground, lit up by a fitful gleam, are other boats hasting to aid the drowning crew; one is almost engulfed in the boiling surge; in the other, the mariners strain hard at the helm to steer clear of their companion. Terror is on every face.

Turner as an artist was quite aware of the greatness of his own powers, and jealous of their proper recognition; many indications of this feeling will occur to those who read his life.

In person Turner had little of the outward appearance that we love to attribute to the possessors of genius. In the last twenty years of his life, during which we knew him well, his short figure had become corpulent —his face, perhaps from continual exposure to the air, was unusually red, and a little inclined to blotches. His dark eye was bright and restless—his nose, aquiline. He generally wore what is called a black dress coat, which would have been the better for brushing—the sleeves were mostly too long, coming down over his fat and not over clean hands. He wore his hat while painting on the varnishing days—or otherwise a large wrapper over his head, while on the warmest days he generally had another wrapper or comforter round his throat—though occasionally he would unloose it and allow the two ends to dangle down in front and pick up a little of the colour from his ample palette. This, together with his ruddy face, his rollicking eye, and his continuous, although, except to himself, unintelligible jokes, gave him the appearance of one of that now wholly extinct race—a long-stage coachman. In the schools his eyes seemed ever in motion, and would instantly spy out any student who was sketching his portrait—which we were all anxious to do on the margin of our drawings, but out of many attempts none succeeded, for he knew, as if by intuition, when any one had his eye on him for this purpose, and would change his posture so as to preclude the chance of its being finished. Thus stolen likenesses of him are rare. On the varnishing days he was generally one of the earliest to arrive, coming down to the Academy before breakfast and continuing his labours as long as daylight lasted ; strange and wonderful was the transformation he at times effected in his works on the walls. Latterly he used to send them in in a most unfinished state, relying on what he could do for them during the three days allowed to the members.

Soon after Turner's death the "varnishing days" were, however, abandoned for a time, and only reinstated in 1862. It had been found in the interim that Turner was right in the value he placed on these days of meeting. The English school is constituted on the system of individual independence ; each artist after having learnt the mere technical elements, the handicraft of his art, practises it almost irrespective of the rules and traditions of his predecessors. In England, the *atelier* system of the Continent—a system where the pupil enters upon all the knowledge of his master and follows all the traditions of the school—is all but unknown ; while even our academic system leaves the student, after he has obtained a command of the language of his art, quite free as to his mode of using it, and has the merit of forming artists of varied originality, because untrammelled by rules and systems ; if it has also the fault of leaving the rising body ignorant of any general code of law or precedent to guide them in their practice.

Now on the "varnishing days," when painting was going on in common, much of precept, much of practice, and much of common experience, were interchanged. The younger members gained much from the elder ones, and many useful hints and suggestions from one another. Who does not recollect the valuable remarks of Wilkie, Etty, Leslie, Constable, and Mulready, and, above all, of Turner? though

R

from him, as has been already seen, it was conveyed in dark hints and ambiguous phrases. A little anecdote of what happened to one of the writers, on his first admission to the privilege of these meetings, which must be told with the singular pronoun, will illustrate what has been said ; at the same time it is quite characteristic of Turner, and of his keen perception of what a picture required to set right an apparent defect, and it is on both accounts well worth insertion here. "The first varnishing days at the Royal Academy to which I was admitted on my election as associate, I was trying to *spoil* my picture of 'The Castle Builder,' when Howard came up to me and said, in his most frigid manner, 'that the bosom of my figure was indelicately naked, and that some of the members thought I had better paint the dress higher.' Here was a dilemma for a new associate. Of course, with due meekness, I was about to comply with his advice, although greatly against the grain, and with a sort of wonder at myself that I could possibly have been ignorantly guilty of sending an immodest contribution to the Exhibition. Meanwhile, Turner looked over my shoulder, and, in his usual sententious manner, mumbled out, 'What-r-doing?' I told him the rebuke I had just received from the secretary. 'Pooh, pooh,' said he, 'paint it lower.' I thought he was intent upon leading me into a scrape. 'You want white,' he added, and turned on his heel. What could he mean? I pondered over his words, and after a while the truth struck me. The coloured dress came harshly on the flesh, and no linen intervened. I painted at once, over a portion of the bosom of the *dress*, a peep of the chemise. Howard came round soon after, and said, with a little more warmth, 'Ah! you have covered it up—it is far better now—it will do.' It was no higher however ; there was just as much of the flesh seen, but the sense of nakedness and display was gone. Turner also came round again, and gave his gratified grunt at my docility and appreciativeness, which he often rewarded afterwards by like hints. Now this was not a mere incidental change, but it was a truth, always available in the future, the value of linen near the flesh—a hint I never forgot, and continually found useful. Many such have I heard and seen him give to his brother landscape painters—either by word of mouth or with a dash of his brush ; and it is a great satisfaction to all that by a fair compromise with the other exhibitors, the Academy has again partially restored the varnishing days, and that members can again interchange opinions and advice with one another."

But we resume. Hitherto Turner has been spoken of principally as an oil painter, and this art has furnished most of our illustrations of his methods and practice. Yet as a water-colour painter, he is, perhaps, even more eminent. It has already been said that his treatment of oil was greatly influenced by his practice in water-colour, and that his success, or the novelty of the results, influenced the whole art of the period, introducing a lighter and brighter scale of painting than had heretofore prevailed. His influence on the growing school of water-colour was treated of in a former chapter; but it is impossible to conclude our notice of Turner and his art, without some more definite account of his works in water-colour. Perhaps it is not too much to say, that he shows even as a greater artist in these works, than in those painted in the nobler medium. In oil he had the body of ancient art before him, and great masters of execution in almost every varied style. But in water-colour, what was there in the beginning to guide him—what had he to adopt—what to improve upon? The art all but began with him; weak and feeble, in its very childhood as to executive means, hardly a resource had been invented by which to express the wonderful qualities which nature presents to the artist's eye, and which Turner, more especially, was gifted to perceive. Nature revealed to him a flood of atmospheric light, a world of infinitely tender gradations of tint and colour, gradations so minute as to be almost unappreciable by other men, and such as it seemed hopeless to realize by the practice which then prevailed; he had, therefore, to invent his own methods.

Turner soon found that an untrue heaviness resulted from the old process of diluting or strengthening a grey tint and treating every part, first as a mere gradation of light and dark, afterwards tinting with colour, thus to represent the hue of the object in the lights, and by passing the same tint over the shadowed ground, the hue as affected or changed by shade. He proceeded, therefore, to view every object and part of an object, the whole surface of his picture, as *colour;* the local colour modified and often absolutely changed by light or the absence of light, by atmosphere, reflection, or distance, but each portion still looked at for its own *colour;* and then, resorting to the pigments which, either separately or mixed, would represent that colour, he would execute the tint or hue at once on the paper. This was a great advance in the true direction, but here another danger was to be avoided, muddiness of tint, and loss of the translucency from the white ground, partly from the imperfection of the pigments, and partly from the needful repetitions of the washes. Hence arose delicate hatchings and stipplings, which in his hands achieved wonderful qualities of broken hues, air-tints and atmosphere; and various modes of removing from the surface any overloaded parts. All these, with numerous other resources, were, if not invented by him, applied so judiciously, and with such consummate manipulative skill, that we never for a moment are led to a consideration of the process by which the effect is produced, being so fully satisfied

R 2

with the truth of the impression it imparts. Water-colour seemed to lend itself readily to the imitation of those effects in nature he so much loved to represent—nature lost in a blaze of light, rather than dimmed with a twilight gloom—and thus it happens that his works in this medium mostly embody some evanescent effect, be it flood of sunshine bursting forth after storms, or careering in ·gleams over the plain, the mountain, or the sea; or some wrack of clouds, some passing shower or rainbow of promise refreshing the gladdened and glistening earth.

Turner's water-colour paintings, indeed, epitomize the whole mystery of landscape art. Other painters have arrived at excellence in one treatment of nature. Thus, Cozens in grand and solemn effects of mountain scenery; Robson, in simple breadth and masses; De Wint, in tone and colour; Glover in sun-gleams thrown across the picture, and tipping with golden light the hills and trees; Cox, in his breezy freshness; and Barret, in his classical compositions, lighted by the setting sun. These were men that played in one key, often making the rarest melody. But Turner's art compassed all they did collectively, and more than equalled each in his own way.

It had been almost a dogma in art that the darkest colour of a picture must, in open-air subjects, be in the foreground. But Turner, by his knowledge in the application of hot and cold colours could place his dark in the distance, and yet be true, although the foreground was glowing with golden sunlight. Thus in the "Heidelberg" (which was in the International Exhibition, 1862), a few small touches of warm dark in the foreground are all that counterbalance a mass of blue dark in the distance.

Turner began in water-colours, as he did in oil, by imitating the art of his predecessors and contemporaries. In many of his early works the inspiration is evidently caught from Cozens. Other works suggest the low tones and broad manner of Girtin, as the "Warkworth" and the "Easby Abbey": perhaps the golden manner which the latter painter adopted·just before he died, led to Turner's rich and golden tones; but if so, he speedily surpassed his early competitor, and began to range over the novel and hitherto untrodden field of fleeting effects, such as painters term accidental; his readiness and boldness in seizing these is as remarkable, as is the fearlessness with which he pushed them to the very verge of truth.

Turner repudiated the *mere* imitation of Nature, and never cared to represent her commonplace aspects: those indeed, which from their abiding, are the only aspects which can be *literally* copied, and although he made hundreds of studies from nature, he never seems to have painted a picture out of doors. He cared only to reproduce those varied effects which are fleeting as they are beautiful—like the passions which flit across the human countenance, and which can raise the most commonplace and stolid face into the region of poetry, or those expressions which, whether on face of man or the wide-spread champaign, pass as suddenly as they arise, and can only be reproduced by the hand of genius, working with the stores of a schooled memory, enriched by the treasures of long and patient study.

Moreover, Turner's art was completely an art of selection : of selection as to time and circumstance, as to effect of light, shade, or colour ; of selection by omission or by the addition of parts.

If we look even to his foregrounds, where, if anywhere, the details of nature would be imitatively rendered, we find no such attempt on his part. Even there he sought to give the impression of foliage, flowers, and fruit, rather than to render them imitatively. We recognize, it is true, some of the typical plants, the leading growths, such as the vine hanging from branch to branch, or the gourd trailing over fallen column or sculptured stone, rendered, it may be, with the utmost truth of *general* effect and of relation to the tone of the picture, whether of grey storm or of golden sunlight. Still never rendered with any curious perception of minute beauties arising from direct individual imitation, but rather with relation to the masses of light and dark in his picture, or to the forms he wished to emphasize or to hide.

If Turner had a defect it was too great generalization ; and, as our defects grow upon us in our old age, his latter works in oil seem rather schemes for pictures—the bold and startling laying-on of masses preparatory to future completion—than attempts at any detailed realization. In many of them we try in vain to make out the minor forms in the masses. It seemed sufficient for the painter that the great truths of sun and shade, of hot and cold were faithfully rendered, and then—did we not know his perfect manipulation in water-colours even late in life—we might think that either his eye failed him, or that the will was wanting to cope with the tedious labour of completing the parts whilst maintaining the requisite breadth. The palette knife, the broad hog-tool for scumbling the broken surface, were the means he employed—means quite incompatible with minute completion.

He ever studied to preserve a sense of *mystery*, a quality which is most valuable to the painter, as Turner very well knew. "Hang that fellow's works," said a great living painter, on looking at a pre-Raphaelite picture ; "one sees them all at once, and there is nothing left to find out." The suggestiveness of a work of art is one of its richest qualities ; and the veriest blot of Turner is suited to suggest more than the most finished picture of imitative details.

The wonderful industry of the painter is apparent even from his exhibited works. Rodd, who published in 1856 a catalogue of the pictures painted by Turner and exhibited at the Royal Academy, gives a list from 1787 to 1850, of 259 pictures; to which he adds sixteen more, exhibited between 1806 and 1846, at the British Institution, making in all 275 pictures. This, which might well represent the whole life of an ordinary man, was but a fraction of Turner's labours. How many fine easel pictures by him were never exhibited? and how shall we estimate the addition which should be made to the list by the drawings made solely for the engraver? In 1808 he commenced his first work of this class, pitting himself against Claude, in his *Liber Studiorum ;* and from that time his engagements with publishers never ceased—his *Southern Coast Scenery,* his *England and Wales, Rivers of England, Rivers of France, Rogers's Italy, Rogers's Poems,* &c.

The large property he had accumulated by his art, and his generous disposal of it (though partially frustrated) for the benefit of his brother artists and his countrymen, are well known.

Of Turner's life, passed entirely in the pursuit of art, enough has been said. He was elected an associate in 1799; a full member of the Royal Academy in 1802. In 1807 he was appointed professor of perspective, the duties of which office he fulfilled for nearly thirty years. Secretive in his habits, he loved to make his journeys alone, and to the last he continued to absent himself for uncertain periods from the knowledge of his household and his friends. His death was as characteristic as his life. Just below the picturesque old timber bridge which spanned the Thames from Chelsea to Battersea the river widens out into a deep bay. In the centre of the curve just at the bottom of a little half-country lane, were two small cottages, such as might be inhabited by the boatmen whose craft lie along the curving shore. These houses looked out on to the broad expanse of river, ever as the day declined reflecting the glories of the setting sun and the evening sky. In one of these cottages Turner died. That he might enjoy solitude and his lonely studies he was accustomed to lodge here under the assumed name of Brooks. Here, evening and morning, he could look out on his beloved Thames, and what was better still, see sky, ever changing, clean down to the hilly horizon. Here, unknown as the great painter, his last illness seized him; from his sick bed he could yet see the setting sun, and here he died on the 19th of December, 1851. His body was conveyed to his house in Queen Anne Street, West, and thence to its last resting-place in the crypt of St. Paul's.

CHAPTER XXI.

HOWARD, HILTON, HAYDON, AND ETTY.

In this chapter we propose to trace the career, marked by struggles and neglect, of four talented men, who devoted themselves to naturalize the grand style in the English school, and to assert its power. They were contemporaries in the schools, and competitors in the race of fame, but one came a few years before the other three, and had a more lengthened career; and to him we give the precedence. *Henry Howard, R.A.,* was born in London, 31st January, 1769. He left school at thirteen with an average education, and a little knowledge of Latin, and then from time to time accompanied his father to and from Paris, and picked up French. Though not intended for an artist, he showed a predilection for drawing, and at the age of seventeen he became the pupil of Philip Reinagle, R.A. In 1788 he was admitted a student of the Royal Academy, and in 1790 he gained the two first medals—the first silver medal in the life school, and the gold medal for his original painting of Caractacus, which the president Reynolds informed him, was the best picture which had been submitted to the Academy.

Having thus distinguished himself, he determined, in pursuit of his art, to visit Italy, and he set off early in 1791. He went by Paris and Geneva over Mont Cenis to Turin, Milan, Parma, Bologna and Florence, seeing and sketching many of the fine works of art in those cities, and finally reached Rome. Here he pursued his studies, and painted in competition for the travelling studentship of the Royal Academy a large composition, the figures life-size, of "The Death of Abel, a subject from the text of Gesner." The treatment, which was hardly Scriptural, was unfortunate, and he was not only unsuccessful in his competition, but his work narrowly escaped rejection at the Academy Exhibition in 1794. He returned by Florence, Venice, and Trieste to Vienna, Dresden, and home by Hamburg. He was now in his twenty-sixth year, and well trained for his art career. His tastes led him to the poetic and classic, rather than to the more severe and grand style, and in 1795 he exhibited three small-sized pictures, "Puck and Ariel," "Satan Awaking in the Burning Lake," and a portrait; and in the following year a finished sketch of the "Planets drawing Light from the Sun,"—

> "Hither as to their fountain, other stars
> Repairing, in their golden urns draw light"—

which, with some modifications, he twice repeated, first as "The Solar System," exhibited in 1823, and later on as the ceiling of the Duchess of Sutherland's boudoir.

He began by painting poetical and classical works from the English and Latin poets, with occasionally a subject from the Scriptures, and at times found much employment as a portrait painter. He also made a few designs for book illustration, and for the ornamentation of Wedgwood's pottery; some of which latter he executed himself on the clay. His classic tastes received further development by his employment in 1799 on a series of drawings for the Dilettante Society, from the antique sculpture in England; a work which he completed with great accuracy and finish. In 1801 he married Miss Reinagle, the daughter of his old master, and in the same year was elected an associate of the Royal Academy. In 1808, upon exhibiting his "Christ Blessing Little Children," the figures life-size (a work which is now the altar-piece of the church in Berwick Street, St. James's), he was elected a member of the Academy; three years later he was appointed to fill the office of secretary, and in 1833 was chosen professor of painting. His pictures are in the collections of the Duke of Sutherland, the Marquis of Lansdowne, and in the Soane and Vernon Galleries. He died at Oxford, where he had gone on a visit to his son, 5th October, 1847.

Howard will not be able to maintain a high rank in the English school. Distinguished in the outset of his career by the highest honours to be gained as a student, he fell short of the genius that will live. His works are graceful and pretty, marked by propriety, pleasing in composition; his faces and expression good, his drawing correct; but his style cold and feeble. As a lecturer he had little originality of thought; his matter wanted interest, and failed to catch the mind or impress itself upon the memory of the student. He is a part of our school—a link in the chain—but he has not exercised much influence either by his pictures or his teaching. His life was uneventful—neither marked by great success nor by failure. He possessed the esteem of his profession.

William Hilton, R.A., was another history painter, whom the Royal Academy may fairly claim as an offspring, and the English school as a representative. With more talent than Howard, and with greater resolution, he devoted himself exclusively to high art, and was neither tempted aside by the gains of portraiture nor of applied design. Yet his works, from their large size and subject, were less suited to the public taste, and had, in his day, little chance of finding purchasers. He was the son of a portrait painter at Newark, and was born at Lincoln, 3rd June, 1786. He early showed a love for art, and in 1800 became the pupil of John Raphael Smith, the mezzotint engraver. He entered as a student at the Royal Academy in 1806, and applying himself zealously to anatomy, soon made himself master of the figure. In 1810 he completed a subject from English history, "The Citizens of Calais Delivering their Keys to King Edward III.," for which he was awarded a premium of fifty guineas by the directors of the British Institution.

He next year attempted sacred art, and in 1811 received from the Institution a second premium of 122*l.* 10*s.* for his "Entombment of Christ." This was followed by "Christ Restoring Sight to the Blind" and "Mary Anointing the Feet of Jesus"; and for this latter picture he was fortunate to find purchasers in the directors of the Institution, who gave him 525*l.* for it, and in 1821 presented it to the church of St Michael in the City. We do not find that he had hitherto sold his pictures, yet he quietly and unobtrusively pursued his own high path in art. His father, who lived till 1822, probably continued to assist him with money, yet in his twenty-fifth year, and after producing so many fine works, he must have bitterly felt, gentle as he was in spirit, that he was neglected—his talent without reward. Haydon says: "Hilton, my fellow-student, had been successful in selling his 'Mary Anointing the Feet of Jesus,' in the British Gallery, for 500 guineas, which saved him from ruin. I told him he was a lucky fellow, for I was just on the brink of ruin. 'How?' said he. I explained my circumstances, and he immediately offered me a large sum to assist me. This was indeed generous. I accepted only 34*l.*, but his noble offer endeared him to me for the rest of his life. A more amiable creature never lived, nor a kinder heart; but there was an intellectual and physical weakness in everything he did." In 1825 Hilton painted his fine work, "Christ Crowned with Thorns." This picture was also purchased by the directors of the British Institution for 1,000 guineas, and was presented by them to the new church of St. Peter, Eaton Square. It has now been bought by the Royal Academy with the money left by the Chantrey Fund.

It is a pity that, of one so talented and so well known to a generation of students—to whom we ourselves are indebted for so much friendly teaching—so few facts have been recorded. In his earlier career, his quiet, homely habits, added to his weak health, kept him from society; and he was by nature opposed to all that brought him into personal notice: he gave the public his works; but he avoided the notoriety which his talents would have gained him. In 1818 he visited Italy, and was at Rome with his friend Phillips, R.A. He was elected in 1813 an associate of the Royal Academy, and in 1820 a full member. In 1827 he was appointed the keeper of the Academy, an office for which he was specially qualified; and in the following year he married. In 1835 he had the misfortune to lose his wife. Her loss, which to a man of his habits was a severe affliction, aggravated an asthma, from which he had some time suffered; naturally silent and pensive, he gave way to great depression, and never altogether rallied. He died 30th December, 1839, in his 54th year, of disease of the heart, and was buried in the churchyard of the Savoy chapel; where his sister—the widow of his true friend, De Wint—has placed a font to his memory.

On his death, several of his finest works remained unsold. His "Christ Delivering Peter," conceived in the same spirit as Raphael's well-known work in the Vatican, was painted during his keepership, and having tempted no purchaser, usually hung in the Lecture Theatre. As students, we recollect it fresh and beautiful, the face of the angel finely conceived and grand in style. Alas! When we again saw it at the International Exhibition of 1862 it was a mere wreck: the face seemed to have been entirely repainted; it looked shrunk and weazened, and the other parts of the picture were either corrugated, or gaping in wide glistening fissures. How much truly has the *brown school* to answer for: how many fine pictures has it brought to utter ruin! Hilton's art was chilled by neglect, and never fully developed. He was a man of more talent than genius, and not inclined to depart from precedent; but his reputation will be maintained if his works endure.

We have regretted the absence of information necessary to do justice to our notice of Hilton; but we have no cause for such remark with regard to *Benjamin Robert Haydon*, who left behind him an autobiography and a mass of journalism, extending to the last hour of his fitful life, which have been published under the careful editorship of Mr. Tom Taylor. He was born at Plymouth 26th January, 1786, and was the son of a bookseller there who claimed a descent from an old Devonshire family. Having gained a little knowledge of Latin and Greek, and made some attempts at drawing, he was apprenticed to his father's trade; but of unsettled habits, and preferring art to bookselling, he determined, in spite of the entreaties of his parents, that "he must be a painter." He started for London in May, 1804, with 20*l.* in his pocket, and set himself closely to his studies. He was by nature obstinately self-willed and self reliant. He had already made anatomy his study, and with the most exaggerated opinion of his own powers he aimed at the highest style in art. He brought with him an introduction to his

townsman Northcote, who cynically said to him :—" Heestorical peinter !
why yee'll starve, with a bundle of straw under your head." But he was
neither discouraged nor depressed, by an opinion which after-experience
proved too painfully near the truth.   In 1805, he was admitted a student
of the Royal Academy.   In the following year, at the age of twenty-one,
he pompously records his commencement :— " Ordered the canvas for
my first picture (6 ft. by 4 ft.) of ' Joseph and Mary resting on the road
to Egypt,' and on the 1st. October, 1806, setting my palette, and
taking brush in hand, I knelt down and prayed to God to bless my
career, to grant me energy to create a new era in art, and to rouse the
people and patrons to a just estimate of the moral value of historical
painting."   Then, rising with calm gratitude, he tells how "looking fear-
lessly at his unblemished canvas, in a species of spasmodic fury, he
dashed down the first touch."

On the exhibition of his picture he went back to Plymouth for a season
" and painted his friends at fifteen guineas a head, a good price, at which
he soon got full employment ;" and he candidly adds, "execrable as my
portraits were, (I sincerely trust that not many survive), I rapidly accumulated money; not probably because my efforts were thought
successful, even by my sitters, but more because my friends wished to
give me a lift, and thought that so much enthusiasm deserved encouragement."   This practice, however, he says, advanced him and gave him
confidence, and he recommends it to the young history painter.   On his
return to town he began his "Dentatus," a commission from Lord
Mulgrave ; and after telling us that he was puzzled to death to reconcile
the antique forms with his anatomical knowledge in his conception of
this figure, he by chance accompanied his friend Wilkie, who had
obtained an order to see the Elgin marbles.   In a fit of vain enthusiasm,
he finds that he has been pursuing the true Grecian road, and exclaims,
"Here were the principles which the common sense of the English
people would understand ; here were the principles which I struggled for
in my first picture with timidity and apprehension ; here were the principles which the great Greeks in their finest time established ; and here
was I, the most prominent historical student, perfectly qualified to appreciate all this by my own determined mode of study."   And then he
tells us, " I drew at the marbles ten, fourteen, and fifteen hours at a time,
holding a candle and my board in one hand and drawing with the other ;
and so I should have stayed till the morning, had not the sleepy porter
come yawning in, to tell me it was twelve o'clock ; and then I have often
gone home cold, benumbed and damp, my clothes steaming up as I dried
them ; and so spreading my drawings on the ground, I have drank my
tea at one o'clock in the morning with ecstasy, as its warmth trickled
through my frame, and looked at my picture, and dwelt on my drawings,

and pondered on the change of empires, and thought that I had been contemplating what Socrates looked at and Plato saw ; and then lifted up with my own high urgings of soul, I have prayed God to enlighten my mind to discover the principles of those divine things, and then I have had inward assurances of future glory, and almost fancying divine influence in my room, have lingered to my mattress bed, and soon dozed into a rich balmy slumber."

Haydon's bane was his inordinate, insupportable vanity. Lord Mulgrave, who had given him a commission for the "Dentatus," was courteous to him, and invited him frequently to his table ; but this was too much for his weak head. He says he talked more grandly to his artist friends (and we may be sure he did, as he owns it), and that he did not relish the society of the middle-classes; then he tells us— "My room began to fill with people of rank and fashion, and very often I was unable to paint, and did nothing but talk and explain. They all, however, left town at Christmas, and I worked away very hard, and got on well, so that when they returned I was still the object of wonder ; and they continually came to see that extraordinary picture by a young man who never had the advantages of foreign travel. Wilkie was for the time forgotten. At table I was looked at, selected for opinions, and alluded to constantly. 'We look to you, Mr. Haydon,' said a lady of the highest rank, 'to revive the art.' I bowed my humble acknow- ledgments, and then a discussion would take place upon the merit and fiery fury of 'Dentatus' ; then all agreed that it was a fine subject, and then Lord Mulgrave would claim the praise of the selection. Then people would whisper, he has himself an antique head, and then they would look, and some one would differ. Then the noise the picture would make when it was out : then Sir George (Beaumont) would say, that he had always said, that a great historical painter would arise, and that I was he."

All this, the poor misguided painter says, he "believed as gospel truth." He believed that the production of his picture "must be considered as an epoch in English art,"and when it proved a failure he laid the blame on the Academy.

In 1810 he began a third picture—"Lady Macbeth," a commission given to him some time previously by Sir George Beaumont, who wished to befriend him ; yet he managed to pick a quarrel with Sir George, and to be sadly, we think, in the wrong. He was in debt and desperate. His father would help him no further, and, "exasperated by the neglect of my family (we use his own words), tormented by the consciousness of debt, cut to the heart by the cruelty of Sir George, fearful of the severity of my landlord, and enraged at the insults of the Academy, I became furious. An attack upon the Academy and its abominations darted into my head. From this moment the destiny of my life may be said to have changed."

In this crooked state of mind he began his large picture, "The Judgment of Solomon," while living in a small confined room, using his blankets or his table-cloth for drapery—suffering from sickness aggravated by dreadful necessities; painting, as he tells us, on one occasion till three o'clock in the morning from ten the morning before, he continued his work, alternating sorrows and suffering with intense enjoyments. But, "after the most dreadful application, influenced by an enthusiasm stimulated by despair almost to delirium, living for a fortnight upon potatoes because he would not cloud his mind with the fumes of indigestion, he broke down." His eyesight failed, and while he was in this sad state, his picture began to make a noise, and "West called and was affected to tears at the mother," and though his income from the King had just been stopped, he generously sent Haydon a cheque for 15*l.*

When his "Solomon" was finished he sent it, not to the Academy, but to the Water-colour Exhibition at Spring Gardens, which then admitted oil paintings; and a prominent centre place was given to the work. He was fortunate. He sold it for 600 guineas, and the British Institution awarded it a premium of 100 guineas. He was raised from the depths of his despair, was at once in the clouds, and again became the fashion. With some money in his pocket he started off to Paris with Wilkie, and enjoyed himself, seeing and commenting upon the great collection of works which then temporarily crowded the Louvre. But returning home, he soon after says in his journal that "not a single commission, large or small," followed his success.

He had, before his journey to Paris, begun his "Christ's Entry into Jerusalem." On his return, by paroxysms of application, and long occasional fasting, his health became deranged, his eyes suffered, and he was unable to work; still in 1816 he continued to labour upon the "Jerusalem," and in the following year he was engaged on the same great work; and again suffering in health, but assisted by a friend, he was enabled to remove to a healthy house, with a handsome studio, at Lisson Grove. Here he was visited by beauty and fashion; and for a time, short indeed, basked in the rays of an illusive prosperity.

Haydon's art, his whole existence in fact, was illusory. He thought his talents should make him the pensioner of the State; and when advised to paint smaller and more saleable works, he said, "All my friends are advising me what to do, instead of advising the Government what to do for me."

In 1820, the "Jerusalem" was completed, and was exhibited at the Egyptian Hall, Piccadilly, and we have again his shout of triumphant success. Money he admits, too, came pouring in, and he kept paying off debts; but not fast enough, for his success brought a multitude of claims, though he received no less than 1,760*l.* in the season. Encouraged by this, he married, in 1821, a widow lady, to whom he had been for several years attached. His picture did not, however, find a purchaser, and a subscription set on foot to present it to the church, failed. Subsequently in (1831) it was purchased for only 240*l.*, and sent to America.

He had, on the completion of the "Jerusalem," immediately begun another great work, on a canvas 19 feet long by 15 feet high. His subject was—"The Raising of Lazarus."

The first impression of the picture is imposing; the general effect powerful and well suited to the subject; the incidents and grouping well conceived; the colouring good, and in parts brilliant. Then the mind, at once fixing upon the chief figure, feels unsatisfied with the Christ. The head is in direct profile and heavy, the eye sleepy and wanting in due expression, and the attempt at calm dignity results in inanition. The drapery is clumsy and loaded upon the right arm and shoulder. The hands are good and are well painted; but the feet, though also well drawn, seem hardly suited in action to the poise of the figure. The head of the Lazarus is finely conceived and painted; the mouth and general expression of the muscles of the face still retain the rigidity of death, but the eyes wide open, and fixed upon the Saviour, are filled with an expressive gaze of wonder. When beginning this head, the painter tells us he was arrested, and that with his mind struggling to regain its power he set to work, and scrawling about with his brush, he gave an expression to the eye of Lazarus. "I instantly got interested," he adds, "and before two I had put it in. My pupil, Bewick, sat for it, and, as he had not sold his exquisite picture of 'Jacob,' looked quite thin, and anxious enough for such a head." The Martha is certainly finely conceived; the face, almost colourless from emotion, is well and brilliantly painted, the feeling of sorrowing resignation beautiful; the whole action of the figure expressive of quiet, subdued grief. The Mary is comparatively a failure. The St. John is rather extravagant, both in action and expression. The father and mother are good in expression and action, particularly the mother, for whom his washerwoman served as a model. The two Jews are contemptuously expressive without loss of dignity, and the group, including St. Peter, piled upon the cemetery wall, is well conceived—the action and expression good, and the colour and general effect brilliant.

The "Lazarus" comprises twenty figures, on a scale of about nine feet high; the composition is natural and original. Each figure has its appropriate action and place in the great story. Some parts possess high merits, and very painter-like qualities, with a peculiar luminous brilliancy of flesh colour unknown in the Engl'sh school since Reynolds. Can we wonder that there are inequalities in this great work when we see the painter hurried on by his necessities—the enthusiasm and thought of to-day damped and obliterated by the trials of the morrow. In March, 1823, his picture was exhibited, and he records, "It has made the greatest impression. No picture I ever painted has been so universally approved of." But the money taken for admission would hardly stop gaps from day to day. Haydon was arrested and thrown into prison, and his picture sold fcr 300*l.*

On his release from the King's Bench Prison, Haydon tried portrait painting, but notwithstanding all his efforts he was reduced almost to actual want.

In 1826 he finished his "Venus Appearing to Anchises," a commission; and after some scruples sent it to the Academy for exhibition. He notes that this gave much satisfaction; that he wished to be reconciled to the profession; and that with a stubborn heart he called upon the members to make peace, and was well received by all. He then began "Alexander Taming Bucephalus," and in the following year his "Euclus" —both commissions—and was again thrown into prison for debt. He appealed to the public through the newspapers, and a public meeting was called and subscriptions were raised to restore him to his art and to his family. After painting small subjects and portraits for daily bread Haydon grew apathetic till his hopes were raised by the King's buying his "Mock Election." Nevertheless in 1830 he was again arrested. He had commenced, while surrounded by distress, a large subject—his "Zenophon," and on his release began it on a smaller canvas; but he was without means, the butcher impudent, the tradesmen all insulting, when Sir Robert Peel gave him a commission for the "Napoleon," but having named what we should think a liberal price, he offended the minister by expressing dissatisfaction on being paid the sum he named.

Stirring political times now arrived. Haydon was much excited by the reform agitation. and under this influence painted "Waiting for the *Times*," which is well known by the mezzotint engraving. In 1832, encouraged by Earl Grey, he began a sketch for the Reform Banquet, for which his lordship afterwards gave him a commission for 500 guineas. During the greater part of that and of the following year he was busily engaged with all the great men of the Reform party, painting their portraits into his picture and journalizing their gossip. He was happy over his work, "a more delightful work an artist never had," when in the midst of all he was arrested, but was soon released by his generous friends. His painting contained ninety-seven heads, all portraits. When finished he exhibited it, but the exhibition did not pay. He was again in difficulties and was again assisted by his friends; the Duke of Sutherland giving him a commission to complete his sketch of Cassandra.

His troubles seem to have culminated in 1835. "The agony of my distresses (he says) is really dreadful; for this year I have principally supported myself by the help of my landlord, and by pawning everything of any value I have left, until at last it has come to my clothing: a thing, in all my wants, I never did before." In 1836 he was prominent before the committee of the House of Commons on the constitution of the Royal Academy, of which body he was again a bitter opponent; and about the same time began his career as a public lecturer, and for the next two or three years, found engagements which materially assisted in the support of his family.

State employment had been the dream of Haydon's life: he had for years persistently teased every Minister who would listen to him. When therefore the opportunity arrived, and a Royal Commission was issued to carry out the decoration of the New Houses of Parliament—which he claimed as his own suggestion—he was greatly excited; and in 1842 he eagerly, but not without some misgivings, entered into the cartoon competition. But great trials and troubles followed; his competition was unsuccessful; the object for which he had all his life contended so ardently was missed; his powers had failed, a life of contention and trouble had at last had its unvarying result.

Meanwhile he was painting for his daily bread; he may be said to have almost lived upon his "Napoleon at St. Helena," which he repeated over and over again; also "Napoleon in his Bedroom"; "Meditating at Marengo"; "In Egypt"; "Musing at the Pyramids"; and we know not in how many other moods. In 1844 he notes, "I have painted nineteen Napoleons, thirteen of them 'At Saint Helena';" and he adds, "By heavens! how many more!"

He had struggled through appalling difficulties. He had known troubles of every complexion; but hitherto his vanity had been invulnerable and had sustained him. He was now deeply wounded in spirit; young men were selected for the work which he had made the ambition of his life, and he was contemptuously passed by. Involved in debt, mortified and depressed, he yet began another picture, "Alfred and the Jury." But the struggle had become too hard; "he sat staring at his picture like an idiot, his brain pressed down by anxiety:" and so his mind gave way; and, without warning, on the 22nd June, 1846, he made this sad entry in his journal, "God forgive me! Amen. *Finis.* B. R. Haydon. 'Stretch me no longer on the rack of this rough world.' —LEAR." And then he died by his own hand.

There can be no doubt of Haydon's true love of his art: it was his ruling passion. He followed it with a fitful enthusiasm, unchilled by the most severe trials; which it would be difficult to say were not, in their excitement, an essential stimulant to his progress and suited to his irritable nature. It may be doubted if under more tranquil conditions he would have done more. He seemed at times to begin his pictures without any plan or forethought, and to begin painting in the fervour of his first conception, without even drawing in; how, then, can it be wondered that the gross faults they exhibit were often very severely commented on? He was a good anatomist and draughtsman; his colour was effective, his treatment of his subject and his conception original and powerful; but his works have a hurried and incomplete look; his finish is coarse, sometimes woolly, and is not free from vulgarity.

William Etty, R.A., was another man of mark in the British school, who formed a style of his own, which, amidst much discouragement in the beginning of his career, he persevered in until he arrived at great excellence; introducing a class of subjects which had hitherto been but little attempted, or attempted very imperfectly by our native painters. In one view of his labours he cannot be said to have greatly influenced the school, since he had but one or two followers, and these did not inherit their master's talent; thus the apparent result of his works has not been large. Yet his influence on the students of his time was really great; as must be that of every earnest and patient labourer who really loves his work and is able to attain mastery in it.

Etty was born on the 10th March, 1787, at York, where his father was a baker, and also owned a mill. He demonstrated his love for art very early by defacing every plain surface. His schooling was short, and he mastered little more than reading and writing; but he was piously taught by his parents who were Methodists. As a boy he was of a reserved and shy, yet affectionate, disposition. In 1798, when in his twelfth year only, he was apprenticed to a printer at Hull, and notwithstanding hard work during long hours, he managed to nourish his love of drawing, conscientiously drudging on during seven years, without giving up the hope of becoming a painter. Then, his printer's work done, an uncle who had settled in London invited him to town, and assisted him in the study he had so zealously commenced. We know, for he was proud to tell us, that his labours during his apprenticeship made future work light to him, and that his late beginning in art only stimulated him to make up for lost time. In 1807, when in his twentieth year, he was admitted a student in the Royal Academy. He was from the beginning one of the most constant in attending the schools, and when he passed from the antique into the life school, he became wholly absorbed in the study of the nude, and permanently formed his style as a flesh painter; for when he had arrived at a proficiency in the study of the figure that qualified him for admission to paint from the life, he took

s

with avidity to the use of the brush and ever after *painted* his studies ; thus he gained a power over the imitation of flesh, both as to colour and texture, beyond that of any other artist of our school.

Traditionally, his progress was slow,—so much so that his fellow-students were rather inclined to say "Poor Etty!" and to think that he had mistaken his vocation ; but his self-confidence never flagged : he went perseveringly onward in the course he had prescribed to himself, and attained such facility and perfection by his persistence, that as new students surrounded him they began to regard him with veneration, and his studies with great admiration ; and, so far as the laws allowed, to imitate his practice. Always among them, and every night during the school sessions, seated with them at their studies, gathering frequently a little party at his home in Buckingham Street to drink tea and to chat over art matters, it is no wonder that his talents and his habits made him a great favourite, and a model for imitation. His first inclination was to paint landscape : he then tried the heroic. In the uncertainty of his aim, he was attracted by the works of Lawrence, and in 1808 became his pupil, by the liberal help of his uncle. His first attempt did not meet with encouragement. He was an unsuccessful competitor for the Royal Academy medals. His works sent for exhibition were returned to him, and it was not till 1811 that he gained a place on the walls of the Exhibition.

Etty's brush in some degree supplanted the crayon, and a great facility in its use became the characteristic of the painters who immediately succeeded Etty. Some of the older members were inclined to disagree with this mode of study, and when, on his election as a member, Etty still continued to frequent the schools as usual, they thought it, to say the least, irregular. But his habits were too confirmed to change, even if he had not been thoroughly convinced of the value of the practice. Hence, almost to the end of his life, he was as constant in attendance as in the days of his studentship. In his studies in the schools he seemed to play rather than to labour, so easy was his brush, and such beautiful colour seemed to flow from it, as if accidentally. This is visible in his studies merely commenced and laid in, as well as in those he had most completed. His practice was very simple. He usually drew in his figure with white chalk or charcoal, on a raw mill-board, which he then inked in and took home to prepare by merely rubbing size over it. The next evening in the school, he dead-coloured his study in the broadest and simplest manner, taking great care to mark in the relief of the figure from the ground at those points where it was visible in nature, by a close appreciation of the light and dark of the contrast ; and these points he constantly kept in view, and renewed as he proceeded, only rubbing them over with some general uniting tint to form the background when the study was completed. These contrasts of dark upon light and light upon dark, or of flesh upon colour, of such value for relief and about which he was so careful, are still to be seen in most good studies from his hand; although it is to be regretted that few remain in an entirely genuine state—many having been altered and completed *pictorially!* for the dealers, by painters who lent themselves to such a practice.

He proceeded to finish his studies by passing over the dead colour a glaze of some brown pigment (asphaltum in early days, latterly we think bone brown), dashing in dexterously bold touches of lake in parts—in parts, ultramarine for greys, and then painting his white, slightly charged with Indian red, into the glaze; often with his scrubbing brush (he loved an old and well-worn hog-tool) drawing in touches of pure madder here and there in the finishing, producing great brilliancy of effect in his studies; and by his dexterous execution, preserving a nicety of tone, beautiful pure tints, and very tender gradations. This is written from remembrance of his manner of working. In his own words, as given in his life by Gilchrist (vol. i. p. 58), it is a little different, yet substantially the same. He writes thus:—"Resolution. First night, correctly *draw* and outline the figure only. Second night, carefully paint in the figure with black and white and Indian red, for instance. The next, having secured with copal, glaze, and then scumble in the bloom. Glaze into shadows, and touch on the lights carefully—and it is done." By his rapid execution he kept his colour pure and unmuddled, never teazing the tints; and from painting so constantly by gaslight, he became accustomed to great breadth of light and shade.

The subjects which he adopted were of a voluptuous character, and arose somewhat out of the nature of his studies, varied by his love of poetry, fairy, and classic lore: such as "Perseus and Andromeda," "Hero and Leander," the "Syrens," &c , mostly chosen with a view to the introduction of the nude. Even when his theme was from history the same feeling prevailed: as in the "Cleopatra," "The Storm," from the Psalms, and "The Eve of the Deluge." Such he delighted to paint. Above all, he delighted in the beauty of women. He was used to say that, "as all human beauty was concentrated in woman, he would dedicate himself to painting her." His first picture exhibited at the Royal Academy in 1811, was "Antiope Rescued by Telemachus from the Wild Boar." His first which gained him reputation was "Cleopatra Sailing Down the Cydnus," now in the possession of Lord Taunton; and to which Leslie refers when he says, "One morning he woke famous, after the opening of the exhibition." This was in the spring of 1821, when this picture was given to the world. From painting direct from nature Etty was apt to introduce some of the false individualities of common life, and the bad proportions of his models; but there was always a superadded grace and style even in their faultiness. The "Cleopatra" is traditionally said to have been painted with a large addition of wax to the medium, and has suffered much since it was first executed. Nevertheless, even now the flesh painting maintains as happy a medium between the silvery hue and the rosy as it is possible to achieve.

But Etty was not content to remain a painter of cabinet-sized pictures. He possessed a strong feeling for the heroic, and early set himself a great task—that of painting a series of pictures of heroic subjects, with figures the size of life. Two years after his fame was initiated by the exhibition of the "Cleopatra," the president, Lawrence, bought his "Pandora Crowned by the Seasons," a work which confirmed his talent, and won his admission to the associateship of the Royal Academy; and now he determined to begin what he had for some time contemplated—the large works by which he hoped to win still higher fame. He commenced with "The Combat—Woman Pleading for the Vanquished." The subject represents two combatants just at the crisis of their struggle. The younger is wounded and is forced on to his knees, his broken sword at his feet, his long hair in the grasp of his terrible adversary, who is about to give him the death stroke. A woman, rushing forward, throws herself at the feet of the victor; clasping him, in the energy of her appeal for mercy—by voice, by look, by action—she restrains him from vengeance.

Here are all the materials for a noble picture, and finely has the painter availed himself of them. The forms are heroic; the drawing is grand and large; there is not the slightest appearance of mere posed models; there is no pause in the action; the muscles are in full play, starting with the energy of the strife. The modelling and painting of the flesh are very fine, and place Etty high as a colourist in a school which is at least a school of colour. In this picture he was the inventor, as well as the painter, of his story.

In the next of this series of heroic works, Etty took his subject from the Scriptures, and treated it with great originality, and in a manner unlike that of any of his predecessors in art. To show that he was prepared to meet difficulties, he chose a continuous action—a drama as it were, in three acts, and requiring three separate canvases to give its beginning, middle, and end. The theme he chose was the delivery of the Jewish people from the armies of Holofernes by the hand of Judith. There is fine drawing and grand action in the figures of these pictures, although they are more especially pictures of colour.

It must be remembered that Etty painted these great works without a commission, and with small hopes of a purchaser. Martin, the painter, himself not troubled with wealth, bought the "Combat," it is said, for

200*l.*, a sum small in those days,—ridiculous in our own, when one of Etty's cabinet pictures, " Perseus and Andromeda," has realized 1,500*l.* ; but it was highly to Martin's honour to have appreciated his brother painter's talent, when the rich and the titled overlooked it ; and it is a great satisfaction that this, with the other nob'e pictures we have mentioned, has found a fitting resting-place in the Royal Scottish Academy.

It cannot be said, however, that Etty's talents, and the beauties so visible in his works, nor even their fine colour (a quality that, as seizing the eye, is more readily appreciated by the uninstructed than those which appeal to the mind) won the painter present fame or profit. There were other causes besides a want of perception of their merits that prevented his pictures from being sought after by the public. Though himself a particularly pure-minded man, with a most chivalrous respect for women, it must be allowed that many of his pictures were of a very voluptuous character, and clashed with the somewhat prudish temper of the age. There has always been a stronger objection to the nude figures of the painter, than to the more tangible works of the sculptor ; this had to be slowly overcome. It was difficult to tolerate such works from a living artist, in pictures in their first glow of beauty and freshness—unspoiled with age and fiddle-brown varnish ; so that those who saw no objection to cover their walls with such subjects as " Lot and his Daughters," " David and Bathsheba," or " Joseph and the Wife of Potiphar," if reputed to be from the hand of a Guido or a Caracci, could not tolerate the nude from a native painter, even when the subject itself was unobjectionable.

Though a great student of nature, Etty's imitation was ever general rather than individual : perhaps no one painted flesh more largely from the living model than he did ; but how unlike it is to the microscopic detail of the works of Denner, or to the ivory smoothness of those of Vanderwerf. His landscape, although but an accessory and background to his groups, is treated with the same largeness of imitation ; no details are there, but the happiest rendering is given of the general colour or tone of nature, in true accord with the feeling of the subject. When his collected works, 130 in number, were exhibited in his honour at the Society of Arts, in June, 1849, he came up to London to be present at the exhibition, and was much moved by the congratulations of his friends. In answer to our inquiries, he then pointed to his " Hero and Leander," as his favourite and best work.

Early in his career Etty paid a short visit to Italy. In 1816, assisted by his brother, he set out on a long-contemplated journey to see the Continental schools. In 1822 he paid a more lengthened visit, and during his eighteen months' stay, saw Rome, Florence, Naples, and Venice, and copied some of the great works of the Italian school, particularly the Venetian. In 1824 he was elected an associate of the Royal Academy, and in 1828 a full member : and he then began the series of large pictures we have mentioned. From 1826 to 1848 he lived in Buckingham Street, Adelphi. Then his health failing, he retired to his own city of York, to which he was fondly attached ; and there he died, 13th November, 1849, and was buried in a quiet corner of the churchyard of St. Olave, almost within the shadow of the old Cathedral he loved so well.

In person Etty was short and thick-set, with somewhat massive features, deeply scarred with small-pox ; he had a face expressive of great benevolence, and a head large—disproportionately large indeed—but tending to a look of power. Slow in speech and slow and measured in action, both rather increasing in late years from an asthmatic affection ; he had a kindly and gentle nature, and an extreme simplicity of character. Such is our recollection of Etty, and we are told further, that his tender nature was shown by his repeatedly falling in love with one fair object after another ; which we can well believe, though he was in his habits decidedly a bachelor, and he died unmarried.

CHAPTER XXII.

TABLEAUX DE GENRE.—WILKIE, MULREADY, AND LESLIE.

IN the English school, *genre* pictures may be said to take their rise from Hogarth, whose works were of cabinet size, and of a dramatic, rather than historic tendency. After his death, although small pictures were occasionally painted by Zoffany, Hamilton, Peters, and others, yet the general efforts of our figure painters, stimulated by the example of Barry, West, and Copley, were for a time directed to works of the scale of life, and to subjects of a religious or historic character, rather than to those domestic and familiar incidents from home life and the affections which in France have obtained the name of *Tableaux de Genre,* and which we, from want of a better, have hitherto consented to call by the same name. It was, however, soon apparent that our countrymen cared little for battle pieces ; nor were they desirous of seeing the sacred subjects of their creed surrounding them in their every day life. In England the churches are not open to the painter's art, and the burgesses and aldermen of our provincial towns were little likely to forego the pleasures of the table at the guild and corporation feasts, that the walls of the guild-halls might be decorated at the expense of their good cheer. Hence the zeal for producing works of heroic size could not be expected to endure, since, even were he disposed to forego the due reward of his labours, the artist could find no place to display them. It was soon found that pictures to suit the English taste must be pictures to live by ; pictures to hang on the walls of that home in which the Englishman spends more of his time than do the men of other nations, and loves to see cheerful and decorative. His rooms are comparatively small, and he cannot spare much wall-space for a single picture. His eye, too, must be pleased before his mind, and colour is to him one of the first sources of gratification.

No doubt our school suffered somewhat by this change from heroic and religious to familiar art—suffered in the grandeur of its attempts at least, more especially in the estimation of Continental nations—and really suffered by adopting too generally subjects of a somewhat tame and familiar class, to the exclusion of the ideal and the poetical. It gained, however, in care, in refinement of execution, in attention to the completion of the parts and in the perfection of the work as a whole. We find that soon after the beginning of the present century, several painters almost simultaneously rose into notice, whose works had at least a common likeness, in that they were of cabinet size and bore somewhat the same relation to historic art that the tale or the novel does to history. It is our intention to take three of these painters who held the highest place in public estimation, and from their practice to illustrate the new direction which art took in their hands.

It is noteworthy that these three artists, whom all will admit to have attained the highest eminence in this class of art, should at the same time represent the three sections of our countrymen; that in Wilkie, Scotland, in Mulready, Ireland, and in Leslie, England, have reason to be proud of men who have left behind them pictures so varied in manner, so original in treatment, and so characteristic of British art as to be wholly different from those of any other country. It will enable us to develop the progress of art of this class if, in the first instance, our attention is confined to the works of these three representative men; afterwards noticing those of their companions and fellow labourers in the same walk who were their contemporaries or successors.

David Wilkie, the Scotch representative of the branch of art we are now entering upon, was the oldest of the three painters whom we have included in this chapter. He was born on the 18th of November, 1785, at Cults, in the county of Fife, of which place his father, also named David, was at that time the minister. The painter was his third son. The minister, it seems, if his own assertion may be accepted, married for his first wife a lady of great beauty; for he enters in his diary of October 18th, 1776, "Was this day married to one of the most beautiful women of Fife." He lost her in the short space of five months, and shortly after married a far away cousin; perhaps from gratitude, since through her father's influence he had received his call to Cults. She, too, was shortly taken from him; and for a third wife the minister took the notable daughter of a neighbouring miller of the village of Pitlassie, of whom the painter was the third child.

It may be presumed that, with an increasing family and the small stipend of a minister of the Scotch Church of that day, the young David would be brought up with the strictest frugality. A few acres of glebe and a stipend of 100*l.* a year must be carefully laid out to secure necessaries, let alone luxuries; and much of the artist's frugality of disposition, many of his acquisitive habits must have been owing to the teachings of his early life—this acquisitiveness, be it noted, was of the best kind, since it led him to gather at all times every sort of material for his art, and to acquire art knowledge as well as riches. As with all other painters, we hear of Wilkie's precociousness ; that he drew before he wrote, which most children do, and that ere his seventh year, when he was sent to the village school of Pitlassie, he surprised his parents by chalking a head on the floor, and by drawing on the walls. While at Pitlassie school he improved in the use of his pencil if he gained little else, and when over-taxed by his schoolfellows with demands for sketches and portraits, he cannily turned his skill to small profit by demanding slate-pencils, marbles, pens, &c. in return.

As he advanced in boyhood, we are told by his biographer that he was a great observer of workmen and their habits and actions; even gaining skill in some handicrafts. This talent of observation will be more especially spoken of when we note his pictures; it is one that in-dicates the true painter more than all the scribblings on the margins of books, or even the portrait-sketches of his schoolfellows ; on which much stress is laid, but which is common more or less to all boys.

In Fifeshire, beyond a portrait or two by Sir Joshua, there were no pictures to inspire the prospective painter, and although he was occa-sionally thrown into the company of David Martin, yet that artist died before Wilkie was twelve years old. As the lad grew in years his love of art increased, and the minister soon felt that his son was set upon being a painter. This choice was hardly one that could be pleasing to the Presbyterian clergyman, who would doubtless consider art as one ot "the lusts of the eye" ; nor was it more agreeable to the lad's maternal grandfather, for the miller and elder had set his heart upon little David's becoming a minister like his father : still, when the parents of the lad saw that his bent was decidedly for art, they cast about for the best means of cultivating his talents, and after some hesitation upon the part of the secretary, who doubted the lad's fitness, he was admitted into the Trustees' Academy at Edinburgh, and studied there under John Graham, in company with William, afterwards Sir William Allan, John Burnet, and Alexander Fraser. Wilkie himself confirmed this doubt, for advert-ing to his having obtained an entrance to the school with difficulty and chiefly through the influence of the Earl of Leven, he says, "I for one can allow no ill to be said of patronage ; patronage made me what I am, for it is plain that merit had no hand in my admission." When admitted, however, the young artist was a most diligent student, readily appre-hending the character and sentiment of what he was at work upon. He speedily sent home to his parents some specimens of his studies from the antique ; which, alas ! were Greek indeed to the village worthies, for when they were shown to one of the kirk elders, taking up a drawing of a foot he inquired of the minister, "And what is this, sir?" "It is a foot," replied the minister. "A foot!" exclaimed the elder, "it is mair like a fluke [a flounder] than a foot." The youth, however, was soon to achieve a work more comprehensible by the elders and villagers of his native place.

Young Wilkie left Edinburgh and the Trustees' Academy in 1804 and returned for a while to his father's village. Unlike many other artists he seems at once to have found the true bent of his genius and the class of subject best suited to his powers. In the adjoining village of Pitlassie, where the family of his mother resided, there was an annual fair held, and the strange characters, the rustic humours, the many incidents of merchandise and barter common to such gatherings, were taken by the young artist for the subject of his first picture, which he began in August, 1804, and finished within the year. Though a work of small size, it contains much subject and many figures, and enables us to see that Wilkie was a diligent as well as a ready workman. As far as execution goes, "Pitlassie Fair" seems painted at once, and in most cases direct from nature. It has little promise of the colour and tone which he subsequently sought and achieved. A red rank hue pervades the picture; and we see the flat manner and want of textural truth, combined with a certain broadness of touch, that prevailed with the artists of the day. The work, moreover, is allied to the Dutch school in some of its incidents, which are such as in after years he would have rejected from his canvas. His early skill in handling is seen in the execution of some of the accessories, the crates of pottery, the tables, and other products displayed in the fair. It perhaps arises from the oneness of execution above alluded to, and the simplicity of his materials, that the picture has stood so perfectly, while others of his works have well nigh perished; and whatever faults or shortcomings it may evidence, it certainly is an extraordinary work for a lad of nineteen years of age.

Wilkie remained some time at Cults, engaged in painting the portraits of persons in the neighbourhood, and even made trips to other Scotch towns in search of sitters. But his ambition led him beyond the narrow bounds of a Scotch village, and he determined to start for London. He had carefully husbanded his gains by portraiture, and having sold his picture of the "Fair" for 25*l.* to Mr. Kinnear, he took his passage from Leith on the 20th May, 1805, to try his fortune in the great city.

Wilkie's first endeavour on his arrival in London was to obtain admission as a student in the Royal Academy. He found the rooms in which the schools are held occupied by the annual exhibition, and it was only on its close, at the end of July, that he was entered as a probationer. Here he became acquainted with Jackson, the portrait painter, who describes him in a letter to Haydon (also a student) as a "tall, pale, thin Scotchman." A lad of delicate health then, he continued all his life to suffer from maladies which baffled the acumen of his physicians, which often interposed to prevent his labours, and which finally carried him off at a time of life when the world might have hoped to see many more fine works by his hand. Wilkie, on his arrival, had taken lodgings in Norton Street, Portland Place, and with the usual providence of his countrymen, he sought to make proper provision for the future. He had brought to London with him the small picture of "The Recruit"; this he found means to display in a window near Charing Cross, where it met with a purchaser at the modest price of six pounds, which our painter was glad to add to his little store. He gradually advanced in the Royal Academy schools from the antique to the life-school, and studied from the living model with great interest and satisfaction, and this while he was at work at pictures which were gradually raising him to great reputation. But at this point we will leave him for a while, to bring the other two painters whom we have chosen as representative men to the same point of comparison.

William Mulready, the Irish representative of the class of art of which we are now treating, was born on the 1st of April, 1786, at Ennis, in the county of Clare. His father followed the trade of a leather breeches maker, and was a master workman in his craft. Shortly after the birth of his talented son, he removed to Dublin with his family, where he continued to carry on his trade for a while; but he passed over to London about the time that the lad was five and a half years old, and took up his abode in Old Compton Street, Soho.

The boy had already shown some aptitude for drawing; having, it is said, at three years old copied a hare with sufficient accuracy to be known without labelling. In 1805 appeared a little book, called *The Looking Glass; a mirror in which any little boy or girl may see what he or she is, and those who are not quite good may find out what they ought to be.* This book is said to have been written by W. Godwin, under the name of Theophilus Marcliffe, and is the history and early adventures of a young artist. It is known that it was compiled from conversations with Mulready, who was then engaged in illustrating some juvenile books for the author; and the facts in it related to the painter's early life. It is now very scarce. It contains illustrations of the talent of the subject of the tale, done at three, five and six, years old, and presumed to be imitations of Mulready's own drawing at the same age. Many children at a like age produce such works, which are made no account of when the after bent of the youth is not to art, but which are looked upon as treasures of precocious genius, when in riper years, study or accident have developed the lad into a painter.

Soon after the arrival of the family in London, young Mulready was put to school. But the parents of Mulready were members of the "old faith," as he used to designate it; and at ten years of age the boy was removed to a school kept by a Roman Catholic, and afterwards placed under the Irish chaplain of the Neapolitan ambassador, who gave instruction at No. 7, Newman Street. Here young Mulready continued nearly two years, learning a little Latin, besides the usual English rudiments. At the end of that time, Mr. Ryan was unfortunately burned to death, and the lad was transferred to another Catholic teacher, who resided in the neighbourhood of Buckingham Gate. It is not possible to say what amount of knowledge the youth obtained under these various masters. In after life he claimed to be able to read the *Æneid* in its original tongue, and was able to detect a false quantity in one, who, presuming him to be ignorant, undertook boastfully to interpret to him a quotation from that work. He, at least, knew the Greek *alphabet*, since on a sheet of sketches and small pen-and-ink hints as to the mode of thinking out his pictures, there are many memoranda written in its characters.

By some means Mulready was thrown into the way of artists, since Mr. Graham, who was engaged in painting one of the subjects for Macklin's Bible, "David Instructing Solomon," exhibited at the Academy 1797, saw the boy, and, struck with his beauty and fair proportions, made interest with the father to let him sit to him as a model for the young prince. No doubt this admission to the study of an artist stimulated young Mulready, already prepared to love and take a delight in art; and this makes the wonder less, that we find him while yet of a mere schoolboy age, endeavouring to get into the only really good school where he could at that time study—the school of the Royal Academy. When only just thirteen he applied to Banks, the sculptor, for a letter to the keeper, in order to gain admission as a student. He took with him a copy in chalk from a cast of the Apollo. Banks saw dawnings of ability in the boy, although the work was hardly sufficient to win him entrance. He recommended him to try again and return in a month—advised him to join a drawing academy in Furnival's Inn Court, and on the failure of that school very shortly afterwards, allowed the young lad to study in his own gallery.

From this time he drew in Banks's studio, and under the sculptor's eye, for nearly twelve months; after the first six his kind instructor thought he might send in a figure to the Council, but his drawing from the Hercules was not approved; at the end of that time, however, the keeper, struck with a drawing the boy had made from a statue by Michael Angelo, admitted him to draw as a probationer with the other pupils; and a few weeks after, when fourteen years and six months old—that is, in October, 1800—he gained his student's ticket. About the same time he obtained the greater silver palette of the Society of Arts; and it is said that from the day he completed his fifteenth year he required no more aid from his parents.

What the works were on which he was employed when he thus went forth to fight the battle of life alone, it is not possible now to tell; he used to say that he had tried his hand at everything, from a miniature to a panorama; we know that all his life he was a teacher, and he declared of himself that he had passed through life as a drawing-master, giving a little of his superfluous time to painting. Perhaps this life-long habit of teaching others may lead to the secret of the careful completion that marked all he did; to that habit of making sure of everything before-hand, of studying out all the parts and details that he might be accurate and assured in all he said, and, moreover, able thoroughly to convince others that he knew to the bottom what he was employed upon.

How Mulready became first acquainted with John Varley, the water-colour painter, is not told; whether during his country journeys to sketch, or at his home in London where Varley gathered many of the rising artists of the day. From that little school, Mulready, Linnell, W. Hunt and others, no doubt learnt much of the love of art. Mul-ready there found his wife, who was a sister of Varley's. The young painter seems to have entered upon his married life with much less thought and prudence than he gave to his art life: before he was eighteen years of age, and when he must really have been *earning* his *daily* bread, he was a husband; before he was nineteen, a father. Four sons were the issue of the marriage, which, to say the least, was not a fortunate one: the pair were early separated and never afterwards lived together.

It has been said that Mulready began, as other young artists have done, and as it is inferred students in the Royal Academy *must* do, by attempting works in the grand style; that among his first productions in this way were "Ulysses and Polyphemus" and the "Disobedient Prophet;" that these were his first offerings to the Academy exhibition, and were both rejected, and that from 1804 till 1807 all his exhibited works are landscape studies. His first attempts in figure painting, which were exhibited, however, were "Old Kasper," from Southey's *Battle of Blenheim,* in 1807, and "The Rattle," in 1808, both sent to the British Institution; and both subjects treated familiarly and founded on Dutch art. The only evidence that Mulready ever contemplated high art was afforded by his picture of "The Supper at Emmaus," painted in 1809, which was never exhibited till 1864.

Thus, at the early age of nineteen, we find Mulready a student of some five years' standing in the Royal Academy, and one who had already " given hostages to fortune " as a husband and a father. We know, from the number of his works of about this period—studies he left behind him, both from the antique and the life—that he was a diligent student then, and that all his life long he continued to work and to take the deepest interest in the schools. His last words in evidence before the Royal Academy Commission, " I have, from the first moment I became a visitor in the life-school, drawn there as if I were drawing for a prize,"—testify to this, if we had not the stronger evidence of the wonderful studies that he wrought on up to almost the last days of his life.

Here, following the arrangement we have adopted, we will turn to the life of Leslie (the third of the trio whom we have classed together), preparatory to entering into some comparison of their labours and the influence they have had on our national art. *Charles Robert Leslie,* the youngest of the three artists, was born in London on the 11th October, 1794. In the short autobiography which he has left, the painter does not give the exact place of his birth, but only tells us that his first recollections were of living in a house in Portman Place, Edgware Road. Though born in our metropolis, Leslie was of American parentage, being the son of Robert Leslie and Lydia Baker, natives of Maryland, both originally of British descent. Robert Leslie, the father of the painter, was a clock and watchmaker, who, settling in Philadelphia, took a partner into his business, and then, in 1793, made a voyage to London with all his family, in order to purchase stock-in-trade on advantageous terms in the mother country. His stay in England extended over several years. Some months after his arrival Charles Robert was born, it is said, in Clerkenwell, where the manufacturers of clocks and watches then, as now, mostly resided. His partner dying, the father was constrained to return to America, taking his family with him.

The journey was in many respects a long and troublesome one. The United States were then at war with France, and the American ship in which the family sailed was attacked by a privateer of superior force, which, though beaten off, inflicted so much damage on their vessel, that it was necessary to put into Lisbon to refit. Battered by fight, and tossed by tempests, the voyagers did not reach Philadelphia until the 11th May, 1800. They had left London on the 13th September, 1799, and had been seven months and twenty-six days on their tedious passage. The watchmaker found his affairs greatly entangled, and he was obliged to begin a lawsuit with the executors of his partner. The trouble and anxiety attendant on this suit preyed upon his mind, and before his eldest son was ten years of age, he was left, with the rest of the young family, to the care of a widowed mother. Leslie ever spoke warmly and tenderly of his father's kindness and affection, and those who had the happiness to know him when himself a parent, can well feel that, if his father resembled him, sad and deep indeed must have been the loss ; for one more tender, or more devoted to his children than the painter, it is hardly possible to picture to ourselves.

At the father's death the widow was left in very straitened circumstances, and was obliged to eke out her means by opening a boarding-house, whilst the eldest daughter aided to maintain the household by teaching drawing in the families of the once capital city. The citizens of Philadelphia seem to have shown much consideration for the widow, and kindliness for her fatherless children. The professors of the university abated their charges in favour of the boys ; although the painter confesses that the liberality of the professor of mathematics was not met by corresponding exertions on the part of his pupil. He felt but little interest in the study, and little power in its prosecution ; the mathematical faculties being, perhaps, those least active of the many qualities that go to make up a perfect painter. Meanwhile the boys, in the summer and autumn, were frequent visitors to the farmhouses in the neighbourhood, where uncles and aunts, both on the father's and mother's side, practised the primitive occupations of farmers and millers, on the pleasant creeks of the Brandywine ; where the painter learnt to enjoy the loveliness of natural scenery, and treasured up for his future years happy memories of the country sports, the free kindly manners, and the harvest frolics of the people.

But life wore on, the boy Charles approached his fourteenth year, and it was time to determine his course in life. He himself tells us his early wish was to be a painter ; but the widow knew that with her straitened means she could not afford him proper instruction. She herself thought of the more business-like profession of an engraver ; but herein, too, the education was difficult, and the success uncertain ; and finally the boy was bound apprentice to the firm of Bradford and Inskeep, booksellers and publishers of the city of his abode. Mr. S. Bradford, the senior partner, was a true man of business, and wished his young assistant to devote his whole heart to his duties. The boy loved painting, and ever lingered at the print-shop windows, or made a hasty visit, when on errands of business, to the open studio of Mr. Sully, the principal painter of the city, whereby not only his love of art increased, but also his sense of what was good and beautiful in its practice. The old bookseller at first repressed his attempts. "If he found me drawing," says Leslie, "he shook his head, and seemed so much displeased, that the most distant hope of his ever assisting me to become a painter, never entered into my mind." But man proposes, and God disposes. What the apprentice wished, and the master objected to, was at length to be brought about by his very means, and he eventually aided, with great liberality, in our painter's art education.

This event happened on the occasion of the visit of George Frederick Cooke, the English tragedian, on a starring engagement to Philadelphia. The young painter—a great lover of the stage—was present at the first representation of *Richard*, and was deeply impressed with the actor's powers. He managed to make from recollection a telling sketch of the tragedian, which astonished the sedate bookseller, who henceforth encouraged him to practise his art. A friend carried this sketch to the Exchange Coffee House, at the hour when it was most thronged with men of business. The work was considered wonderful for so young a lad, and the good bookseller, contributing liberally himself, found no difficulty in raising a fund sufficient to enable the young artist to visit Europe for two years' study.

Before leaving America, Leslie received some instructions in the use of his materials from Mr. Sully, to whom he had been introduced. Copying part of a picture in Leslie's presence, the painter put his palette into his pupil's hands, and required him to proceed as far on another canvas. This he continued from day to day until both copies were finished, and the pupil had learnt at least the accidence of his art, and understood what was meant by scumbling, glazing, and other executive processes. Leslie's execution continued throughout life to be of the simplest character ; his vehicle, latterly at least, was merely linseed oil, and he rejected systematically those executive processes which serve to enrich and give brilliancy to the pigments, and to produce variety in the handling of a picture : but this we shall have to speak of more fully in treating of his art.

Leslie sailed from New York on the 11th of November, 1811, provided with letters of introduction to West, Beechey, and other artists. He took lodgings in Warren Street with a Mr. Moore, who had also come from America to study, a youth but two years older than himself, and the two began to devote their days to painting, their evenings to the Royal Academy.

West and Allston opened their studios to one they looked upon as their countryman. They permitted him to see their works in progress, aided him with counsel and advice, and introduced him to society. In West's gallery he made several copies, but whether of the president's own works he does not give us to understand. The British Museum contained the Townley collection of marbles, and these Leslie studied, besides rising at six in the morning to join his friend Moore in working from the Elgin collection, at that time at Burlington House.

Leslie placed little value on instruction, and thought that, given the materials for study, every man will best instruct himself. He found that Fuseli paid little attention to the students, and he approved of this course ; telling us "that under Fuseli's *wise neglect,* Wilkie, Mulready,

Etty, Landseer, and Haydon distinguished themselves, and were the better for not being made all alike by teaching." He says, "Art may be *learnt*, but cannot be *taught*," a maxim that sounds well, but puts a part for the whole ; for though invention and feeling cannot be taught, the language in which they are to be expressed may : young painters have many difficulties as to drawing and the executive processes of painting, which may be cleared away by judicious advice and teaching without in the least interfering with that originality or invention which is the true gift of nature to the born artist.

While following out his studies in his own manner, Leslie did not forget that he must find means to live, and he seems early to have gained employment in portraiture of the small size, which he continued to adopt through life. Allston introduced him into society, and he soon threw off the gloom that had gathered around him at the first feeling of the loneliness of his situation ; while his cheerful nature, always highly appreciative of wit and humour, seems to have made all who came near him fast and constant friends.

Here, then, we find the three painters whom we have chosen as representative men in this class of art, past the first period of study, and coming before the public with their works ; let us, before proceeding with their career as individuals, endeavour to compare them with each other, to arrive at their several characteristics, and the points in which they advanced British art.

We may safely say that the education they received, while it armed them with technical knowledge and executive power, did not in any way interfere with their originality. If we compare the methods of the three in the conduct of their pictures we shall find their practice very diverse. Wilkie began by a rough blot of the treatment, afterwards preparing a somewhat finished sketch in oil. He at times made a few studies of the action of the hands, but his real work was direct from the life on the canvas ; and, although he altered and changed the action of the hands, the inclination of the head, or the attitude of a figure, or even substituted a more for a less characteristic model, yet he retained the general grouping and arrangement, the general effect and composition of his sketch. The blots of colour in his sketches were at times somewhat arbitrary, and it was difficult to assign them to any definite object or form ; but having pleased him in the sketch, he was very solicitous to keep them in the same place and of the same quality in his picture, and often took much pains to invent suitable details for the purpose. The young artist, to whom such hints are most valuable, may study the ingenious way in which the small blots of red have been carried round the somewhat grey and slaty picture of "The Blind Fiddler." As to the alterations Wilkie made in the progress of his pictures, we find frequent

T

allusions in his diaries such as, "Rubbed out to-day what I did yesterday." "Made several alterations in my picture," &c.

As he advanced in art and obtained more power, he seems to have
made his previous sketches slighter, and to have painted more at once
on the panel or canvas. In "The Sacrament of John Knox," left unfinished at his death, and of which a previous sketch exists, heads and
hands, painted at once to a very low key consistent with the chiaroscuro
of the finished work, are surrounded by the colour of the raw canvas,
and no doubt would have fallen properly into their places as the work
proceeded ; as it is, they show the certainty with which he latterly carried
on his pictures.

Mulready appears to have begun his works after much more preparation even than Wilkie. Before beginning a picture, we find "first
thoughts" for it in pencil, blots in pen and ink, larger sketches in chalk,
and then frequently a small completed sketch in oil. After this stage
Mulready often made slight sketches of individual figures ; studies for
varied actions of the hands or the head, changed attitudes, variations in
character or expression. At times when he had found a characteristic
model, Mulready still further enlarged and thought out a study from it
in pen and ink, or in chalk ; and after all, more especially for his later
works, put the whole together in a most elaborate and highly finished
cartoon—finished with such care and anxiety that these works are almost
equal in beauty to his pictures. He seemed to have a great dislike to
losing his *ground*, and always to have drawn his picture most carefully
on the panel or canvas before commencing with colour. If, which was
rarely the case, he did alter after the work was begun, the part changed
was carefully removed to the ground. The habit of preparing careful
cartoons, and of drawing the work elaborately on the canvas, grew on
him latterly, and his cartoons became more elaborate, as may be seen in
his unfinished one of "The Bathers with Lizards."

Leslie in his mode of beginning his pictures differed widely from both
Mulready and Wilkie. His practice was the very opposite of Mulready's ;
Wilkie's being as it were between the two. We may presume that
Leslie made some sketch of the arrangement of his picture previous to
beginning to paint, although there is little or no material of this kind by
his hand. Certainly he did not like to exhaust himself by making previous studies either for the whole picture or separate parts. He mostly
painted direct from the model on to his canvas, seizing any happy
attitude or expression that arose naturally ; consequently he often made
changes in the progress of his work, and removed and destroyed very
beautiful passages in his pictures, to adopt some better or more graceful
action that arose as he proceeded, and pleased him by its novelty. He
is said not to have given much trouble to his sitters, often hardly re-

quiring them to pose for him, but merely referring to nature at various points of his work, or when difficulties occurred. From these two causes his pictures generally seem produced without labour ; they delight us by their freshness and ease, and are the very opposite to the elaborate and somewhat over-studied excellence of Mulready.

In one respect Leslie differed wholly from Wilkie and Mulready in the choice of his subjects. The two latter, as soon as they had emerged from historic art, began by inventing the incidents which they painted. Such were " The Village Politicians," " The Card Players," " The Barber's Shop," and " The Fight Interrupted," subjects in which truth of character, humour, and close observation of nature were the great requisites. Leslie, on the contrary, passed from the " grand historic period " of the student, to the illustration of incidents in the works of the poets and classic writers, and continued through life to choose such subjects for his pencil. They presented to him an added difficulty which did not lie in the way of those chosen by his two contemporaries ; since all who have read Goldsmith or Sterne, Cervantes or Shakspeare (but especially the latter two), have formed for themselves special ideas of the principal characters in these works, and are apt to object at once to a new or tangible representation of them, either by the actor or the painter. In this very difficult position, Leslie was pre-eminently successful in realizing characters in harmony with the general idea ; and entering into the true spirit of the poet or writer, has placed before their eyes a bodily presentment of the being with which the author had filled their imagination.

As a painter, Mulready almost wholly avoided this difficulty, his principal pictures being subjects and incidents of his own invention. It is true that after the publication of Van Voorst's edition of the *Vicar of Wakefield*, which Mulready illustrated, he was induced to carry out some of the designs into pictures, and also true that one or two of these rank as his best works ; but it is more for their beautiful art, their colour and completion, than from his having mastered the characters of whom Goldsmith wrote. No one can accept the figure making hay, in the " Haymakers "—almost a portrait of the painter himself—as the Burchell of Goldsmith ; or the young lady with the rake in the same picture as the simple-minded Sophia. Like Mulready, Wilkie took few of his subjects from writers or poets, although he did paint a few historical incidents. Were we to judge him by his " Alfred in the Neatherd's Cottage," we should not rank his realization of historical characters very high. " John Knox " was better, but it is known that it was founded on that true orator and divine, Edward Irving. And his " Columbus," although really a noble picture, and a fine rendering of the intense self-occupation of the world-discoverer in the demonstration

T 2

of his thesis, has yet but little of the Genoese, and less of the seaman in its presentation.

The subjects chosen by Leslie were of a higher class than the early works of either Wilkie or Mulready. He seems from the first to have had an innate refinement in his choice, and to have thrown a sense of gentle blood into all he did. His works abound in beauty, elegance, character, and quiet humour, which make them irresistibly pleasing. Take as an instance the picture of "Sancho Panza in the Apartments of the Duchess," in the National Gallery, a repetition of an earlier picture at Petworth. How lovely is the duchess, how perfectly at her ease, how truly one of Nature's gentlewomen as she sits listening to Sancho's tale! What a round full form! The light of a happy smile in her eyes; the amused satire of her dimpling mouth, pleased at the simplicity of the peasant squire who takes her into his confidence, and binds her to secrecy as to his master's escapades, putting his finger to his nose as he tells his tale. Contrasted with the rare beauty of the lady, and serving as its foil, is the stately, frigid duenna, drawn up to her full height, her hands crossed in front, her keen, observant eye seeing all that is going on; but no smile is ever likely to twinkle there nor to part her thin dry lips. What a contrast to the laughing black damsel on the opposite side of the picture, who grins and shows a mouthful of teeth, at the unconscious assurance of the garlic-loving Sancho in relating his adventures to her noble mistress. Even when Leslie deals with rogues and the simpletons they prey on, it is not the common rogue he represents; and Autolycus, with his ballad "on the hard heart of maids," sung by the great fish "that appeared on Wednesday the fourscore of April," is still Shakspearian as a vagabond, while the straw-hatted shepherd, brown with toil, is far removed from the clodhopper of to-day, who has lost all development of calf from stiff-soled boots, and looks to end his days in that parish paradise, the union. Even Leslie's servants are raised above the common household drudges who are expected to be perfection on 10l. per annum: Leslie raises them up to dramatic equality with the other characters of his tale; and whether it be "Toinette," the cleverest of abigails, circumventing M. Purgon in the Sheepshanks Gallery, or "Nicole" pinking M. Jourdain in the same collection, they seem the very individuals the author dreamt of, and the spectator anticipated. In this latter picture, M. Jourdain himself is the model of pompous ignorance and weakness; his two legs planted in the due attitude of fence, but so thoroughly weak in the knees, so thoroughly wrong from their very rightness; the hand with the foil so attemptedly correct, but so hopelessly out of place; the left hand raised as that defence which is hopeless from the foil, all fill us with a full perception, a thorough representation of the plebeian citizen trying to remedy the defects of his early education, and are so full of character that it may be doubted if the dramatist could have been better illustrated by one of the cleverest of his own countrymen.

Mulready, as we have already said, mostly invented his own subjects, and sometimes without any great subject-matter in them. It has been objected that his irascible disposition and love of fighting is shown in too many of his pictures, and that most of them have some tendency to brutality and cruelty : but this is surely very unfair towards him. Five or six of his pictures out of the eighty or hundred that he painted may be amenable to this criticism : a lad detected at playing "fox and geese" instead of doing his sum. Then, again, in "The Fight Interrupted" and "The Wolf and the Lamb," we have a well-told tale of a coward and a bully ; and in these, as well as "The Careless Messenger" and "The Dog of Two Minds," the fighting element prevails. Moreover, there are episodes of the same nature in "The Convalescent," in "The Seven Ages," and even in "The Last In," where we are well assured that the ironical politeness of the master will end in a good caning to the truant scholar : but this is all ; and besides these we have numerous pictures turning on some simple domestic incident, oftentimes well told, as in "The Travelling Druggist," "Train up a Child," "Village Gossips," "The Widow," &c.

Mulready's first subjects were evidently chosen in emulation of Wilkie, who preceded him by a year or two in public favour ; and in his "Carpenter's Shop," painted in 1808, and "Barber's Shop," in 1811, he had an eye to the popularity of his Scotch rival. This feeling even lingered in his "Punch" and his "Fight Interrupted" ; after which pictures he began gradually to develop a style of his own, and to adopt a changed manner of execution, while the character of his subjects also changed slowly, and tended to a higher class ; some degree of sentiment being added to his domestic drama, as in "The Gamekeeper's Wife," and still more fully in "First Love," one of the best of all his invented subjects.

Wilkie had little sense of beauty. The lady in "The First Ear-ring," in "The Spanish Mother," or the two females in the group in the left corner of "John Knox," represent as much perhaps as he was capable of, and this much is small indeed. The proportion of his typical female face is long, particularly in the nose, the eyes are too small and too close together, the lower part of the face round rather than oval ; neither, as a rule, is there much elegance in his female figures : the rollicking action of the Spanish mother is about one of the best things he painted. To the homeliness of the female in the "Refusal," he might, if beauty was denied to his pencil, have added a little more comeliness ; as it is, we feel that Duncan Gray has on the whole the best of it, and that the lady has no loveliness, and little lovableness that he need regret. Nor had Mulready any very great feeling for female beauty; although, from his great power of drawing, he was able to represent, much more perfectly than Wilkie did, what beauty he found in nature.

If we compare the power of perceiving and delineating character and humour in the three painters, they each possessed it in a remarkable, although in a very different degree. In Wilkie and Mulready, character and expression formed the basis of their first works, and they both rather abandoned it in after life for other qualities of art; while Leslie, in his later pictures, studied character and individuality perhaps more than even in his early works.

Leslie never had a strong innate feeling for colour. He says of himself, "It was Allston who first awakened what little sensibility I may possess to the beauties of colour. For a long time I took the merit of the Venetians on trust, and, if left to myself, should have perferred works which I now feel to be comparatively worthless. I remember when the picture of 'The Ages,' by Titian, was first pointed out to me by Allston as an exquisite work, I thought he was laughing at me." Yet Leslie's taste and feeling generally led him right in the end, and few of his pictures are really ill-coloured. In the general opinion of his contemporaries his colouring was best while he was under the influence of his friend Newton, with whom he was very intimate. Newton had a fine eye for colour, but he was fettered by his feeble power of execution; whence he was ever feeling out his pictures rather than painting them, and was prevented from achieving those precious qualities which arise from a proper preparation of the ground, and after paintings with transparent colour, glazing, &c., as seen in the noble works of the Venetian school.

When Newton ceased to paint, about 1834, Leslie fell under the influence of Constable, and a marked change took place in his pictures.

Wilkie's natural feeling for colour was far more acute than Leslie's, if less so than Mulready's. As soon as his residence in London gave him an opportunity to consult the works of the old painters, he began by founding himself on Teniers. Cunningham says Wilkie gathered his leaden hues from setting his palette by Ibbetson's work on oil painting, but rather perhaps from his study of Teniers; and Wilkie probably afterwards inclined to the brown key from the continued admonitions of Sir George Beaumont, who certainly was a kind and warm friend to the young artist, helping him at times of much difficulty, and giving him advice which he often remarks upon as valuable and judicious.

Wilkie gradually began painting as much as possible at once, and finishing the part he was at work upon while wet, without any interval for drying. During his travels in Italy he continually spoke of the *starved* lights and opaque shadows of the English school, and said that our works were chalky and white; and that water-colour drawings had tainted our exhibitions. Writing to Collins from Florence, he says, "perhaps I say more for colour than I ought," and again from Spain, "with me no starved surface now ; no dread of *oil*, no perplexity for fear of change. Your manner of painting a sky is the manner in which I try to paint a whole picture," that is to say, at once and while the whole is wet. We have even heard from Mr. Stonhouse, who joined him while in Spain as a pupil, that on his return so anxious was Wilkie to carry out this practice, that he would make a wall of wax round a head unfinished during the day's work, and laying the panel flat, cover the uncompleted part with oil, to enable him to continue his work in the same state on the morrow.

"The Parish Beadle," if rather black in the darks and shadows, is one of the best coloured pictures of Wilkie's early class of subjects, and a good specimen of his ability as a colourist. It is mainly painted direct from the ground into a brown uniting colour. The shadows in most parts of the picture seem laid in with some brown pigment made fluent with abundant medium. Into this brown the white lights appear painted, and over them, while still wet, the local colour has been rapidly manipulated with a soft brush, a little white being added for half-tints or high-lights. No doubt the painter has seized the happy moment when, at the latter part of the day, the work has in some degree set, before applying the local colour as a secondary painting ; but, under the best circumstances, such execution would require great skill and rapidity of touch to prevent muddiness from the mixing of the upper and under painting, and the medium or vehicle would require to be abundant and flowing. Notwithstanding Wilkie's constant apostrophes to colour, and his assertion that "no master has as yet maintained his ground without it," we cannot but think that his tendency as he advanced in art, was to tone rather than to colour.

We have seen him, even before his Italian and Spanish journey, tending to the over use of a brown key in his pictures ; and after his return our own experience is that this practice greatly increased upon him. He used asphaltum as his universal shadow, and even mixed it with all his lights to take off that chalky crudity which he found in our English works. Thus he killed the brilliancy of his local colour, although at the same time, by this simple expedient, he increased the tone of his works. As colourists, however, neither Leslie nor Wilkie had the same innate perception as Mulready.

There is yet one point on which these painters may be compared before we proceed to the history of their individual art progress, that is, their acquaintance with the art of other countries. Wilkie, as we have seen, made diligent study of such foreign art as was accessible to him in his own country, and as soon as opportunity offered, visited the schools and collections abroad. Partly from ill health, and partly with a view to improvement, he spent some years of his art-life in Italy and Spain ; and we have the evidence of his works, as well as of his letters and diary, that Italian and Spanish art, but more especially the latter, greatly influenced his work, and, indeed, ended in his thorough change of style ; although it must be allowed that the change was not wholly beneficial, and that his fame will rest on his English, rather than upon his Spanish pictures. An admirer of the great Venetian colourists, he never attained to those executive processes to which their works owe so much of their lustre and richness, but continued to paint to the last as at first ; varied in his method, however, after his Spanish journey.

Leslie, although full of admiration for the best works of the old masters, never visited the great seats of their art ; his knowledge of the Continent was limited to France and Belgium ; the monumental art of Italy or Germany he never saw ; nor was his practice much influenced by the fine works of the old masters that did come within his observation at home. Mulready never visited the Continent at all, or at most only the French coast, and was wholly unacquainted, except from prints and copies, with the mural works of the great painters. Encumbered with difficulties at the time of life when most young artists travel for improvement, he arrived at eminence without having seen the great Continental schools, and seemed latterly rather to pride himself upon never having left his own country, and upon being unindebted to foreign travel. From his birth a member of the Romish communion, had he in his youth seen the simple art of the fifteenth century, it might have influenced his practice ; but art would have been a loser thereby. Possessed of little imagination, and not very refined in choice of subject, he was content to labour on the repetition of his own thoughts. Had his art been turned to religious subjects, he might have laboured on the thoughts of others, and realized the letter without the spirit of religious art ; so that we should have lost what little originality he possessed. Although he never visited Italy, he understood well the principles of the great colourists ; and it were to be wished that, for their rich and varied execution, his own works should influence the British school, and lead to a better understanding of the preparatory processes which give lustre and variety to painting.

CHAPTER XXIII.

DAVID WILKIE, R.A.

WE have been led into a somewhat long digression in the preceding chapter, in order to bring into direct comparison, the art of our three great *genre* painters. We left Wilkie simply a student of the Royal Academy, but as yet he was without patronage, and dependent on himself for his future. Like many other young artists, he resorted to portraiture for his subsistence, and to gain the means to enable him to work for fame ; but, with the peculiar forethought of his countrymen, he borrowed for a time his first work, which, as we have already said, he had sold before leaving his native place ; and had " Pitlassie Fair " sent up to London to show as a specimen of his powers, to those who sought the aid of his pencil. He was fortunate in making the acquaintance of Stodart the pianoforte-maker, who recommended him sitters ; and fortunate also in the choice of the next subject for his pencil. Lord Mansfield, who had seen his " Fair," encouraged him to proceed with a picture of " The Village Politicians," giving him, however, no distinct commission when Wilkie named the modest sum of fifteen guineas as the price of the work. When exhibited in the Royal Academy it attracted much notice, and Wilkie was advised to ask for it a larger, but still very inadequate sum ; to which the earl demurred, and claimed the picture at the first-named price ; but as no acceptance on his part had been given, Wilkie maintained his ground, and the earl finally sent him a cheque for the full sum, thirty-five guineas. In the May of this year, the painter, not yet of the mature age of twenty-one, but full of exultation at his success, writes to his father, " My ambition is got beyond all bounds, and I have the vanity to hope that Scotland will one day be proud of David Wilkie."

Wilkie was not a man to be made idle by success. He set to work at once upon a picture of the same class, yet of even more interest. " The Blind Fiddler " was finished by the middle of August, 1806, while the painter was yet in his twenty-first year, and it deserves careful examination as an evidence of the amount of real knowledge, in many qualities of art, he had thus early achieved.

The painter's next work was not a fortunate one. Mr. Alexander Davison, of St. James's Square, commissioned pictures from various artists to form a gallery of English history, and applied to Wilkie to paint one of the series. It was hardly to be expected that the young painter, at a time when commissions were not too frequent, would decline such an offer; the more especially as he was allowed to choose his own subject for illustration. He selected the well-known incident of King Alfred and the cakes, but as far as we can learn from his diaries, the picture appears to have given him much trouble, and, in the end, after many changes, was certainly not a success, and was never exhibited.

In the spring of 1807, Wilkie revisited his native village, there to enjoy the gratifying approval of his parents and the reputation that had already preceded him. Shortly after his arrival, however, he was seized with an attack of fever, from which he but slowly recovered, and although carefully nursed by his affectionate mother and sisters, it was not until October that he was able to return to London and to the work of his easel. This susceptibility to disease and the slowness with which his constitution acted to throw it off, is a marked feature of his life, and shows some innate weakness which neither change of air, diet, nor scene could readily overcome. On his return, he proceeded with a picture of "The Rent Day." It is a characteristic incident of English life, characteristically rendered; the story is well told, the grouping and arrangement excellent, and the execution an advance on his former works. Wilkie was elected an associate member of the Royal Academy on the 10th November, 1809, when he yet wanted eight days of completing his twenty-fourth year, the prescribed age for admission to that body.

On the 29th September, 1809, Wilkie tells us in his diary that he began "The Village Festival," which was at first called "The Alehouse Door." He says, "After employing some time in preparing colours, I chalked it out on the canvas, to assist me in which I dotted out the picture and the sketch into several compartments. I began with rubbing in all the shadows with umber, and the lights with white, and succeeded in getting in the principal group." He afterwards tells us that he used the sweetener to prevent the surface interrupting him in the finishing. We find him continually removing the work he had done during the day, rubbing out heads, hands, and whole figures, notwithstanding he had prepared a careful sketch beforehand. Many other details of the progress of this picture are noted by him; but unfortunately he has omitted to name the vehicle with which it is painted. Haydon, however, who was intimate with him at this time, says that it was pure oil. Yet notwithstanding this assertion, we are inclined to think that magylph was really used. "The Blind Fiddler" stood perfectly until it was varnished about twenty-five years ago, and then in the course of one short month it cracked in widening hair cracks down to the white ground ; and "The Village Festival" also cracked in like manner.

It will be seen that in our opinion pictures painted in mastic magylph do not crack when left unvarnished, but are liable to fail when this is done ; yet it must be confessed that it is very doubtful if the "Fiddler" had been left unvarnished until the time spoken of above. Wilkie was evidently accustomed to have his pictures varnished very soon after their completion ; perhaps agreeing with West's maxim, that you should "lock them up" with varnish as soon as possible. Thus we find an entry in Wilkie's diary in May, 1808 : —"Accompanied Seguier to the Admiralty to varnish the picture of 'The Rent Day' ;" and again in July, "Seguier varnished for me 'The Village Politicians,' and the sketch of Miss Phipps." So that without it was a particular wish of the owner not to have a work varnished, it would appear to be the usual practice of the painter to varnish. "The Village Festival" is differently executed from those works which preceded it, the flesh and the draperies being made up of broken tints, although the general tone is grey. Wilkie had now mastered all the varied modes of execution, such as thick and thin painting, painting into a glaze, glazing, &c., although he ever used the latter quality very sparingly. The improvement in execution as well as in expression is very marked.

"The Village Festival" was a picture containing too many figures and too much material to permit of the painter's finishing it in time for exhibition in 1810, and Wilkie, perhaps somewhat too hastily, painted a small work to keep his place on the walls. This he called "No Fool like an Old Fool," but subsequently changed to "The Wardrobe Ransacked." His friends in the Academy thought it did not maintain his reputation ; they advised him to withdraw it, and he reluctantly complied with their wishes. His biographer seems to lean to the opinion that there was some jealousy on the part of the members in this, but although the painter was ill-represented in their exhibition, the Academy elected him in the ensuing spring to the full honours of their body.

In this year (1810) Wilkie had the first serious attack of the illness which afterwards distressingly haunted him. He complained to Dr. Baillie that he could neither paint nor think for a quarter of an hour consecutively without experiencing a giddiness almost amounting to fainting. This ended in fever, which prostrated him for many weeks, and prevented his painting ; indeed his weakness lasted almost to the end of the year. He had long been meditating upon a scheme for profiting by the exhibition of his own works. He thought—as Fuseli and others had done before him—that the public, which took especial pleasure in his pictures when seen with others in the Academy exhibition, would flock to a collection brought together for his own profit. He took a house, No. 87, Pall Mall, and in May, 1812, opened a collection of his own pictures, partly new and partly borrowed from his patrons.

It is not to be wondered at that the members were vexed to see their new colleague diverting his chief works from their walls, but if so, they had their revenge. Wilkie, though sufficiently a man of business and canny at a bargain, as his diary shows, was at least not fitted to puff an exhibition of his own works; and the time was yet distant when this was to become a profitable business to middle-men and dealers, who, given a banquet scene, the entry of a royal personage, or indeed any *outré* or singular work, can, by dint of sheer advertising puffery, draw large sums of money from the public, whether the art is good or bad. We are not surprised, therefore, that the attempt was unsuccessful and a loss. Wilkie was accustomed to shake his head when the affair was mentioned. A distraint was made on his pictures for rent due *from* his landlord for the premises sublet to the painter; "The Village Holiday," as it was then called, was seized, and had to be redeemed. The only benefit accruing to the artist was that it suggested the fine subject, "Distraining for Rent," which the painter shortly commenced.

In December of the year 1812, Wilkie's father died, having lived long enough to witness the full reputation of his son. This caused a great change in the painter's household; eventually his mother and sister came to live with him at Kensington. This must have put an end to the affairs which we trace him relating with much simplicity in his journal for 1810 :—" Had a valentine to-day, from whom I know not, but certainly in the same handwriting as one I formerly received," and shortly afterwards :—"A young lady called and made use of the name of one of my friends to see my pictures; she expressed in strong terms her regret at not finding any picture of mine in the exhibition, and said she had seen a print of me, but it looked much too youthful. Though she said nothing at all improper, I am inclined to doubt her character, as well as her motive for calling on me. It is altogether a strange matter." We fancy we can see the sedate young painter of twenty-five bowing out the somewhat bold lady who would have liked to remain to share his home. Now with his mother and sister at hand to add to his comforts and to keep off such visitors, Wilkie was able to resist all such attractions; and having passed through his period of temptation he remained single to the last, devoting himself wholly to the art he loved.

He had exhibited his picture of "Blindman's Buff" (which he had taken in hand after "The Village Festival") among his other works in Pall Mall. He finished it for the Academy exhibition of 1813, where, according to the rules of that body, he was on this occasion to act as one of the members of the hanging committee. Wilkie says on this occasion, " We had many a squabble, as you may suppose, during the arrangement, about who should have the best places ; but as no one was admitted, this was all confined to ourselves, and although we had the interests of all the members to balance and take care of, as well as those of our own particular friends, and those of the many poor fellows who had no friends, we have adjusted them all so well that there is not a single complaint : " but he also adds with much *naïveté*, " The first persons we thought of were our own three selves, as you may suppose ; and, acting on this principle, my picture of ' Blindman's Buff' was accordingly placed *in the principal centre in the great room* "— showing that he also knew how to take care of his own interests. Not that this is characteristic of the members of hanging committees, who often sacrifice their own works for those of their brother artists. When one of the writers was on the hanging committee with Leslie, the latter withdrew a picture of his own to make way for one that, if not more deserving, would have injured its author more, if misplaced, than could be the case with the work of a painter so distinguished as Leslie. And it is pleasant here to record that on a similar occasion the same writer was assured that when a place could not be found on the line for his picture of " Ellen Orford " Wilkie took down a picture of his own from the line, to give it a place.

Wilkie's next important pictures were " The Pedlar," " The Letter of Introduction," and the " Duncan Gray." These two latter are of the same size, and originally the " Duncan Gray " was painted in the same thin delicate manner, and of the same silvery tone, as " The Letter of Introduction." Mulready, however, who was well acquainted with the painting of " Duncan Gray," used to say that when nearly finished, Wilkie became enamoured of tone, and went all over the picture with asphaltum, painting into it, and repeating this process even a second time. The result was fatal to the picture ; it cracked and went into a very sad state, of which a photographic record has been preserved. It is now in the South Kensington Museum. Mulready himself sat to Wilkie for the " Duncan Gray," Mulready's father for the father of the unwilling damsel ; and for her Wilkie's sister sat.

In 1814, Wilkie made his first trip to the Continent, remaining five or six weeks in France, where he visited the schools and galleries, but seems to have come back without being much impressed by French art. On his return he commenced the picture of " Distraining for Rent," a work of great dramatic merit. " The Penny Wedding " followed in 1819, and in 1820, " The Reading a Will," a very characteristic subject, said to have been suggested to him by Jack Bannister, the comedian ; it was a commission from the King of Bavaria, and almost the only instance in which a British painter has been asked to paint for a foreign gallery. When Wilkie visited Munich in 1826, he naturally wished to see his picture, which was understood to have been hung with the works of the older masters, and to note how it stood in their company.

But he found the king who had given him the commission, dead, and the picture sealed up with the other royal treasures, preparatory to their sale. An application to see his own work was, however, favourably received, and the seal of the apartment broken in the presence of a commissioner, who accompanied him for that purpose. Wilkie says of the work, "its look and hue gratified me exceedingly: it looked rich and powerful, and remarkably in harmony with the fine specimens of Dutch art which surrounded it:" he adds, "observed the picture had been varnished about a twelvemonth ago, on looking narrowly I could discover the beginning of small cracks in the varnish." These cracks subsequently enlarged greatly; thirty years after they had become wide and deep; but in a second visit to Munich lately made (1888), on a careful inspection of the picture, the evil did not seem to be progressing. It is now among the modern works in the new Pinacothek.

He was now about to begin one of his most important pictures, one that eventually became almost historical, although not undertaken with that idea. He tells us that "in the summer of 1816, the year after the Battle of Waterloo," the great duke requested to have a picture by him, the subject to be "British Soldiers Regaling at Chelsea"; and he adds, "in justice to the duke as well as to myself, it is but right to state, that the introduction of the *Gazette* was a subsequent idea of my own to unite the interest, and give importance to the business of the picture." Above the soldiers a jovial group, from the windows of the "Duke of York," listen eagerly to catch the words of the reader. The composition is filled up with many figures—the negro bandsman, the one-legged veteran now turned civilian, the oyster wife opening her luxuries for their delectation, the Scotch Highlander, and the figures that lead the eye away into the picture and the distance. The features of the background, while they are felicitously pictorial, are literally exact.

This picture greatly advanced the painter's fame. High and low flocked to see it. The soldiers to find out their comrades in arms, who in India, in the Peninsula, and finally at Waterloo, had fought with them under the command of the great captain. The public were delighted with it, the artists were equally delighted, and the visitors to the exhibition had to be railed off from it, waiting *en queue* their turn to pass in front. It is one of Wilkie's best pictures; in it he carried his early style to its completion.

It is delightful, after seeing the decaying state of so many of Wilkie's works, to find this one, "Reading the Gazette of the Battle of Waterloo," uncracked and sound. It has been what is technically called "painted into a glaze" throughout, apparently bone brown, with perhaps, from the greyness of the half tints when they melt into the shadows, the addition of a little black. The heads have the appearance of being completed at once, and not gone over and over in seeking expression. It is worth noting that this Waterloo picture, which has stood so well, has certainly been varnished.

Wilkie's next picture was a commission from George IV., the " Parish Beadle," a beautiful picture for character, expression, and colour, although a little black in the shadows. It was to be a companion to the " Penny Wedding" and "Blindman's Buff." His early art culminated in this work, still in the Royal Collection.

In 1883, Sir Henry Raeburn, who had been the King's limner for Scotland, died, and Sir Robert Peel recommended Wilkie to his Majesty for the appointment. The painter then began to work diligently on his historical picture of "The Royal Entrance into Holyrood." His Majesty was pleased to approve of the choice, and promised to sit for it when the work was sufficiently advanced. But the King had his own idea of a dignified attitude, and posed to show how he received the keys of the seneschal : much to the distraction of the painter. Courtly sitters also troubled him, and the work proceeded slowly ; nevertheless he laboured on, paying another visit to Scotland to sketch the details for the picture, and at the same time having an eye to the subject on which he had set his heart, " The Preaching of Knox." While in Scotland he was induced to undertake a life-size whole-length portrait of Lord Kellie—wishing, as he says to his brother, "to have the practice of painting large, in case I should have anything to paint for the King in the same way."

An accumulation of family sorrows weighed heavily at this time on the sensitive mind of the painter, already overtaxed by his art labours, and, tried by undeserved pecuniary troubles, this caused his old malady to return upon him ; he managed to finish some small works for the exhibition, and then was advised to seek a renewal of his health in foreign travel and an entire cessation from his art.

Wilkie set out for Paris, wintered in Rome and Naples, visited Germany, and tried the Teplitz baths in the summer, and the following winter revisited Rome, where he found himself once more able again to paint about the end of the month of April.

During the summer he made some short stay in Geneva, still progressing with his art, and then resolved, instead of returning, to pay a visit to Spain, almost an unknown land to that generation of artists. He arrived in Madrid early in October, 1827, was delighted with the novelty of Spanish art—looked much at Velasquez, an artist but imperfectly known out of Spain—painted several pictures, now in the Royal

Collection—and writing home to his sister, says :—"Will the London public, with my former style in recollection, judge of these new subjects, and new manner of treating them, with the same favour as those who see them now for the first time? This is what I mean to try. I have now, from the study of the old masters, adopted a bolder and more effective style; and one result is rapidity. The quantity of work I have got through, all seem surprised at. If it excites the same interest in London that it does here, it will probably bring better times." On leaving Spain, he said :—"I return highly satisfied with my journey. The seven months and ten days passed in Spain I may reckon as the best employed time of my professional life."

Wilkie's illness, and the foreign journey that it necessitated, brought to a close the first period of his art. The position he now occupied as King's limner opened up a new species of labour, and a new source of profit, which he would no doubt have followed out, even without the stimulant of his foreign observations. As his difficulties increased, arising from his long abstention from painting, his losses from over-trading capitalists, or from the misfortunes of his relatives, he began to find his early art too laborious; he felt, as Cunningham says, "that if he continued to work in his usual laborious style of detail and finish, he should never achieve independence;" and while these thoughts troubled him, he saw the master works of Velasquez, and instantly became a worshipper.

Most of the pictures actually painted in Spain are in the possession of her Majesty. They are all treated in a brown key, and they seem completed at once; they are fine in general effect and tone, and have a Spanish air about them, but are more defective in drawing than his earlier works. The best of the series is, however, that of the "Two Spanish Monks in the Cathedral of Toledo," which he painted in England. The Queen's Spanish pictures are much loaded in the brown darks, but not so much so as "The Confessional," and they are all equally uncracked. Painted in Madrid, as we find from the journal, and from the painter's signature to the works, he was perhaps out of the way of colourmen's materials—and his pictures are the sounder for it.

When these pictures were exhibited, they raised a storm of criticism; all reverted to his early art, and to the class of subjects which had won him fame, and few were ready to admit that the change was for the better. But although the art-world, true to its first love, hesitated to consider Wilkie's change of style an improvement, we, who at a distance of time compare the two, are able to give a less biassed judgment, and can find many beauties in these works. It is rarely that an artist goes so completely out of himself as did Wilkie; between Mulready's first and last style there was almost as great a change, but it was very gradual.

Wilkie made the contrast far more startling by the sudden change. He had begun to loosen his hand before leaving England, as we see by "The Pensioners," but on and after his Spanish journey he not only ignored all executive finish, but considered it as tending to bad art.

It must be allowed that there is great beauty in the rich tone, and the mellifluent melting of the colour into it, in these latter works; and we have already said that the subjects chosen are of a higher class; but the rich tone was obtained at too great a sacrifice of permanency; and in choosing historical rather than merely dramatic subjects, Wilkie shut himself out from his strongest quality—character. Moreover, there can be little doubt that the change led him out of his depth and beyond his powers. Although he drew readily and imitated his model well, he never was a good draughtsman, and when he attempted beauty his defects became apparent; still more so when he increased the size of his pictures, and introduced figures of the scale of life.

For a time after his return Wilkie was much occupied in painting portraits, many of them being of the Royal Family. In the early part of the year 1830, Sir Thomas Lawrence died, and many thought Wilkie ought to be his successor, but it is said that only one vote, that of his devoted friend Collins, was given for him. Wilkie himself was wise enough to swallow quietly his disappointment, if it were one, and to busy himself with his portraits, and his long-delayed picture of the preaching of the great Scottish reformer. It proved one of the most successful pictures of his second style.

At the time the Knox was on the easel, the celebrated Edward Irving was pouring forth his fervid eloquence to warn a London audience of the second advent of our Lord. Hurried away by his own earnestness, his action was often perfectly unrestrained. Wilkie studied him for the great reformer; the action he has chosen we have often seen when Irving in Regent Square was preaching his sermons on the "perilous times," and he even sat to Wilkie for the expressive head.

As usual the painter visited the locality of his picture. He found the pulpit of the great reformer stowed away, in company with the gallows, in a cellar of the old town; and one of Wilkie's young friends made a careful drawing of it for his use. For this picture Wilkie resorted to another expedient to enable him to get the fullest impression of his subject. To study the light and shade, and the relative relief of the several groups and figures, he modelled them small, draped them, and placed them in a box fitted up to represent the interior of St. Andrews.

As a portrait painter, Wilkie succeeded worst in the most important part. When first painted, his portraits looked well as pictures; the colour and general distribution being mostly agreeable; but the heads wanted drawing, and worse still, high character. Wilkie had not the

U

power of either Reynolds or Gainsborough to seize the mental characteristics of his sitter, or to give the best expression ; in some cases the heads
look as if the painter had in vain endeavoured to coax the paint into a
reluctant likeness : the hair is also a difficulty, it seems full of a fatty
pomade, stiff and colourless. No doubt portraits added greatly to his
income, but as surely little to his fame. In 1836, William IV. bestowed
on him the honour of knighthood, and when he died, and our present
beloved Queen came to the throne, Wilkie retained his office in the
household, and was required to paint her Majesty's first council ; a subject
of high interest, but carried out too quickly to be entirely satisfactory :
the present state of this work, we grieve to say, is most deplorable.

In the autumn of 1840, Wilkie suddenly determined on a voyage to
the East. In the full practice of his profession, with commissions for
pictures and portraits uncompleted, he resolved to visit the localities
of the sacred narrative, and, as a painter, to try to realize for himself, as much as possible, the scenery and accessories of Scripture
history.

He started by way of the Hague, Cologne, Munich, and Vienna, and,
dwelling with renewed pleasure on the works of art in the countries he
passed through, he reached Constantinople on the 4th of October, 1840.
Here he was delayed some time on account of the war in Syria, and
made use of his somewhat enforced leisure to paint the Sultan. He
reached Jerusalem on the 27th of February ; there, and in the neighbourhood, he remained about five weeks. On his return, while at Alexandria,
he began a portrait of the Pasha of Egypt, and after his long absence
wearied for home.

Wilkie left Alexandria in the Oriental steamer, apparently in his usual
health. He had had occasional attacks of illness on his voyage, but
nothing serious ; at Malta, however, he committed an imprudence in
eating fruits and ices, and had an attack of some complaint in the
stomach ; it yielded apparently to the care of the surgeon, but recurred
during the night previous to the vessel's leaving the island. Wilkie was
found fast sinking when the ship cleared the harbour, and died within an
hour, on the 1st of June, 1841. The vessel put back, but the authorities
would not allow the body to be landed ; and that same evening it was
committed to the deep with all due rites and honours. His fame and
its due commemoration was left to the care of his countrymen ; but his
mortal remains it was not given to them to enshrine.

Had Wilkie lived to return to England with the sketches he had made
during his visit to the East, we may presume that he would have again
changed his class of subjects and his style of treating them, if not his
mode of execution. He would not only have painted Oriental but most
likely religious subjects. But it was ordained otherwise, and we can only

speculate upon the effect his new views on these subjects might have had on the world.

In person, Wilkie was tall and somewhat ungainly in figure, and he was ever of a pale and colourless complexion. His art was of a character particularly laborious, and his health was unequal; this, and perhaps his native temperament, made him frugal; but he was very just, and generous even in his justice, in fulfilling his engagements.

Wilkie's mind was very slow, but fixed itself pertinaciously on any subject, and this led him to brood on whatever struck him. Like all Scotchmen, he was not alive to pun or equivoque. We have heard Callcott tell curious stories of this lack of readiness. On one occasion, when they had been at an evening party at Sir John Swinburne's, and came away together, Wilkie sat in the cab, entirely absorbed and silent. After some time he suddenly cried out, "Verra good! Verra good!" and on his companion asking him what was very good, Wilkie spelt out and put together a little witty equivoque whose sparkle had amused the company in the early part of the evening, and of which Wilkie had been chewing the undigested cud, unable to comprehend it, until he was half way on his road home from the party.

He was fond of society—especially the society of his brother artists, and he entered with great earnestness into any amusements connected with art ; we frequently find him masquerading while in Rome.

His early art certainly made a great impression on the English school ; showing how Dutch art might be nationalized, and story and sentiment added to scenes of common life treated with truth and individuality. As to his middle time, such pictures as the "John Knox" also had their influence on the school, and the new mode of execution as supported by Wilkie's authority, had a very evil influence ; bringing discredit upon English pictures as entirely wanting in permanency. His methods and the pigments he used were soon discarded in England ; but at the time they influenced, and have continued to influence, his countrymen long after his death.

CHAPTER XXIV.

WILLIAM MULREADY, R.A., AND THOMAS WEBSTER, R.A.

WE resume the narrative of Mulready's art from the completion of his student career. As far as we can trace him by the pictures he exhibited, he first came before the world as a landscape painter, and for some time exhibited such works rather than subject pictures. We find his name in the Royal Academy catalogue for the first time in 1804, appended to three landscapes. In 1805 he exhibited three landscapes; and in 1806, four. But in this year there was a great change in the execution of his pictures: the careful, precise, and rather minute execution of his former works was changed for one somewhat larger and broader, but approaching mannerism in the use of the browns, and in the mode of painting into a brown key. It is evident that he was not satisfied with this new manner—no doubt adopted from some of the more advanced painters of the day—as he soon reverted to his own elaborate mode of viewing nature, and with slight modifications he persevered to the end in this treatment of his art.

In 1807, together with one or two landscapes, Mulready exhibited his first subject picture, "Old Kaspar," from Southey's poem of *The Battle of Blenheim*. It is a small work (about 10½ inches square) on panel, and has an interest from being his first figure picture, rather than from any intrinsic excellence as a work of art. It is solidly and crisply painted, with the evident want of knowledge of a beginner, but showing that the painter had looked to his Dutch predecessors. It has stood well, and it is still fresh, although it has failed a little in the darks. The composition, light and dark, and even the colour, have been well considered; but there is a great want of truth and of knowledge of the constructive details in the parts of the cottage shown in the background: a want soon overcome by the painter's great perceptive imitation. There is a foreshadowing of his future finish in the hair and beard of the old man.

In 1808, Mulready was again a contributor to the exhibition of the

Royal Academy, both of landscapes and figure pictures ; and one of these, " The Rattle," is painted very much in the manner of Teniers, except that the background is more solid. It is executed with a flat crisp touch, very little glazing or scumbling, and with no appearance of the stippled manner of his latter years, but a dexterous oneness, such as the Dutch master was so well skilled in. The scheme of light and dark is like Teniers, and all the colour is focussed to a single object in the foreground. Though a small work, it ranks him at once as an artist.

But at the time this was exhibiting Mulready had a work of yet more importance on his easel, perhaps far advanced, his first large picture, which he sent to the British Institution : induced to do so, most probably, by the prizes offered by the directors on this occasion.

This picture of Mulready's, to which the directors of the Institution preferred one by Sharpe, is "The Carpenter's Shop and Kitchen," and it is the painter's first important figure picture. The story told is very simple. The wife of the workman, neither pretty nor young, sits beside the fire in the living room ; her little son is asleep on her lap, and the father has come from his work-bench to have a loving look at his youngest child ; on the other side of the fireplace is an older boy, with his back to the spectator. These constitute the materials of the picture, which is a little history of a workman's life, true from its very homeliness, and touching, because without any false sentiment.

In this picture the system and principles of the Dutch masters Jan Steen and Teniers are seen to have been well studied and clearly understood. How well has the painter appreciated their principle of giving great breadth to the light, and accumulating it round his principal group. Also that of spreading his warm colour, his reds by yellows into light, as in the red dress of the carpenter's wife and the yellow frock of her sleeping child ; while the cooler light of the fireplace expands and enlarges that of the group ; the red also is sedulously carried round the picture by all the little art devices of the masters whose works our painter had so far built upon, and which they knew so well how to use, and how to conceal. The execution of the picture, still of the same character as "The Rattle," is sincere and masterly, painted at once, and with a degree of easy freedom, and great completion in the accessories ; which indeed are carried further than the figures in point of finish, and speak the future art of the painter : thus the texture of the coarse shawl of the woman, the cradle, the old worsted stockings turned into sleeves for the working waistcoat of the carpenter, are wrought like miniature painting, while they have also the higher finish of keeping. The picture in its present state looks a little spotty, as the darks have somewhat lost their richness ; but when painted it must have been thought a striking picture for a young man of twenty-two.

Mulready's "Carpenter's Shop" was an attempt to compete with the popular favourite Wilkie, and, as far as it went, was a very successful attempt; but as yet he had not sought to give character, expression, or even much action, all of which are to be found in the pictures of his rival, such as the "Blind Fiddler" and the "Rent Day."

We may very well suppose that Wilkie's friends, one of whom does not hesitate to call him "a consummate dramatist—the only one who had appeared since the days of Hogarth," had not failed to make these objections against Mulready, for we find him in his next pictures making an effort to show that he was quite capable of achieving these qualities also. In 1811, he produced his picture of "The Barber's Shop," in which the execution is perhaps less refined than "The Carpenter's Shop," while it has less apparent finish with far more of local truth; but the great advance is in character and expression.

During this period the painter must have had a hard struggle to live. His family was increasing (all his four sons were born before Mulready was twenty-four years of age), and there were times when—the country at that time being engaged in a long and costly war—the necessaries of life were at famine prices; while the purchasers of pictures were few in number, and the prices obtained insignificant as compared with those of our day. It must have been about this period that the painter assisted Sir Robert Ker Porter in getting up his panorama of Seringapatam, and occasionally painted on the scenery of the Lyceum, then under the management of Arnold. He also found purchasers for his landscapes. No doubt Mulready also taught at this time, as in later days; and from all these sources he managed to make a sufficient income to support his rising family.

It is not our intention to give a description of the many fine works of this great painter, but simply to describe his progress in art; and perhaps it may be as well, before proceeding further, to advert to his power as a landscape painter, the direct practice of which art he almost concluded at this period. In landscape, as in figure subjects, he would no doubt have attained to the first rank had he continued to practise it; but after the picture of "Boys Fishing," painted in 1813, we have no pure landscapes by him for nearly forty years, till in 1852, he painted the "Blackheath Park," being the view from the front gate of the house in which Mr. Sheepshanks then resided.

Though he would no doubt have achieved excellence as a landscape painter, he would perhaps have been rather imitative than inventive. The "Boys Fishing," the background of the "Punch," and of "The Fight Interrupted," show his best early manner: broad, flat, and somewhat empty. Mulready's works at this time are very highly finished, but all the finish is thoroughly subservient to breadth and general effect.

Callcott used to say :—" Finish as much as you please, if you can keep the parts of your picture in their right place." And Mulready, who was his neighbour, and no doubt had often heard this doctrine laid down, had felt its truth, and duly attended to it. In his latter days Mulready changed his views somewhat, and the finish in his landscapes is rather too apparent.

Passing over his " Punch," we come to the "Idle Boys" and "The Fight Interrupted," produced in an important year of the painter's life. The first of these pictures, which from the greater facility of the execution might be thought the later of the two works, were it not for the order in which they were exhibited, was sent to the Royal Academy in 1815, and was no doubt the cause of his being chosen an associate at the election which took place in November. It is a perfect work for arrangement, strong action, expression, and suitable colour. The schoolmaster seated at his desk, to which he has summoned the two offenders, has a very characteristic head (the painter's father sat for it); his face is red and angry, his appearance that of one who would rule by fear rather than by love, and he has just administered a tingling blow on the palm to one of the urchins who has been detected playing in school hours. There is a slight change in the execution of this picture ; in some places the ground is seen through a semi-solid painting, as in the coat of the boy who waits for punishment, the master's desk, and in parts of the background ; true glazings also are adopted, as in the master's cap, the green breeches of the beaten boy, and the green back of the master's chair. "The Fight Interrupted" was in a forward state at the time of Mulready's election to the associateship : it was ready to exhibit in 1816 as a justification of the Academy's choice. But higher honours awaited him : the members, alive to the talent of the young painter, selected him for the full membership of the Academy in the February following his election as associate ; a course of which there is no subsequent instance.

It was fortunate that he was ready with the most perfect picture in his first manner, to justify to the public the wisdom of the choice. In "The Fight Interrupted," the story is well and simply told ; the big bully of the school soundly thrashed by one of the lesser boys, over whom he had endeavoured to tyrannize, is but too glad of the opportune arrival of the Dominie. Mulready's children were by this time grown into boys and did their part in standing as models for this fine work.

The execution and handling are the same as in his earlier pictures ; it is true there are some indications of glazing, but it is used to enhance and enrich colour rather than to produce it. The red cap of the boy addressing the master is the only instance of colour produced direct from the white ground, as in his later pictures ; but this bit of painting was renewed in 1861, when Mulready had the picture in order to restore one or two injuries it had received before it came into Mr. Sheepshanks's possession. From this time we begin to trace a change towards a manner far more peculiarly his own ; gradual at first but afterwards more strongly marked.

It is unnecessary to follow Mulready year by year, and picture by picture ; we rather propose to show the changes that took place in his art as he advanced in life and increased in knowledge.

Between 1822 and 1832 the painter seemed to be feeling his way to a new mode of execution. Hitherto he had painted at once and from the object ; now he began to work from drawings and studies. Although the change resulted in giving us a number of pictures of a character wholly different from any others in the English school, it did not at first appear one for the better. Of the transition time there are three illustrative works, "The Travelling Druggist," "The Origin of a Painter," and "Firing the Cannon." In these the crispness of al-primo painting is almost gone, and a degree of woolliness throughout has resulted from the mode of execution. The colour is obtained by glazing over a prepared ground, as in the robe of the rhubarb merchant, the leaves of the vine over the door, or the yellow shawl in which the sick boy is wrapped. Some process has been used to give texture to the prepared ground, either by stabbing, pressing cloth on the wet layer of paint, or some such means. On this the design seems made out in brown ; Mulready's son Michael said bone-brown was used, and that himself and his brother burned the bones to make it : the brown ground in all the three pictures predominates too much. The ground in "The Druggist" is very thin, and has gathered up into small pin-holes ; and in "The Origin of a Painter," into sharp, wiry cracks. This failure may be noticed in the other works, and seems to result from the vehicle used, since "The Druggist" has failed also in the solid painting ; as in the breeches of the sick boy, and the dress of the mother. The use of bone-brown to lay in the chiaroscuro of the picture, is one of the features of his new mode of working. The weakness arising from painting from drawings is most evident in the girl with the skipping-rope, in the sick boy, the dog, and the foliage over the door.

In 1828, Mulready exhibited the picture of "The Interior of an English Cottage," in which he seems to have completely overcome the difficulties of the new methods he had adopted. He had obtained a perfect vehicle and durable pigments ; the textural preparation of the ground has been laid aside and a semi-solid execution direct from the white ground is substituted. This picture deserves great study : the treatment of the interior is wonderfully luminous, and the look-out from the window into the open beyond is very true to the effect of light ; the cottage is full of material, all adequately finished without over-apparent labour, all truly in keeping and properly subordinate to its position in the picture and the general effect. The light in the distance is very low in tone, yet it looks brilliant ; the greatest dark, clearing up all the darks in the picture, is that of the black cat in the foreground : the scale of light and dark, from the sky to the black of the cat, is very much diminished by this lowness of tone, but there is no light at all approaching that of the sky in brightness, no dark equal to the cat in intensity. This is one of the few pictures of sentiment which Mulready painted, and it is full of beauty and the pleasant quiet of the sweet evening hour.

"The Seven Ages," which shortly followed, is the picture of the greatest pretension that the painter undertook ; but it can hardly be called a success, nor does it form a mark in his practice : nevertheless, being incomplete, it is a picture that reveals some of his methods. All the work seems carried out from drawings, or completed without referring direct to nature; but this procedure is more concealed than in his former works. The colour is produced by transparent painting over a slightly prepared ground, on which the lights are heightened and rendered with impasto; or by painting solidly a pale version of the colour sought, and then glazing it into richness. The mode is best seen on the left of the picture (the spectator's right), where the work is not carried so far as on the right. Thus the hose of the lover have been laid in of a reddish hue, then delicately glazed, and some of the colour wiped off, leaving it in the texture of the painting, and afterwards the folds enriched by the same means. The buildings on the left, the cap of the bowing pantaloon, and the ground on that side of the picture are evidently unfinished ; while the justice, the flitting peasants, the buildings, and landscape on the other side of the picture, are perhaps carried up to the tone and strength to which Mulready would have wrought the whole had he taken up the picture again. This he much wished to do after the picture left Mr. Sheepshanks's possession, but time and opportunity never served. The pictures of "Bob Cherry" and "The Sonnet," which followed, are painted on a white ground so thinly that in many places the pencil lines by which the parts are drawn-in show through the painting. Mulready had now arrived at the perfection of his second manner. The works completed by him between 1839 and 1848 are the most perfect in story, colour and execution of any of his productions. The chiaroscuro is excellent, the colour rich and jewel-like, the execution refined and perfect of its kind. "The Whistonian Controversy" is somewhat hot, but it is most agreeable as a whole, full and harmonious, and in the furthest possible way removed from paintiness. An autumnal hue seems to pervade the picture, suitable to the ease-loving age of the disputants ; while "Choosing the Wedding Gown" is fresher and more spring-like in colour, agreeing with the opening life of the young vicar and his fair and notable wife. In this picture the full force of the palette is given—the brightest vermilion, the richest green, the purest ultramarine; yet all are thoroughly harmonized. Some of the colours are obtained by rich glazings; some by painting the semi-solid pigments directly over the pure white ground of the panel; and the Venetian methods have been better understood than by any painter of our school. The discrimination of the textures, also, as seen in these two pictures, is well worth a careful study. The parchment books and table-cover in the first, the rich stuffs at the foot of the tradesman's counter in the second; while the end of the counter itself is curious, and shows that it is an imitation of imitative mahogany; what a nice distinction to achieve in its pictorial reproduction! But the picture by which the painter himself considered he had arrived at the greatest excellence is the "Train up a Child," painted in 1841, just before "The Whistonian Controversy."

After 1846, Mulready's art increased in finish, but decreased in power. "The Mother and Child," his last completed work, is timid and inclined to prettiness, and his "Toy Seller," left unfinished at his death, is an evidence of labour wrongly applied.

It would be very desirable to have a thorough record of Mulready's vehicles, and his methods of using them in the production of his pictures. Having early become convinced of the danger of using asphaltum, he wholly abandoned it after 1816; he also gave up the use of mastic magylph, and, latterly, painted with copal, and he was extremely careful that one painting should be dry before another was placed over it. He was very minute in his execution, using a powerful glass to look at his work. His palette was of the smallest dimensions, and often contained only the one or two colours or tints of the drapery on which he was working. In his early pictures he used the colour freely, and with a broad, flat manner of handling; but in his later works he inclined more to stippling, although he managed to hide the method when the work was complete.

We must not overlook his remarkable powers as a draughtsman. This is evidenced in his early studies for his pictures, his sketches for backgrounds, and details of birds, plants, foliage, &c.; but latterly he gave great attention to drawing the figure, and developed a remarkable style. It has already been said that Mulready made careful cartoons, finished in black and red chalk, for some of his works. These drawings led the painter to the use of the same means in working from the living model, and resulted in a series of studies made after 1846. It was the painter's view that all the characteristics of the model chosen should be strictly attended to, and that it was no part of the student's business in drawing from the nude, to mould it to some preconceived idea, to the proportions or idealization of the antique. Yet in religiously following out this plan of study, nature is rarely represented otherwise than beautiful.

Mulready was ever a willing and diligent visitor in the life-school, and, like Etty, was always a worker there. The earnest and careful study which these drawings evidence, many of them made before the eyes of the students, should lay the foundation for better drawing in the British school. During the painter's life-time the Department of Science and Art purchased several of the best of his life-studies, for the use of the schools of art throughout the land, and both the Royal Academy and the Department were purchasers at the sale after his death. The sight of such earnest works ought to be extremely useful, and it is to be hoped that students will not merely copy the manner, but be led to imitate the deep study by which such excellence was achieved.

All the painter's last years were passed at Kensington, first in the Mall, and afterwards at No. 1, Linden Grove, Bayswater, which he moved into when these buildings were erected in 1827 by Mr. Allison, who built a painting-room according to Mulready's plans and directions. Here he resided until his death in 1863, leading a sort of half-hermit life, latterly with his son Michael, who tended him to the last, was with him when he died, and was no doubt the chief depository of all his views and wishes.

But if his life was a solitary one, and a life of labour, he had at least the happiness of working at his beloved art to the very last ; and may, to the very last, have been said to have extended some section of art-practice. Thus his wonderful life-studies were almost entirely the work of the last ten or twelve years. When above seventy-five years of age, he set himself to practise drawing hands and heads rapidly in pen and ink, at the little life-school, held by the painters of the neighbourhood at Kensington. "I had lost somewhat of my power in that way," said he, "but I have quite got it up again : it won't do to let these things go." Large canvases were in his rooms, and during the last two or three years of his life he laboured diligently on his large repetition of the "Toy Seller"; laboured, it may be truly said, for his art was not fitted for works of the life size ; as this picture most clearly shows, both in its execution and in the wonderful studies he prepared for it.

He died with his mind clear, and his faculties unimpaired ; perfectly aware of the insidious disease to which he was subject, he yet hoped to fight off its attacks by his resolute will, and did not consider his end so near. The week before he died he attended a committee meeting of the Royal Academy, and took an active part in some animated discussions ; we accompanied him on his way home, and in crossing Waterloo Place, Mulready had one of his spasmodic attacks ; seizing our arm, he remained motionless in the middle of the road for about two minutes, regardless of the vehicles that thronged by. After a period of apparently absolute powerlessness, he exclaimed—"It is all over now ; I know well when I have conquered it : 'tis all right, I shall have no more ; " and when we reached the corner where our roads diverged, he was deaf to our request to allow us to see him home. That night week he was again at the committee, apparently well—at least without pain. Again we proposed to walk away together, but he remarked that Hardwicke was such an invalid, that he thought it right to convoy him on his way, and they left together. This was at eleven o'clock at night ; at seven the next morning, the 7th July, 1863, Mulready was at rest.

Perhaps we shall be pardoned for including here a notice of Thomas Webster, R.A., and deferring our return to Leslie till the next chapter.

A younger man than Mulready by fourteen years, *Thomas Webster, R.A*, was still, in an art sense, his contemporary, though he long survived his friend. Webster was born in Pimlico, 20th of March, 1800. His father was a member of George III.'s household, and resolved that his son should become a musician. But, though young Webster began his musical career as a Chapel Royal choir boy, he never took to music as a profession, and decidedly preferred the sister art. When his voice broke, his father, who was a trusted servant in the royal household, procured for his son a place at Windsor as "Clerk of the Buttery." His duties here were cut short by the death of George III., when he narrowly escaped receiving a pension for life of twenty pounds a year. This he always looked upon as a very fortunate thing, as he at once resolved to set to work to become a painter. He was a great favourite with the Princesses Mary and Sophia. They had already noticed his powers of drawing, in fact he made all the patterns for Princess Sophia's embroidery, which he found not a little tiresome ; he also tried her portrait, when, as he used humorously to relate, he was obliged to make her sit on the arm of the sofa, as his powers of drawing were not strong enough to enable him to place her on the sofa itself ! The Princess however kindly forwarded his wishes, and by introducing him to Fuseli probably decided for him the best way of learning his art. Fuseli was at this time keeper to the Royal Academy, which was located at Somerset House. He approved of young Webster's works on their being shown to him, but told him he was not sufficiently forward to become a student in the Academy schools. Fuseli, however, gave him permission to draw in the great hall from the antique models placed there, and in due time Webster gained his studentship. Besides this in 1824 he took the gold medal in the school of painting for an oil painting from a Vandyck lent by the trustees of the Dulwich Gallery for the students to copy. Webster used to tell how John Jackson, R.A., who was then visitor in the school, and a painter of great merit, helped him much with his work, actually painting on it a good deal himself; this in those easy times was considered no bar however to young Webster's taking the medal for his copy.

On beginning his art career Webster painted life-sized portraits, exhibiting a portrait group in 1825, while he was still a student. Rather a curious incident led to his first undertaking those subjects of schoolboy life for which he afterwards became so celebrated. He had an artist friend who was a great colourist, but who had no invention, and he confided to Webster that when he had to set about a design for a picture, he was, notwithstanding his powers of colour, at a dead loss, he never could arrange his composition. On hearing this Webster offered to make him a design, and setting to work produced a sketch of a scene of mischief (boys firing a toy cannon at a girl's doll). Webster was so pleased with this sketch, that instead of giving it to his friend he resolved to paint it himself. When completed, the picture was exhibited at the British Gallery in 1827, under the title of "Rebels Shooting a Prisoner," and at once made a mark. He followed it up the next year by a companion picture, and always afterwards devoted himself to that particular kind of subject—the frolics and mischievousness of the British school-boy, whose varied moods Webster depicted with much genial humour and a thorough appreciation of the vagaries, tricks and games of his model. Perhaps the two pictures by which the artist is best known to this generation are "The Smile" and "The Frown," exhibited in 1841, taken from Goldsmith's familiar lines on the schoolmaster in the *Deserted Village.* Other well-known works are "The Village School" exhibited in 1833, "Foot Ball," 1839, "The Boy with Many Friends" sent to the British Institution in 1843. In 1840 he exhibited "Punch," which is full of individual character and much quaint humour; this probably gained him his associateship, for he was elected an A.R.A. in 1840, and always afterwards sent his principal pictures to the Academy exhibitions, such as "The Truant," "A Dame School," and "The Village Choir," which latter is in the Sheepshanks Gallery, and is an admirable bit of quiet humour.

In 1849 he exhibited at the Royal Academy "The Boys on the Slide," he was, while at work on this picture, laid up with gout, his great enemy, in consequence of standing in thin shoes upon the pond's brink to study the effect of reflections on the ice. Just as he was getting a little better, another frost set in, which, as the season was mild, he feared might be the last. How to obtain one or two more studies was the question; at last he hit upon the expedient of being wrapped up in blankets, tucked into a Bath chair, and wheeled to the pond's side. There from the little window of his narrow vehicle he made some useful memoranda which enabled him to complete his picture.

On the occasion of his parents' golden wedding Webster painted a charming little portrait of them side by side on a small canvas. This is to our thinking one of his best paintings, and it was a great satisfaction to learn that on his death he had bequeathed it to the National Gallery.

Webster's method of painting was the same as that practised by Wilkie and Mulready, and by the artists of that day, who took Teniers and the Flemish school for their models. He painted on a white ground, and laid in his shadows in the first place with umber or some brown, he was careful to keep his shadows transparent, and to preserve his ground, especially in the lights. When he had to make any alteration, he scraped down at once to the panel or canvas, so as to avoid in repainting any loss of the whiteness of his ground. But in his best days he painted with exceeding facility and was extremely expeditious with his work. He made, as before stated, a sketch of his subject, frequently in oil, and a careful drawing of his model, which he transferred to his canvas and painted in almost at once. Of course as he grew older, and suffered much from gout in his hands, his pictures grew more laboured. He did not excel as a colourist, and some of his drawing is a little wooden. As a rule in his works he avoids strong colours and any violent contrasts, this may be because he was a little doubtful of his own powers. He warmly advised keeping a good picture, if possible by some great master, in the studio while painting, both as a rest and a guide to the eye while at work. Webster was elected a full member of the Academy in 1846. At this time he was living in the Mall at Kensington, at one time he had the house next to Callcott's there, and not being then acquainted with the landscape painter, acknowledged that he felt a trifle jealous at the number of carriages waiting before that academician's doors on the show days before the pictures went into the Royal Academy. Later on, however, they became friends, and Callcott showed him many kindnesses. Webster found the year of the Reform Bill, 1832, a very trying one; the depression in trade reacted upon the artists, and they found it difficult to sell their pictures; when, however, Webster's fame was more surely established, he made large sums by his works. He left London in 1856 for Cranbrook in Kent, where he resided till his death, a period of nearly thirty years. His health was at first much benefited by a country life, and he painted away with great vigour. He lost his first wife in 1857, but remarried shortly a lady who, besides making him an excellent wife, watched over his declining years with the greatest kindness and devotion.

In disposition Webster was the most amiable and genial of men, a true friend, and much beloved by his brother artists. He delighted in anecdotes of himself and other people, which he told with lively humour unalloyed by sarcasm. He was a member of the Etching Club, and his stories at their meetings were a source of great amusement to the members. He was also one of a band who after the pictures were sent into the Academy, used to go off for a day's pleasure in the country. On one occasion he related an amusing incident which had happened to himself when a youth while out for a day's ramble with his brother at Dorney.   At that time the old stocks, stood before the village inn ; down sat Webster on the vagrant seat and thrust his feet fairly into the stocks, aided by his brother, who raised the upper bar for him, and then letting it down found too late that the whole fastened with a spring.   Behold the future painter made fast in the stocks, where he had to remain one hour and a half, as the village constable who had the key was nowhere to be found, and they had at last to have recourse to the blacksmith ! Webster recalled the gibes and jeers of the village boys who gathered round the unwilling prisoner with the greatest gusto, and probably treasured up many actions for future use.

Webster resigned his membership of the Academy in 1876, and was placed on the retired list. He died at Cranbrook 23rd September, 1886, aged eighty-six years.

CHAPTER XXV.

LESLIE, NEWTON, AND EGG.

In concluding the early life of our three drama-painters, we left Leslie, a student of the Royal Academy, using his best leisure to perfect his art-education; and adding to his means by painting the portraits of his American friends. The art of his two countrymen, Allston and West, had so impressed him that his first attempts were in the grand style; and even when descending from "Saul and the Witch of Endor," to Shakspeare, he turned to the historic plays rather than to the comedies, his subject being "The Death of Rutland." The former of these works the governors of the British Institution, with their usual sagacity, turned out of the gallery; the latter, after exhibition at the Royal Academy, where Leslie tells us it had an "excellent situation," was purchased for the city of Philadelphia, his American home. In 1817 he paid a visit of two months to Paris, Brussels, and Antwerp, making diligent study of the pictures by the old masters; and in 1818 he made a journey into the south of England, where he obtained much insight into the characteristics of rural life. As the year advanced he began to find that the true bent of his genius was neither for historical nor religious art, but for humorous comedy; which he treated with beauty and character of a far more refined kind than either of the distinguished painters we have classed with him.

The same year he painted a small picture of "Slender and Anne Page," from the *Merry Wives of Windsor;* a comedy which afterwards afforded subjects for some of his finest works.

He tells us that on his return from Devonshire in 1818, he painted for his friend, Mr. Dunlop (to whose then residence in Dawlish his visit had been made), the picture of "Sir Roger de Coverley going to Church accompanied by the Spectator," which was very popular in the exhibition of 1819. That Washington Irving, his great friend, suggested the subject, is more than likely. Perhaps there is no scene so full of episodes of peaceful beauty and kindly feeling as the gathering to-gether of a rural population to the service of a village church ; no doubt Irving and Leslie in their rambles through the land had seen many similar scenes ; and it was a happy thought that led the painter to a kindred subject from one of England's classic authors, and including in the Bachelor Knight one of the most genial creations of his pen. Leslie's kindliness, his sweet nature, general feeling of humour and fine taste, well qualified him for this class of subjects. He was a true gentleman, and therefore could thoroughly enter into and represent scenes in which humour is subordinated and refined in its display, as exhibited by the educated and gentle class.

Leslie was not slow to perceive the impression these subjects had made, and followed up his success by painting in 1820, "Londoners Gipsying," and in 1821, "May Day in the Time of Queen Elizabeth." Much of our success in life arises out of apparently fortuitous circum-stances : thus it happened to Leslie. Lord Egremont, one of the kindest and best friends of artists, and a true lover of art, had a little grand-child at the point of death, and asked Phillips, R.A., the portrait-painter, to go down to his country seat to make a sketch of the dying child. Phillips's engagements, however, prevented him, and he proposed Leslie, who was thus introduced to his lordship. Leslie only reached the seat of the child's relation after the little sufferer's death, but sat up all night making sketches of her really beautiful features. The sketches and the picture he painted from them gave great satisfaction to the owner of Petworth, and resulted, in the first instance, in a commission for a picture, and afterwards, in a friendship that lasted until the death of Lord Egremont.

The picture commissioned was painted and exhibited in 1824, "Sancho Panza in the Apartment of the Duchess," from *Don Quixote.* Sancho is telling the graceful Duchess, as a great secret, that he considers his master as no better than a madman—" as mad as a March hare "—and is bragging that, knowing well his master's blind side, "whatever crotchets come into his own crown, though without either head or tail, he can yet make them pass on him for Gospel." This picture, full of beauty, elegance and humour, was so great a favourite that Leslie repeated it with variations no less than three times : the replica painted for Mr. Vernon is now in the national collection, and Leslie always attributed much of his success to this commission. He was at this time paying his addresses to Miss Harriet Stone, one of six sisters, spoken of from their personal attractions as the "six precious stones" ; and the success of "Sancho Panza " and a further tentative commission from its owner, together with the various demands on his pencil that it called forth, enabled him to terminate his engagement by marriage. He writes

x

to Irving in the ensuing January, " I have (as you know) made the greatest change in life that it is in our power to do, and find myself so much the happier, and I trust the better for it, that I scarcely seem to have lived before. All the evils of matrimony that I have heard or read of appear to me to be slanders, and all the blessings to be underrated ; " the language of the early days of married life it may be said, but as far as our own personal experience of Leslie goes, he felt and said the same to the end.

In February, 1826, Leslie was elected a full member of the Royal Academy, and that season exhibited " Don Quixote in the Sierra Morena, deceived by the Curate Barber and Dorothea." It was not equal to " Sancho and the Duchess " ; landscape was not an art in which Leslie excelled ; indeed those pictures in which a landscape background forms an important part are weaker than others, at least as far as the background is concerned. Yet he was a great observer of nature, and of natural effects ; and his friends will remember with pleasure his constant remarks on light and dark, on colour and reflection, as he walked beside them. Often has he stopped us in the midst of some artistic colloquy, to look at a changing effect that had struck him ; sometimes in the most public thoroughfares—standing shading his eyes with his hand, and looking over his spectacles, he would reason of the cause, wholly regardless of the passers-by. Yet he was not made for a landscape painter, as the two or three small landscapes which he painted sufficiently testify ; and even before he was intimate with Constable, his greys were cold, and his greens unnaturally vivid.

Leslie's life passed on smoothly and with few incidents. First one child was added to his household, and then another, greatly to the increase of his pleasures ; for he was very fond of his family and very indulgent to the whims and ways of children. In 1828, he joined the Artists' Sketching Society, which widened the circle of his friends, and brought him into constant fellowship with the two Chalons and Stanfield ; with all of whom he continued, till parted by death, on terms of kindliest intimacy. In 1831 Leslie painted " The Dinner at Page's House," from *The Merry Wives of Windsor,* he afterwards repeated it on a smaller scale for Mr. Sheepshanks. The first picture was painted under the influence of Newton, the second after his death, when Constable was the great crony of the painter. The first picture of " The Dinner at Page's House " is certainly one of his finest works. The execution is broad and easy, the drapery quite free from the tendency to raggedness observable in some of Leslie's works, and there is an absence of any sense of paint.

Those who had been accustomed to Leslie's first manner, felt a change for the worse in the pictures painted under the Constable influence. At the time of the change we had the same feeling ; but after-judgment does not entirely confirm this. Thus there is a great sense of daylight and air in the second "Page's Dinner," which we look for in vain in the first ; in the second the light throughout is pure, cool, and grey, the outlook through the window very truthful, and there is far more atmosphere than in the earlier work ; there is not an inch of hot or foxy colour, the oak panelling of the room has the true grey of old oak upon it, so seldom given, a clammy varnished brown being usually substituted for it. Some figures in the first are left out in the second—Pistol for instance, who is rather forced in character, and has too much of the theatrical make up : a rare fault in Leslie, whose innate sense of delicacy rather led him to refine than exaggerate characteristics. This has prevented him giving much of the libidinous side of Falstaff's character. In the Sheepshanks repetition this is admirably illustrated in the females, and shows an improvement upon the first in taste and delicacy. Mrs. Page is a charming matron and mother, Mrs. Ford has not an atom of evil in her hearty jollity, but a sense of fun in her smiling half-opened mouth, showing a range of fair white teeth, and speaking of sport with the fat sack-loving knight. In their full matronly beauty they contrast happily with Anne, come forth for the first time into society, and also more lovely, more girlishly innocent and timid in the latter than in the former work. The earlier picture has been painted with a vehicle that has failed in the browns—the repetition, painted with pure linseed oil, is as fresh as from the easel.

It is not necessary to describe the causes that led Leslie's friends to obtain for him, or Leslie to accept, an appointment from the American Government as teacher of drawing at the Military Academy of West Point on the Hudson. We can well recollect how much regret was expressed, both by his companions in art and by the public when, in 1833, it became known that Leslie was returning to America. With that honest right-mindedness which ever characterized him, he offered, before leaving, to resign his membership of the Academy. From this course, however, he was dissuaded by the president.

It is strange that Leslie, who it is well known thought any kind of art-teaching unnecessary, and who himself, though richly accomplished as an artist, was not much grounded in the elements of art—painting from feeling rather than from knowledge—should have undertaken the office of teaching elementary art to others. To those already sufficiently advanced to appreciate his advice and instruction, they would have been indeed invaluable ; but for the routine of elementary instruction he was of all men the most unfitted. It is no wonder, therefore, that the task was wearisome and his duties irksome ; but when to this was added letters, reports, and attendance at long sessional examinations, he soon found the post a burden not to be borne, and that the irksomeness of his duties quite overbalanced his pleasure in the society of affectionate relatives, the fixity of his income, or the hopes of future advantages to his children. Moreover, the climate did not prove so healthy as had been anticipated, and the change was not agreeable to Mrs. Leslie ; what wonder, then, that ere six months had passed he was again on ship-board to return to England? He had quitted it in September, 1833, and he left America in April, 1834.

He returned to England in the full vigour of his art powers, and with plenty of encouragement to use them. He found on his arrival that a sad change had taken place in his former intimate, Newton ; whose mind had given way, and it had become necessary to place him in a private asylum.

From this time as we have seen Constable mainly influenced Leslie's art. In 1838, Leslie had a commission to paint the Coronation of our beloved Queen, and produced a picture bright with sunshine and female love-liness, and of a far different character to what is usually the result of such commissions. In 1841, he again received a royal commission ; this time to paint the "Christening of the Princess Royal." His friend Constable had died in 1837, a great grief to Leslie, who says of himself that before he knew Constable he really knew nothing or worse than nothing of landscape ; for, he adds, " I admired as poetical, styles which I now see to be mannered, conventional, or extravagant."

There are few more very marked incidents in the life of our painter. His powers were now fully estimated and his works were eagerly sought for. He was active in his duties as a member of the Academy, and in 1826 was elected professor of painting, a post which he held for five seasons. In his early years he had opposed the admission of engravers to the full honours of the Academy, but latterly being convinced of their claim, he re-opened the question before the general assembly and became one of the warmest advocates of the measure ; which he had the satisfaction of seeing carried and approved by her Majesty, as it was by the profession and the outside public. His children grew up around him and his home life was a very happy one ; and in this respect we may fairly contrast him with Wilkie and Mulready, as we have no doubt that his home life greatly influenced his art. Wilkie lived and died in the coldness of celibacy. Mulready, though married early, had little of happiness in his family circle. But Leslie, surrounded by sons and daughters, exceedingly fond of their childish fun and humour, and a great observer at all times, has given us pictures illustrative of the simple happiness of child-hood, which stand quite apart from the recipe notions of second-rate painters.

And as the painter's children grew to maidenly years and to manhood, we often see in his pictures glimpses of their forms and faces; and we know that many graceful actions in his best works arise from the hints obtained from his family circle.   But this happiness was to have a rude shock and a sad termination : early in 1857 the painter's second daughter, Caroline, was married, greatly to the satisfaction of her parents ; but she died a year later.   Leslie did not long survive the blow occasioned by her death.   He paid a visit to Petworth to seek relief in change of scene, but he seems to have found none, and although at first his complaint was not thought fatal, he sank by degrees and died on the 5th of May, 1859.

It is somewhat singular that his last entry in his pleasant gossiping diary was a story of Mr. Rogers, that " those who go to heaven will be very much surprised at [the people they find there, and very much surprised at those they do not find there ; " and on a slip of paper attached to his will he writes, "I trust I may die as I now am, in the entire belief of the Christian religion, as I understand it from the books of the New Testament, that is, as a direct revelation of the will and goodness of God towards the world, by Jesus Christ the Saviour and Judge of the world." So lived and so died this rare artist and good man. Those who read his diary and letters will feel how full he was of true Christian charity—how prompt to speak well, how slow to speak ill of others—how glad to find beauties rather than to criticize defects : while those who had the happiness of knowing him will treasure in their memory the pleasant recollections of a kind friend and a man of true genius, and hope at least to find him there ; if, through God's mercy, they should obtain entrance to His future kingdom.

Leslie was an artist from feeling rather than from instruction ; he had little early grounding in his profession, yet he drew correctly, from an innate perception of form and a sense of grace ; and he painted well from having obtained a simple method for the expression of his first thoughts, to which he remained constant to the finish. He was happy in his choice of subjects, and his own good taste and sweet nature led him to treat them suitably.   He was far beyond either of his competitors in his sense of beauty.

Leslie's embodiment of female beauty was not of that eclectic kind sought for by the artists of Italy, who aimed to present to us the purity and excellence of divine or saintly persons; it was rather the fullest embodiment of the loveliness with which we are surrounded in our daily life.   Theirs was an abstract beauty, cold and impassive, removed from the sphere of human passions into the calm atmosphere of holiness, and hence their beauty had little variety ; while his was but true English flesh and blood, not glorified—for it is hardly possible to add to the beauty of the race—but lighted up by passion, feeling, and the nobler sentiments and affections, and enhanced by purity and truth. Thus his beauty was varied in every character; first, from being individual, and further, from the varied characters he had to delineate.

Leslie was very happy in his illustrations of Shakspeare, the more so that he has made the poet's characters individuals, rather than abstractions. It was from his sense of beauty and grace, his individuality in the treatment of his characters, and his fine appreciation of humour, that Leslie approximated to the spirit of his author, and has given us more pleasure in his pictorial illustrations of Shakspeare than those whose works were of far greater pretensions.

Before his time, little attention had been paid to costume, and though we cannot praise Leslie for any amount of accuracy in this respect, yet his dresses have at least an air of truth; look as if they were made for the wearers, and are far beyond the vapid conventionality of Peters, Hamilton, Wheatley, and others, whose costume seems to have been devised at second-hand from the stage dresses of their own period. In painting his costume, Leslie used drapery, but rarely dresses: he had the happy art to improvise them from scanty materials. He tells us that he "made them up from old prints and pictures," and we know that he was able so to dispose loose drapery on his model (for we believe he never used a lay figure), as to enable him to represent his costume without the aid of the milliner. Thus he managed to clothe his figures without detracting from their grace and elegance, and without the passing peculiarities of fashion. In his art there is nothing stilted, nothing extravagant, and it is without the slightest taint of vulgarity. The treatment of his subjects is so simple, that we lose the sense of a picture, and feel that the incident is presented to us as it must have happened; fashion had no part in his works, and we have no doubt that a future age will own them as true as the present, and will love them equally well: it may be said that he popularized the class of refined drama-pictures.

Without being too imitative, Leslie was true to nature, and has left us this example: that a work which is generally true as a whole, is far more true than that which is built up from an exact imitation of the several parts. As an instance of this, his treatment of utensils of glass or silver in his dinner scenes may be quoted; thus the vessels on the table in "The Dinner at Page's House," or "The Duke's Chaplain Enraged and Leaving the Table;" or again the jewellery and trinkets in "The Pack of Autolycus." In all these instances, by means of a very few touches, more effect of truth, more real glitter and sparkle is given, than by the most elaborate imitation. The same may be said of the treatment of candlelight effect in his picture of "Trissotin reading the Sonnet, from *Les Femmes Savantes*," now in the Sheepshanks collection; there a truer effect is given of the brilliancy of candlelight by the slightest means, than in the most laboured works of Schalken or Honthorst.

Leslie was an agreeable companion, full of anecdotes of his brother painters, and of others who had been thrown into his company; the sense of humour so prevailed in him that a story with little real point became interesting from his mode of telling it. As a writer on art he is pleasant, intelligent and kindly, if not very deep. His life of Constable is a picture not so much of that painter as others saw him, but as clothed with the kindlier nature of Leslie. Of the three painters we have classed together, we value a picture by Wilkie; we are surprised by a picture of Mulready's, but we love a picture by Leslie.

The art, as practised by Leslie, naturally leads us to that of Newton, who was so closely linked to him both by ties of country, friendship, and by the class of art which both followed. There are, in fact, so many points of resemblance, that much of the criticism on Leslie applies equally to the art of his friend and companion.

Gilbert Stuart Newton, R.A., was born at Halifax, Nova Scotia, 2nd September, 1795. He was the son of an officer in the British Commissariat Department, or, according to other authorities, of an officer of Customs in that province, who had left Washington when the British were driven from Boston by General Washington. His uncle, on his mother's side, was Gilbert Stuart, distinguished in America as a portrait painter; and after his father's death his widowed mother returned with him in 1803 to Charleston, near Boston. Dunlop, the American biographer, says:—"Newton congratulated himself upon being born a subject of the king and aristocracy of Great Britain, and on one occasion in New York, at a large dinner-party, got up and disclaimed being a citizen of the United States;" but he adds, "Newton cannot, however, shake off the stigma of being an American painter."

Newton was "reared" at Boston, and intended for commercial life, he was placed with a merchant; but art prevailed. We do not know from his early history what led him to foster this desire, unless it was the reputation of his uncle Stuart, under whom he was early placed for study. Stuart himself had practised his art for some years in England, from whence he returned in 1805. One of his countrymen tells, that he left the brightest prospects in England, and returned to his country from his admiration of her new institutions, and a desire to paint the portrait of Washington. "On hearing this" (we quote from Leslie's diary), "Sir Thomas Lawrence said, 'I knew Stuart well, and I believe the real cause of his leaving England was his having become tired of the inside of some of our prisons.' On which Lord Holland remarked, 'After all, then, it was his love of freedom that took him to America.'"

In 1817, one of Newton's elder brothers, who was engaged in commerce, brought the future painter with him to Italy and left him at Florence, that he might see some of the master-works before finally settling down to his studies.

He remained some months in Italy, and then repaired to Paris, where he met Leslie ; they travelled together through the Netherlands, arriving in London in 1817, and from that time were firm friends.   Leslie introduced him to Washington Irving on an excursion to Richmond, and tells that the three passed a day of such frolic and fun as became such men ; and from that time they were three inseparables.   Irving says in one of his letters that on Newton's arrival in London, " he did nothing for three days but scamper up and down like a cat in a panic ; " and in the same letter adds, " Newton's manikin has at length arrived, and he is to have it home in a few days, when it is to be hoped he will give up rambling abroad and stay at home, drink tea, and play the flute to *the* lady."   He made many visits to Sloane Street, which were in pursuit of " the lady " with whom he was much smitten.   Irving again alludes to this in 1820. " I find," says he, " the Sloane Street romance is still unfinished . . . . Newton is busy with a brush in each hand, and his hair standing on end, turning Ann's portraits into likenesses of Mary Queen of Scots, General Washington, and the Lord knows who."

Newton, however, settled down to work in 1820, and became a student of the Royal Academy ; although, as we find from the same sources, he was very fond of society and naturally formed for it ; hence we may infer that he was not very constant in his attendance at the schools, which may account for his weakness and want of skill as a draughtsman.

But, although Newton loved society, he had real genius, and made rapid improvement in his art.   In 1821, he painted and exhibited at the British Institution a small head, which he called the " Forsaken," and a picture of " Lovers' Quarrels," and about the same time his clever picture of " The Importunate Author."   This was a most successful work, and gave evidence of his great observation of humour and character.   Two figures are pacing up and down a raised terrace ; the victim, manly and erect, of a noble presence, but with a look of the deepest disgust and weariness, holds his watch in his hand, as if to intimate in the most marked manner, that the time of another and more pleasant appointment is passing away.   The poet hangs on him and holds him fast ; reading as they walk along, he is determined to inflict on his companion every stanza of his dreary and tedious composition : he heeds not—he will not heed—the expressive hints of impatience and contempt it calls forth. Leslie tells us, incidentally, that Peter Coxe volunteered to sit to Newton for the poet : he was the author of the *Social Day*, a poem which he victimized artists to illustrate, and certainly he must have looked the character.   Wilkie relates that Coxe came to him to read some of his poetry, and being interrupted by a visit of Lord Mulgrave, he waited for his departure, and then resumed and read the remainder; Wilkie, most likely to get rid of him, proposed a walk, and bored, no doubt, went into a house which had a notice of being to let, to inquire about it: "When," says he, " Mr. Coxe pulled out his manuscript and began to read it to the woman who had charge of the house." Such a man needed no "making up" to sit for "The Importunate Author."

In 1821, Newton was for the first time an exhibitor at the Royal Academy, where he sent two portraits; and again in 1822, he exhibited two portraits: one of them, of his friend Irving, was engraved for *The Sketch Book*, which Murray published in 1823. In his dislike for the labour of study, Newton took to portrait-painting as requiring less exertion of mind. Irving, who felt his talent, remonstrated with him; but as he defended a weak part of his picture, so he defended the propriety of his choice, talked of Vandyck and of Reynolds, and parted with his friend in a huff. Some time after Irving called, and finding him at work on his poet reading his verses to an impatient gallant, complimented him on being in the right road; and from that time Newton devoted himself to those subjects in which he became so eminently successful.

From 1823 till 1833, Newton was a continuous exhibitor at Somerset House. In 1823 he sent the first subject picture, " M. Pourceaugnac, or the Patient in spite of Himself." In 1828, he was elected an associate of the Royal Academy, his picture of that year having been "The Vicar of Wakefield reconciling his Wife to Olivia." This picture, as treated by him, is of touching interest, and he well deserved the honours it won for him. The impasto of the picture is excellent, and the colouring very perfect.

Newton justified his election as associate by his picture of "Camilla Introduced to Gil Blas at the Inn," exhibited in 1829. He had previously painted in 1827, "The Prince of Spain's Visit to Catalina": indeed his taste seemed much directed to Spanish subjects; and as Leslie was at the same time painting from *Don Quixote*, Irving, then at Madrid, congratulated them on their choice, and regretted that, as they were now painting Spanish pictures, they could not get a peep at the Spanish people. This has become a common journey with our painters since Wilkie led the way; but it may be doubted if the pictures of either Leslie or Newton would have been much improved by a more direct Spanish flavour. In the years 1830 and 1831, Newton painted and exhibited some of his finest works: namely, in 1830, "Yorick and the Grisette," now in the National Gallery, "Shylock and Jessica," and the "Abbot Boniface" from Walter Scott's novel of *The Abbot*. Leslie says that Newton took the idea of the figure from Sydney Smith, whom he met when on a visit to Walter Scott. In 1831, Newton's pictures were

" Portia and Bassanio," with " Cordelia and the Physician." The former is in the Sheepshanks collection, and although sadly injured by the use of asphaltum, it deserves attention as exhibiting some of the painter's best qualities. It shows Newton's great feeling for colour, expression, and beauty, but also his small power of drawing, and his weak execution. These pictures had made a great impression in Newton's favour, and in 1832 he was elected to the full honours of the Academy.

He now sought to establish a home for himself, and, the romance of Sloane Street forgotten, he made a voyage to America to find a wife, with whom he returned to this country at the end of the year. Newton had so continually painted the same type of beauty in his pictures, that his brother artists thought he must be favoured with sittings by some female friend with whom they were unacquainted. On his return from America with the lady whom he had married, her features were so like the face he had usually pictured, that those who were unaware of the circumstances thought they had at length discovered the hidden beauty he had so long worshipped ; but it was afterwards understood that this was not the case, his acquaintance with the lady not having dated previous to his journey.

During Newton's American visit slight symptoms of insanity had manifested themselves; unhappily, these rapidly increased soon after his return. He painted no more pictures of any importance after his election, and it was soon found necessary to place him in a private asylum, where he died on the 5th of August, 1835, and was buried in Wimbledon Churchyard. Leslie tells us in his diary, that Newton's mind seemed somewhat restored a few days before his death. During the rapid consumption that ended his life he read only the Bible and Prayer-book, and when he became too weak to read, they were read to him by an attendant. The day before he died, he desired to hear the funeral service, saying, " It will soon be read over me." He listened to it with great attention, and remarked that " it was very fine." His wife and son returned to America shortly after his death, and the widow soon married a second time.

As a painter, Newton was sadly deficient in executive power, and as he also drew timidly he worked out his pictures from feeling rather than with knowledge. His sense of colour was far greater than Leslie's ; and, as we have seen, Leslie was much influenced by him. Newton displayed great beauty and loveliness in his females ; there is a peculiar tender innocence of expression in his Sophia, Cordelia, and Portia, as well as in the fancy heads which he painted. He had some humour, though not nearly so much as his friend Leslie, and a tolerable appreciation of character. Unfortunately, Newton did not exclude asphaltum from his palette, nor confine himself to simple vehicles for his pigments, and the result has been that all his works have more or less suffered, while some are in danger of perishing altogether. He was not a prolific painter; and we should judge from his pictures that, though working rapidly, he arrived at their completion after many changes and much elaboration. From his first picture in the Academy, in 1821, until his last in 1833, he only exhibited thirty-three works; of which eight were portraits, three only heads, and twelve subject pictures.

Many stories of Newton's conceit and vanity were current at a time when the narrators little dreamt of the sad calamity in which they were to end. Thus it is said that on a brother artist pointing out some strange mistake in one of Newton's pictures, he replied, "Yes; it is purposely left so; every picture should have a fault, this is the *one* fault of mine."

Newton loved to have it thought that he lived expensively and kept a *recherché* table. An artist calling on him just as dinner was served was invited to partake of it. It consisted merely of some mutton chops, but when these were removed, Newton asked the servant, with an air of surprise, why there were no ices? as if these luxuries formed part of his daily meal, and had been strangely overlooked on this occasion.

From the shortness of his life, and the few pictures he painted, Newton's art was eclipsed by Leslie's, and he left very little impression on our school: yet, had he lived, his art would most probably have diverged from that of his friend, and his colouring and his sense of beauty would have obtained for him a far higher reputation than he even now enjoys.

Augustus Leopold Egg, R.A., was born in Piccadilly on 2nd May, 1816, the son of the well-known gunsmith. Showing a desire to follow art, on leaving school he was placed in 1834 in Sass's academy; there he made such progress that in the succeeding year he was admitted a student of the Royal Academy. In 1837 he exhibited his first picture at the gallery in Suffolk Street, and in 1838 at the Academy, "A Spanish Girl," which was much praised. After this time, we find his name, with but few intervals, as an annual exhibitor on the walls of the Royal Academy; his pictures increasing in interest and excellence. In 1849 he was elected an associate, and in 1861 a full member of the Academy. His health had for many years been delicate, his lungs were weak and he suffered from chronic asthma, which obliged him, in the latter years of his life, to retire to the warmer climates of Italy or the south of France to avoid the rigour of our winters. The winter of 1862-3 was passed in Algiers with the same object, and his health seemed so much benefited by the climate of Africa, that he resumed his painting, and there was every prospect of his return to England and the practice of his profession, when his imprudence in taking a long ride on a bleak day caused a renewal of the worst symptoms of his disorder, to which he succumbed on the 25th of

March, 1863, and was buried in the immediate neighbourhood of the city of Algiers.

Egg's range of subjects was in many respects somewhat similar to that of Leslie and Newton ; but his vein was oftener sad than humorous, and he was without the abiding sense of beauty and gentleness that characterize the females of both of these painters. Egg's first pictures were painted with a broad and free pencil and a clear touch, and his execution gave the sense of great ease and facility. The picture, " A Scene from *Le Diable Boiteux*," painted in 1844, and now included in the Vernon collection, is an example. It shows his ready handling, his delicate appreciation of harmony of tint and general tone, and from his simple manner of painting it stands well. As he advanced in art he became impressed with the manner of the pre-Raphaelites ; he purchased some of their pictures, and encouraged them by his own example, giving to his own works more laborious completion and greater force of colour. Of these, the best specimens of his pencil are " Pepys's Introduction to Nell Gwynne," painted in 1852 ; and a scene from Thackeray's *History of Henry Esmond, Esq.*, illustrating the following passage :—" ' Kneel down,' says Mrs. Beatrix, ' we dub you knight with this,' and she waved the sword over his head." This was exhibited in 1858. We miss in the " Pepys " the beauty Leslie would have given to Nelly, whom Pepys takes care to tell us was "a most pretty woman ;" adding, "I kissed her, as did my wife, and a mighty pretty soul she is."

CHAPTER XXVI.

OLD CROME AND THE NORWICH SCHOOL.

THE landscape painters of whose art we have hitherto treated, were men, whatsoever their birth or origin, who eventually established themselves in London to take part in the fierce struggle for reputation with which artists have to contend in that great city. We have now to notice the labours of a painter born in a county town far distant from London, where he chose to remain, seeking fame in his own lesser world, satisfied to be first there rather than second in the metropolis. *John Crome* (generally called Old Crome to distinguish him from his son, who also became an artist,) was born in Norwich on the 22nd of December, 1768. He was the son of a journeyman weaver, and first saw the light in a mean public-house in that city. We have no account of his childish years, but the elder Mr. Bacon of Norwich tells us that he could hardly be said to have enjoyed even the common instruction of the most ordinary schools. At twelve years of age he was placed as a servant in the house of Dr. Rigby, where his principal duties consisted in carrying out the medicines prescribed and prepared by the doctor. He was a boy of a lively and enterprising disposition, and when of the suitable age apprenticed himself to Frank Whisler, a house and sign-painter of Norwich ; partly, it is said, moved by a love of art and a desire to make himself acquainted, however roughly, with art processes.

Thus far, then, we find the future painter wholly without those advantages which now lie at the doors of people of all ranks. Day and night-schools for elementary education abound in all cities, and there are few towns which do not—none which cannot—have a well-appointed school of art, wherein the artisan and the mechanic, the tradesman, and the children of the resident gentry, may obtain sound instruction in the rudiments of art, and be taught to overcome the difficulties of execution which beset the beginner. In Crome's time this was not the case. Before the age of railroads, Norfolk and its capital city were outlying districts as it were ;

rarely visited by the curious—rarely subject to change or improvement. The city itself was picturesque, full of antiquarian interest, and seemed as if it had slept while other cities of the kingdom were up and at work. The lanes in the suburbs, the banks of the river, the heaths, the commons, were wild, untrimmed, and picturesque ; the old labourer's cottage with its thatched roof, the farms with their rural homesteads, were scattered close around the city ; villas and terraces had not yet, like drilled intruders, broken in upon their picturesque decay ; the river as it wound with silvery surface through the fat meadows, or stretched away towards the sea, widened into lakelets called broads, and bore on its way, inland or seaward, the picturesque barges, or wherries as they are locally called, whose tanned sails, ruddy in the sunlight, contrasted so well with the green of the landscape. Thus the very sleepiness of the land, not yet awakened to afford instruction to its children, was yet peculiarly fitted to call into life an instinctive love of art such as that with which young Crome was gifted.

Meanwhile, Crome followed his trade as a house painter, painting, as he advanced in skill, signs as well as houses, and in his leisure hours sketching the local scenery we have just described—scenery he loved through life, and which forms the subjects of some of his best works. He early formed an acquaintance with a fellow-townsman of the name of Robert Ladbrooke, then a youth of about his own age, and the two lodging together, sketched and painted for their mutual improvement. Many tales are told of the poverty of our painter, of his having manufactured his own brushes, and used his mother's apron as a canvas whereon to practise his art ; such tales are common to other painters as well as to Crome. No doubt he had his difficulties ; no doubt, coming somewhat irregularly into art through the introduction of house and sign-painting, it was hard to obtain his first footing ; but friends generally are found when the man is resolved and in earnest, and Mr. Thomas Harvey, of Catton, is spoken of as one who aided the young artist with his advice (for he was himself a painter) and introduced him to others as a teacher of drawing, by which he obtained means of following art in the intervals of his teaching. Better still, Mr. Harvey had a small collection of Dutch and Flemish pictures, and to the study of these Crome diligently applied himself ; and through them we may no doubt trace the affinity many of his pictures have to those of Hobbema.

Mr. Harvey gave young Crome an introduction to Sir William Beechey ; who, his biographer states, also commenced life with a house painter of Norwich, but was then in the height of his reputation as a portrait painter. Be this as it may, Beechey felt an interest in the young landscape painter from the first interview, as he himself tells us. "Crome," says he, "when first I knew him, must have been about twenty years old, and was a very awkward, uninformed country lad, but extremely shrewd in all his remarks upon art, though he wanted words and terms to express his meaning.   As often as he came to town he never failed to call upon me, and to get what information I was able to give him upon the subject of that particular branch of art which he made his study.   His visits were very frequent, and all his time was spent in my painting room when I was not particularly engaged.   He improved so rapidly that he delighted and astonished me.   He always dined and spent his evenings with me."   Beechey had gone to Norwich in 1781, and lived there four or five years, painting portraits of the clergy and gentry of the town and neighbourhood.   Shortly after Crome's introduction to him, which must have been about 1790, Beechey was elected into the Academy ; he was a rising man, and soon to become the court painter, so that Crome, through him, would no doubt learn much of the art and artists of the metropolis.

Crome married early in life, and having to struggle to maintain an increasing family, he gave himself up largely to that branch of his art yielding the most steady and certain remuneration ; teaching drawing both in the families of his townsmen and of the neighbouring gentry, as well as in the surrounding schools. Teaching brought him many friends, and gave him local fame, but it did not provide purchasers for his pictures. At that time purchasers, or as they then proudly termed themselves, "patrons of art," were few, and it was only when a reputation had been already won, that an artist was likely to have his works sought after. During his lifetime this was hardly the case with Crome : he sold his pictures it is true, but at low prices, and it is only since his death that his talent has been appreciated.

We have seen that he paid many visits to London, but that he continued to reside in his native city.   He was not even an exhibitor at the Royal Academy until 1806, in which year he sent two landscapes, and continued to exhibit occasionally until 1818.   Yet in all these years he only contributed eight times, and the whole number of his works seen in London was only fourteen ; what wonder, then, that before the age of railroads, an artist working locally in a remote angle of the kingdom seldom visited for its scenery, should achieve only a local fame.

But there were other causes besides the occupation of his time in teaching, that prevented Crome being an exhibitor in London.   He had gathered around him the artists of his native city into a little fraternity, and in February, 1803, they formed themselves into a society for their mutual benefit and improvement, and eventually for the public exhibition of their works.   The society was called "The Norwich Society, for the purpose of an inquiry into the rise, progress, and present state of Painting, Architecture, and Sculpture, with a view to point out the best methods of study to attain greater perfection in these arts." It was something of the nature of a joint-stock association, since every member on his election had to contribute his proportion of the value of the property of the body. It was not confined to artists by profession, but every member, prior to his election, had to submit to two tests—one of his ability, by submitting his works to the general body; the other, of his personal popularity; each member was balloted for, the votes of three-fourths of the members present being required to secure his election. Out of this institution arose the Norwich Exhibition of Works of Art, whose first exhibition was in 1805, and the earliest, we believe the first, annual exhibition of pictures in a provincial town. Crome was naturally a large contributor. It is a strong indication of his love for the scenery of his native county that so few of his subjects are derived from places he visited. He made journeys to Wales and to the north of England, and we find a few pictures and sketches from Wales and the lake country. He visited Paris and the Low Countries, and we have three pictures from these places; but the great mass of his works are from the lanes, the heaths, the rivers and shores of his native county.

It was not Crome's practice to paint his pictures on the spot; he made drawings and sketches, and occasionally painted before nature in water-colours; but his pictures, the result of careful study and observation of nature, were painted in his studio. He wanted but little subject: an aged oak, a pollard willow by the side of the slow Norfolk streams, or a patch of broken ground, in his hands became pictures charming us by their sweet colour and rustic nature. He was very facile in his execution, painted with a full brush and very much at once: and often, under the pressure of necessity, produced slight works or repeated others, to supply an immediate demand upon him. Moreover he was fond of society, and, latterly, was apt to indulge a little too freely. He loved boating, and no doubt frequented the regattas and water-frolics on the Waveney, the Yare, and the Bure; he was fond of the pleasant idleness of watching the boats and boating parties as he took refreshment and repose with good companions in the Hinsby Gardens at Thorpe, and other like resorts for citizens' ruralities. His palette and canvas were often in demand to meet the wants arising from such outbreaks, and his talents as a teacher were in constant requisition. Had his art been laborious, the production of so long a list of works would have been an impossibility. The elder Mr. Bacon even says that he was through life a drawing-master, that his fine landscapes were painted in his holiday leisure, and that he was a wine-bibber and improvident, often receiving money on his unfinished works. We are told also that very many of his pictures were never exhibited at all, and that amongst such, several of his very important subjects were included.

Crome seems to have founded his art on Hobbema, Ruysdael, and the Dutch school, rather than on the French and Italian painters ; except so far as these were represented by our countryman Wilson, whose works he copied, and whose influence is seen mingled with the more naturalistic treatment derived from the Dutch masters. He had less *finesse* of execution, and paid less attention to details than the Dutchmen, but he had a fine sense of generalized imitation. His picture of " Mousehold Heath," painted probably in 1816, is a good example of his style. It shows how very little subject has to do in producing a fine picture. A sky, a barren heath spreading away into the far distance, a bank in the foreground, with a few weeds, are all the materials the painter had to treat ; but the manner of treating them has resulted in a beautiful work. The sky is very luminous, with grand rolling clouds, accidental shadows from which are thrown over the distance and the foreground, leaving the middle distance luminous, clear and cool, though rich and full of colour. A few thistles and large weeds in the foreground, and some small figures going away into the picture, complete this interesting work ; interesting from its painter-like treatment, certainly not from its subject. This picture has a curious history, illustrative of the art of the picture-dealer, which has been already alluded to. It was bought by some sacrilegious brother of the craft, and cut down the middle to enable him to sell it as two pictures—indeed the work was, we believe, sold separately in this state. Some more reverential possessor of pictures then repurchased and reunited them ; and the picture has now found its final resting-place in our national collection.

Another fine picture by this master is " A Clump of Trees, Hautbois Common," probably that in the Norwich Society's catalogue, in 1810. In some of his small pictures of heath scenes and broken ground, Crome closely approximated to his Dutch prototypes. We ourselves saw one of his pictures of this class sold at Christie's as a Wynants. Yet in his more important works there is great breadth of treatment, largeness of manner, and mastery of execution, and, in all, a fine eye for the general colour of nature.

The Norwich Society, which had established itself successfully as a public institution of the city, continued its exhibitions until the year 1816, when a split in the body of artists caused a separation. While many continued to exhibit in the old rooms—some, under the leadership of Ladbroke, opened another exhibition in the Assembly-rooms Plain. Crome, however, remained true to the old party, and although he had of late years decreased the number of his contributions, he sent, in 1816, eighteen works to their exhibition, among them one of his few foreign pictures, " Bruges River—Ostend in the Distance—Moonlight ; " the result of a visit to the Continent in the previous year. He continued to

Y

exhibit with the society until 1821, but died on the 22nd of April in that year, previous to the opening of the exhibition. His last illness was of an inflammatory nature, and carried him off in the short space of seven days ; his constitution having it is said been somewhat impaired by his early labours as a house painter. He was buried at St. George's, Norwich, and a large number of artists of his native city as well as others attended his funeral.

Crome etched many plates of the scenery of his native county, which, however, were not published until the year 1834. After his death, also, an exhibition of his works in the hands of his relatives, friends, and neighbours, took place. One hundred and eleven pictures and studies were collected, the catalogue of which will be found in Wodderspoon's brochure. Crome not only painted landscapes, which since his death have obtained increased and increasing reputation, but he may claim to be the founder of a provincial school of art at Norwich ; a school with peculiar characteristics, and in some respects differing from metropolitan practice. His influence and maxims had great weight with his contemporaries and friends, and of his pupils, two at least, Stark and Vincent, deserve some notice at our hands ; while his brother artist in the society, John Sell Cotman, has obtained a distinguished name both at home and abroad.

Of Crome's two pupils, *James Stark* is the best known in London. Like his master, he was a native of Norwich, born in the year 1794. He was the son of a dyer in that city, a man well to do in his trade, into which he had introduced many improvements, who was much respected in his native city, and honourably mentioned by the local press at his death. Young Stark early indicated a love of art, and in 1811 he was articled for three years to John Crome. He must already have obtained some proficiency, since in the same year he contributed five landscapes, in oil, to the Norwich Exhibition, and in 1812 he was elected a member of the society, exhibiting in that year several works. On the completion of his articles with Crome, young Stark came to London in 1817, entered the schools of the Royal Academy, and soon became an exhibitor at the British Institution, where he was successful in selling his works, and even received a prize of 50*l.* from the governors. From some unexplained cause he returned to Norwich, where he settled for a time, married, and remained nearly twelve years. In 1827, he issued proposals for the publication of a work on *The Scenery of the Rivers of Norfolk ;* this was completed in 1834, when, notwithstanding a good list of subscribers, it is understood that his enthusiasm in producing a work of such merit and interest led to little adequate reward. This publication gives us a good insight into the rural beauties of this somewhat neglected county— beauties that must soon pass away in this age of improvement. It does much credit to the painter's talent, and to the school of art in which he was educated. In 1830, Stark returned to London, where he remained ten years. In 1840 he went to live at Windsor, finding many subjects for his canvas in that beautiful locality. After many years' residence there, he returned to London for the advantage of educating his son in art, and he died on the 24th March, 1859, in the sixtieth year of his age.

Stark exhibited at Suffolk Street, with the Society of British Artists, intermittently from 1824 to 1839, and at the Royal Academy, with intervals, from 1831 to 1859, besides contributing frequently to the British Institution. His works are simple, but very truthful and unobtrusive. His *Rivers of Norfolk* give a favourable impression of his talent as an artist ; the character of the local scenery is well preserved, the scenes are full of appropriate figures and incidents, and the individuality of each subject makes us feel sure of the painter's truth. Stark founded his art on the principles of Crome, and the study of the Dutch landscape painters ; but his treatment of his subject, his handling and execution are *petite* and mean when compared with his master's— thin, and wanting in the impasto and richness of Crome ; while in seeking the quiet tone of colour of his Dutch examples he has failed to obtain their brilliancy and richness. His pictures have few faults, at the same time there is little in them to warm into enthusiasm or to awaken delight.

Of Crome's other pupil, *George Vincent,* we have very scanty information, although he is an artist of far higher powers than Stark, and does honour, or might have done, to his school and his master. He was born on the 27th June, 1796, and was a pupil of Cromes', with Stark, and with him first appears as a contributor to the Norwich exhibition in 1811, his works being evidently quite elementary. In 1812, he again sent two pictures, still showing a state of pupilage, since they are described in the catalogue as "after Crome." He made rapid progress from this time, in 1814 exhibiting no less than fifteen pictures. He exhibited two landscapes in the British Institution in 1817, and four in 1818, at which time he seems to have finally left Norwich to reside in London, as his direction is given —"Wells Street, Oxford Street." In 1820, we find him contributing to the Exhibition of the Society of Painters in Water-Colours, "London from the Surrey Side of Waterloo Bridge." (The society had thrown open its exhibition to others than members, and did not confine itself to drawings in water-colours.) But the work which places him very high as an artist, and shows that he would have proved a worthy rival of the great landscape painters of his day, had he persevered in his course, is the large picture of "Greenwich Hospital" ; a commission from Mr. Carpenter.

Vincent executed this work thoroughly, giving all his powers to the

task, and he produced a noble picture. The subject chosen is the
hospital as seen from the river, the sun being in the picture. The river
at full tide is crowded with craft and shipping, the sky pearly and luminous, the sun obscured by the vessels, and the light dispersed. When
again seen in the International Exhibition of 1862, this fine picture was
greatly appreciated for its talent and art. Latterly, Vincent painted
subjects seen under the sun, as did Constable, but his treatment was
wholly different ; broad masses of greyish shadow were tipped and fringed
with the solar rays.

Soon after the date of the "Greenwich Hospital" picture, Vincent fell
into bad habits and money difficulties ; his pictures were to be seen in
the shop windows of dealers, and gradually became more slight and less
studied. He had married a daughter of Dr. Cunoni, and furnished a
good house at Kentish Town, but when he fell into difficulties he was
gradually lost sight of by the art world. The time of his death is
unknown ; his widow afterwards married Mr. Murphy, a writer for the
public press.

John Sell Cotman, another of the friends and associates of Crome, and
one who has won for himself a reputation in art far more than local, was
born in Norwich on the 16th of May, 1782. He was the son of a linen-
draper who carried on his business in London Lane, and sent his boy to
be educated at the Norwich Free Grammar School, when Dr. Forster,
who afterwards became the first vice-president of the " Norwich Society,"
was principal. On leaving school young Cotman evinced a great love for
art, much it is said to the annoyance of his father, who wished the good-
looking youth to take his place behind the counter and to follow him as a
draper. We have little account as to the early life of young Cotman ;
but have been informed by Miss Turner, the daughter of Dawson Turner
who was associated with Cotman in several of his works, that much of
the artist's early life was spent in London, studying design, in company
with Turner, Girtin, and Munn, and that with them he used to frequent
the well-known meetings at the house of Dr. Munro—whence so many
artists who afterwards reached the goal of excellence, made their first
start in the race of art.

Cotman must have returned to Norwich soon after the foundation of
the Norwich Society of Artists, which he joined in 1807. He then styled
himself a portrait painter ; and in 1808, when he contributed no less
than sixty-seven pictures to the exhibition, several of them were portraits;
while others were in that class of art in which he afterwards became so
distinguished. Cotman married early, and soon learnt that neither
portrait nor landscape painting yielded him sufficient means to maintain
his increasing family. He therefore found it necessary to become a
drawing-master ; and being a young man of very gentlemanly appearance

and agreeable manners, he was welcomed at the houses of the surrounding gentry, whose children he taught, whose parks and country seats he sketched and painted, and from the study of whose pictures he drew knowledge and pleasure. He left Norwich and settled at Yarmouth, where, in the capacity of drawing-master, he made the acquaintance of Mr. Dawson Turner, and taught his children.

As all the early water-colour art arose out of the practice of the antiquarian draughtsmen, the painters at the beginning of the century were still imbued with somewhat of the spirit. Dawson Turner found in Cotman a congenial worker, and he soon began to concert with him works illustrative of his own antiquarian pursuits. In 1811, Cotman commenced publishing a series of etchings of *The Architectural Antiquities of Norfolk*, and *Engravings of the Sepulchral Brasses.* In 1817 he accompanied Mr. and Mrs. Turner, and their three daughters, on a tour in Normandy, which country he again visited in 1818 and in 1820; and the result was a work in two folio volumes, written by Dawson Turner, and illustrated by Cotman, called *Architectural Antiquities of Normandy*, published in 1822. In 1825, although still continuing to reside in Norwich, where he had again returned, he appears as an associate exhibitor of the London Society of Painters in Water-Colours, contributing to their exhibition continually until 1839. Obtaining the appointment of drawing-master in King's College School, he removed to London about the year 1834, and lived in Hunter Street, Brunswick Square. Here his health began to decline. He was afflicted with severe nervous depression, which gradually terminated in mental aberration, and his death took place on the 28th of July, 1842, at the age of sixty.

Cotman not only painted in water-colours, but in oil also; in this medium, however, he was hardly successful, and his works are solid and heavy. As a painter in water-colours he adopted a manner of his own, somewhat derived, perhaps, from the art of Turner, but without his refinement. He was a master of the principles of light and shade, but at times made his knowledge too obvious. His masses of light and dark were broad and simple; and he managed to indicate with little labour the smaller forms in the masses without losing breadth in his lights, or leaving his shadows sombre and obscure. His smaller forms were sometimes added with the reed pen. There was but little of literal imitation in his pictures, which latterly became mannered, and showed a want of renewed reference to nature. His mode of treating his subject was well suited to advance his pupils; to enable them to see nature as a whole, capable of being easily rendered on the reduced scale usually attempted in water-colours. One of his critics said justly that "he had the happy and unusual gift of converting the dryest architectural subjects into pictures by an artist-like disposition of the light and shade, by the arrangement of subordinate objects, and by the pleasing introduction of accessories." His figures are generally well-placed, and carry brilliant spots of light or colour into the dark parts of his picture. He was, above all things, ready with his pencil : it shows through all his colour ; it supplies the detail and drawing of his architecture, giving its sharp angles or its mouldering decay, and when used without colour, giving the masses of dark, the greys, and almost the colour of his subject ; yet in colour itself he was defective, and merged all the *finesse* of broken tints and of gradations in the broad hue of sunlight or shadow. His architectural works led the way to the pictorial study of the Norman towns, and the rich and picturesque structures with which they abound.

It remains for us to add a few words on the Norwich Society of which these men were members. While those who still remained true to the old society, Crome among the number, continued in their old premises in Wrench's Court, the seceders who formed the new society in 1816, did not long maintain it ; not that they deemed it a new society, for their first exhibition in 1816 was called the twelfth, the last, apparently, in 1818 being named the fourteenth. Nor is it to be wondered at that it was unsuccessful. Norwich citizens and Norfolk gentry did little for the arts, if we may judge from the circular of the old society when it also was removed to Exchange Street. " They had taken upon themselves," they say, "a responsibility equal to about 200*l.* per annum, for the charges incidental to their exhibition, in the conviction that the taste of the county and city would not be backward to assist their efforts for the promotion of art." But their hopes were unfounded. Norwich might support a few portrait painters, and require the services of some score of drawing-masters, but patrons and purchasers of pictures did not abound ; a local historian records "that since their establishment the Norwich Society of Artists have exhibited about 4,600 pictures, the production of no fewer than 323 individuals, while scarcely a single picture has been bought in the Norwich rooms ; and the receipts at the door have never amounted to a sum sufficient to meet the expenses." After Crome's death, and the removal of Stark and Cotman to London, the exhibition ceased to be mainly supported by artists of the Norwich school, but it was largely supplemented, as are those in other provincial towns, by works of metropolitan artists who are invited to contribute ; and the Norwich school as a peculiar provincial confraternity ceased to exist.

CHAPTER XXVII.

WE will in this chapter return to our practice of dealing with one
branch of art at a time, and we will give a brief notice of the portrait
painters who, since the death of those whom we have classed as contemporaries of Lawrence, have added lustre to this branch of the profession in England. In doing this, though the chronological order of
painters is somewhat violated, we have followed the most satisfactory
arrangement, and keeping to our fixed purpose, we will only mention
those whose art we consider to have had an effect upon the art of the
time, and whose work will live, from its own excellence, as well as by
the interesting characters it has been called upon to depict.

Henry William Pickersgill, R.A. was a portrait painter whose works
are distinguished more by their being satisfactory likenesses than for any
artistic qualities they possess. Still, he was at one time the fashionable
portrait painter of the day, and he was called upon to paint all the celebrated people of his time. He was elected an associate in 1822, and
an academician in 1826. There is a half-length portrait of Mr. Vernon
by him in the National Gallery, in a puce dressing-gown, holding a small
spaniel on his knee. It is a tame portrait, without individuality. Pickersgill's fame may be said to have departed during his lifetime. He was born
December 3rd, 1782, and died April 21st, 1875, aged ninety-three years.

The portraits of *Sir William Boxall, R.A.*, claim a much higher
place in our regard. Boxall was born at Oxford, January 23rd, 1800, and
became a student of the Royal Academy in 1819. In 1827 he started
for Italy, where he remained three years, and on his return exhibited a
subject picture, "Milton's Reconciliation with his Wife." Nevertheless
his bent was for portrait painting, and he devoted himself to it during
many years. His colouring was rich and harmonious, and he was fastidious and careful in his method of work. This very over-scrupulous-

ness sometimes marred the effect of his pictures and made him a very uneven painter. He was elected an A.R.A. in 1851, and an academician in 1863, in which year he painted his really admirable portrait of John Gibson, R.A., which he presented to the Academy as his diploma work. In 1859 he executed a fine portrait of the Prince Consort for the Trinity House. Boxall was a man of much artistic culture, and he was eminently fitted by his literary taste and knowledge of the works of the old masters for the post of director of the National Gallery, to which he was elected in 1865 on the death of Sir Charles Eastlake. It was he who negotiated for the Government the purchase of the Peel collection, though this was subsequent to his retirement from his post in consequence of failing health. Boxall was knighted by the Queen in 1871. He was never married, and died in London from congestion of the lungs, December 6th, 1879.

Sir Francis Grant, P.R.A. succeeded better in female portraits than in giving the sterner characteristics of the male sex ; but his future fame will more probably depend upon his hunting scenes, in which his figures, though of small size, are yet very capital likenesses, than on his life-sized portraits in oil ; still these latter had one most excellent quality— Grant was always able to paint a *lady*, and to make you feel that his subject was a high-born dame ; it is the same with his men, who are emphatically gentlemen. This power is not granted to some who are much greater painters than Grant. Grant was the fourth son of a Perth-shire laird whose tastes led him to prefer art to the dryer study of the law. He was born in 1803, was educated at Harrow, and after having run through his patrimony, began to try his hand at painting portraits, and became ere long quite a fashionable portrait painter, to whom many of the most beautiful women of his day sat for their likenesses. One of his portraits of most marked excellence is that of his daughter, Mrs. Markham, a full-length of a lady in a walking dress, looped up over a brilliant red petticoat. The colour of his later works is too apt to be leaden. He was elected a full member of the Royal Academy in 1851, and on the death of Sir Charles Eastlake he was chosen president of that body, receiving the honour of knighthood. Perhaps his handsome person, kindly nature, and natural qualities, fitted him better for this office than did his artistic ones. He died rather suddenly at Melton Mowbray, October 5th, 1875, and was buried there, his family having declined the honour of a public funeral.

John Prescott Knight, R.A. was another portrait painter of much merit, born at Stafford, the same year as Grant, 1803. He was the son of Knight the comedian, and was placed by his father in a merchant's office. The firm having failed, Knight was allowed to follow his own inclinations, and in 1823, after having studied under G. Clint, A.R.A., and in Sass's art school, he entered the Royal Academy as a student, and the next year exhibited his first work, a subject picture. He devoted himself to this class of art for many years, but his chief reputation will always rest upon his portraits. They are characterized by excellent drawing, are ably placed upon the canvas, and are good in colour and masculine in execution. Knight was elected an associate of the Royal Academy in 1836 and a full member in 1844, in which year he sent six portraits to the exhibition, among them those of Sir E. Paget and David Solomons. He acted as secretary to the Academy for nearly thirty years, and made a very energetic officer. On his retirement it was deemed wiser that his post should be filled by one who is not a member of the body. Knight was once credited with more power than his office entitled him to, and he was knocked down in one of the exhibition rooms of the Academy by an offended artist whose pictures had been turned out. Knight was a small man, very lively and witty, and gifted with a delightful tenor voice, with which he would charm his brother members at certain council dinners. He once made a happy remark to the mother of a young painter who considered her son's works badly placed, and who was animadverting to Knight, one of the hanging committee, on the badness of the arrangement of the pictures. " Well," said the portrait painter, pleasantly, " we did make one mistake, certainly." " What was that? " inquired the enraged lady. " That we did not get you to help us." Knight was teacher of perspective for many years to the Royal Academy, and made an excellent professor. He died in London after a long illness, 26th March, 1881.

We must not pass over without mention the name of *Sir Daniel Macnee, P.R.S.A.,* who was born in 1807, and studied his art at the Trustees' Academy in Edinburgh, under Sir W. Allan. He was elected a member of the Scottish Academy in 1829, and became its president in 1876, after the death of Sir George Harvey, when he received the honour of knighthood. He lived principally at Glasgow, but often sent portraits to the exhibitions of the Royal Academy in London, many of them being female portraits of excellence, though he was more successful with those of the male sex. His portrait of the Rev. Dr. Wardlaw gained him a gold medal at the Paris Universal Exhibition of 1855. In 1845 he contributed to the Academy a vigorous portrait of Colonel Burns, the son of the poet. He died in Edinburgh, 17th January, 1882, in his seventy-sixth year.

Of late years the English school has lost but one great portrait painter, but that has been a loss indeed. A true artist has been only too prematurely withdrawn from our midst. *Frank Holl, R.A.,* was the elder son of Holl the engraver and was born in Camden Town on the 4th July, 1845. Being a very delicate child, and so unable to mix with other children, his pencil, and, as a great treat, a brush and a few penny cakes of colour, were his chief playthings. At the age of eight his parents fearing that he might be suffering from want of companionship, sent him as a weekly boarder to a school in Hampstead. While there, he so far defeated the object for which he was sent that instead of playing with his schoolfellows, he drew their portraits, or his school house, or anything in sight of the playground, and his great ambition was to have fresh drawings to take home each Saturday to his parents to prove to them that he was not wasting his time! His wife preserves now some of these careful drawings done when a little over eight years of age, and she has often heard him say that he never had any other idea of his future life but that he was to be a painter. He was a most anxious-minded child, and used to worry himself with his anxiety to begin to paint, in order to earn money for his father, when he saw him overworked at engraving. This acutely sensitive disposition is demonstrated by the following anecdote; having when quite a small boy induced his father to buy him a large ball for the great sum, as the child thought, of eight-pence, remorse, when he had obtained this long-coveted plaything, produced by the thought of how hard his father had had to work to procure him this gratification, quite took away all the pleasure in it!

At twelve years old he went to University College School, and while still at this school he received his first commission in art, it was to paint ten farms belonging to a gentleman, which were all in the neighbourhood of London. These he managed to execute in his half holidays, and he received for them ten pounds! He indeed felt that he had started as an artist, and during the three years he remained at University School he devoted all his spare time to drawing. Having at the age of fifteen obtained his probationership at the Royal Academy, he persuaded his father to let him leave school and begin his art work in earnest. At the Academy he was a most successful student, gaining a silver medal in 1862, a gold medal and scholarship in 1863, and in 1868, the year after his marriage, the travelling studentship. Holl and his wife set out on their travels, fully intending to remain a year abroad, but at the end of two months he became quite convinced that English life, which he said he understood and sympathized with, was what he ought to paint, and not foreign life and ways, which were inexplicable to him and even distasteful. So he returned home, and as the travelling studentship could then be only held while abroad, he resigned it.

The picture which had gained him the studentship was called "The Lord gave, and the Lord hath taken away; Blessed be the name of the Lord." It depicts the interior of a modest room, two young women and a sailor lad are seated at a table, at which a little girl kneels; a young clergyman stands at the end of the table, on which are some cups and saucers ; the death of the head of the family being probably announced in the words of the text ; in the background is an old serving woman. The sombreness of the whole work is redeemed by the brick floor and red cushion of the chair. The scene tells with terrible earnestness that it is the solemn moment just after death, when all the care and watching are at an end, and when the family may give way to its very natural sorrow.

It was shortly after this that Holl began drawing on wood for the *Graphic*, or rather making black and white drawings for reproduction on the wood. He for some years did a good deal of this work, besides his painting, and he always attributed his success in dealing with light and shade to the education he thus obtained. It also served as a correction to what might have proved a defect in him. Like many another painter he felt an extreme dissatisfaction very often with his work, and this involved constant changes in the course of the painting of a picture, changes too which were not always improvements. This hesitation and indecision were greatly lessened by getting into the habit of finishing rapidly, for he was obliged to work up to time for the *Graphic*, and it afterwards proved invaluable to him in portraiture, when a promptness in quickly seizing the characteristics of your sitter, and acting upon the conception at once, are so important to the success and life-likeness of a portrait.

Holl shows in his portraits much sympathy with the characters of his models ; they are something beyond mere likenesses, and will depict to posterity something of the mind of the men of the day as well as their outward semblance. Let us take for instance his portrait of Lord Spencer, one of his finest works. We see the earnest resoluteness of the face, though rather worn with care, and the calm repose of the attitude, as well as pictorially the fine treatment of the red beard, and the masterly handling of the brush. Equally characteristic are his portraits of Captain Sim in his ninety-fourth year, of John Bright seated in his study, of Lord Dufferin and of Piatti with his violoncello. Holl's backgrounds are as a rule very dark, he leans to them as simple as possible, he cares little for the environment of his sitter, or for any pictorial arrangement of background as such, he loves to throw the subject out into the strongest relief of light and dark, he enhances his lights by dashes of the whitest of whites. His local colour is finely given, though sometimes rather harshly expressed. It is curious to note the refined finish, not unmixed with timidity, of his portrait of himself at the age of eighteen, then to remark the more confident handling of his portrait of Samuel Cousins, R.A., which, by the applause it met with from his brother artists and others, first induced Holl to take to portrait painting. In fact the only person who disliked it perhaps was the veteran engraver himself, who we believe was actually much offended by it, and who certainly disagreed with Mr. Gladstone, who opined that it had immeasurably increased his (Cousins') chances of immortality. In some few of his portraits Holl's handling becomes coarse, and he is inclined to load on his colour too much ; but in his last pictures he returns to a greater refinement of brush-handling. With regard to his method of work, he himself when asked about it, would say, " I am sure I don't know how I do it. I just look at my subject, and then try to drag him, himself, on to the canvas before me. I know nothing hardly of what colours I use, except as they represent what I see." For his subject pictures he made a rough sketch in colour, very rough, but for his portraits he never thought out the idea until he started on his painting, though he would occasionally make a trifling pencil sketch on the back of an envelope ; the only exception to this was in the case of two or three of his full-length portraits, which he treated more as pictures, and for which he designed a slight notion in colour.

In our preceding remarks upon his art, we have considered Holl merely as a portrait painter ; but his subject works shown in 1888, after his death, at the Royal Academy Winter Exhibition, are full of interest, as for instance, "The Pawnbroker's Shop," 1873, where the young mother is sacrificing her wedding-ring for the sake of her child. "Newgate," 1878. In this picture there is no strong colour, but the effect of the cold, dull prison-light is very striking. Then there are the two funeral pictures, particularly the one called " The Firstborn," where the children are carrying the little coffin, which is especially gracefully grouped ; the mother so desperate in her sorrow, the old grandfather calmly resigned, and the father moody in his grief ; all are full of dramatic pathos. A much earlier picture, " The Ordeal," where a gentleman and his wife are examining a picture they have commissioned, while the artist and his wife, one full of his picture, the other more concerned as to whether the patron will buy the work, is a very minute bit of finish. This was probably executed when Holl painted very slowly, and it is carefully elaborate. In his later work, and more especially during his portrait career, he was wonderfully rapid, and almost daring in his attack of the subject, scarcely ever making an alteration. It seemed as if his picture was so impressed on his brain that to place it on canvas was only a reproduction. He threw the full vigour and energy of his character into his work, and sacrificed his life to his devotion to his art.

Holl became an associate of the Royal Academy in 1878, and a full member in 1884, and he always took great interest in the working and the schools of the Royal Academy. He died at his house, The Three Gables, Hampstead, at the height of his fame, from heart disease, aggravated, no doubt, by overwork, at the early age of forty-three, on the 31st July, 1888. His brother members, admirers and friends, combined to erect a memorial to him in St. Paul's Cathedral. It has been objected to nearly all Holl's subject pictures, that they are of such sad subjects; perhaps the very force of his character and the remains of his youthful sensitiveness, gave him a keen perception of the sadder elements in human life.

We must just mention, in concluding our chapter on portrait painting, the small water-colour portraits of *J. C. Moore* (B. 1829, D. 1880) which are very true to nature, quiet and delicate in tone, and pure in colour, having an original character of their own which call for some remark. Being precluded by the limits of our work from mentioning living painters, we can only add here, that in portrait painting our school, though it may not be equal to the times of Reynolds and of Gainsborough, has yet, of late years, made a very distinct advance, and that the portrait painters of this day will probably more than hold their own in the opinion of posterity.

CHAPTER XXVIII.

TURNER, of whom we have already spoken, was not without comtemporaries, distinguished men practising the same branch of art, yet in a manner quite their own, and aiming at original excellence. Of these *John Constable, R.A.*, was remarkable as the first who wholly emancipated himself from the schools. His art is purely and thoroughly English. Turner, in his early works at least, built much on the art of Claude and Poussin; so did Callcott. Gainsborough, English as he was in almost every phase of his art, was not clear of the dark masters and the "brown tree" school. Morland was a Dutchman in subject, and in the mode of composing his pictures. Crome built upon Ruysdael and Hobbema. But Constable began with studying nature; he was ever deep in the love of it, and ended as he began. His nature, too, was English nature; he never visited Italy; he did not even care for the mountain and the torrent of his own land, but he loved the flat pastures and the slow streams of his native Suffolk.

Constable was born at East Bergholt, Suffolk, on the 11th June, 1776. He was the son of a wealthy miller, who had inherited considerable property. He was first intended for the Church. Then his father tried to make a miller of him, but he had a loving preference for art, and after a year he was left to follow his own bent. In 1795 he came to London. In 1799 he was admitted a student of the Royal Academy; and in 1802 we find him exhibiting his first picture. Soon gaining confidence in his own powers, he wrote in the following year, "I feel now more than ever a decided conviction that I shall some time or other make some good pictures—pictures that shall be valuable to posterity if I do not reap the benefit of them." He made one or two attempts at history, then lost much time in painting portraits, the only art which he found paid, and at last settled down to his true art, as a landscape painter.

In 1819 he gained his election as associate, and ten years later his full membership.

The banks of the Stour made him, he owns, a painter. He treated the nature which he saw in a thoroughly original manner, and he chose it under an aspect that had previously been overlooked. Landscape painters had hitherto usually painted with the sun at their backs, to the right, or to the left, out of the picture, looking to the landscape as the sun looks on it. But Constable took another view; he loved to see his subject *under* the sun. Many had painted the sun *in* the picture gradually sinking in the low horizon, and casting a dreamy mist and glow over all the earth. Such treatments Claude loved and painted finely; Cuyp also loved them, and gave them with unequalled breadth and beauty. But Constable chose the time when the sun was high in the heavens, far above, out of his canvas, but still in front of him, and painted almost always under the sun; and much that is peculiar in his art arose from this cause.

Moreover, he fully appreciated the special characteristics of the English climate of our sea-surrounded land; its moisture causing all that wealth of foliage unknown elsewhere, that lovely verdure which foreigners so deeply admire and wonder at. Its breezy freshness delighted him, the rolling clouds drifting tender showers over the rich meadows, and giving those accidental gleams of light mingled with shade, so lovely to watch, as their shadows slowly float over hill and plain. He never thought nature *too green*, nor left the full foliage of summer for the brown tints of sun-dried autumn. Was not England above all things green? was it not so distinguished from other lands? So he thought, and so he ever painted.

Thus his skies were generally masses of warm grey clouds rounded off with edges of silver; here and there a rift opening through them into the blue depths of heaven beyond. Such skies he knew produced those flying shadows and the contrasts of warm sunbeams and cool greys, of deep blue under the emerald foliage, which he felt to be the character of our scenery. But his greatest peculiarity in the eyes of his critics arose more particularly from the habit he had adopted of painting *under the sun*— that glitter and sparkle of white lights on his foliage, which by those who had never observed nature, or who had no eyes to read her aright, was nicknamed "Constable's snow"—was laughed at as spotty, and ever treated with ridicule by those who loved the patina of brown pictures, and in whose eyes all freshness was a sin against both taste and truth. It is told of Chantrey—who, as having begun art as a landscape painter, ought to have had some sense of nature—that he took the brush out of our painter's hands on one of the varnishing days, and as poor Constable said, "brushed away all his dew;" passed a dirty brown glaze over all his truthful sparkle, to tone it down to the dull hue of conventional *truth*. And his friend Leslie, speaking of his fine picture "The Opening of Waterloo Bridge," says, "What would he have felt could he foresee that in little more than a year after his death, its silvery brightness was doomed to be clouded over by a coat of blacking, laid on by the hand of a picture dealer; yet that this was done by way of giving tone to the picture, I know from the best authority, the lips of the operator; who assured me that several noblemen considered it to be greatly improved by the process. The blacking was laid on with water, and secured by a coat of mastic varnish."

Now, to convince one's self of the true and original view of nature that Constable took, it is only necessary to look at nature, and we shall find that all leaves more or less, when not grimed with smoke, or foul with dust, are fitted to reflect light, and when so seen between the sun and the spectator do, like mirrors, reflect light from their surface—rays of crystal as from bright jewels, which can only be represented, if at all, by pure white. Still more do they sparkle and glitter when the dew of morning, or the freshness of summer showers is upon them, and this Constable as a painter was the first to treat. This original view of nature led him to depict many other beauties, which he rendered most truthfully; thus, seen under the sun, the shadows are broad and liquid, with fulness of rich colour in them; at the edges of trees the true local colour in all its fulness is found, while in other parts where the sun-rays pass through the thinner foliage, the colour is enriched by transmission, as it is through stained glass, and is in vivid contrast with the full shadows. But this is never the case opposite the sun, where the colour is modified and somewhat neutralized by the reflected grey or blue of the heavens. All this the painter has felt, and much more, has taught us to feel also; but it required a generation to do so. Fuseli, whose pictures are, as to colour, but honey and treacle, could see in him nothing but a painter of watery skies and coming showers, and thought it witty to call to the Academy porter, "Stroulger, bring me my umbrella, I am going to see Mr. Constable's pictures."

But Constable himself was satirical by nature, and could justly be so on the connoisseurs who asked, "Where is your brown tree?" or who would lay down rules of what "foregrounds should or should not be." He well knew what they should be; that they should be carefully studied from nature; that water-weeds should grow on the banks of his streams, and not on high uplands; that each plant had a separate individuality, characteristics different from all other plants; and that weedage should not be done to pattern, as was rather too much the case even with Claude. He was accustomed to say, "Paint your foreground well and truly, and the middle distance will take care of itself," showing at least how much he valued his foreground. To him painting was wholly a matter of feeling, not of rule; he was heard to lament after a visit from one of the tribe of small critics, who had assured him that *this* was wrong and *that* against all rule, that he wanted a tree here, a light there, and changes everywhere—"Ah! there is my day's painting done; that little fellow with his cocketyhoop manner has taken away all my feeling."

Free from the shackles of the schools, Constable was free also to choose his own mode of execution. With him the tool was nothing, nor the workmanship, but only the effect produced. There was on his part no wish to astonish by eccentricity of execution—like the painter in Queen Elizabeth's day, who, affecting to find painting with his fingers too easy, took to working with his toes—but simply as setting up feeling and truth above labour and execution. He mostly laid in his works with the palette knife, thus obtaining great flatness and breadth of touch; and avoiding all littleness of execution and attention to mere details, he was enabled to treat the general truths of nature as to colour and chiaroscuro largely and simply. A minor beauty arising from this practice was the full purity of white or other solid pigments, or tints mixed with them, as left by the flat knife, unchanged in the slightest degree by the greyness occasioned by the texture of brush-marks.

What he really sought, however, was the thorough abstraction of his attention from details, to concentrate his whole feeling on the general effects of nature; to allow his memory to recall those deep impressions of beauty, often most evanescent and transient, but which, as delighting the painter, it is his peculiar province to produce for the delight of others. Constable's practice thus wholly differed from the later school of landscape painting which arose out of what is called pre-Raphaelism. That system inculcates the exact and literal imitation of parts, gradually merging them into a whole; while Constable viewed his work from the first as a whole, afterwards adding just sufficient detail to give truth of form without destroying the higher qualities arising from generalization. The P.R.B. system is admirably adapted for study, for the early practice of the young painter; but really fine art, such as the art of Turner, of Gainsborough, of Wilson, of Claude, or of Cuyp, will never be achieved if literal imitation becomes the end instead of the means. Mere imitation, bit by bit, is certain to produce works less like nature than when its general expression is sought after.

Painting is, and must be, a sacrifice of less significant truths in order to obtain truth as a whole. How can we, with our poor pigments, represent the luminousness and the infinite gradations seen in nature, either of light and dark or of colour? Black and white, for instance—the pigments which represent for us the extremes of light and darkness—what relation has white paint, seen in the subdued light of room or gallery, where pictures must be seen, to the bright light on the rolling cumulus in the summer heavens; let alone the sun, the source of light, or its reflection on stream or from polished surfaces? or black, to that intensity of darkness when from sunny daylight we look into some deep cavernous gloom? The same may be said of all the pigments which represent colour; they are but sorry substitutes for nature's hues. The infinite gradations that exist in nature are almost unattainable in art; so refined and delicate are they that the coarse media of pigments and varnishes cannot produce them. What pigments, what execution will render such delicate transitions? Certainly not the crude colours at our command, or the oil vehicles with which we temper them. Hence the painter has to substitute other truths, and resorts to "breadth," whereby he masses the parts and loses the gradations; suppressing details, he makes the general colour of the mass to include the many minor forms and hues which his limited means prevent him from producing with adequate truth. For such as are important to retain he reserves his palette; refusing for a while to avail himself even of the full purity of the pigments he has at his command, in order that he may have means, by enhancing points of light or of colour higher, purer, and brighter than the rest, to make some object of interest sparkle and glow on the spectator's eye.

Again, reduction in size compels the painter to the same expedients. Objects in nature that tell palpably on the eye, are, when reduced to the relative scale of our picture, so microscopically small, that we must either unduly enlarge them, or suppress them, and seek compensation in that "breadth" which includes them. In working direct from nature these minute beauties enchant us, so affecting the painter that he can hardly avoid the endeavour to imitate them, and thus the whole is sacrificed to the parts. It must be remembered, also, that what may appear to the painter, when in face of nature, almost faithful imitation of the scene before him, becomes tame and changed when his work is brought into the subdued light of his own room. It is said that the Dutch painters of candle-light effects wrought by daylight, looking through a small aperture into a room where their subject was seen illuminated by candle-light. Now, whether true or not, this is the effect to be obtained—the candle-light must appear to be candle-light when seen by daylight; and the sunny landscape must not merely be bright and glowing when the painter is on the field of his out-of-door labours, but must bring the sun and the glow of daylight into our rooms: and as every painter must be aware of the change that takes place when out-of-door work is seen indoors, he will be aware that some treatment must be adopted to insure that his work when examined indoors shall have the effect seen out-of-doors.

All these considerations, joined, no doubt, to a fine perception of truth and an accurate memory of form and colour, led Constable to forego painting direct from nature, which he was so well qualified to excel in, and to form instead, a style and manner built on careful studies ; by which he was better enabled to place before us all those large truths of landscape scenery, which had impressed him with their poetry and beauty, and could thoroughly enable us for all time to enjoy them through him.

There are commencements for two of Constable's pictures, which are invaluable, not only for their intrinsic qualities, but as illustrations of his mode of conducting his pictures. They are studies for " The Hay-wain," one of his finest works, and for " The Jumping Horse," sometimes called " The Canal," exhibited in 1825. The canvases are the size of the completed works. The subjects are laid in with the knife, with great breadth and in a grand and large manner. Various glazings have then been passed over the parts, to bring together and enrich them (even the skies are glazed) ; and then the whole has again had enhancing points of colour added, brightness and daylight being obtained by further draggings and knife touches. With the exception of the glazings, it would seem as if the brush had not been used upon them ; hence there is a complete absence of any sort of detail.

When Constable had carried his study thus far, and was pleased with the indications it contained, he would leave it without further completion, perhaps fearing to lose what he was so satisfied with—for it must be confessed that Constable was a man who had sufficient self-esteem, in the language of the phrenologists, to think well of his own works—he would leave it without completion, and begin again on a new canvas, endeavouring to retain the fine qualities of the studied sketch, adding to it such an amount of completeness and detail as could be given without loss of the higher qualities of breadth and general truth. How completely this was effected would be at once seen by comparing the incomplete with the completed work. There was an opportunity for doing this during the International Exhibition of 1862, when the two studies were hung for a time on loan in the Sheepshanks collection, and the two pictures were placed in the adjacent gallery. It was a lesson that might be most valuable to young artists if they could read it aright, and to the despisers of the method followed by the older masters of our school. Constable himself knew the value of such studies, for he rarely parted with them. He used to say of his studies and pictures that he had no objection to part with the corn, but not with the field that grew it.

Because Constable despised the painters who were content to see nature only through the eyes of others, it must not be presumed that he did not feel the merits of the great painters among the old masters, or was untouched by the beauty of their works. He was a great admirer of all that was truly good in landscape art; he made studies from Ruysdael's pictures, pointing out their merits with great delight, and the power of observation they evinced.   Even the landscape art of the higher schools was fully appreciated by him; and one of his latest labours was to lecture upon the beauties of the landscape of Titian's "Peter Martyr."

Moreover, it is rather contrary to the usual practice of the Royal Academy that a landscape painter should be a visitor in the life-school, but at Constable's desire he was elected to that office. He selected for study some of the finest figures from Raphael, and from Michael Angelo in the Sistine Chapel, posing the models in the life-school in like attitudes; an excellent mode of study, enabling the students to see how these great masters had treated nature. Among other figures, he placed one in the attitude of a well-known Eve, and he thought it would be useful to the students to contrast the flesh with real foliage. Accordingly he had a large laurel bush cut down from his garden at Hampstead, to stand in the place of the tree of knowledge. Unfortunately (as his visitorship was just at Christmas time), the man employed to convey it to Somerset House was seized by the police as a garden robber, who had stolen the tree for Christmas decorations; and notwithstanding his protestations, both he and the tree were carried to the station-house, which Constable had to visit in order to redeem them from durance. Finally, the bush with a few oranges tied on to give colour, and to represent the forbidden fruit, did service as a support to the female representative of Eve; much to the satisfaction of the students, and also to the gratification of Etty's love of colour, he being, as usual, at his post on this occasion.

Constable has been most fortunate in his biographer, but Leslie has painted him *couleur de rose*, and transfused his own kindly and simple spirit into the biography. The landscape painter, though of a manly nature, was eminently sarcastic, and was very clever at saying the bitterest things in a witty manner. This had no doubt been increased by the neglect with which the would-be connoisseurs had treated his art, and by the sneers of commonplace critics. He may be said to have been born a little too early; before the time when nature was appreciated rather than pictures, and within the period when Dutch finish was thought indispensable to a fine work. Yet he certainly was the forerunner of the race of artists who, about the period of his mid-career, began to rely upon their own impressions of nature in the treatment of their subjects, and to reject the traditional dogmas of art.   There can be no doubt that Constable had great influence on the landscape art, both of his own country and that of France, inducing much of that candid acceptance of nature, as contradistinguished from *compositions*, which some of the artists who succeeded him here, affect to follow even too minutely. Yet his peculiar treatment of his subject has not been followed up by any. One painter only of his own time, whether from original observation, or following in Constable's footsteps, adopted the same practice; this was George Vincent, of whom we have already spoken, who almost invariably practised painting "under the sun." As to Constable's influence on French art, arising from the picture of "The Hay-wain," which he sent in 1824 to the Paris Exhibition, and for which he was honoured with a gold medal, it is acknowledged even by their own art-critics; and there is no doubt that the school of which Troyon was so able a representative, was initiated owing to the admiration of these fine works. Constable's influence upon Leslie and his art has been spoken of in the account of that painter's career.

Constable died in Charlotte Street, Fitzroy Square, on the 1st of April, 1837. He had worked hard for appreciation and fame, and it must have been with pain that he said of himself in reference to a work of his engraved by Lucas—"The painter himself is totally unpopular, and will be so on this side of the grave; the subjects nothing but art, and the buyers wholly ignorant of that." Again—"My art flatters nobody by imitation, it courts nobody by smoothness, it tickles nobody by petiteness, it is without either fal-de-lal or fiddle-de-dee: how can I therefore hope to be popular?" But his conviction that his pictures would be valued by posterity soon found its fulfilment. His friends purchased his fine work, "The Cornfield," and presented it to the National Gallery. A better feeling for his art at once arose, and his pictures are now treasured in all collections, and prized at their proper worth.

Augustus Wall Callcott, R.A., was born on the 20th of February, 1779, in the quiet suburb of Kensington Gravel Pits, not as now abounding with art and artists, but a rural neighbourhood separated from London by green fields and workmen's villages, by the parks and gardens, in our day so trim and well-frequented, but then neglected and run to waste— the park stocked with deer, the gardens tangled and unhealthy; but from which "dogs and livery servants" were rigorously excluded. Callcott's family had resided long in the neighbourhood; his elder brother had adopted the profession of music, in which art he developed rare genius, and became the celebrated Dr. Callcott. He had studied under Dr. Cooke, at Westminster, and his younger brother, the future artist, was in his boyhood a chorister in the Abbey, until his voice broke, and his desire for art outweighed his love of music. In 1797, he was admitted a student of the Royal Academy, and became for a time a pupil of Hoppner. Following the direction of his studies he began life as a portrait painter, and we find him exhibiting in 1799, for the first time, a "Portrait of Miss Roberts." In 1802, he exhibited a portrait of Dr. Gray, the father of the distinguished naturalist, Dr. Gray, of the British Museum; it is now in the Royal Society, and is a work of much merit for so young a painter. But Callcott's natural bent was evidently in another direction. In the same year he exhibited five landscapes; and landscape art constituted the labour of his life until a late period of his career.

In 1811, the year after his election to the associateship of the Academy, he exhibited ten landscapes, and in 1812 six; but whether it had been whispered to him that his art was not up to his early promise, or that with his sound judgment he felt such to be the case; or, it may be, struck with the grand works of Turner, or the rising talent of Constable, he seems from this time to have determined to limit his appearances in public. For the next two years he exhibited nothing, and thenceforth, for the period of twelve years, he put all his strength into a single picture for the annual exhibitions. During this interval he painted his finest pictures and undoubtedly raised his reputation to the first rank. His best works were mostly English landscapes; "The Entrance to the Pool of London," exhibited in the Royal Academy, in 1816, and "The Mouth of the Tyne," in 1818, both of which were in the International Exhibition of 1861, are evidences of his claim to this distinction; they had an individuality of their own, and showed an appreciation of English atmosphere and English scenery not to be found in the works of his later years.

Callcott and Mulready were neighbours from early times, and being seven years the elder, Callcott was a little looked up to by his junior. Varley also was intimate with them. A curious story used to be told among the members of Callcott's family, and during the lifetime of both parties, relating to Varley's practice of, and belief in, astrology. Varley asked Callcott to give him his exact age, and having obtained it, he cast his nativity, sealed it up and gave it to Mulready, charging him to keep it safely until Callcott was fifty years old. The paper, it is said, was laid aside and forgotten until Callcott, then in his fiftieth year, wrote to Mulready, to invite him to his wedding, which was about to take place with Mrs. Graham, the widow of Captain Graham. Mulready recollected Varley's sealed paper and his injunction, and took the document with him, opening it in the presence of the assembled company; the contents ran thus—"Callcott will remain single until he is fifty, and then will marry and go to Italy." As the painter really was to make a trip, shortly after his wedding, to that country, it was thought a wonderful coincidence. Over and over again have we heard this tale told, with many other of Varley's wild fancies; but if our dates are accurate, Callcott was married on the 20th February, 1827, his forty-eighth birthday, and he started for Italy on the 12th of May following, so that we have a false date, or Varley made a false prediction. This was Callcott's first journey to Italy, but he had previously been in Paris and in Holland.

On Callcott's return from Italy in June, 1828, he seems to have entirely changed his views as to exhibiting; perhaps it was necessary, as he was now married, to provide for a larger establishment. His wife also assisted with her pen; and her work on early Italian painters added to her husband's reputation from his pencil. His studio in "The Mall" was frequented by the titled and the rich; his art became fashionable; the painter himself was courteous and somewhat of a courtier—far different from his great competitor, Turner. His pictures, bright, pleasant of surface, and finished in execution, were suited to the appreciation of his public, and not beyond their comprehension; commissions poured in upon him. In the week before the pictures were sent in to the Academy, the occupants of lines of carriages usually waited their turn to be admitted to see his works before they left the painter's easel. Instead of the one picture of rare excellence which he had formerly shown as the public pledge of his improvement, he began to send the full number allowed by the Academy laws; instead of the careful study of nature and nature's effects, which he made with a view to perfect such works, he began to rely on sketches and on his memory—to rely on his art-knowledge, his composition, his sweet execution; and his works increased in art, or what is called art, and decreased in nature.

In 1837, on the accession of her Majesty, he received the honour of knighthood, and this year, reverting rather to his early art, he sent to the Academy a picture of "Raphael and the Fornarina," the figures life-size, the whole finished with the careful execution of a cabinet picture.

Callcott's health was not strong as he advanced in years. Lady Callcott's, after a time, wholly failed; and for many years before her death, which happened in 1842, she was a complete invalid, confined to her chamber, almost to her bed. Yet in that sick chamber she managed, in the intervals of her suffering, to draw around her a circle of friends, of literary companions, of artists young and old; to learn of, and be interested in, the advance and social progress of the outer world from which she was so much cut off. In the long summer evenings, when these occasional gatherings took place, as the sun declined in the west and the day faded into twilight, the room and the company formed a picture such as memory reverts to with many regrets, and we are reminded of our own art aspirations, and the subjects of interest there discussed. The little bed on which the lady sat, partly dressed and propped up with pillows, covered with rich draperies, was placed before one of the windows of a room in the old house—a copyhold tenement of the Callcotts —in which the painter lived and died. Vines were trained across and across the window, and through their leaves the rays of the setting sun came tempered and moderated into green coolness. Inside the room here was usually a small selection of rare plants in pots, and little bouquets of choice flowers were on the tables. Two or three dogs formed part of the company—one of large size was a great favourite with the mistress; while the visitors, seated about on the old furniture of a quaint, picturesque, and irregular room, gave the painters of the party many hints of colour and effect as the light sank away into gloom. Lady Callcott mostly supported the conversation. She was somewhat imperious in her state chamber; the painter being more of a silent listener, until some incident of travel, some question of art, roused him up to earnest interest or wise remark. He was a kindly-hearted man, and always seemed interested in the progress of the young; being quite willing to communicate to them his art-lore, and to advise with them on the progress of their pictures; and for his sake the young painters made it a rule to take their works on the morning of sending in to the Academy, and to range them before the sick lady who could not leave her chamber, that she might have a sight at least of some portion of the coming exhibition.

Some time prior to the excitement which pervaded the whole art world when the commissioners for decorating the Houses of Parliament called for competitions in historic painting, Callcott, incited perhaps by the success of "Raphael and the Fornarina" (for in the eyes of many it was a success), again came forward as a history-painter, and sent to the Academy, in 1840, a picture, with the figures rather larger than life, of "Milton dictating *Paradise Lost* to his Daughters." It was a large picture, rather than a great one; a picture that would have taxed the strength of a man in the prime of his art to produce, and was too much for one enfeebled by illness, and in the decline of his powers. It impressed the spectator with an oppressive sense of the labour that had called it forth, and of the labour that had been given to its completion, rather than with the grandeur of the subject or the severity of its treatment; yet it satisfied most of the conditions and rules of art, and wanted but the fire of youth and genius to make it a real and impressive work. It was indeed too much for the physical powers of the painter, whose health rapidly declined from this time. On the death of Mr. Seguier, he was appointed to the duties of surveyor of Crown pictures, but was prevented from entering upon the active discharge of his office. In the same quiet nook in "The Mall, Kensington Gravel Pits," in the house wherein he was born—with the same clipped old elms in front of it that he had looked on when a child, but which were shortly after to be removed from the face of the earth by the buildings rapidly advancing from the outskirts of the metropolis—he passed the short remainder of his days, and he died, regretted by many, on the 25th November, 1844. He was buried at Kensal Green.

Callcott early became aware that with the limited scale of light and dark, of colour and negation, at the command of the painter, as compared with that of nature, a compromise must absolutely be made, and he adopted the principle of reducing the positive tints of his pictures to negative ones, diffusing light pretty generally throughout the whole, and making the figures, which he introduced with great skill, the telling points of the composition; both the strongest lights and darks, and the purest hues of colour, being focussed in their draperies. As these were naturally the points of most interest the system was a sound one; the picture gained great breadth, and was from its lightness and the salient brilliancy of the figures, always pleasing in our dark rooms. By this system the secondary green of trees became, as treated by Callcott, a tertiary citrine; his skies rarely contained azure blue, and his buildings were varied hues of brown. It is not so obvious in his early works, since in them his reference to nature modified it; but when in after-life his works were in great demand, and he was obliged to produce them by system rather than by immediate reference to nature, the principle of his composition became very apparent, and was apt to be a little vapid and empty in larger pictures; while, carried to excess in his latest works, it resulted, as was naturally to be expected, in weakness and insipidity. This was the case with his last large picture, painted in 1842, "An English Landscape;" the subject being a group of cows standing in a pool of water under some trees, of which an eminent figure painter, who was asked what he thought of it, answered, perhaps even more wittily than justly, "I should say it was milk and water." In his early pictures he painted with a firm and manly execution; latterly, when his works became, as we have said, more conventional and less realistic, and when he was influenced, perhaps insensibly, by the practice of Turner, he endeavoured to achieve air-tint—infinity of parts combined with breadth of light—by scumblings and by scraping the surface, by glazings and thin paintings, which further contributed to give his pictures an artificial look. We greatly prefer the English landscapes of the period already named; but some of his Italian compositions have an air of classic grandeur, which, if we cannot place him near Turner, at least induces us to regret that such art is fast dying out of our school : dying out before those merely imitative landscapes which are painted out of doors and direct from nature. The "Italian Landscape," exhibited in the British Institution in 1863, is among the best of this class.

With all the faults of this picture, and of the school to which it belongs, how much is the loss to be deplored of the talent which produced it! What a refined art! What an attempt to lift us out of the commonplaces of nature! Callcott himself never painted directly from nature, but from drawings and studies; his art would have been better had he *studied* nature more by colour, his pictures wanted this. Callcott's early study enabled him, as we have seen, to paint the figures in his landscape well; but it did not fit him for a figure painter. His weakness is shown in his smaller figure pictures as much as in his larger. They are weak and tame, and have rather the appearance of being painted from the lay figure than from nature.

While it is given to but few, very few, artists to attain the highest rank in art, it is an honourable end to have stamped a marked individuality on any of its varied modes of appealing to mankind. If the former was denied to *William Collins, R.A.*, it at least was given to him to find a somewhat untrodden path in art for himself, and to make the latter success his own by the way he treated his subjects. William Collins was born in Great Titchfield Street, on the 18th September, 1788. Although an Englishman by birth, by parentage he was allied to each of the sister kingdoms; his mother being a native of Edinburgh, and his father born at Wicklow in Ireland. The elder Collins had settled in England as a writer and journalist, and to these, considering them as precarious means of supporting his family, he added the business of a picture dealer. The love of landscape scenery in the younger Collins might be derived from both parents, born as they were in places remarkable for picturesque beauty. The two sons, William and Francis, moreover, were from their father's business early thrown among art and artists; and brought up in its very atmosphere, what wonder that William, the elder, chose it for his pursuit in life. His first studies, we are told, were from the objects around him, and these alternated with " copies of pictures and drawings for the small patrons and dealers of the day."

Collins's father was intimate, among others, with George Morland (an intimacy which subsequently led to his writing the life of that artist); and the son was very anxious to be introduced to a man who was everywhere spoken of as a wonder of erratic genius, and who had promised to admit the lad to his studio, that he might at least see the conduct of his pictures. It so happened that the boy's first sight of the famous animal painter was at his father's house, under very questionable circumstances, sleeping off, in the kitchen, a fit of filthy intoxication; this may have been a lesson for our young painter, who was through life a man of the most correct habits. From this time Collins was a visitor at Morland's painting-room as often as the irregularities of that painter would permit. He seems to have had a high sense of his talents, and to have taken great interest in the places where he had been in company with Morland when in after-life he revisited them. We are told, however, that he did not consider that he gained any remarkable advantage in the practical part of his art from the kind of instruction which Morland was able to convey; but those who examine the works of the two men will see that the early impression made by the art of the eccentric painter had a marked influence on the future art of Collins, and perhaps first led him to those rustic subjects which he handled so skilfully, and treated with a refinement which was denied to the man of gross sensuality and intemperate habits.

Pursuing his desultory studies under his father's superintendence, alternately painting from a group of objects, perchance jars or blacking bottles, with his friend John Linnell; sketching from nature and copying pictures spurious and original, with the advantage also of seeing the rapid pencil of Morland at work to produce means to continue his excesses, young Collins reached his nineteenth year, and was sufficiently advanced in 1807 to obtain admission as a student in the Royal Academy, and also fortuitously to become an exhibitor on its walls. Of these first pictures, "Two Views of Millbank," there is no record further than their insertion in the catalogue.

In 1809, Collins was advanced to the life-school, and in the same year his pictures, both in the Academy and in the British Institution, obtained some share of public notice; and, what was even of more importance to a struggling artist fighting his own way in life, they found purchasers also. As years passed on, young Collins improved in his art, though not rapidly; his works had little of the richness and less of the free handling he arrived at afterwards. Early in the year 1812, Collins lost a father to whom he seems to have been tenderly attached; a short diary of this period, preserved by his son, very touchingly paints the few anxious days which preceded his death, and the destitution of the family now left wholly dependent on the young painter. But friends rose up to help, as they mostly do for those who are true-hearted, and we find one kind friend coming forward to assist them with furniture in lieu of that which the creditors had laid their hands on; while another, Sir Thomas Heathcote, one of Collins's first patrons, not only paid him half the price of a picture in advance, but offered a loan of money in addition. From this time, in young Collins's pictures, the figures were more predominant than the landscape; his subjects, mostly the joys and sorrows of children, won their way in public estimation, and seem to have found ready purchasers.

It shows how popular were the subjects of his choice, and how true it is that the quality of colour in art is the most attractive to the public; and when joined to subjects appealing, as did those of Collins, to the heart and understanding of all, is sure to win an early success. Both these qualities were united in a work of this period which became very widely popular, and is a representative work of the painter's, "The Sale of the Pet Lamb," which, painted in 1812, united very happily the best characteristics of the painter's art.

The incident is one of frequent occurrence in rural life, where the

cade lamb, as it is called—a lamb which by accident has lost its dam—-
is given away to the cottager, that it may be petted into life, if possible,
by the active sympathy of his children : it gradually grows into their
young hearts as companion and playmate, until its age, or some pressing
need, gives it up to the usual fate of its kind.   In the painter's treatment of the subject, the butcher-lad has come to lead away the
unconscious victim ; he does his duty kindly for the children's sake,
although (as labouring in his vocation) *he* is untouched by any sentiment
the others feel.   One of the children pushes him away from their
playfellow, another feeds it for the last time, while a little girl clings to
the mother, who is receiving the price of the lamb, tearfully urging that
it should not be taken from them.   This picture, with one or two
others of the same class, so advanced Collins in the estimation of his
brother artists that in November, 1814, he was elected an associate of
the Royal Academy.

The painter having obtained his first promotion in art, had taken a
new and larger house ; but although his works were popular and many
were purchased, he had still difficulties to struggle with ; in subsequent
years fortune was not equally favourable, and we find an entry in his
diary in the spring of 1816, " A black-looking April day, with one
sixpence in my pocket, 700*l.* in debt, shabby clothes, a fine house, and
a large stock of my own handiworks."   It must be remembered that
the young painter had his mother and his brother at this time to
provide for, that he had entered upon the responsibilities of a larger
establishment, and also that, on looking down the list of pictures and
their prices, recorded in his *Life*, it is evident from statements in his
diaries, that some of the pictures were not purchased at the time they
were painted, but afterwards, when he was growing still more into fame
and notice.

In the troubles of this period of his life, he cast about for some new
class of subjects to attract the attention of the public, and made journeys
to the sea-coast, painting first at Cromer, and afterwards at Hastings,
coast scenery, enlivened with groups of fisher-boys, boats, fish, &c. ;
these he treated with great freshness and truth, and having made
himself a place of his own in art, he was elected a full member of the
academic body in February, 1820.   In 1822, during a visit to Scotland
in company with his friend Wilkie, Collins completed a long-standing
engagement by marrying Miss Geddes, by whom he had two sons.
The elder has written a life of his father, full of matters of interest both
to artists and to the general public.

Collins was now well established, having obtained the highest
honours of the profession, and having in his particular branch of
landscape art, as Wilkie told him, the ball at his feet, he had but to

paint as he had begun, to widen his popularity. There was no fear of any lack of subjects in the inexhaustible field he had chosen, nor of their palling on the public taste. Such subjects he continued to paint until the year 1836, when he produced two of his very best works— "Sunday Morning," and "Happy as a King." This latter picture is full of life and action, the landscape is broad and simple in manner, and is beautifully suggestive.

Wilkie, while on the Continent, had in his letters repeatedly urged his friend to see the beauties of Italy; recounting the many subjects he would find there for his pencil, and the desirableness of filling his mind with new ideas; and at length Collins made up his mind to the journey, and on the 19th September, 1836, he left England to spend some time in the South.

To us who look back over his whole course and review his art life, it may be permitted to doubt if the Italian journey was at all beneficial to his reputation. It is true that some beautiful landscapes resulted from it; such as that seen "From the Caves of Ulysses at Sorrento, Bay of Naples," a work of great truth and beauty. But Collins was essentially an English painter; from his youth up he had lived among the rustic children he loved to paint and the rural scenery in which he placed them; and although Italian mendicants, priests, and lazzaroni might be a change to the public, yet even at the time, they were hardly thought a change for the better; while to ourselves, one such picture as "Happy as a King" is worth all the figure pictures, the fruits of his Italian journey. Nor can we forget that to the treacherous smiles of an Italian sun we ultimately owed the loss of the artist. While at Sorrento, he could not be persuaded that it was dangerous to paint out of doors in the heat of the day. The temptation to do so was great; the artist was incapable of idleness, and continued against the remonstrances of his friends to work at all hours; the result was a severe attack of rheumatic fever, which lasted many weeks, and left behind it a disease of the heart, which troubled him during the remaining years of his life, and finally resulted in his death on the 17th February, 1847.

As a landscape and figure painter, Collins was not of that imitative school who paint directly from nature; his practice was to make drawings of all the parts and details which he intended to use in his work, to study the effects of air and light on the spot, and then to paint his picture in his studio from these materials. He sketched in, first the general composition of his picture, the disposition of the parts, the rack of clouds, the figures he intended to form part of the composition; often arranging and re-arranging, until he was satisfied with this stage of his labours. From this he proceeded to the dead colouring. He began, as is usual, with the sky, which he endeavoured to finish at once, and, failing to do so, would hang a wet sheet before it during the night, to keep it wet for the next day; and this part of the work he finished with the sweetener. He then painted from the horizon forward, finishing the various distances towards the foreground. To secure the true light and shade of his figures, he adopted at times the method of his friend Wilkie, grouping clay figures or dressed dolls in a box lighted for that purpose. His son tells us that he was ever most anxious to execute his works with such durable materials and pigments as would ensure their preservation, not only during his own lifetime, but to posterity. He does not appear to have given in to the use of asphaltum, which his friend Wilkie used so largely to the destruction of his own pictures, and recommended so warmly to others; he used magylph, it is true, but with proper restraint.

In his diaries he has left us some valuable records of the vehicles with which various of his pictures are painted—records well worth careful investigation by those who have the opportunity of comparing them with the several works. In some of his pictures he has used his vehicle too freely, and cracking has been the result; while in those where he has used copal largely, we should expect the lights to have become somewhat *horny*.

Much of Collins's reputation was derived from his happy choice of subjects. These, in many respects, correspond with the subjects chosen by Morland, but they are treated with far more refinement; and as many of his actors are children, and as he entered thoroughly into their sports and habits, they interest us much more. His landscapes are always an important feature of the picture; the handling and execution are a little akin to the art of Gainsborough, having his freshness and a little of his case, with greater finish.

Collins was a devout imitator of nature, but in its generalities rather than in details. He had a strong feeling for colour, but he was a very indifferent draughtsman. He painted his Italian sketches in this country, away from the models that had suggested them, and in such works his drawing and execution were still more timid and feeble. Then again his draperies are often merely rags, suggestive of pleasant colour it is true, but distasteful to those who desire somewhat of form or fold and flow.

CHAPTER XXIX.

John Linnell, perhaps the most thoroughly English of our landscape painters, was born in Bloomsbury, 16th June, 1792. Unlike Constable, who revelled in the flat pastures of his native Suffolk, Linnell seems, as a rule, to represent a glorified Surrey. The scenery of that county and of Kent in passing through his mind reappears upon his canvases, shorn of all littleness—treated with great impressiveness under the happiest effects, and surmounted by the most splendid skies. It is curious that this master of landscape art began his career by painting portraits, but they were, in one sense, merely "pot-boilers," as our painter only looked upon them as subservient to landscape, his real love; and while he painted portraits for money, he worked away at landscapes till he had secured a fame and reputation in his cherished art.

He seems, from the account of those who knew him best, to have begun to draw from his earliest years, and he painted his first work in oil when only twelve years old. While quite a boy Linnell was articled to Varley, where one of his fellow pupils, his senior by seven years, was Mulready. The two became great friends, and Linnell probably learnt most of the technical part of his art from him. The lad also obtained an introduction to West, who treated him kindly, criticized his drawings, and even worked upon some of them, and advised him, as did Mulready also, to enter the Academy schools. He was admitted as a student in his thirteenth year, and not only carried off a silver medal for a drawing from the life in 1809, but in 1810 successfully competed with sculptor students and took a medal for the best modelling in bas-relief from the life model. Already in 1809 he had been awarded a prize of 50*l.* by the directors of the British Institution for his landscape "Removing Timber in Autumn," exhibited in their gallery. This delicious little painting, which remained in the artist's possession, is a curiously finished work for a boy of sixteen to produce, and it shows a thorough insight into the beauty of cast shadows upon grass. The figures are happily grouped, and the old, bare-headed man in the foreground is, we believe, a portrait of Mulready's father. As portraits were not admitted to the British Institution, Linnell sent his portraits and miniatures to the Academy exhibitions. His activity did not stop here, for not only did he paint many well-known people of the time, but he also engraved their likenesses in mezzotint. John Varley's "Burial of Saul" too was engraved by him, and various works of the old masters. He also, like Mulready and other artists of that day, gave lessons in drawing. One of his miniatures of three of his children playing with a kitten, with their abundant golden locks and rosy cheeks, dwells on the memory as a richly-jewelled bit of colour. His portraits though faithful and characteristic likenesses are less good as works of art. It is by his landscapes that Linnell's fame will live, and even in these there is sometimes a great difference in quality, for while we yield to none in admiration of his best work, we cannot close our eyes to the fact that there are pictures by his hand which fall below his reputation, where his usually fine colour becomes hot and unpleasant, his touch uneven, and his clouds woolly in texture.

Linnell lived for many years at Hampstead; he then built himself a house in Porchester Terrace, from which he retired in 1852 to the crest of the hill in Redstone Wood, near Redhill, in Surrey, where, environed by the scenery he loved, he continued to live for thirty years in a patriarchal manner, surrounded by his family, and with his sons settled in houses near him built on different parts of his property. Linnell was a devoted friend to William Blake, whose genius he recognized, when others could not see it. He was not only his friend but his patron, as he bought several of his works; and one of the pleasures of a visit to Linnell at Redhill, was the permission to have some of these interesting Blakes brought out for your delectation. Moreover Linnell preserved the features of his friend in an excellent portrait which was afterwards engraved as a frontispiece to Gilchrist's *Life of Blake.*

Linnell's method of work was to lay in his subject on a white ground in brown; this brown he allowed occasionally to appear through all the richness of his future colouring. He painted many of his pictures with a medium probably prepared from amber varnish, which has well stood the test of time. He seems to have made innumerable studies and sketches, but never to have painted his finished pictures directly from nature. Sometimes he found it unnecessary to draw the object he wanted to place in his picture; he looked at it well instead, or he watched an effect with the deepest attention, and his eye and mind were both so well trained, that he was able to reproduce exactly what he required. His studies from the antique and what Stephens in his biography in the *Art Journal* happily calls "the stringent influence on his mind of the Elgin marbles," together with the maxims of his master, Varley, led him to eschew a merely realistic copy of nature; he always desired to see her in a poetic mood. He replied to a lady who inquired of him in his studio from whence a landscape on his easel was taken, "Madam, I am not a topographer!" His pictures are thus entirely raised above the commonplace, and bear a distinctive character of their own, in which the mind of the great painter may be perceived inspiring the efforts of his hand. Linnell seldom worked for more than two hours consecutively at one subject, he then either changed his picture or engaged in some other occupation. In painting he sat at a good distance from his easel with his brush well held out at arm's length, and he laid on his touches with a firm and vigorous hand.

A collection of his works was shown in the Winter Exhibition of the Royal Academy in 1883, and here were gathered some of his finest pictures, "St. John Preaching in the Wilderness," "The Disobedient Prophet," "The Last Gleam before the Storm," "The Eve of the Deluge," "The Timber Waggon," "Barley Harvest," and many others, with portraits and miniatures, and above all a most interesting collection of sketches, some of which show his minute power of finishing to the smallest details when occasion required it. "The Last Gleam before the Storm" is perhaps one of our painter's noblest works. On the right a thinly-wooded slope, below which is a pool and near it a gipsy tent. There is a hill in the mid-distance, on which is a windmill. A boy drives cattle in the foreground, while a stormy sky above the whole scene is relieved by a gleam of sunshine on the left. The whole is instinct with the solemn shiver and hush of nature before the rain pours down.

Linnell never, we believe, visited the Continent, but gained his knowledge of the old masters from those of their works which he could see at home, and from engravings and copies. He was very friendly with the best painters of his day, and it is much to be regretted that he was never elected with others among his companions to the honours of the Royal Academy. His name was down for many years, but from some unaccountable reason he was passed over, and he then withdrew it, and would not allow it to be replaced, though much solicited to do so by a member when an alteration took place in the rules of electing associates. He thought he was entitled, as indeed he was, by his fame, to a *full* membership, but the rules of the Academy did not allow of his being offered this at once, and though the probation of the associateship would have been the shortest possible one, he was still bound to pass through it. Linnell was a Baptist by persuasion in early life, but afterwards found more sympathy with the Plymouth Brethren. He held his religious views very strongly, and fortified them by searching study of the Greek and Hebrew Scriptures. He published some pamphlets on

A A

polemical and theological subjects ; and could give in a discussion on religious topics a full reason for the belief that was in him. He held Popery and the Church of England in almost equal detestation. He was married the second time when already in advanced years. He died at Redstone, January 20th, 1882, and was buried in Reigate Cemetery.

Thomas Creswick, R.A., was a landscape painter who had a great appreciation of rural scenery and much taste in the arrangement and composition of his pictures. He was accustomed to paint only what may be called the eye of his pictures out of doors, and on the spot, and having done this and attacked what he considered the most valuable point of his work direct from nature, he would finish in the studio from sketches and from his own observation at other times. To secure exactly what he wanted he would brave cold and wet, and all other trials incident to painting in the open air. He had a true feeling for the elegance of foliage and for graceful passages of interest in a landscape, but his touch is inclined to mannerism, and there is a good deal of sameness in his work. His colour is apt to be rather cold and somewhat monotonous. This is most felt in his later works. This defect in colour was very visible in an exhibition of his works which took place in 1873, in the galleries of the International Exhibition, South Kensington, where they were hung with the collected works of John Phillip, R.A. Creswick was born in Sheffield, February 5th, 1811, and gained some knowledge of art in Birmingham. In 1828 he settled in London, and began at once to exhibit both at the British Institution and the Royal Academy. In 1842 the directors of the former gallery awarded him a prize premium of eighty guineas for the general merit of his works, and in the same year he became an associate of the Royal Academy. It was not till nine years later, in 1852, that he was elected a full member of the body.

Creswick especially delighted in painting water, in delineating lakes and brooks and streams crossed by picturesque bridges, or forded by quaint carts ; his water is always fresh and limpid and true. In the National Gallery there is a small picture by him, "The Pathway to the Village Church," a sunny, wooded landscape, and a fieldpath leading to the distant church, whose tower is seen peeping between the trees. The central object is a young girl, who is somewhat disproportionately tall, and who is about to cross a stile.

Creswick was an etcher of much merit, and also a designer on wood. His vignette illustrations are particularly full of taste. He lived many years in Linden Gardens, at that time called Linden Grove, in Bayswater, where he had built himself a house, and after a long failing in health he died there on the 28th December, 1869.

Frederick Lee, R.A., was an older man than Creswick by many years, and in his early pictures he took rank with some of the best landscape painters of his day. In those works which he painted direct from nature he was an artist of real merit, but the canvases which he worked on only in his studio, his more usual productions, were not pleasing. He entered the army as a young man, and retiring from it on account of ill health, became in 1818 a student of the Royal Academy. He was elected an associate in 1836, and became a full member in 1840. He spent most of his time latterly on board his yacht. He died at Viesch Bank Farm, Cape Colony, South Africa, in 1879, aged eighty-one. He was a great lover of the sea, and some of his best works are marine subjects; he had a peculiar faculty for depicting a wealth of beauty in natural landscape which gave a charm to his early pictures of Devonshire valleys and Cornish coasts. Lee painted many pictures in conjunction with S. Cooper, R.A.

A man who will leave a much more lasting impression upon the art of his time is *George Hemming Mason, A.R.A.,* whose works, while they have a truthfulness of feeling, characteristic of the life of rural England in its most straightforward simplicity, combine with it an idealism which renders them while perfectly true, yet perfectly idyllic. Painting the commons, fields, and country roads of our native country with their primitive peasant groups, he is yet able to appeal to the most poetical feeling of the mind; and his art has exquisite qualities of pastoral rest and beauty; his subjects a pathetic tenderness, a sense of sweetness and sadness, quite peculiar and original to himself. He was a man who throughout life struggled with bad health, and this almost seems as if it had evoked in his work a singular sentiment for a quiet kind of poetic beauty which a painter in rude health could perhaps not have produced.

Mason was born at Witley in Staffordshire in 1818, and was intended for the medical profession, but he was attracted to art, and went to study and to paint in Rome, in which place after travelling about for some time he settled and lived for several years. His first picture exhibited at the Academy was "Ploughing in the Campagna," in 1857. The next year he returned to England. His Roman pictures are powerful and rich in colour, depicting the brilliant effects of Italian light. He seems in them to delight in the clearness of a Roman atmosphere as much as in his English works he revels in the mists and vapours of our sea-girt land. Some of his best pictures are "Mist on the Moors," 1862, "The Unwilling Playmate," 1867, "The Evening Hymn," 1868, "Girls Dancing," 1871, "Crossing the Moor." His last picture was the fine "Harvest Moon" exhibited in the Royal Academy in 1872. About seventy works, many of these merely sketches, represent the whole of Mason's art, yet though it only depicts one side of nature, not its rugged

A A 2

grandeur or its rude power, it will always make a deep impression on those capable of appreciating the finer subtleties of art. His pictures have a very harmonious sense of keeping, and true originality of feeling. Mason lived for some years in Hammersmith, and died there 22nd October, 1872, from heart-disease, when only fifty-four years of age. His works were collected and exhibited the following year by the Burlington Fine Arts Club.

Three years after the death of Mason a still greater painter was carried to an early grave. It is very sad for a great genius to be taken away in the midst of his career, when under ordinary circumstances a noble future would be opening before him, and a prospect of delighting the world by further proofs of his striking originality might be confidently predicted. This was the sad case with *Frederick Walker, A.R.A.* He was born in Marylebone, in 1840, and began very early to show a great predilection for art. His first school was the British Museum, where he studied the antique, and at sixteen he was placed for more than a year with an architect named Baker. When he left him he studied at Leigh's evening classes, and soon after he entered the schools of the Royal Academy. Before this, though, he had begun to draw on wood, and to improve himself in this branch of art he placed himself with a wood engraver, and remained with him for three years, drawing three days in the week. This was probably, though a laborious training, yet an excellent way of becoming a practised draughtsman ; at any rate, it helped on Walker's original genius, by perfecting his eye and giving confidence to his hand. An introduction to Thackeray led to his illustrating that author's works in the *Cornhill Magazine.* Thackeray began by supplying Walker with rough sketches of his own, to show him how he wished his story illustrated, but he very soon allowed the young man to design and execute the illustrations himself, saying that Walker's ideal entirely pleased him.

The young painter also drew largely for several other periodicals, such as *Good Words, Once a Week,* &c. In 1869 he became an associate of "Old Water-Colours," and a full member two years later ; and, while still a member of this society, he was elected an associate of the Royal Academy in 1871, being the first painter to whom this had ever happened. Four years later he died at S. Fillan's, Perthshire, of consumption, June 5th, 1875, aged thirty-four. His father had died young, and it is probable that from him Walker had inherited the seeds of this fatal disease. He tried a winter in Algiers for the sake of his health, but as he came back to England to face a very cold spring, he found no real benefit to result from it. A cold caught in going down to Scotland hastened his end. He was buried at Cookham, on the Thames, a place which in life he had had a great love for ; and there, in the village church, his brother painters erected a tablet to his memory.

Walker's art is peculiar to himself both in method, drawing, colour, and execution. He was a most fastidious painter, and he always found it exceedingly difficult to please himself with his pictures; perhaps there is scarcely one of them which has not been often repainted before he considered it completed. He was not a very assiduous sketcher, for he had such a retentive memory that perhaps his sketches were taken more mentally than by hand. His figures are beautifully drawn, and combine a true feeling for rustic life with the grace of the antique. His colour is harmonious and subtle; he sees nature through a mood of his own, generally gentle and pathetic; yet he is able also to revel in her great effects, as, for instance, in the grand clouds and ruddy sunset in "The Plough," exhibited in 1870.

Ruskin, in a letter addressed to Marks, R.A., has rather unjustly accused Walker of being fond of *mud*-coloured skies, though he attributes this quality of subdued colouring, not to the fault of the young painter himself, but to the depressing effects of our present life, "the passionate folly and uninstructed confusion of modern English society." Notwithstanding this criticism, we feel that Walker's work, entirely apart from its powerful artistic merit, will be interesting in the future just because it illustrates so exactly the life of the time. Many of his subjects are taken from novels which depict the customs and habits of the day, and as such will be delightful to a future generation as characteristic of the date at which he lived. Perhaps his finest oil pictures are "The Bathers," "The Plough," 1870, "The Old Gate," 1869, and "The Harbour of Refuge," 1872. In the background of this latter picture is an old almshouse, with its grey creeper-clad walls and red roofs. The youthful mower with his scythe is in strong contrast to the creeping age of the almsmen, and yet, somehow, he reminds us pathetically of death, who will shortly mow down these old people. In this, as in all Walker's works, the figures form an integral part of the subject, and combine in rustic grace with the poetry of the landscape. "The Vagrants," 1868, is now in the National Gallery. It depicts a tender autumn evening sky, with a moorland landscape and a bushy foreground. A gipsy with her baby sits over a fire just kindled in the open-air, which a boy is feeding with dry brushwood. On the right stands a tall, handsome, melancholy gipsy woman watching the blaze; on the left a small girl shelters her little brother. The figures are very beautiful in their perfect keeping with the landscape background; the action of the boy is specially graceful. Walker took a gold medal for his water-colour paintings at the Paris Universal Exhibition of 1867. They are, as a rule, lovely harmonies of colour, delicate in tone and gradation, and exquisitely finished like the best miniature work. "The Fishmonger's Stall," "Philip in Church," and "The Chaplain's Daughter," are perhaps among his finest productions.

Cecil Lawson was another clever young landscape painter, whose premature death is much to be regretted. He was born at Wellington in Shropshire, in 1851, and learnt the rudiments of his art from his father; otherwise, he was mainly a self-taught painter. He died of an affection of the windpipe, combined with congestion of the lungs, when only thirty years of age, on the 11th June, 1882. He may be said to have risen to fame through the Grosvenor Gallery, for his pictures had been placed so high at the Academy exhibitions that they had attracted little notice. His work is founded on a great appreciation of, and the power of reproducing, without any servile copying, what other great landscape painters have achieved before him. His art has a poetic complexion, and seems to have made a short cut to what other men arrive at by slow degrees. He had one great merit—that he always strove to paint an effect rather than a scene. His colour is harmonious, rich, and deep, but his handling is inclined to be coarse. His two pictures first exhibited in the Grosvenor in 1875 were, "The Minister's Garden," and a "Pastoral in the Valley," but he had had a picture in the Academy Exhibition as early as 1869; and his "Hop Gardens of England," exhibited there in 1876, was very highly thought of. "The Wet Moon, Battersea," and "The Road to Monaco," by him, are both fine works. "The August Moon," presented to the National Gallery by his widow, depicts the moonlight flooding low-lying meadows in which cattle are standing. In the foreground are fir trees, not too happily grouped. The whole scene is wanting in delicate appreciation of the tender hues of moonlight, and is too evenly brown. The colour is so loaded, and the handling so coarse, that it interferes with the proper enjoyment of the spectator.

John W. Oakes, A.R.A., born 1820, died 1887, was another landscape painter, whose handling was crisp and refined, and his drawing good. As he usually worked entirely out of doors, his pictures give truthfully the relationship of light and shade and colour. He tries, notwithstanding his realism, to unite with these qualities a poetical effect.

CHAPTER XXX.

IDEAL LANDSCAPE.—MARTIN, DANBY, AND POOLE.

In our preceding chapters we have given some account of the contemporaries and successors of Turner, who were purely landscape painters, relying on natural scenery as influenced by storm and sunshine, by noonday or twilight, their figures being merely accessories to give life and interest to the scene; but Turner himself, in addition to his art as a landscape painter, depicting the scenery of the present age and of classic antiquity, of plain and mountain, of ocean and river, painted works wherein the scenery was subordinate to the subject, such as the pictures of "Ulysses Deriding Polyphemus," the "Jason," &c.

This chapter will treat of painters whose works are wholly of the latter class; who rarely painted realistic landscape, but occupied themselves largely with the poetical and ideal. Of such was John Martin, who studied nature not to realize her pastoral or rural aspects, but to embody for us, subjects derived from history and poetry, in which the landscape is made to sympathize with the story, and is equally necessary with the figures to the effect on the spectator.

John Martin was born in the North of England, at a house called Eastland Ends, Haydon Bridge, near Hexham, on the 19th July, 1789; as he reached the age when it was necessary to settle his future career in life, his taste and inclination were so decidedly towards art, that his father adopted a somewhat practical application of it, and determined to make the lad a herald-painter. The family having removed to Newcastle, he was apprenticed at the age of fourteen to one Wilson, a coach-builder of that town, and, with little inclination to the branch of art he was to pursue, continued to labour as an apprentice for twelve months. At that time, by the terms of his apprenticeship, he was to begin to receive a weekly payment for his work; but his master asserting that three months of the period had been passed as on trial, demurred to the payment, wishing to postpone it yet three months longer. Martin, who disliked his work, ran away from the workshop; his father approved the step, and supplied him with colours and materials to practise art. He had just begun to feel happy in his emancipation from trade drudgery, when he was brought before the alderman of the town as a runaway apprentice; but his answer to the charge, showing that his master had himself broken the contract, was upheld by the town authorities, and from the ability with which he conducted his case, his indentures were given up, and he was set free to follow the art he loved.

His father then placed him under the instruction of an Italian practising art in Newcastle—Bonifaccio Musso, the father of Charles Musso, or Muss, afterwards well known as an enamel and miniature painter. At the end of the year, Charles Muss, who had settled in London, and was gradually making his way, invited his father to town to reside with him, and asked Martin to accompany him. After a few months' delay, Martin, with the permission of his father, repaired to London, where he arrived in September, 1806. After some time he left Muss, and, as he tells us, worked hard during the day to support himself; while at night he diligently studied architecture and perspective, by the knowledge of which he was hereafter to achieve so much of the reputation he enjoyed. Muss had introduced Martin to Collins, a glass manufacturer, who resided at No. 106 in the Strand, and much of Martin's employment at this time consisted in painting in enamel colours on glass and china. At the age of nineteen, as the painter has himself recorded (although other authorities say twenty-two), Martin married, and he says that he had to use every available means for his support, teaching, painting small oil pictures, glass and enamel painting, water-colour painting, &c.

In 1811 we find him for the first time an exhibitor at the Royal Academy; his work is described as "Landscape, a composition;" and his residence, "Thanet Place, Temple Bar," shows that he was living near the scene of his daily labours. Speaking of his marriage, which, if it took place when he was nineteen, must have been in the year 1808 or 1809, the painter himself says, "It was now indeed necessary for me to work, and, as I was ambitious of fame, I determined on painting a large picture, and in 1812 produced my *first* work, 'Sadak in Search of the Waters of Oblivion,' which was executed in a month;" and he adds, "You may easily guess my anxiety when I heard the men who were to place it in the frame, disputing as to which was the top of the picture:" it was, however, to the inexpressible delight of himself and his wife, sold for fifty guineas, so that his first start in life was of good augury.

His next year's work was "Paradise, Adam's first sight of Eve," exhibited in 1813, and also sold, as was the "Clytie," exhibited in 1814. The "Paradise" was exhibited in the great room of the Royal Academy, but when, *the next* year, the "Clytie," and subsequently the "Joshua," were hung in the ante-room, he considered himself insulted by the place allotted to them. The "Joshua" was afterwards exhibited at the British Institution, and obtained one of their prizes of 100 guineas, but continued unsold for many years. A conversation with Allston, in which Martin wholly differed from that painter, led him to paint "Belshazzar's Feast." Leslie, he says, spent a morning in attempting to convince him that his treatment was wrong, but he persevered, and in 1821 completed his subject, and exhibited it at the British Institution; on this occasion he was rewarded with a prize of 200 guineas; the picture was considered a new mode of treating such subjects, and created a sensation among the general public.

Wilkie, writing to Sir G. Beaumont in 1821, says, "Martin's picture is a phenomenon. All that he has been attempting in his former pictures is here brought to maturity, and although weak in all those points in which he can be compared with other artists, he is eminently strong in what no other artist has attempted."

The painter made use in this picture of all the properties at his command—the hanging gardens—the tower of Babel—range upon range of massive columns, and terraces one above the other, are there, and made clever use of by the aid of perspective; the light which lights the impious feast is derived by the painter from the letters of light, the handwriting on the wall, which the prophet is explaining to the terrified king—the light, hot and fiery, is shed on the hurrying group of frightened revellers who are expressing their alarm in a somewhat melodramatic manner. The seven-branched candlestick from the holy place is over the throne of Belshazzar: but if the ornaments on the banqueting table are intended to represent the other sacred utensils of the temple, they are anything but oriental in their fashion, and might well have been lent for the painter's use by some of the great silversmiths of that day. The hot brown of the foreground is carried into the sky by the clouds of the rising storm, so that the hanging gardens and the monster tower, with all the range of impossible buildings and the mountains of structure, are of a hot, foxy hue. On the left the young moon is seen in the heavens. A better artist would have improved the picture by spreading its cool light through parts of the work, contrasting it with the supernatural illumination of the foreground, and bringing out from the dark solid masses tower and column, lighted as in nature by its beams. Martin, who was still connected with glass-painting, repeated the subject on a sheet of plate-glass. This was shown in the Strand, inserted in a wall, so that the light was really transmitted through the terrible handwriting; the effect was startling, yet it was surely allied more to the diorama than to fine art.

After the "Belshazzar's Feast," which many thought his best picture,

Martin continued to cover large canvases with poetical and scriptural subjects, such as "Adam and Eve entertaining the Angel Raphael," "The Deluge," "The Eve of the Deluge," "The Fall of Nineveh," "Pandemonium," &c. Many of these works were engraved, and as that art was peculiarly suited to display his pictures, the impressions had a large sale both at home and abroad, and greatly spread his reputation. Some of the plates he engraved himself, and complained before a Committee of the House of Commons of the injury that he, in common with other artists, sustained by the insufficient protection against piracy afforded to such works. Martin had an eye to other subjects besides art, subjects of public utility ; such, for instance, as the supply of pure water for the metropolis, which engaged the painter's attention in 1827, 1828, and 1829. In view of this, it is evident that he visited all the water sources of the surrounding country ; we fear that it never advanced his pecuniary interests, but to these visits must be attributed many of the very clever studies in water-colours of the valleys of the Thames, the Brent, the Wandle, the Wey, the Tillingbourne, as also from many of the hills and eminences within a circle of twenty or thirty miles. Though nature in these works is treated with the peculiar manner he has adopted, there is in many of them a poetry that elevates them out of the region of commonplace.

He was yet labouring assiduously at his art, with large pictures in various stages of progress on his easel, when, on the 12th of November, 1853, while at work on a picture, he was struck with paralysis, which rendered him speechless and deprived him of the use of his right hand. From the first there was no prospect of his recovery ; but he lingered on, and was taken to the Isle of Man in hopes of some improvement. He seemed, however, to have entertained an idea that abstinence was a remedy for his complaint, and to have resisted taking sufficient food ; so that he sank rapidly, and died on the 17th of February, 1854.

We can hardly agree with Bulwer, who said that Martin was "more original, more self-dependent than Raphael or Michael Angelo ;" but if, in his lifetime, Martin was overpraised, he was certainly unjustly depreciated afterwards. Many, both of his brother artists and the public, when the first astonishment his pictures created had passed away, called his art a trick and an illusion, his execution mechanical, his colouring bad, the figures he introduced vilely drawn, their action and expression bombastic and ridiculous. But granting this wholly or partially, it must also be remembered that his art was thoroughly original, and opened up a new view, which, in his hands, yielded glimpses of the sublime, dreams, and visions the art had not hitherto displayed, and that others, better prepared by previous study, working *after* him, have delighted, and are still delighting, the world with their works.

The repetition of quantities in the architectural structures he loved to introduce, was one of the great elements of the grandeur, space, and magnitude of his scenes; but applied to figures, it was less appropriate and less successful. Even the details of his architecture, too often repeated, occasioned the remark that his pictures were done by recipe; and St. John Long, who, before he took to curing consumption, was in search of some wonder to advertise himself, was led to ask Martin if he would "sell him his secret." It was even said at the time that these multiplied forms were done by stamp and stencil.

In his colouring, Martin was not successful; gay colours, and want of tone and harmony, he never overcame, and there was somewhat of a sense of the china-painter to the last. A straining after startling effects by wrong opposition of colours, by extreme opposition of light and dark, and by forced and contorted action of the figures introduced, was but too apparent in all he did. His earlier pictures have sadly failed from the faulty pigments and vehicles used; but in this he is no worse than the greater number of his contemporaries.

One of the Martins, in conversation with a great statesmen of the past on whom he had forced himself, said, "There are four brothers of us,—one is a soldier; one is a painter, that is my brother John; one is a philosopher, that is myself; and one is a church reformer, that is my brother Jonathan:" the same whose first act of church reform was the burning of York Minster. Martin's desire to reform the Academy, certainly was not to burn them out, but to turn them out. It is satisfactory, however, to see by his evidence, before a committee of inquiry, that he was on terms of friendship with, and admired many individual members, if he disliked them as a body.

Francis Danby, *A.R.A.*, was another of the disappointed sons of genius. He was one of twin brothers, born near Wexford, on the 16th of November, 1793. His father, James Danby, was a farmer and small proprietor of that neighbourhood. About the time young Danby arrived at an age to prepare himself for the active duties of life, his father, who had removed to Dublin with his family, died. Francis Danby had been placed in the drawing classes of the Royal Dublin Society, and showed such a desire to follow art as a profession that his mother was induced to consent. He afterwards studied under O'Connor, a landscape painter whose works have hardly been sufficiently appreciated. They have a certain massive and somewhat melancholy character, that may have influenced his pupil in the choice of the peculiar phase of landscape art which he adopted, and in which he was, during his lifetime, without a rival. Thus Danby's first work, publicly exhibited in Dublin in 1812, was a "Landscape—Evening." The bias had already been given towards that period of the day when breadth of effect and colour predominate, and the mystery of gloom and twilight divests even the most homely scene of its commonplace, and clothes the tamest forms with grandeur and ideality.

After painting some time with O'Connor, master and scholar managed between them to make up a purse to enable them to visit London, and to see for themselves the state of art in the capital. If Danby was an exhibitor in 1817, this journey most probably took place in 1816. It is related of them that they soon exhausted their means, and finding themselves almost penniless, they started on foot to Bristol, hoping to make their way back from that port to Dublin. When, however, they reached Bristol, they had difficulty, on the first night of their arrival, in paying for their night's lodging. In the morning Danby set to work, and made three drawings, which he carried for sale to a fancy stationer on College Green, and was fortunate in selling them for seven shillings each. By similar exertions he was soon enabled to provide a passage for his friend O'Connor back to Ireland. Danby, struck with what he had seen in London, and with a desire to enter the lists where he had such powerful competitors to stimulate his exertions, determined to remain in England. We know from the pictures he exhibited in the Royal Academy that he stayed some time in Bristol. In 1817, we find a picture, "A View in Scotland," exhibited at Somerset House, by G. Danby, of Clifton, and there is every reason to suppose that the initial of the christian name is a misprint, and that the picture in question was really by Francis Danby.

It is usual for his biographers to refer to "The Disappointed Love," which was exhibited in 1821, as his first picture. But the first really important picture—if, as we have surmised, it was not the second—was "The Upas, or Poison Tree of the Island of Java." (It is on a large canvas, 5 ft. 6 in. by 7 ft. 6 in., and was exhibited at the British Institution in 1820). This fabulous tree was said to grow on the Island of Java, in the midst of a desert formed by its own pestiferous exhalations. These destroyed all vegetable life in the immediate neighbourhood of the tree, and all animal life that approached it. Its poison was considered precious, and was to be obtained by piercing the bark, when it flowed forth from the wound. So hopeless, however, and so perilous was the endeavour to obtain it, that only criminals sentenced to death could be induced to make the attempt, and as numbers of them perished, the place became a valley of the shadow of death, a charnel-field of bones. To succeed in such a subject required a poetical mind, joined to powers of the highest order: no mere landscape painting, no mere imitation of nature, would suffice to picture to us the gloomy horrors of this land of fear. Danby's interesting picture represents a deep chasm in a valley of dark slaty rocks, into which the pale light of the hidden moon only partially penetrates. Above the black crest of the gorge is a space of star-lit sky, with the pointed summits of a mountain range stretching away into the distance. The sides of the cleft are rugged, full of rifts and seams, and wholly bare. Vegetation there is none, but the solitary Upas growing out of the thin soil at the bottom of the valley. The whole rests in the silence of death, broken only by the dripping of a little fall of water from the gloomy rocks. The poison-seeker is in the foreground, about half-way down into the cavernous pit, and has just arrived within view of the tree and within the influence of the pestiferous vapour. He turns sickening from the sight: for at his feet are the bodies of several of his latest predecessors, while around the fearful tree the ground is white with the dry-bleached bones of multitudes who have gone before him, and perished at the moment they had reached the goal. Animals there are none, instinct has warned them from the fatal spot; but a vulture, flying over the chasm, has fallen with extended wings almost at the feet of the fainting poison-seeker. The story has been vividly told, and yet the horrors do not painfully obtrude. It is a wonderful first attempt, and shows the original poetry of Danby's mind.

In 1821, Danby, then living at Kingsdown Place, Bristol, exhibited "Disappointed Love," now in the Sheepshanks collection. This also serves to show how from the first the painter had a higher aim than mere landscape painting; he sought indeed to treat his picture as a poem, and to give ideal interest to his works. The full effect of the work is marred by the want of beauty in the girl who is going to drown herself.

In 1824 Danby exhibited his "Sunset at Sea after a Storm." Forty years have passed since we saw this picture, yet we could almost describe from memory the lurid red of the setting sun, the broken waves of the subsiding storm, the few survivors of the wreck, alone on a raft on the limitless ocean; perhaps if we saw it now we might think it less impressive than its memory, yet it was a work that made the painter's reputation. Lawrence, the president, purchased it, it is said, at a much higher sum than the painter's price, and the world of artists and the outer world of art-lovers were so struck with it, that in the next year, when he followed up his success by a still greater effort, "The Delivery of Israel out of Egypt, and Host of Pharaoh overwhelmed in the Red Sea," the Academy elected him an associate of their body, and the road to wealth and fame seemed to lie open before him.

The road to fame seemed open before him. Why, then, was he disappointed? why was Danby never elected to the full membership of the Academy? It is a story ill to tell, with faults, and no doubt recriminations, which the grave has partly closed over, and which we will not venture to re-open; suffice it to say, most emphatically, it was not for want of a sense of the great merit of the painter : not that his art was unappreciated by his brother members ; hardly even that he made a false step involving the council of that day in many annoyances, and bringing disgrace on art ; since this might have been overlooked as time dimmed its recollection, had not Danby defended the fault to the last rather than regretted it.

It has been said that in "The Delivery of Israel out of Egypt," and in pictures of that class, Danby was but an imitator of Martin ; and certainly it is true that the multitude of figures, and the vastness of the scene, have some of the characteristics of that master. But the grand ideality of his treatment was truly Danby's own, and was kindred to the feeling which had already produced "The Upas-tree," the "Sunset at Sea," and "Disappointed Love ; " and was afterwards to inspire the "Solitude," the "Enchanted Island," "The Spring," and numerous other works that have little in common with those of Martin, except that they are ideal landscapes. Even in this "Passage of the Red Sea" there is far more of colour, far more of terrible grandeur, and less of the tricky and mechanical qualities of art than in Martin. Danby drew the figure better, had far more feeling for form, and we find little of the over-strained theatrical action which is so frequent in the figures of Martin. Of course, in subjects like this by either painter where multitudes of figures have to be introduced, and the impression has to be made by numbers, rather than by passion and by individual expression, the grandeur and solemnity of the general effect has to be relied on. In this we feel that Danby was far more of an artist than Martin. The effect in the above picture is wonderfully attained ; the pillar of fire looks like a real lambent flame, putting out the dim crimson sunset, lighting up the massive clouds and the rising storm that is to dash the waves of the Red Sea over the hosts of Pharaoh.

The rupture between Danby and the Academy was one of the causes which made him leave England for the Continent in 1829. During the next eleven years he resided principally in Switzerland, boat-building, yachting on the Lake of Geneva, making studies and drawings, and painting some few works on commission. It is understood, also, that he visited Norway ; but of this period and its labours we have little knowledge. About 1841 Danby returned to London, residing for a time in its immediate neighbourhood. He again renewed his contributions to the exhibitions, both at Trafalgar Square and Pall Mall ; and his pictures exhibit the same characteristic style, the same power, and the same poetic feeling. Among the best works of this latter period are, "The Grave of the Excommunicated," 1846 ; "The Evening Gun," 1848 ; and "A Wild Seashore," 1853. Such works quite upheld Danby's former reputation, although occasionally his pictures were fatiguing in execution, and the intention not always realized. In 1847, he retired to Shell House, near Exmouth, to enjoy the neighbourhood of the sea and the rich foliage of Devonshire. His early error had separated him from his brother artists, whom he rarely saw except on varnishing days; and he remained apart from them until his death, which took place at Exmouth, the 9th of February, 1861.

Whatever were his failings as a man, as an artist Danby should take high rank. His pictures are true poetry as compared with the prose— noble prose it may be—of many who have great reputation as landscape painters. The very list of his works shows the imaginative aim of all his labours. Of forty-six pictures, mostly landscape in their general character, registered in the Academy catalogues between 1817 and 1861, there are only three whose titles bear any relation to actual scenery; and of the large number exhibited during the same interval at the Institution, only one is a view.

Danby's art was totally opposed to that of the realistic school. He was not one to sit down to imitate nature leaf by leaf, to photograph her maze of branches, to count the myriad blades of grass, or the wildflowers she strews with so lavish a hand. His effort was rather to combine the large general truths of nature—her grandest, saddest aspects, with the imaginative and ideal creations of poetry.

Paul Falconer Poole, R.A., can scarcely be held to be a painter of ideal landscape, for his figures are always so prominent that he should perhaps by rights have found a place with the subject painters of his day; nevertheless we have mentioned him here on account of the intense ideal interest of his landscape art, and the subtle power he shows of amalgamating its poetical effect with the figures of his work. He is scarcely to be judged from an ordinary standpoint of art, for he owed nothing to the training of academies or schools of art; he is deficient in power of drawing, careless in modelling, and demonstrates sometimes a singular neglect of the very elements of the technicalities of painting; yet perhaps there are few painters whose works show such a delightful combination of art and poetry, such originality of conception, and such a strong feeling for colour and chiaroscuro as Poole.

He has a dramatic instinct for the terrible, and enforces it upon the beholder with a singular power, and such strength, that even a person ignorant of the title or subject of the work cannot fail to be impressed; on the other hand some of his pictures, though supreme bits of tragedy, are without anything terrible, and are stately in the quietness of their pathos.

Poole was born in Bristol in 1810, and was entirely self-taught in art. The first picture which he exhibited at the Academy was "The Well," 1830. This was a scene at Naples, and as he had not been abroad at that time, he must have composed it from sketches or prints. For seven years after this date his name does not re-appear in the Academy catalogue, but in 1838 he contributed "The Emigrant's Departure," and in 1840 "Hermann and Dorothea."

His earlier works, of which there are but few examples, were simply landscapes with figures, and, though they are refined in colour, they are apt to be a little weak and confused in character. Perhaps the first picture of his which attracted considerable attention was "Solomon Eagle Exhorting the People to Repentance during the Plague of London," exhibited in 1843. The subject is taken from Defoe's *History of the Plague*, and depicts the wild enthusiast almost stark naked, calling down judgment upon the stricken city, the pan of burning charcoal upon his head throwing a lurid light around. This picture was followed in 1844 by "The Beleaguered Moors," and in 1846 by "The Visitation of Syon Nunnery," in which year he became an associate of the Royal Academy. Poole was never a very prolific painter, his pictures being the outcome of much thought and conscientious endeavour. He entered into the competition for historical designs exhibited in Westminster Hall, and gained a second prize of 300*l.* for his large painting of "Edward III.'s Generosity to the People of Calais," which is not at all so unsuited, as one would naturally imagine it might be, for the decoration of the Houses of Parliament.

He was elected a full member of the Royal Academy in 1861. Among his later works may be mentioned "Philomena's Song by the Beautiful Lake," from the *Decameron*, a most delightful and romantic idyll, "The Escape of Glaucus and Ione," "A Midsummer Night"—a lovely effect of moonlight upon the water, and "The Last Scene in *Lear*," now in the South Kensington Museum, &c.

Poole and Danby both lived in Bristol, and were at one time a good deal together, and though they both paint an ideal subject, their inspirations are not in the least alike. Nearly the last of Poole's pictures was "Ezekiel's Vision," which by the bequest of the painter has become the property of the National Gallery. It is unfortunately not a good specimen of his powers; the figures are small and indifferently grouped, and the execution is feeble. In 1878 Poole was elected a member of the Institute of Painters in Water-Colours, and the next year he died at Hampstead on September 22nd, 1879, aged seventy-three.

CHAPTER XXXI.

ROBERTS, NASMYTH, BONINGTON, MÜLLER, AND LEWIS.

It is not intended to include in our work every painter who has produced meritorious pictures. Many have taken good rank in art whose
works are a delight and a pleasure, yet possess no marked character of
their own. It is only those who have enlarged the scope of British art
by the originality of their manner, their choice of subject or novelty of
execution, that claim a particular notice at our hands. Such a one was
David Roberts, R.A., whose works we are about to review. He was
born at Stockbridge, near Edinburgh, on the 24th October, 1796. His
parents, though in a humble sphere of life, gave him, as is usual with
his countrymen, an education beyond that which would have been the
lot of a youth of the same class in England. Before the usual age he
was apprenticed to a well-known decorator and house painter in Edinburgh, whom he served for seven years, learning all the trade processes
—the rapid execution of the decorator, and the mere mechanical
appliances which shorten labour. This gave him great readiness of
hand, as well as a simple and somewhat matter-of-fact mode of using
his pigments, which he retained during life.

By an innate feeling for art, Roberts was easily led to apply his trade-
knowledge to something beyond house-painting, for we learn that he
had tried scene-painting, and perhaps with the varied practice of his
'prentice training, completed before he was nineteen, he was better prepared for the branch of art he adopted, than half the artists of his age,
when schools of design were unknown in England and schools of art
gave little instruction in the use of the brush and the palette. It is true
that Roberts entered as a student at the Trustees' Academy, when
Andrew Wilson was at its head—a master under whom many of the
Scotch artists who afterwards attained eminence were formed—but
Roberts was either satisfied with what he knew and preferred his own

methods, or he found it necessary to seek employment for his maintenance. He remained in the school only one week.

He was engaged in 1820 in scene-painting at the Glasgow and Edinburgh Theatres. In 1822 he found employment in the scene-room at Drury Lane Theatre. For this art his great rapidity of execution peculiarly fitted him, but scene-painting did not satisfy him; he aimed at distinction as a painter in oil. He had, in 1820 and the following year, sent pictures to the Edinburgh exhibition; and in 1824 his works first appear on the walls of a London exhibition. He joined the Society of British Artists in Suffolk Street, of which he was one of the foundation members, and at first contributed more pictures to their annual exhibitions than to any other. In fact he became the first president in 1831. We find that he sent to their first exhibition three small views, "Dryburgh Abbey," and "The East Front" and "South Transept of Melrose Abbey." In 1824 he strayed to France and visited the coast towns of Dieppe, Havre and Rouen, in pursuit of a class of art the scenic picturesqueness of which had already possessed him. In the year 1826 Roberts exhibited his first work at the Royal Academy, "A View of Rouen Cathedral," having been attracted by the greater distinction which the exhibitions at the Royal Academy afforded.

He was now advancing in art, and his interests led him to seek admission to that body, of which he was elected an associate in 1838, and an academician in 1841. He had already, in the pursuit of his art, travelled in France, Belgium, Germany, Spain, Morocco, and Holland. Then seeking novelty in more distant lands, in the autumn of 1838 he started for Egypt and Syria, and for the ten following years his works, with only an occasional return to his former subjects, were Eastern. He was now at the height of his reputation, and producing his best pictures. Among them, in 1840, "The Greek Church of the Holy Nativity at Bethlehem;" "The Statues of the Vocal Memnon on the Plain of Thebes—Sunrise." In 1841, "Jerusalem, from the Mount of Olives, with the return of the Pilgrims." In 1843, "Ruins of the Island of Philoe, Nubia;" "Gateway of the Great Temple, Baalbec." In 1849, "The Destruction of Jerusalem by the Romans."

In 1851 he visited Italy for the first time, returning by the way of Vienna, and from that year to 1860 his themes were Italian; the decaying grandeurs of Rome, Venice, Pisa, and Milan were the inspirations of his pencil. Then as age crept on and the desire of travel was satiated, he found his subjects nearer home, and began a series of pictures of "London from the River Thames." This was a fine theme, and well suited to his pencil. It was commenced at a time when the banks of the river afforded the most picturesque combinations; these, if they are now rapidly disappearing, to give place to the nobler works of the architect, yet have cherished associations in connection with our great city, which we rejoice to see preserved in the works of such a painter. He had completed several and was painting on another of the series on the morning of the 25th November, 1864; towards the afternoon of that day he left his home apparently in perfect health, but was seized with an apoplectic attack in the street, was brought home speechless and unconscious, and died the same evening.

Roberts's choice of subject, its picturesque treatment, and the characteristic groups with which his pictures were filled, eminently fitted his art for publication. In 1837 he published, in lithography, his *Picturesque Sketches in Spain;* and in 1842 commenced his well-known work, *Roberts's Sketches in the Holy Land and Syria,* which was completed in 1849. In 1859, he published *Italy, Classical, Historical, and Picturesque.* These had an extensive sale; and from them and from his paintings, the artist realized a considerable fortune.

It is hardly correct to call Roberts a landscape painter, in the sense in which we should apply the term to Turner or Constable. The art as practised by Roberts was essentially scenic; his pictures almost always consist of buildings, towns or ruined cities: of exteriors or interiors of palaces, cathedrals, or temples; these he treated less with a view to those atmospheric effects which are the delight of the true landscape painter, than with the desire to give us an idea of the splendour and magnificence of his structures, by simplicity and largeness of parts, by breadth of daylight, and by enriching his subjects with groups of accessories. His early labours for the theatres formed his style, and he clung to it through life; or, might we not rather say, that his art was naturally fitted for the subjects on which he began to exercise it? He had no sympathy with the imitative or realistic school; in all the hundreds of sketches by his hand, there is not one that indicates an attempt at individualized realization. Broad, simple and very conventional, with the details suggested rather than given, his pictures charm us by their onceness, their direct appeal to the eye, and the extreme ease with which they are executed. The colour is agreeable, though not like nature, but generalized to what he thought best suited for the scenic display of the class of subjects he loved to paint; so that whether his buildings are on the banks of the Clyde or the Thames, the Nile or the Tiber, there is a sameness of tint and hue pervading them which is quite independent of the dingy tones of our own city, the damps of Venice, or the clear sharpness of the dry atmosphere of the East. His conduct of his picture was very simple, it being little more than an enlarged sketch. He saw his subject complete from the commencement—the quantities and masses —even the general effect of the figures which were to enrich it, being laid in with the dead colouring. On the clean canvas he drew very carefully with his pencil all the lines and forms of his work, using the ruler as freely as an architect would; such ornamental details as he intended to admit were also boldly sketched, as were the figures, both near and distant; the perspective of his work being most fully and carefully considered. Over this pencil outline the general masses of local colour and shadow were laid in with a full pencil and a facile hand, rather negative in tint than otherwise; the general light, shade and colour of the groups of figures being laid in at the same time.

It is to be observed that, consisting as his pictures generally do, of large masses of cool stone colour, the figures form an important part of the composition; enabling the painter to introduce strong contrasts of light, dark, and colour to give life and animation to the work, and to draw the eye at once to the principal object—the altar, the tomb, or monument, which forms the point of the picture. Up to his intention he drew figures easily and well, and had a picturesque eye to groups and processions of priests or soldiery; though it must be confessed that they remind us somewhat of stage supernumeraries, and green-room properties. His first painting when completed, showed much of the firm pencilling with which he outlined his work, still remaining; in the second, the masses are again gone over with semi-solid tints to break them up, to enrich them, and to bring the parts together; the details and ornamental parts are touched cleanly, and the forms defined, sometimes by the use of the end of the brush-stick, drawing firm lines of light in the wet colour. The drawing of the figures completed, and the colours and draperies enriched, then a few slight after-glazings and touches to heighten the lights completed the picture.

Roberts's manner throughout his career varied but little. Latterly he no doubt obtained greater facility, and learned exactly how little would suffice for the expression of his work, how much he might afford to leave out. In his art and his method of painting he was like Canaletti; in the choice of architecture and buildings as the subjects of his pencil; in his love of a firm, decided outline and the use of the ruler; in precision of hand, and the ready way in which he touched in his accessories; and the scenic groups of figures, &c., with which he animated his pictures. He was less precise than the Venetian, less minute in his details, but also less conventional.

The art of *Patrick Nasmyth* is a complete contrast to that of his countryman Roberts, being chiefly remarkable for its homely imitative truth, and the absence of all accident or effect. His father, Alexander Nasmyth, was a pupil of Allan Ramsay, and became a landscape painter of much merit. He was born in 1758, and settled in the Scotch capital, where he died in 1840. Young Patrick was born in Edinburgh in 1786, and early showed a great love of nature; playing truant from school to idle in the sunny fields, and to sketch, or attempt to sketch, the scenery of that beautiful neighbourhood. As he had little aptitude for learning, and paid little attention to his books, he was gradually allowed to take his own course, and to follow his disposition for art. His father no doubt helped his studies, and seems indeed to have made all his children love and follow art. Young Nasmyth came to London at the age of twenty, where his talents were soon appreciated and his works found ready purchasers. In 1812 we find him for the first time exhibiting at the Royal Academy "A View of Loch Katrine in Perthshire;" but it is by more simple and rustic scenery that he is generally known, and his best landscapes are essentially English.

In early life an injury to his right hand obliged him to learn to use his left in painting, and when about seventeen years of age, having had the misfortune to sleep in a damp bed, it brought on an illness which resulted in deafness, by which, and by his want of taste for literature, he was shut out from many sources of enjoyment; and in his solitude he early addicted himself to habits of excess, indulged in with low company. We are not told where he obtained his knowledge of Dutch art, but his works show that he founded himself on that school, and imitated the execution, while he adopted the class of subjects of Hobbema and Wynants; delighting in lane scenes, hedgerows, the skirts of commons, and village suburbs, and choosing the dwarf oak with its contorted limbs and scrubby foliage, in preference to other trees. He is said latterly to have painted to live rather than lived to paint, working from necessity and to supply his actual wants; yet he painted to the last, and his last illness arose from an attack of influenza caught in sketching, which his frame, enfeebled by his bad habits, was not able to resist. He died at Lambeth on the 17th of August, 1831, during a thunderstorm, which, at his own request, he was raised in bed to contemplate. He was buried in St. Mary's Church.

His art was popular at first, from its likeness to the Dutch school, then in high favour with art patrons. This school had some small tendency to lead our young painters to a closer imitation of nature; but with all its excellences, and it has many, it has little originality. Nasmyth's manner is rather mean, his foliage over-detailed, and his work somewhat black in the shadows, but the execution is solid and satisfactory, and his paintings stand well; painting in rather a low tone, his skies look fresh and brilliant, but they show the simplest effects of cloud and daylight. No tendency to poetry or invention is found in his works; but he wisely confined himself to painting that in which his strength lay.

The genius of *Richard Parkes Bonington* inclined him to the same class of art as Roberts, and would probably, had he lived, have led him to higher excellence. He was born at Arnold, a village near Nottingham, on the 25th October, 1801. His grandfather was the governor of the county gaol at Nottingham, and on his death he was succeeded by his son, the father of the painter; who seems to have been one of that unhappy class born to be the torment of others. He soon lost his appointment in the gaol, and then, with what previous acquirements we know not, attempted to earn a living as a portrait painter; he also published some prints of little merit in coloured aquatint. His wife meanwhile kept a school.

Under such influences the young painter was passing his boyhood. His first inclinations were divided between art and the drama, and his future career for a time hung in the balance, when his father's imprudence, love of low company and violent political opinions, broke up his wife's school, which was probably the mainstay of the family, and they fled to France and made their way to Paris. Young Bonington was then fifteen years of age; he gained permission to study in the Louvre, and began most diligently to improve himself in art as his profession. He made rapid progress; though we know little of him in his student days. He became a pupil at the Institute, drew in the *atelier* of Baron Gros, and gained a gold medal in Paris for one of his marine views. About the year 1822 he went to Italy, and we have some fine subjects by him, which have the true impress of that glowing land.

He was rising into reputation in Paris; his works both in oil and water-colours, were sought after and commanded large prices. He was even claimed by the French artists as belonging to their school, in which he had surely developed his genius, while he was unknown in his own country. In 1826 some longing desire of fame among the artists of his own land, induced him to send for exhibition to the British Institution two views on the French coast, and their high merit received the most cordial recognition. Gratified by this, he sent in 1827 and 1828 four pictures to the Royal Academy. He had now attained a reputation in both capitals; his genius attracted commissions which overwhelmed him. Sketching imprudently in the sun in Paris, brought on brain fever, and subsequent severe illness. He came to London for advice, but was seized by rapid consumption, which terminated his life on the 23rd April, 1828. He was buried in a vault at St. James's Church, Pentonville. We are indebted to a writer in *Arnold's Library of the Fine Arts* for these facts; but some other accounts say that Bonington died in Paris, which we think improbable, as he certainly came here for advice, and was buried in London.

Bonington's works were specially marked by originality. He was a master of the figure, which he painted with much grace. He succeeded equally in his marine and coast scenes, and his picturesque architecture of the Italian cities. His drawing in these various classes was characteristic; his light and shade powerful, his colour rich and pleasing. His works differed from those of his countrymen mostly from the simple breadth of the masses, both of light and of shadow, and from his appreciation of the change which shadow induces on the local colour ; the handling and execution is very broad and flat, and presents a happy union of the best qualities of the French and English schools : it is curious that the only marked impression made on the French school by English art has been through two landscape painters, Bonington and Constable. It is difficult to say to which particular class of art Bonington might have devoted himself had he lived. His genius promised success in all. His appearance was that of a man of genius. We are told that he was affectionate and generous, with a countenance bearing an expression of melancholy thought.

We must include in this chapter *William J. Müller*, whose art possessed much in character with that of both Roberts and Bonington. His father was a German, who settled at Bristol, was curator of the museum there, and was known as the publisher of some works of a scientific character. In this city the painter-son was born in 1812. From his birth he had the character of a genius. He early showed a taste for botany and natural history, and was an apt scholar ; but his strongest inclination was to drawing. He received some instruction from J. B. Pyne, a fellow-townsman; but self-reliant, he soon left him, and began to study from nature alone.

In 1833-34, he visited, for his improvement, Germany, Switzerland and Italy, and then returning to Bristol, resumed his profession there, and worked for some time without much encouragement. In 1836, he exhibited for the first time in London, sending to the Academy, "Peasants on the Banks of the Rhine, Waiting for the Ferry Boat," and to the Society of British Artists, "Venice," and "Hoar Frost— Autumn Scene near Monmouth." He exhibited for the next three years with the British Artists alone. In 1838, probably induced by the example of Roberts, he visited Greece and then Egypt, and, with his sketch-book stored with rich material, he returned again to Bristol. He made but a short stay, however, in his native city, for about the end of 1839, he had settled himself in London. Here he soon found purchasers for his works, which he was able to finish with great rapidity, realizing the fruits of his travels. He appears again as an exhibitor in 1840, at the Royal Academy; in the following year he sent to the Academy his "Slave Market, Egypt," and "The Sphynx ;" and also published his *Picturesque Sketches of the Age of Francis the First.*

Soon after Government projected the Expedition to Lycia. This he solicited and obtained permission to accompany, and that he might be at full liberty to follow his own art he defrayed his own expenses;

making the voyage from his own resources. He found abundant materials peculiarly suited to his art, and on his return home he painted "A Turkish Burial Ground," and a "Zanthian Tent Scene," both highly meritorious works. But he complained that he was not appreciated; that his paintings were badly hung at the British Institution, and that he fared no better at the Royal Academy. He returned to Bristol dispirited and unwell, and was advised that his heart was diseased. His merits were acknowledged; he had many commissions to execute, but he was unable to work. His disorder gained ground; he was weakened by repeated attacks of bleeding from the nose, and though he continued to paint occasionally, his health gradually succumbed, and he died at Bristol on the 8th of September, 1845, in which year he sent more works than in any other to the Royal Academy.

Müller had a large and simple manner of his own, with a somewhat glittering feeling for colour, without a full sense of space, keeping, or distance. "The Baggage Waggon," which is one of his best works, is fine in composition, and sparkling in colour; the figures are appropriate, and lead the eye well into the picture; but the various distances seem a little too much cut out, and have not those refinements of space which belong to our best landscape painters, and of which in the works of Turner, Müller must have had so many examples before his eyes. His pictures of Eastern scenery are truthful, and carry us away to other climes: his "Rhodes" has a truly Eastern look, and if a little too white, is broad and luminous, and a work that could hardly have been painted, had not the painter studied on the spot the peculiar aspects of nature in the Mediterranean isles.

John Frederick Lewis, R.A., is another painter of Eastern scenes whose work may appropriately be commented on here. His pictures have a richness of colouring and a brilliant perfection of completeness which seem almost peculiar to himself; his drawing is so exceedingly accurate, and his manual dexterity is so great, that he is able to combine the utmost finish without oppressing you with any sense of the labour of execution. In the modern French school, where his branch of art is more pursued than in our own, there is scarcely a painter who can rival Lewis's work in beauty of colour or in exquisite dexterity of handling. John Lewis was the eldest son of Lewis the engraver, and was born in the same house as Sir Edwin Landseer, 14th July, 1805, and was thus Landseer's junior by three years. Like Landseer he was devoted to animals, and when quite a child began to draw them with great accuracy. There is an anecdote of him that having played truant from his school in order to go out sketching, his master, taking a walk with some friends, found the little boy the same afternoon busily engaged, sitting under a hedge, drawing a cow, when he was so pleased with his pupil's performance that he presented the small truant with sixpence notwithstanding his delinquency.

Lewis used to accompany Landseer to the menagerie of Exeter Change to sketch the lions which were at that time kept there; and when one of these animals happened to die, he and Landseer bought it, and preserved it so long for purposes of drawing and dissection that at last their neighbours, whose artistic sense was less developed perhaps than their olfactory one, were forced to complain.

Lewis was intended for an engraver, and actually studied under his father, who only allowed him to paint one day in the week; but having at a very early age—about fifteen—sent a picture to the British Institution, which was well placed, his father withdrew his objection and allowed him to become a painter. His first efforts were devoted to animal painting, and by these works, when still quite young, he realized a very sufficient income.

There is a very early picture by him in the royal collection—the portrait of "Old Clark of the Sandpit Gate"—in which deer are introduced; and in the year 1821 he exhibited in the Royal Academy "Puppies : a Study from Nature." In 1825 he published a collection of etchings. Ruskin speaks very highly both of his power of drawing animals and of his water-colour painting. He says: "I believe John Lewis to have done more entire justice to his powers (and they are magnificent) than any man among us."

An accident turned Lewis from working in oil to the practice of water-colour painting. Being asked to do some illustrations to Shakspeare, he became fascinated with the ease and with the simplicity of the tools required for working in water-colours, and was very soon so successful that he was elected an associate of the Society of Painters in Water-Colours in 1828, in which year he contributed an important picture, "Highland Hospitality." In 1835 he went both to Spain and Italy in the pursuit of his art, and remained away two years. His visit produced a series of water-colour paintings, in a large and bold manner, rich in colour, and varied in character. The picturesque Spanish costume and the incidents of the Civil War provided him with many interesting subjects; and on his return he published *Sketches in Spain*, lithographed on stone, which was very successful. He also made sixty-four water-colour copies of pictures by old Spanish and Venetian masters, which are now in the Edinburgh National Gallery. In 1843 he went to Cairo, and remained in Egypt eight years, having found a land exactly suited to his art, and in depicting which he seems once more to bring the *Arabian Nights* before our eyes. His manner became more minute in detail, and brighter in colour. Perhaps one of the finest of his pictures sent home from Egypt is "Interior of a Harem," a work of most elaborate finish, great purity of colour, and most careful and learned drawing. As an accident had caused Lewis when a young man to take to water-colour painting, another accidental occurrence led him to resume oil painting. One of his brothers in passing through Cairo, *en route* for India, by chance left his oil-colour painting-box behind him. Lewis took it up and began playing with the colours, and finally used them, painting three small oil pictures on three little panels. One of these, "The Armenian Lady, Cairo," which was exhibited in the Royal Academy Winter Exhibition in 1888-9, still retains all its brilliancy, and is in the finest state of preservation, though painted thirty years ago. The lady's dress, the narrow stripes of which are foreshortened with the most accurate draughtsmanship to accommodate themselves to the limbs they enfold, is a marvel of delicate execution; and, though the picture is small and painted with the utmost minuteness of execution, it does not lack breadth or solidity.

Lewis was very particular both in the preparation of his colours and in the choice of his panels, which latter he generally used in preference to canvases. He used to keep them a long time by him before painting on them, after having had the grounds laid with great care by his colourman. His colours were mostly mineral, and were selected with much caution. He used, as a rule, exceedingly small sable brushes, hog tools only for backgrounds or scrubbing in. Nevertheless, we must admit that though the process of execution may have been prolonged by the smallness of the tool, that there is not one touch too much or one thrown away in his work, and that the result is always very perfect, conveying an impression of power without too great a sense of labour.

He worked hard throughout the day, and would be in his painting-room by eight every morning, rigidly excluding every one except his wife —without whom he seemed scarcely able to get on—and, of course, the model, if he was painting from one. A difficulty in his work only roused him to more energy, and he would never leave a picture till he had overcome it, whatever it was; then, having done so, he would perhaps set the picture aside for months before finishing it. He altered his work a good deal. This habit, perhaps, arose from his long practice of water-colours, when he declared that by washing out he got a better face upon his paper; at any rate, he would occasionally in his oil painting scrape parts out to the ground and repaint. If he thought of an alteration or of an improvement to a picture he would get up in the middle of the night and would go down to his studio to set about it, for his love for his art was an intense passion with him; and during his latter years his devotion to it was so great that he rarely passed a night away from home, always preferring if he dined out to drive home many miles, however late in the evening, in order to sleep at Walton, so as to be ready for his painting the next morning. Lewis became president of the Society of Painters in Water-Colours in 1857, and a year after he was elected an associate of the Royal Academy. He became a full member in 1865, in which year he exhibited "A Turkish School in the Vicinity of Cairo," and "In the Bey's Garden, Asia Minor." Lewis delighted in the brightest flowers, and his painting of lilies and tulips is most delicately truthful and rich in gorgeous colouring.

About the spring of the year 1876, Lewis, in consequence of failing health, had to place himself on the retired list of the Royal Academy, but he did not long enjoy repose. He continued painting until almost the last—in fact, till his brush would fall out of his hand, when he would beg to have it replaced, remarking how true it was that it was the head which painted and not the hand. He died at Walton-on-Thames, 15th August, 1876, and a brass has been placed to his memory in the church there.

CHAPTER XXXII.

ANIMAL PAINTERS—LANDSEER AND ANSDELL. MARINE PAINTERS—
STANFIELD, COOKE, AND HOLLAND.

WE have described in an earlier chapter the great merit of J. Ward R.A., as an animal painter. He may be said to have been the successor in that branch of art of Morland and Stubbs, both clever artists of very opposite characters. In our present chapter we have to deal with another animal painter, who enjoyed an almost unparalleled reputation, and whose works are perhaps even at present a little too near to us to enable us to criticize them quite dispassionately. *Sir Edwin Henry Landseer, R.A.*, sprang from a family of artists, and occupied an almost unique position in the art world from his babyhood. He was the third and youngest son of John Landseer, the engraver, and was born in Queen Anne Street, London, 7th March, 1802. His father taught him to draw in company with his two brothers; and some of Edwin's sketches, or, rather, portraits of animals, made at five, seven, and ten years of age, are shown at the South Kensington Museum. Hampstead Heath was his first studio, and it is recalled that his father *lifted* him over the stiles of the fields leading to it to enable the future painter to reach his sketching position. He also visited the Tower and Exeter Change at an early age to sketch and to etch—for he began, too, to etch, when quite a boy—the animals preserved in those menageries. F. G. Stephens, in his excellent *Memorials of Landseer*, relates an anecdote which Landseer took for the subject of one of his sketches, reproduced with three others by Thomas Landseer in *Twenty Engravings of Lions, Panthers, &c.* " A lioness—an orphan of course—had been captured in very early cubhood, and brought on board ship, and was suckled by a bitch for whom, although she soon surpassed her nurse in size and strength, she ever retained the utmost affection and some respect. The attached couple were shown in Exeter Change menagerie, attracted much admiration, and were the source of unmitigated delight to many

thousands of good people." Here was a subject Landseer could delight
in. Unlike other animal painters, he infused into his creatures an
almost human element which, while it did not interfere with the finest
perception of animal nature, added a tender sentiment or a delicate
humour to the subjects of his brush wanting in the pictures of other
artists in the same line.

But to return to Landseer's studies. He actually began to exhibit at
the Royal Academy before he was admitted as a student to their schools,
sending his first work when only twelve years old, and figuring as an
honorary exhibitor. His brothers were pupils of Haydon, but Edwin
does not seem to have received anything beyond advice from that
painter, who recommended him to dissect animals, which advice the
young man acted upon. He certainly understood the anatomy of the
lion well—taking advantage of the death of one in a menagerie, as we have
already seen when speaking of Lewis, he thoroughly studied its anatomical construction, and it was of great use to him in his future work.
He entered the Academy as a student at the age of fourteen, and
became a great favourite with Fuseli, who, on coming into the schools,
would say, "Where is my little dog boy?" The graceful and curly-
headed lad sat at this time to Leslie as the hero in his picture, "The
Death of Rutland," taken from Shakspeare's *Henry IV.* (Part III.).

Landseer continued his studies and exhibited at the same time. In
1817 he sent "Mount St. Bernard Dogs" to the Water-Colour Society,
oil paintings being at that time admitted there: and to the Academy,
"The Heads of a Pointer Bitch and Puppy." In 1822, the directors of
the British Institution awarded him a premium of 150*l.* for "The Larder
Invaded," exhibited there; and in 1824 he contributed to the same
gallery his celebrated work "The Cat's Paw," a monkey making use of
a cat's paw, having first seized the unfortunate animal in his strong
grip, to take the roasting chestnuts off the fire. This is the first of his
paintings in which a well-known moral is happily combined with humour.
He was elected an associate of the Royal Academy in 1826, when only
four-and-twenty, which is the earliest prescribed age, and had even at
that time a great reputation. He became a full member five years later.
Already, when only twenty-two, he had entered upon the trials of a house-
holder by taking the house at St. John's Wood, in which he lived till his
death, surrounded, though he never married, by various members of his
family. In 1835 he sent to the Academy "The Drover's Departure,"
now in the Sheepshanks gallery. This picture contains a host of incidents arising from the departure of the herds from the Highlands to the
south. In the same gallery, which contains sixteen of the painter's
works, is to be seen "The Old Shepherd's Chief Mourner," perhaps the
most pathetic picture Landseer ever painted; and said by Ruskin to be,

"One of the most perfect poems or pictures (I use the words as synony-mous) which modern times have seen." Every one will remember the faithful dog pressing its breast lovingly against the coffin of the master so steadily served in life, so truly mourned in death; the rosemary sprig spread on the coffin lid, telling of old-world customs now passed away, or only held sacred in the solitary hills; the clasped Bible and the spec-tacles, reminding us of reverence and age; while the stick and bonnet are thrown carelessly on the floor to denote that their use has come to an end.

If we want to see Landseer in a comic vein we have only to turn to "A Jack in Office," in the same collection. Even the mere title is a happy bit of humour, and, by the way, the translation of this into French proved a difficult question when the picture was exhibited in Paris in 1855. It is too well known to need description, especially as it was treated as a political caricature by H. B., which was almost as clever as the work which originated it. It was exhibited at the Academy in 1833. All the accessories in this picture are painted with a wondrous appreciation of their various qualities, the copper scales, for instance, seeming thin from constant wiping!

Our painter visited the Highlands when quite a young man, and ever after found in them many attractive subjects for his pencil—revisiting them again and again for the purposes both of sport and painting, though, as the artist ever came first, the gun was often laid aside for the sketch-book. The knowledge of Landseer's art has probably been more widely spread by engraving than that of any other painter, perhaps because his father and brother were both engravers, perhaps because in a country such as ours, where a hardy open-air life and a love of field sports fosters a great attachment to animals, Landseer's subjects natu-rally excited much admiration. Hardly a household in which engravings are to be found but what owns one from a picture by Landseer; and it is certain that not only do his works lend themselves happily to engrav-ing, but that they have also been fortunate in finding excellent engravers to interpret them.

Landseer's method of work is characterized by great facility of execu-tion. So much so is this the case in his pictures that it is curious to read of Wilkie's warning him against "niggling;" but it is evident that his quite early work was carefully and minutely finished, and that the rapidity of his later execution came from his perfect mastery and power over his brush. He had been so early trained to accuracy in the minutest details that his long life of exact draughtsmanship resulted in the hey-day of his powers in a matchless rapidity and facility of execution.

Landseer's maturity, as we know, came when he was still quite a young man; and his early pictures, while they appear imitatively perfect, are a wonder of light-handed execution. Take, for instance, his "Tethered Rams," painted in 1839, where the fullest truth of woolly texture is obtained by simply applying with a full brush the more solid pigment into that which has already been laid on as a ground, with a large admixture of the painter's vehicle; days might be spent in striving after a result which the painter has achieved at once.

We remember in the famous collection of Mr. Wells at Redleaf a fallow deer, the size of life, by Landseer, painted down to the knees. Mr. Wells used to relate that on leaving the house to go to Penshurst Church the panel for this picture was being placed on the easel by his butler, and on his return in less than three hours the picture was complete. Under Landseer's able hand a single drag of the brush gave a more effective rendering of the coat of the animal than could be achieved by a painstaking imitation of each single hair. There is, too, a portrait by him of Lord Ashburnham completed in a single sitting. There is an anecdote current concerning him that once at an evening party, a lady having made a careless remark that no one had ever drawn two things at once, Landseer immediately drew simultaneously the profile of a deer with antlers with one hand, and the profile of a horse with the other. If true this speaks of a most remarkable power of both hand and brain.

Landseer's colour is, unfortunately, apt always to be unduly heavy, and in his later pictures it became grey and leaden. As a portrait painter, when his model was to his taste, he was very fairly successful; but when he was oppressed with the sense of an uncongenial task, perhaps only undertaken from good nature, he was less happy in the results. In later life, after many attacks of illness, though Landseer would still paint with the same extreme facility, he would touch and retouch upon his pictures while they remained in his studio and would often quite spoil their first perfection. He was fortunate in gaining all the honours which art could give him. The Queen bestowed on him a knighthood in 1850; he was awarded the gold medal at the Paris Universal Exhibition in 1855; and on Eastlake's death, in 1865, he was offered and refused the office of president of the Royal Academy.

In appearance Sir Edwin was small, but he was energetic, quick in speech, frank and full of wit; he was also an excellent mimic. It is related of him that once while dining with Sir Francis Chantrey, he imitated him so well as to deceive the sculptor's own servant. Chantrey had been speaking of some very choice wine which he only brought out on his birthday, or on some other like great occasion. Soon after Chantrey happened to leave the table for a few minutes, and as he passed into the inner room he rang the bell for more wine. Landseer slipped into the sculptor's high-backed chair, behind which was the door. When the man entered, Landseer imitating Chantrey's voice, his person being hidden by the chair, said, "Thomas, what day is this?" "Wednesday, Sir Francis," was the reply. "Ay, ay, but what day of the month?" "The 20th, Sir Francis." "Well, then, bring up a bottle of *that* port." "Yes, sir." "You know which, that particular port." "Yes, Sir Francis." In rushed the real Sir Francis with a "Stay! Stay!" but it was too late to recall a bottle so fairly earned, and the wine came and was enjoyed the more for the wit that won it.

In society Landseer with his many gifts was a great favourite. The Queen was one of his chief patrons. Her Majesty bought several of his best pictures, and commissioned him to paint in fresco for her summer house in Buckingham Palace from the subject of *Comus*. With all these advantages he was from his youth up liable to severe fits of depression. He was nervous and acutely sensitive, these causes led to an illness in 1851, which prevented him from painting for nearly two years. In fact, merely to sign an engraving or to see one of his own pictures was too much for him. Happily he rallied, and again took to painting, but his works never quite attained their former excellence. Landseer's portrait of himself, sketching-block in hand, with two favourite dogs looking over his shoulders at his work, called "Connoisseurs," is well known through the engraving. We have heard that a patron of the painter's was so much struck with this work while in the studio that he asked him if he was going to part with it. "Of course, I am," replied Landseer. "Then," said he, "I will give you 2,000*l.* for it; the picture shall remain with you during your lifetime, and the copy of it shall be yours." "No, no," said Landseer, "you sha'n't have it." Some time afterwards the Prince of Wales being in the studio, asked the same question whether the picture was engaged, whereupon Landseer immediately replied that it was not, and begged him to accept it.

Many funny stories have been told about Landseer and his animals, as, for instance, one which Dickens was fond of relating, that when the painter was in the midst of the entertainment of a circle of friends, his manservant, with the stolidity of his class, opened the door suddenly, and said, "Did you order a lion, sir?" Great were the fears expressed by the guests, but it soon turned out that a lion having died at the Zoological Gardens, the manager with kind forethought had despatched the carcase, thinking Landseer might like to sketch it. Frith, in his recollections, tells us of a comic though very natural mistake to one speaking in an unfamiliar tongue, made by the late King of Portugal, who, when Landseer was introduced to him at a party, said, "Oh, I have so wished to make your acquaintance, I am so fond of beasts."

Towards the end of his life his nervous state of health was aggravated by a railway accident, which befell him going north, in November, 1868, and which left a scar on the forehead, visible in his coffin. For the last two or three years of his life he was a great sufferer; he passed away on October 1st, 1873, and was buried in St. Paul's Cathedral, his pall being held by the six senior members of the Royal Academy. A memoir of his life would be incomplete which does not mention his great achievement in sculpture in modelling the four lions round the base of Nelson's column in Trafalgar Square, remarkable more for their truth and accuracy as portraits than as ideal works in sculpture.

Richard Ansdell, R.A., was another animal painter whose reputation was great in his day. He was born in Liverpool in 1816, and first exhibited in the Royal Academy in 1840. He visited Spain in 1857 with J. Phillip, R.A., for the purpose of sketching, and on his return to England his Spanish subjects became very popular. He was a facile and ready draughtsman, picturesque in his groupings, and he readily seized the characteristics of animals. His pictures were very well composed, and his first charcoal outlines of his subject on the canvas were full of vigour and excellently conceived, but his colour was not good, and his finished works lack what the painters call "quality." He was a most industrious painter, and his works are very numerous.

He painted several pictures in conjunction with his friend, T. Creswick, R.A. His works, which were much sought after in the north of England, have been very frequently engraved. Ansdell was a man of most generous nature, and very popular with his brother painters. He died at Farnborough, in Hampshire, 20th April, 1885, aged sixty-nine. He had not Landseer's unique power in the choice of a subject, or his sympathy with the instincts of animals, but his works appealed to the true English love of sport, and were accordingly much admired.

It is curious that in a country surrounded by the sea so few of our painters should have devoted themselves to marine subjects. In the first half of the eighteenth century Charles Brooking, born 1723, acquired great skill in painting scenes of naval tactics, but he died early at the age of thirty-six. He was followed in the same line of art by Dominic Serres, R.A., and his son, and though some of Turner's finest pictures are sea pieces and Callcott and Collins both painted subjects taken from the sea, yet they are scarcely to be called marine painters, and it was left to *Clarkson Stanfield, R.A.*, to consecrate himself almost entirely to subjects of this class. He was the son of a writer of some reputation, and was born at Sunderland in 1793. Here he lived during his early boyhood, till he entered the marine service, where he had Douglas Jerrold for a shipmate, and while the one got up plays on board ship the other painted the scenery for them. These two met later on, Jerrold as professed dramatist, Stanfield as scene painter at Drury Lane Theatre. An accident which

c c

befell Stanfield caused him to leave the navy, and to take to scene painting. While at work thus at Edinburgh he made the acquaintance of David Roberts, who was occupied in a similar manner, and the two became friends for life. We hear of them next in London, at the Cobourg Theatre and Drury Lane, for which latter theatre Stanfield painted two or three fine drop scenes, besides contributing to the dioramas exhibited there, which made at the time a great sensation. His scene painting was vigorous, and remarkable for boldness of execution and rich colour, and he effected very great improvement in that branch of the art. He continued scene painting for some years, and at the same time produced in oil some small marine views, and in 1827 he exhibited " A Calm " at the Royal Academy, though three or four years before this he had contributed to other exhibitions, and actually took a premium of fifty guineas for a picture, "Wreckers off Fort Rouge," awarded to him by the British Institution that same year.

In 1831 William IV. gave him as a commission " The Ceremony of Opening New London Bridge." The painter took for his point of view the scene above the bridge on the Surrey side of the water. He has given us the representation of a fine pageant, but there is a slight doubt as to what the group of people in the centre of his picture are standing upon. The following year he was elected an A.R.A., and a full member of the Academy in 1835, when he exhibited a large work, " The Battle of Trafalgar," painted on commission for the United Service Club.

Stanfield very generally made his landscapes and marine pictures serve as illustrations of some historical or dramatic event. He was naturalistic in his treatment of a subject, and though trained as a scene painter he avoids in his work coarse or strong effects, erring possibly a little in the opposite direction of staidness and coldness. He was a firm and vigorous draughtsman. Ruskin, in the first volume of *Modern Painters*, speaks highly of Stanfield's thorough knowledge of his subject and of his power both of wave and cloud drawing—in this latter indeed he places him next to Turner. Yet the author of *Modern Painters* complains of his being wanting in impressiveness, wishing him to be "less clever and more affecting," less wonderful and more terrible, and as the first step to such an object " to learn how to conceal." This want of mystery in his pictures may have partly arisen from his early labours as a scene painter ; we imagine the influence of stage effect would cling round him to the last ; still his later pictures would seem to have acquired more imagination, and his sense of colour became more delicate and refined. His works show a great sense of aërial perspective, and his knowledge of seamanship gives truth to the grandeur of his marine subjects. The drawing of his marine architecture will be interesting as the years go on, when the picturesqueness and grace of the sailing ships of the early part of the century will contrast favourably with the ironclads and torpedo vessels of the later part. We believe that Stanfield had perfect models of all his shipping craft, boats, oars, sails, rigging, &c., made in a small size for his studio, in order to ensure an entire correctness of detail in his pictures.

In 1833 he sent to the Academy the first, the only one he exhibited, of a series of ten pictures painted for the banqueting room at Bowood. These pictures were completed in 1840, and almost at the same time Stanfield was at work upon a series of Venetian subjects for Trentham. In the collection at Windsor Castle is a painting of "The Royal Yacht off Mount St. Michael, Cornwall," which Stanfield was commissioned by the Queen to paint for her in 1846. The forms of the sky are beautifully rendered, it depicts a bright and cheerful day, the usual " Queen's weather," and the painting of the water, the one part of his picture which Stanfield under all circumstances made prominent, is translucent and clear.

In 1829, just after he had given up scene painting, our painter paid a first visit to the Continent, and again in 1839 he made a long stay in Italy, and from this time the greater number of his pictures are of foreign scenery, such as "The Castle of Ischia," "Beilstein on the Moselle," "Vesuvius and the Bay of Naples," 1864, together with many marine subjects painted off the Dutch coast.

Stanfield was a member of the Sketching Society of which we give an account elsewhere. He retained to the last his friendship for his dramatic friends, and used often to meet them at the Garrick Club. In 1865 he went with Roberts to Edinburgh, where "Stanny," as his old friend loved to call him, was made an honorary member of the Scottish Academy. He had been for some time in declining health when he died at Belsize Park, Hampstead, 18th May, 1867. He was a Roman Catholic by religion, and was buried in St. Mary's Cemetery, Kensal Green, his funeral being attended by many admirers and friends.

Edward William Cooke, R.A., was another painter who throughout his art career devoted himself to marine subjects. He was born in London, March 27th, 1811, and was the son of an engraver. He early showed a great taste for drawing, and began to use his pencil deftly when little more than a child of four, and when quite a boy, he modelled a deer in high relief most correctly and accurately in black wax on a slate. Cooke never attended the Academy schools. His father taught him both to draw and to engrave, and sent him up to town, from Hackney, to take perspective lessons from Augustus Pugin ; but after young Cooke had paid two visits, Pugin begged his father not to send him so far again, saying with great honesty the boy knew as much as he did. Cooke's father intended him to be an engraver, and he continued to assist him in his art till he was nearly twenty. When only in his fourteenth year he made and etched drawings of Old and New London Bridges, which his father published. He also illustrated Loudon's *Encyclopædia* and the *Botanical Cabinet*, while yet an engraver, for which work he was eminently fitted, as he was a good botanist. In fact he became a man of many scientific attainments, and was elected a Fellow of the Royal Society.

His first oil picture was painted from Broadstairs on a panel given him by his father, and with colours set on a palette the gift of James Stark. He sold it for eighteen guineas, and it was re-sold during his lifetime for seventy-eight. Before he settled down to oil painting, he practised in water-colours, which was a favourite medium with him. His first pictures exhibited in the Academy were " Honfleur Fishing-boats Becalmed," and "Hay Barge off Greenwich," in 1835. In 1845 he set off for Italy, where he remained a year and three months, painting ninety pictures during the time, besides making innumerable drawings. It is as a draughtsman that Cooke's greatest talent was manifested. He made most accurate and carefully detailed drawings of almost everything he saw ; his hands were never idle, and even at a party he would bring out a little sketch-book and begin to take artistic notes. The number of his sketches must have been enormous. As a rule he painted his small pictures on the spot, assisted by these very accurate drawings of details. His palette was always most carefully set, and every colour was well ground and in its proper place, and he kept them very fluent by adding oil with his brush as he painted. There is scarcely any impasto in his work. He delighted in a smooth surface and in an almost mechanical correctness of outline. His skies he never permitted to dry while he painted on them, and he was careful therefore to finish, if possible, in a single day. His colour is rather wanting in warmth and tone, and except in some of his Venetian subjects, his pictures lack imagination.

Cooke was elected an associate of the Academy in 1851, and a full member in 1864, in which year he exhibited his large work "The Goodwin Lightship." Another picture much praised for its geological accuracy of detail was "Catalan Bay, Gibraltar." Many of his best pictures are of Dutch subjects. Cooke died at Groombridge, near Tunbridge Wells, on the 4th January, 1880. He was of a lively and genial disposition, restlessly active, a great talker, and full of anecdote.

James Holland, who was born in Burslem in 1800 and died in 1870, can scarcely be called a marine painter, yet some of his views of Venice are marked by great delicacy and poetry, and are remarkably tender and glowing in colour. A very fine work by him was shown in the Manchester Exhibition of 1887. It is not our practice to mention living men, but we may be allowed to say that our present marine painters perhaps excel their predecessors, and will no doubt maintain the reputation of the British school for works which illustrate the element by which these islands are surrounded.

CHAPTER XXXIII.

THE SCHOOL OF WATER-COLOUR PAINTERS.

THE foundation of the Society of Painters in Water-Colours was the means of establishing the art on a firm footing; and while uniting its members, made them emulous of progress, and zealous for the interests of the body to which they belonged; which was for many years the sole representative of water-colour art. Some two or three men of talent, it is true, never joined the society, and there were some seceders from the body. This chapter is not, therefore, devoted exclusively to its members; indeed the artist with whom it commences was a seceder, who turned early in his career from the practice of water-colour to oil.

John James Chalon, R.A., was born at Geneva in 1778; he was the elder brother of Alfred Edward Chalon, a distinguished painter, in our notice of whom we have already told such particulars of the family as were known to us, and of the early days of John James, of whom we are now about to speak. His first appearance as an artist was in 1800, when he exhibited "Banditti at their Repast," at the Royal Academy, followed, but not till 1803, by two pictures, "A Landscape," and "Fortune-telling." Up to 1805 John Chalon's exhibited works had been in oil; but in 1806 he became a "fellow-exhibitor" of the Water-Colour Society, and then turned to water-colour art. In 1808 he was elected a member of the society, and in that year exhibited, with other pictures, his "Shorwell Rocks on the Wye," a work which gave him a distinguished place as a water-colour painter. It was exhibited in the International Exhibition of 1862. On the alterations which took place in 1813, when it was proposed to dissolve the Water-Colour Society, John Chalon was among the members who seceded.

It is probable that John Chalon's withdrawal from the Water-Colour Society may have been influenced by his desire to become a member of the Royal Academy. In 1812 his brother Alfred was elected an associate, and many of the contemporary artists thought even more highly of

John's abilities than of Alfred's. When in 1816 the younger brother was advanced to full honours, John made great efforts to appear well on the Academy's walls, sending his "Napoleon on board the *Bellerophon*," now in the gallery at Greenwich Hospital. The brothers were deeply attached to one another, and having attained rank in art himself, Alfred was most anxious for his brother's advancement also; but although he exhibited from time to time works of great merit, it was not until 1827 that John Chalon was elected an associate, and he continued in that rank until 1841.

It has been said of John Chalon, and this within ten years of his death, that "during a long life, he painted a multitude of pictures mostly in water-colours," so little is really known of his art; yet Leslie who knew him well, and who was at least a competent judge, thought him a man of great and original powers. "Few painters," he said, "had so great a range of talent." Moreover, his principal works were in oil, although he was in early life an accomplished water-colour painter; and we can admit that, if invention were the great qualification of an artist, few better deserved that title than John James Chalon.

A picture exhibited at the International Exhibition in 1862, and called "The Gravel Pit," is, on the whole, one of John Chalon's best works, broad, simple, and manly in treatment, square and facile in handling, and free from faults of colour that overtook him in later practice: it is really a finely-coloured picture; the sky is a luminous mass of rifting clouds through which a sun-ray breaks and lights up lines on the distant plain, while the flat cutting of the steep side of the gravel-pit is lighted with warm rich sunlight, telling against the neutral green in the foreground, which is all in shade; two or three female figures at the foot of a tree on the right sparkle like jewels against the negative masses.

Another very masterly work by the painter is a "View of Hastings," exhibited in 1819, and now in the collection at South Kensington Museum. Chalon's faults of blackness were more apparent in his water-colours than in his oil pictures. He made beautiful studies from nature, both in oil and water-colours; and had it been the fashion in his day to paint direct from nature, would have produced very fine imitative landscapes. In his early days much of his time was given up to teaching, and although he was an exhibitor for fifty years his works are comparatively few.

In 1847, while walking with his brother, he was suddenly seized with paralysis, and lost the power of supporting himself. His disorder gradually increased; and with his physical, his mental powers also declined. The attentions of his younger brother were unremitting, until his tedious illness terminated fatally on the 14th November, 1854, when in his seventy-sixth year. The brothers Chalon were the mainstay and support of the Sketching Society, were inseparable during a long life, and equally steadfast in their friendships and hospitality.

In our list of artists, who in the early part of the century obtained reputation as painters in water-colours, *Thomas Heaphy* must be included as one of the best of those who painted figure subjects. He was born in London, in the parish of Cripplegate, 29th Dec., 1775. His father, John Heaphy, was descended from a French family, who in the seventeenth century had settled in the eastern part of London, where his countrymen who fled on the revocation of the Edict of Nantes, had introduced the manufacture of silk, which then took root in our city. John Heaphy took Katharine Gerard, a Frenchwoman, to wife, and the taste characteristic of the race, descended to their son Thomas, who early in life showed a predilection for art. His father apprenticed the boy to a dyer, perhaps hoping that his art-feeling might tend to improve the silk dyes of the district; but the occupation was very distasteful to the youth, and his evident dislike led to his indentures being cancelled within a few months, when a new direction was given to his life. He was now articled to an engraver of the name of Meadows, who obtained some reputation by engraving book plates from the designs of Richard Westall. There was, at the time we are writing about, 1796-7, an art-school of some repute in Finsbury, conducted by a painter of the name of Simpson, who numbered among his pupils Thomas Uwins, Ross the father of Sir William, and others who afterwards became known in the arts. Heaphy, who was more inclined to painting than to engraving, after his master's work was finished, attended in the evening very regularly at Simpson's school, and studied diligently with the view of fitting himself for future practice as an artist.

Before his apprenticeship to Meadows expired, Heaphy, with the improvidence characteristic of artists, had married Miss Stevenson, the sister of one of his fellow students at the school, and to enable him to support her he had recourse to colouring prints after Westall and others, works at that time of ready sale; he also began to paint portraits. In the year 1800 we find him exhibiting at the Royal Academy for the first time, two of these portraits, one of his young wife, and one of Mrs. Meadows, doubtless the wife of his master. When little more than twenty-one years of age, he painted his first subject picture in water-colours, a girl stooping over a river bank to gather a water lily; and having completed his time with Meadows, he obtained admission as a student of the Royal Academy. There also, he continued to exhibit—principally portraits—ending in 1804 with one subject picture, "The Portland Fish Girl." He did not join the Water-Colour Society on its foundation, although we learn that he was already a somewhat popular favourite; but in 1807 he was admitted as an "associate exhibitor," and contributed three subject pictures.

Pyne tells us that when Heaphy's picture of "Juvenile Poachers Disputing for their Stolen Game" was exhibited, the then president of the Academy, West, pointed it out before a room full of persons of rank and position as a work of great merit and original talent. This criticism of course spread from one to another and greatly increased the young painter's reputation. His "Fish Market," exhibited in the Water-Colour Exhibition of 1809, raised him to the summit of success; it was painted with great care, full of truth and character, the colour tender and delicate, the hues of the fish rendered with great purity. His pictures found ready sale at prices high for our own day; but remarkable for his time, if, as has been said, his "Hastings Fish Market" was sold for the sum of 500 guineas. But Heaphy was versatile and somewhat volatile. In 1807 he was appointed portrait painter to the Princess of Wales whom he painted in miniature, as he did many other persons of rank and fashion. His subject pictures having less of his attention, the sale of them about this time began to decline, and many remained on his hands. Soon afterwards he left the Water-Colour Society; exhibiting there for the last time in 1811.

He now gave himself up to portraiture, and with this view he quitted England for the British Camp in the Peninsula, where he occupied himself in painting portraits of the principal officers. Here he must have led a life of adventure, since he continued with the army throughout the rest of the campaign and until the war ended with the Battle of Toulouse. On his return to England he painted a large picture of the Duke of Wellington, and the officers of his staff, some of whom had fallen victims in the strife, and their memories are thus preserved to us. The work was engraved, and had much success.

Heaphy was mainly instrumental in founding the Society of British Artists. To its first exhibition in 1814 he contributed nine pictures, and he was elected the first president of the society, though he only held office one year; after the second he ceased to be an exhibitor, and his connection with the society terminated. Years passed away during which Heaphy contributed little to art; but he was still interested in all new associations of artists. He was again active in the formation of the new Society of Painters in Water-Colours, of which he became a member; but died shortly after its foundation on the 19th November, 1835, aged sixty years.

Heaphy's works won upon the public by their truthfulness and direct reference to nature. His brother painters had attempted fashion, false rusticity, and classicality; he went to nature both for his character and expression, and did not scruple to represent her as he found her. Of this his best picture in the South Kensington Museum, "The Wounded Leg," is an example. It is not an agreeable subject to choose, but Heaphy made no compromise in representing it; the wounded leg forms a prominent feature.

Practising his art in the cottage, the field, or by the sea-beach rather than in the studio, it is little to be wondered that he habitually undervalued what he termed academic art; using the phrase in reference to the mode of study adopted by the old masters, whose works he probably persuaded himself he held in less estimation than was actually the fact; for on visiting Italy towards the close of his life he evidenced his true appreciation of their power by the earnestness with which he made copies from their works. Heaphy's life illustrates the necessity of unceasing practice on the part of him who would continue to improve; for Heaphy having for several years painted only occasionally and at long intervals, when he again desired to assume the active practice of his profession, although still in the prime of life, was led to feel that he had fallen off rather than improved, and he exclaimed with grief, "My art has gone from me!"

David Cox, an eminent water-colour painter, was born in Birmingham on the 29th April, 1783. His father was a blacksmith, a healthy handicraft which has been the specialty of the town and neighbourhood from time immemorial; the whole population being more or less workers in metal. The mother of the painter, a woman of strong good sense and deep religious feeling, gave their only son David such an orderly and careful training in his childhood, as served to guide him aright in the difficulties and dangers to which he was exposed on his entry into life, and to form the sincere character of the man. While yet a child the boy had the misfortune to break his leg; this, joined to a somewhat delicate constitution, obviously unfitted him to follow his father's trade. While laid up from the effects of the accident, a box of colours and some paper provided for his amusement was a source of such unceasing delight to the invalid, that his father, on his recovery, sent him to a drawing school in the town, conducted by Mr. Barber, Sen., a local teacher of the day. Here he must have made great progress, and showed a true vocation for art; since, when not yet sixteen years of age, he was apprenticed to a locket-painter, to paint the devices and ornaments of various kinds, which, mounted in metal, form what is called toy jewellery, for which Birmingham is almost as much noted as for its coarser works in iron. He lost his master at the end of about eighteen months, and was obliged to seek other sources of improvement and employment: a locket of his painting still in the possession of his family shows that he had obtained great mastery of his work, even during the short time he had been engaged in it.

Not readily finding other employment in art, to which he instinctively clung, he undertook, like his great predecessor Claude, to grind colours ; and in this way he laboured for the scene painters at the Birmingham Theatre ; gaining at the same time, from his habits of observation, a knowledge of their art and art processes. Macready, the father of the tragedian, was then stage manager, and wishing to improve the scenery of his theatre, he sent to London and engaged De Maria, who at that time was painting scenes for the Italian Opera, to come and prepare a set for him. Of this artist we have no records, but his works seem to have awakened in Cox the desire to become a landscape painter. He used to compare the ready handling and broad manner of his scenes to Wilson's landscapes. De Maria, who soon perceived young Cox's talent for the art, set him to carry on the less important parts of his own works, and to paint side scenes. Shortly after, Macready, who accidentally found out the skill and readiness of the young assistant, employed him to copy, on his own account, a set of scenes for the Sheffield Theatre. Of scenic art, more than any other art, the essential object is to please the eye— to make effective points tell, and to express the intended effect with facility and ease. It may be presumed that young Cox, during the four years he remained with the company as scene painter, laid the foundation of those very qualities which are so characteristic of his works, and which, added to his refined sense of the colouring of landscape, of the effects of air, and the fresh atmosphere of English scenery, make his pictures such favourites with all who love art.

The management, as is customary with most provincial companies, moved from place to place, and the scene painters travelled also. This unsettled life was very distasteful to Cox. After remaining the time we have named, he left and proceeded to London ; where, in the first instance, he sought and obtained employment in the scene-loft at Astley's Theatre. In his journeys to and from his labours there, he was attracted by the water-colour drawings in Palser's well-known shop, then on the Surrey side of the river ; the works there exhibited determined Cox to become a water-colour painter. He was fortunate enough at some of his subsequent visits to Palser's to make the acquaintance of John Varley, who invited him to his painting room, and introduced him, no doubt, to the clever knot of rising artists who assembled in his studio, and who profited so largely by the maxims and methods inculcated there. Colonel Windsor, afterwards Earl of Plymouth, struck with some of Cox's works, which he saw at Palser's, obtained many pupils for our artist ; who was thus enabled to leave the theatre, and to take more entirely to the art he loved.

In 1805, Cox made his first visit to North Wales, and on his return he exhibited first in Bond Street, and on the breaking up of that society, with the one in Spring Gardens. Residing on Dulwich Common, then somewhat of a sequestered nook, though in the immediate vicinity of London, Cox made a diligent study of nature ; not by elaborate imitation, but, as he said, always with some direct purpose—to learn to render the aspects of some one of the several periods of the day, with its varied effects and the incidents and characteristics suitable to it. He also studied the old masters—Velasquez and Ruysdael being his chief favourites. He copied Gaspar Poussin for his improvement ; nor were the works of Girtin, Turner, Havell, and Varley without their direct influence upon him : thus he searched the art of the past and the practice of his contemporaries, to give himself a foundation on which to form his own style direct from the observation of nature.

These studies were for a time suspended by his being appointed, in 1814, teacher of drawing to the senior officers of the Military College near Farnham ; but finding the duties irksome and unsuited to his disposition, he resigned after a few months, and retired, in 1815, to Hereford ; visiting London usually in the spring, at the exhibition season, to keep up his acquaintance with art and artists, and to prevent that falling-off which is too apt to arise when an artist secludes himself from his brethren. At Hereford he continued to reside until 1829, when he returned to the vicinity of London, and lived at Kensington until 1840. Then, weary of teaching and making small drawings, and wishing to practice art for itself and to indulge in his own feeling for it, he retired to Harborne, a village in the neighbourhood of his native city, and devoted himself almost entirely to painting in oil. His works in this material were rarely seen in London, remaining principally in the hands of his friends ; but he continued to contribute to the Water-Colour Society's Exhibition in Pall Mall until his death, on the 7th of June, 1859.

In 1816, Cox published a *Treatise on Landscape Painting in Water-Colours*, containing progressive lessons, with examples of the various effects of morning and evening, of storm and calm, of winter and summer. He gives us his own views of the aim of the landscape painter. "In the selection of a subject from nature," he says, "the student should keep in view the principal object which induced him to make the sketch. The prominence of the leading feature should be clearly supported throughout ; the character of the picture should be derived from it ; every object introduced should be subservient to it."

Cox's *handling* in water-colours was peculiar to himself, and was somewhat analogous to that adopted by Gainsborough and Constable in oil painting. He worked with wet colour, repeating broken tints loosely hatched over one another until the local colour was obtained. From the fluency of his brush, and the liquidity of his tints, they dry with richness and fulness, the gum rising to the surface. Many of his best works are wrought in this manner, the knife being sparingly used to give glitter and sparkle. We have already said that a painter's peculiar execution is part of his idiosyncrasy ; that it has less to do with his education than with his feeling. It is the readiest way by which he can express to others what he feels in art, or sees in nature—it is personal, and could hardly with advantage to his art expression be changed for any other mode of execution.

It has been objected to great completion in art, that it leaves nothing to the imagination of the spectator. This is certainly not the case with the works of Cox. Like the two great painters we have quoted, he seems more intent upon obtaining the exact tone and colour of nature, than in defining *form ;* which is gradually developed in his pictures by the juxtaposition of hues and tints rather than by drawing. Apparently simple transcripts of nature, his works are yet cunningly dominated by art. The light and shade are well distributed, the figures in the most appropriate place, the keeping always excellent. His great characteristics are a generalized treatment of nature rather than individualized imitation ; breadth, luminous freshness and breezy motion. He had a true genius for landscape art, a thorough perception of the colouring of nature ; but, unlike Turner, who mastered the whole realm of landscape, Cox was contented with a more limited range, in which, however, he reigned almost without a rival. No painter has given us more truly the moist brilliancy of early summer-time, ere the sun has dried the spring bloom from the lately opened leaf. The sparkle and shimmer of foliage and weedage, in the fitful breeze that rolls away the clouds from the watery sun, when the shower and the sunshine chase each other over the land, have never been given with greater truth than by David Cox.

Many of his works are truly imaginative ; the very looseness of the handling already adverted to adding to their sentiment. His noble picture of " A Welsh Funeral," is characteristic both of his modes of execution, and of that highly imaginative feeling, which he added to truth, of the general impression of nature. It is one of his largest and most impressive works. The time chosen is twilight—day, just dying out into the gloom of evening—an hour so full of mournful impressions, so suitable and so in harmony with the subject. The picture is nevertheless full of colour and freshness, and not by any means heavy or grey. The funeral procession moves away into the picture, along a road bordered with stone dykes, and overhung with trees ; these contrast with the barren stony hills in the near background, the desolate stony region onwards to which they are bearing the corpse. The backs of the throng of mourners are all turned to the spectator ; going away, as it were, from life into the gloomy solitude of death : to the grave in the little hill-side churchyard, a sepulchre in the rocks seen beyond. A gleam of light illuminating the belfry shows the bell on the swing; we seem to hear its mournful knell, while over the path of the funeral, above the chapel and the desolate hills, a rift in the dark clouds opens up to us a glimpse as it were of the calm heavens, the glorious home and future rest of the departed.

Latterly Cox used at times a low-toned paper, coarse in manufacture, with fragments of straw appearing on the surface, and he freely resorted to wiping out the lights, and even to the use of body colour; glazing over it, to give richness, but reserving points of pure light, to focus and give requisite tone to the whole. The "Funeral" is painted in this manner; the execution is loose and apparently undecided; when seen near, it is a mass of blots and scratches, but from a few feet distant we feel that any further completion would take from the perfect impression it makes on us, and deprive the picture of the solemn truth of dim imaginative twilight which hangs over the whole. The scene is from the neighbourhood of Bettws-y-Coed, which was latterly as much Cox's country as Dedham and Flatford were Constable's. There he painted many of his finest works; and it shows how readily genius finds a subject, where others only find tameness and the commonplace, that many of his pictures are from a single field. As a painter, he had a marked individuality, and his pictures are an honour to the water-colour school.

Samuel Prout adds another name to the long list of Devonshire artists. He was born at Plymouth on the 17th September, 1783. When barely five years old he was smitten with a sun-stroke, carried home insensible, and not only suffered much at the time, but in all his after life he was subject to constantly recurring attacks of headache, so severe as to confine him to his bed and wholly to prevent any labour while they lasted. He early showed a great fondness for drawing, but as he advanced in years his father proposed that he should follow him in his own profession; though we are not informed what that was. The lad, however, had heard of the fame of his townsmen and of their success in the great metropolis: the love of art had taken possession of him. His kind-hearted schoolmaster, too, had somewhat encouraged the pupil's propensities; he used to set young Prout beside him to make pen and ink sketches of the pedagogue's favourite cat, and thus that predilection for drawing, which the parent had thought a mere devotion to an idle amusement, was silently fostered and gradually became the fixed wish and decided aim of the future artist.

The Rev. Dr. Bidlake was then master of the grammar school. Placed under his instruction Prout became the schoolfellow and companion of his townsman, Haydon, whose hopes and aims were of a like character; and on their half-holidays the two lads used to wander forth together to enjoy nature. No doubt their early efforts were very different; Prout's careful and imitative, Haydon's bold, hasty, and sketchy; but they were at least united in their love of art. It will be remembered that Payne, holding some office in the dockyard, was a resident of Plymouth and enjoyed a local reputation for his water-colour drawings of scenery in the vicinity; his works seem to have stimulated the exertions of Prout in the same art, and he was allowed to have a few lessons from S. Williams, a local teacher. Hence he had obtained some skill when, in the winter of 1801, Mr. Britton, journeying westward in search of materials for his forthcoming work, *Picturesque Beauties of England,* was introduced by Dr. Bidlake to young Prout. Britton saw, or he thought he saw, promise in the lad, and offered to take him on his journey into Cornwall, and to pay all expenses in return for his assistance in sketching objects of interest for the forthcoming work. The offer met with a willing assent on the part of the elder Prout; but the journey was very unpropitious: it began with wet and stormy weather, the accommodation at the little country inns on the route was the reverse of comfortable, while Britton tells us that he soon found the youth was unable to render him the assistance he expected and was depressed at his own deficiencies and want of success. When they reached Truro they parted for the present, Prout to return to Plymouth, Britton to continue his journey to the Land's End; their connection, however, did not end here. Prout had found his deficiencies and set himself diligently to conquer them. He studied and sketched all ancient buildings within his reach, and in 1802, was able to send up a folio for Britton's inspection, sketches in which were found sufficient excellence to permit of their being engraved for Britton's work. This led to a renewal of intercourse between them, and resulted in an invitation to the young painter, who came to London, and lodged with Britton for nearly two years in Wilderness Row, Clerkenwell; employed, greatly to his improvement, in copying the best sketches and drawings of Hearne, Alexander, Turner, Cotman, Mackenzie and others.

In 1804, we first trace Prout as an exhibitor in the Royal Academy, and here he continued to exhibit until his election into the Water-Colour Society in 1815. Much of Prout's time—as, indeed, was the case with many of his brother water-colour painters—was devoted to teaching; this led him to publish on his own account many educational works. *Studies for Learners* was published by Ackerman in 1816, and followed in 1818 by a set of *Progressive Fragments,* by *Rudiments of Landscape, Views in the North and West of England,* &c. The early works are executed by soft-ground etching in a simple and large manner.

Though born in a country richly wooded, and with an abundant weedage, Prout seems to have been naturally deficient in the power of representing foliage, and he rarely introduced trees into his pictures. His style was simple and large, without imitative details; the picturesque effect of the whole being sought somewhat at the expense of the individual parts. Having passed his early years in the neighbourhood of our great naval arsenal; conversant from his childhood with the beach and cliffs of Devon, and the boats and craft that people its shores, it would have seemed, that with the above-named deficiency, he would have become a marine painter; and this probably would have been the case but for his early introduction, through Britton, to employment on subjects connected with architecture. Many of his early pictures are marine subjects, and those who have seen his fine painting of "The Indiaman Ashore," exhibited in the Society's rooms in 1819, will feel Prout's great qualification for such works. This picture probably arose from the impression made on him by the wreck of the *Dalton*, East Indiaman, on the rocks under the citadel of his native town. The crew were saved by the great personal exertions of Sir E. Pellew, afterwards Lord Exmouth, and the hull held together on the sands for hours after the wreck. Prout and Haydon are said to have watched it as it rolled in the surf and spray, and gradually broke up. Both at the time attempted pictures of the subject, and both failed; but the scene seems to have made a great impression upon Prout, and served to incite him to the fine work he afterwards produced.

But circumstances turned him from marine subjects to architecture, and it is as the painter of churches and cathedrals, of picturesque Norman cities and market places, that Prout is most celebrated. Yet we cannot feel that Prout had any particular qualification for such labours beyond his great sense of the picturesque. It is true that he seldom misses the general proportions of his buildings, or the relation of the several parts to the whole, yet that want of knowledge of construction which Britton complained of, he never overcame; and he hid his lack of perception of beauty and refinement of detail, under the broad markings of the reed pen. In all that related to the "making up" of his picture, Prout was unrivalled in his own art, and may be compared to Roberts as an oil painter, whose art his own in many respects resembled. Like Roberts, Prout was skilled in the appropriate introduction of figures, and peopled his pictures with a host of living accessories, for which Normandy and Venice amply supplied him with picturesque materials. The crowded market-places of Normandy are usually under the shadow of the cathedral; there are gathered in masses, fruit and vegetables, screened by huge coloured umbrellas; the market people in quaint costumes, rich with many dyes: the outskirts crowded with cumbrous vehicles drawn by horses under a panoply of harness studded with brazen nails and jangling bells, gay with tassels and fringes; the colour of the groups below carried upwards into balcony and window by flowers and draperies, by gaily painted signs and lattices. Such material, in Prout's hands, produced pictures that make us overlook their paucity of details, and the sacrifice of individual realization at the shrine of the picturesque.

Prout's election as a member of the Water-Colour Society in 1815 brought him fully before the patrons of that art, and when in 1818, in search of health, he visited the Continent and began to paint the picturesque towns of Normandy, so well suited as subjects for his pencil, he had made a manner of his own and taken an acknowledged rank in his art. In 1824 he visited Venice, a city filled with subjects for his brush, and extended his journeys gradually to other Italian cities, to Germany, Bohemia, &c. The invention of lithography about this time introduced an art admirably fitted for the dissemination of Prout's works, and by its means he was enabled to publish *Fac-similes of Sketches made in Flanders and Germany, Views in France, Switzerland and Italy ;* with others of the like nature.

During the latter years of his life he was a frequent sufferer from ill-health ; he died at his residence in Camberwell, 10th February, 1852, aged sixty-eight. We have already said that Prout, as an architectural draughtsman, aimed at generalization rather than at that precise imitation which characterized the well-trained pupils who were formed by the elder Pugin. Yet he brought before us admirably, if with a degree of *chique,* the general aspect of the ruined buildings, the churches and towns he so loved to paint ; his art was that of the period, and had little relation to the precision required by the new school. His reputation in his own day was greatly extended by his numerous publications ; but there is no doubt that the brilliancy of his colouring, the apparent ease and freedom of his execution, and the largeness of his style, will always make his pictures sought for, and retain for them a place in the folios of collectors.

The De Wints, as their name imports, are of Dutch origin, and the family had long been wealthy merchants in Amsterdam. Considerably more than a century ago, while the population of New York still consisted largely of the descendants of Dutch settlers, one of the De Wints left the sleepy canals and slow counting-houses of Holland, to try his fortune among the more active settlers of the new country, and in the young city of New York, Henry De Wint, the father of the painter, was born. He was the second son of a merchant of ample fortune, and in due time he was sent to Europe to study physic in the university of Leyden ; there he took a doctor's degree and went to London to complete his medical education. His father had determined, on his return to New York, that he should marry his cousin, that the family wealth might continue with the name; but this was not to be; young De Wint fell in love with an English lady of good family but no fortune, and married her at the early age of twenty-one. The father, offended with the step, withdrew the allowance of 300*l.* a year which he had hitherto paid his son, and never again saw the young physician. He received an injury shortly afterwards from the overturning of his carriage, and died, leaving all his wealth to the eldest son. No doubt the struggle of the young couple was for a time severe; youth is no recommendation for a physician, nor was the matter improved by his being a foreigner. He fixed his residence in Staffordshire, where he gradually established himself in practice, and where he continued to reside until his death in May, 1807. *Peter De Wint* the painter was the fourth son of the physician, and was born on the 21st of January, 1784. He was at first intended for his father's profession, but showing a great dislike to it as he grew up, and at the same time a great love for drawing, his father consented to his being an artist, and placed him, in 1802, with John Raphael Smith, the crayon painter and engraver. Here he met with a fellow pupil in William Hilton, the future historical painter, and a friendship was formed by the two lads that ended only with their lives. About the year 1807 the two young men entered as students of the Royal Academy during the keepership of Fuseli; the one to follow history painting to his life-long cost, and the disappointment of his best hopes; the other to practise landscape and to achieve competence and reputation from the new art of water-colour painting. In the year 1810 we find De Wint for the first time making his public appearance as an exhibitor. He sent three works to the Royal Academy, two being views in Staffordshire, and one in the neighbouring county of Derbyshire.

The intimacy of the two students soon ripened into a closer connection. De Wint visited the home of his friend. He found in Lincoln and its neighbourhood numberless subjects for his pencil: some of his best pictures are of the noble cathedral, towering high above the town which nestles at its foot. Better still, he found in the only sister of his companion—the daughter of the clergyman—a congenial nature, suited to the serious earnestness of his character; and in 1810, Miss Hilton became the wife of De Wint. The union was a happy one for all parties, but especially for Hilton. Years were to elapse ere history painting would afford an establishment for him; meanwhile, in his sister's house he found a happy home. He only left it when his election to the keepership of the Royal Academy obliged him to reside there: and after his late marriage and the loss of his wife, he returned to die at his sister's in Gower Street.

In 1810, De Wint became an exhibitor with the Society of Water-Colour Painters, and eventually a member of the body; and, though

D D

from time to time he sent a picture to the Royal Academy, he contributed for nearly forty years to the annual exhibitions of the Society. It is not to be supposed that De Wint's course was without its trials and difficulties. His father's death had occurred while the painter was yet a student. Marrying young, and at a time when art-purchasers were not so numerous as at present, he had to take to teaching—the usual resource of his brethren. This gradually introduced him to a wider circle : his pleasant manners and kindly nature made attached friends of those who had at first been pupils. He loved his art, particularly that branch of it he had made his own. He loved to paint direct from nature, making sketches and studies for his more elaborate pictures : he was never so happy as when in the fields. The scenery of his native country was so congenial to his taste, and his love of home so strong, that, except for a short visit to Normandy, he never left England. And after a happy life with those he loved, he died of disease of the heart, on the 30th June, 1849, leaving a widow, to whom we are indebted for many of the above facts, and an only daughter. He was buried near his friend and brother-in-law, in the ground of the Royal Chapel in the Savoy ; and his widow subsequently erected a handsome altar-tomb in Lincoln Cathedral, to the memory of the two friends who loved each other in life, and in death were not divided.

As an artist, De Wint formed a style of his own, sufficiently marked and distinct from his contemporaries to prove his originality. His art was neither realistic nor ideal ; but he had a fine sense of colour, and truly appreciated the tints and harmonies of natural scenery. He was a very indifferent draughtsman, and had little executive handling. Thus, in his trees, the delicate forms against the sky, the intricate mystery of boughs, the multitudinous leafage are all merged into masses, yet so locally true that we hardly regret the omission of details. The figures also which he introduces into his landscapes, though well placed and effective as to light and shade, and as enhancing points of colour leading the eye into the picture, are clumsy and feeble in their forms. He frequently used a drawing paper with a coarse surface ; partly to give texture to his flat masses, partly to hide his deficient handling, as well as for its value in giving the appearance of finish with little labour. From his habit of laying in his effect at once in broad, flat washes, his works have great freshness and purity. He avoided those executive processes to which others resorted. He occasionally *took out* his high lights, but did not make liberal use of the process ; when he did, the forms are still large and clumsy, and do not improve the *handling*, but merely tell on the general effect of the work. He rarely flattened his tints by stippling, though he occasionally resorted to broad hatchings in his skies. Like most of the artists of his period he objected to the use of white or of body colours in his works; though in some few instances we find his figures a little forced into sharpness by touches of solid white, as on the cattle of his picture of " Nottingham," in South Kensington Museum. He belonged to the middle period of water-colour art, to a school whose representatives have, alas, departed from amongst us.

George Fennel Robson was the son of a wine-merchant of Durham, in which city he was born in 1788. In early childhood he showed a power of imitation that seemed in the eyes of his friends to indicate the future artist. When only four or five years of age he made careful outlines from Bewick's woodcuts, and, as he grew in years, was fond of loitering in the company of any artists who were attracted by the picturesque scenery of Durham; while in school hours he was apt to devote himself to miscellaneous sketching rather than to his tasks. His father, seeing the bent of the boy's inclinations, placed him for instruction in drawing with a local teacher of the name of Harle, with whom his progress was so rapid that the teacher soon found himself distanced by the pupil. In the spring of 1805, the year of the first Water-Colour Exhibition, young Robson came to London, with five pounds in his pocket, lent by his father to enable the lad to see the art and artists of the metropolis. Robson was so delighted with the works of Varley, Hills, Havell, Glover, and other of the exhibiting members of the society, that to rival them became his highest aim, and he decided to practise as a water-colour painter. He remained in London, and was so successful in the sale of his drawings that he was enabled to maintain himself, and at the end of twelve months to return the five pounds to his father.

It may truly be said that Robson was a citizen of no mean city; he came to London with a portfolio of sketches of his native place, as a part of his stock-in-trade. In 1808 he published a view of Durham, which was so successful as to afford him the means of making a journey in the Highlands of Scotland, the Grampians and the fine scenery of the Lake district, laying up stores for future pictures, and studying nature under all the varied aspects of mountainous districts. The climate of England is peculiarly suited to the landscape painter: the moisture of its atmosphere induces those hazy mists that give breadth and size to our mountains, diminutive as they are when compared with those on the Continent. In the clear atmosphere of Italy and the East, hills, a day's journey in advance, seem to the traveller as if close at hand; and the distant town, the monastery, or the ruin, have their sharp clear lines defined to his eye. But in our cloud-land, vapour, even in the day-time, interposes its blue veil between him and the distance; and as the sun declines, the hills—not hidden as are Alps and Apennines by rounded spurs, the outworks of their range, but starting almost at once from valley and plain—are shrouded with a dim mystery of purple haze that elevates them, and gives them the apparent magnitude of the mountains of other lands. This effect of the atmosphere of our climate Robson diligently studied, and it became one of the distinguishing features of his art.

In 1814 Robson was elected a member of the Water-Colour Society; and his works being much admired, they began to be eagerly sought for by patrons and collectors: in 1820 he was for one year president of the Society. After his election he was ever an active member, and in the years 1828, 1829, 1830, and 1831, contributed nearly two hundred works to the exhibition. In 1826, Britton published *Picturesque Views of English Cities*, from water-colour paintings by Robson. Later than this, it became the fashion for ladies to have a scrap-book or album on the table of the boudoir. The Countess Demidoff while in Paris determined to have a superb work of this kind, and gave commissions to the principal French artists for sketches and studies. Mrs. Haldimand, the wife of the London banker, followed in the same path; Robson was intrusted by her with the selection of contributors, and the sum of ten guineas was named as the limit for each painter's work. This was thought liberal, and it served to increase the general popularity of the art; many charming works being executed for the album and subsequently exhibited. Years afterwards, when these books were broken up and the works dispersed, many of the sketches doubled and trebled their original value.

Robson painted many pictures in Scotland, and at times worked in conjunction with Hills, the animal painter, painting the backgrounds and scenery to Hills's animals. In the autumn of the year 1833 the two made a journey to Jersey, and after a short stay in that island, Robson took passage on board a Scotch smack for the north. He was landed in a distressing state of sickness at Stockton-on-Tees, and notwithstanding every care and attention, after a week's illness, he died on the 8th of September, 1833. A *post-mortem* examination failed to reveal the cause of his death. He himself in his last agonies declared that he was poisoned; and it was thought that his decease was to be attributed to his having, while on ship-board, eaten of food cooked in unclean copper vessels.

William Henry Hunt was born at 8 Old Belton Street, Long Acre, on the 28th of March, 1790, the son of John and Judith Hunt, and was christened shortly afterwards in the church of St. Giles's in the Fields. His father carried on the business of a tin-plate worker; but we have no record of the artist's mother, of her influence on his childhood, or of the instruction which he received in his youth. Judging from his letters in after-life, it must have been scanty; for though the matter of his correspondence is well expressed, it was said to be with difficulty, and after many corrections.

When the time arrived for settling the future vocation of the lad, his own inclination was decidedly towards art, while his father is said to have been strenuously opposed to it. Whatever had been the boy's education in other respects, he had certainly made some progress in art early, and must have had some encouragement from his parents in his pursuit of it; since we learn that his early friend, Mr. Linnell, who was intimate and worked with him at the time, possessed paintings by him made in the year 1805, months previous to his beginning regularly to learn art as a profession.

When about sixteen years of age, young Hunt was bound apprentice for seven years to John Varley, then living at 15, Broad Street, Golden Square. In our account of water-colour painting, we have already noticed Varley's influence on the rising school. In his house, Hunt met with many fellow-students, among others, with Mulready, who no doubt contributed to Hunt's future career by that example of careful and earnest study which has made his name so well known in art; and, most probably by his advice, Hunt sought and obtained admission as a student of the Royal Academy in the year 1808.

Hunt must have made rapid progress under John Varley's instruction, since in 1807, when little more than seventeen years of age, three of his pictures, which appear to have been works in oil, were hung in the Exhibition of the Royal Academy; and he continued to exhibit there during several following years. Hunt became a visitor at Dr. Monro's house in the Adelphi; followed, no doubt, the practice of the other painters who assembled there; and on the summer evenings, after their study at the Academy, in company with his friend Linnell, used to go forth to make those sketches, whose production the doctor encouraged by his purchases of the young students, or to copy Gainsborough's drawings, it is said, for the sum of one shilling and sixpence each. Doctor Monro, who saw young Hunt's docility and talent, took him down to his house at Bushey, near Watford, to paint from nature under the doctor's own instruction; who, we are told, did not hesitate to sponge out large portions of these sketches when their execution or colouring did not meet with his approval. Hunt often stayed with him for a month at a time, and was paid at the rate of 7s. 6d. per diem for his labours for the folio of Monro.

While sketching in the neighbourhood of Watford, the young student became known to the Earl of Essex, and was invited by him to paint some of the scenery of the park at Cashiobury. His name first appears in connection with the Water-Colour Society in 1814. In this year the society had been nearly broken up by a change in its objects—its exhibition being opened to works in oil as well as in water-colours, and Hunt's contributions as "fellow exhibitor" were most likely pictures in oil. In 1824, when the society had resumed its original character, Hunt was elected an associate, and in 1827 a full member of the body; and he continued to be a constant exhibitor with them to the last, one of his latest contributions being his own portrait.

He was throughout his life more or less of an invalid, and was never strong. For his health's sake he resided many years at Hastings, and by great care he continued to live and paint until nearly his seventy-fifth birthday. Attending at the rooms of the society, to examine the paintings of the candidates for its membership, he caught a violent cold, which terminated in apoplexy, and caused his death on the 10th February, 1864.

The works of Hunt differ widely from those of his contemporaries : they have a character of their own, and many qualities which place him as an artist, in his somewhat narrow range, on a level with the highest. He painted landscapes, figures, and, latterly, fruit and flowers equally well. His great characteristics are perfect imitation, without littleness or mean details; truthful colouring, never overcharged, never meretricious; a remarkable power of rendering the effect of daylight on the surface of objects, giving each the greatest textural truth, and marking its distinctive qualities of absorption or reflection. His sense of daylight was equal to that of De Hooghe, with the greater truth that arises from more luminous materials. Though a close imitator of nature, it was never without selection ; and if he made no attempt to add those effects which give ideality or poetry to his subject, yet even his objects of still-life were raised almost to the dignity of fine art by the taste with which he rendered them.

As a figure painter, Hunt drew passably well and rendered rustic nature with truth both of character and expression. If he is at times vulgar in his humour, and in the choice of his subjects, he at least avoids the vapid prettinesses from poets and novelists, of the Stephanoffs, or the sleek, mannered, china painted tableaux of Richter. There may be a smell of the barn or the stable, the aroma of the labourer's cottage about his boys and bumpkins ; but they are the children of the soil, the rustics of real life and not of the stage or the studio. Such are "The Attack," a young lout sitting down to feast on a huge pie ; "The Defeat," the same youth overcome with food fast asleep, the almost emptied dish beside him.

In the pictures of Hunt we find every variety of execution ; from tinted drawings, such as those of the early water-colour painters, to the thorough adoption of the pigments and processes of the present school. In "A Boy with Goat," in the South Kensington Museum, the colour is produced by tints coarsely hatched beside and over one another, the flesh finished by stippling, and the knife freely used throughout to give texture to the various surfaces. In some parts advantage is taken of the roughness thus obtained to give texture by tinting over it.   The hair of the goat is wholly made out by scratching up the paper with the knife. Very little body colour is used, and that merely to give absorbency to some of the surfaces; the work is well worth careful examination for the great effect obtained by the use of what would appear very incommensurate means.   "The Monk," in the same collection, shows the same handling, with a larger use of body colour, as in the high lights of the flesh, the cover of the book, &c.   It is curious to notice, in parts of his picture of "The Brown Study," how indifferent the painter was to the surface of his paper being kept intact; large portions in this picture have been destroyed by changes and the very roughness made to assist the required effect.

In his last manner Hunt entirely left the transparent system of the founders of the society; his works of this period are wonders of colour and imitative execution, but they have not the excellence of his middle period. The man of true genius easily adapts himself to new processes: and his later works are purely works in body colours, for such is the modern practice as opposed to the past; works by our present school actually approach what in old times would have been called tempera painting. To the end Hunt worked on with little apparent decline in his powers, little feebleness of eye or hand. The old painter continued to labour and to love his labour till the last.

We are obliged to pass over the names of many men whose works are creditable to the school and would claim place for them in dictionaries or in memoirs of artists, but who have not contributed sufficiently to the progress of art to have place in this work. Such were François Louis Francia, Francis Stevens, James Holmes, John Byrne, and some others. *Copley Vandyke Fielding*, however, must be noticed here not only for his art, but also for his influence during many years as the president of the Water-Colour Society; and as the fashionable teacher of the day, whose pupils swelled the crowds who visited the exhibition and purchased the pictures from its walls. He was one of four sons of Theodore Nathan Fielding, an artist of considerable local reputation who resided near Halifax, painted in oil with the careful finish of Denner, and was much patronized by the gentry of Lancashire and Yorkshire. Copley, his second son, was born in the year 1787, and showing in due time a liking for art, he received an early education from his father; who seems to have been more careful than most parents in instructing his children, since Theodore, Copley, Thales, and Newton, his four sons, were all either artists by profession or practised art with success.

We are not informed at what period Copley left home, but early in the century he was placed with John Varley, and with his master and fellow-pupils, was a constant visitor at Dr. Monro's, and there formed those friendships which connected his future with water-colour art. Not that he neglected entirely the nobler medium of oil; but his reputation wholly rests on his water-colour painting. Intending to follow landscape art, he refrained from the labour necessary to obtain admission as a student in the Royal Academy; hence the figures he introduces in his pictures do not reach beyond the usual properties of the landscape painter. In 1806 Fielding married the sister of Mrs. Varley. In 1810 we find his name for the first time as an associated exhibitor of the Water-Colour Society, contributing five landscapes, and he continued to exhibit through all the changes of the society until his death. In 1818 he was treasurer, and in 1819 secretary of the society; and during this period, when the society was in some difficulty, he seems to have made great efforts to support the exhibition, sending in 1819, forty-six frames containing seven-one paintings, and in 1820, forty-three frames, with fifty-six paintings. Most of these must have been such as he executed in lessons before his pupils, works of slight merit which had perhaps better not have been exhibited. In 1831, on the resignation of Cristall, Fielding was elected president of the society; a position which he held until his death, which happened on the 3rd March, 1855, in his sixty-eighth year. He was buried at Hove, near Brighton, where he had lived for many years.

Fielding's art also gradually suffered from his practice as a teacher. Obliged to make showy drawings before his pupils, and occasionally to indulge them with special "fireworks," in the shape of rapid and dexterous execution, methods of obtaining texture and handling by working on wet paper, by breading-out, or by the free use of the sponge; these manipulative tricks gradually became too apparent in his pictures, and individuality and truth are sometimes sacrificed to them.

Space is one of the qualities Fielding obtained in his pictures: he delights in distances, extensive flats, and rolling downs. It is true that while space is often attained the result is emptiness.

Fielding painted many marine pictures. From his long residence on the coast, constantly in presence of the ocean under every effect of calm and storm, some of these are among his best works. But they have too much of recipe in them; too much of that power of achieving at once a pleasant respectability which is so fatal to improvement. We have constantly the same alternations of sunlit sea with ranges of shade; the same ochrey sail contrasted with the spreading rain-cloud; varied and shifted in position, no doubt, in different pictures, but essentially the same. Though not wanting in truth, and agreeable and pleasant to the eye, his works rarely excite us with the feeling of any new combination or novel treatment of natural effects.

On the whole, it must be said that Fielding influenced the social status of art, rather than advanced it, by his own powers. His pictures show much talent, arising more from his adoption of the progress made by others than from any large share of natural genius of his own. He was a man of kindly nature and gentlemanly manners, and promoted the interests of water-colour painting by his practice, though he did not advance the art.

The art of *George Cattermole* (B. 1800, D. 1868) is more dramatic and pictorial than really artistic, yet he was versatile in his powers and learned in costume, and his best figure subjects are full of vigour, and dashing in colour and effect. He became a full member of the Society of Painters in Water-Colours in 1833, and for the next few years produced some of his best works, such as "After the Sortie," "Pilgrims at a Church Door," "The Armourer Relating the Story of the Sword," &c. In 1850 he withdrew from the society. He received a first-class gold medal for water-colour painting at the Paris Exhibition of 1855. He painted principally figures, and chose picturesque and romantic subjects, such as brigands, armed robbers, knights errant, and fair ladies. He had stored his mind with all the necessary material, and worked from memory without the intervention of a model, but with a facility of execution which gave great freshness and vigour to his compositions. His figures are rather types of their class than possessed of any distinct individuality, and in his later work they incline to tameness.

He very early adopted the use of white, and his pictures are solid or semi-solid throughout ; his rich transparent colour he reserved solely for the draperies of his foreground figures.

Louis Haghe (B. 1806, D. 1885) was another vigorous painter, combining figures with excellent interiors, especially of Flemish towns. He was by birth a Belgian, and painted with his left hand. He was for some years president of the Institute of Painters in Water-Colours.

Edward Duncan (B. 1803, D. 1882) had a great reputation in his day. He was intended for an engraver, but soon abandoned engraving for painting. He became a full member of the Society of Painters in Water-Colours in 1849. His marine subjects are the more important of his works, and have a distinct freshness and charm. He painted a good deal in transparent colour, but also used body colours in his lights.

George John Pinwell, born in London 26th December, 1842, was a painter whose water-colour method may be said to have been entirely opaque. His art was in some respects analogous to that of Walker. He obtained his first reputation as a book-illustrator, and was decidedly a brilliant draughtsman. He was elected an associate of the Society of

Painters in Water-Colours in 1869, and a full member two years later. In 1872 he exhibited the "Pied Piper of Hamelin," a composition with many figures happily grouped, and very pure and delicate in colour. He was cut off prematurely by death at the early age of thirty-three, 8th September, 1875. Had he lived longer he would probably have made for himself a name in art.

In coming nearer to our own time, though many names occur to us of those who have more or less affected the art of our day, want of space compels us to pass them over, while there are others who will doubtless extend the reputation of our water-colour school, who as they are still living are out of our sphere. It would seem almost invidious during their lifetime, when we consider the immense spread of water-colour art, to extol, at the expense of their brethren who are still with us, those artists who have been taken from us, but in 1881 there was removed from our midst a truly original and poetical-minded painter, whose art has till now found no follower, though it must have influenced many, but without such a notice any work treating of a century of English art would indeed be incomplete ; we mean the art of *Samuel Palmer.*

His life was a long study of the varied aspects of nature, and having mastered all imitative detail, and having a mind filled with the study of classic poetry, and deeply imbued with the noble imagery of the most classic of our English poets, Milton, he acquired the power of rendering nature in her grandest phases, and of painting her as she appeared to his original and learned mind. Palmer was born at Newington, 27th January, 1805, and was educated at home. At the early age of fourteen he exhibited and sold his first oil picture at the British Institution. He became at this time known to Linnell, who introduced him to Blake. Blake's influence fell on a congenial soil, and Palmer ever acknowledged his deep obligation to him, and spoke of him with the greatest veneration. Palmer drew from the antique at the British Museum, where he had his life-long friend, G. Richmond, R.A., for a companion, and his work was then distinguished by its accuracy and elaborate finish.

Always delicate. Palmer soon after his first success in art went to live at Shoreham, in Kent, with his father, as his health required country air. Of this time he ever afterwards spoke as one of deep enjoyment and rapid growth. He looked back to the sunsets of Shoreham, its hollow lanes, and wondrous woods, its golden harvests, its wealth of pastoral beauty, and glorious effects of storm and darkness, as to a land of pure delight, investing its real natural beauty with a still more vivid glory culled from the wealth of his own imagination. In 1839 he married the eldest daughter of his friend John Linnell, who was herself an artist, and went with his wife and the Richmonds to spend two years in Italy, a time of hard and untiring study, and of rich artistic develop-

ment, which coloured the rest of his life. On his return he settled in
Marylebone, and painted mostly in oil. His pictures in that medium
were very truthful and careful, but not boldly conceived. In 1842 he
made his last appearance at the Royal Academy, for the next year he
was elected an associate of the Old Society of Painters in Water-Colours,
and from this time painted entirely in water-colour.

Palmer took infinite pains in the preparation of his pigments, and
would use several palettes in order that he might not be tempted to mix
those colours together which did not properly assort, or whose
juxtaposition might lead to serious consequences. It is therefore more
than probable that his pictures, brilliant as is their colour, will stand
well, for Palmer left out no step in the proceding, and he was equally
anxious in the preparation of the cardboard on which he painted.

In 1848 he removed to Kensington, where, besides pursuing his art,
he gave lessons in drawing to schools and private pupils. The death
of a little daughter had induced him to leave Marylebone for Kensington, and in 1861 a still sadder cause, the death of a son of great promise,
made him leave Kensington for Reigate, in which place he lived till his
death. His younger and sole surviving son, A. Herbert Palmer, has
written a most interesting memoir of his father, containing also a list of his
works and an account of his method of painting, which is of the greatest
technical value. We recommend it, too, to those of our readers who
are anxious for more details of a highly intellectual, simple and noble
life, devoted to art, literature and music. Unfortunately our space only
allows us to comment on the work of a painter, and not upon his
domestic life.

Palmer's early water-colour paintings are, we think, perhaps more
like his oil pictures, that is to say more conventional and less lustrous
than his later work. As his art grew, so did his power of design, his
love of mystery in landscape art, his feeling of tone, and his delight in
dazzling effects of brilliant sunlight. "St. Paul landing in Italy," 1850 ;
"The Dell of Comus," 1855; and "The Brothers Discovering the
Palace and Bower of Comus," 1856, are among the finest works of his
transition stage, but his art culminated in the noble series of eight
water-colours illustrating Milton's *L'Allegro*, and *Il Penseroso*, which he
painted for Mr. L. Valpy. Palmer's etchings, too, are gems of imaginative art. These harmonious renderings of light and shade carry out
even in black and white his fine sense of colour. He was a member of
the Etching Club, and during the last years of his life worked upon a
series of etchings to illustrate Virgil's *Eclogues*, which have been
finished and published by his son. He became a full member of the
Water Colour Society in 1854.

Palmer retained the old traditions and rarely used body colour in his water-colour pictures, he kept his highest lights of the pure white of his paper ; indeed, if he wished for a sparkling light in his foreground, he would cut it out with his knife. He loved to paint light, and it has been objected to his art that he was too much devoted to subjects involving the representation of the sun and moon. In preparing his cardboard for work, he would give it a slight wash of Chinese white with perhaps a little cadmium to obtain a warm ivory tint, on this he drew in in red chalk. A swan quill was with him a very favourite tool, and he used it frequently during the progress of the picture. Though a most conscientious painter, his art was entirely free from " niggle," and had a grandeur and style of its own. He made designs for each picture both in charcoal and pen and ink, and used to speak highly of the tone he could produce with simple writing ink. He had a great appreciation and love for Claude's pictures, and had been an attentive student of the old masters.

Palmer was always a great sufferer after his return from Italy from spasmodic asthma, and during the last years of his life he was very much confined to the house, and endured many severe attacks of illness. He died 24th May, 1881, and was buried in Reigate Church-yard. He was a most delightful companion, abounding in humour, and rich in anecdote, proceeding from a mind stored with interesting know-ledge. He was a fine reader, and in his youth was very musical. The Fine Art Society held an exhibition of his works after his death, by which, as Sir F. Burton well observed, " the present generation had an opportunity of showing their own worth, by their appreciation of his."

CHAPTER XXXIV.

IN tracing the progress of the arts, we have noted the formation of various societies for their promotion; both by the King, by the artists themselves, and by amateurs and patrons of art. Two other institutions connected with the spread of art yet demand notice at our hands.

When the long period of almost universal war had ended, and a general peace had restored the finances of our country and increased the wealth of individuals, our countrymen, always the most prone to travel, resorted in great numbers to the Continent. In all the great cities of Europe they found, not only museums of works of art, but picture galleries containing the easel pictures of the great masters, freely opened for the instruction of their artists, and the use and pleasure of the public. Returning, they noted that our artists, our public, had no such advantages, and they the less wondered that our country enjoyed no reputation on the Continent for the talent of its artists, or the taste of its manufactures. The public taste wanted cultivating to appreciate works of higher art and nobler aim, and to create a desire for manufactures decorated with less pretence and more refinement. This feeling, which arose among the more travelled and educated, rapidly spread through all classes. Public opinion, gradually awakened, influenced the Government of that day, and when, on the death of Mr. John Julius Angerstein, his collection was for sale, the opportunity was taken, by its purchase in 1824, to begin a National Gallery of Pictures.

The Angerstein collection contained many very choice works, and since it became the property of the nation, it has been gradually added to by gift and by purchase; it has been of great benefit to art, a source of great instruction to the public, and the pictures, especially by masters of the Italian school, have been increased to form a collection of which the nation may be justly proud. For many years British art found no real place in the collection. Mr. Wornum tells us in his catalogue that " up to the year 1847, nearly a quarter of a century after its foundation, the National Gallery contained only forty-one pictures of the British school," mostly the irregular gifts of individuals. In 1847 Mr. Vernon bequeathed his collection ; and in 1856 Turner bequeathed 108 pictures ; and the gallery consists now, it having been increased by pecuniary bequests for the purchase of pictures by four generous donors, of nearly 1,280 British pictures. Still it cannot even now be considered, much as it has improved, to include an entirely satisfactory representation of British art. The water-colour collection at the South Kensington Museum is perhaps more chronologically perfect, and it contains some beautiful specimens of English art in oil pictures by the gift of Mr. Sheepshanks.

About the year 1823, the Water-Colour Society having ceased either to admit oil paintings, as it had done for a short time, and closed its doors against every one but its own members ; and the spring exhibition of the British Institution, as managed by lay directors, being unsatisfactory to the profession, while the number of painters had much increased, the time seemed ripe for change, and a number of artists met together to form another society to promote the better exhibition of their works. Preliminaries having been discussed, premises were secured and suitable galleries erected in Suffolk Street, Pall Mall East ; and in 1824 the new " Society of British Artists " opened its first annual exhibition.

On the first opening the new galleries contained 754 works by two hundred and fifty-six exhibitors. A plan somewhat analogous to that of the British Institution was adopted to provide funds for the new society. Donations were sought for, and annual subscriptions, while sums were requested on loan at five per cent., with contingent advantages of admittance to the exhibitions. Among the first members of the society were some men already eminent, and others who soon became so. Heaphy, of whom we have already given a memoir, was the first president ; Hofland, the landscape painter, the first vice-president, while the list also contained the names of J. Glover, P. Nasmyth, D. Roberts, C. Stanfield, and J. Wilson the marine painter. Among the contributors to the first exhibition (beside the above) are Haydon and his pupil G. Lance ; Martin, and Rippingille ; together with six others, who subsequently became members of the Royal Academy.

It seems to have been the principle of the British Institution at its first formation to change its officers annually, if with occasional re-elections. The new society had to contend with a difficulty to which the founders of the Water-Colour Society had not been subjected. They had no speciality, the scheme of their exhibition was only supplemental to that of the Academy, and it was inevitable that the older institution should offer attractions to painters of talent that would make them at times unfaithful to their first engagements. As its members rose into distinction, some of them left the society to seek admission into the Royal Academy. Stanfield and Roberts paid a pecuniary fine, and seceded. In 1841, a charter of incorporation was obtained from the Crown, and shortly after, in 1847, schools were opened for the study of art. In 1848, the society announced that 100 students had entered, and that the schools were well attended : this congratulatory notice was repeated in 1849 ; but the Academy schools retained their old prestige, and the new school of design at Somerset House attracted all those who found difficulty in obtaining admission at Trafalgar Square, so that after 1849 the schools of the society were closed. But while some of the members seceded from the body, and many of those who were only exhibitors were led there rather by interest than by gratitude, there were still those who remained staunch to their membership. Still the Society of British Artists though it has not always prospered, has outlived one or two other attempts at active competition, and, as managed entirely by artists and in the interests of art, we trust that it has obtained a footing, which for the future will ensure its prosperity and success.

We have already written of some of those who were connected with the early history of the society ; of Heaphy and Glover, in our account of the Water-Colour School ; of Martin and Haydon, of Nasmyth and Roberts. Hofland, one of the first presidents, deserves some notice as a successful landscape painter; John Wilson, as a painter of marine pictures ; George Lance, the pupil of Haydon, as a constant exhibitor for the first ten years of the society's existence, after which, as rather a favourite with the directors of the Institution, and usually finding his pictures well hung on the walls of the Academy, he ceased to be an exhibitor with the Society of British Artists.

Thomas Christopher Hofland was born at Worksop, in Nottinghamshire, on Christmas-day, 1777, the only son of a cotton manufacturer. The father removed to London in 1780, and, after struggling some years in his business, eventually failed just as his son had attained his nineteenth year. Young Hofland had now to settle upon some occupation for life, and he devoted himself to landscape painting. Beyond a few lessons from Rathbone he had to struggle on unassisted, and to obtain knowledge as he best could, by examining such pictures as came in his way. Like most other young artists in the branch he had chosen, his chief dependence for subsistence was on teaching ; but in 1799 we find him for the first time in the Academy catalogue.

In the early part of the present century, when our land was continually threatened with the French invasion, men of all ranks and all ages enrolled themselves as volunteers, and young Hofland joined the King's Own company at Kew. The King took much pride in the loyalty displayed by his people, and frequently reviewed his volunteers. Hofland had the good fortune to attract his particular attention as fugleman of the corps, and was employed to make drawings of the rare plants in the collection at Kew, the King also seeking to promote the painter's interests in other quarters; but illness frustrated his Majesty's kind intention.

An opening for a teacher of drawing at Derby led Hofland to settle there for a time. After living there several years, he came up to town to take the opportunity of copying some landscapes by the old masters at the British Institution. His love of art influenced him to remain, and he settled in London at the close of 1811. He was very successful as a copyist, finding ready purchasers for his repetitions of Claude, Wilson, Poussin, and Gainsborough. He painted a large landscape, "A Storm off the Coast of Scarborough," obtained a premium of 100 guineas for it from the British Institution, and sold it to the Marquis of Stafford. His smaller pictures of lake scenery, founded on the studies he had made, were admired and purchased, and he became established in reputation as a landscape painter.

With a view to his art, he removed in 1816 to Twickenham, and was employed to paint a series of pictures for the Duke of Marlborough of his estate of White Knights, to which work he devoted several years. He became responsible to the engraver employed to engrave these pictures, and disputes arising, the painter was exposed to cruel disappointment and heavy loss, through confiding in the duke's promises. Hence he was obliged to return to London, and to renew his engagements as a teacher; occupying his spare time in painting, and producing at this period some of his best pictures, among others, "A View of Lake Windermere," purchased by Lord Durham, and which was exhibited in the International Exhibition of 1862. We have already seen that he was a promoter of the Society of British Artists, and one of the first members. From the time of its foundation until his death he remained true to the society, and was a regular exhibitor at Suffolk Street. In his sixty-third year he was enabled by a commission from that true friend of art and artists, the late Earl of Egremont, to fulfil a long-cherished wish to visit Italy. He reached Naples, made many sketches at Pompeii and other spots, but on his return was seized with a fever at Florence, and reached home with his health thoroughly broken up. He lingered about two years, and journeying to take the advice of Dr. Jephson, died at Leamington, of a cancer in the stomach, on the 3rd January, 1843. His widow, who obtained some celebrity as a writer, did not long survive him. To the Suffolk Street exhibition of the year he died, he contributed three pictures. Singularly enough the last in the catalogue is the same subject as that by which he made his fame, No. 480, "A Storm off the

Coast of Scarborough ; " it was not quite finished, and was accompanied by a very appropriate line, " Here the last touches fell from Hofland's hand."

Hofland's landscapes were not of the imitative or realistic school. They are mostly studied compositions ; he aimed, at least, at treating nature under a poetical aspect and divested of commonplace. But the tone he adopted throughout gave great monotony to his works ; while his handling wanted variety, his surface lacked texture, and the softness with which the parts too often melted into one another, added to the prevailing want of colour, gave a feeling of insipidity to his pictures. As a painter he never rose to the first rank, since propriety rather than genius was his great characteristic.

John Wilson was another of the original members of the society who remained true to the institution, and continued to exhibit there to the last. He was born at Ayr on the 13th of August, 1774, and like his countryman and friend Roberts, was, in his fourteenth year, apprenticed to a house painter and decorator. He served his master, Mr. John Norie of Edinburgh, duly and truly, and attained at least a knowledge of the processes of painting as adapted to larger surfaces than the usual canvas pictures of the artist ; this knowledge he afterwards found highly useful, when, as an artist, he gained employment in the scene-loft of our London theatres. When he left Mr. Norie he took a few lessons in oil painting from the elder Mr. Smith, which were his only direct art-teaching. From Edinburgh he turned his steps northward, and for more than two years he resided in Montrose, practising as a drawing-master. But the prospect of wealth and fame which London holds out would not allow him to remain satisfied with such unimproving drudgery. He journeyed to the metropolis, and soon found an engagement as a scene painter at Astley's Theatre in the Lambeth Road.

In 1807, we find his name for the first time as an exhibitor at the Royal Academy. In 1810 Wilson married, and was fortunate in his choice. Of a genial nature himself, fond of the society of his friends and countrymen, his married life was a happy one while it lasted ; Wilson having survived his wife more than twenty-four years. In 1813, the painter exhibited at the British Institution, " The Aqueduct on the Kelvin near Glasgow," and was afterwards a frequent exhibitor ; in 1826 the directors awarded him 100*l.* for a sketch for the " Battle of Trafalgar," which he had exhibited in response to a prize offered by the institution. We have seen that he was one of the prime movers in founding the Society of British Artists, and after the formation of the institution he continued to be a constant contributor to their exhibitions.

During the latter years of his life he lived at Folkestone, where he was constantly within view of the ever-changing sea, whose moods and motions were his constant study; there he died on the 29th April, 1855, having contributed to the exhibition of that year five pictures: thus he laboured on his beloved art to the last. Wilson's education as a decorator did him good service when he turned to scene painting, and his qualities as a scene painter pervaded his easel pictures. They are bold, free, and unlaboured. The pictorial feeling was strong in him; his works want refinement of execution and are not very varied in range, but they present themselves agreeably to the eye, and render nature vigorously and with rude truth.

George Lance, the painter of still-life, was born on the 24th March, 1802, at the old manor-house of Little Easton, in Essex. His father, who had previously been an officer in a regiment of light horse, was, at the time of young Lance's birth, an adjutant in the Essex Yeomanry. A handsome young man and a soldier, he won the heart of his future wife while she was yet at boarding-school, and used to relate that he eloped with her from one of the school windows. She was the daughter of Colonel Constable, of Beverley, in Yorkshire, and if the match was a hasty one, she made a good wife and mother. The elder Lance afterwards held for many years the office of inspector of the horse patrol, who were so useful in ridding the environs of London of the daring highwaymen and footpads in that day infesting the roads leading to town. As young Lance grew towards manhood, his parents determined to bring him up as a manufacturer, and placed him with some relations at Leeds; but the boy, who in youth had loved picture-books in preference to all others, had a great distaste for his new labours, and his friends soon perceived that they were not suited to him. He was allowed to return to London, and soon found a profession for himself. Walking through the British Museum, where young artists were then, as now, permitted to copy from the marbles, he was struck with the work of one who had written on his study, "pupil of B. R. Haydon." Lance mustered up courage to ask him if Mr. Haydon would take other pupils. It was Charles Landseer whom he thus fortuitously addressed, and he told him he had better make the inquiry of Haydon himself. Thither, full of trepidation, the young painter took his way, and admitted to the presence of the historical painter, faltered forth the question, "I am anxious to become an artist, and want to be one of your pupils—I am come to ask your terms." "Terms, my little fellow," answered the impetuous but generous painter,—"when I take pupils, I never look at the fathers' purses; bring me some of your works, and if I think they promise success, I will take you for nothing." And Haydon did become his master, and under him, and as a student in the Royal Academy, he learnt his art.

The adoption of his future walk in art was the result of an accident.

Being set to paint some still-life as a means of improving his execution, the work was good enough to find a purchaser in Sir George Beaumont ; other patrons gave like commissions, and the young artist, finding the work profitable, was gradually confirmed as a painter of still-life. In this class of art Lance was for a long time unrivalled, not only for truthful imitation of fruits, foliage, flowers, and all the varied accessories of vessels of glass, rich plate and draperies, with which they are grouped ; but for most delicate execution and pleasing arrangement. To these qualities he added a strong feeling for colour, yet at times verging on meretricious vividness. His renderings of dead game and birds of rare plumage have rarely been excelled in any school. In his picture of "Melanchthon's First Misgivings of Rome," wherein a young monk, painted of the size of life, regards with pain the sensuality of an elder brother sleeping off the effects of his attack on the banquet beside him ; and "The Seneschal," executed to fill one of the compartments in the dining-room at Somerleyton, he has shown powers of higher order than those of a mere painter of still-life. He died on the 18th of June, 1864, at Sunnyside, near Birkenhead.

His pupil, *William Duffield*, died before him—died just as he was developing even higher powers than his teacher. Born at Bath, he entered the schools of the Royal Academy, and afterwards studied his art under George Lance. As he advanced, he gradually adopted a larger manner than his teacher. Of this, his last exhibited picture, a "Swan and Peacock," at the British Institution in 1865 (the background painted by his friend and fellow-pupil, Gilbert), is a good example, and is a work of great merit. Lying right across the front of the picture is a dead peacock, his head resting on the snowy bosom of a swan. The contrast between white and colour, light and dark, is most artistically treated without the appearance of artifice. The colour and tone are good, the execution excellent in finish, yet without the sense of tedious labour. Gilbert's share in the work which is wholly confined to the background is well defined, and is happily suited to support that of his friend. Duffield died on the 3rd of September, 1863, in his forty-sixth year. He owed his last illness to the earnest pursuit of his profession. He was painting a dead stag, which remained in his studio for that purpose until it became extremely decayed. Unfortunately the painter, from a prior illness, had lost his sense of smell : and in the absence of the organization given to warn us of the presence of miasma he continued to work unconscious of the danger, until the infection took place which caused his death.

CHAPTER XXXV.

FRESCO-PAINTING AND STATE PATRONAGE.

In a previous chapter we have traced the attempts made by the lay directors of the British Institution to foster and promote art in England. The scheme of our work now leads us to consider the efforts which have been made by the State with the same great purpose. The first attempt of the State to patronize art, was the employment of our sculptors to commemorate the heroes of the French revolutionary war, by the erection of public monuments in St. Paul's Cathedral and Westminster Abbey; but the great and primary object really was to distinguish the brave soldiers who had fallen, irrespective of any scheme for the advancement of art. There was little difficulty in giving commissions to our most eminent sculptors, and appointing places for their works in our two great national mausoleums; and having done this the public purse-strings were again drawn tight, and art and its interests were overlooked and forgotten.

When one evening in October, 1831, the Houses of Parliament burst into flames, and the trusty porter of the Royal Academy thus announced the event to the students in the library—"Now, gentlemen; now, you young architects, there's a fine chance for you; the Parliament House is all afire;" he only expressed what soon became the received public opinion. The extensive destruction caused by the fire was looked upon by all as affording a large opportunity for the development of native art by State patronage; and accordingly when Sir Charles Barry's great design began to assume completeness in its magnificent proportions, the House of Commons (on the motion of Mr. Benjamin Hawes, an independent member), without explanation or discussion, appointed, in April, 1841, "a select committee to take into consideration the promotion of the fine arts of this country in connection with the rebuilding of the Houses of Parliament." This committee sat nine times; they examined Sir Charles Barry (then Mr. Barry), Sir Martin Shee, president of the

Royal Academy, Mr. Dyce, the superintendent of the Government School of Design, Sir Charles Eastlake (then Mr. Eastlake), Mr. Fradelle, an artist, and two or three well-known amateurs.

The committee had not time to consider the plan by which the great national work they enquired into should be carried out, but they thought that a Royal Commission might be appointed, and that the advice and assistance of persons who were competent from their knowledge of art and their acquaintance with great public works, both at home and abroad, should be called in to propose, in conjunction with the architect, the most effectual means of attaining the chief object aimed at—the encouragement of the fine arts of the country. The pattern presented to the committee by the dilettanti was Munich. Fresco-painting which had been revived there, was to be introduced and naturalized here, and the committee recommended it for adoption. Yet they did so, quite unsupported by the distinguished artists whose opinions they had sought. Eastlake, in fact, saw from the first the necessity, if fresco were to be used, of adopting the *atelier* system, a plan which has never found favour among the artists of the English school.

When the new Parliament met, Sir Robert Peel, then prime minister, stated that instead of re-appointing a select committee, he purposed to recommend the appointment of a Royal Commission for the completion of the inquiry ; and no time was lost. Her Majesty's commission was opened in November, 1841. It comprised twenty-one members, none of them artists except Eastlake who acted as secretary.

Expectation was on tip-toe, and it was soon gratified. Within six months the commissioners made their first report. They, of course, expressed their opinion, echoing the words of their commission, "that it would be expedient that advantage should be taken of the rebuilding of the Houses of Parliament, for the purpose of promoting and encouraging the fine arts of the United Kingdom." And then with regard to the employment of fresco, they cautiously say, "They have not yet been able to satisfy themselves that the art of fresco-painting has hitherto been sufficiently cultivated in this country to justify them in recommending that it should be so employed ; and in order to assist them in forming a judgment, they proposed that artists should be invited to enter into a competition by cartoons ; " and they announced premiums chiefly, but not exclusively, in reference to fresco ; explaining that oil painting and sculpture would receive further consideration. The conditions of competition were appended to the report. The premiums offered were three of 300*l*. each, three of 200*l*. each, and five of 100*l*. each. The time named for the reception of the works was the first week in May, 1843. There was also appended, among other matter, a valuable report by the secretary in which it was argued that high art is best displayed in large works; that large paintings have not met with encouragement from private patronage; and that fresco is the best material for the display of high art on a grand scale.

In France, where the national art was better suited to fresco, it had also been tried : the Church of St. Vincent de Paul was decorated in fresco-painting before the year 1825 ; but the French artists have reverted to oil, and few great works in their capital have been executed in fresco. Our own artists had long admired the fresco works of the great Italian painters, which are well known to them : but they had not thought fresco suited to the qualities in which they excelled, or to the expression of their art ; though some exceptional attempts had been made by them. While nothing could be more foreign than fresco to the art which Wilkie practised, its merits and advantages were well understood and described by him. Its processes are, we assume, generally known to consist in the application of the colours on the surface of a wall newly plastered, in which they are imbibed by the chemical action of the lime in drying ; and that so much of the surface only is prepared from day to day as may be finished at once by the artist, who traces such daily portions of his work from a prepared cartoon-drawing of his whole subject, removing after the labour of the day is completed, all the plaster that he has not had time to finish completely.

The commission had adopted the principle of competition ; but that system in art has, we fear, been generally prejudicial. We believe that the true mode of obtaining a good work of art is to select the artist of the highest acknowledged ability, and, after explaining fully the object desired, to leave the work as much as possible to his unfettered judgment and skill ; relying rather upon his reputation, which is at stake, than upon the conflicting opinions, and, too frequently, the crude notions of a committee. Their powers would be sufficiently exercised in the selection of the artist whose talent most specially fits him for the production of the particular work they contemplate.

But to return. In July, 1843, the commissioners made their second report. They stated that the competition in cartoons had taken place, "and that they are satisfied with the evidence of ability afforded," and they add, "we now propose, in pursuance of the plan before announced by us, to invite artists to exhibit specimens of fresco-painting of a moderate size, which, by being portable, will enable all candidates for employment in that method of painting to send in works exhibiting their qualifications therein as painters and colourists, and which, taken together with their larger compositions in drawing which they have exhibited or may exhibit, and with other existing evidences of their talents, may enable us to proceed to the selection of artists for the decoration in fresco of certain portions of the palace." To this second invitation many of the artists again responded, and a second exhibition of their works took place in Westminster Hall in the summer of 1844. Omitting sculpture, which is outside the scope of our work, we find that eighty-four works were contributed by fifty-six painters. They were chiefly by young artists rising into note; and by men who had been long known for their large historic compositions which they had not found a public to appreciate; with some few crude attempts by men hitherto unknown.

The commissioners were again "satisfied." In their third report, dated 9th July, 1844, they state: "We propose to commission six artists, selected by us from among the present exhibitors in Westminster Hall, to furnish designs, coloured sketches, and specimens of fresco-painting, for certain subjects proposed by us to be executed in the House of Lords, at the same time not binding ourselves to employ such artists finally."

The commissioners had already allured the profession into two competitive displays of their works. First, of cartoons drawn to a large scale, and necessarily involving the cost, not only of much thought and labour, but also of models—always a serious expense to the young artist. Secondly, of specimens of fresco-painting — a new material requiring some experimental practice, and, while attended by expense, leading men aside from the direct pursuit of their own art, the promptings of their own imaginings. Yet, after these labours and trials, the commissioners proposed, not to select the painters for employment on the great works in the expectation of which they had been stimulated to make such costly efforts, but to select six, and to require these fortunate men to furnish cartoon-designs, specimens of fresco-painting, &c.; and still to undergo another ordeal, for the commissioners "did not bind themselves to employ such artists finally," and, in fact, did not.

It was not till after four years' gestation that among the competitors the commissioners resolved that one fresco—the "Baptism of St. Ethelbert," by Mr. Dyce—should be completed; and they deferred for one year, till June, 1847, the competition for oil painting.

Thus her Majesty's commissioners were appointed in 1841, and were commanded to report to the Queen, "the mode in which, by means of the interior decoration of the palace of Westminster, the fine arts of this country can be most effectually encouraged;" the sole object of the commission was assuredly the encouragement of the fine arts, the decoration of the Houses of Parliament as surely only the means to that end; yet in 1846, after five years of sittings and deliberations, her Majesty's commissioners were only able to report that one painting was finished and three others commissioned. Dire and bitter disappointment was experienced — disappointment founded on just expectations unfulfilled.

In the interval, the works of the painters in oil, invited by the commissioners in 1845, were received and exhibited in Westminster Hall; forming the fourth competitive exhibition. The oil medium was the practice of the English school, and many artists had lain by to make their powers known in this long-promised competition; and, stimulated by the national work before them, which all hoped to share, the profession once more with unchilled enthusiasm, though with abated confidence, submitted their works. We are not told how many were rejected—for the commissioners reserved this right—but the catalogue shows that 124 paintings by 103 painters " were deemed by the commissioners to possess sufficient merit to entitle them to the *privilege*" of exhibition.

The paintings were, with few exceptions, of unusually large size; the canvases averaging more than 100 square feet, but many exceeding twice that size. The competitors were chiefly ambitious, young and rising men; but there were several of the elder men well known in the profession, and among them, this time, two members of the Royal Academy. Then followed the commissioners' judgment in their seventh report, dated July, 1847. The nine premiums of 300*l.* were awarded to nine of the competing exhibitors by a committee of three members of the commission, with whom were associated three Royal Academicians; and the commissioners announced that they were desirous that some of the paintings should be preserved to the nation.

We believe that the proceeds of the exhibition, 1,300*l.*, were devoted to the purchase of four of the works. This seems but a poor return or encouragement for all the labour and all the outlay of time and money that the competitors had expended upon their pictures.

In their eighth report, September, 1848, they state that three more frescoes in the House of Lords are to be executed, and they announce the employment of Mr. Dyce, R.A., to decorate the Queen's Robing-room with the "Legend of King Arthur;" having stipulated that he should receive 800*l.* a year for six years, within which time the work (which his death in 1864 left unfinished) should be completed; and further, that they had authorized four artists, whose designs they had approved, to begin their frescoes in the Upper Waiting Hall. These frescoes, illustrations of our great poets, are, alas! at the time we write, complete wrecks! A lapse of eighteen months ensued before the next report. It was dated in March, 1850, and proclaimed the completion of the two remaining frescoes in the House of Lords; it said they were highly satisfactory, and indicated increased skill on the part of the artists in the management of the material : it also announced the completion of the four smaller frescoes in the Upper Waiting Hall. The commissioners, moreover, had selected Sir Edwin Landseer, R.A., to paint in oil three subjects connected with the chase, for the three compartments of the Peers' Refreshment Room, naming 1,500*l.* for the three paintings : a price which proved that the painter's motives in accepting it were far other than pecuniary ones.

The expectations with which the first proposal to promote art and to decorate a palace for the Legislature had been received, could hardly have been satisfied ; but they had long since been chilled by protracted delays, followed by small performances ; while the profession had been wearied out by fruitless competitions and contests. It was as difficult to understand the proceedings, as the objects and aims of the commission.

In the four frescoes completed, the artists, with probably one exception, had not succeeded in adapting their art to the peculiar conditions demanded in fresco decorations. They had been told in the admirable reports by the secretary, that imperfect light requires magnitude and simplicity of parts, that distinctness may be attained by light and shade, form or colour ; but they had missed these essential qualities, the principal figure in one being absolutely invisible ; and they had failed to attain that dignity and repose which belong to fresco, and that subordination and symmetry of composition which are indispensable when the painter's art is employed in the decoration of the architect's. It is true that the painters had to contend with insuperable difficulties. The situations selected for them by the commissioners were quite unsuited to the proper display of high art in any medium. The three paintings opposite the throne are so deeply recessed, that they are seen as in a dark hole, and with the three opposite to them, have to contend against a side light, admitted on their level, and through richly stained glass ; and they also suffer from the great absence of repose, arising from the extensive employment of colour-gilding throughout the forms in the general decoration of the chamber. Tapestry would have been a far more suitable decoration. These works are at the time we write in a sad state arising from neglect, decay and dirt.

Meanwhile the public lost patience ; they thought that little had been done, and that little unsuccessfully, and the failure of the whole scheme was already predicted. The House of Commons had, in the previous session, with grumbling and grudging, voted the sums asked for the commission. They were irritated with the absence of responsible control over the moneys when voted, and dissatisfied with the work they had got for their money ; upon which they turned very critical, and when the Government asked the sum of 1,500*l.* to pay for the three oil-paintings by Sir Edwin Landseer, the House by an adverse vote, while expressing the highest estimation for the artist's talent, made him the scapegoat, and struck that amount out of the estimates. This was a very plain expression of want of confidence in her Majesty's commissioners, and a rude check to their proceedings. They had till this reported their doings yearly, but now, above four years elapsed before another report appeared. Their tenth report was dated July, 1854, and announced the completion of eight frescoes in the Upper Waiting Hall. These eight are crammed into the four corners; two in each, at right angles, and so close that the frescoes actually meet in the angles : an arrangement which is not only utterly opposed to the architectural decorations of the chamber, but to every principle of true taste ; and the lighting indeed needed the apology they made for it. The " local circumstances " to which allusion is made must truly have been a crucial test to the painters : a worse place could hardly have been found for their works, which, after above ten years' deliberation, are cruelly called "experimental." Then, as to the works themselves. They were hardly completed when decay seized them ; the colours underwent destructive changes, flesh tints became painfully livid, greens disappeared, blues and browns changed places—a general mildew seized the whole. The ground itself was soon destroyed, it blistered, became loose and disintegrated, and these eight works are now beyond the reach of criticism.

The commissioners also reported that four of the frescoes proposed in their seventh report for the Queen's Robing-room had been finished, and that they considered them altogether satisfactory in regard to their general treatment, and as examples of the method of fresco-painting. And further, that they have commissioned J. R. Herbert, R.A., to prepare designs for a series of frescoes in the Peers' Robing-room, according to the scheme of their seventh report; that they have assigned subjects to C. W. Cope, R.A., and E. M. Ward, R.A., in the corridors ; and propose to employ D. Maclise, R.A., to paint the " Marriage of Strongbow and Eva," in the Painted Chamber.

Then again a long silence intervened ; public opinion had not changed or moderated, when in June, 1858, the eleventh report appeared. It commenced by the announcement of error and want of judgment. Bad as had been the spaces already selected by the commissioners, for decoration, that assigned to Maclise in the Painted Chamber was absolutely unfit ; and the commissioners, with many words, say, " Some difficulties having been found to exist with regard to the lighting of some compartments in that locality, the work was postponed, and the artist was, at his own request, finally released from such undertaking, and the grant of public money amounting to 1,500*l.* which had been voted by Parliament for this object, was, with the consent of the Lords Commissioners of the Treasury, appropriated to the painting of twenty-eight whole-length portraits of personages connected with the Tudor family; " and of these works her Majesty's commissioners say, " Being taken from authentic sources, and executed in methods fitted to produce the style of the original works, they at once serve a decorative purpose, and constitute trustworthy resemblances of the historical personages represented."

It was clear from this report that matters had not mended. However, in lieu of the work and the locality that Maclise had abandoned, the commissioners proposed that he should paint in fresco one of the subjects in the Royal Gallery for 1,000*l.*; and they reported that Mr. Herbert had completed to their entire satisfaction a large cartoon of " Moses bringing down the Tables of the Law to the Israelites."

Hitherto the reports of the commissioners had been made in a style of the most strict official brevity; but the current of public opinion and criticism ran strongly against their doings; the completed frescoes had most of them failed, and those which afforded the most promise, if completed, stood still : so in the face of these difficulties, an altered manner was adopted in the twelfth report, dated in February, 1861, and the commissioners, feeling themselves on their defence, began to reason and to explain. In Herbert's fresco there has undoubtedly been unnecessary delay; Dyce's, " to their extreme mortification, is still unfinished." It was not possible for Cope and Ward to paint their frescoes on the walls, and an "expedient of painting them on movable frames was necessary." But Maclise's work was the bright spot, and "his unremitting industry" was, as it richly deserved to be, the subject of the commissioners' especial mention. Then after all that had been said of the prominent merits of fresco, which was to create a new art in England, the commissioners quietly add : " Finding that the process of fresco-painting is imperfectly adapted for subjects containing a multiplicity of details, Maclise, with the sanction of the commissioners, or rather by the personal intervention of the Prince Consort, proceeded in the autumn of 1859 to Germany, in order to make researches into the practice of the stereochrome or water-glass method of painting. The result has been that he adopted that method in the execution of the large wall-painting referred to, ' The Meeting of Wellington and Blücher after the Battle of Waterloo,' and also in his second large work ' The Death of Nelson.' Ward too practised it with success on his last two corridor subjects, and the method has also found favour with Mr. Herbert, who having, after repeated experiments, modified it according to his own views, professes his entire satisfaction with it."

Surely though, the first question to have been solved should have been whether fresco was the best method to be adopted. Did the commissioners, in the first instance, take the trouble to examine those examples of wall painting within their reach, in order to test the durability of the methods employed upon them? We had lately an opportunity of closely examining the ceiling of the Queen's bed-chamber at Hampton Court, the work of Verrio. It is painted in an oil medium on the plaster; yet it is fresher, brighter, and in better condition than pictures on canvas of the same period. The flesh is pure and rosy, the whites extremely bright, the ultramarine draperies, which seem thinly laid on over a white preparation, are most brilliant; the yellows (ochre), painted with some degree of impasto, are hard and strong when touched with the knife, the gilding in the decorative parts is wholly unaltered; the only failure is in the browns, which have been thinly painted, and have partially cracked; but, as a whole, no work in fresco could have shown greater brilliancy and purity. Of course the art is meretricious and flashy, but the execution, vigorous, free and facile, is perfect. From below, it is so bright and luminous, that it looks like water-colour or tempera. We must also recollect the pictures by La Guerre, on the staircase and the walls of the hall at Marlborough House, which have been subjected to all kinds of ill-treatment and injury, yet are, after a century and a half, much sounder than our newly painted frescoes.

Having, as we have shown, upon the principle of "the least said the soonest mended," abandoned their dearly cherished fresco scheme, the commissioners prepare for the winding-up of their commission, and admit that the artists employed might have been more profitably, if not more honourably employed, in less arduous undertakings. Their thirteenth and final report bears date in the succeeding month, the 11th March, 1861, when they say they are "of opinion that the term of their prescribed duties has now arrived, as the whole scheme of decorations for the palace of Westminster has been considered and decided."

The artists had a ground of distrust in that it was entirely without professional opinion when the commission was issued, but they looked forward to its acts with a hope that had no foundation. Its failure was generally pronounced and admitted. After several years lost in expensive experiments fresco was found to be unsuitable; competition did not act favourably on the artists as a body, nor was it found to be wise that a body of laymen should attempt to control and direct the painter, by requiring the repeated submission of his works to their judgment at every stage of progress. In the selection of the localities best adapted for decoration, which the commissioners considered their especial province, they were, as we have shown in respect to the Upper Hall, the Prince's Chamber, and, in the important consideration of light, in the House of Lords itself, singularly unfortunate; and no less so in the two corridors, mere ill-lighted passages, quite unworthy the talents of the two able painters to whom they were assigned. In these and in many minor matters, the commission would have been better advised had art been duly represented.

The sole object really entrusted to the commission by her Majesty was the *inquiry* how the fine arts of the country might be encouraged and promoted. But the commission proceeded to attempt to carry out the plans they recommended ; and the attempt proved disastrous.

The commissioners were, in one respect, unfortunate. They terminated their own existence before the completion of some works in which they might have found just cause for exultation. But these works are not in fresco. They are in the new water-glass process, by which a silica surface is given, by means of a fine syringe, to a painting in water-colours. There is some ground of hope that Maclise's works by the new process will prove more durable. They have already stood for many years without much change or need of repair, though it is a question how long they will defy the deleterious effects of the London atmosphere, unless they are put under glass. The frescoes in the Peers' Corridor have been restored, those executed in fresco with distemper, those in water-glass with the same material, and having been carefully glazed they are confronting time without serious loss, for it is London smoke and London dirt which are such destroyers of colour. Dyce's frescoes have also been repaired with water-glass, though executed in pure fresco ; one or two of these now greatly require attention. The frescoes in the House of Lords are, as we have said, in a sad state, while those in the Upper Waiting Hall are past restoring.

CHAPTER XXXVI.

MACLISE, WARD, EASTLAKE, PHILLIP, ELMORE, AND O'NEIL.

WE propose to devote the first part of this chapter to two painters who gave up much of their time to fresco-painting, while carrying on the pursuit of *genre* and historical painting in England, and whose work made a great impression upon the art of the day, and we will begin with

Daniel Maclise, R.A., who was born in Cork on the 25th January, 1811, or 1806, he himself always adhered to the first date as the correct one. His father was of Scotch extraction, and his mother the daughter of a Cork merchant. Maclise showed an early taste for art, and as a child drew pen and ink sketches all over his own copybooks and those of his schoolfellows. His father however placed him with a banker, but at sixteen he managed to leave this, to him, distasteful employment, and to enter the Cork School of Art. While still quite a boy he made a portrait of Sir Walter Scott, who happened while visiting in Cork to go into a bookseller's shop. Maclise, who was concealed in the back of the shop, in a short time made three outline sketches of his face, and working up the best one in the night, carried it the next morning to the bookseller, who was so pleased with it that he placed it in his window, where Scott saw it, and being also much struck with it, not only appended his autograph to it, but congratulated the young artist warmly. While in the Cork Academy Maclise was a diligent student, and he at the same time made a practical study of anatomy. He found profitable employment in sketching the portraits of the officers stationed in Cork, and in 1826 he made a sketching tour in Wicklow. With the money he saved from the sale of his sketches, and with that he derived from his portrait painting, Maclise made up a purse to come to London, and shortly afterwards he entered the schools of the Royal Academy. Here he immediately gained honours, taking a silver medal both in the antique and the painting school, and in 1829 the gold medal for the best historical composition, the subject being " The Choice of Hercules." This gave him also the right to the travelling studentship, although he did not avail himself of it, but continued working in the metropolis. On his first arrival in town he had, on the occasion of Charles Kean's acting young Norval, made a most successful sketch of him in that character, done in the theatre itself; this was published, and gained Maclise many commissions for portraits both in pencil and water-colours. But he was not anxious to devote himself to this branch of art, and he very soon began to take up subject pictures, sending "Malvolio affecting the Count," to the Royal Academy exhibition in 1829. In 1832 his picture of "All Hallows Eve," a composition depicting the games and ceremonies which in Ireland are carried on on that evening, made a great impression on the public. The subject had been suggested to him during a visit to Cork, where he had enjoyed "Snap-apple Night," at the house of the parish priest; the picture contains portraits of his sisters and friends. In consequence of his connection with *Fraser's Magazine*, for which journal under the name of "Alfred Croquis," Maclise etched a series of seventy-two small portraits of men of the day, which were very popular, he was led to devote himself to literary composition, and contributed to it a clever poem and several sonnets. In 1835 his picture "The Chivalric Vow of the Ladies and the Peacock," produced his election to the associateship of the Royal Academy when only twenty-four years of age. He became a full member in 1840, when he exhibited "The Banquet Scene in *Macbeth*."

About the year 1845, he entered the lists as a competitor for the great work of decorating the palace of Westminster, and after many wearying delays received a commission for two frescoes—"The Spirit of Justice" and "The Spirit of Chivalry." Maclise's great faculty of invention and powers of execution, together with his extreme vigour of conception, eminently fitted him for the task of decorating the houses of Parliament, nevertheless, eventually this work for the nation proved a task and a burden too much for his strength. He was of a generous and noble spirit, and ill-adapted to contend with the worrying vacillation of the commission, who treated him, after the death of the Prince Consort and of Eastlake, with, to say the least of it, considerable meanness. It was not till 1851 that he undertook the decoration of the Royal Gallery, beginning with two subjects, the "Interview between Wellington and Blücher" and the "Death of Nelson," each work was to be forty-eight feet long. By the original agreement, Maclise was to fill in all the sixteen compartments of the gallery, and he had prepared designs for three of these, and made sketches for the rest, but these were destined never to be carried out, as the engagement was rescinded by the committee. Maclise set to work with great vigour upon the meeting of the two generals, and in 1859 completed the cartoon for his "Wellington and Blücher," which is now the property of the Academy, and is a crowded composition full of life and incident. His brother artists were so delighted with it that they clubbed together to present him with a gold portecrayon and an address, which says the trifle was given "not so much as a token of our esteem and admiration, as of the honest pride, which, as artists and fellow countrymen, we feel in the success of the cartoon you have so lately executed."

When Maclise came to the carrying out of the work, he found himself hampered with many difficulties; the light was bad, and the medium unsuitable, so that he resigned the task of executing it in fresco, but he offered to do it in oil. However, following the advice of the Prince Consort, he went to Berlin to investigate the water-glass process, and having made himself master of the method he returned, and after destroying the portion begun in fresco, he worked incessantly under most depressing circumstances, and finished the design in water-glass by 1861.

He was then entrusted with the companion picture of the "Death of Nelson," which he completed in 1864; but his energies, great though they were, had been completely exhausted by these heavy labours, and though for a few short years he returned to his studio in Cheyne Walk, and contributed pictures to the Royal Academy exhibitions, yet his health being materially weakened, he succumbed to an attack of pneumonia 25th April, 1870, and was buried in Kensal Green Cemetery, where his grave was surrounded by friends. His great friend Dickens, who was so shortly also to be laid in the grave, pronounced an eloquent eulogy on him the same evening at the Academy banquet, finishing with these words—" In art a man, in simplicity a child; no artist, of whatsoever denomination, I make bold to say, ever went to his rest leaving a golden memory more pure from dross, or having devoted himself with a truer chivalry to the art goddess he worshipped."

Maclise, like Landseer, refused the presidentship at Eastlake's death, a post which his brother members hastened to offer him. He was always much beloved by his friends from his frank-hearted, generous and simple nature. In youth he was very athletic, and of a tall and handsome person; he never married, one of his sisters always lived with him, and he was devotedly good to the members of his family. Maclise did a great deal of work as a book illustrator, he also designed the Turner Medal for the Academy and the Swiney Cup for the Society of Arts. He was a master of form, for which he had a marvellous memory—a memory so great that he was often able, alas! unwisely, to work without making use of the living model. His sense of colour was very imperfect, though he studied the old masters with great attention, and tried to admire their works, and devoted himself to the galleries during his trips abroad, yet he really could get little from them. His compositions, while remarkable for richness of incident and accuracy of detail, are apt to be over-crowded, and from the very vigour of their conception are sometimes wanting in repose, while the colour is inclined to be crude and harsh. Yet in many ways he was very fitted for historical painting, for his style was spirited and his handling bold. In considering his two pictures of " Waterloo " and " Trafalgar," entirely the work of his own hand, whether we reflect merely on the size of the works, forty-five feet by twelve, or on the masculine energy of their drawing, the knowledge displayed in their grouping, especially, for instance, that of the horses in the " Waterloo," a finer work than the " Trafalgar," for the painter has been trammelled in his second subject by the dark blue jackets of the sailors, which do not compose so well as do the more varied colours of the soldiers' uniforms, we are bound to confess that he has brilliantly carried out the commission confided to him, and that, besides reflecting the greatest credit on the painter himself, both these fine works are fit objects of national pride.

We must now turn to the consideration of a painter who throughout his art career had this distinctive characteristic, that as a whole he devoted himself to depicting scenes from the history of our own country. He was not a history painter in the true sense of the term, his pictures are rather illustrations of historical scenes, and fall more under the class of *genre* paintings, but Ward always seizes on a definite story to tell, he is fortunate in the dramatic interest of that story, and he has plenty of antiquarian knowledge to help him in the composition of his subject, and skill in rendering the diversified qualities of human character. His draperies are apt to be too ample, and in his flesh colour he is inclined to be chalky. His women are more stage beauties than refined ladies, and in this latter point he contrasts badly with Leslie, compared with whom his art is scenic and, we think, a trifle meretricious.

Edward Matthew Ward, R.A., was a nephew, on his mother's side, of Horace and James Smith, the authors of *Rejected Addresses,* and was born in Pimlico in 1816. He used to relate that as a child he was fond of drawing and painting everything he could get hold of, and even " coloured all the joints in the cookery book." His mother, to whom he was devotedly attached, fostered his love of art, and under the advice of Chantrey and Wilkie, Ward became a student of the Royal Academy in 1835, though he had had some art instruction previously from a Mr. T. Cawse, who kept a drawing school at that time, and was reputed to be a good teacher; from him, however, Ward declared he learnt little.

In 1836 Ward went to Rome, remaining three years, and gaining the silver medal of the Academy of St. Luke, and on his way home he stopped in Munich for some months to learn the art of fresco-painting from Cornelius, for like all the painters of that day Ward hoped to be employed in mural decoration by the Government. The first picture he

F F

exhibited on his return from abroad, was inspired by the scenes he had so recently left, and was called "Cimabue and Giotto." In 1843, his cartoon of "Boadicea," sent in to the competition for the decoration of the Houses of Parliament, though commended, did not obtain a premium; but in 1852 he received a commission to paint eight historical pictures for the corridor of the House of Commons. Some of these were painted in oil and afterwards re-executed in fresco, and two are in "water-glass"; perhaps "The Last Sleep of Argyll" is the best of the eight, which were painted under the most disadvantageous circumstances, and are in a very bad light. These pictures cracked and gave way, as did all the frescoes executed in the Houses of Parliament, but were repaired and glazed rather more than ten years ago, and have since stood well.

Ward exhibited in 1845, "Dr. Johnson Waiting in the Ante-room of Lord Chesterfield for an Audience," depicting the neglect of Dr. Johnson by that nobleman after he had promised to be his patron, and to help forward the Dictionary. This picture probably led to Ward's election to an associateship in the Royal Academy; it is now in the National Gallery, and is a little black in the shadows, thin in treatment, and inclined to be hot in colour. The best group is on the right, where the fine lady, whose attention is drawn to Dr. Johnson by a worldly-looking beau, gazes rather contemptuously at the great lexicographer, seated sad and gloomy, waiting to be sent for by his capricious patron. Ward became a full member of the Academy in 1855, and the next year exhibited one of the best and most popular of his pictures, "Marie Antoinette parting with the Dauphin." In 1859 he completed a commission for her Majesty, "The Emperor of the French Receiving the Order of the Garter," and "Marie Antoinette Listening to her Act of Accusation." Here Ward is very happy in his treatment, the sitting figure of the Queen is full of dignity, the hands are meekly folded together, she has just laid down her *livre d'heures*, and listens to what she knows to be her death-warrant, not only with pious resignation, but with the bearing of one who is a queen still in spite of outrage and contempt.

Ward was a tall man, inclined to stoutness, with black hair and a powerful voice. He was indifferent to personal appearance, of a most genial and tender disposition, full of kindness, a good mimic, and most amusing companion, a fond husband and father, and of an honourable and sensitive character. For some years before his death his health was very indifferent, and though naturally of a gay and cheerful temperament, he became through illness very depressed, and in a fit of aberration hastened his own end. He died at Windsor, January 15th, 1879, and was buried in Upton old churchyard, his funeral being attended by very many academicians and personal friends. Ward married the granddaughter of James Ward, R.A., who is herself a painter. A sympathetic memoir of him has been published by J. Dafforne.

There have been a few exceptional painters who have served the art they loved better by their lives than by their brush. Such an one was *Sir Charles Lock Eastlake, P.R.A.*, who was the son of a lawyer, and born in Plymouth the 17th November, 1793. During the best part of his life, he was so occupied with onerous engagements in the service of art—such as acquiring pictures for the National Gallery, conducting the business of the Royal Academy, investigating the principles of art, writing upon the subject, giving his judgment on disputed points, for which his great art knowledge and kindly impartiality peculiarly fitted him— that little time was left to him for the practice of painting. Thus it is not astonishing that his maturity did not carry out the promise of his youth ; and that, though his works proceed from an elevated conception and a high ideal, and are graceful in arrangement, and laboured and refined in execution, yet they do not exhibit any largeness of method, and they often seem to fall short in their fulfilment of what his cultivated taste required.

Eastlake first learnt the principles of his art under Prout ; but in 1809 he entered the schools of the Royal Academy, where he was a very conscientious and diligent student. His father also sent him to study in Paris, where he worked for some months ; after which he returned to Plymouth, and began to paint portraits, his most celebrated sitter being Napoleon I., who was brought into port on board the *Bellerophon.* Soon after this, young Eastlake went abroad, and made an extended tour on the Continent. Returning a second time to Rome, in 1818, purposing only to make a short stay, he remained twelve years in that city, sending some of his best works, such as, "Pilgrims Arriving in Sight of Rome," for exhibition in the Academy.

In 1827, he gained his election as associate, and was made an R.A. in 1830, when he thought it right to leave Rome and to settle in England, where for some years he remained devoted to his art ; but gradually, his duties as secretary to the Royal Commission for the Decoration of the Houses of Parliament, his directorship of the National Gallery, and his labours as president of the Royal Academy, to which he was elected in 1850, induced him to lay aside his brush. He married the daughter of Dr. Rigby, whose literary tastes and art knowledge coincided with his own. He died at Pisa, December 24th, 1865 ; but his body was brought to England, and, his widow declining for him a public funeral, he was buried in Kensal Green.

As a writer and a critic, Eastlake greatly promoted the interests of art, and he ably seconded every effort to advance the love of art and the fortunes of its professors in this country : an account of the art of the century would be very incomplete which did not fully acknowledge his merits in this respect.

We will now turn to a painter, one of whose great merits is, the richness and force of his colour, and who attained by the power of his original talent to a high place in the art of his day. *John Phillip, R.A.*, was the son of a soldier, and was born at Aberdeen, 19th April, 1817. He delighted in painting from his earliest days, and, when quite young, produced without any teaching a good likeness of his aged grandmother. Phillip was apprenticed to a house-painter, and while seated apparently only occupied in diligently grinding up the workmen's colours, he applied himself to painting small subjects, which he hid away in a drawer from his master's sight, though he showed them occasionally to his brother workmen. So highly did these men think of his productions, that when a perplexing order for the painting of a " sign " arrived at the shop, they unanimously recommended that young Phillip should try his hand upon it. In this he was so successful that he was always afterwards employed on such work.

The boy's one ambition, however, was to see the Royal Academy Exhibition in London, and to buy some real painter's tools. To effect this he first saved up money enough to buy brushes, paints, &c., and then getting on board a granite brig, the owner of which was known to his father, and having provided himself with a letter of recommendation to a friend in London, he hid himself till the vessel was fairly on its voyage. The owner of the ship scolded him well when he discovered his presence on board, and made him work for his passage ; but little did Phillip care for that, and one morning very early, long before the doors were open, he found himself waiting eagerly at Somerset House for the fulfilment of his long-cherished desire. He remained the whole day, and used to say in after years that he distinctly recollected each picture and the spot where it hung. Having carried out his plan Phillip returned to Aberdeen in the same vessel, and began the practice of his art by painting portaits, for which he received the handsome remuneration of half-a-crown apiece. Where are those portraits now ?

A figure subject painted by Phillip being shown shortly after this to Lord Panmure, he was so struck with it that he sent young Phillip to London to study, and in 1838 he entered the Royal Academy schools, and the next year he exhibited a portrait at the exhibition. Phillip's first pictures were mostly of Scotch subjects, and he made periodical absences from London in order to paint them and to catch sight of his beloved Highlands, away from which he always experienced a certain home-sickness. In 1847 he sent to the Academy Exhibition " Presbyterian Catechising," in 1850 " Baptism in Scotland," followed in 1851 by "The Spae Wife" and "Scotch Washing." Phillip was accustomed to get in his subjects in brown on a grey coarse canvas. He made this brown of Indian red and black, and as he mixed them together on his palette as he painted, he has not always been successful in tempering them quite equally, and the black being the stronger colour has impinged on the brown and white, and has caused a blackness in some of the shadows of his pictures which was not there when they left his easel. In this first painting he got in his high lights with a warm white, producing his cool grey half-tints by overlapping this solid colour into the warm browns of his shadows. His second process was over this first painting to sweep a rich glaze of transparent colour, diluted with Roberson's medium, turpentine and oil, and to paint solidly into it. He was a dexterous and ready painter, and was wont to turn to account in his work the accidents of a rapid execution. There is a picture of his in the Edinburgh National Gallery, which, being left unfinished at his death, is very useful in showing his mode of work.

Phillip's health giving way in 1852 caused him to seek a warmer climate in Spain. Here, filled with admiration for the works of the Spanish painters, especially for Velasquez, with whose work his own genius was akin, Phillip's art found a new inspiration. He delighted from henceforth to paint the picturesque peasantry of Seville, their rural customs and celebrations; his eye for colour revelled in the rich harmonious colouring and wealth of brilliant sunlight to be found there, and he returned three times to Spain. On his third visit he remained four months, and brought back forty-two canvases, and no doubt overworked himself. He was a generous man and paid his models well, and the consequence was that the courtyard of the house where he lived in Seville was always thronged with picturesque idlers only too delighted to act as models for the English artist, quite unaware that their loitering habits and the amusing scenes with their fellows in the *patio* spurred on the ardent painter, to an incessant and too arduous exertion in order to record these characteristic bits of Spanish life. Phillip was elected an associate of the Academy in 1857, and a full member in 1859. In 1860 he painted by command of the Queen " The Marriage of the Princess Royal," a group of portraits glowing with brilliant colour. This was followed in 1863 by a portrait subject of the greatest interest and excellence, " The House of Commons." The following year Phillip exhibited one of the finest of his Spanish subjects, " La Gloria," which is really a wake. In Spain the people think it wrong to mourn the death of a young infant, considering it rather a cause for rejoicing. The mirth of the neighbours and relations in this noble picture, who are dancing and singing and summoning the reluctant and despairing mother sitting beside the poor little corpse to join them, is very finely given. Another very beautiful Spanish subject is " Murillo in the Market Place of Seville." In 1857 he painted "The Prison Window" and "Charity," both in Seville. These pictures are well known by their engravings. All Phillip's pictures show a keen discrimination of character, and of moods both pathetic and humorous. The vigorous and strong mind of the man shows forth in his work. He used to say of his brother painters, that if he couldn't like the man, he couldn't like his art, and also just the reverse, that is, he could not separate the man and his art; and this is quite true in his own case. Phillip went to Rome in 1866, which resulted in his painting two pictures of "The Lottery." He was suddenly struck with paralysis and died prematurely at Kensington, the 27th February, 1867. His collected works were shown at the International Exhibition in 1873, and made a great impression from their firm and broad execution, their vigorous drawing and powerful and mellow colouring.

Alfred Elmore, R.A., is another subject painter whose works are very varied in idea, and exceedingly well thought out and composed, and evidently produced by a cultivated mind. His pictures are both rich in colour and good in drawing, they are more academic than Ward's, but have not the same feeling for character. Elmore's father was a doctor in the 5th Dragoon Guards, and our painter was born at Clonakilty, Cork, in 1815. He was admitted to the Academy school in 1832, and afterwards studied in a French *atelier* and in the galleries of the Louvre. After exhibiting in London he returned to the Continent, and studied at Munich, after which he went to Italy, and remained two years in Rome, where he diligently examined the works of the old masters. He became a full member of the Royal Academy in 1857, having obtained his associateship as far back as 1845, ten years after he first began to exhibit at the Academy exhibitions. As early as 1841 he had sent to the Academy Exhibition "The Murder of S. Thomas à Becket," which was bought by Daniel O'Connell, and presented by him to a church in Dublin. Another of Elmore's best pictures was "The Origin of the Combing Machine." In 1860 he exhibited "The Tuileries, 20th June, 1789," a fine picture. Marie Antoinette is facing the mob protected by the presence of her children, the Dauphin sits on the council table before her, and her daughter stands by her side. The young girl to whom the Queen has been speaking stands there, already softened by remorse. Elmore died in London, after a long and painful illness, 24th January, 1881, and was buried at Kensal Green.

Henry O'Neil, A.R.A., who had been a fellow student with Elmore at the Academy, and had travelled with him in Italy, had died on the 13th March, 1880. O'Neil was born in St. Petersburg in 1817, and was a man of varied accomplishments, which, perhaps, interfered with his attaining to the highest rank in art. His pictures "Eastward Ho!" and "Home Again!" were exceedingly popular, especially as engravings, and after these he produced a really fine work in " The Wreck of the *Royal Charter.*" He was deficient in the power of composition, and his colour is a little garish, but he chose good subjects, and in this, in common with many of the artists of his day, he presents a lesson to our more recent painters, with many of whom the subject of their pictures seems quite a secondary consideration.

CHAPTER XXXVII.

W. DYCE, R.A., AND SCHOOLS OF DESIGN.

William Dyce, R.A., was not only eminent as an artist and as a representative of the new school of fresco-painting, but he was engaged in initiating the system of Government art-teaching, intended, in the first instance, to provide instruction for our artisans, and designers for manufactures ; but which, under the direction of his successors, has been extended to provide sound elementary instruction open to all.

William Dyce was born in Aberdeen, on the 19th September, 1806. His father was a physician in extensive practice in that city. It is not recorded whether young Dyce was from the first intended for the arts, but he received a liberal education, fitted to form his mind and to qualify him for any future pursuit or profession. He early graduated at the Marischal College in his native city, and at the age of sixteen took the degree of Master of Arts. Soon after, having adopted art as his profession, he left Aberdeen and in his seventeenth year entered the schools of the Royal Scottish Academy. Whether from any cause other than the desire of improvement in the metropolitan schools we know not, but he came early to London, and obtained admittance as a probationer at the Royal Academy. He himself tells us that he was dissatisfied with the instruction in these schools ; and as he did not obtain his admission as a student, he determined to avail himself of opportunities afforded him of visiting the Continental schools of art.

In 1825, Dyce, being then only nineteen years of age, made a journey to Italy, to prosecute his studies amidst those great historical and monumental works which can only be fully appreciated *in situ*. On this occasion he spent nine months in Rome. In thus early visiting the great seats of art, he differs from most of our British painters, and we can trace the influence of this early visit on all his future career. With a cultivated mind, but as yet unfettered by the prevailing tastes of his brother artists, he was brought face to face with the great works of the masters of the fifteenth and sixteenth centuries, and the impression made on him was deep and enduring. The "propriety" and refinement of Raphael's labours seemed congenial to his taste, and gave aim to his future efforts. For a time, perhaps, the veneration with which the early masters were regarded by him, led rather to imitation than to originality, but as strength and confidence increased with years this was cast aside, and he sought rather to work in their spirit, and to sacrifice whatever was meretricious to the higher qualities of simplicity, feeling, and expression which he found in their works.

There was another result arising from the young painter's visit to Italy, and his study of the great lunettes of Raphael, the arabesques of the Vatican, the Farnesina, and generally of the palaces and churches of Italy. He early learnt to appreciate the decorative nature of the art of the great Italian fresco painters, and to understand, as it had not yet been understood by the great body of his brother artists, that the painters of the *quattro* and *cinque-cento* were ornamentists as well as historical painters, and thought it a part of their labours to give unity to the whole scheme of decoration, by controlling the design and execution of the ornamental as well as of the pictorial parts.

This led young Dyce on his return from Rome in 1826 to prepare a set of arabesque designs, and to decorate a room in his father's house in Aberdeen ; and this was, no doubt, the introduction to that fuller study of ornamental art which conduced so largely to his future fame and his future usefulness. While working at this labour of love, Dyce was also employed in painting his first picture, "Bacchus Nursed by the Nymphs of Nyssa," a bold attempt as a commencement. It was exhibited in 1827 in the Royal Academy, and in the autumn of that year he again set out for Rome to continue his studies under the inspiration of the great works of Raphael, which had deeply impressed him ; and which, with those of Raphael's precursors, remained throughout the rule of his faith, and the models for his imitation. Endowed with a congenial mind, he delighted in their simplicity, earnestness, and truth. On this, his second visit, Dyce remained in Italy the greater part of three years, studying diligently the frescoes and wall decorations of the earlier masters ; the purity of their pictorial art, and the elegance and simplicity of the ornamental accessories with which it is often surrounded.

The great monumental works, the wall paintings at Padua, at Pisa, at Florence, at Assisi at Rome, and a host of other Italian cities, had not been properly studied for their unity with the walls of the edifices they adorn, for the monumental character which attaches to them, or that peculiar treatment which makes the spectator, in a measure, a party to the scene and subject represented. Dyce had not failed to appreciate these qualities, and if he was constrained to paint nymphs and madonnas, it was because the opportunity was as yet wanting to work out the larger views these studies had opened up to him : nay, so little encouragement was there at that time for the art he desired to follow, that on his return to Edinburgh in 1830, he passed several of his best years as a portrait painter, exhibiting, both in that city and in London, many portraits of children and others; hoping for the advent of the future when he should be called to nobler labours. Meanwhile, in 1835 he was elected an associate of the Royal Scottish Academy.

In 1836, Dyce sent to the Royal Academy a large picture of "The Descent of Venus," which attracted much notice, as, since his first work already mentioned, he had contributed only portraits to our exhibition. About this time many voices were raised to call the attention of our Government to the want of taste in the designs for our staple manufactures, and the loss consequently sustained by our manufacturers in the markets of the world. Among others, Dyce, who was interested in the Trustees' School at Edinburgh, published, in conjunction with Mr. Charles Heath Wilson, a letter addressed to Lord Meadowbank, suggesting means for improving the course of instruction given there, and making it bear more fully on design, as applied to manufactures. This pamphlet led to Dyce's appointment as secretary and director to the schools just opened in London at Somerset House, and in connection with them, to his being sent to visit and report upon schools of the same character in France and Germany. His report, dated April 27th, 1838, was published in the parliamentary papers of the year 1840, and contains much valuable information as to the then state of the Continental schools, and the deficiency in all of them, except that of Lyons, in any actual production of patterns or designs for manufactures; and he infers the necessity for such instruction, and for the production of designs in the schools newly founded in this country. This report led to the remodelling of our schools in conformity with Mr. Dyce's views. He undertook to prepare proper elementary works for the students, but soon found that this, together with his duties as superintendent and secretary, intrenched too much on his time to allow of the practice of his profession; and when urged in 1843 to give up more of his time to the schools, he declined to do so, and resigned his appointments in May of that year; accepting instead the office of inspector of the provincial schools, with a seat in the council, which offices he also resigned on the 10th of June, 1845.

In 1844, Dyce was elected an associate of the Royal Academy, consequent on his exhibition, in that year, of his picture of "King Joash Shooting the Arrow of Deliverance;" a picture of singular severity of style and simplicity of parts. In 1848, he was raised to full Academy honours. When the competition took place for the decoration of the

Houses of Parliament, he was one of the first five commissioned to prepare cartoons for the frescoes to fill the spaces in the House of Lords, and his work, "The Baptism of King Ethelbert," was the first one selected for execution on the walls.

He was also commissioned by the Prince Consort to paint a fresco on the staircase at Osborne, of "Neptune giving the Empire of the Sea to Britannia," and also to fill one of the lunettes of the decorated summer-house in the gardens at Buckingham Palace. The former of these frescoes—a work of importance, the figures being life-size—has remained unchanged, and may lead us to infer that those in the Houses of Parliament have suffered from acids in our gas-charged atmosphere, rather than from bad materials, imperfect execution, or an ill-constructed wall.

In 1847, Dyce again resumed his connection with the Government School of Design, being appointed one of three head masters, among whom the instruction was divided. But with great abilities he was somewhat impracticable, and constitutionally unfitted to fill any position of joint authority. He again, and finally, resigned his duties in 1849, and henceforth devoted himself almost exclusively to fresco-painting; for, although he continued occasionally to contribute works to the exhibition at the Royal Academy, his attention was almost wholly occupied with mural painting and decorative art. During this period he made a design for a window to be executed in stained glass for Ely Cathedral, and another as a memorial to the Duke of Northumberland for Alnwick. He also designed the decorative and mural paintings for the church of All Saints, in Margaret Street, Cavendish Square, and he executed them in fresco on the walls; it is to be regretted that the "dim religious light" admitted into the edifice hardly suffices for their examination. But the great labour of Dyce's latter years was the preparation of cartoons for the decoration of the Queen's Robing-room in the Houses of Parliament; the subject given him by the royal commission being the mythical legend of King Arthur. The painter himself was not well pleased with the choice; but he engaged to finish the series in eight years, and during that time received the whole sum agreed upon for its completion. It no doubt is true, that the time likely to be occupied in such works was not properly ascertained when the engagement was made, and that the remuneration for artistic labour had greatly advanced during the period under review: yet the House of Commons, irritated by the non-completion of the work and the incessant delays of the painter, arising partly from causes beyond his control and partly from ill-health, complained loudly of Dyce's shortcomings, as well as of the inertness of the commission in not enforcing the engagement. The clamour was a source of great irritation to the painter, and no doubt increased a wasting illness which had seized him. He gradually grew worse ; to relieve his mind of the anxieties of the position, he wished to throw up the commission, and offered to return the amount which had been overpaid him in advance ; but meanwhile he rapidly declined, and died on the 14th of February, 1864. A committee of the House reversed the whole of the engagements made by the Fine Arts Commission with the several artists employed, and the Government more than justified Dyce by the additions they made to the prices to be paid to the other artists for the works they were engaged upon on the walls of the national building.

Dyce drew the figure correctly and with grace, but without much originality of style ; indeed in his work generally, he rather founded himself on the style of others than formed a style of his own. After he had passed his imitative period, his colouring was pearly and agreeable ; yet we cannot rank him as a colourist. Generally his works are learned rather than original, and call forth our approval in a greater degree than our love.

We have noted that the best years of Dyce's life were occupied either in fresco-painting, or in forwarding the new art movement in the establishment of schools of design ; but though winning great reputation in both directions, in both he failed to carry out his own views. With great art knowledge, and much real talent in its application, together with methodic habits in matters of mere business, so seldom found conjoined with art, some quality was wanting to enable him to achieve complete success : he seemed ever right in theory, but in practice he fell short of full fruition. He did not possess the power of controlling other men to work in harmony with him, nor of subjecting his own will, in things indifferent, to those who were his colleagues in labour or in aim. This is evidenced in both the great undertakings he was engaged upon.

His labours connected with the first effort on the part of the Government of this country to promote the spread of art were also most important ; they have too intimate a connection with the future, and thus with the subject of this work, to be dismissed without a somewhat lengthy notice. In the foundation of Government schools of art, perhaps the more important work of the two in which Dyce was engaged, he was continually contending with a committee which he had not the art to lead nor the power to convince ; thus his wise suggestions were either disregarded or only partially adopted, and finally it was left to others to carry into execution what he had proposed, and to enlarge on the basis he had endeavoured to prepare. Dyce's first contribution to the new movement was his valuable report on the Continental schools. His first labour was in preparing a set of examples for school use, and he proceeded so far as to produce an elementary work of the greatest merit.

Dyce reported that in the best Continental school, that of Berlin, instruction in art, and instruction in the processes of those manufactures which required art for their decoration, was given, but that no school existed for the actual production of patterns or designs for manufactures ; this third element Dyce sought to introduce into our art schools. But neither manufacturers, artisans, nor the public were prepared to meet the effort. .

When the Department of Art was formed and placed under a minister of the Crown, her Majesty permitted it temporarily to occupy Marlborough House.   Sir Henry Cole was appointed general superintendent, and R. Redgrave, R.A., art superintendent, under the president of the Board of Trade ; and the Board at once passed a minute providing for the extension of art schools—for opening them to all classes—and making instruction in drawing a part of the teaching in schools for the poor ; thus preparing the children of the artisan for a higher future training in schools of art. In connection with this extension of art teaching, provision was made for forming a collection of works wherein the best art was allied to handicraft-skill ; historical, but chiefly of those periods when the union of art and manufacture was most perfect, and the taste exercised in such productions of the highest ; the museum thus formed was to be opened to the public. The success of the poor-school teaching may be estimated by the number at present under instruction (806,048 in 1888) ; while the museum now at South Kensington has already become a great national institution, and has had immense influence on general art, as well as on the public taste.

Thus two objects which Dyce had thought desirable, but had been unable to accomplish, have been fully carried out. Hitherto the teaching afforded by the art schools had been expressly confined to artisans and designers, and every effort upon the part of others to participate in the instruction was systematically discouraged ; but the general superintendent wisely perceived that it was necessary to extend the instruction, so as to improve the knowledge of the manufacturer by whom the skilled artisans were to be employed, and the taste of the consumer who was to purchase the results of their skilled labour.   Under the new department the schools, formerly called Schools of Design, were now named Schools of Art, and the teaching they offer is thrown open to all.   The result has been the increase of the art schools in the country to 213 ; while their pupils during the last year have reached above 41,000.

On the formation of the department a great effort was made to produce original designs suited to the manufacturing processes by which they were to be executed.   In the end this attempt temporarily failed—partly from the jealousy of the manufacturers, who dreaded lest the special designs of their own workshops should be betrayed ; and partly because designers, when fully educated, had for a time difficulty in obtaining employment on remunerative terms.   The effort was not laid aside, but only postponed, and the great aim of the central school in London directed to the thorough training of teachers to take charge of the various art schools throughout the country. For this purpose the first labours of Redgrave were concentrated upon laying down a course of instruction suitable for all schools, and the selection or preparation of examples of a high class for the use of the students; with, at the same time, a mode of examination, both to test the instruction given, and to justify the department in certifying the ability of its teachers when trained, as well as that of the general pupils, who were admitted to share the instruction offered in the schools.

The course of instruction is based on a careful and rigid training in *form;* the student commences from examples of mere abstract symmetrical forms, and is led up through ornamental forms and foliage to the highest aim of the draughtsman, the human figure; at each step in the course the student alternates examples from the flat with fuller practice from "the round," and from "the life" drawn, modelled, or painted. The next effort is to exercise the invention of the student. In a conversation with the then president of the Scottish Academy, Sir John Watson Gordon, wherein the necessity of exercising the inventive faculties of the student was dwelt upon, and of leading him on to the preparation of new designs, he wholly discouraged the attempt, saying,—"Teach invention—the thing is impossible." This, at first sight, appears a self-evident proposition; but it does not contain the whole truth, either in reference to art or to manufacture. If the student cannot be taught invention, he can be led up to it; he can be taught where to seek materials for new ideas, to store them up, and to arrange and combine them in a novel and effective manner. For this purpose the students were required at stated periods to produce collections of careful sketches of the best ornament of all periods, noting the source whence it was obtained, and the material it decorated, to improve them in the history of styles, and to give them an insight into the best practice of the best artists.

To exercise their invention, the following method was devised by Redgrave—a method wholly new in the use thus made of it. It consisted first in the ornamental analyses of plants and flowers, displaying each part separately according to its normal law of growth, not as they appear viewed perspectively, but diagrammatically flat to the eye; so treated, it was found that almost all plants contain many distinct ornamental elements, and that the motives to be derived from the vegetable kingdom were inexhaustible. Moreover, this flat display of the plant was specially suitable to the requirements of the manufacturer, to reproduction by painting, weaving, stamping, &c., to which naturalistic renderings do not readily lend themselves; while this treatment of the plant is also in conformity with that followed by the Oriental nations, and by the best artists of the middle ages. The third part of the course of elementary design was also entirely new in its application. It was intended to teach the pupils the laws of distribution, and the rules best adapted to cover given spaces with ornamental forms and colours. A bounding form being given, such as a circle, a lozenge, a hexagon, triangle, &c., the students were first required to place simple spots of black or white with agreeable inter-spaces over the surface. Afterwards some simple floral, or leaf, form is given, then a flower, or a flower combined with suitable foliage ; or the students are allowed to use any ornamental forms obtainable from a given plant, to vary the colour, the colour of the ground, &c. From year to year these forms and fillings were changed throughout the schools. The plan has had a valuable effect in stimulating invention, and leading on to designs for fabrics, wall papers, carpets, &c.

In the annual display in London of hundreds of studies of the same form filled in with the same plant, many of them of very great merit, sent up from all the schools of the department, it is hard to find any two that approach to sameness. All the students have sound instruction in geometry, perspective, the anatomy of the bones, and the exterior muscles, &c. ; and those training for masters are also taught mechanical and architectural drawing. They are required to use the museum as a field for study, and thus are prepared not only to teach others, but to produce designs for manufactures in accordance with the principles of the best artists of the best times. This sound course of instruction, coupled with the teaching of the noble museum which has sprung up at South Kensington, has already made great impression on the manufactures of this country, and on the public taste by which they must be stimulated and encouraged ; and we find that some of the best authorities in France united to urge on the Emperor the necessity of new efforts to improve the Continental schools, if their manufactures were to hold their acknowledged place in the markets of the world.

When Redgrave retired in 1876 his successor E. Poynter, R.A., said of him that "he was the author of the most perfect system of national art instruction ever devised—a system unique in Europe and the value of which had been recognized in many countries."

Many others bear testimony to the influence on manufactures of the schools and their teaching. Our work relates rather to their bearing on art-teaching generally. The effect of opening the schools of art to all those who are willing to enter them, and receive a thorough grounding in the language of art, has been to prepare a generation more competent to enjoy and to appreciate it ; especially in cases where genius and talent were latent, and opportunity of instruction only was wanted to give that which, while it is as necessary as "the accomplishment of verse" to the poet, is far more difficult of acquisition than *his* language ; more opposed, in the labour of acquisition, to the higher mental qualities which alone constitute the true artist ; and which many, no doubt, lacking these opportunities, faltered and fainted in the strife to achieve.

CHAPTER XXXVIII.

It has been said that "pictures have strong constitutions," which, if true, is a wonder, considering the evils they derive from their parent, the painter, who indifferently employs in their production bad materials, bad vehicles, and bad execution ; clothes them in bad varnishes, and gives them over to the care or carelessness of guardians or keepers, without one word of advice as to their treatment : perhaps even without the knowledge to give it. Passing out of the hands of the painter, what perils beset the after-existence of his works; how indifferently are they sheltered and preserved ! Exposed to every variety of light and temperature ; to the careless broom of the housemaid, to smoke, and dust, and gas ; as premature old age and decay come upon them from all these causes, shrivelling their skins and drying up their juices, quack renovators and conceited restorers are called in, who make it a boast that ignorance of the first principles of art fits them especially for their office, and that from their hands a picture comes forth "better than new." In a work like this, it will not surely be out of place, and most probably it will be acceptable, if we point out some of these sources of evil, examine how they arise, show how they may be avoided, and how they may be alleviated, if they cannot be wholly cured.

First, as to bad materials. The painter of the last century took very little thought for the immortality of his own progeny, and from its birth trusted its well-being more to chance than to care. The old painters, as we have already described, would seem always to have prepared their own panels or canvases; that is to say, their preparation was carried on by pupils or apprentices under the painter's eye, and according to recipes handed down from age to age. The pupils carefully ground, washed, and tempered the colours for use, the resins, oils, and varnishes with which the colours were mixed, or which were passed over the master's work when completed, to give it proper lustre and to defend it from injury. They often also laid in the work in dead colour preparatory to the hand of the master, according to simple rules which obtained in the various schools, and of which experience had tested the value. Any new colour was thoughtfully tested before it was added to the approved stock ; and the traditions of the school to which the artist belonged, and of the master under whom he received his instruction, were treasured up and transmitted to his pupils and successors.

But when the old art died out in Lely and Kneller, and a British school arose, it deserted the "traditions of the elders," when it repudiated their works ; and our great painters began to seek new pigments, new vehicles, and new methods of using them. Up to the time of Kneller, the old practice had prevailed ; but when he came to this country, he brought with him a servant whose employment was to prepare all the colours and materials for his work. Northcote tells us this, and adds that Kneller afterwards set him up in business as a colour maker for artists, and that from this man's success—he being the first that kept a colour-shop in London—arose the trade of artists' colourman. Henceforward, the preparation of panels and canvases, and the grounds that cover them, the washing, grinding, and tempering of colours,—the oils and varnishes to use as vehicles, or to protect the surface of the finished work,—passed out of the hand of the painter into that of the colourman, and the former blindly used what the latter had prepared. This is a state of things to be deplored for many reasons ; amongst others, that the artist is now too often ignorant of the commonest facts relating to the pigments and vehicles he uses, and so long as they are brilliant in themselves, dry rapidly, and mix well in tints with other pigments, he makes little inquiry into their durability or permanency, and uses indifferently those which have received the sanction of the past, with those yet untested, because newly brought into use and notice.

Sir Joshua Reynolds was undesignedly the author of much of this mischief; deeply interested, as we have already seen, in ascertaining the methods of the great masters of colouring, he was continually seeking new and more brilliant pigments, to enable him to rival theirs ; new vehicles to give his pigments increased body ; using not only the various siccative oils and resinous varnishes, simple and compounded ; but the essential oils, wax and asphaltum, were also pressed into his service, to give brilliancy, impasto, depth, or richness. Of course many of his pictures at the time of their production astonished his brother artists by their surpassing force and beauty of colour, and of course the host of admirers hastened to become imitators, and were prompt to follow his practice. The artists' colourman was called on to supply the demand for orpiment and carmine, for vegetable yellows and pitchy browns ; and after a while these fugitive pigments, included with others in his lists, became accepted as of the same value as those sanctioned by use for centuries.

The subject of grounds is of the greatest importance to the future of the picture. Many of our finest works are suffering from want of due care in their preparation. If on canvas, it is essential that the ground, though firm and hard, should have due toughness and flexibility; to which end it should be thin, and have sufficient oil in its composition, and, whether on canvas or panel, just such an amount of absorbency as will admit of the proper union of the picture with it. If too absorbent, it is troublesome to the painter, and apt to make the picture heavy in the darks, while it prevents, in a degree, the use of the ground as a source of illumination to pigments used over it transparently. If too hard and impervious, the picture is apt to divide from it and blister off. This is often the case with Turner's pictures. "The Regatta at Cowes," and the "Fishing Boats at Yarmouth," in the Sheepshanks collection have both a strong tendency to rise from the ground; as have also many other of his works, such as "Pope's Villa at Twickenham," the "Mercury and Herse," "The Beach at Hastings," besides many in the national collection, all which require great care on this account. The fine landscape by Callcott, "Southampton Water," the property of Mr. Gibbs, has suffered largely, and is likely to suffer from this cause; indeed it is a source of evil to many other English paintings of the period. Pictures thus endangered should, if the size permits, be covered with glass in front, and at any rate, be lined behind with painted cloth, to render them impervious to the damp; and they should be kept away from the wall against which they are hung by small blocks of cork at the four corners.

Reynolds's works are some of them liable to suffer from this cause, more especially those most free from the injurious use of asphaltum. Moreover, he was careless in overloading his pictures, repeating his work over and over again when dissatisfied with his previous labours, thus losing the benefit of a pure ground. This is exemplified by the answer he is said to have given to one who asked how a certain head had been painted. "How can I tell?" replied Reynolds; "there are at least six others under that one." Again, we are told of his turning a whole length, partly painted, upside down, and beginning the face of another portrait between the legs. Such stories, whether exactly true or not, will serve to illustrate his known carelessness in these matters.

But the works of Reynolds and of his followers, and indeed almost all the pictures of the English school up to the end of the first thirty-five years of the present century, have suffered more from the use of improper pigments than from bad grounds; amongst these the worst is bitumen in all its varied forms of asphaltum, mummy, bitumen, &c. These pitchy colours never thoroughly harden: they are readily affected by heat and change of temperature, and as they remain soft beneath the surface, any harder dryer imposed over them, either as a vehicle for the last glazings of the picture, or as a securing varnish, is certain to draw the work together, and to result in deep separation of the parts. Reynolds used this pigment mostly in the darks, for which its luminous richness so well adapts it : indeed its place can hardly be supplied by any known brown ; from this cause many of the pictures of our greatest portrait painter have failed terribly in the darks, and every fresh varnishing increases the evil. It is a misfortune to pictures painted with preparations of bitumen, that the evil does not always display itself at once : indeed, under favourable circumstances, they will remain very many years without disruption ; but a change in hanging, or in the temperature of the room or gallery, an exposure to the sun's rays, and above all varnishing, will, though they have been heretofore free from harm, crack them in a few weeks.

The works of some of the contemporaries (as Wright of Derby), as well as those of the pupils and followers of Sir Joshua, have suffered from the like cause, and many of the pictures of Northcote, Opie, and Fuseli have, as to their finer qualities, perished from the use of asphaltum. Opie, when asked what medium he had used in painting a certain picture, sarcastically replied *brains ;* the retort was cutting, no doubt, but ill-placed ; he wished to rebuke the littleness that thought of the *means* rather than the end of art ; but a little more attention on his part to these means would have saved his works from early decay, and have prevented his being an example of bad practice to the rising school.

Notwithstanding that the evils arising from the use of bituminous pigments must have already made great progress in destroying the works of Reynolds and his immediate followers, the artists who succeeded them employed these pigments still more unreservedly. Wilkie and Hilton are notable examples, as their decaying works painfully testify. Wilkie began with simple pigments and vehicles ; his "Pitlassie Fair," painted perhaps with linseed oil, still remains in sound condition, as do many others of his early and careful works ; even before he went abroad, however, he began to use asphaltum, but after his return from Spain he attempted more tone and richness, and for this purpose used asphaltum not only in his darks, but mixed even with his solid lights. The manner of working with it was this :—About equal quantities of boiled oil, mastic varnish, and liquid asphaltum (asphaltum melted into the oil), were mixed together, forming a magylph that solidified or "stood up," as the painters called it, and this was the vehicle used throughout the picture, of course mixed with more asphaltum in the darks. He recommended that the dead colour of flesh should be light and grey, and in the second painting he gave the low tone he required by mixing asphaltum largely with the white to form flesh tints, semi-transparent, and obtaining some share of their luminousness from the under-ground. When visitor in the painting school, he asserted, and Hilton supported his opinion, that Titian could only be so copied. A careful study of the "Venus and Adonis," from the Dulwich Gallery, was made by one of the most talented students of the day, under their joint direction; and however beautiful at the time of its production, it now shows only a network of dark seams and corrugations. Wilkie's own picture of "The First Earring," and "The Peep of Day Boys," in the Vernon collection, are other fast decaying evidences of this dangerous practice.

Strange to say, Wilkie's pictures painted while in Spain are uninjured and in sound condition; for which there seem to be two or three reasons. It is probable that the painter was out of the reach of the objectionable pigment, and was obliged to use some other; it would seem bone-brown. Moreover, the pictures are evidently painted at once, many of them being little more than sketches; nor does it seem as if they had as yet been varnished. Several of those which are the property of her Majesty certainly have not, nor apparently that fine work, "The Confessional."

We have already referred to this picture and the manner in which it and others painted at Madrid have been carried out. And it may be noted here, how much better pictures stand which are painted with freshness and facility and with little or no repetition, than those in which the dissatisfied or fastidious artist repeats his painting many times, over work perhaps already too loaded and not sufficiently dry to receive the new layer of colour. It is this facile execution that has preserved the fine works of Gainsborough, when so many of those of his great rival are far advanced on the road to destruction. "The Blue Boy," "The Cottage Girl," the portraits of Mrs. Sheridan and Mrs. Tickell, of Mrs. Siddons, of Mr. and Mrs. Hallett, of Lady Ligonier, of Dr. Fisher, and a host of others painted almost at once, have come down to us nearly without injury. Of Gainsborough's facility and rapidity these works give abundant evidence to the painter who examines their execution; but there is a curious collateral proof in the seventeen beautiful portraits (head and bust life-size) of the children of George III. now at Windsor; these are all dated on the back as being painted in one month, September, 1772, and have most of them the appearance of little more than a single sitting. There are also at Windsor two studies of the Duke and Duchess of Cumberland, life-size, painted on half-length canvases, but only the head completed, and these also seem the work of one sitting each; yet the colour is fresh and clear, has not changed or darkened, and except a few hair-cracks the pictures are perfectly sound. Compare these with some of the noble works of Reynolds, and the latter are seen to be but wrecks of what they were; while the works in our National Gallery by Hilton (to whom allusion has also been made as one of the great authorities for the use of asphaltum) have had to be removed from time to time, in order to reverse them, that eyes and limbs may float back again to the places from which they had slipped whilst hanging on the walls !

What is best to be done with pictures cracked and flowing from the use of asphaltum? No doubt many repairers will readily undertake to bring the parts together with the pressure of a heavy iron over a strong glue, and then with a *little* repainting, and not a little varnishing, the picture for a short time will appear perfectly renovated ; yet this is but a fallacious cure. New rents will soon open, all the sooner for the strong varnishing ; and the *little* repainting will be mixed up with the original, to be again *cured* by the same process. Far better is it to abstain from any attempt at repair, to cleanse the surface with fastidious care by means of cotton wool, and then to preserve the picture from dust (which sticks so readily to the pitchy surface) by means of glass, and from damp and change of atmosphere by covering up the canvas behind.

The use of improper vehicles is another cause of injury to pictures, either from cracking the colours or darkening. Most of the works of the early part of the century are painted with a magylph composed of half mastic varnish and half boiled oil ; a pleasant medium to paint with, and one that stands well when sparingly used, until the picture is varnished ; but, it is to be feared, not longer. With this Wilkie's " Village Festival " and " Blind Fiddler " are painted ; the latter was perfectly sound until varnished some forty years ago, when it immediately cracked down to the white ground ; the same, it will be seen, has taken place in the " Parish Beadle ; " and also in many of Lawrence's portraits, as well as in other pictures of that period. These cracks, however, are narrow, and look like wholesome wounds as compared with asphaltum cracks, and they may be stopped by a careful restorer ; the repainting, which should be with colour ground and used with spirit varnish, being religiously confined to the white lines of the stopping, and not spread over the adjoining parts to hide the bungling clumsiness of a bad workman. But there are pictures where this mastic magylph has been used almost as freely as asphaltum was, and with some of the same evils. As a rule, mediums should be sparingly used ; but Wilkie, admiring the beautiful amber tone of the jelly-like vehicle, exclaimed, as if he had made a discovery, " Magylph is a colour ! " and used it as such. This was the case with the picture of " John Knox Preaching," in which what were beautiful luminous golden lights when the work left the painter's easel, are now brown horny dirty darks. Turner practised the same folly at times ; and in the sky of the " Beach of Hastings," the once brilliant lights on the edges of the rolling cumuli have become darks ; and in other places there are dirty brown spots instead of fleecy golden cloudlets ; formed, no doubt of luscious touches of magylph, perhaps snatched, on the varnishing days, from some neighbouring artist's palette, where it had tempted the eye of the great landscape painter.

Fortunately a change for the better has taken place in art, and those who use the old magylph use it sparingly and with care ; while the greater number of our artists paint with a harder and firmer mixture, formed of copal combined with mastic varnish : some use copal alone ; and some content themselves—as did Leslie in many of his finest works—with simple linseed oil.

Such are a few hints at the causes of the decay but too visible in many of our English pictures : and it must be remembered that pictures, so sickly from their birth, require continuous nursing and careful attention to preserve them in any sort of sound condition ; yet it too often happens that when once arranged on the walls, either very little further attention is paid to them, or the care and superintendence are of the worst kind. When the pictures were received for the Paris International Exhibition of 1855, and our own of 1862, it was curious to note the condition of such valuable property. Some works had evidently never had any cleansing of their surface since the time they were painted, although they had hung during the whole period of their existence in the heart of this or other smoky towns. The tops of the frames of some and the lower interstices between the canvas and stretcher of others were the harbourage of thick layers of dirt ; while the curiosities in the shape of wedges, nails, screws, and filth of all kinds that were gathered between the stretcher and the canvas would have served to furnish a little museum. In many respects the loan of works formed a fortunate epoch in their condition ; as while deposited in these exhibitions they were most carefully looked after and attended to, and the dust of years removed. Moreover, as to some, the possessors on their return—for once while in their possession —minutely looked them over ; and if they attributed the evils that had been progressing for so many years to those who had had them temporarily in charge, they were at least awakened to the sense of their decay, and likely to take better measures to preserve them in future.

Pictures belonging to the proprietors of more than one mansion are very apt to suffer, since they should as much as possible be kept in an equable temperature ; but in the absence of the owner the house is closed, the rooms in which the pictures are hung are left without fires, and the pictures thus subjected to sudden changes of atmosphere, the panels alternately shrink and swell, causing them, if tight in the frames, to warp and split. Windows are opened on improper days, and shut when they ought to be opened ; the direct rays of the sun are allowed to rest upon the pictures, or, what is nearly as bad, no light at all is admitted to them. It is not sufficiently known that *oil* pictures require abundant light, and that they darken and get yellow in rooms with shutters constantly closed and blinds drawn down. The following is a case in point :—

Callcott sent home his picture of "The Mouth of the Tyne" to Sir M. White Ridley, and the family leaving town shortly after, the housekeeper covered it up wholly with a coarse yellow canvas such as is used to cover the frames of pictures against the flies. On the return of the family, when the picture was uncovered, the sky was found to be changed throughout to a golden yellow. Callcott was sent for and was quite unable to account for the change ; attributing it to bad oil or bad pigments. He desired to have the picture home, and in despair of any other mode of treating it, was preparing to scrape out the sky and repaint it, when by accident the picture was placed in the sun on the lawn at his house in the Mall, where it remained some hours, at the end of which time such a visible improvement had taken place that he ventured to continue the treatment, and in three or four days the picture had returned entirely to its pristine freshness : the light had bleached it.

Almost as much mischief arises from ignorant care as from want of care. The mere dusting of pictures is a work requiring some judgment ; it should be done with the softest of feather brushes, and even these are dangerous when the picture has a tendency to scale or blister. Pictures are often carelessly wiped, many persons believing that a silk handkerchief can do no harm ; but a glance at any old collection, and even at some of our own public ones, will show how this has been abused : in many pictures, scales have been torn off, the canvases are cracked all round the edges, the corner pieces and the bars of the stretcher marked on the surface, by undue pressure of the hand of the careless operator as he polishes them ; at times rubbing even the paint away, but at least rubbing in the dust rather than removing it. Perhaps the best preservative for old pictures beyond dusting them with the feather brush, is to have them tenderly wiped with cotton wool about once a year, by the hands of some person qualified to do this with care and judgment. The backs of all pictures, whether oil or water-colour, should be covered with painted cloth to exclude air and dust.

Ill-ventilated rooms are another source of mischief to works of art. Hundreds of fine pictures are hung in close rooms lighted with numerous candles or with gas, yet without the slightest means of ventilation. It was shown in the careful report on this subject by Professors Faraday, Hoffman, and Tyndall, that the proceeds from the combustion of coal gas, unless wholly removed from the apartment, are most deleterious to pictures ; but that gas unburnt was almost innocuous, and its combustion might be made most useful in promoting an active ventilation sufficient to remove all the resulting evils ; and with them, those almost equally deleterious excretions arising in crowded rooms, from condensed breath and an unchanged atmosphere.

While there are those who leave their pictures from year to year untouched and unnoticed, there are others who are continually incrusting them with coats of varnish. Under the dust or dirt of years, the picture may remain intact, and be brought, simply by careful washing, to its first purity and freshness; but those who cover their pictures with numerous coats of varnish, either lock up numerous coats of dirt also, or, if the varnish is continually removed for new applications, remove with it the last tender and most precious finishings of the painter. And here let us again add our warning, at least in respect to British pictures, against the new invention of solving the coats of varnish on a picture, and letting them subside into a new surface. Mastic varnish enters so largely into the vehicle with which such pictures are painted, that under this treatment varnish and pigment may be found floating into one common mass.

It only remains under this head to remark upon a few of the avoidable dangers to which pictures are liable on their occasional removal from place to place. And first as to marking pictures. A practice, but too common, has been to *paste* paper labels on the back of the canvas or panel indifferently. In the latter case, it is harmless; in the former, the moisture of the paste shrinks the spot of canvas to which it is applied, and the result is a permanent lump on the surface. Again, in passing through the hands of upholsterers or packers, pictures are often numbered or marked with chalk on the back of the canvas—a still more dangerous practice—for in the hurry of so marking them, a little extra pressure cracks the picture, which as it ages, takes that singular form of crack so like a caterpillar with many legs, becoming visible as dirt or varnish gradually fills the lines. On one occasion we saw a large number of works which had been just returned to a London agent from a provincial exhibition, all so marked on the back of the canvas by the local authorities. Again, blows or pressure from behind should be scrupulously guarded against: the projecting corners of frames, for instance, dragged against the canvas, will result in the crack above described; and a thrust from any bluntly pointed object—from the finger or the shoulder in carrying—will produce the circular crack so often seen in old pictures, and which, from its regular web-like appearance, Turner used to express his belief was occasioned by an insect.

Great care also should be taken not to over-drive the wedges of the stretching frames, more especially when the pictures are liable to any sudden alternations of damp and dryness. Any one who has noted the great shrinkage that takes place on damping the fibres of a stretched string or cord, will be aware that some play must be allowed for these alternations, or the canvas will be torn from the stretcher, and the surface of the picture be broken up into fine hair cracks. These variations of temperature are much guarded against by lining the back of the picture with painted cloth, as already advocated.

Other injuries arise to pictures from careless or improper packing. One of the commonest errors, and certainly one of the most dangerous, is the practice of screwing the picture to the top or bottom of the case; or, when two pictures are in the same case, screwing one to the top, the other to the bottom: this should never be done; they should be slung on battens within the case. Two battens, crossing the back of the picture, should be carefully secured by screws to the most solid part of the back of each frame, the screws being of sufficient length and depth of cut to allow of the picture hanging beneath the batten without fear of its weight drawing the screws. The ends of these battens, projecting somewhat beyond the frame or frames, should drop, and be carefully secured, into notched racks or ledges, well fastened to the sides of the case; so that the picture should be slung within it, free everywhere but at the end of the battens. Pictures thus packed are partly on springs, and any shock on the outer case is distributed and dispersed without injury. If the case is large and deep enough, a number of pictures may be packed within it in the same manner, merely by placing the racks or notched ledges at proper intervals to keep the pictures well apart.

Before placing the battens across the frames, the wedges should be looked to and slightly tightened, and what is of still more importance, the picture properly nailed into its frame, otherwise the picture may get loose, although the frame remains secure, and rub itself to pieces with the motion in carriage. So carelessly in this respect are pictures sent away by their owners that valuable works are often received at public exhibitions quite disengaged from their fastenings. Another danger to which pictures are exposed in travelling arises from the bad construction of the frames; the flat or inner portion being mostly a separate piece, merely bradded in, or slightly secured by glued wood blocks. Such a construction, although sufficiently strong while the picture hangs on the wall, is most dangerous when it travels horizontally, exposed to the jolting of the railroad; when even if the picture is carefully fastened into the flat, the two break away from the other part of the frame; or when the picture is very heavy—as for instance a lined picture, or a picture on panel—the thin rebate of the flat gives way, and the picture falls through, with the splintered remnants to increase the mischief. The best precaution is, in all such cases, to screw pieces across the back angles of the frame, and to screw the stretcher of the picture to them, which removes the pressure entirely from the flat; but this will not do when the picture is on panel.

Thus a few of the most obvious sources of injury, and of the causes which lead to the premature decay of pictures have been slightly glanced at ; it only remains to allude to the doings of those who undertake, qualified or unqualified, to repair their injuries, to renovate their fading glories, and even to restore them to their first freshness and brightness.

Wrong, indeed, would it be to throw discredit on *all* who practise the restorer's art. Some few there are who are duly qualified, but for our own part we would put up with many blemishes ere we trusted a work we loved out of our own hands. For as in the healing art there are quacks and nostrum-mongers, and shallow or incompetent practitioners ; who are always the boldest in their pretensions, and the most boastful of the universality and infallibility of their cures ; so it is with the renovators of pictures ; and many a one whose qualifications consist only in the reckless impudence with which he dares to use the spirit or the alkali to scour off dirt and art together, places a half-washed portrait in the window and dubs himself a restorer. Some of these boast that their very ignorance of drawing is one of their best qualifications, since they must of necessity follow the leadings of the painter whose work is under their hands ; which is about as logical as it would be to say that we are more fully qualified to decipher a half obliterated inscription by ignorance of the language in which it is written. Too often such *renovators* use strong detergents, and wash away all the last and delicate heightenings of the painter, together with the dirt and varnish that had accumulated over his works ; and then reduce the whole to a meaningless uniformity by a universal coat of stippling : perhaps at the same time heightening the *expression*, in their idea, by darkening the eyes, the eyelids, the corners of the mouth, and the nostrils, to give the vigour their labours had destroyed. In the case of injuries or blisters, a common fault is, after stopping the holes, to paint over the part with colour ground in oil. Then, in order to hide the spot, the retouching is spread far and wide round the original injury ; nay, it often happens, that, led on by their conceit or their audacity, an entire face or hand is repainted, much (in their eyes) to its improvement, and the whole, highly varnished, comes back to its possessor, reputed as in the finest state. Sad it is that such evils perpetuate themselves, and the injuries of a picture come to be considered its greatest merit. To hide these wholesale restorations, a dark brown varnish is resorted to, and what is hence called "the fine golden tone " of a picture—a golden tone neither the work of the original artist, nor of the gradual mellowing influence of time, but really a false incrustation—becomes one of the sources of its estimation.

It is true that, backed up by the folly of would-be connoisseurs of the last age, "the golden tone " was so coveted that it was added as a necessary flavour to all pictures. This perhaps arose in the first instance from the importation of smoke-browned altar-pieces, and other second-rate pictures of the Bolognese school, the fashionable school at that time

—works painted on a dark ground which had greatly failed in the "darks," and thus the solid whites and lights had to be toned down to bring lights and darks together. Once accepted as the true tone of a fine picture, all must be heightened or lowered to the same standard of excellence. The late Mr. Uwins used to tell of a visit he paid to De la Hante the dealer, when the fine picture of St. Nicholas, by Paul Veronese, was in his hands for sale. When he found who had come to see the picture, he took Mr. Uwins into the gallery where it was, and after they had looked at it awhile, said—"Now I will show you what this picture really is," and taking a sponge, he removed a dark coat from its surface, leaving the picture in a beautifully pure, cool, and fresh state; a state they both could fully appreciate. After they had admired it awhile, he remarked, "I may show it thus to you, but it will not do for the world to see it without the tone being renewed." Ere Uwins left, a party of dilettanti were announced; but De la Hante would not let them see it until "the golden tone" was restored. Here was a dealer who well knew what a fine picture should be, obliged to conform to the prevailing dilettantism; but to the host of vampers-up of brown masters, this "golden tone" was a true god-send, and far too valuable an agent in their mysteries, not to be upheld with all their influence.

Goldsmith—the learned simpleton, as he was thought by the clever but shallow wits of his own day—must have been admitted behind the scenes, or he could not so well have described the audacity of these gentry. Speaking in the person of the vicar's son, he says of one of these oracles, "There was sometimes an occasion for a more supported assurance. I remember to have seen him, after giving his opinion that the colouring of a picture was not mellow enough, very deliberately take a brush with brown varnish, that was accidentally lying by, and rub over the picture before all the company, and then ask if he had not improved the tints." The application of such a tone of course hid all the scrubbings and over-cleanings of the ignorant restorer; and when the repairs made in oil, which have been already described, changed, as they must change, to dark spots or extensive patches on the original tints, a still deeper shade of this coveted tone hid all their blotchings, and like charity, covered a multitude of sins.

Though the practice of toning pictures was mostly resorted to to enhance the beauties of the old masters, yet under the enthusiastic patronage of the dilettanti of the day it was extended to more modern works, and the ignorance of the painter as to what his picture should be, was supplied by their care. Many Wilsons, Gainsboroughs, and Reynolds, bear present testimony to their superiority of judgment. There can be no doubt that pictures were, and are, constantly over-toned as well as over-cleaned, and that pictures in our national collections have, in past days, been so treated; but, in view of the terrors of that body of experts the House of Commons, who would venture to bring them back to what the painter thought they ought to be, or he himself would have toned them? To remove such additions would raise up a storm of virtuous indignation that few would be willing to face. This, it is true, is not to be wondered at, in face of the wholesale scrubbings that have taken place abroad, as many even of the works in the Louvre testify; whilst at Dresden, the world-famous Correggios, instead of the delicate, refined, yet luminous glazings which characterize the master's works when in a genuine state, have become solid, dry, and insipid under the hands of the restorer, who has gained fame and reputation at the expense of the poor painter; born, it would seem, only that Palmaroli might be glorified in him. At Rotterdam also the true Dutch spirit of cleanliness has reduced some of the pictures in the public collection to the mere panel.

As individuals, however, will require medical and surgical aid, so occasionally must pictures, whether from accident or premature decay; it may be difficult in an age of quacks to choose a skilled physician, and it is an equally anxious affair to have to make choice of a good restorer. Enough has been said to induce us not to resort to him on slight occasions. On more grave ones, seek out the man of the highest reputation; him, moreover, who promises the least, who has a wholesome dread of doing too much, and the strongest objection to doing anything at all. If the canvas want lining, or the panel parqueting, have it done in the best manner and by the best craftsman; but do not allow the work to be varnished, so that you can see your face in it as in a looking-glass.

Thus much as to pictures in oil; but something must be said as to works in water-colour, in order to complete this section of our labours. In oil or water alike, many of the radical defects arise from the materials used. This is especially the case with the drawings of our first water-colour painters; whose art stimulated the manufacture and improvement of papers suitable for its use, till great excellence has been attained. Originally the paper was deficient in its dimensions and surface; but it concealed more dangerous defects. Sometimes made in mills whose water-supply was impregnated with iron, ferruginous spots of foxy tint develop themselves over the surface of the drawing. Sometimes unequally or imperfectly sized, the whole surface is covered with spots of a darker tint than the colour used; or the drawing has a sunk-in woolly appearance, destructive of all sharpness and brilliancy. Again, the colours used by the early water-colour painter were no less immature. Suited only to the mere tinter, they were quite unfitted for the artist who would contend with the brilliancy and power of the oil painter. Earths (ochre, umber, and sienna), have been now supplemented by brilliant mineral or chemical products; and Prussian blue and reds of a fleeting weak character, have given way not only to better colours, but to better modes of preparation.

When, therefore, we would judge of the durability of a water-colour drawing, we must not bring the works of our early artists into comparison with the perfected excellences attained in the present day, and ascribe their weak washed-out appearance, their want of brilliancy and sharpness, to decay alone, but rather to their original and inherent defects; among which may be classed the practice of passing a uniform tint, or wash of warm colour, often of much power, over the whole surface. Some of the early drawings, however, exhibit great freshness and colour, undimmed by eighty years of exposure. We see this most in the water-colour works of men who practised chiefly in oil—Ibbetson and Hamilton, for instance—whose drawings may be cited as proof of the durability of the art. Of the great works of Turner, in the two mediums, it may be safely said that up to this time his water-colour pictures, delicately beautiful as they are, have, under average treatment, suffered less than his oil paintings. We are told that on the establishment of the British Institution in 1805, the reason for the exclusion of water-colour drawings, was their want of permanence; a mere presumption, if the reason given is true, as time had not then been given to test the new art.

The two great enemies of water-colour art are exposure to sun, or the glare of strong reflected light, or to damp. Nothing so surely destroys as the sun : the colour is burnt off the paper ; even the forms disappear, and every quality which gave pleasure is hopelessly destroyed. Damp is likewise destructive ; but while generally affecting brilliancy, its effects are chiefly evidenced by spottiness, dark spots in the light parts, and light on the dark parts : this is often increased by bad paste used in the mounting, which gives rise to a fungous growth highly destructive to such works. In addition to these special ills, drawings are of course subject to all the mischiefs common to their fragile nature.

There is not any mystery in the due care of water-colour drawings. They require only security from sun, and damp and dirt. When kept in a portfolio, or in closed drawers, they will, if such receptacles are constructed properly, be safe from these united evils ; but whatever may be the temperature in which they are maintained, it will be found necessary that they should from time to time be subjected to light, and warmth with its ventilating influence. When exhibited in frames their charge is no less simple. They are then always defended by glass, which should be gummed or pasted to the frame, so that the drawing may from the front be impervious to the subtle permeations of a London atmosphere. They should also be exhibited in sunk mounts to keep them from touching the glass, and should not only be pasted into the frame at the back, but additional security from damp walls, against which they may be hung, should be obtained by the use of the patent painted cloth. In moving drawings from place to place, when in folios or boxes, care must be used that they do not rub one another.

It may be proper to add a few rules as to the hanging of pictures in rooms or galleries. A small frontage to the street is one of the necessary conditions in planning London houses, and houses in most of our large towns ; hence the rooms are deep in proportion to their width, and the light from narrow windows is often insufficient, they being mostly too near the side-walls, which are always dark at the end furthest from the front. This darkness is increased on one side by the usual projection of the chimney breast, and on both by the curtains and furniture, which fashion and the necessities of our climate cluster round our windows ; while projecting frames to the pictures too often add to the obscurity. The wall opposite the windows, even if not too far removed from the light, is unsuitable for pictures, because the glass over water-colour paintings, or the varnished surface of works in oil so placed, must always mirror the windows opposite, and the glitter and reflection of their light hinder any pleasure in viewing them. Hence, where any available space can be found for the purpose, most of those who love art, and collect pictures, build top-lighted galleries for their reception. It is only in such galleries that pictures can be seen to the best advantage.

The conditions for such galleries are simple and are as follows :— First, abundance of light perfectly under control, so that by blinds or shutters it can be readily increased or diminished at pleasure. Second, the skylight of the gallery should be so placed that when the spectator is in the best position to view the pictures, they shall not glitter with the reflection of the window or skylight : a condition determinable by fixed laws of optics ; so that no gallery need be ill-constructed in this respect.

As a general rule, an oblong parallelogram on plan is more suitable than a square room ; and in such cases it will be found that the height of the skylight should be equal to the width of the room. Thus, twenty feet wide by thirty or forty feet long, and twenty feet high, will light well, if the skylight be properly arranged. The proper amount of light will be admitted through an opening about equal to half the superficial area of the floor, and should be as little as possible interrupted by ceiling joists, rafters, or beams. If light is too high above the pictures, as it diminishes rapidly in proportion to its distance from the source of admission, the pictures will be in half-shadow, as if in a well. If the light is too low down, glitter from the surface of the picture is unavoidable. If the pictures are to be lighted at night, the artificial light should be so placed as to correspond in the angle of its rays with those of the natural light.

Air for ventilation should be admitted near the floor, and have abundant exit at the roof : this rule, desirable even where artificial light is not used, is an absolute necessity where it is used, if pictures are to be preserved from injury. It is most desirable, for all these reasons, that beneath the skylight, glass sashes or a glass ceiling should be introduced.

It must be repeated, however, that as the laws which regulate the proper proportion and angle of light can be laid down with absolute certainty, no gallery should be constructed without the lines having been determined by those who have studied them, and are competent to advise on the proportions adapted to a gallery of the size to be erected.

CHAPTER XXXIX.

IN all schools, individuals from time to time arise who carry some phase of art to a high degree of perfection, and the danger is that their contemporaries and successors neglect to study nature for themselves, and become followers and copyists of the manner or art of these master spirits. When this occurs, the decadence of the school is rapid. The nature of English habits, and the independence of the English character, are in this respect favourable to art progress, since each man loves to think for himself. Had the landscape painters of the past generation been content to follow the manner of Wilson or Gainsborough, we should not have seen the noble works of Turner and Constable. Novelty in aim or treatment seems necessary to art progress. Wilkie, Leslie, and Mulready, with characteristic differences in their art held its great principles in common; their reputation and the beauty of their works gathered around them imitators, while their living influence was in the schools; but, as the half-century in which they had produced their best pictures drew towards its completion, the painters of the rising school abandoned the rules of art which had guided these great landscape and figure painters, and adopted principles apparently the very opposite of theirs.

The poets of the beginning of the nineteenth century had rebelled against the conventionalisms of their predecessors both as to metre and manner, but more particularly as to their choice of subjects. They had reverted to a degree of realism which was then stigmatized as sheer puerility, and severe was the criticism that Wordsworth and his followers had to endure at the hands of critics and reviewers. Yet the rebellion against old forms of thought was on the whole healthy, and when the first reaction had somewhat subsided, it introduced new beauties, with fresher views of life and springs of thought. Music also had its rebels against authority : and art, although with us at a later period, was to experience a movement of the like nature, and to have its outbreak of realism as had poetry. First the young Germans studying their art at Rome, disgusted, no doubt, with the tame proprieties of the modern Romans—Cammuccini and his followers, whose art was built upon rules and precedents with little reference to nature and truth—broke loose from the fetters of the schools.

So earnest were these young artists in following the religious art of the early Italians, which they considered defiled by the Paganism of the Renaissance and despoiled of all fervour by Protestantism, that, headed by Cornelius and Overbeck they went over in a body to the Church of Rome, and henceforth devoted themselves to the restoration of religious art on the basis of its pre-Raphaelite practice. Later the movement spread to France, but under a different phase; Courbet and his followers adopted realism, repudiating beauty and selection, and copying nature as she is found, rather in her meanest than under her noblest aspects.

About the year 1850, seven young Englishmen, five of whom were artists just completing their studies, banded together under the name of the pre-Raphaelite Brethren; a term which they adopted to signify that henceforth they would take their stand on the art of the painters prior to Raphael, as opposed to the conventional art, as they termed it, of his school and followers. They began by publishing a weekly magazine called *The Germ*, intended to set forth their peculiar views in art and poetry. Though it is difficult to find any clear statement of what these views were, originality and truth seemed to be pointed at in the verse which accompanied the first number, and which was printed as a motto in black letter upon the wrapper; it is as follows:—

> " When whoso merely hath a little thought
> Will merely think the thought which is in him—
> Not imaging another's bright or dim.
> Not mingling with new words what others taught.
> When whoso speaks, from having either sought
> Or only found, will speak, not just to skim
> A shallow surface with words made and trim,
> But in the very speech the matter brought ;
> Be not too keen to cry, ' So this is all !—
> A thing I might myself have thought as well
> But would not say it, for it was not worth ! '
> Ask, ' Is this truth ? ' For is it still to tell
> That, be the theme a point, or the whole earth,
> Truth is a circle, perfect, great or small ! "

If the publication had contained nothing more intelligible than the verse which heralded it into the world, there had been need of little wonder that its career was ended after the fourth number. This, however, was not the case, since some of the contributors gave promise which their pens have since fully redeemed. Still it is to their own statements at the time, and to the works they produced in the first fervour of their brotherhood, that we must look for the *principles* of the school; unless so far as we may accept them from the pen of one who has ever been their eloquent, if at times, their injudicious champion. Their first great principle was truth rather than beauty; and, therefore, non-selection in treating their subjects. Thus it was said by their able expositor, in his lectures on architecture and painting delivered at Edinburgh, 1853, that "pre-Raphaelitism has but one principle, that of absolute uncompromising truth in all that it does, obtained by working everything, down to the most minute detail, from nature, and from nature only. Every pre-Raphaelite landscape background is painted to the last touch in the open air, from the thing itself. Every pre-Raphaelite figure, however studied in expression, is a true portrait of some living person. Every minute accessory is painted in the same manner." Further that the pre-Raphaelite disciples rejected "that spurious beauty whose attractiveness has tempted men to forget or to despise the more noble quality of sincerity;" and also with the further uncomplimentary addition, that, "in order to put them beyond the power of temptation, they are, as a body, characterized by a total absence of sensibility to the ordinary and popular forms of artistic gracefulness."

It would appear that the protest of these young painters—and it was so far a right protest—was against worn-out conventionalisms, stale repetitions of other men's modes of thought and modes of treatment; although at that time such art was not particularly characteristic of our school. In the spirit of youth and enthusiasm this protest was, in some of their number—for the seven original members soon had a large following—accompanied by an indiscreet self-assertion, and an amusing despisal of all art since the end of the fifteenth century, calculated to call forth some bitterness in contemporary criticism. But on the whole it has had a good result, and art has benefited by their earnestness, and by the works they have produced; even if these have been achieved rather by overlooking their own early dogmas, than by rigidly enforcing them. The three principles which have been enunciated in the above quotations, and which are found in the first works of the brotherhood are :—The rejection of beauty, or non-selection; imitative finish of the details from nature; and equal completion of all parts of the picture. We are told that their first object is truth. "What is truth?" was mournfully asked by one who did not clearly see his way between two conflicting courses; and we may still say, what is truth? Each may decide, as he believes sincerely, but his decision will be warped by his education and his prejudices. We are also told that in pre-Raphaelite pictures each figure is a true portrait of some living person. Now as to this being one of the pre-Raphaelite efforts after truth, are not all artists accustomed to work from models? When the great Leonardo wished to paint into the " Last Supper" the head of Our Lord, he was for months seeking a model whose head might suggest to him features that he could clothe, alas! he knew how faintly, with the deep impression of Him who sat at meat. Surely this was a right step on the part of the painter in *his* search after truth. Far more so than was his, who, painting the husband of the blessed Virgin, chose a mechanic with corny hands and sun-stained arms as a true representative, because, like the holy man of old, he was a carpenter; rather than sought out one, whatever his rank of life, whose features might somewhat realize the noble and trustful nature of him who was to shield and shelter from the distrust and scandal which were likely to be her lot, the mother of Our Lord.

Then as to backgrounds. Surely in looking at the touching and earnest expression the painter has given to one who seeks to save her lover from danger and death, we do not wish to be called upon to examine how minutely he has rendered, brick by brick, the wall behind her, with its rotten mortar and crumbling surface. We are not to be provoked into admiration, even though assured that it "is painted to the last touch in the open air," from the wall itself. We rest our eyes on the earnest action, the sweet pleading expression of the woman, and feel that attention to the wall would indicate about the same amount of obtuseness on our part, as on his who, invited to see a picture, should turn aside to praise the frame. Or let us look to the landscape painters of this school, carrying out the " one and only principle of absolute and uncompromising truth obtained by working everything, down to the minutest detail, from nature and from nature only." From such a principle, what is the result? certainly not art, but merely topographical truth. As well might the poet, from some hill-top, catalogue the meadows and cornfields, the hedgerows, the villages, mansions, and churches he sees before him, and call it poetry.

Rather than criticize the works of the living, let us take the picture of " Jerusalem and the Valley of Jehoshaphat," by Seddon (b. 1821, d. 1856), in the National Gallery, as a type of the class. It is painted by one who travelled far and endured much to produce it, and it is worthy of our admiration for its fidelity, if we cannot praise it for the art it displays. The " Jerusalem" is highly interesting; but merely for its topographic accuracy. It is a photograph with colour, containing every—even the minutest—detail of the scene: the walls of Jerusalem seem piled up stone by stone; outside are the few scant houses of the village suburb with their narrow openings to shut out the eastern sun; square in form and with flat roofs, they look like blocks of stone which have rolled down from the arid hills behind, so similar are they in colour to the rocks themselves. There, feeding on the scant herbage of thistle and teazle, painted as if from a *hortus-siccus*, are the sheep and the goats together; the shepherd, meanwhile, his long gun beside him, lying under a flowering pomegranate. The little patches of soil on the sides of the valley kept up by walls of stone; the olive and fig trees, each are given by number so that the owner of each might recognize his own tree, his own patch of arid earth. The deep blue heaven of unclouded noon is above, the all-penetrating glare below. Jerusalem is before you—Jerusalem as it is—as it may be registered, mapped and catalogued; but the poetry of Jerusalem is not there : it must come, if at all, from our own hearts and not from the picture. The sheep and the goats feeding together may suggest the great day when the angel of the Lord shall come and divide, setting the one on His right hand, the other on His left; the flat house-tops in the Valley of Jehoshaphat, His command that on that day they who are on the house-tops shall not go down to find their clothes : but all these suggestions are from within. This is, and is not, the Jerusalem that He wept over : this is, and is not, the valley of decision, wherein the multitudes shall be gathered on that day : it suggests nothing to us but a barren valley, a hill fortress, a place of stones.

It is true we are told of the pre-Raphaelites that "as landscape painters, the principal of that division of them who do not trust to imagination, must, in great part, confine themselves to mere foreground-work ; they have been born with comparatively little enjoyment of those evanescent effects and distant sublimities which nothing but the memory can arrest, and nothing but a daring conventionalism portray." Rather disparaging admissions if true. But it is also said "for this work they are not needed; Turner, the first and greatest of the pre-Raphaelites, has done it already." Turner a pre-Raphaelite! Turner, who passed his life in studying nature under her varied aspects that his memory of her might be sure; who left us thousands of his studies, yet repudiated the practice of painting *his pictures* at all out of doors, and would have laughed at the "one principle, the uncompromising truth of working everything from nature and from nature only, painting to the last touch in the open air from the thing itself." Turner a pre-Raphaelite! he who repudiated topographic imitation when it had served his purpose, and made selection of the beautiful and characteristic in nature his principle ; idealizing the commonplace of every-day nature, which the laborious idler, painting from " the thing itself," can never do ; and adding to it, from the ample stores of his well-filled memory, every evanescent beauty arising from sun and shade, and the thousand changes with which they glorify the common aspect of things !

But if Turner had been a pre-Raphaelite, let us imagine how he would have painted Jerusalem, " the city of the Great King," had he undertaken to realize it on canvas. Let us notice his treatment of Venice, as an instance in point. We many of us know the actual prose aspect of that city of waters ; most of us may have seen the aspect realized, the buildings ruled out with precision, the canals with their regular wavelets as painted by Canaletti; but Turner, despising this matter-of-fact view of the city of the sea, realizes to us rather what the poet saw.

> " The fair city of the heart,
> Rising like water-columns from the sea,
> Of joy the sojourn, and of wealth the mart."

He lighted up her palaces and towers into jewelled richness with the bright rays of an Italian sun, filled her courts with pageants, her canals with rich argosies, her wharves with gondolas draped with broideries of pearl and gold. Had he treated Jerusalem, would he not by his art have clothed her with some of the glories promised to her by the sacred poet ? " I will lay thy stones with fair colours, and thy foundations with sapphires, and I will make thy windows with agates, and thy gates of carbuncles, and all thy borders with precious stones "—some such glorious city has he made of Venice. And such, but far more glorious, we long to picture Jerusalem.

Let us pause, however ; lest, in objecting to the principles they propounded, or which were propounded for them, we are thought to depreciate the men who held them. Be this far from us. Some of the followers of this school have attained, and are universally allowed to have attained, the first rank in art ; and have painted pictures which all true lovers of art must admire. Some have avowedly repudiated the early principles of the brotherhood ; and all who have gained eminence have more or less ignored them. We are also willing to admit that the principles themselves have a great value, if not observed to the exclusion of others, in enforcing constant reference to nature and greater imitative truth.

At first the rigid carrying out of the " one principle of non-selection and exact copying from nature " obtained more among the landscape than the figure painters. Some landscape painters there were who assured us that all the landscapes painted prior to their own advent— not even excluding the works of Turner—if preserved at all, would only be so as curious specimens of what in ignorance was aforetime called art, and in order to compare them with the wonderful works of the painters of the future. We may well have been amused with such conceit, as we were well convinced that painting landscapes " to the last touch direct from nature," will not produce noble but rather mean art; and that, however useful at the beginning of an artist's career this mode of studying nature may be, it will be dropped by the true artist as soon as he arrives at greater power, and realizes to himself that true art is the *poetic* representation of common nature.

The guiding spirit in the brotherhood as first formed was *Gabriel Charles Dante Rossetti*, who is usually called by his last two names. He was the second child and eldest son of Gabriel Rossetti, the eminent commentator on Dante and Italian patriot, for many years a professor in King's College, London, and was born in London, 12th May, 1828. He was, perhaps, the most remarkable member of a remarkable family, and it would be a difficult matter to decide whether he is greater in poetry or in painting; at least, it is certain that for both he was specially gifted, and in both he manifests a quite original and unusual force of genius. He joined Cary's Art Academy in 1843, and entered later the antique school of the Royal Academy, but this latter he attended very irregularly, and he never studied in the life school.

After leaving the Academy he was for a while a pupil in the studio of Ford Maddox Brown, and on leaving this painter he joined Holman Hunt in leasing a painting room in Cleveland Street, where he began his first picture (if we except a portrait study of the head of his father), "The Girlhood of Mary Virgin." Before this he had written his poem of *The Blessed Damozel*, a much more complete work of art than is the picture, which, though a very striking effort for a young painter, scarcely comes up pictorially to what Rossetti achieved in his later works. In this picture, and another very pathetic and dramatic work, called "Found," and in the "Ecce Ancilla Domini," now, we are glad to say, in the National Gallery, Rossetti's colour is cold and tame when compared with the splendour and wealth of rich colouring displayed in "The Bride," "Dante's Dream," "Venus Verticordia," and other pictures, but these early pictures, notwithstanding angularity of form, show a purer conception and more sincere earnestness and greater dramatic simplicity of subject than do his later works, which are marred by mannerisms and peculiarities.

On the proceeds of the sale of this first picture Rossetti went for a short time to two or three old Belgian towns, where the works of Memling and Van Eyck had a great effect upon him. On his return from this trip, while he was painting in Newman Street, the pre-Raphaelite Brotherhood was first formed, and its principles were enunciated in *The Germ*. Rossetti at this time was devoting himself more to water-colour than oil pictures, though he considered the latter medium to be the real vehicle for his expression. In 1860 Rossetti married, only to lose his wife after rather over a year's married life. In the first impulse of violent grief he laid the MSS. of all his poems with her in the coffin, and it was not till ten years later that they were exhumed and afterwards published. Rossetti's wife was a most frequent model for his pictures, and we believe his fine picture of " Beata Beatrix," though painted after her death, is a very exact portrait. " Beata Beatrix " is intended to illustrate symbolically the death of Beatrice as related by Dante in the *Vita Nuova*. Beatrice is in a trance, and seated in a gallery which overlooks the city of Florence, her figure is life-sized, and about two-thirds is represented on the canvas. The face is quiescent, the hair of a rich auburn. She is dressed in a green bodice with purple sleeves. In front of her is a sun-dial, a crimson bird is bringing her a white poppy, an emblem of the sleep of death, and behind her Dante and the Angel of Love are shown watching in the background. This is one of Rossetti's best works, though for gorgeous colour we prefer " The Bride," the subject taken from the Song of Solomon ; a group of five female figures round a centre one, the bride, dressed in a robe of figured green, one of the most lovely of Rossetti's female figures, whose beauty is set off by a swarthy young negress in the front of the picture holding up a golden vase full of pink and yellow roses. " Dante's Dream " illustrates another passage from the *Vita Nuova*—Beatrice lying dead upon a couch, before which two green-clad ladies hold the pall full of may-bloom. Dante in a dream is led into the chamber by the winged figure of Love in red drapery. The picture is full of poetic details of imagery. It was bought by the corporation of Liverpool.

In about six months after his wife's death Rossetti removed to the house where he passed almost all his remaining life, 16, Cheyne Walk, Chelsea ; here he lived in a more and more retired manner, latterly only seeing a few faithful and devoted friends. He varied his life by occasional visits to Scotland. Between 1872-74 he passed much time at Kelmscote Manor in Gloucestershire. In 1872 he had a severe illness, though from this he perfectly recovered. It was partly induced by his habit of taking chloral as a remedy against insomnia. The fatal effects caused by a constant use of this dangerous drug are very much to be deplored, it led to a decay of his bodily energies, and gradually a weakening of his constitution. He was again in 1881 attacked by illness, but nevertheless his death came rather unexpectedly on Easter Day, April 9th, 1882, at Birchington-on-Sea, to which place he had removed by his doctor's advice, as he had been suffering from partial paralysis of the left arm. Rossetti's art, by his persistent dislike to having pictures exhibited, could, during his lifetime, only be known to a small circle, if we compare the few people who could see them in his studio, or at their owners' houses, with the numbers of those who frequent an exhibition. It was therefore a pleasure to many when the

Royal Academy resolved to include a collection of his pictures with their Old Masters Exhibition in 1883.

As during his lifetime the opinions on his art varied very considerably, so the controversy continued during this exhibition, and it is rather difficult to pass a fair judgment upon it, as we are too near to him to be quite dispassionate in our criticism. Rossetti's art was that of a mystic deeply imbued with the study of Dante, and of the Arthurian legends. He owed nothing to foreign travel, academic study, or to artists in general, for though he was greatly admired by many painters, he was personally known to but few, and over these he exercised more sway than they did upon him. In the great point of originality, his works are therefore very unique. We have had few artists of such distinct individuality. His pictures betray a decided exuberance of fancy, they are rich and splendid in colour, and in some cases very fine in execution ; on the other hand they are apt to degenerate into a wholly sensuous feeling for beauty, they show a lack of drawing or of a want of any appreciation of what is classical in form. He paints too much from the same model, whose too rich lips and large throat he exaggerates and overdoes. His intention is always earnest, and his work is carried through with the same arduous effort of the mind which is apparent in the poetically thought-out details of all his pictures.

He ever strove to realize his ideal. Whether this ideal was as pure and elevated in conception as we should like the ideal of a great painter to be, whether it was not sometimes marred by a passion for a certain kind of beauty not of the highest order, a beauty more sensuous than spiritual or intellectual is a matter perhaps for each person who thinks over the subject to decide for himself. To our mind it detracts from the otherwise high poetic grace and value of Rossetti's work.

Again Rossetti's admirers seem to have a blind partiality for all his art, but we should call him an uneven painter. There is a great difference in his work, and while some of his pictures, such as " Found," " Dante's Dream," " The Blessed Damozel," " The Bride," are most powerful creations, there are water-colours by his hand that might have been produced by an inferior imitator of his pictures.

James Collinson, another original member of the brotherhood, but who seceded from it in 1852, was born at Mansfield in Nottinghamshire, 1825, and died in London 24th January, 1881. His picture of " St. Elizabeth," which was an illustration of a portion of Charles Kingsley's *Saints' Tragedy*, was painted while he was contributing to *The Germ*. He afterwards became a Roman Catholic, and in future exhibited pictures of domestic subjects.

Among the landscape painters who founded the P.-R. B. *John W. Inchbold* was throughout his life the one most influenced by pre-

Raphaelite principles. He was born in Leeds in 1830, and died there in 1888 suddenly from heart disease. His pictures were very careful and minute copies of nature, his subjects were chosen apparently without selection, and though his colour was very brilliant and yet delicate, his work was wanting in atmosphere and in sense of proportion. " The Moorland," exhibited by him at the Royal Academy in 1855, is perhaps his best picture.

On the whole English art was improved rather than injured by what was called the pre-Raphaelite " heresy," the zeal and earnestness of its followers served to counterbalance the evil caused by the numbers of meretricious pictures, which the newly-awakened interest of the public in art, the formation of art-unions all over the country, led those painters to produce who only cared for money and who painted with no end but to sell. It is curious that the ebb and flow which seems to obtain in all the circumstances of human life has now apparently washed away the sincere, earnest, and minute endeavour of the pre-Raphaelite after truth, bringing in his place the ardent Impressionist who, though affecting the same zeal for reality, presumes it can only be attained by dash and vagueness, by slashing on masses of untempered colour upon a canvas in any state of unfitness for its reception, and who, though trained in the French school, begins where he ought to finish, and, without the genius of his masters, believes that if he is able to imitate their faults he may count himself a sharer in their perfections.

Some time ago, another source of danger to true art arose out of its very prosperity. Rumours of the large sums paid to living artists for commissioned work, the rise of prices in pictures of merit when sold at Christie's and other public sales, was looked upon by painters as a proof that art had a brilliant future for all its members ; whereas a more wholesome view to take would have been that the rise in prices came from the general prosperity at that particular time of the middle classes, and from the abundant capital at that moment in the hands of our large manufacturers, who, unlike our nobles with large estates, family encumbrances and numerous dependents, had but to spend or re-invest their gains. Art affords both these opportunities ; it gives pleasure and delight in possession, and rising prices show that the best art is a safe investment. But how obtain the best art ? Want of knowledge on the part of the purchasers has raised up a class of middlemen and dealers ; these again add largely to prices for their necessary profits. It would be wrong to say that many of this new class of purchasers were not genuine lovers of art, or that those who began with small knowledge or appreciation, did not learn by possession of fine works to love art for its own sake.

Still, with the many, art is no more than a source of self-glorification in possession, and a safe and improving investment for the future. The true painter should resist the spirit of covetousness. It is right that artists should be paid at least as well as other professors who require no higher endowments, no longer previous study, nor harder probation ere reputation is achieved, than those who, if they are true artists, must also be favoured with natural gifts. But art must be practised for the love of it, and not for gain, if art is to make true progress. The artist should love his labour, and no work should leave his easel that is not the best he can make it. This is hard, when dealers and purchasers wait, money in hand, hungry for possession, and caring little for subject or for excellence, so that they get an undoubted work of a favourite painter: hard indeed to resist the temptation of ready profit, though perhaps indifferently satisfied with the success of his own labours. Thus the very prosperity of artists may be a source of danger to true art-progress. There are other causes that may affect the future of art, either for its prosperity or decay. We have shown its progress, from small beginnings until it is almost co-extensive with society. Some knowledge of it has spread among all educated classes, the Government taking in hand, as we have shown, to instruct the artisans, and even their children, in its rudiments.

At the beginning of our history, one exhibition of modern works was a novelty; now all classes have opportunity of seeing not only modern pictures, but the noblest works of art. The National Gallery opens its treasures, not to the rich alone, but freely to the poor; Hampton Court is the resort of the poor man on his holidays; South Kensington in his leisure hours. The great International Exhibitions have afforded means for the multitude to see and enjoy the best modern art of all countries. The winter exhibitions of the old masters now held in London bring the fine works of bygone art before the public. Illustrated works issue from the press at prices within the reach of all; and so the workman has learnt to love art, and has had it brought near to him by various societies.

During the latter part of our century, hopes have been realized which were the life-long dreams of our predecessors. Our early academicians offered to devote to them their unpaid labours. Barry struggled through life in an endeavour to realize them. Haydon saw these hopes at the point of realization, and died. Our churches even have opened their doors to the painter, and works have been produced that may well vie with anything that has been done in modern times in other lands. It remains to be seen whether this step in art-progress will be continued, but our faith is yet strong in the progress of art; we know that the English school has much to achieve, and we do not believe in our brethren flagging in the race. The talent rising up to succeed that which is passing away is abundant ; and, if with a difference, is it not desirable that it should be so ? All originality consists in a difference. Even as we write we read in the press the successes of our painters, at the Paris 1889 Exhibition, and though our work does not permit us to mention *living* painters, we have every confidence that British artists will continue to produce works worthy of record in a future century of painters of the English school.

INDEX.

ILLUSTRATED BIOGRAPHIES OF THE GREAT ARTISTS.

*Each Volume contains many illustrations, including, when possible, a Portrait
of the Master, and is strongly bound in decorated cloth.*

Crown 8vo, 3s. 6d. per Volume, unless marked otherwise.

ENGLISH PAINTERS.

WILLIAM HOGARTH. By AUSTIN DOBSON. From Recent
Researches. Illustrated with Reproductions of Groups from the celebrated En-
gravings of the Rake's Progress—Southwark Fair—The Distressed Poet—The
Enraged Musician—Marriage à-la-Mode—March to Finchley—and ten other
Subjects.

SIR JOSHUA REYNOLDS. By F. S. PULLING, M.A. From
the most recent Authorities. Illustrated with Engravings of Penelope Boothby
—The Strawberry Girl—Muscipula—Mrs. Siddons—The Duchess of Devonshire
—Age of Innocence—Simplicity—and ten other Paintings.

GAINSBOROUGH and CONSTABLE. By G. BROCK-
ARNOLD, M.A. Illustrated with Engravings of the Blue Boy—Mrs. Graham
—The Duchess of Devonshire—and five others by Gainsborough ; and A Lock on
the Stour—Salisbury Cathedral—The Cornfield—The Valley Farm—and four
other Pictures by Constable.

SIR THOMAS LAWRENCE and GEORGE ROMNEY.
By LORD RONALD GOWER, F.S.A. Illustrated with Engravings of the
Duchess of Sutherland—Lady Peel—Master Lambton—and Nature, by Law-
rence ; The Parson's Daughter—and other Pictures, by Romney. Price 2s. 6d.

TURNER. By COSMO MONKHOUSE. From Recent Investigations.
Illustrated with Engravings of Norham Castle—The Devil's Bridge—The
Golden Bough—The Fighting Téméraire—Venice—The Shipwreck—Alps at
Daybreak—and eleven other Paintings.

SIR DAVID WILKIE : A MEMOIR. By J. W. MOLLETT,
B.A. Illustrated with Engravings of Groups from the Rent Day—The Village
Politicians—The Penny Wedding—Blind Man's Buff—Duncan Gray—The Cut
Finger—and four other Paintings.

SIR EDWIN LANDSEER : A MEMOIR. By F. G.
STEPHENS. Illustrated with seventeen Facsimiles of Etchings after Landseer's
designs : among others, Low Life—A Shepherd's Dog—Four Irish Greyhounds—
Return from Deerstalking—Mare and Foal—Sheep and Lambs—and Facsimiles
of the Woburn Game-cards.

DAVID COX and PETER DE WINT. Memoirs of the
Lives and Works. By GILBERT R. REDGRAVE. [*In preparation.*

WILLIAM MULREADY, Memorials of. Collected by FREDERIC
G. STEPHENS. [*In preparation.*

GEORGE CRUIKSHANK, His Life and Works : including a
Memoir by FREDERIC G. STEPHENS, and an Essay on the Genius of
George Cruikshank, by W. M. THACKERAY. [*In preparation.*

*Full List of the other Volumes—Italian, Spanish, German, Flemish,
Dutch, and French Painters—on application.*

" Most thoroughly and tastefully edited."—*Spectator.*

LONDON :
SAMPSON LOW, MARSTON, SEARLE, & RIVINGTON, LIMITED,
St. Dunstan's House, Fetter Lane, E.C.

R/.

GX 464

9 781362 989691